Public Policies Toward Business

The Irwin Series in Economics

Consulting Editor **Lloyd G. Reynolds** Yale University

PUBLIC POLICIES
TOWARD BUSINESS

William G. Shepherd
Professor of Economics
The University of Michigan

Clair Wilcox
Late Professor of
Political Economy
Swarthmore College

1979   Sixth Edition

RICHARD D. IRWIN, INC.   Homewood, Illinois   60430
Irwin-Dorsey Limited,   Georgetown, Ontario   L7G 4B3

© RICHARD D. IRWIN, INC., 1955, 1960, 1966, 1971, 1975, and 1979

ISBN 0-256-02183-X
Library of Congress Catalog Card No. 78–70003

Printed in the United States of America

4 5 6 7 8 9 0 K 6 5 4 3 2 1

*To those of our students
who have warmed our hearts by
becoming economists*

Preface

This sixth edition continues the form and content of earlier editions. The main types of American policies toward business are presented both in breadth and in some detail. Attention is drawn primarily to the economic content of policies, as they evolve in parallel with market conditions. The causes and effects of policies are resolved into their parts.

Our aim in this book is, as before, to help readers to analyze; to think for themselves and to make their own evaluations. We have provided a road map for the subject and filled it with many details. These facts are not important for themselves, for few students will remember more than the main lines and some details. It is the method, the independent and objective cast of mind, that matters. As the whirligig of time spins out more cases and problems, we hope that our students will be able to evaluate them with X-ray eyes and a fair mind.

Our format is much as before, though there have been extensive revisions. With the methods in hand (as presented in Chapters 1–3), one then proceeds through the three great categories of policies. As always in the United States, antitrust is the central policy. The coverage of it in this edition has been enlarged by about half, even though the whole book has been slimmed down by one fifth.

Regulation of utilities, a more specialized topic, comes next. It has recently undergone some changes, with effects that are still uncertain. We have tried to place them within a good long-range perspective. Public enterprise is of growing importance, and we continue in this edition to give it close attention. The special cases in Part V have been trimmed down, but they still offer a good deal of variety.

Broadly, we have enhanced the antitrust coverage, while condensing the last two parts. This fits the balance of interests of most teachers in a variety of courses. We have carried further the effort to make the text more concise, while still comprehensive. This edition is also a better teaching book. There is an appendix (to Chapter 2) on writing term papers, and some 300 review questions are placed at the ends of the chapters.

To help decide the balance and scope of this edition, there has been much valuable advice from colleagues and students. Yet no single treatment could please everyone in the diversity of courses in which the book is used. By providing more than a bare minimum of content, we have left room for teachers to try differing emphases among the parts. As always, we will be grateful for readers' advice of all sorts on ways to improve later revisions.

The question of what to include is especially marked for new cases and writings. Each may seem to be a "landmark," but it usually takes time, perhaps decades, for the effect to show through. Our treatment of recent developments reflects our best judgment, tempered by a sense of historical proportion. Such judgments are hazardous and often debatable, but we have tried to reach them fairly. We have also given copious footnote references, so that students can work up their own judgments.

Our whole approach is meant to be objective and unbiased. It fits, we believe, the mainstream of scientific study in the field. There are divergent opinions on many parts, and a variety of splinter groups. Our focus on competition—as a beneficial process which needs protection—fits both the weight of research and a deep tradition in U.S. social values.

The book is designed to fit a one-semester or two-quarter treatment of industrial policy at the upper college level. It is also intended to be useful in law and business courses that deal with competitive issues and the economic content of antitrust and regulatory law. Although the book's format gives a natural sequence, it can be used flexibly.

This book is designed to be used effectively with two companion volumes. One is William G. Shepherd, *The Economics of Industrial Organization* (Englewood Cliffs, N.J.: Prentice-Hall, 1979). That volume presents in detail the topics which are here outlined concisely in Chapter 1 (section B) and Chapter 2. Together the two books fit a two-term course sequence on Industrial Organization and Public Policy (or three quarters devoted to Industrial Organization, Antitrust, and Regulation). The other complementary book is William G. Shepherd, *Public Policies Toward Business: Readings and Cases,* rev. ed. (Homewood, Ill.: Irwin, 1979). Its selections give depth on many issues, putting the student more directly into the literature. It provides flexibility, by letting the teacher and student choose which points to probe in more detail.

The analysis presented in these pages is an outgrowth of many years of teaching by Wilcox at Swarthmore College and by Shepherd at the University of Michigan. It also reflects extensive service by both authors in various public agencies. The content of the book further reflects research by both authors on a variety of issues in industrial economics and policy effects. We are aware that policies often have defects but also that they can on occasion be highly effective. The concepts we present here for analyzing policies are meant to reflect such distilled wisdom as the field has evolved, as best we can convey it.

In the years since 1960, the usual healthy rethinking of policies and the emergence of new industrial problems appear to have quickened. The older policies now appear to be under unusual strain, so that the present period may be a watershed for new industrial policies. Still, old policies have remarkable inertia, and so the basic policies in 1985 or 2000 may be little changed from those now in being.

In any case, these are exciting times in this field, and this book is meant to convey that excitement as well as to encourage clear thinking. It is meant also to display the sheer zest of the subject, where tricks and absurdities abound and all acts are only too human.

February 1979   *William G. Shepherd*

1, 2, 3, 4, / 5, / 6, 7, / 17, / 9, 10, / 17, / 11,

Contents

xiii

Part I

THE SETTING FOR POLICIES

chapter 1

Public Control: The Basic Issues

Public policies toward business are of three main kinds: antitrust, regulation, and public enterprise. This book will train you to analyze them and to judge their effectiveness.

Policies are what policymakers do. They evolve in thousands of offices, especially in Washington, D.C., and in state capitols. Policy choices are made, fudged, or postponed "for more study." A few officials or agencies seem, at any one time, to be important. But the scene shifts, now to antitrust, next to a regulatory commission, then to the Supreme Court, perhaps to the Pentagon or the Postal Service, and back to antitrust.

"Good" policies are effective treatments, like medication or surgery for good health. The main condition they treat is market power. The laws and agencies can have nearly any effect—creating, preventing, reshaping or ignoring market power. The social objective is to develop an optimum set of treatments and to keep them attuned to changing real markets.

These tasks are ancient and often sophisticated, going back into the mists of early history. In these modern times we speak scientifically about "optimizing" the levels and designs of policies. Yet the problem existed in prehistoric tribes, in ancient Sumer, and under the Pharoahs, centuries before the ancient Greeks named it *monopoly*. Monopoly also flourished in Medieval Europe, in the Tudors' and Louis XIV's monopoly grants, and under the Shogunate in Japan, well before Adam Smith prepared *The Wealth of Nations* to strike off the fetters of Mercantilism.[1] To gain control over a market has been a leading way to found a family fortune, and it still is.

Every day, the market economy is an arena for moves in countless real games of monopoly. All of them are played in earnest, some of them for stakes running into billions of dollars. In many markets, this striving for wealth results in a continuing stand-off, with no final winner taking all the

---

[1] Adam Smith, *The Wealth of Nations* (New York: Random House, Modern Library, 1937); see also Joseph A. Schumpeter, *History of Economic Analysis* (London: Oxford University Press, 1954), and Fritz Machlup, *The Political Economy of Monopoly* (Baltimore: Johns Hopkins Press, 1952), for reviews of the early conditions and doctrines.

cards and cash. That is what competition means: The game goes on, fairly, among equals. Such competition prevails in large areas of the modern economy, in the United States, Western Europe, Japan, and others. But in some markets, monopoly may be required by large-scale technology, or it may be created by strategy or by exploiting the political process to gain a dominant position. Adam Smith and Karl Marx pointed it out quite clearly: the structure of the economy and how the society treats monopoly help to define each civilization. Monopoly is closed, exclusive, unequal, rigid. Competition is— usually—open, inclusive, fair, flexible; efficient, and equitable.

Yet that contrast does not translate into a simple policy rule, such as: *Always Maximize Competition.* Technology sometimes makes a degree of monopoly advisable, in order to achieve economies of scale. The recurring riddle is: how much monopoly is justified, from market to market? Even where economies of scale are absent, it pays aspiring and actual monopolists to claim that scale economies exist and require monopoly.

Your task is to treat such issues and claims skeptically and skillfully. They will crop up many times during this course and the rest of your life. The objective is to learn to judge them with logic, good sense, and good humor. Logic alone will not do, for one must weigh up complex matters of degree: how much monopoly, economies of scale, inequality; changing at what rates; and so on. One must be wise, not doctrinaire, both logical *and* sensible.

The basic questions are simple: What is to be done about monopoly? What treatments have been used, or could be tried anew? What have the results been? To answer, one must cut beneath the words and formalities, to see what really happens. One looks for the historical and social roots of policies, and also compares them with what is done abroad. One learns details *and* how to compare the results with the standards for good results. That is, *positive* knowledge is used to make *normative* appraisals.

Behind these dry concepts lie great social interests. How monopoly was treated in 1870–1920 has shaped the corporate structure and social structure that we have now. How it is treated now will influence future generations. How other countries manage *their* industrial policies explains much of their distinctive economic performance and social structure (contrast Japan, China, Sweden, Britain, and the United States of America).

Indeed, the stakes are more fateful. Shall the State control markets, or shall private monopolists, or shall free and fair competition? The answer defines much of a civilization; compare Athens and Sparta, or Soviet Russia and the United States. How deeply should some citizens be permitted to exploit the others? The answer reflects the ethics of the people. These values shape the policies, and the policies shape the economy and the social structure. The subject is in the warp and weft of society.

The topic has a simple core of ideas, surrounded by layers of intricate fine points. One must start simply, with clear concepts and a good grasp of the basic processes at work.

A. BASIC CONCEPTS: (1) PUBLIC (2) POLICIES (3) TOWARD (4) BUSINESS

The four words of the title fit four main features of the subject.

A1. PUBLIC Policies toward Business: The Public Interest

The public is, of course, the whole community; individuals sharing citizenship, responsibilities, and benefits. The economy can do the public much good by providing abundant goods and services, fair shares, interesting work, a minimum of pollution, and so forth. There are other goals too, such as a rich culture and social cohesion. The economic goals are important, and often they make the wider values possible.

The economic goals divide into two main categories: efficiency and equity. The goals recur throughout the book, and they are the main purposes of public policies.[2] A short summary follows. More detail is given in Section B on "Competition and Performance."

1. Efficiency. This means, basically, that there is no waste or avoidable destruction; the use of resources cannot be improved. There are two main categories of "static" efficiency:

1. Efficient management within the firm so that no slackness or mistakes occur. This is often called "X-efficiency."
2. Allocative efficiency. Resources are allocated so that their value at each margin of production just equals their cost. (Price equals marginal cost) for each good and each firm.

"Dynamic" efficiency—or the optimum rate of technical change—is also a criterion. It occurs when the resources needed for invention and innovation are allocated efficiently, and when innovations are not retarded for private gain.

2. Equity. Equitable means fair, so equity means a fair distribution of economic benefits among citizens. "Fair" has many meanings, going straight to the heart of ethical standards of decency and a good society. Some citizens are very rich, while many are poor. Is the fair basis to each according to (a) Effort? (b) Merit? (c) Luck? (d) Birth? (e) Marginal value product? (f) Equal shares? (g) Need? (h) Two or more of these? (i) Some other? and from each according to (a) Ability? (b) Equal effort? (c) Some other? Each criterion has validity, but they can clash sharply in practice. They are of utmost importance to each society, and much political activity arises purely from the struggle over distributive "fairness."

---

[2] The proper goals are a matter of rich debate. Here we touch only on the economic ones which industrial policies might affect. Yet even these go deeply into the character of society. See Schumpeter's *History of Economic Analysis* for some of the classic issues.

Fairness relates to three dimensions of economic rewards:

1. *Wealth:* the assets we hold (cash, bonds, stocks, houses, land, gold, and so forth) *minus* our debts.
2. *Income:* the yearly flow of net purchasing power.
3. *Opportunity:* the chance to gain wealth, income, status, or other good things in life, *in the future,* by dint of one's effort, talent, or luck.

3. Others, Including Social Values. These include reasonable security, cultural richness, a high degree of freedom of choice, and many other broader social conditions. A key one is the sense of identity and fulfillment in one's work. An efficient and monetarily "fair" society could still have everybody in jobs (and/or home chores) which they detest.

These other "social" goals may outweigh the economic ones in the end. Keep that in mind as you proceed, for competition is so economically fruitful that its social ambivalence is easy to forget.

On the whole, *competition usually induces or compels firms to behave in line with these criteria.* It enforces efficiency and stirs innovation. It spreads the rewards fairly, and it nourishes an open, free society. By contrast, *monopoly tends to distort the economy from these goals.* It usually restricts output, raises price, breeds inefficiency, retards innovation, and reduces choice. Only if there are large economies of scale might monopoly give better results. These effects and contrasts are analysed in detail below.

The "public interest" is to see that the economy attains these standards as closely as possible. If there is waste or unfairness or other deviance, the public interest lies in removing it. This happy result is often difficult to reach, for three reasons.

1. The public policies themselves absorb resources, which can exceed the benefits they yield.
2. Waste and inequity in markets are often hard to measure, for lack of facts or because there are honest differences about what is efficient or fair.
3. Some groups usually have an interest in averting an efficient policy, and there are many ways of doing so. The groups are often powerful, skillful, and large.

The public interest is therefore easier to define in theory than to apply in practice. In practice, public policies can and often do work *against* the true public interest. The costs from bad policies and the gains from good ones can be large.

A2. Public POLICIES toward Business

There are many kinds of policies, but in the United States several types are prominent. Their basic format is shown in Figure 1–1. Markets are on

FIGURE 1–1
Policies act upon markets (but are also acted upon)

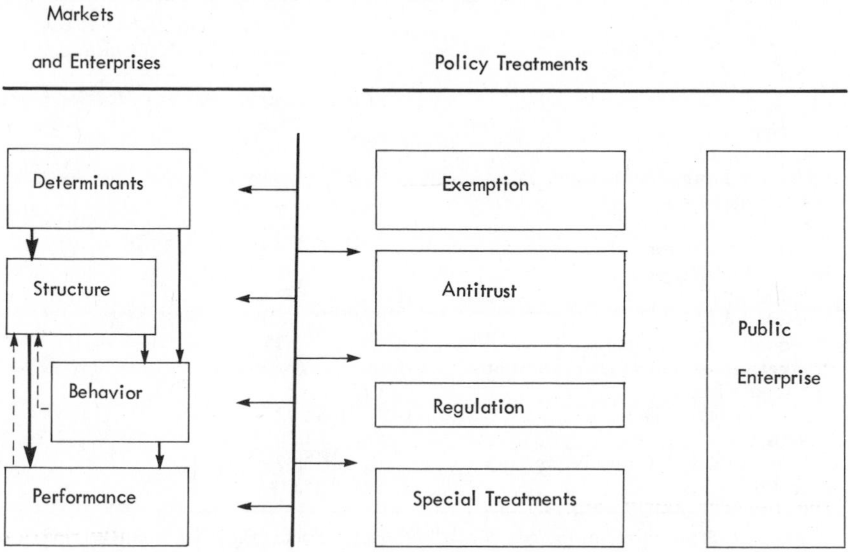

Markets

and Enterprises   Policy Treatments

the left-hand side; policies are on the right.[3] Ideally they act upon industry, as a doctor treats a patient. The leftward-pointing arrows illustrate such control. But industries also act upon the agencies, by resistance, persuasion, lobbying to cut budgets, publicity campaigns, and so forth. Therefore, the arrows of "control" go both ways. The balance of this mutual control will differ from case to case.

The resources used for policies are summarized in Table 1–1. The conventional policy tools have become: *antitrust* for the "naturally competitive" sector (which is primarily industry and trade), *regulation* for "utilities," and *public enterprise* for certain economic sectors and many social services. There have also been a wide range of special cases—weapons, farming, oil, shipping, health, sports, and so on. Table 1–1 summarizes the public funds used directly on policies. It understates, for some of the costs (such as for court hearings of antitrust cases) are indirect, though real. Table 1–1 also indicates some of the *private* resources employed in anticipating and responding to the public actions (including 11,000 lawyers specializing in antitrust, 3,000 in regulation, and 5,000 in patents).

Table 1–2 shows the incidence of these policies, sector by sector. The patterns reflect both the formal domains and simple usage. Though many

---

[3] The analysis of market conditions is presented in W. G. Shepherd, *The Economics of Industrial Organization* (Englewood Cliffs, N.J.: Prentice-Hall, 1979), and F. M. Scherer, *Industrial Market Structure and Economic Performance* (Skokie, Ill.: Rand McNally, 1970). The political power of business is explored in Charles E. Lindblom, *Politics and Markets: The World's Political-Economic Systems* (New York: Basic Books, 1978).

TABLE 1–1
Policy Resources under Selected Programs, United States, Fiscal 1979 (projected)

	Estimated Levels of Public Resources Used in 1970–71 ($ million)	
	Public Agencies	Private Units
Antitrust		
Antitrust Division	46	(400+)
Federal Trade Commission	66	
Utility regulation		
Federal commissions	246	(400+)
State commissions	45	(75)
Public enterprises		
Postal (deficit)	784	
Federal courts	(80)	
Federal prison systems	315	
Product safety and other regulations	(630+)	(700+)
Public purchases		
Department of Defense	31,927	
NASA	3,307	
Atomic Energy Commission	2,829	
Subsidies	(95,000)	

Source: U.S. Government, *Budget, Fiscal 1979* (Washington, D.C.: U.S. Government Printing Office, 1978), Appendix volume; annual *Reports* of state commissions; and various financial and legal references. Some figures are estimates, shown in parentheses.

areas are debatable, the main outlines are clear enough. There have been changes. Antitrust has extended its coverage to nearly one third of the economy. Regulation and public ownership have almost doubled their scope, while special cases (subsidies, cartel support, and public purchases) have more than doubled in share. Meanwhile the scope of exemption—of laissez-faire—has shrunk markedly, to less than one third of the economy.

The Principal Policies

1. Antitrust is the main U.S. policy. It has three main parts. *(a)* It tries to abate *existing* market power. Though its focus is in industry and trade, it can also reach into certain regulated sectors. *(b)* It screens *mergers* between firms and stops some of them. And *(c)* it attempts to reduce *cooperation* among competitors. Its tasks are large, its resources are small. (See Part II.)

2. Regulation involves ratifying one or several firms as a "utility" and, in return, putting it under some degree of constraint by a commission. Price changes—either up or down—must be approved by the commission. The criteria are *(a)* the profit rate is to be "fair" (not too high nor too low) and *(b)* the price structure is to be "just and reasonable" (price discrimination is to be limited). Federal, state, and local commissions exist, overlap, and fight each other in many sectors. (See Part III.)

TABLE 1–2
Estimates of Policy Coverage by Sectors, U.S. Economy, 1924 and 1978

Sector	Total	Percent of National Income					Public Ownership (percent of national income)
		Subsidy or Cartel Support	Public Purchases	Exempt	Antitrust	Regulation or Other Control Device	
1924							
Finance, etc.	15.1	2.0		13.1			0
Manufacturing	21.9			9.9	12.0		0.4
Utilities	3.3			2.0		1.3	0.5
Transport	7.5			5.5		2.0	0.7
Government	9.6		9.6				9.6
Wholesale and retail	13.6			9.6	4.0		0
Services	11.6		0.6	11.0			0
Construction	4.4		0.4	4.0			0
Mining	2.5			2.5			0
Agriculture, etc.	10.5			10.5			0
Rest of world	0			0			
Total	100.0	2.0	10.6	68.1	16.0	3.3	11.2
1978							
Finance, etc.	11.2	5.1		2.2	3.9		1.4
Manufacturing	26.1	1.0	3.5	8.8	11.8	1.0	0.9
Utilities	4.0		0.5	1.3		2.2	0.7
Transport	3.6		0.2	1.5	0.8	1.1	1.2
Government	16.0		16.0				16.0
Wholesale and retail	15.8			6.0	9.8		0
Services	13.6	3.0		5.3	5.3		2.0
Construction	4.5		0.7	3.0	0.8		0
Mining	1.5			0.8	0.7		0
Agriculture, etc.	2.7	2.2		0.5			0
Rest of world	1.0			1.0			
Totals	100.0	11.3	20.9	30.4	32.1	4.3	22.1

Sources: W. G. Shepherd, *The Treatment of Market Power* (New York: Columbia University Press, 1975): U.S. Census Bureau, *Historical Statistics of the United States* (Washington, D.C.: U.S. Government Printing Office, 1957); and U.S. Census Bureau, *Statistical Abstract* (Washington, D.C.: U.S. Government Printing Office, annual).

3. **Public enterprise** exists in a variety of sectors, but in the United States it is relatively least common in industry, finance, and utilities. The United States is unique in its reliance on the regulation of private utilities in place of public ownership (Table 16–2 in Chapter 16 below compares the United States with other countries). The public corporation has become a standard form for public enterprises, but other varieties (joint ventures, holding companies, and so forth) are being increasingly tried. (See Part IV.)

4. **Other special policies** (covered in Part V).

Pseudo-regulation. Many sectors are permitted to engage in "self-regulation." This tends to raise industry profits, to limit competition among members, and to erect barriers against new entry. *Purchases by public agencies* impinge strongly on many sectors, such as weapons, R&D activity, nuclear development, construction of schools and highways, and medical services. The buying is often done in ways which permit—even foster—market power for the suppliers. *Trade barriers.* Tariffs and quotas are high for a variety of industries. *Patents.* These grant a monopoly on new inventions for 17 years. They are critical in a few industries, and significant for many.

Taxes, expenditures, and subsidies can set controls, as well as feed in public funds. *Investigations and publicity* can apply pressure on behavior, by means of hearings and reports. But they are often empty or stir meaningless controversy. *Emergency controls* during wars and crises have been of many kinds.

Constraint and Ownership

The policies all contain two main dimensions. One is the *degree of constraint* on the firm. This is measured by the effect on profits, either reducing them under tight regulation (to the left) or raising them via subsidy (to the right).

The Effect of the Constraint on Profits

$$\longleftarrow \text{Regulation} \longrightarrow \qquad \longleftarrow \text{Cartel support} \longrightarrow$$

$$\text{Antitrust} \qquad\qquad \text{Subsidy}$$

$$\longleftarrow\longrightarrow \qquad\qquad \longrightarrow$$

$$(-) \qquad\qquad\qquad\qquad\qquad\qquad (+)$$

Antitrust lies in the middle, usually reducing the profits which some firms gain from market power. It overlaps with regulation; both have a range of effects from plus to minus. We will be asking again and again in this book what the effects of each policy have really been.

The second dimension is *ownership,* which ranges from totally private to totally public.

Ownership

Private	Mixed and nonprofit	Public

The two polar cases are easy to understand; for example, General Motors Corp. is wholly private, and the Government Printing Office is entirely public. There is also a large middle range, of joint or mixed ownership, which is more common abroad than in the United States.

Figure 1–2 combines these two dimensions in a box diagram. Virtually

FIGURE 1–2
The Two Dimensions of Policy Choices

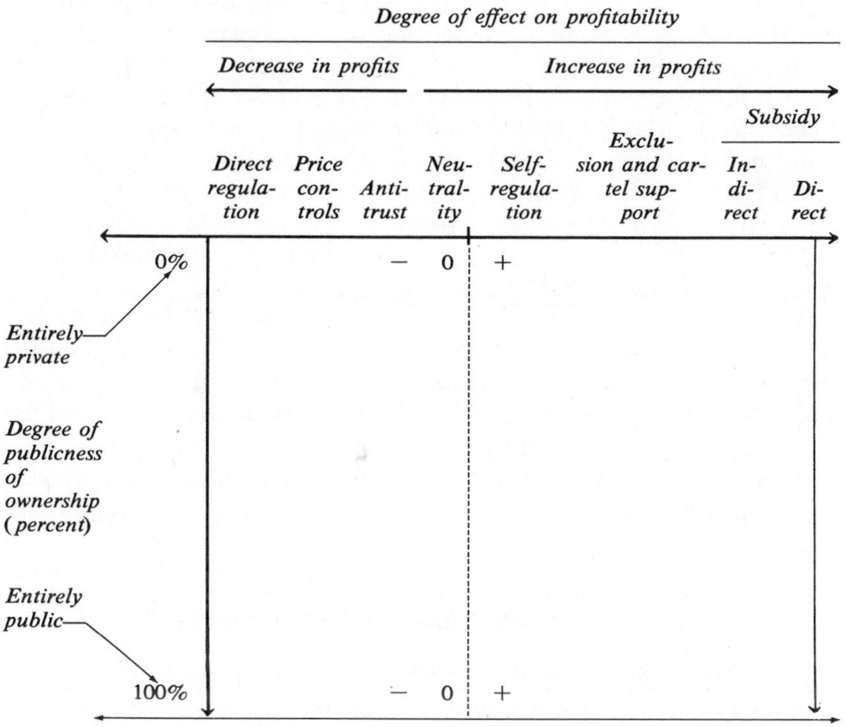

Degree of effect on profitability

	Decrease in profits			Increase in profits				
							Subsidy	
						Exclu-		
	Direct regula- tion	*Price con- trols*	*Anti- trust*	*Neu- tral- ity*	*Self- regula- tion*	*sion and car- tel sup- port*	*In- di- rect*	*Di- rect*

$$0\% \qquad - \quad 0 \mid + $$

Entirely private

Degree of publicness of ownership (percent)

Entirely public—

$$100\% \qquad - \quad 0 \mid + $$

any enterprise or product can be located in the box according to its policy status. Figures 1–1 and 1–2 clarify the fact: *public* enterprise is a substitute for *private* enterprise, rather than for regulation or antitrust. This point is often mistaken. It is often thought instead that each of the main policies—antitrust, regulation, and public enterprise—is mutually exclusive with the others. And, so it goes, antitrust gets the mild cases, while the most difficult ones are given the drastic treatment—public enterprise—as a last resort. But in fact, these choices are along two different dimensions, which can and do overlap. Public enterprises can be, should be, and often are, under antitrust and regulation; an example is the U.S. Postal Service. A free economy—and an energetic and innovative one—can have a lot of public enterprise in it.

Though partly substitutable for each other, the policy treatments are *complementary* over wide ranges. Public firms routinely need a degree of antitrust and regulatory treatment. Regulated firms usually do best when they face a degree of competition. And private firms are often actually under close public constraints on, or get subsidies for, much that they do. Moreover, many public firms behave as if they were private companies, as we will see in Part IV.

The present coverage of the policies (shown in Table 1–2) seems traditional and even natural to many observers. But *(a)* It has changed since 1900–30 (with some major shifts since 1960); *(b)* It may not be working well; and *(c)* It will evolve and perhaps change markedly in the future. Moreover, it differs sharply from the policies used in most other countries. The United States makes more use of antitrust and utility regulation, and less use of public enterprise. Therefore, it is an open question how well these United States policies have worked, and how (if at all) they could be improved. Is the United States abberrant, or is it the best archetype? In thinking about this, foreign experience can provide a useful perspective.

The basic American trait is to prefer open, arm's-length, formal dealings between policymakers and enterprises. Much transpires behind the scenes, but less than in Western European economies and Japan. In these countries, informal controls and public enterprise are more routine, with little pretense at formal antitrust or regulation.

A brief history of policies is presented in the Appendix to this chapter. Current policies and issues often make sense only as phases in a long process of change, growth, and struggle.

A3. Public Policies TOWARD Business: How Policies Are Applied

The naive image is that the legislature writes laws which (after testing, if necessary, in the courts) are *applied to* private firms by executive agencies. "The State" stands outside the economy, acting—or "interfering"—to change markets from their natural course.

Reality is more complicated (as Chapter 3 will explore). The policy setting has two basic elements: *(a)* a *political* process (democratic or otherwise) which carries out the evolving will of the people; this process is parallel to *(b)* the *economic* process. **These two interact, shaping each other.** And:

The political process is not perfect. It has pockets of political monopoly, ignorance, and delay. It may be the best there is, but it reflects the underlying power structure rather than strictly equal voter power.

The influence goes both ways, between the economic and political process. Policies toward firms A . . . F are shaped *by firms* A . . . F themselves as well as by firms G . . . Z, and perhaps by others. Indeed,

Democracy moves slowly and openly, and so those affected can usually influence policy. And firms adversely affected by Policy X will have strong incentives to shape policies their way. In doing this,

The rational firm will spend (on experts, lawsuits, lobbying, advertisements, and other persuasion) *up to the dollar amount that is at stake, in order to get its way* (see Chapter 3 for details). Therefore in fact

Policies are evolved under pressure from all sides, rather than applied unilat-

erally. Policy actions usually strike reasonable balances, rather than push to logical extremes.

And policies take time to evolve. Therefore, they usually lag behind events and needs, often by many years. Policy treatments are not usually "done to" or "applied to" firms, as an autocratic doctor might decide that a gall bladder must come out. Rather the policy move is usually by consent, including the reluctant consent (if not the virtual direction) of the firm itself. This reality differs from the high school civics view that a problem is "solved" by passing a law or taking a public action against it.

A4. Public Policies toward BUSINESS

The businesses affected by public policies are diverse and fascinating.

a. There are conflicting interests *among* businesses. The business community is like a continent full of warlike tribes. There is strife among firms, among industries, among sectors, big versus small, local versus international, Main Street versus Wall Street, and so forth. Firm A's gain usually causes a loss to some firm B, C, H, or Z. Good public policy recognizes these natural contraries, and it often puts such opposed private interests to work. The deepest single contrast is between established firms and newcomers: between old-line, blue-chip, establishment firms, and new outsiders.

b. Industries differ greatly in their ages and styles. Examples: steel and meat-packing are old; cable TV and hand calculators are young. Age can strongly influence structure and performance.

c. Enterprises include the conventional private firms and banks, *plus* (1) Public firms of many types and degrees, (2) Partnerships (lawyers, doctors, small business), (3) Non-profit and charitable units (hospitals, universities), and (4) Cooperatives, mutuals, and other hybrid forms. All of these units produce and sell under some forms of financial constraint. All of them can monopolize, or conspire, or compete, and can innovate or stagnate. Public policies need to deal with them all, not just the standard private corporation.

d. Private firms often have deep public effects. Large firms commonly use the capital of thousands of investors, employ thousands of workers, buy from hundreds of suppliers, and sell to thousands or millions of customers. They affect jobs, prices, local prosperity, future resources, national security, and often the quality and meaning of life. The behavior of many private firms is properly a matter of public concern.

e. Firms should not be expected to be "socially responsible" on a conscious basis. Frequently it is argued otherwise; that large firms can and do serve as social stewards, doing "good" things that are not profitable. This may happen occasionally in private firms, but it is not frequent or consistent. Such acts go against the grain of training, belief, and stockholder pressures in private management. And the diverse social impacts of larger business choices often embrace so many elements and groups that Solomon himself could not find the best solution. Such impacts properly require explicit public policies.

f. Business is resilient and inventive. Its managers and legal advisers can devise ways through—or around—almost any obstacle. This "adaptive response" often frustrates public policies; if tactic A is prohibited, the firm can try similar tactics B through Z instead. But it also means that business can bounce back handsomely from almost any treatments, even "radical" ones (though of course it will try to persuade us otherwise).

B. COMPETITION AND PERFORMANCE

The degree of competition is a spectrum, with pure competition and pure monopoly at the two ends.[4] In between are many shadings and varieties of market power. We will consider performance under the two extreme cases, using the tools of introductory economics. The comparisons also shade across the middle range between pure competition and pure monopoly.

		Oligopoly			
Pure competition	Monopolistic competition	Loose oligopoly	Tight oligopoly	Dominant firm	Pure monopoly

B1. Pure Competition and Efficiency

Defining "the market." Each market is an area or set of arrangements where sellers and buyers interact in exchanging a product. The workings of supply and demand set the product's price at each point. An ideal market has a well-defined edge. Inside is one homogeneous product, with instant communication among well-informed sellers and buyers. Outside the edge are all other products, none of which is substitutable for the good.[5] Actual market edges are usually shaded, not sharp, because there is a range of partly substitutable products. Experts often disagree in defining the scope of actual markets, and this can decisively affect policy choices (see especially Chapter 5). A narrowly defined market will look more monopolistic than a broadly defined one.

Pure Competition. At any rate, consider a well-defined market with a swarm of sellers in it, all of them with insignificant market shares. Each firm has cost curves like those in Figure 1–3. Average costs first decline,

---

[4] For a full treatment of these issues, see Shepherd, *The Economics of Industrial Organization*, chap. 3 and 4.

[5] The cross-elasticity of demand between this product and others is therefore zero. Market definition is a crucial question for many policies. The concepts are discussed in detail in Chapter 5.

FIGURE 1–3
Cost and Output for a Purely Competitive Firm in the Long Run

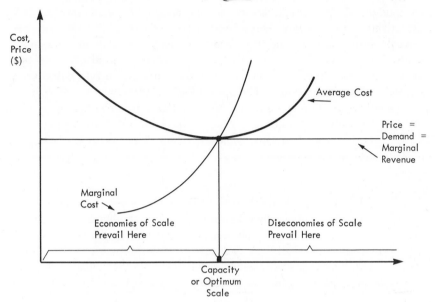

reflecting economies of scale. They reach a minimum at optimum size or capacity and then rise, as diseconomies of scale set in. In this market, optimum size is only a tiny share of the market. Being so tiny, each firm is a price taker, not a price maker (like a Kansas wheat farmer, who merely finds out what the current price is). Also it must be well-run internally, in order to survive.

With its flat demand curve, the firm's only task is to choose its level of output. This it does where its marginal costs equal the going price (this is the firm's demand curve which, being flat, is also its marginal revenue curve). The firm's profits are at a maximum, given the cost and price conditions. And the suppliers' marginal cost curves sum up to give the market supply curve.

Meanwhile, the many buyers are choosing so as to maximize their welfare. Their actions set the demand curve for the market. The process yields a market-clearing equilibrium, with demand equalling supply at the going price. In the long run, this brings the firms to or near their lowest average cost, so that their marginal cost is just equal to price.

The profound lesson of this is that in a well-functioning competitive system, *marginal cost*—the social sacrifice necessary to produce another unit of input—*just equals price*, which measures how valuable that output is believed to be. Social sacrifice is brought into line with value, and so a social optimum is reached. This is the familiar efficiency condition, in which consumers, input suppliers, and producers interact to reach the best allocation of resources among diverse uses. Behind each of the individual demand and supply curves lies equilibria in individual choices, so that each of the economic actors is maximizing its own welfare. This all adds up to the "invisible hand" metaphor of Adam Smith, whereby the entire economy reaches an economic optimum.

Limits. But there are limits. *First,* there may be external effects in production or consumption. If these are large, the private choices will diverge far from the social optimum. The *second* limit is that dynamic efficiency is not assured. Innovation and other forms of technical progress may lie outside the pure competitive equilibrium result. *Third,* efficiency does not assure equity. The efficient outcome may yield something close to Utopia or, instead, gross unfairness.

B2. Monopoly's Effects

We now introduce monopoly into this competitive equilibrium, by merging together all of the firms in this market. The new monopolist now faces the *industry* demand curve, and there is also a marginal revenue curve, as shown in Figure 1–4. This marginal revenue curve intersects the summed marginal cost of the monopolist's plants at an output level well below the competitive

FIGURE 1–4
The monopolist reduces output and raises price.

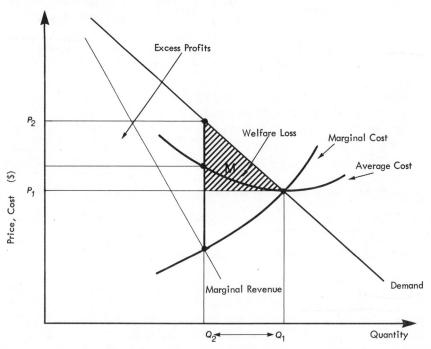

FIGURE 1–5
Monopoly may breed X-inefficiency

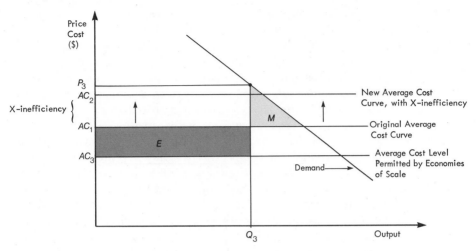

level. Output is cut, price is raised, and excess profits are earned. Since price now exceeds marginal cost, people are willing to pay more than the true cost of added output in the range between Q_1 and Q_2, *but the monopolist will not let them do it.* That is the crux of inefficient allocation.

Also, the monopolist cuts back on inputs, so that the values of their marginal products are well above their wages. To this degree the inputs are exploited; they produce more value than they are paid for. Others of them are now out of work; they will have to try for other jobs at lower wages in other industries.

The burden of misallocation is shown by the triangle M in Figure 1–4. It is, roughly speaking, the consumer surplus lost by the shift from competition to monopoly.

From its affluence, the monopolist may now develop a degree of internal slack or X-inefficiency.[6] The monopolist's employees know that the profit flow gives the firm some elbow room. Pressure from stockholders and financial markets can limit the slack, but perhaps not tightly. Actual profits may fall short of the potential monopoly profits. Costs rise, as from AC_1 to AC_2 in Figure 1–5.

The monopoly has caused a degree of *allocative inefficiency* and *X-inefficiency.* Its excess profits have also enriched the few owners at the expense

---

[6] The phrase "X-inefficiency" was coined by Harvey J. Leibenstein; see his *Beyond Economic Man* (Cambridge: Harvard University Press, 1976), for a full analysis. Slack and sluggishness have long been recognized as possibilities in monopolies. Thus, Adam Smith long ago wrote of "the negligence, profusion and malversation" of workers for monopolies *(Wealth of Nations,* p. 712).

of many customers. This disequalization of wealth can be a sharp shift away from a *fair distribution*.[7]

These effects of pure monopoly hold pro rata over the middle degrees of market power. If there are several main oligopolists, they may cooperate or compete. On average, oligopoly will cause some effects of market power, the severity of effects varying directly with the degree of concentration.

Monopoly's effect on innovation is more ambiguous. A monopolist will tend to delay innovations which make obsolete its existing investment. By contrast, a competitive firm has no choice but to put them in posthaste. Yet big innovations may require big firms, perhaps with substantial market shares. The balance of these effects can go either way. Schumpeter carried the point further, saying that competition is really a process of turnover among temporary monopolists, who generate rapid innovation as a side effect of their dynamic struggles.[8] This innovation might be more important than the slight inefficiency and excess profits which the successive monopolies cause. Schumpeter's disequilibrium process contrasts point-by-point with the traditional static analysis of pure competition, and it is akin to the common business image of competition as rivalry among a few firms.

Your task is to understand both models and then to judge how well they apply to actual markets. Some sectors may be more turbulent, along Schumpeterian lines, but many are not.

B3. Economies of Scale

If economies of scale extend up to large sizes, then a monopoly share of the market may be inevitable. Moreover the "excess" profits may merely reflect the lower costs, rather than a higher price. The market share, and the profits, would then appear to be socially justified. In Figure 1–5 the net effect on cost would be a move from AC_2 to AC_3. A triangle of misallocative loss would still exist, but the resources saved by the economies of scale (the rectangle labeled E) would easily exceed it.[9]

In judging actual cases, one must ask three main questions. First, how big are the scale economies? The firms will naturally assert them to be large,

---

[7] For example, imagine a firm with 10 owners whose market power enables them to extract merely $1 of excess profit per year from each of one million customers (on a toy, perhaps, or rock music record, T-shirt, earth shoes, or poster). Each buyer's loss is small. But the $1 million flow of excess profits will have a capitalized value of perhaps 6 to 15 times as great. This could give each owner $600,000 to $1.5 million in wealth, enough to guarantee $30,000 to $75,000 in yearly income for a lifetime (and more!). None of the owners would have to work for a living. Evidently, even small price effects can create a sizable wealth effect.

[8] Joseph A. Schumpeter, *Capitalism, Socialism and Democracy* (New York: Harper, 1942), pp. 86–107.

[9] See also Oliver E. Williamson's statement of this "trade-off" in his "Economies as an Antitrust Defense: The Welfare Trade-Offs," *American Economic Review* 58 (March 1968), pp. 18–36, and "Correction and Reply," ibid. (December 1968), pp. 1372–76.

but objective facts are needed and are often not available. Note that the down-slope in average costs must be steep, if it is to yield important benefits. Second, are the economies pecuniary rather than technical? Pecuniary gains come strictly from cheaper inputs. Only technical economies, from improved arrangements in the actual process of production, are of social value.

Third, who gets the benefits from the economies? If the monopolist keeps them all in its profits, society as a whole has scarcely benefited from them. Only if they are passed on should they count fully as an offset to the social losses from monopoly. Note, finally, that these losses still occur (the welfare triangle, X-inefficiency, inequity, and so forth), even though scale economies may also be achieved.

In short, the social value of economies of scale are smaller than the simple extent of the observed economies. And the economies are usually difficult to observe.

The basic policy task is to compare the net social economies with the social costs of monopoly, in actual markets. Where economies are slight, then firms with small market shares can be efficient. In turn, concentration can be low and competition can be relied on. High concentration is excessive and costly. Only if economies of scale are deep and wide may society need to accept monopoly, dominant firms, or tight oligopoly. Even then, the economies must be steep, technical in origin, and passed on to consumers.

In fact (see Chapter 2), such cases are the exceptions in the large U.S. economy. Market structure is normally more concentrated than social economies justify. Therefore, policies to increase competition are correct and important for the great majority of U.S. markets.

B4. Competition Is Powerful but Can Be Overdone

It is true that competition is the best general process for getting efficiency and equity. Efficient producers can undersell others, who must cut costs or be weeded out. The fittest survive. Competition also forces sellers to advertise their wares informatively. Competition fosters progress, by giving a free run to new blood and new ideas. It rewards the innovator and compels the others to imitate rapidly. It spreads income and wealth widely, by averting monopoly profits for the few, and by feeding rewards to new operators and innovators. It provides the widest opportunity for seeking success. Competition enlarges freedom of choice for most citizens. It also gives a certain cultural richness by catering to the full range of consumer wants.

Yet competition can run to excess, and if the pre-existing distribution of wealth is unfair, competition can tend to worsen it, or at least not correct it. Competition can seem a grueling and heartless way of life, lacking in warmth and charity. It is stressful and divisive, pitting people against each other. It can glorify the ruthless operator, the Gradgrind and Babbitt, the sharks of society, who gain by suppressing or exploiting human motives. The tyranny of the bottom line can be immune to decency, kindness, forgiveness. Business life usually expresses the underlying culture, or lack of it: it also shapes that culture.

Since competition can be pressed too far, a wise policy does not just blindly maximize it. Policy needs to bear down hardest on those tight markets with slight economies of scale, where a shift toward a healthier degree of competition is clearly warranted. In all but the natural monopoly exceptions, some degree of competition is better than none. At its best, competition operates within a decent, fair, and rich culture.

For the common run of markets, competition is the best all-round economic optimizer. Promoting competition is the first great task of policy in this area. Those who would abridge competition bear the burden of proof.

C. PERSPECTIVE AND FORMAT

This book is about urgent and fascinating issues, which inspire a diversity of opinions and proposals. At one pole are the backers of the status quo, property rights, and laissez faire. At the other extreme are critics eager to replace the whole economic system with a better one.[10] You already inhabit a place somewhere on this spectrum, and your views are likely to change as you learn more, grow older, and watch the changing scene.

C1. Perspective

Chapters 2 through 26 aim to help you develop your views intelligently, by thinking for yourself, not just by taking on others' ideas. You will also need to develop a clear sense of priorities among the parts of the economy, among the economic problems, and among the policy tools. You need to sort out which ones matter the most and how they interrelate. The images you form on these matters will then shape your judgments about which policies are best.

Writers on the subject naturally have their own personal views about the nature of the economy and how to treat its problems. Some writers strive to be strictly scientific in their research and debate, but others are self-serving apologists or evangelists with a story to sell. The facts about the true underlying conditions are often uncertain or obscure. Accordingly, advocates and zealots can flourish, and even objective scholars often exaggerate points as they warm to the debate.

---

[10] One can distinguish four main classes of views. "Optimists" regard current policies as being just about right. Those managing the policies are prone to this view. "Removers" are classical liberals who think most policies are harmful or irrelevant. Competition prevails, they believe, unless the State intervenes to prop up monopolies. Most policies should be withdrawn. "Reformers" want policies improved and expanded. More antitrust and regulatory resources and tougher enforcement, they expect, will promote more competition and guide industry better. "Radicals" regard the core of the system as the problem. Reforms will not do; the whole system must be changed. Monopoly is prevalent, both in economies and politics, and moderate policies cannot resolve the deep conflicts within society.

Therefore, the wise student treats each point skeptically, alert for bias and error. Yet one should not just sink into disbelief. There is much honesty and reliable evidence on the subject, if one takes care to sift them out. Be cautious and good-humored, not cynical.

The cast of characters is remarkable: officials and scholars of all kinds, magnates, judges, plucky small business managers, great inventors, lawyers, and the like. The scene ranges from city offices, to State houses, hearing rooms, and the marble halls of justice. We will get to know them all in this book. They—and we—all operate within a grand historical process which seems to move glacially but inexorably to the Left. Yesteryear's "radical" idea is often today's law, and in a few years it may be the rallying point for conservatives.

C2. Format of the Book

The Contents gives the sequence of topics in detail. The format is a natural one. Part I presents the main concepts and tools. Chapter 2 summarizes the conditions in modern markets: structure, economies of scale, effects of market power on performance, and so on. The standards for rational policy choices are set forth in Chapter 3. The rest of the book then reviews the actual policies and discusses how sound they are.

We begin with the main U.S. policy set—antitrust—in Part II. The tools are reviewed in Chapter 4. Then the two "structural" parts, toward existing structure and mergers, are presented in Chapters 5 and 6. Policies toward conduct (or "behavior") are given two full chapters, and then Chapter 9 draws together the main lessons.

Part III then takes up the second distinctive U.S. policy method, public regulation of private "utility" firms. The basic issues are given in Chapters 10 and 11, followed by three chapters on specific sectors (electricity and gas, communications, and transport) and a summary chapter.

Part IV then addresses the third major policy approach: public enterprise. Its fields, forms, and guidelines are presented in Chapter 16. Public enterprises in industry and finance are analysed in Chapter 17, and those in utility and social sectors occupy Chapter 18. Chapter 19 sums up the lessons about public enterprise as a policy tool.

With the core of the subject in hand, you will be prepared to treat most policy questions: to analyse a market, compare policy tools, and define a wise set of policies. Part V then presents the small galaxy of special cases around this main body of policy. They range from finance (Chapter 20), to health care (21), conservation (22), and other consumerist and safety regulation (23). Chapters 24 and 25 outline the remaining special cases and policies, such as official cartels, agriculture, patents, subsidies, and military supplies. They are important in themselves, and in the eccentric way they help put the mainstream sectors in perspective. At the end, Chapter 26 reassesses the balance among policies and the likely trends in the subject.

APPENDIX: A BRIEF HISTORY OF POLICIES

Modern policies have roots and antecedents in the past.[11] The current versions are often just more detailed, cover bigger industries, and in some cases are *less* sophisticated. Tariffs, limits on monopoly, regulations, public ventures, almost all have been tried before.

A look backward helps clarify *(a)* the nature of present treatments, and *(b)* where the trends in policies are heading. (More detailed histories are given in Chapters 4, 10 and 16.) Is public control on the rise? Is antitrust— or regulation, or public enterprise—an experiment or a fixture?

Early Origins

One goes back well beyond the Renaissance, to three early areas in which policy came to be important: usury, guilds, and food supply.

Usury was the practice of charging high interest rates on loaned capital. It often touched closely on royal power and finance, as well as on the wider use of capital throughout society. Therefore there was a chronic struggle— with religious and ethnic overtones—over the rate of interest and other terms of loans. From scripture were derived rules limiting the interest that could be charged.

Guilds were the cartels set up by master craftsmen to control their trades and the entrance of new talent. This too was important to the structure of power and wealth, for guild membership was widespread and the use of guilds' products was virtually universal. As the Middle Ages blended into the preindustrial growth period, the power of the guilds to control competition receded.

The third policy area was agricultural supply to the towns. It was natural for the suppliers or middlemen to try to restrict supply and raise prices, at the expense of the city dwellers. In various forms, this was called forestalling, engrossing, and regrating. It too involved basic social struggles, affecting the well-being and power of major social groupings.

To 1890

By the 16th century, early industrial development was stirring in Western Europe. There were many pockets of monopoly, some stemming from powers of the nobility to exact tolls or other privileges. While the early economic growth was beginning to dissolve and bypass some of these powers, monarchs were—on the contrary—resorting to grants of monopoly as devices to foster new industrial growth. The technique reached extensive scope under the

---

[11] Excellent references include Machlup, *The Political Economy of Monopoly;* J. M. Clark, *Social Control of Business* (Chicago: University of Chicago Press, 1926); and Joseph A. Schumpeter, *History of Economic Analysis* (New York: Oxford University Press, 1954).

Tudor monarchs of England and under Louis XIV in France.[12] In addition, these royal promoters also used public enterprise of various sorts, to manage key parts of the economy and to start others. During this mercantilist period, statecraft was deeply involved in the deliberate restriction of competition in various directions, by what we would now call an infant-industry strategy. The restrictions affected not only production but also trade, imports, and other sectors.

It was against this that Adam Smith and other classical economists strove, in order to clear away barriers and controls so that private interests could operate freely to maximize true national wealth (as measured in real productive capacity, not gold). Tariffs, controls on movement of goods, and monopoly grants were the main targets. This effort coincided with the main eruption of industrial growth in Britain during 1780–1840, which we now call the Industrial Revolution. Whether the reduction of controls caused the growth, or vice versa (or neither) is a matter of much debate. In any case, they both occurred, enough to mark the 19th century distinctly off from the earlier two centuries.

Yet even in this heyday of free-enterprise classical liberalism there was much state promotional activity. Late in the 19th century, the common-law reliance on open competition and unfettered private property rights had crystallized. But it was not the only trait. In addition, there was a willingness to mark off some markets as "affected by the public interest." Also, public involvement in infrastructure was large, both in the United States and elsewhere.

The ascendancy of the Manchester School, the assertion of unfettered power of those with capital, was waning by 1890 in England. But its legacy was strong: private enterprise had become the basis for most of the economy in both the United States and Britain by 1860. Other European countries remained more willing to create economic capital directly by the state.

From 1860 to 1900 the beliefs of Social Darwinism crested in the United States. With much pomp and rhetoric, the survival of the fittest was said to occur in industrial markets as well as in the population. Out of the ferment of this period grew most of those policies which now prevail. Modern markets were widening and deepening, so that the range of structures and constraints on them offered a wide area of choice. Turbulent events were creating not only industrial unrest but also massive changes in the structure of industry. Moreover, these industrial shifts and new monopolies were generating large fortunes, some of which still loom large in the structure of society.

In short, the period from 1860 to 1900 was a watershed for industrial policies throughout the modern world. The policies themselves took form in the decades from 1900 to 1920. The United States made decisive choices

---

[12] See W. H. Price, *The English Patents of Monopoly* (Cambridge: Harvard University Press, 1913), and Charles W. Cole, *Colbert and a Century of French Mercantilism* (New York: Columbia University Press, 1939).

about antitrust, regulation, and public enterprise. And in Europe too occurred major changes.

Antitrust and Regulation Are Established in the United States

In the United States the decisive changes were two: antitrust—under Theodore Roosevelt, Taft, and Wilson before 1916—was applied with some strictness, and private utilities were franchised under regulation rather than being converted to public enterprise. By contrast, in Europe the reliance on public enterprises increased, both in cities and nationally, and both in industry and utilities.

The U.S. move toward antitrust and regulation was primarily a conservative shift, a choice *against* more ambitious methods.[13] Antitrust enforcement was sharp in several directions: price fixing was outlawed in 1899, and a spectacular "trust-busting" campaign came to a climax in 1911–15. The Federal Trade Commission was created in 1914. But with the onset of World War I, antitrust activity was virtually halted after 1915. Likewise, the creation of state commissions regulating utilities seemed to be a progressive move. But instead it was often sought by the utilities themselves as a way of heading off public ownership. The 1920s brought a growth of federal regulation in a few utility sectors, but a fading away of antitrust activity.

In the 1930s, the Great Depression ushered in several varieties of policy activity. The basic American patterns of antitrust and regulation were hardened and extended during this decade. There was a massive cleaning up of holding-company abuses in electricity, gas, banking, and securities markets. There was the experiment in industry cartels under the National Recovery Administration. The Reconstruction Finance Corporation, a large public banking agency, restored credit to some farms, banks, and industries. Basic new agricultural policies were created. TVA was begun, as a major symbol of public enterprise. Perhaps most important, antitrust was reborn under Thurman Arnold during 1938–44.

The 1940s brought the rise of large new gray areas, in which the now-conventional policy controls were blurred and weak. The purchasing of weapons was a prime case, but the oil industry, insurance, and shipbuilding also posed new problems. Antitrust and regulation were ripe for reassessment but continued in the old patterns. In short, by 1952 policies were overdue for basic reappraisal.

Recent Patterns

Instead, the development has only been moderate. During 1952–68, there was nearly a moratorium on antitrust treatment of established market power.

---

[13] See Donald J. Dewey, *Monopoly in Economics and Law* (Chicago: Rand McNally, 1959), and Hans Thorelli, *The Federal Antitrust Policy* (Baltimore: Johns Hopkins Press, 1954).

Merger policy was tightened during 1958–66, to proscribe nearly all horizontal mergers. Regulation continued in a passive stance until the 1960s, when there was an increase of quality and vigor in some federal commissions. Weapons and space expenditures were high, and remained largely outside settled policy treatments. Other agencies had various impacts in the area of public ownership, but there was no marked refinement of public enterprise nor a clear understanding of the public enterprise that already existed.

In a longer perspective, the antitrust and regulatory experiments may have now reached maturity or perhaps run their course.[14] The 1970s appear to have brought some big changes. A few efforts at restructuring dominant firms have begun. Severe energy problems have shaken the old ways of regulating electricity and gas. Competition is being reintroduced into several regulated sectors. Public enterprise has revived as a matter of debate and practical experiments (for example, railroads). Public controls on safety, pollution, and products have grown.

The ferment of the 1970s is fascinating and perhaps a source of big changes. Its ultimate effects are not yet clear, and many present changes may be reversed in the 1980s. Still, U.S. policies have had a rare upheaval in the 1970s, which makes the issues more interesting and urgent.

In Europe, recent decades have brought some contrasts with American policy. British reliance on public enterprise shifted upwards during 1945–50 when a brace of new public enterprises were created, primarily in utility sectors. Since then, public enterprise has grown only marginally. Meanwhile, a distinct growth in British antitrust activity has occurred since 1955, so that its policies are now nearly as firm as are those in the United States. In a few antitrust areas, in fact, British policy is now stricter.

In other European countries, the development of public enterprise has been more fertile since the 1930s. Especially in Italy, public enterprise has gone beyond the older type of utility monopoly, into a more luxuriant growth of public holding companies. These have become increasingly related to national economic planning in Italy, France, and Germany. Both Germany and Japan underwent bouts of Allied antitrust restructuring after World War II. These had limited but real effects.

In this whole sequence, there appears to be no major trend toward increasing government interference.[15] Rather, there has been increasing variety, in a continuing process of trial and error. At any time, each country has a portfolio of current policies, some of which are major and some minor. Over time, this set evolves, as new treatments are tried and old ones fade out. This shifting is also caused by the rise and fall of individual sectors, for which the suitable policy treatments differ.

---

[14] See Dewey, *Monopoly in Economics and Law,* and William G. Shepherd, *The Treatment of Market Power* (New York: Columbia University Press, 1975).

[15] Some observers see, instead, a large rise in public regulation since 1965, especially in the areas of job safety, product quality, and pollution; for a representative statement, see Murray L. Weidenbaum, *Business, Government and the Public* (Englewood Cliffs, N.J.: Prentice-Hall, 1977).

There is also a mixing of motivations for actual policies. Not only do policies often follow strange paths, but frequently the "reasons" given for policies are quite different from the real ones. Drastic policy steps turn out instead to be conservative. And conservatives often impose drastic new policies. Countries regarded as reactionary often are radical.

Altogether, the evolution of policies reflects *(a)* the past, *(b)* the national culture, and *(c)* the political economy of struggles among various private interests. Whether this evolution mainly fits or strays away from an efficient set of policies is, of course, the core question around which this book turns.

chapter 2

The Conditions to Be Treated: Market Structure and Performance

This chapter gives a compact summary of real market structures and policy yields in the modern economy.[1] These conditions define the needs for policies: market power may be treated by antitrust, regulation, or some other approach. But how extensive is monopoly, and how severe are its social costs? How strict should policies be, and which policy tools should be used?

First we set the background scene by reviewing the nature of the firm and of aggregate concentration in the economy (Sections A and B). Then we turn to individual markets, asking the four basic questions: How competitive is market structure (Section C)? Does structure reflect scale economies (Section D)? How does structure affect behavior and performance (Section E)? These topics fit Figure 1–1, and readers who have had a course in Industrial Organization may pass this chapter over lightly. After the chapter-ending Summary, an appendix gives brief rounded reviews of seven important industries, to show how the concepts can be used in evaluating real cases. Long though it is, the chapter is a mere capsule of a very large subject.

A. THE FIRM

We must try to understand the firm well, for it is the main economic actor and the target of whatever public policies are applied. Throughout the many sectors of the economy—as outlined in Figure 2–1—firms are the economic building blocks. Firms are often highly complex organisms, in their structure, goals, incentives, and patterns of behavior. But the basic activity

---

[1] It summarizes parts of the field called "industrial organization." For thorough coverage, see William G. Shepherd, *The Economics of Industrial Organization* (New York: Prentice-Hall, 1978); or Joe S. Bain, *Industrial Organization,* rev. ed. (New York: Wiley, 1967). F. M. Scherer, *Industrial Market Structure and Economic Performance* (Skokie, Ill.: Rand McNally, 1970), provides a graduate-level survey of concepts and methods. Richard E. Caves, *American Industry: Structure, Conduct, Performance,* 4th ed. (New York: Prentice-Hall, 1977) gives a brief review of the essentials.

FIGURE 2–1

An Outline of the Main Sectors in a Modern Economy

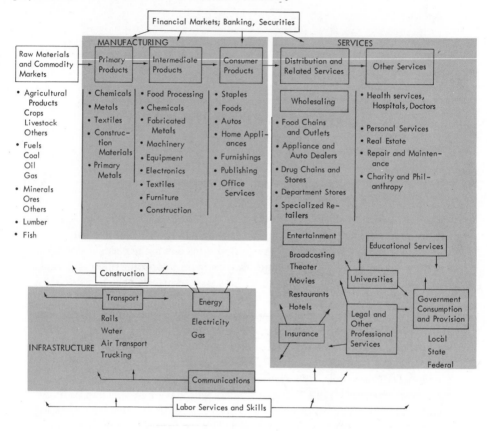

is simple. The firm acquires inputs, uses them in some production process, and then sells the outputs. The firm's opportunities are set by the nature of the market and the state of technology; by the degree of competition (which depresses the firm's demand curve); and by public policies. In most private firms, the managers maximize long-run profits on behalf of the owners. Such firms are the main focus of the policies in this book. In other types of firms (such as public and quasi-public enterprises, cooperatives, nonprofit units, and worker-managed firms), there may be other goals and revenue targets. For nearly all firms, the physical output is just a side effect of the pursuit of the financial goals.

Firms are started and run by people, of course, and they are merely devices used to serve purposes. They can be bought or sold, reorganized, divided, augmented, terminated, or absorbed into other firms. Such actions are the normal stuff of business life, occurring freely and frequently. The firm's structure may range from unified (with one chain of command) to diversified (with many separate divisions, each specializing in one product or task).

A1. Basic Anatomy of the Firm

The parts of a typical firm are shown in Figure 2–2. Several main groups in the firm—managers, owners, and directors—bear attention, for their actions often determine how effective public policies will be.

FIGURE 2–2
The Firm and Its Setting

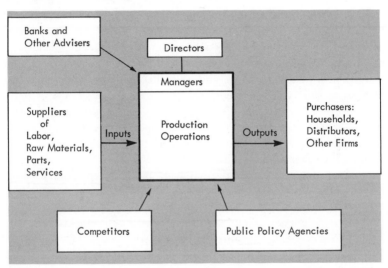

Managers are the pivotal group. They make the firm's choices about prices, outputs, investment, competitive strategies, and the rest. The top echelon is a small group, with a brief tenure—perhaps three to five years—in the topmost positions of power. Authority is delegated in varying degrees, and often there are layers of bureaucracy between the executive suite and the factory floor. Top managers are usually promoted from within, chosen in a process of rugged individual competition. Operations are often controlled by middle managers, while the top officers deal with larger issues and strategies. In diversified firms, the upper managers are more remote, dealing mainly with financial matters, enforcing profit standards, and allocating investment funds.

Managers are often less powerful than they seem. They are the focus of many interest groups, each of which wants more benefits from the firm.[2] Indeed, managers often are able only to mediate and conciliate among these

---

[2] Workers want higher wages and easier work loads. Suppliers of inputs want larger sales at higher prices. Shareholders want higher profits and dividends. Towns want factories to be built and jobs expanded in their locales. Buyers want lower prices.

interests, rather than to issue orders. Also, the firm usually has a certain momentum and character, which the leaders can modify but not reverse during their short time at the top. And, of course, the managers are supervised by their directors, stockholders, and bankers.

Owners are primarily the shareholders, whose shares of stock carry voting rights. (Bondholders have claims, but they have no role in setting policy.) The stockholders' votes elect the directors and decide on formal proposals made by the managers. By maximizing profits, the managers are maximizing the current value of the firm's shares in the market.[3] The share price is rightly regarded as a crucial index of the firm's performance. It can be affected *inter alia* by managers' performance, by events in the economy, *and* by public policies. Any rise in the share price increases the wealth of the shareholders, and the managers are under pressure to deliver such rises. Conversely, any threats to share prices (including those from strict public policies) will be stoutly resisted. The owners range from small investors up to large institutions (pension funds, insurance firms, and so forth), and the larger units usually have superior skills and knowledge.

Owners are numerous and often seemingly passive, so that managers may appear to hold all real control.[4] Yet the larger owners can exert direct pressure. And the stock market as a whole exerts pressure on managers to keep their performance up (see Section A2).

Directors formally supervise the managers, in the interests of the shareholders. They meet monthly to hear, discuss, and vote on the main actions of the firm. The board includes "inside" directors (usually several top managers of the firm) and "outside" directors (drawn from executives, lawyers, bankers, or others). Boards usually ratify the managers' plans, intervening only if serious troubles have developed. Some boards are forceful and thorough, but the degree of control varies over a wide range.

Firms' *banking relationships* are often more important in supervising the managers. The firm usually develops a close relationship with a bank, which provides the firm both money and advice. The bank comes to know the

---

[3] A rising profit flow makes the shares more valuable, for they will perforce provide greater dividends and/or capital gains. Maximizing long-run profits is therefore identical with maximizing the present value of the firm at each point.

Analytically, the present value depends on the expected flow of future yearly profits:

$$\text{Present value} = \text{Profit}_1 + \frac{\text{Profit}_2}{(1+r)} + \frac{\text{Profit}_3}{(1+r)^2} \cdot \cdot \cdot \frac{\text{Profit}_n}{(1+r)^{n-1}}$$

where 1, 2, 3 . . . n is the number of years within the time horizon and r is the rate of time discount. Obviously, estimates of the future profits can vary, as do the time-discount rates which are applied. There is no unique present value for a real-world firm. For typical values of r (10 percent) and n (20 years), present value is about 10 times the yearly value of a constant profit flow.

[4] The divorce of ownership from control was first urged in 1932 by A. A. Berle and Gardiner C. Means in *The Modern Corporation and Private Property* (New York: Macmillan, 1932), reissued with additional material in 1968 by Harcourt, Brace & World; yet the divorce is not complete, as reviewed in Shepherd, *Industrial Organization*, chap. 6.

firm intimately, and it often sets limits on what the firm's managers can do. The firm gets financial backing and also supervision. Often a competitive battle between two firms is really governed by their banking support. These relationships are usually stable and long lasting. They are not easily measured by outside observers, but they do exist and are often a key fact for public policies to deal with.

Other groups impinging on the firm include: customers, suppliers, employees, competitors, and public agencies. They all help to determine the cost and demand conditions of the firm.

A2. Performance

Profitability. The private firm's success is measured by profit (net income after tax, the bottom line of the income statement, as shown for two familiar firms in Table 2–1). The degree of profitability is usually measured by profit as a rate of return on the firm's equity investment.[5] A firm must earn profit that is at least as great as the cost of the capital it uses. Otherwise, the firm cannot renew its capital and the firm will fail. The cost of capital is usually in the range of 6 to 12 percent.[6] The "normal" or "minimum" rate of return is usually thought to be about 8 to 12 percent; effective competition usually keeps profitability down in that range. Everything above that is an extra benefit. A sustained 12 percent rate of return is good, 16 percent is very strong, and over 20 percent is high indeed. (The two firms in Table 2–1 are large, but which was more profitable in 1977? Which is the more capital intensive?)

Share Price. Profits are a single main outcome of the myriad choices made by managers about *(a)* current production levels, *(b)* prices, *(c)* level and forms of investment, and *(d)* many other items, such as wage bargaining, methods of financing investment, and location of plants. The managers strive to reach and sustain high profitability. The flow of expected future profits in turn influences the present value of the firm; a high flow means a high present value. Investors on the stock market do the evaluating, and their choices drive the firm's stock price up or down. The market value of the firm then is the going share price times the number of shares outstanding. This value reflects both *(a)* real factors, such as the firm's market position, capacity, product design, and management caliber, and *(b)* expectations about

---

[5] Profits are not easy to measure reliably. Recorded profits reflect many choices among accounting methods. Depreciation can be figured by different concepts, which can sharply alter accounting profits. Inventory valuation and the handling of special write-offs also give room for choice. Firms' reported profits are therefore often not comparable; Firm A reporting a 15 percent rate of return may be less truly profitable than Firm B which reports 12 percent. Also, profits can be taken as a rate of return on total assets or on stockholders' equity. There too the results can vary.

Still, these problems largely wash out if profits are averaged over five or more years and then compared carefully. On these issues, see any good accounting textbook.

[6] In recent years, one can get about a 6 percent return on "riskless" securities (U.S. Treasury bonds). Any other use of capital which incurs any risk must presumably offer at least as good a return as that.

TABLE 2–1
Basic Financial Statements for Two Large Firms, 1977 (in $ billion)

GENERAL MOTORS CORPORATION
Income Statement

Revenues	$ 55.3
Expenses	
Operating	46.6
Depreciation, etc.	2.4
Net income	$ 6.3
Taxes	3.0
Net income after taxes	(3.3)

Balance Sheet

Assets		*Liabilities*	
Plant and property	$ 20.9	Equity	
Depreciation	12.7	From issuing shares	$ .8
Net plant and property	8.2	Retained earnings	15.0
Investments, etc.	2.4	Total equity	(15.8)
Current Assets	16.0	Debt	1.1
		Current and others	9.8
Total Assets	$ 26.7	Total Liabilities	26.7

Return on equity Capital = 20.9%

AMERICAN TELEPHONE AND TELEGRAPH COMPANY
Income Statement

Revenues	$ 36.5
Expenses	
Operating	20.4
Depreciation, etc.	5.0
Net income	$ 11.1
Taxes and related	6.6
Net income after taxes	$ (4.5)

Balance Sheet

Assets		*Liabilities*	
Plant and property	$101.9	Equity	
Depreciation	19.5	From issuing shares	$23.1
Net plant and property	82.4	Retained earnings	17.8
Investments, etc.	5.0	Total equity	(40.9)
Current assets	6.6	Debt	32.5
Total Assets	$ 94.0	Current and others	20.6
		Total Liabilities	$94.0

Return on equity Capital = 11.0%

Sources: Annual reports of the two companies.

the firm's future prospects. The share price is not a perfect guide to the firm's present or future conditions; yet it is the best single approximation, based on "the market's" judgment.

Moreover, it applies very real pressure to the firm's managers. They must reach the expected future levels, or the stock price will fall. A sharp fall may so anger investors that it endangers their jobs. The stock market anticipates and discounts performance ahead of time. Therefore:

1. Managers are on a form of treadmill, in order to meet the expectations of investors in the market, and

2. Excess profits are capitalized immediately, as stock prices rise at the new prospect of future extra profits. The original owners will cream off the excess value of a monopoly (or innovation or bit of luck) in the form of capital gains. The firm's market value rises above the book value of actual investments made by the firm. Those who buy the stock later must pay the higher price, at which the firm's earnings will provide only the low normal rate of return. Therefore, the present returns on all shares tend down to normal levels, even if the firm continues to earn high rates of profit on its capital.

Internal efficiency.   Competitive pressure forces a firm to cut costs to the bone, in order to survive. But a highly profitable firm has elbow room, and some of its profits may be absorbed by a degree of slack, extra expenses, or other forms of X-inefficiency. The treadmill effect can restrict the X-inefficiency, but in a big, lucrative firm, it may take extraordinary efforts to keep costs down. X-inefficiency can arise wherever discretionary resources are large, either in private or public firms. Bureaucracy too is found in both private and public enterprises, as a common result of large size.

A3. Variety

Corporate life is highly diverse and changing. Two directions for this variety deserve special note.

Insiders and Outsiders.   At any time, there is a set of older leading firms with settled market positions and banking relationships. They form part of the "business establishment," or "corporate power structure." There is also a set of "outsiders," new entrepreneurs challenging the "old guard." The outsiders may start up direct competition or new entry against the established firms. Or the newcomers may try to capture old-line firms by take-overs. This healthy process of renewal and innovation is essential to a competitive system. Naturally this infusion of new blood will provoke resentment and exaggerated criticism, especially against the outsiders. Yet all firms were new "outsiders" once, and the outsiders which succeed will soon become part of the establishment. Good policies will avoid being manipulated by older interests in order to keep out the newcomers.

Industry Life-Cycles.   There are natural life-cycles for many products, firms, and industries. *Product* life-cycles are a standard concept in the business-management literature. *Firms* do not trace out rigid life-cycles, and yet the age and growth experience of a firm will often explain much of its current behavior. *Industry* life-cycles are of special interest, for they can closely affect the success of public policies. What works in treating a new formative industry may fail on an old, "mature" industry.

An industry commonly passes through four stages. First there is *birth*, when the technology is created and production becomes economic. Second,

2 the industry *grows rapidly,* spreading from a few elite customers down to mass production for the whole range of consumers. Third, the industry
3 *matures,* as the technology reaches its limits and demand grows slowly. This
4 phase is usually the longest one. Fourth and last, the industry *declines,* as other products and technologies displace it. The sequence varies from case to case, and some industries deviate sharply, but the basic process is common.

During stages 1 to 3, the industry often becomes less concentrated. Also, the industry usually becomes more fixed and resistant to policy actions as time passes. Preventive policies during stages 1 and 2 are easier and more effective than restorative actions in stage 3. Of course, each industry may depart from the sequence, and some industries are "reborn" several times. Most utilities trace out a clearer life-cycle than do the standard manufacturing and service industries (see Chapter 10). Knowing an industry's stage of life can often clarify its behavior and help to identify which policies will work best.

B. THE LARGER SETTING

Before turning to individual markets, we need a bird's-eye view of the whole setting. There are several key items: the role of corporations, trends in aggregate concentration, peaks in merger activity, and the spread of diversification.

B1. Types of Firms

Since 1890, the corporation has become the standard form of industrial enterprise. But other forms of business far outnumber it, and in some sectors they have a large share of sales. Many of your direct personal dealings (purchases, jobs, and so forth) are with retail proprietorships, rather than corporations. Still, corporations do the lion's share of economic activity.

B2. Levels and Trends in Aggregate Concentration

Though it means little for competition, aggregate concentration is an important fact about the economic system. One needs to know the share of the largest firms in the entire economy, as a rough measure of overall economic and social concentration. Several sticky technical problems make it hard to show aggregate concentration in one definitive index.[7] But the data used in Figure 2–3 are a starting point.

---

[7] The main problems are:

1. Which group of firms is included: the largest 50, 100, 250, 500, . . .? The largest 100 is the most frequently noted group, but the others are also plausible.

2. Are assets, sales, or employment the best unit for measuring size? Assets show the ability to deploy capital. Sales reflect the firms' scope in the nation's marketplaces. Employment reflects power over jobs and perhaps votes.

3. Should firms' foreign branches be included in their U.S. totals? The foreign operations are outside the United States. Yet they can affect the firms' overall economic power.

FIGURE 2–3

Trends in Aggregate U.S. Industrial Concentration since 1909.

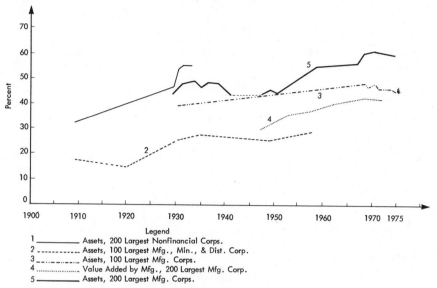

Legend

1 ————— Assets, 200 Largest Nonfinancial Corps.
2 ------------- Assets, 100 Largest Mfg., Min., & Dist. Corp.
3 –·–··–··– Assets, 100 Largest Mfg. Corps.
4 ·················· Value Added by Mfg., 200 Largest Mfg. Corp.
5 ————— Assets, 200 Largest Mfg. Corps.

Sources: Adapted from John M. Blair, *Economic Concentration* (New York: Harcourt, Brace, Jovanovich, 1972), chap. 4; and David W. Penn, "Aggregate Concentration: A Statistical Note," *Antitrust Bulletin* 21 (Spring 1976), pp. 91–98.

The share of the largest 100 firms in the manufacturing sector clearly is large, at about 47 percent of the total. This share has stabilized since 1965, after rising gradually but strongly for about 50 years.[8] Manufacturing is only about one third of the whole economy. Regrettably, no measure for the entire economy is available. One would have to lump together utilities, banks, insurance firms, and other diverse units, for which there is no best single measure of size.[9] Lacking exact comprehensive evidence, the consensus is that aggregate concentration is probably: *(a)* substantial, with the largest 100 firms holding perhaps 25 to 30 percent of all assets, and *(b)* stable, with no strong trend either up or down.

The large corporation does not dominate the economy, for the great mass of small and medium-size firms—up to, say, $100 million in sales—do most of the nation's business. And the truly "giant" firms are even more unusual

---

[8] These measures include the firms' foreign operations. It is not known whether those operations are a growing share of the firms' total activities. If they are, then the strictly domestic share of the largest firms might be declining.

[9] The assets of banks and insurance companies, for example, are portfolio values, not comparable to the largely physical assets held by industrial firms. One might instead use the stockholders' equity of financial firms, but that *understates* their true assets. Likewise, sales are not equally valid in comparing the economic power of retailing and heavy industrial firms. Since the raw numerical aggregates would be of dubious meaning, it is understandable that they are not found in the literature.

TABLE 2–2
The Largest U.S. Firms, Ranked by Sales in 1977 ($ in billions)

Company	Main Products	Sales	Assets
General Motors	Motor vehicles	$55	$27
Exxon	Oil and products	54	38
Ford Motor	Motor vehicles	38	19
AT&T	Telephone service	36	94
Mobil	Oil and products	32	21
Texaco	Oil and products	27	19
Sears, Roebuck	Retailing	22	23
Standard Oil (Calif.)	Oil and products	21	15
IBM	Computers	18	19
Gulf Oil	Oil and products	18	14
General Electric	Electrical goods	18	14
Chrysler	Motor vehicles	17	8
ITT	Diversified	17	20
Standard Oil (Ind.)	Oil and products	13	13
Safeway Stores	Groceries	11	3
Atlantic Richfield	Oil and products	11	11
Shell Oil	Oil and products	10	9
K Mart.....................	Retailing	10	2
U.S. Steel	Steel products	10	10
E.I. du Pont.................	Chemicals	9	7
JC Penney	Retailing	9	4
Continental Oil	Oil and products	9	7
General Tel. and Elect.	Communications	8	15
Tenneco	Diversified	7	8

Source: *Forbes* magazine, *The Forbes 500s* 121 (May 15, 1978), 201–85, and annual reports of the firms.

in the larger picture. The 25 largest U.S. firms include mainly: *(a)* AT&T, *(b)* the three automobile firms, *(c)* nine oil companies, and *(d)* several electrical-electronic conglomerates and retail chains (Table 2–2 shows these leading firms). They are a rather specialized group, not a normal model for the rest.

In most other countries, aggregate concentration is much higher. This befits the smaller size of most other nations (though concentration in all Western Europe together would be lower than in the United States). In Western Europe, concentration has been rising since 1955, rather than stabilizing. Also, the ties between banks and companies are tighter than in the United States, and so the fundamental degree of concentration is higher than it seems.

The array of large United States firms has become more stable in recent decades.[10] The turbulence of the late 19th century has gradually faded, and turnover among the largest firms has slowed. This reflects, among other factors, *(a)* less disparity in the growth rates of major industries, and *(b)* diversification, which enables firms to move into new industries. Conglomerate mergers and fluctuations in military spending have caused some sharp shifts

---

[10] This is made clear in Norman R. Collins and Lee E. Preston, "The Size Structure of the Largest Industrial Firms, 1909–1958," *American Economic Review* 51 (December 1961), 986–1011.

in the size distribution of firms. Yet for the rest there is a remarkable stability, which belies the common rhetoric about "business dynamism" and "slippery foot-holds at the corporate peak." Table 2–2 shows the patterns for the very largest firms. The contours of corporate capitalism are clear and steady to those who study them carefully.

Yet there are large risks and shocks for prices, profits, output, and stock values on the industrial scene.[11] The real world is a rugged place, and participants in it routinely accept high risks and, occasionally, large losses. Therefore public policy is not bound to avoid causing any risks or financial losses. Policies should not be capricious, of course, and impacts should be carefully weighed. But reasonable policy risks and impacts are quite natural and acceptable.

B3. Mergers

There have been three main waves of mergers as shown in Figure 2–4. They have added to the rises in aggregate concentration at the turn of the century, in the 1920s, and in the 1960s. The first wave created dominant firms in scores of industries, and some of these firms still loom large.[12] The second wave mainly combined *(a)* second-level firms, thereby tightening oligopoly structure in many markets, and *(b)* local utility firms into wider holding-company pyramids. The 1960s wave was mainly conglomerate mergers, uniting firms whose activities were not closely related. Even during the 1970s lull in mergers, there have been several thousand each year, a few of them very large indeed.

Take-overs have continued as an important route for new outsiders to gain access to established markets. In contrast to the common run of friendly mergers, a take-over is a seizure of a "target" firm by an "aggressor" firm. The aggressor expects to make the target firm more profitable, often by raising the quality of management. Among the fascinating technical issues (see Chapter 6) stands the basic fact: take-overs are a normal activity in the market for corporate power.

B4. Diversification

All sizable firms make more than one product, and some firms are exceedingly diverse. Most large firms operate in more than 10 separate industries,

---

[11] For example, during 1972–78, commodity prices tripled and then fell by 50 percent; oil, coffee, uranium, and gold prices rose more than fourfold; the U.S. stock market fell by half (wiping out $300 billion of stock values), then recovered the lost ground, and then fell again; new stock issues by small firms virtually ceased; sugar prices went from 10 cents/pound to 66 cents and then down to 9 cents; job lay-offs for some workers were severe.

[12] The reader should look through John Moody, *The Truth about the Trusts* (Chicago: Moody Publishing, 1904), for a detailed and sympathetic review of scores of the new trusts. More statistically complete is Ralph L. Nelson's excellent analysis, *Merger Movements in American Industry, 1895–1956* (Princeton: Princeton University Press, 1959).

FIGURE 2–4
Mergers in U.S. Mining and Manufacturing, 1895–1973

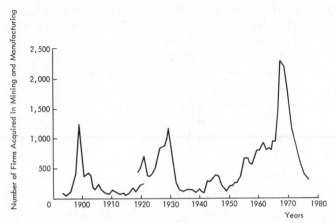

Sources: Data for 1895–1920, Ralph L. Nelson, *Merger Movements in American Industry, 1895–1956* (Princeton: Princeton University Press, 1959), Table B-7; for 1919–1940, Willard L. Thorp, "The Merger Movement," in *The Structure of Industry,* Temporary National Economic Committee, Monograph No. 27 (Washington, D.C.: U.S. Government Printing Office, 1941), Part III, pp. 231–34; for 1940 to the present, U.S. Cabinet Committee on Price Stability, *Studies by the Staff* (Washington, D.C.: U.S. Government Printing Office, 1969); and Federal Trade Commission, *Statistical Report on Mergers and Acquisitions* (Washington, D.C.: U.S. Government Printing Office, 1977).

some in more than 50 industries.[13] Diversified firms are not new (the East India Company in the 17th century was one), but they have recently gained in prominence. The "pure conglomerate" became highly visible in the 1960s. Often such firms have a good deal of common technology or other unity under the surface. The degree of diversification in U.S. industry has probably been rising in recent decades, but not sharply. It goes outside market edges, and so it may usually be irrelevant to competition within markets.

Yet "conglomerate power" may be a real phenomenon.[14] Diverse firms might be able to deploy resources strategically among their parts, in ways which create market power. The "cross-subsidizing" of predatory pricing has been said to be a danger, but so far it has scarcely ever been shown to have occurred. Whatever the actual effects, diversification is extensive and might need policy treatment (see especially Chapter 6 on mergers).

So-called multinational firms diversify across national borders as well as across product markets. They too have long been familiar; by 1929 there were over 187 U.S. multinational firms with over 470 foreign branches. Some large firms seem almost able to dominate some of the smaller countries in

[13] For further analysis, see Charles H. Berry, *Corporate Growth and Diversification* (Princeton: Princeton University Press, 1975).

[14] See Shepherd, *Industrial Organization,* chap. 19, and Scherer, *Industrial Market Structure,* chap. 11.

which they operate. Concern over this power has grown since 1960, often amid exaggerated estimates of the actual power.[15] Most large U.S. firms do have extensive foreign operations, and they are able to deploy resources among countries and to exert bargaining power. Analogous foreign branching into the U.S. economy has been much slighter and more recent. The main important foreign moves have been by imports into some industries (steel, autos, cameras), rather than by branching into production in the United States. Most multinationals, of whatever home base, are beyond antitrust or regulatory controls.

C. THE STRUCTURE OF INDUSTRY

Now we look at the degree of competition in individual markets. How much market power is there? What is its trend? Does it tend to last or to erode? Without a grasp of these conditions, one cannot evaluate the proper role of policies toward these markets.

C1. Elements of Structure

The first task is to define markets accurately. This is not easy, for most markets have shaded edges. In the few cases where cross-elasticities of demand can be measured, they show middle-range values, not sharp differences which define clear market edges.[16] Since good measures of cross-elasticities are rarely available, one must usually rely on "reasonable judgment" to decide whether good A is a close substitute for goods B, C, and D. This leaves room for debate over each market and over the degree of competition in the whole economy.

Still, experts do make judgments about markets and their structure. The consensus is roughly as follows. Market power reaches high levels in a sizable minority of industries. The most direct indicator is the **market share** of the leading firm. Market shares are near 100 percent in most "utility" sectors and are over 50 percent in a number of industrial and financial markets. Table 2–3 gives some of the known cases: secrecy hides many others, especially within diversified firms and in regional and local markets.

Concentration in the largest several firms is the next most accurate measure of market structure. It reflects the degree of oligopoly. The standard concentration ratio covers the four top firms; properly applied, it is a good all-round index. Ratios are published for the 436 separate manufacturing industries, as defined by the Census Bureau. About 200 of the ratios are seriously in error, because the Census defines the product or geographic scope of the

---

[15] See Raymond Vernon, *Sovereignty at Bay* (Cambridge: Harvard University Press, 1970) for a judicious review of the issues.

[16] If goods A and B have positive and high cross-elasticity of demand, then they are close substitutes and should be regarded as in the same market (see any good microeconomics textbook).

market wrongly.[17] Properly adjusted, these ratios do give a fairly clear picture. Table 2–3 shows some leading cases, and Figure 2–5 presents the contours for all manufacturing industries. The average degree of four-firm concentration—properly measured—is about 55 to 60 percent, which is a moderately tight oligopoly.[18] There is a wide dispersion around this average, but concentration below 20 percent is rare. Most lasting firms have some standing and identity in their markets. The policy lesson is clear: policies will mainly need to deal with high concentration, rather than attempt to press markets toward extremely low levels of concentration.

Barriers to entry are the third main element of structure.[19] They are like a wall, keeping potential competitors out of the industry. Barriers can arise from several sources: *(a)* A specific device (patent, ore rights, key location, and so forth) can exclude new competitors; *(b)* Product differentiation can make it difficult for new firms to force their way in; *(c)* If entry must be on a large scale, the large volume of capital may be hard for the entrant to raise. There may be other sources of barriers as well, but the uniform result is the same: a high entry barrier gives the established firms room to raise price without suffering new competition. High barriers breed high concentration and shared-monopoly pricing. Low barriers may set a lid on the monopoly effects, as new entrants move in quickly to beat down prices that go too high above costs.

Actual barriers range from very high to low, as Table 2–2 notes. They cannot be precisely measured, because the barriers factors are hard to estimate and to combine in a single index of "height." Still they do reinforce high market shares or concentration in a number of large markets. Many barriers

---

[17] See Shepherd, *Industrial Organization,* chaps. 9 and 10, for extended discussion of these issues.

Official concentration ratios published by the Census Bureau are based on national totals. But many industries have distinct regional and local markets within them, where true concentration is higher. Also the industry definitions tend to be too broad. Imports also need to be adjusted for in a few industries. The net effect is that official ratios seriously understate true concentration, probably by over 20 percent on average. Examples: newspapers are listed at 14 percent concentration, but are really near 100 percent in most markets. Bread, milk, bricks, ready-mix cement, and so on, are all similar. The ratios are available for 1935, 1947, 1954, 1958, 1963, 1967, and 1972. Data on less than four firms per industry are kept permanently secret by the U.S. Census. Other data on structure and financial ties are either not collected or are kept under strict secrecy. Figure 2–5 reflects adjustments to match the correct product and geographic conditions. For similar findings, see Carl Kaysen and Donald F. Turner, *Antitrust Policy* (Cambridge: Harvard University Press, 1959).

[18] This average concentration in individual markets is an entirely different concept, of course, from aggregate concentration in the whole economy. If you are in doubt on this point, review it carefully.

[19] The seminal discussion of them is Joe S. Bain, *Barriers to New Competition* (Cambridge: Harvard University Press, 1956). For another attempt to measure barriers, see H. Michael Mann, "Seller Concentration, Barriers to Entry, and Rates of Return in Thirty Industries, 1950–1960," *Review of Economics and Statistics,* 48 (August 1966), pp. 296–307.

TABLE 2–3
Leading Cases of Substantial Market Power

Industries (principal firms)	Approximate Shares of the Largest:		Height of Entry Barriers
	Firm	Four Firms	
Utilities			
Telephones (AT&T)	100	—	High
Electricity (local firms)	100	—	High
Gas (local firms)	100	—	High
Water and sewage (city units)	100	—	High
Urban transit (city units)	100	—	High
Manufacturing			
Computers (IBM)	60	85	High
Telephone equipment (Western Electric)	95+	100	High
Automobiles (GM, Ford)	50	85	High
Heavy electrical equipment (GE)	50	100	High
Drugs	(50)*	(90)	High
Photographic film (Eastern Kodak)	70	100	High
Copying equipment (Xerox)	70	95	Medium
Industrial chemicals (du Pont, Union Carbide)	45	80	Medium
Soaps and detergents (Procter & Gamble)	50	95	Medium
Aircraft and engines (GE, United Tech.)	50	100	High
Iron and steel (U.S. Steel, Bethlehem)	(35)	(70)	High
Petroleum refining (Exxon, Mobil, Texaco) ...	(35)	(70)	High
Cereals (Kellogg, General Mills)	45	95	High
Locomotives (GM)	75	100	High
Flavoring syrups (Coca-Cola)	50	90	Medium
Soup (Campbell Soup)	70	95	Medium
Others			
TV broadcasting (NBC, CBS, ABC).........	35	90	High
Newspapers (NY Times, LA Times)	40+	95	High
Banking			
San Francisco	44	83	High
New York	19	58	High
Chicago	19	49	High
Los Angeles	32	77	High

* Parentheses indicate an average of regional and product submarkets.
Sources: John M. Blair, *Economic Concentration* (New York: Harcourt Brace Jovanovich, 1972); W. G. Shepherd, *The Treatment of Market Power* (New York: Columbia University Press, 1975); and various other industry sources.

are actually created by public policies themselves (for example, patents and licensing laws), as we will see in later chapters.

Countervailing power (or monopsony power) is a fourth possible element of structure. A strong monopsonist buyer can keep oligopolist sellers from exerting market power, by playing them off against each other and by threatening to integrate vertically so as to produce for itself. Some cases of this are known (such as large buyers who neutralize some of the power of the leading tire companies), but the full range of countervailing power is unknown. It is not widespread, but it may limit a minority of tight oligopolies in some degree.

FIGURE 2–5

Concentration Patterns in U.S. Manufacturing Industries in 1972

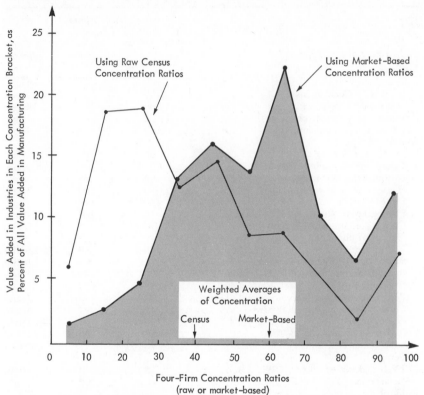

Source: U.S. Census Bureau, *Concentration Ratios in Manufacturing, 1972* (Washington, D.C.: U.S. Government Printing Office, 1975), as adjusted.

Altogether, perhaps 30 to 40 percent of U.S. industrial markets have extensive market power. Leading cases are shown in Tables 2–3 and 2–4. Various utilities are genuine monopolies. No clear estimate can be made for the rest of the economy. Retailing and services are usually highly competitive, though there is also a great deal of petty market power in small-scale local trades. In all, the monopoly problem is serious, though not rampant.

This structure is embedded in tissues of informal agreements and ties among competitors, which add to the effective degree of market power. These ties include trade associations and other forms of cooperation. They are especially hard to evaluate, but they are often strong.

Concentration in U.S. markets is probably about as high as is found abroad. Smaller countries might tend to have higher concentration because their small markets might have less room for efficient-sized firms. Yet import competition is also usually much greater into just those smaller nations. The net effect on concentration varies from country to country, but U.S. markets are not

TABLE 2–4

Leading U.S. Industrial Dominant Firms as of 1977, and Their Background

Sales Rank 1977	Firm	Principal Markets	Estimated Average Market Share (percent)	Entry Barriers	Average Rate of Return on Equity, 1970–77 (percent)	Present Position Dates Back to about
1	General Motors	Autos, locomotives, buses, trucks	50	High	19	1927
7	IBM	Computers, typewriters	60	High	19	1954
18	Western Electric	Telecom- munication equipment	95+	High	9	1880s
9	General Electric	Heavy electrical equipment	50	High	15	1900
20	Procter & Gamble	Detergents, toiletries	50	Medium	17	1940s
29	Eastman Kodak	Photographic supplies	55	Medium	20	1900
34	United Tech- nologies	Aircraft engines	50	High	12	1950s
39	Xerox	Copying equipment	70	Medium	20	1961
61	Coca-Cola	Flavoring syrups	50	Medium	19	1920s
143	Campbell Soup	Canned soups	70	Medium	13	1920s
157	Gillette	Razors, toiletries	60	Medium	19	1910
165	Kellogg	Dry cereals	45	High	22	1940s
219	Times Mirror . .	Newspaper	60	High	17	1960
385	New York Times	Newspaper	60	High	15	1966
	Various drug firms . .	Drugs	50–70	High	21	1950

Source: *Fortune, Directory of the Largest 500 Industrial Corporations,* yearly; Shepherd, *Treatment of Market Power;* and various other references.

sharply less concentrated than others. U.S. antitrust policy probably does keep informal ties lower than in most other countries.

C2. The Trend

The average degree of concentration in industry probably rose smartly during 1890–1904, in the 1930s, and during 1945–65. More recently the average seems to have stabilized. Behind the average lie some offsetting rises and declines in individual sectors. The trend in the rest of the economy is virtually unknown, but there has probably not been a marked change. In

Founders of Four Firms with High Market Shares

Courtesy of Culver Pictures

*Courtesy of Eleutherian Mills
Historical Library*

John D. Rockefeller (1839–1937) founded the Standard Oil monopoly during 1870–80 by a variety of pricing tactics, railroad debates, and astute buying out of competitors. By 1900 he had retired from direct management and moved into other financial activities. These developed into parity with the Morgan group. (Shown about 1910).

Pierre S. du Pont (1870–1954), a pivotal figure in modern industrial organization. He developed du Pont's gunpowder monopoly and then negotiated a mild divestiture in 1911–13. During 1915–25 he guided General Motors' rise to dominance in the automobile industry. (Shown 1902.)

*Courtesy of Eastman Kodak
Company*

Courtesy of Wide World Photos

George Eastman (1854–1932) founded Eastman Kodak Company in 1892, which dominated the industry by its celluloid film and convenient small cameras. Brilliant, urbane, solitary, and meticulous, he introduced profit-sharing and set high standards while establishing the firm's leading position. He is shown in 1890, already the leader in his industry.

Thomas J. Watson (1874–1956) established International Business Machines as the dominant tabulating-machine firm by 1930. In the early 1950's, his sons overcame his opposition to IBM's shift into electronic computers. (Shown in 1951.)

Western Europe and Japan, the averages have risen since 1960 or so, from a number of causes (including government policies, technical change, and growth rates).

C3. Erosion of Structure

Market power might fade away naturally, either by voluntary choices or under fierce competitive inroads. If so, high market shares and concentration would be self-curing, and policy action might not be needed. If not, policy treatments may be urgently in order. The point is crucial. Your view on it will shape your whole outlook on monopoly and the need for policy steps.

In fact, a moderate process of erosion does appear to operate.[20] Market shares above 50 percent probably tend to decline by as much as one point per year (for example, from 80 to 60 in perhaps 20 years). The decline is usually sharper for producer goods than consumer goods (where advertising helps maintain market share). A high and lucrative market share will normally last only a decade or two at most. Yet some of the leading dominant firms in the United States stand out as exceptions. Most of those in Table 2–4 have held their positions for decades, some even since 1900. The natural rate of decline of such firms was much more rapid during the 1910–35 period. This rising stability of the leading dominant firms accords with the rising stability of the whole distribution of large firms (noted in Section B2). Abroad, the dominant positions are often much less secure than these American ones. In short, high concentration in the United States is a serious problem, some of which is not self-correcting.

D. ECONOMIES OF SCALE

The concentration might merely reflect the economies of scale, as has been debated since before 1900. We need to review how important such economies are, for they may make concentration necessary. The social benefits of the economies might outweigh the social costs of the market power.

First we must define economies carefully. *Economies of scale in production* are the most basic possible factor. They arise both within the *plant* and at the *firm*—that is, multiplant—level. They reflect *(a)* the technology at the factory floor, *(b)* transport costs (if high, they inhibit centralizing in one big plant), and *(c)* problems in coordinating multiplant operations. Scale economies may be either technical or pecuniary. *Technical* economies are real, arising from the actual organization of production in the firm. *Pecuniary* economies are strictly monetary, stemming merely from obtaining lower prices on inputs. Only technical economies count as a social justification for market power.

---

[20] See W. G. Shepherd, *The Treatment of Market Power* (New York: Columbia University Press, 1975), chap. 4, for a review of this process. The rest of this section draws on that source.

FIGURE 2–6

The Common Shape of Costs, with Minimum Efficient Scale at a Low Market Share

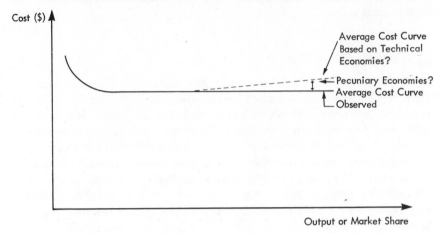

The present research consensus is that technical economies of scale are real but, in most industries, limited to rather small market shares.[21] As illustrated in Figure 2–6, minimum efficient scale (MES) is usually reached at a 2 or 3 percent market share in most industries. Moreover, at lower sizes the cost gradient is usually not steep. Above MES, costs may be flat for a range, although diseconomies may set in quickly.

Large firms now commonly expand not by enlarging old plants but by building new ones, and the newer plants are not built on an ever-larger scale. Indeed, there is a trend toward smaller size. In many fields, new developments in technology appear to make for operation on a smaller scale. Transport by truck and the ability to transmit electricity over long distances permit decentralization. So does the spread of computer controls.

There are new materials, such as the light metals, alloys, and plastics, and new processes, such as molding, welding, stamping, and die-casting. They require less heavy machinery than did the older materials and processes. Light, multipurpose machines—independently operated, readily transferred from product to product and moved from place to place, run at varying speeds and turned on an off at will—displace the massive, rigid installations of an earlier day. The growth of technology, in the past, made for greater size. In many cases, now, it works the other way. In nearly all industries, plants with less than 1 or 2 percent of the market are quite as efficient as larger ones, and often they are more efficient.

At the level of the firm as a whole, the evidence is less one-sided. Both Bain and Scherer have found "multiplant economies"—the advantages of

---

[21] Leading studies include Bain, *Barriers,* and F. M. Scherer and others, *The Economics of Multiplant Operation* (Cambridge: Harvard University Press, 1975). For a "Chicago School" counterview, see John S. McGee, *In Defense of Industrial Concentration* (New York: Praeger, 1971).

running many plants as a group—to be slight or absent in most cases. There are obvious bureaucratic problems in managing large firms, as layers of authority and coordination pile up above the basic plant operations. Still, modern techniques and a computer may make close controls possible. And there may be economies in other company activities.

Economies of scale in innovation might favor high market shares. Technical progress usually involves three basic steps: *invention* (the new idea), *innovation* (the first practical application), and *imitation* by other firms. An intense debate in the 1950s first suggested that large firms generally, and oligopoly in particular, are more innovative.[22] But research in the 1960s has reversed the burden of proof. Small scale and independent conditions appear to be best for *invention*.[23] And though some *innovations* have required massive resources, many can instead be financed from outside by small firms. Also, market shares above about 20 percent tend to retard innovation. Dominant firms commonly have incentives to follow and *imitate* the innovations of others, not to lead.[24] And this is borne out by practical experience.[25] In any case, only a narrow set of industries have a high degree of innovation (aerospace, drugs, and so forth), and so the issue is specialized. Moreover, public grants pay for much of the cost of innovation in most of those industries, and so the underlying economic factors are not clear.

Advertising may also provide economies of scale, as national advertising is spread over high sales volume. Yet much advertising is merely persuasive, not informative, and so that part has little or no social value. And advertising is a large factor in only a small group of industries (toiletries, cereals, drugs, beer, cigarettes).[26] Presently, proven multiplant economies are slight in most industries; Figure 2–7 illustrates this common pattern. But there may be exceptions.

---

[22] Recall Schumpeter's view from Chapter 1; and see J. K. Galbraith, *American Capitalism* (New York: Houghton Mifflin, 1956). The 1950s flowering of discussion was not the first; earlier versions were in vogue in the 1890s and 1920s.

[23] A theoretical basis for this is given in Kenneth J. Arrow, "Economic Welfare and the Allocation of Resources for Invention," in *The Rate and Direction of Inventive Activity,* National Bureau of Economic Research (Princeton, N.J.: Princeton University Press, 1962). A persuasive review of practical instances is in J. Jewkes, R. Sawers, and R. Stillerman, *The Sources of Invention,* rev. ed. (New York: St. Martin's Press, 1968).

[24] For a technical analysis, see F. M. Scherer, "Research and Development Resource Allocation under Rivalry," *Quarterly Journal of Economics,* 1967, pp. 359–94.

[25] See Edwin Mansfield et al., *Industrial Research and Technological Innovation* (New York: Norton, 1973); and F. M. Scherer, *Industrial Market Structure,* chap. 15. There is room for debate. A "Chicago School" view is that good performance and innovation tend to cause the high concentration, as successful firms come to dominate their markets. See Shepherd, *Industrial Organization,* chaps. 12, 13, and 21.

[26] For fuller analysis, see William S. Comanor and Thomas Wilson, *Advertising and Market Power* (Cambridge: Harvard University Press, 1975); for a counterview, see Jules Backman, *Advertising and Competition* (New York: New York University Press, 1967).

48

FIGURE 2–7

The Common Shape of Average Costs for the Firm (including Both Plant and Multiplant Conditions)

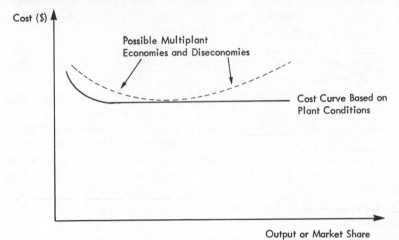

To Sum Up. All of these factors provide little or no social justification for more than a scattering of market shares above 15 percent in industry, trade, and banking. Nor do they justify high barriers to entry in most industries. In smaller economies abroad, a slightly higher degree of market power may be justified.[27] Research on these determinants is still in progress, but its findings so far place the burden of proof against the market power. The old cult of bigness is now reduced to faith, for the facts do not broadly sustain it.

E. EFFECTS OF MARKET POWER

The effects were stated broadly in Chapter 1. Now they will be analyzed in some detail.[28] These effects define the yields for public policies; if market power had no effects, policies to treat it could have no positive social yields.

E1. Behavior

Three main classes of monopoly behavior—collusion, price discrimination, and exclusion—emerge as market power arises. Here we merely outline them; see Chapters 7 and 8 for more detail.

[27] There has been good research on this. See Joe S. Bain, *International Differences in Industrial Structure* (New Haven: Yale University Press, 1965); C. F. Pratten, *Economies of Scale in Manufacturing Industries* (Cambridge: Cambridge University Press, 1971); and Scherer, *Economics*.

[28] On the details and research methods, see Shepherd, *Industrial Organization*, chaps. 14, 21, 22, and 23.

Collusion includes price fixing, market sharing, profit pooling, and other devices. All competitors have mixed motives to collude and to compete. Tight structure can let collusive motives prevail. Generally, successful collusion requires: *(a)* a short time lag in discovering price cutters, and *(b)* effective penalties to inflict on them. Actual conditions vary, and so actual collusion displays all manner of ingenious devices. Cooperation ranges from unstable, weak agreements up to official cartels with comprehensive, legally enforced controls over their members' prices, outputs, and profits. Most common in the United States is the price-fixing agreement with some penalties (explicit or implicit) against "cheaters."

Price discrimination occurs when the seller sets varying price-cost ratios to different customer groups. It can be procompetitive, if done sporadically by firms with small shares. At the other extreme, it is anticompetitive when done systematically and rigidly by a dominant firm. Tight structure opens up a wide scope for discrimination, which both *(a)* extracts monopoly profit, and *(b)* helps to maintain or increase market power.

Exclusion of competition can be done by many tactics. Exclusive contracts or refusals to deal are one category. Vertical restrictions on retailers' sales are another. Tight structure makes these and other devices more effective.

In short, tight structure influences behavior, by unleashing a range of actions which competition otherwise holds tightly in check. The influence is not microscopically exact. As always, human behavior has much variety around the norm. Competitive behavior can break out even in very tight structures. Yet the basic pattern is clear: tight structure normally breeds anticompetitive behavior, in the form of collusion, price discrimination, and exclusion. In turn, the market's performance is affected.

E2. Financial Effects

Two key financial variables—price and profit—are altered. **Prices** are raised above costs. The effect can be very sharp, in some cases multiplying the price to 5, 10, or 20 times cost, or even higher. Pure monopoly gives the highest rises, but even loose cartels such as OPEC (the Arab oil countries) can have spectacular effects. Thus, OPEC is an imperfect cartel, but its effect is colossal; the price of oil was multiplied more than five times in 1973–74, and over $50 billion per year in monopoly profit is flowing to OPEC members. Across the range of more normal markets, the average effect of tight structure is probably about a 15 to 30 percent rise in price, but there is wide variation.[29] New competition in tight markets has frequently caused price levels to fall by 30 to 50 percent.

Price discrimination also emerges sharply under tight structure, especially as the leading firm's market share goes over 50 percent. Price-cost ratios

---

[29] The issue is warmly debated, but this consensus is firm; see Shepherd, *Industrial Organization,* chap. 14.

FIGURE 2–8

How the Elements of Structure Appear to Relate to Profitability

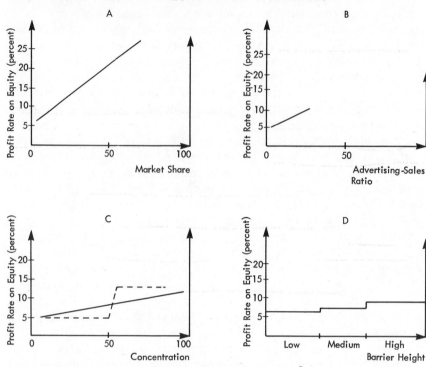

Source: Shepherd, *Treatment of Market Power*, chap. 4.

for customers with inelastic demand have been multiples of those for custom-ers with elastic demand (that is, who have competitive alternatives).

Profitability is increased by market power. The effect is outlined in Figure 2–8, with a separate part for each main element of structure. For each 10 points of market share, the profit rate usually rises about 2.5 points. This reaches about a 20 percent rate of return for market shares of 50 percent, and at 70 percent of the market, a typical firm's profits may reach 25 percent of the firm's capital, nearly triple the competitive rate.[30] This actual profit yield is lower than it could be, because X-inefficiency usually absorbs some profits. Concentration is also related to profit rates, but of course more loosely. Each ten added points of concentration goes with about one extra point of profit rate. Some researchers report a stair-step rise at about 50 percent concen-tration (shown by the dashed line in Figure 2–8C). In any case, concentration is related to higher levels of price and profit.

Intensive advertising seems to yield higher profitability. Yet advertising's

---

[30] See also Robert D. Buzzell, Bradley T. Gale, and Ralph G. M. Sultan, "Market Share—A Key to Profitability," *Harvard Business Review* 53 (January–February 1975), pp. 97–106.

punch is limited, as Figure 2–8C shows. Even at extreme levels of advertising intensity (20 percent of sales) the rate of return is not much higher than the competitive rate. Therefore advertising is a lesser influence on profits than is market share.[31]

More generally, entry barriers do not seem to be central elements of market structure. They matter somewhat, but they are weaker than market share itself (see Figure 2–8D). High barriers typically add only about two points to the profit rate.

These effects confirm the central role of market share. It is the key to excess profits, and so businessmen are sound in focusing their efforts on it. Wise public policy will deal primarily and precisely with market shares, rather than trying only to control concentration or entry barriers. There will be exceptions to this, of course, where a specific barrier is clearly important, owing to a key patent or mineral right, for example. But these are departures from the rule.

To some extent these profit yields might reflect economies of scale, as was discussed in an earlier section. But as we have seen in the section on economies of scale, these economies usually are relatively slight. In another vein, there might be a "risk" justification for the higher profits. But this has not been borne out by objective research.[32]

E3. Real Effects

Market power also reduces efficiency. A degree of internal inefficiency usually emerges in secure firms, reaching perhaps 3 to 5 percent of costs on average when market shares reach 70 percent. Allocative inefficiency also occurs (the triangle in Figure 1–3), but it is diffuse and has proven difficult to measure. These two types of loss, plus the share of advertising which is merely persuasive, probably total to about 3 percent of national income.[33]

---

[31] Also, only a few industries have intensive advertising. In recent years the highest advertising-sales ratios were: perfumes 15 percent, cereals 10 percent, drugs 10 percent, soaps 9 percent, beer 7 percent, pop 6 percent, clocks 6 percent, wines and cigarettes 5 percent. All others are less.

[32] Higher profits might be socially justified as a premium for greater risk. Capital theory and portfolio analysis have both suggested this for a long time. (See F. M. Knight's classic, *Risk, Uncertainty, and Profit* [New York: Houghton Mifflin, 1921].) Some industries *are* much riskier; that is one reason why managerial styles are so diverse (recall the first section).

The hypothesis of a positive general risk-return relationship has been tested in several ways, but so far with little success. These include I. N. Fisher and G. F. Hall, Jr., "Risk and Corporate Rates of Return," *Quarterly Journal of Economics,* 1969, pp. 79–92; and Shepherd, *Treatment of Market Power,* chap. 4. Risk is inevitably hard to measure, but several reasonably good indexes of it show little or no association with company rates of return. And in large stretches of industry—and on the over-the-counter stock market—returns are clearly *lower* where risk is *higher.* The risk-return hypothesis therefore does not dilute the observed link between market power and profit rates.

[33] On these estimated losses, see Scherer, *Industrial Market Structure,* chap. 17, and Shepherd, *Industrial Organization,* chap. 21 and 22.

Technical progress is also probably retarded in dominant firms. Research suggests that innovation is fastest in firms with modest market shares. At high market shares, the firm slips more into an imitator's role. We do not know this precisely, for innovation eludes easy measurement. Also, federal research payments have affected it artificially.

E4. Equity

The effect on *equity* arises from the profit effects shown in Figure 2–6. The flows capitalize directly into wealth and can be realized immediately. The whole impact is large and has shaped wealth and social status, especially since 1890–1910. These excess returns are no longer available direct to new investors nowadays. The market power was capitalized when it arose, often decades ago.

And as structure has stabilized in recent decades, the structure of wealth also has hardened. Most of this family wealth has long since been detached from its original monopoly sources. And many heirs have had favored access to positions in financial firms. Therefore, the older equity effects are deeply set and immune to action toward the markets themselves. Fairness in employment opportunity has also been lessened. Most minority groups and women appear to face job discrimination at managerial levels in most firms holding market power.[34]

Altogether, the marginal social costs of market power are high. As a firm's market share goes above 20 percent, the social costs begin to accumulate. For monopolists, the costs are usually large. They may be offset in unusual cases, where technical scale economies, the conditions of innovation, or managerial skill depart from the norm. But the basic patterns hold.[35]

---

[34] This is increasingly clear both from research and from a series of cases and settlements involving job discrimination in a large number of the largest corporations. See also W. G. Shepherd and Sharon G. Levin, "Managerial Discrimination in Large Firms," *Review of Economics and Statistics,* November 1973, and W. G. Shepherd, "Market Power and Racial Discrimination in White-Collar Employment," *Antitrust Bulletin* 14 (Spring 1969), pp. 141–61.

On the wealth effect, see William S. Comanor and Robert H. Smiley, "Monopoly and the Distribution of Wealth," *Quarterly Journal of Economics,* 89 (May 1975), pp. 177–94.

[35] Consider, finally, whether the system is some degree of "monopoly capitalism" in the Marxian sense. The answer is both yes and no.

Some perceptive observers have long regarded the U.S. economy as dominated by powerful firms under a financial plutocracy. In these views, capitalists control power and wealth, while workers barely subsist because a reserve army of unemployed keeps wages down. Monopoly rises. Depressions grow more severe, and the disparity increases between the moneyed few and the propertyless many. The economy is driven toward militarism, and the nation attempts to dominate and exploit underdeveloped lands abroad. In short, there is Monopoly Capitalism and Imperialism.

In fact, market power is serious—much more serious than is commonly recognized—but it is not pervasive. There is a gentle trend toward greater aggregate concentration, but the economy is still in more than a few hands. High finance does exert some control. Wealth holdings are highly skewed and the disparities are not narrowing,

F. SUMMARY

In this chapter we have analyzed the firm, its setting, and its motives. The common life-cycle of industries was described. Next we reviewed the role of large firms, as it has evolved and stabilized. Aggregate concentration was shown to be fairly great and increasingly stable.

The rest of the chapter was about individual markets. High degrees of market power—of excess market power—do exist in an important group of industries, utilities, and financial markets. Yet economies of scale require much less concentration than this. The problem is chronic. Some leading cases now appear to be nearly immune from the normal decay of market shares. Such market power has a sizable social cost, in inefficiency, retarded innovation, and inequity.

There is thus a serious problem for policy to resolve, in many parts of the economy. The need is to protect or increase competition in tight markets, not to pursue extreme "perfect" competition. The needs are practical and sensible, not idealistic or farfetched. Market power's forms, causes, and effects are reasonably well understood. The problem is manageable and important.

QUESTIONS FOR REVIEW

1. "Managers are supervised by their Board of Directors, by their bankers, and by the stock market generally." True?
2. "By maximizing long-run profits, managers maximize the firm's present value." True?
3. "The stock market helps to enforce efficient business management." True?
4. "There is a clear life-cycle which every industry traces out." True?
5. Aggregate concentration is measured by (a) sales, (b) assets, (c) leverage, (d) employees, (e) none of these. Which?
6. "Corporations do only 20 to 25 percent of the economy's business." True?
7. "The rise in aggregate concentration has been caused entirely by mergers." True?
8. To measure market power, one must consider (a) market shares, (b) profit per worker, (c) entry barriers, (d) concentration, (e) growth rate. Which?
9. "Once concentration occurs, it stays for good." True?

on the whole. It is possible to go from poor to rich, but not easy or common. Fluctuations now are milder than depressions, but they are not small. And there is now chronic underemployment, especially among a "reserve army" of unskilled minority groups and women. The degree of reliance on military spending and exploitation of foreign resources may not be full-blown imperialism, but (especially in the 1960s) some element of it has existed. And the political process ("the State") is swayed by financial and industrial interests, of the upper middle classes generally.

In these matters, one can select out facts for almost any viewpoint. But many conditions of monopoly capitalism are present in some degree. Some of them can be abated by public policies; some of them feed upon policies.

10. "Plant-level economies usually justify a high market share." True?
11. "As concentration rises, prices tend to be higher and more discriminatory." True?
12. If true concentration can't be precisely measured, does that make it less important?
13. Why are imports a factor which would affect concentration ratios in the United States less than those in other countries?
14. How could aggregate concentration rise if average concentration in markets is constant?
15. Why might the natural rate of erosion of market shares have declined since 1930 or so?
16. If managers were free from outside control, would that affect the behavior and performance of their companies?

APPENDIX: MARKETS ILLUSTRATING MARKET POWER AND COMPETITION

This selection of "leading" industries is meant to help the reader learn to judge real markets, fitting the parts together.[36] The selection includes five leading cases of market power, where competition is limited, plus two cases of effective competition.

Telephones.[37] American Telephone and Telegraph Company (AT&T). Holding company for the Bell System (see Chapter 3), has owned, supplied, and operated the main telephone system in the United States since the 1880s. It is the largest private firm in existence, with over 1 million employees and nearly $90 billion in assets. It is also the largest monopoly. Formed soon after Bell patented the telephone in 1876, it adroitly used the Bell patent to gain dominance. By 1910 it covered most cities and all long-distance traffic in the United States. Its Western Electric Co. subsidiary has supplied virtually all Bell System equipment and materials since 1881. In 1913, AT&T agreed to stay out of telegraph activities and interconnect with smaller systems, as part of an agreement letting it retain Western Electric as its exclusive supplier. The Federal Communications Commission was created in 1937 with power to regulate interstate telephone operations. In 1948–50, the Bell System gained exclusive control of microwave transmission, which carries much intercity traffic.

Bell's share of telephones has tapered down to 80 percent, because some suburban growth has been in independent company areas. But the hold on large cities and all trunk traffic remains. FCC rulings since 1968 are leading to a degree of competition in data transmission and customers' equipment. AT&T has responded by demanding control of the entire sector. Its basic monopoly position in operations and supply of apparatus remains. The rate

[36] For a wide range of excellent case studies of individual industries, the student should consult Walter Adams, ed., *The Structure of American Industry*, 5th ed. (New York: Macmillan, 1977).

[37] See Chapter 13 for more detail and sources.

of return, regulated by the FCC and state commissions (see Part III), is about 10 to 12 percent on equity. Rate structure has been only loosely regulated. Bell Laboratories has a notable research record. Certain research, construction, and operations are done for the U.S. military (at about $200–300 million yearly). The Bell System draws political influence from its size and operations in nearly all locales. Also, its stock is held by nearly 3 million citizens and most large institutional investors.

Computers.[38]   International Business Machines Corporation (IBM) is the leading firm. Formed in the 1920s, it has sold 90 percent of tabulating equipment and, since 1953, about 60 to 70 percent of computers (plus a comparable share of electric typewriters). Its share in most foreign markets is nearly as high, and it generates much of the firm's total profits. Now the fifth largest U.S. industrial firm in assets, it has assets of $18 billion and 310,000 employees. It capitalized market value, however, has recently been over $40 billion, well ahead of the next firms. This reflects its steady profit rate of 18 to 20 percent on equity and its strong future prospects.

IBM has cultivated a high technical reputation, but it is said by many industry experts to be imitative rather than the leader. IBM has not been able to keep up with Control Data and Amdahl in the large computer end of the market. Successive computer generations (the third IBM generation was the 360 line, introduced in 1964) have raised computing speed and capacity by orders of magnitude. Founded by T. J. Watson (his ubiquitous THINK motto and company pep songs were famous), it was run by his sons Thomas, Jr., and Arthur during 1954–72.

Competitors have been numerous, but many have failed (for example, General Electric and RCA exited in 1969–70, and Xerox in 1972, after incurring large losses). Presently the next largest firm has only 8 percent of the market, and several are still unprofitable. IBM has been sued for monopolizing by the Department of Justice in 1932, 1952, and 1969 (the latter case is in mid-trial in 1978), and by many private firms since 1967. Its position, reinforced by a superb sales network and a thorough system of price discrimination, still appears to be secure.

Pharmaceutical Products.[39]   Numerous firms, including American Home Products, Warner-Lambert, Bristol-Myers, Pfizer, Merck, Eli Lilly, Sterling, and Upjohn are prominent. The drug industry is a mosaic of submarkets, with varying degrees of competitiveness. Several major submarkets are virtual monopolies, based on patents. The industry has arisen mainly since the 1930s,

---

[38] Sources include Gerald S. Brock, *The U.S. Computer Industry* (Cambridge: Ballinger, 1975), and, for a mass of detail and issues, Subcommittee on Antitrust and Monopoly, *The Computer Industry,* Part 7 of *Hearings on the Industrial Reorganization Act,* U.S. Senate, 93d Cong., 2d sess. (Washington, D.C.: U.S. Government Printing Office, 1974).

[39] For contrasting views of this industry, see Milton Silverman and Philip R. Lee, *Pills, Profits, and Politics* (Berkeley: University of California Press, 1974), and David Schwartzman, *Innovation in the Pharmaceutical Industry* (Baltimore: Johns Hopkins University Press, 1976).

led by penicillin and then other "wonder" drugs, including antibiotics and contraceptives. There is much research and product development, aimed at finding patentable new drugs and modifications of old ones. Since 1960, the rate of actual discovery and innovation in the industry has declined. Patents are fully exploited, and the profit rate on equity is over 20 percent for most firms. Production cost is often one tenth or less of the price of a drug. Price discrimination is extensive, and the sales forces are large. The industry's social impact is greater than its size alone suggests.

Automobiles. General Motors Corporation (GM) has been the leading U.S. automobile, bus, and locomotive producer for five decades. Its sales are $50 billion, assets $25 billion, and employees 750,000. Formed in 1910–15 and under Pierre du Pont's leadership during 1918–24, it gained over half the U.S. car market by 1927 and has held it since.[40] It now has about 50 percent of new-car sales revenue in the United States (over 70 percent of luxury-class cars), over 50 percent of bus sales, and over 80 percent of locomotives. During the 1920s, it established frequent model changes as the industry practice.

GM has five car-producing divisions—Chevrolet (much the largest; itself equal to Ford Motor Company's car production), Pontiac, Buick, Oldsmobile, and Cadillac. Operating more than 22 major plants in many states, its traditional method of decentralizing management was partially reversed in 1969. Much larger than most estimates of minimum efficient scale, it has extensive overseas operations. Its profit rates on equity have averaged 18 to 20 percent in recent years.

Copying Equipment. Xerox Corporation's dominant position is based on the patented selenium drum technology and a marketing strategy much like IBM's. The basic technology, originated by Chester Carlson in the 1930s and 1940s, was finally applied by the small Haloid-Xerox company in the late 1940s and 1950s. Since 1961 Xerox has gained phenomenal growth and over 85 percent of the market, in the United States and abroad (for example, 95 percent in Britain). Sales are now $5 billion yearly, employees 104,000, and profit rates on equity have averaged over 20 percent since 1961.

Xerox machines are almost exclusively rented, not sold, as part of a brilliant strategy of promotion and price discrimination. Around the basic patent the firm has accumulated nearly 2,000 interrelated patents to secure and extend its position. Recent entry by IBM, Eastman Kodak, and Savin has dented Xerox's position, but the long-term effects are not yet clear. A major FTC action against Xerox was started in 1973 but settled in 1975 with moderate provisions to give rivals access to patents.

Restaurants. This industry is honeycombed with submarkets, including (a) "fast-food" service and (b) traditional restaurants of many kinds. Most

---

[40] This is covered in the excellent volume by A. D. Chandler, Jr., and S. Salsbury, *Pierre S. du Pont and the Making of the Modern Corporation* (New York: Harper & Row, 1971). See also Lawrence J. White, *The Automobile Industry since 1945* (Cambridge: Harvard University Press, 1971).

of these submarkets are highly competitive, and no one firm dominates. The fast-food part has boomed since 1960, with McDonald's, Kentucky Fried Chicken, Burger King, and Dairy Queen in the lead. If one defines submarkets strictly (for example, hamburger, fried chicken, and pizza stores as separate submarkets), then some market shares are fairly high. But the true market probably includes all of these parts, and so McDonald's has no more than 20 percent of sales, Kentucky Fried 8 percent, Burger King only 5 percent, and so on. Entry is still easy for local shops and small chains.

Therefore the industry is still highly competitive. The chains have innovated strongly and enforced higher levels of efficiency throughout most of the sector. Some of them have had high profits, but these have faded as the industry has matured in the 1970s. In short, the market exemplifies a stable competitive structure, with some dominance present but held in check and channeled toward efficiency and innovation.

Clothing. Similarly, the clothing industry is composed of many parts (men's, women's, children's; suits, shirts, underwear; and so on). Some firms hold established positions in some submarkets (such as Pendleton's in woolens, and Levi Strauss in jeans), but the majority of the trade is a highly competitive loose oligopoly. Production and pricing are responsive to changing styles. Some brand names do gain higher price-cost margins, but these are exceptions and consumers generally have a wide range of choice. Imitation of styles is quick. The retailing side is fragmented and highly competitive. It does not impose monopsony power, but it assures relatively easy access to outlets for new producers.

The industry has matured to a flexible competitive structure, which permits some pockets of market power but keeps them under pressure.

These cases illustrate the sharp contrast between a tight structure with monopoly or dominant firms and a loose structure with continuing striving by many more-or-less equal competitors. The one is unbalanced, closed, and often rigid, tending toward monopoly or shared-monopoly results. The other is balanced, open, flexible, and efficient in performance.

chapter 3

Policy Choices and Biases

Policies are formalized in law: in legal prose, powers, and public agencies. Yet their essence is economic. And they are applied by people, working under strong pressures from real interest groups. The social aim (or hope) is to get good economic results even under the stresses of the rugged political process. This chapter trains you to define "good" policies and to anticipate the ways that the political process may distort real policies.

"Optimal" policies can be defined, by comparing the costs of policy actions with their benefits. The general rule is: extend each policy action until its marginal social benefits just cover its marginal social costs. In common sense terms: take actions that are "worth it." The rule applies equally well to antitrust, regulation, public enterprise, and other policy tools. Rather than divide sectors into separate policy areas, we can approach them all on a common economic basis. We want to define the good economic effects that policies should have and then compare them with the economic effects which actual policies have. Where divergences are large, we then consider what better policies might be tried.

First we review some basic facts about policies (Section A). Then we present the concept of "optimal policy," as a set of choices by public agencies (Section B). Private firms also are optimizing their choices, in ways which influence policies (Section C). On both sides, there may be factors which bias the outcome away from the optimum (Section D). There is an imperfect political setting for policies, which also affects the outcomes (Section E). Certain features of the executive, legislative, and judicial branches also influence industrial policies (Section F). Finally, the main points are summed up in Section G.

A. BASIC CONDITIONS OF POLICIES

A1. Resources

Each public agency has certain **tools**, of two sorts: *(a)* resources (such as budget, staff) and *(b)* legal powers. Each agency also has certain **tasks,** which are defined by *(c)* its area of coverage (or "jurisdiction"), and *(d)* the severity of the problems to be treated. For an agency to be effective, these four must be in balance. A large jurisdiction, embracing severe problems, requires abundant resources and/or powers. Resources and powers are often substitutable in some degree. For example, with wider powers (for example, to have final power of decision), and agency may need fewer resources (for example, skilled lawyers to persuade an outside court). An agency with large problems and small tools will usually be ineffective; indeed, it will also stand in the way of other effective treatments. At the same time, however, resources and powers can be wasted if an agency is inefficiently operated (for example, makes the wrong internal choices and develops internal bureaucratic slack).

The policy resources are of several main kinds. **Public supervision.** The most basic resource of all is the scarce ability of the political process to evaluate and to exert control in the public interest. Information is costly, and the ability of citizens to acquire it, weigh it, and act upon it has high opportunity costs. The social control process, such as it may be, is of course the only one we have. It needs to be used sparingly, in ways which fit its strengths. **Staff talent** ranges from high orders of creative professional and strategic skills down to routine clerks and typists. Some of these people are entrepreneurs managing public enterprises; others are financiers, or civil servants, lawyers, engineers, theorists, economists, jurists, and technicians. This pool of talent also is limited. **Public funds** are also of several sorts. Most obvious are the *budget levels* of expenditure; $27 million for the Antitrust Division, $1.4 billion in postal subsidies, and so on. Another cost is *tax abatement* to specific groups. Less obvious but equally real is the *public* absorption of *private* risks, such as loan guarantees to house buyers, international firms, and farmers. These latter two costs are as real as the direct spending of public funds.

Certain other control devices do not entail costs in quite the same sense. Legal powers of compulsion—such as eminent domain to condemn land, or simply the powers contained in the Sherman Antitrust Act—can simply be written into law, at relatively little direct cost. The courts and, ultimately, the armed forces enforce these, though they usually are not required to act to do so.

These resources help to define the policies. There are also other surface dimensions of policy, such as the supposed severity of the constraints as claimed in formal rules, and the asserted degree of public benefits. These are often trivial or deceptive. One needs instead to dig deeper and analyze the real properties of policies. The supposed intent of a policy can be irrelevant to its nature and effects.

The proper focus of analysis is the *net* change caused by any policy, compared with inaction or with specific other actions. Often the status quo would change if left alone, so that what looks like a drastic policy action will in fact yield only small real net effects. Also, good analysis looks ahead, dealing with the *future* effects of policies. We wish especially to understand *preventive* treatments, which anticipate problems and often have higher yields than *restorative* actions.

A2. Basic Features

Public policies toward business involve five special features.

1. Policies often do two or more things, rather than just one. These components are often counterpoised and tilted in surprising ways. For example, antitrust policy in the United States has at least three main parts; preventing collusion, preventing certain mergers, and abating existing market power. The net effect of these parts—as they are actually done, with checkered emphasis—may be to harden structure and to benefit dominant firms (see Chapter 9). This would be the opposite of the supposed effects. Or instead, the effects may be the opposite, to reduce market power and encourage innovation. Another example is regulation. It has two main elements: giving a franchise and constraining profit rates. The one raises profitability, the other reduces it; the net effect depends on the balance among the parts (see Chapters 10 through 15).

2. Sectors change over time, so that the effects—and appropriateness—of given policy tools also change. There are few fixed points or boundaries, and the rate of change in markets can exceed the rate at which policies are applied. Some market changes are predictable and could be anticipated. But all require looking ahead and aiming at moving targets. An example: utilities go through phases which—unless obstructed—commonly end back in competitive status (Chapter 10). The most basic instance of this is the natural rate of decay of market power (recall Chapter 2). Monopoly will often dwindle, unless it is fortified by extraneous devices. If market power lasts, even slow treatments may have high yields. But if monopoly will disappear quickly, any but the speediest treatments will be superfluous. The rate of decay is therefore central to optimal policy choice, in antitrust, regulation, and other areas.

3. Policies also evolve and cause adaptive responses in markets. This evolution is, in some cases, contrary to the optimum direction (utility regulation is an example; see Chapter 10). In other cases, the adaptive response by private firms can anticipate or deflect the intent of the policy. The policy choice often needs to be dynamic, or at least time-related, in order to allow for the inner complexity and time lag in actual policy tools.

4. Policies apply incentives. They either constrain or subsidize, or frequently they do both. The marginal incentives may be deep, even where their average effects are not. The firms affected (who have often also helped to design and enact the policy in the first place) then either have reduced, or increased, profit opportunities. There is probably no significant industry or firm that is not both constrained and subsidized by two or more public policies.

5. Optimal policy treatments require both (a) information and (b) rational analysis. Each is necessary but not sufficient. Most policy resources are used to gain information, by hearings, investigations, and so on. Information is not only critical but often costly. Also, the processes for gaining it may themselves contain biases. Even the wisest and most rational policy choosers will err if their information is incorrect. Indeed, they will fail even to consider problems if they—and/or the political process which guides their activities— are kept in the dark.

B. CHOICE BY PUBLIC AGENCIES

B1. The Problem

An "optimal" policy serves the public interest by promoting efficiency, equity, and related benefits, as stated in Chapter 1. It yields the maximum of these benefits for any given level of policy costs. The benefits of competition may need to be balanced against any technical economies of scale. Policies also need to be well *designed,* to get maximum effect for their effort. This means applying the right incentives to private firms, so that they align their choices to the public interest, rather than resist it. Too, good design often means early *preventive* policies rather than *restorative* actions; and it often means *therapy* to modify behavior, rather than *surgery* to force changes in structure.

The purpose of this section is to define optimum public choices, in a system where private firms are—as is true in fact—also optimizing *their* choices. As is usual in economics, there are two parts to the optimizing problem: *(a)* to get the right level of *total* policy resources, and *(b)* to allocate resources across the range of markets and policy types so as to maximize the net public benefits yielded by any *given level* of policy resources. Each policy is to be pursued quantitatively in each direction to the point where its marginal returns in net benefits are equal to the marginal returns on alternative actions. Each policy is also to be designed so that the benefits-cost gap is as large as possible for every given level of expenditure.[1]

Such rules may seem like truisms, but they can have great power. They are a consistent basis for thought, and they correctly require choices to be made among multiple alternatives. But there are important complications.

---

[1] Benefit-cost techniques and difficulties are surveyed in Alan R. Prest and Ralph Turvey, "Cost-Benefit Analysis: A Survey," *Economic Journal,* 1965, pp. 683–735; Peter O. Steiner, *Public Expenditure Budgeting* (Washington, D.C.: Brookings Institution, 1970); and E. J. Mishan, *Cost-Benefit Analysis* (New York: Praeger, 1971).

Specific policy choices can be framed in two alternative ways. Where there is a straight choice between types of policies, then the one with the highest *ratio* of total benefits to costs is to be chosen. Alternatively, and more generally, one may regard policy resources as investments, and seek to optimize their allocation in terms of *internal rates of return* on the resources committed. In that case, each policy would be pursued to the point where the net internal rate of return on its resource investment just equals the marginal opportunity cost of public-sector funds. Normally these approaches will yield similar policy choices.

B2. General Public Choice

Consider a public decision-making agency whose tools and problems are in reasonably balance at the start. Suppose that setting a specific policy j at a level L will incur certain direct Costs$_a$ (a for agency), perhaps like those summed up in Table 1–1. These actions may yield certain benefits by improving efficiency and equity. These costs and benefits may be stated as dollar values which will occur over time t, from the present to some distant horizon n. The general expression for determining the economic returns to this set of policy resources is the present-value expression:

$$\text{Net benefits}_j = \sum_{t=1}^{n} \frac{\Delta \text{Efficiency} + \Delta \text{Equity}}{(1+i)^n} - \sum_{t=1}^{n} \frac{\Delta \text{Costs}_a + \Delta \text{Costs}_p}{(1+i)^n} \qquad (1)$$

where i is a rate of time discount. Costs$_p$ are the private costs which occur because of the agency action. The agency has other policy tools to use its resources on, and it can also vary the levels in each direction. An optimum is reached when all policies are adjusted so that their net marginal yields are just equal to the true opportunity cost of the agency's resources, defined by some social rate of return (r_s). A necessary condition for efficiency is therefore that policy returns be in line with policy costs:

$$\frac{\Delta \text{Benefits}}{\Delta \text{Costs}_j} = b_j \geqq r_s \qquad (2)$$

Thus if policy j at level L yields a marginal return greater than r_s, then its level should be increased, and vice versa.

One does not really expect precise figures to be available in evaluating most actual choices. One can only make predictions, in a world full of blurs and guesses. Good judgment will be needed; cost-benefit analysis faithfully carries out the mistakes of those using it. Yet it does clarify the elements of choice directly.

B3. Specific Discounts

The components in this simple model need discounting in three ways.

Time. *A neutral treatment avoids putting time on the side of either the agency or the firm.* The usual sequence is costs first, benefits later. Where resistance by private interests lengthens the time lag of benefits, it reduces the present value of the benefits. This in turn normally reduces the efficient level of the policy. A correct choice will be free of any such time bias. Otherwise, the ability to control the pace of action may decisively distort the outcome, by stalling or by railroading.

The correct discount rate is not easy to specify exactly, as an extensive literature attests. Higher i values shrink the benefits from actions which take a long time to run their course. A higher i may reflect a true government-wide high rate of time preference on social expenditure, but short-run fluctuations in i (as urgency comes and goes) are assumed away.

Probability. Future outcomes are always uncertain in some degree, and so the cost and benefit magnitudes need adjustment to reflect these probabilities. Two inherent causes of this uncertainty are involved.

1. Economic effects are not certain. Research has established several broad relationships between elements of market structure and performance, as Chapter 2 noted. But *(a)* these are soft relationships, not clad in iron certainty, and *(b)* the specific case at hand may deviate from the general rule.

In short, any policy choice contains a weighing of probable effects on both sides. A correct weighing procedure will pose the burden of proof evenly. This neutrality is often difficult to achieve.[2] Stated more generally: *policy choices not to make changes should have as robust empirical support as any other choice.*

2. Even where economic effects are probable, their normative yield may be doubtful. Choice A may make benefit X sure to happen, but X might come about even without A. This is the question of natural rates of decay (recall Chapter 2 and the first section above). And it is of course precisely the defense offered by most targets of policy actions: that the goals are, or will be, gained as well or better without the policy step.

Correct policy choices will therefore be prospective, time-discounted, and probability-adjusted, and *will make comparisons with the results which could otherwise be reasonably expected to occur.* These uncertainty factors can be included by adjusting the best estimate values by probability factors. These will be set between zero for impossibility and one for certainty. For simplicity, the notation here will include all such factors in a single summary multiplier p attached to each element. Thus an estimated net benefit of $10 million at a p of .04 (a 40 percent chance) would have a value of $4 million. Obviously p is itself a matter for subjective estimate, and in most cases it cannot be known precisely. But large differences in the odds can usually be perceived, and there is value in making these factors explicit. It enables the arguable to be argued more clearly.

Precedent. Each policy choice may set precedents which then settle other cases. A single decision may therefore have an additional policy yield which, in landmark instances, can go very high. In such cases, an evaluation of just the one case's own yield is too narrow. Some sort of precedential multiplier m should be applied.

---

[2] For example, courtroom standards of proof for criminal cases will be inappropriate for settling the optimum structure of an industry, since the courtroom burden of proof—beyond reasonable doubt—is one-sided. The law of private property ordinarily sets the burden of proof against changes in the status quo; this is true also of much recent regulatory law. In principle, this will lead to incorrect decisions.

In routine infra-marginal cases, based on settled law, m will approach 1 (standard price-fixing cases are now of this sort). In marginal cases, which extend or retract the law, m may be more or less than 1.[3]

With these additions, the general model of agency choice now takes the form:

$$\text{Net benefits} = m \sum_{t=1}^{n} \frac{(\Delta \text{ Efficiency})p_e + (\Delta \text{ Equity})p_d}{(1 + i)^n} \tag{3}$$
$$- \sum_{t=1}^{n} \frac{(\Delta \text{ Costs}_a)p_{ca} + (\Delta \text{ Costs}_p)p_{cp}}{(1 + i)^n}$$

which looks much more complex than it really is.

In terms of rates of return on policy resources, the efficiency condition at the margin now is

$$b_j = m \frac{(\Delta \text{ Benefits})p_b}{(\Delta \text{ Costs}_p)p_{ca}} \gtreqless r_s \tag{4}$$

The objective is still to reach equal marginal yields among all policies. Roughly speaking, those whose benefits are definite and are landmark cases will be favored over others.

C. CHOICES BY PRIVATE FIRMS

Meanwhile, the firms affected by public policies are busy making their own best choices. The result is commonly a series of choices and actions on both sides. Issues are usually not settled "for good." The process continues with compromises or battles, and the underlying conditions also evolve.

We start by noting that firms generally maximize profits. For the entire firm, for any planning period n, profits simply equal revenues minus costs:

$$\text{Profit}_n = \text{Total revenue}_n - \text{Total cost}_n \tag{5}$$

For any specific project or direction of expenditures, the firm's expected rate of return (π) on investment must equal or exceed its opportunity cost of capital (r_c):

$$\pi_n = \frac{\text{Revenue}_n - \text{Cost}_n}{\text{Investment}_n} \tag{6}$$

and

---

[3] A special twist is what lawyers call *estoppel*. Bringing an action at one point often gives a period of grace during which the action cannot be brought again. For example, IBM was regarded as free from further antitrust action for at least a decade after the 1956 consent decree settling an earlier case. Therefore the estoppel effect amounts to an internal precedent factor which is less than one.

One must bear in mind, however, that precedents frequently arise from the structure of the law, which can be revised. For example, FCC decisions on cable TV can be superseded by new laws from Congress on the matter. In certain cases, m itself is subject to a probability factor, if revision of the law is in prospect!

$$\pi_n \geq r_c \tag{7}$$

One direction of company expenditure is to anticipate or prevent the constraints which public agencies try to apply. Another is to try to increase the subsidies obtained from agencies.

Generally, a public policy which would reduce profits will be resisted up to the point at which the marginal return on resistance expenditures just equals the cost of capital. At the extreme, the profits at stake will all be used up by the firm in resisting the public agency, since otherwise the profits would be lost to the firm in any event.

D. THE MAIN CAUSES OF BIASED CHOICES

D1. On the Public Side

Several conditions may tilt public choices away from optimal patterns.

Information Bias.   Public agencies need complete and timely information on sensitive variables (market shares, prices, costs, innovation choices, competitive tactics, and alternative treatments), both past and future. But they often lack it. Such information is known intimately by firms, and when it endangers their profits, it will naturally be secreted. Because firms also try to influence public fact-gathering policies, the data put out in the public realm are often scanty. This can cause a bias in specific policy choices, as well as in the general evaluation of policy needs and urgency.

The degree of monopoly and its social costs are probably underestimated, because full information is lacking (as Chapter 2 noted). To that extent, the general benefits of policies would be understated. Meanwhile the costs of treatment are more directly measurable. In contested cases, they are fully asserted by the target firms, often with some exaggeration. Therefore, bias is likely to be present in specific cases as well as in the general setting of policy lines.

These biases have three effects. First, industrial policies are less complete than they would otherwise be, because the problems and potential yields are underestimated. Second, whole problems, areas, and cases are probably slighted, because of ignorance. Third, more agency resources have to be spent on mere fact-gathering than a neutral information state would require. These biases may cumulate to large distortions.

Time Bias.   Several time biases are common. When one side can impose delay and gain benefits by doing so, then time is biased in its favor. This bias can be decisive (as we will see in Chapters 5 and 6). The bias often stems from specific procedures or rules, which could be altered.

The time bias is strengthened by the brevity of most policymakers' tenure. New policies usually require at least three years to prepare and at least 10 years (often 20 years or more) for benefits to be fully harvested. Yet most top antitrust and regulatory decisionmakers are in office less than four years (see Chapters 4 and 10). Their inexperience often neutralizes them for the first year or two. They commonly apply a high rate of time preference in their eagerness to get results. This myopia favors quick, visible, and shallow steps, rather than basic ones. It also makes the firms' advantage of having time on their side particularly strong.

Probability Bias.   Two important biases in the probability factors often recur.

The procedure itself may tilt the odds. Courts may be too slow on some matters, or too fast on others. This is accentuated if the passage of time raises political uncertainty. As elections come and go and governments change, the direction of policy may be reversed from above, and then reversed once again. Long-term actions are liable to be stopped, even though the conditions justifying them are unchanged.

An uneven burden of proof can bias the outcome sharply. Thus, the laws and traditions of private property rights normally set the burden of proof against changes in the status quo. This basis often departs from an even choice among alternatives. An even burden of proof presumes, of course, that there is equal access to the critical data. Without such equality of access, the actual burden of proof may be sharply tilted. In fact, the burden of proof is decisive in a wide range of cases.

Private costs.   Public policies usually lead to private resistance costs, which may mushroom to high levels. Should public agencies include these private resistance costs in appraising the real total costs of public actions? Perhaps yes: the costs are real and often predictable. Yet they are also often fully discretionary with the firm. Any smart firm will threaten large or unlimited resistance, if doing so would tip the agency's choice toward weaker actions. To this extent, the firms themselves could control the public policy. This would distort the public choices. Perhaps one could compromise by including only the "nondiscretionary" resistance costs in the public-agency evaluation. But this distinction is not easy to make in practice. A reasonable method is to leave private costs out on first-round evaluations and then put them in only if nondiscretionary costs are large, highly probable, and easy to identify.

D2. On the Private Side

The narrowness of the firm's evaluation will not necessarily cause it to be biased away from the social optimum, under ideal conditions. But lapses from these ideal conditions can be frequent and important. Bias can then arise because private firms are indifferent to precedential effects and external effects.

Also, private firms will often apply different rates of time discount and probability factors than do the public decisionmakers. These can distort firms' choices away from a balanced response to public actions. The normative effect will vary from case to case, depending on the direction in which public policies are pressing.

Two other biases are quite systematic: taxes and speed of action.

Tax bias is embedded deeply in the system. Resistance costs ordinarily are tax-deductible, so that the firm's opportunity cost from resistance will usually be well below the true cost of the real resources absorbed. If the corporation income tax rate is T, then the profit-maximizing marginal condition of resistance costs and after-tax profits at stake is

$$\text{Resistance expenditure} = \text{Pre-tax profit} = \frac{\text{After-tax profit}}{(1 - T)} \qquad (9)$$

The present T of about .5 means that resistance costs would be extended until they are at *twice* the level of the after-tax profits at stake. If, for example, the after-tax profits at stake *(P)* are \$1 million per day (as they are in some cases; see Chapter 5), then the rational firm will spend up to about \$2 million to achieve each *day* of delay. A significant corporation profit tax rate therefore enlarges the resistance to policy constraints, perhaps well beyond a neutral outcome, because it makes resistance dollars seem "cheaper" to the firm.

Firms benefiting from the status quo (and its continuation in the future) will devote resources to retarding any change caused by public policy. If the time yield of delay is high, the stalling effect may be large, again possibly dissipating the whole sum of private and social benefits which the agency is seeking to achieve.

Speed.   Public choices are often made and applied at slower rates than are private ones. This reduces the range of public choice. The lags may cause the public actions, *when they take effect,* to stray from the optimum levels. One instance of this is the antitrust restructuring case which, after many years of trial and appeal, is finally won *after* the industry has changed. Strict optimizing requires that public actions be as rapid as private ones, even if they are not immediate.

Summary

In combination, these biases on the public and private sides can be strong. Occasionally they may offset each other, but that would be a fluke. Frequently they reinforce each other, causing extra distortion. The reader can derive cases in which the biases would cause severe welfare loss, or nicely balance each other out. The essential fact is that the biases are numerous and can be powerful. "Good" policies need to allow for them. *Special care is needed in* (a) *setting the time discount rate,* (b) *avoiding letting time be on the side of one party,* (c) *posing the burden of proof evenly,* (d) *allowing for precedential effects, and* (e) *neutralizing the biases in private-firm choices (from taxes, better information, and speed of action).*

So one analyses policy yields and choices with care.[4] The hope is to avoid large errors and omissions, rather than to reach perfect, comprehensive appraisals.

E. THE POLITICAL SETTING

Having learned how to define optimum policies, we now need to look closely at the processes shaping actual policies. They are rough and imperfect, like most human activities, and they may cause further distortions. Or, perhaps, they broadly press policies toward optimal patterns.

A democratic process has great optimizing power, for it makes government officeholders subject to the preferences of the people. Such a process is analogous to a perfectly competitive economic system.[5] Politicians compete for official jobs by perceiving which policies the public wants and then promising them. Voters decide by strictly equal votes. Once in office, politicians must carry out the preferred policies, or they will lose office at the next election. Policies are just a byproduct of the politicians' efforts to gain and hold office (though they may also express personal beliefs).

They are led toward optimality by individual maximizing choices, as if guided by a political Invisible Hand. There may be much muddling through, or instead a series of crystal-clear choices. There may also be a degree of leadership, or instead a lot of bland, small-scale compromises. The optimizing tendency is there, all the same.

This optimum has limits, some of them analogous to the economic optimum under perfect competition:

1. Preferences may differ in intensity, but the vote weights them equally. Some voters may care acutely about one or all issues, while many others

---

[4] Other policy criteria are often presented as alternatives to benefit-cost analysis. But on inspection, these turn out to reduce to nothing but benefit-cost statements in disguise. Such alternatives include:

1. *Incipiency:* monopoly should be stopped at the earliest possible point in its growth. This is an important criterion used in preventing certain horizontal mergers. It embodies the benefit-cost evaluation that the discounted benefits from preventive action against increasing market shares via merger exceed the discounted costs sufficiently to justify drawing the line at low market shares.

2. *Competition* is the objective pure and simple, even apart from its economic results. Actually, this just says that the total discounted benefits of competition are likely to be very large, so much that there is a rebuttable presumption against market power. That is: the burden of proof should strongly favor competition.

3. *Laissez-faire.* Let markets work freely to erode monopoly, and virtually all public efforts to restore or supplant it will be unnecessary and/or harmful. Translated into benefit-cost form: market power decays so rapidly that policy measures to reduce or constrain it have little or no net benefits.

[5] For detailed analysis of democratic choice, see Anthony Downs, *An Economic Theory of Democracy* (New York: Harper & Row, 1957); K. J. Arrow, *Social Choice and Individual Values* (Chicago: University of Chicago Press, 1951); R. A. Dahl and C. E. Lindblom, *Politics, Economics, and Democracy,* rev. ed. (New York: Harper & Row, 1968); and R. A. Dahl, *A Preface to Democratic Theory* (Chicago: University of Chicago Press, 1956).

will be nearly indifferent. Democratic choices may therefore fail to fit true preferences.

2. Preferences may be sharply divided, rather than converging on moderate, middle-of-the-road policies. The solution will then offend a large minority, perhaps even one with especially intense concern. No consensus may exist.

3. A party may gain and hold office with a package of policies, *some* of which are sharply nonoptimal.

These problems occur even if the process is *perfect.* If it is *imperfect,* more difficulties occur.

1. Preferences may be unclear or easily swayed.
2. Issues may be too technically complex for citizens to comprehend.
3. Information may not be fully available to all. It may be scarce, too costly for many citizens to bother to get. We have all faced lists of candidates we neither knew nor cared about. And access to information may be controlled by specialized interests.
4. Resources for persuading voters may be unequally held.
5. Policy actions may lag behind events.

All of these do occur in some degree, and their effects can reinforce each other. Therefore—from these causes alone, in addition to those in Chapter 2—policies may depart and remain away from the optimum.

Industrial policies are especially vulnerable to these imperfections. The issues are complex and often obscure. Most citizens neither understand nor care about them. Access to key data is not neutral. Those who hold market power largely control the facts about it and its effects; and subsidies are often hidden. Industrial policies are not a central election issue, and so voters do not directly pronounce on it in party elections. Policy processes are slow, often because legal procedures can be used to cause delay.

There are a formidable set of defects. Perhaps the wonder is that industrial policies are not worse than they actually are. The political system may foster more harmful policies than good ones, and be a prime source of monopolies.[6] The realist need not abhor all policies; indeed, that is not possible, for inaction is often a positive choice. Rather, one must learn how these economic and political defects relate. Between naiveté and nihilism there is much room for intelligent policy choice.

F. AGENCIES AND PROCESSES

No general review of the organs of government is in order here, of course. This section treats only those features of the executive, legislative, and judicial branches which strongly affect industrial policies.

---

[6] This view was carried to its limits by 19th century Manchester School (Nassau Senior, and others) and by neo-Chicago School analysts since the 1950s (George J. Stigler, J. F. Weston, and others). The original Chicago mentors (Frank H. Knight and Henry S. Simons) were more moderate and realistic.

"The Law."   Laws are simply rules of the game. They *(a)* define actions, *(b)* attach rewards or penalties to them, and *(c)* specify the means for enforcement. All three branches often share in the origins of law, and all three are involved in applying every important law. The executive agencies choose how—and how extensively—to enforce it (total enforcement is commonly impossible or absurd). Legislatures control the funds for enforcement and modify the laws repeatedly. The courts interpret, and often reject, parts or all of a law.

Therefore "the law" is often a core of legal phrases embedded in a tissue of informal customs and actions which really control what is done. The bigger the stakes, the more complex are the controversies about what the law "really is." The struggles often shift freely among the governmental units, as the parties at interest seek their best changes one way and another, skirmish by skirmish.

So the formal divisions among the three branches of government often obscure the real interactions. A large degree of overlap and clashes among official bodies is quite natural. Moreover, most agencies are managed by lawyers. They have been trained to *advocate* one side and win, rather than to weigh social interests and create balanced solutions. They often slight economic analysis and a balanced evaluation.

Executive Agencies.   These units apply the policies, using resources and powers voted by the legislatures. Their heads are usually political appointees, with only modest technical experience. They hold office only briefly, usually less than three years. Many decisionmakers are unable to understand or develop actions, though many of them take office eager to do so.

The body of the agency is staffed by career experts, who provide continuity. Their salaries are modest, markedly lower than those of the private lawyers they contend with. On occasion, agency staff members are skilled, ample in numbers, and tenacious. But often, instead, career staff members are outnumbered and passive.

Agency resources come from the legislature, which can exert control by the purse, by hearings, or by changing the law itself (perhaps even abolishing—or reorganizing—the agency). These resources are usually scarce, and so it is important to allocate them carefully. Yet most allocations evolve by muddling through from case to case, not by a clear analysis. Such muddling can give the optimal results, by trial and error, but clear tests to verify that are lacking. Much agency effort goes to persuading the legislature and higher executive officials, as well as to making formal presentations in the courts—and simply to the minutiae of keeping the agency in being.[7]

Two semiexecutive agencies—independent regulatory commissions and public enterprises—share many of these features (see Chapters 10 and 16).

---

[7] Usually, small matters with deadlines force aside large issues which can be postponed. This Gresham's Law of Public Policy appears to be universal and will recur throughout this book.

Legislatures.   Legislators are politicians, whose trade is compromise and whose aim is to get re-elected. They are part of an imperfect process.[8] Legislators' formal actions (votes, bills and so on) are always for public display, and their real intent and effect are often hidden. Bills or votes *to do X* are often done really *to prevent Y* (a bigger step) from being done. New laws are given honorific titles which frequently have little to do with the actual effect. And actions are often taken—or blocked—not for themselves but as part of some larger political or personal strategy. Moreover, action is piecemeal. Rarely are industrial policies appraised and revised broadly. Finally, legislative rules provide many points for applying influence: at the committee stage, in one house, in the other house, in joint committee, at final votes; *and* then in authorizing funds; *and then* appropriating funds in both houses. Legislatures therefore strongly *reflect* the established pattern of interests, especially in dealing with industrial policies.

Courts.   The three tiers of the federal courts—90 district courts (499 judges), 11 appeals courts (97 judges), and the Supreme Court—handles most of the important industrial policy cases.[9] Judges have small resources (their clerks do much research and drafting). Their chief resource—courtroom time—is freely available for hearing and settling disputes.

An aggrieved party (the plaintiff) files suit in the appropriate district court. Major cases are usually tried in New York, Chicago, or Boston, where the defendant's company headquarters are. Trial is held after all issues and facts needed in the case have been prepared. The basic rule is: there are to be no surprises at trial, only reasoned arguments and facts. All facts and arguments to be used by either side are disclosed *before* the trial itself begins. In such pre-trial discovery, the two sides fire lengthy lists of questions ("interrogatories") at each other, both to get facts and often to confuse or delay. This pre-trial activity often takes even more than the usual three-year delay on most federal court calendars. Either side can demand a trial by jury rather than by the judge alone. Complex cases usually are tried and decided by judges, but in damage cases (for example, claims of unfair competition or monopoly damages) one side usually prefers appealing to a jury.

Trial may be lengthy, involving masses of documentation and ranks of expert witnesses on both sides. It is supposed to cover all issues of fact. Economists are frequently brought in to testify that the market is (or isn't)

---

[8] Many districts have a degree of political monopoly, which is reflected both in the membership and in the management of the federal and state legislatures. Committees shape actions toward industrial laws and agency budgets. Older members dominate the committees, commonly in sympathy with the older industrial interests. Committee hearings provide a forum for airing issues. But these are often timed and prepared to make a point or favor one side, and the committees and legislatures are free to go their own way in actually framing new laws. Committee staffs prepare weighty reports, often of value but usually meant to support a pet position of the chairman or majority.

[9] A clear introduction to the topic is given in C. Auerbach, L. Garrison, W. Hurst, and S. Mermin, *The Legal Process* (San Francisco: Chandler, 1961). See also the section in Chapter 18 on courts as public enterprises.

competitive or that scale economies are (or aren't) important. For reasons we saw in Chapter 2, it is not hard to locate witnesses for either side. In major cases, decision by the judge often takes another several months.

Either side may appeal. The appeals court hears only a brief restatement by both sides; the original trial record (often running to thousands of pages) contains the facts. Further appeal to the Supreme Court is also possible. The delay is often a year before each appeal hearing, and half a year more before the decision is given out.

The upper courts can declare for either side, revise the issues, and/or send the case back down to the district court for *(a)* retrial on some or all points, or *(b)* a practical remedy. The whole sequence can take 10 or 15 years in complex cases, as each side exhausts its chances to win or delay; see Figure 3–1. At any point, a compromise may be reached or relief be obtained from some other quarter (for example, getting Congress—or a city council—to change the law directly).

Throughout, the judges strive to attain "perfect justice": ample time for preparation, for all sides to be heard fully, for avoiding mistakes of procedure, at virtually any cost.[10] Courts are liberal in letting virtually all suits be heard and in letting both sides use all possible tactics.

Lower court judges are former lawyers, most of them ambitious to reach still higher judgeships. To be reversed on appeal is therefore a setback, and this insures that the lines laid down by the higher courts will soon be applied generally. Lower courts send up a wide range of "fact situations" and doctrines, from which the upper courts select some to change or establish precedents. The really critical, divisive cases are usually declined, in favor of a political resolution in Congress. Generally, lower-court judges are more conservative, since they are usually drawn from local commercial-legal life. Higher-court judges usually take broader views and often try new departures.

Decisions are guided by precedent and usually turn upon a crucial legal phrase or point of fact. The economic optimum is often not defined or applied. Each party continually assesses the probability-adjusted value of its choices (to sue, to countersue, to appeal, to compromise) and takes the best one. Virtually all law reduces to arguing: "My client's situation is *like* these others," or "My client's situation is *not* like these others." Every possible distinction can be wrung dry over and over, and every fact can be challenged.[11] The only limits on advocacy are *(a)* the English language, *(b)* rules of evidence and procedure, *(c)* fears of offending the courts' sense of fair play, and *(d)* money to cover legal fees.

This slow and unruffled process is superb for airing facts, probing issues, and resolving many disputes. But it is slow, and it can be abused. There are many ways of stalling for tactical advantage. The merits of the two sides

---

[10] M. Fleming, *The Price of Perfect Justice* (New York: Basic Books, 1973).

[11] Thus a lawyer does not see a white horse in a field. He sees only a horse that appears to be white *on this side*.

FIGURE 3–1

The Basic Policy Sequence

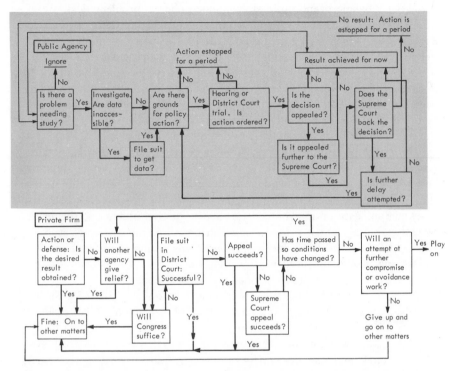

often do not relate to their relative ability to finance a court fight: a deep pocket can win a weak case or crush a small opponent.

Even without these defects, the decisions can ignore optimal economic criteria. The process is legal: run by lawyers and reaching legal answers. As in other branches, the underlying social yields—efficiency, fairness, and so on—may come to be ignored during the strife.

Three Features of the Policy Process. In these various forums, the very substance of policies evolves. Three special features of the process need to be stressed.

1. The law grows. The economy evolves new business methods and new social interests. New ways are devised to get around old rules. "The law" must grow, to deal with these and to reconcile new clashes of interests. This growth can occur by rewriting the laws or by new actions in enforcing the old ones. Agencies and courts usually have discretion in applying the laws. Their new interpretations, in response to changing issues, are a natural and proper source of growth and freshness in public policies.

2. Agency power is less than it seems. Many laws set absolute prohibitions on activities, results, or states of being. But the limits are usually diluted in practice. The agency's powers will always be tested, if they challenge important private interests. Even with full resources, the agency will need support from above, and this often wavers. Therefore the ultimate *power* to carry out a balanced and optimal economic policy is problematical.

3. Due process. Due process is the phrase covering all those customs and explicit rules which try to give every side its say. But due process is not a magic wand. *First,* the hearing itself does not guarantee a fair result. A process which seems to air all interests may instead be simply a device for deflating social protest, or deceiving the parties into believing that they have been listened to. *Second,* due process takes time. There often are time biases, favoring one side or the other. Therefore due process can inherently tip the outcome, or be deliberately abused. To study further is to delay.

Third, due process is not free. It takes resources, including legal talent, research efforts, and simply the time and attention absorbed in mounting and winning one's fight. One side or the other may be better able to bear these costs, or use them to have its way. *Fourth,* due process does not inherently guarantee the optimal outcome. It does regularize and extend the process of fact-gathering which precedes a social decision. But the end result can still be defective. Further, due process proceeds within the setting provided by existing law. If the need is to go outside current law and develop new treatments, due process in itself does not bring it about.

Pressure Groups in the Process.   Interest groups are part of a healthy, pluralistic process. Yet there is a basic source of bias among them: *producers generally have more than their share of power.* Producer groups are focused on high stakes, while consumer groups are diffused. Companies are playing for big money, and they develop skills and continuity in dealing with public officials. They often tilt elections to "their" representatives, and they also lobby more effectively. Their activities are professional, unremitting, and usually unobserved. Precisely those firms with the highest profits at stake will be the ones spending heavily to get their way. Despite surface successes of consumer groups since 1965, major industrial power blocs still have great influence where it matters most.[12]

All this assumes honesty on all sides. Of course, plain corruption can also occur. The stakes are often huge, and officials are only human. Corruption is more common at the local and state levels, but some degrees and forms of it are endemic on the national scene too.

Comparing Formal with Actual Policies.   Given such biases and intricacies in the policy process, actual policies will often diverge from their formal roles. A genuine social need often causes a formal treatment to be put on the books. But enforcement is less than complete, and the true effect can be well short of the supposed effect. Figure 3–2 illustrates such a divergence.

---

[12] The success of corporate political activity appears to be related positively to the market power of the firm. For recent research on this, see Lester M. Salamon and John J. Siegfried, "Economic Power and Political Influence: The Impact of Industry Structure on Public Policy," *American Political Science Review* 71 (September 1977), 1026–43.

FIGURE 3–2
Formal and Actual Policies Can Diverge

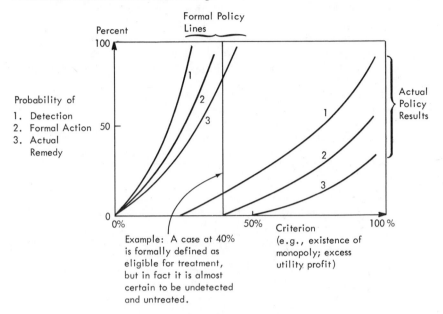

Though monopoly (or excess utility profits, or price fixing, or patent abuses, and such) is illegal, it is only partly likely to be detected, treated, and remedied. How likely? That is what you will learn to evaluate for yourself in the following chapters.

SUMMARY

This chapter has presented the ideal and the real. Optimal policy choices can be defined, using cost-benefit analysis. Several special elements (probability, time discounts, and precedential effects) need to be allowed for. Also, the burdens of proof and of time need to be poised evenly. Private firm choices are biased by several factors, including their narrowness and the role of profits taxes.

The real-world political process sets further limits on policies. Issues may be muddied, ignored, or slanted. The primacy of lawyers in all parts of the process tends to divert attention from economic issues. Moreover, industrial groups tend to have disproportionate influence on the promoting of their focused interests. Therefore, there may be large divergences between optimal policies, formal policies, and actual policies.

QUESTIONS FOR REVIEW

1. "An agency's ability to act depends on its legal powers as well as its resources." True?

2. "Monopoly is against the law, just as speeding and shoplifting are. Therefore, monopoly has been eliminated." True?

3. "If a policy offers social benefits, then it certainly should be carried out." True?

4. Among the possible biases in policies are (a) an uneven burden of proof, (b) having time on one side, (c) taxes on private profits, (d) lack of information about market conditions, (e) intensive private lobbying. Which?

5. "The slower the rate of decay in high market shares, the more beneficial will be Section 2 action to eliminate monopoly." True?

6. " 'Optimal' policies simply have marginal social benefits in line with marginal social costs." True?

7. Cost-benefit analysis usually provides officials with precise answers to policy questions." True?

8. "A precedent-setting case can have much larger ultimate benefits than its own pay-off provides." True?

9. "Profit taxes encourage firms to resist public policies much less fiercely." True?

10. "All lobbying by business groups tends to distort public policies away from good patterns." True?

11. "Lower courts are usually less conservative than higher ones, because district judges have so much leeway." True?

12. "The law grows only when Congress passes a new law." True?

13. Is slowness in court processes always bad?

14. How might one judge if an agency's tasks were in line with its resources?

15. What main defects is cost-benefit analysis likely to have in guiding industrial policies?

16. Would a "perfect" democratic political process yield optimal policies, or at least reasonable approximations of them?

APPENDIX: *TERM PAPERS*

Usually, the good term paper focuses on a specific topic, which you are interested in and willing to explore. You define the issue, read the main sources in the literature, decide what you can add by new analysis or measures, and then write it up in some 10 to 20 pages. The project is a smaller version of the professional research and writing which appear in the literature itself. Your aims are (a) to think for yourself, reaching your own conclusions, and (b) to show your skill in using the concepts fluently.

There are three main kinds of topics: general issues, specific policy tools or cases, and specific industries or sectors. Every part of this text offers issues that need further thinking and debate. Part of your task is to pick out an issue which stirs or irritates you, where new points or facts are needed. *General issues* include such points as: Has antitrust reduced industrial concentration? How does one define a "public utility"? What concept of "predatory pricing" is valid for use in antitrust actions? *Specific tools* or cases might be approached as follows: Was the *Alcoa* decision economically sound? What types of conglomerate mergers should be prevented? What economic effects has the FCC's decision in *Carterfone* in 1968 had? Do patents promote competition or monopoly, ultimately? *Specific industries* might be treated in this way: To what extent is the telephone industry a "natural monopoly"? What policies are appropriate toward the copier industry? Has banking grown more competitive since 1965?

The main research sources for your papers are precisely those references which are given in the notes. They in turn often cite other books, articles, and reports which would be helpful. Usually it is better to focus on one or two main books and a few articles, rather than try to read all possible references. Your teacher can often suggest which references are most valuable. Good general sources include Walter Adams, ed., *The Structure of American Industry*, 5th ed. (New York: Macmillan, 1977); Simon N. Whitney, *Antitrust Policies* (New York: Twentieth Century Fund, 1958), 2 vols.; W. G. Shepherd, *The Economics of Industrial Organization* (Englewood Cliffs, N.J.: Prentice-Hall, 1979); Alfred E. Kahn, *The Economics of Regulation* (New York: Wiley, 1971), 2 vols.

There are a great many possible topics, for there are many important cases, industries, and issues. The following list of suggestions is only a start.

1. **Antitrust cases.** Review the economic content and effects of any of these: *Standard Oil* (1911), *U.S. Steel* (1920), the *Meatpackers* decree (1920), *Addyston Pipe* (1897), *Alcoa* (1945), *American Tobacco* (1946), *United Shoe Machinery* (1954), the electrical equipment price conspiracy cases (1960), *Brown Shoe* (1962), *Von's Grocery* (1966), *P&G-Clorox* (1967), *Utah Pie* (1967), *IBM* (filed 1969), *Telex* (1973), *Xerox* (1975).

2. **Regulatory decisions.** Review the economic content and effects of any of these: *Hope Natural Gas* (1944), *Permian Basin* (1968), *Carterfone* (1968), *MCI* (1969), *Ingot Molds* (1968), *El Paso Natural Gas* (1964), *Otter Tail Power* (1973).

3. **General issues:**
   What biases do operate on actual antitrust policies?
   How could the courts improve their methods for defining markets in antitrust cases?
   Is U.S. merger policy now too strict?
   Is de-regulation a good idea in most regulated sectors? Which ones?
   How might regulation cause inefficiency in utility firms? Does it actually do so?
   What changes toward marginal-cost pricing by utilities are in order?

4. *More specific questions:*
   Has Section 2 action toward dominant firms ceased to be effective? What new methods might be justified?
   Analyse whether de-regulation of natural gas production is a good idea.
   What economic effects will the CAB's flexible policy toward airline competition after 1976 probably have?

Evaluate the U.S. Postal Service's social performance, objectively.

Can price controls substitute for Section 2 actions against tight oligopoly? How would you apply them to accomplish this?

Should the courts soften the per se rule against price fixing, now that penalties are heavier?

For a specific "utility" sector (for example, telephone, electricity, gas, railroads), show how regulatory policies should be altered.

Analyse the performance of public enterprise in one of these cases: TVA, Port of New York Authority, National Coal Board (Britain), Renault (France), others noted in Chapters 16–18.

In what ways should regulation of U.S. banking be revised?

Is there a "new wave" of regulation which is excessive" What criteria can decide that issue?

Part II

POLICIES TO PROMOTE COMPETITION

4.
Antitrust Tasks and Tools

5.
Monopolization

6.
Mergers

7.
Restrictive Practices: Collusion

8.
Restrictive Practices: Price Discrimination
and Exclusion

9.
Antitrust Appraised

ANTITRUST

The powers of antitrust seem all replete
To make great businessmen, and small, compete.

No miscreant's too slight to catch and charge,
But action slows when market shares are large.

This corporal's guard with continents to rule
Strives mightily but often seems the fool.

With meager means, yet lordly aims and bold,
Is antitrust controller or controlled?

chapter 4

Antitrust Tasks and Tools

Antitrust is the generic name for laws, agencies, and actions to promote competition. The American experiment with it began with the Sherman Act in 1890, and interesting hybrids have sprouted abroad since 1945. The economic aim is clear in concept: to bring about the optimal degree of competition in the economy. How and whether this occurs is the question before us in the next six chapters.

There are many antitrust tools to choose among. American antitrust policies are just one special combination which is still evolving. It is a thriving legal industry, with roots lying deep in American economic and social history.[1] Yet nobody really knows what effects it has. It treats, not solves, its problems, and new situations are always arising for it to cope with. It is here to stay: like most social policies, it is travelling (sometimes backwards) but rarely arriving.

This part of the book presents the policies applied by the two mainline U.S. antitrust agencies: the Antitrust Division and the Federal Trade Commission. We begin with the tasks and laws, and then analyze the agencies' inner processes.

A. THE ECONOMIC TASKS

As Chapter 3 showed, a correct or optimal policy will increase competition up to the margin at which the benefits of extra competition are just offset by any lost technical economies of scale. Perfect competition is not sought or expected. Rather, agencies are to operate in the great middle range, where a higher degree of healthy competition and rivalry is usually worth seeking. The rationale for antitrust is firmly grounded on research and experience in real markets, not just on the analysis of perfect competition.

Antitrust is to have optimal *design,* applying the right incentives, and

---

[1] For a review of antitrust origins and scope, see Donald J. Dewey, *Monopoly in Economics and Law* (Chicago: Rand McNally, 1959). See also Hans Thorelli, *The Federal Antitrust Policy* (Baltimore: Johns Hopkins Press, 1954); and William Letwin, *Law and Economic Policy in America* (New York: Random House, 1965).

operating leanly. And in each market, antitrust is to be applied just to the *extent* and intensity where marginal social benefits equal costs. The two basic classes of industrial pathology are (recall the structure-behavior-performance triad in Figure 1–1):

1. Market dominance (a tight *structure,* plus certain types of behavior). This occurs when a firm gets and holds a large share of a market. The dominant firm can do internally what smaller firms could do only by collaboration. Mergers which would increase market power are also part of this structural problem.
2. Collusion among firms and other anticompetitive *behavior,* or *conduct.* This takes many forms, including direct collusion among competitors, informal ties, tacit collusion, price discrimination, exclusion, and so on.

An effective procompetitive policy will try to treat these conditions in all markets, including finance, utilities, professions, and services, as well as the main stream of industry and trade.

B. ANTITRUST LAWS

The basic American laws are firmly set, after 85 years of use. Their language is wide: they flatly outlaw collusion and monopoly. Yet their reach has been held back in practice to "reasonable" levels, and many sectors have been exempted. We consider first the laws, next their background, and then their coverage. An appendix at the chapter's end presents the terms most commonly used in antitrust law.

B1. The Laws

The Sherman Act of 1890 is the first and basic law outlawing monopoly and collaboration in broad terms. In 1914 the Clayton Act made certain specific acts illegal: it was amended in 1936 on price discrimination and in 1950 toward mergers. A trickle of small amendments continues. In practice, the laws have become a well-knit body of rules and precedent, as summarized in Table 4–1.

The **Sherman Act's** two main sections are:

Section 1. Every contract, combination in the form of a trust or otherwise, or conspiracy, in restraint of trade or commerce among the several states, or with foreign nations, is hereby declared to be illegal. Every person who shall make any such contract or engage in any such combination or conspiracy, shall be deemed guilty of a misdemeanor. . . .

Section 2. Every person who shall monopolize, or attempt to monopolize, or combine or conspire with any other person or persons, to monopolize any part of the trade or commerce among the several states, or with foreign nations, shall be deemed guilty of a misdemeanor. . . .

TABLE 4–1

Milestones of Antitrust

1870s	Agitation grows against railroad monopolies and financial and industrial power.
1890	Sherman Antitrust Act passed.
1897–99	*Addyston Pipe* decision against restraints of trade.
1902–04	*Northern Securities* case: the first "trust-busting" action.
1906–15	Major wave of investigations and cases against leading industrial monopolies.
1911	*Standard Oil, American Tobacco,* and *du Pont* gunpowder; the three large restructuring actions. The "rule of reason" is read into Section 2.
1914	Clayton and Federal Trade Commission Acts passed.
1915	International Harvester convicted in District Court.
1920	U.S. Steel acquitted 4–3 by the Supreme Court.
1920–35	Antitrust activity recedes.
1927	*Trenton Potteries* confirms that price fixing is illegal.
1933–35	The National Recovery Administration experiment: antitrust is suspended.
1936	Robinson-Patman Act passed.
1938–52	Antitrust is revived by Thurman Arnold and then others.
1940	*Socony* reaffirms that price fixing is illegal per se.
1945	*Alcoa* decision rejects the "rule of reason" for monopolies.
1945–48	Allied restructuring proceeds partially in Germany and Japan.
1948–49	Basing point systems are declared illegal.
1950	Celler-Kefauver Act passed, closing the merger loophole.
1949–51	Two major Section 2 cases are filed: *Western Electric* (1949) and *IBM* (1951).
1950	*American Can* settlement gives modest relief.
1955–56	*Western Electric* and *IBM* cases are settled by compromise.
1956–62	Explicit collusion is largely eliminated in Britain.
1958	*Bethlehem-Youngstown* decision begins tight merger policy.
1960	Electrical equipment price-fixing cases.
1962	*Brown Shoe* tightens horizontal and vertical merger limits.
1963	*Philadelphia National Bank* applies merger limits to banks.
1966	*Von's Grocery* proscribes nearly all horizontal mergers.
1969	Section 2 suit against IBM is filed. Major conglomerates ITT and LTV are also sued.
1970–78	The Supreme Court relaxes the strict lines of the "Warren Court."
1971–72	FTC initiates action toward cereals firms and Xerox. Conglomerate merger suits are settled before appeal.
1973	Antitrust limits on mergers and restraint are applied to electric utilities: *Otter Tail Power* and *American Electric Power.*
1974	Major case filed against AT&T.
1975	Government's IBM case finally begins trial. The FTC settles the Xerox case with mild limits. Price fixing of stockbrokers' fees is ended by SEC order.

Section 1 is against cooperation. The key words are "Every . . . conspiracy . . . in restraint of trade . . . is . . . a misdemeanor." The classic Section 1 target is price fixing. Section 2 makes market dominance illegal: "every" monopolization or "attempt to monopolize" is a misdemeanor.

The **Clayton Act** outlawed four specific practices, and added a general rule against unfair methods of competition. Particular devices that were outlawed by the Clayton Act included discrimination in prices, exclusive and tying contracts, and interlocking directorates. None of these prohibitions was absolute; the practices were forbidden only where their effect, in the words of the law, "may be to substantially lessen competition or tend to create a monopoly. . . ." The broader prohibition contained in Section 5 of the accompanying Federal Trade Commission Act provided, simply, "that unfair methods of competition in commerce are hereby declared unlawful."

In 1936 the **Robinson-Patman Act** amended Clayton Section 2 to limit price discrimination in more detail. In 1950, the Celler-Kefauver Act amended Clayton Section 7 to prevent anticompetitive mergers.

Certain other more specific laws cover procedural points and penalties. From 1903 to 1974 an expediting act provided for government appeals directly to the Supreme Court. The agencies can invoke either civil or criminal proceedings, seeking fines and/or jail terms. The maximum fine has risen from $5,000 in 1890 to $50,000 in 1955, and then to $100,000 for individuals and $1 million for firms in 1974. Maximum prison sentences were one year during 1890–1974, then raised to three years. The FTC itself can only impose maximum fines of $5,000 (per day if the offense continues). An injured private party can sue to claim treble damages as long as it can show direct injury. By a 1977 decision, an "indirect purchaser" cannot claim damages from a manufacturer because of over-pricing.[2]

If a defendant is found guilty in a public-agency case, that becomes a *prima facie* basis for treble damage claims by private parties. A consent decree does not provide that basis, and a *nolo contendere* plea is regarded as a consent, not a proof of guilt. A judge can reject a *nolo contendere* plea, especially if the offense has been flagrant.

The two agencies largely share the application of the basic antitrust laws, invoking them freely as the case at hand may warrant.

B2. History of the Laws

These laws derive from traditions and precedents rooted deep in the past. In earlier centuries, economic power has been woven into the cultural fabric, especially where the economy was feudal and agrarian. The rise of mercantile trading eventually challenged this structure in the later Middle Ages. The "industrial revolutions" in Britain (1780–1840) and then the United States

---

[2] *U.S.* v. *Illinois Brick,* U.S. Sup. Court, ¶61,460, *Trade Reg. Reports,* No. 285, June 13, 1977, pp. 1–2.

(1850–1900) made it both a more separable and a more urgent problem. The policy treatment of it which took form in the U.S. during 1890–1920 reflected a long competitive tradition.

The Common Law.   In England, during the 17th century, grants of monopoly by the Crown were held illegal under common law by the courts and were voided by Parliament in 1623.[3] The abolition did not extend to grants conferred by Parliament, to monopolies acquired through individual effort, or to those resulting from private agreement. In the 18th century, however, monopolistic agreements came usually to be condemned, unless they were merely ancillary to some innocent action and were judged by a rule of reason. A single person could still monopolize, but not a group. The courts had also refused since the 15th century to enforce contracts which restrained trade. This refusal was narrow at first but gradually broadened.

During the 19th century, the doctrine of restraint of trade was extended to cover any arrangement whereby competitors sought to exclude outsiders from the market or otherwise to limit freedom to compete. In most jurisdictions the courts came to reject all contracts that involved such practices as curtailment of output, division of territories, fixing of prices, and pooling of profits. Here no rule of reason was applied: these practices were held by their very nature to harm the public interest, and contracts that required them were not enforced.

The maintenance of competition was thus supported by the common law. But as an instrument of public policy the common law was of limited effectiveness. If all conspirators stayed in line, and if no victim sued, the action went scot free. If competition were to be restored in such cases, public action was needed.

The Antitrust Movement.   In the United States, during 1865–1900, the pattern of industrial organization was rapidly changed. With the growing network of railways, local and regional markets broadened to national scope. In these larger markets, the scale of industrial operations was increased, production was mechanized, and small shops were displaced by large factories. Large, capital-intensive corporations arose, able to sweep away or absorb small firms. Deflation and depression aggravated the tendency for larger firms to cut prices. During the 1880s, efforts to contain "cut-throat" competition—and to gain monopoly profits—led to agreements or mergers in scores of industries from petroleum, to meat packing, to coal, whiskey, and gunpowder.

As this process continued, many groups in the community—farmers, producers of raw materials, small businessmen, and laborers—suffered injury. The farmers, in particular, experiencing a persistent decline in farm prices, complained of high freight rates charged by the railroads, high interest rates charged by the banks, and high prices charged by the makers of agricultural

---

[3] On the extent of these monopolies, see W. H. Price, *The English Patents of Monopoly* (Cambridge: Harvard University Press, 1913). The leading court decision was *Darcy* v. *Allein,* 11 Coke 84, 77 Eng. Rep. 1260 (K.B. 1603), striking down a monopoly on playing cards.

implements and other manufactured goods. Producers of raw materials, where manufacturing was monopolized, found themselves selling to a single buyer who manipulated the market to depress the prices they received. Independent businessmen, if they refused to be absorbed, were often driven out. Workers were crowded into growing cities, made dependent on industrial employment, and faced with increasing competition for uncertain jobs.

These conditions gave rise to a strong political movement against monopoly, uniting Populists, Grangers, and many other groups. It arose among farmers in the West and South, and among the nascent labor unions and many small businessmen. The movement bred farmer-labor parties, ran an antimonopoly candidate for the presidency, elected a number of members to Congress, and came to control the legislatures of several states. As it grew in strength, the older parties sought to win the votes of its adherents by themselves professing opposition to monopoly. In this way, the movement soon achieved part of its purpose: toward the end of the 1880s, antitrust laws were enacted by state and federal governments.

Since the new monopolies were "trusts" (rather like holding companies), the actions and laws against them were called "antitrust." The trust as a legal device was soon abandoned, but the name has stuck. Led by Kansas in 1889, 18 states enacted antitrust laws by 1891 and most states now have them. These "baby Sherman Acts" vary in detail, but most have proven to be weak and little used, partly because the major cases reach far beyond state boundaries.

In the national election campaign of 1888, both major parties sought the farmer vote by pledges against monopoly. The Democrats, then in office, denounced the tariff as the mother of the trust. The Republicans, proposing higher duties, replied that they could compel competition at home while preventing competition from abroad. Following the Republican victory, President Harrison sent a message to Congress, in 1889, asking that this pledge be redeemed. A number of antimonopoly bills were introduced, one of them by Senator Sherman of Ohio. There was little popular interest in the legislation at the time. Attention was centered, rather, on the effort to grant business and labor further protection against competition by raising the tariff and on the effort to assure farmers higher prices by passing the Silver Purchase Act. The antitrust law was included in the legislative package to quiet the critics of these measures. No hearings were held; the bill that finally emerged from the Congressional committees was enacted, following a brief debate that raised no fundamental issues, with only one dissenting vote in the Senate and without a record vote in the House. It was signed by the President on July 2, 1890. Bearing little or no resemblance to the bill originally introduced by Senator Sherman (and later said by him to be of little consequence), the law was given his name.

The Sherman Act. The act contained little new doctrine. Its real contribution was to turn restraint of trade and monopolization into offenses against the federal government, to require enforcement by federal officials, and to

Senator Sherman of Ohio was only a lesser figure among those working out the final Antitrust Act in 1890. Brother of General William Tecumseh Sherman, who "marched through Georgia," the Senator himself regarded the Sherman Act as of little importance.

The Bettmann Archive Inc.

provide for the imposition of penalties. The penalties were small, and during 1890–94 the Act was used mainly as a weapon to break strikes. Then in 1897 it was used to convict a price-fixing ring, and in 1904 Theodore Roosevelt started "trust-busting" with Section 2. Since 1911, the Sherman Act has been the fulcrum of all U.S. competitive policy. Senator Sherman is a ghostly board member of most large firms and many small ones.

The Clayton and Federal Trade Commission Acts.   There was increasing dissatisfaction, in the years before 1914, with the operation of the Sherman Act. During the administrations of Cleveland and McKinley, the laws had scarcely been enforced. Powerful new combinations had been formed in steel, tin cans, corn products, farm machinery, and many other industries. During the administrations of Roosevelt and Taft, monopolistic abuses had been disclosed in hearings before committees of Congress, in the reports of public agencies, and in the evidence presented in cases brought before the courts. Though it was shown that competition had been eliminated by particular business practices, these practices had not been held to be in violation of the law. And in 1911 the Supreme Court had declared that "reasonable" trusts would be allowed to stand. Following these developments, the trusts again became an issue in the national campaign of 1912. Monopoly was denounced and further legislation promised by the Democrats, the Roosevelt Progressives, and the Republicans.

In 1913 the new Democratic Congress reduced the tariff, set up the Federal Reserve System, and inaugurated the income tax. In 1914 President Wilson turned it to the problem of monopoly. Hearings and debates were now more

TABLE 4–2
Summary of the Main U.S. Antitrust Laws

A. It is illegal:
  1. To enter into a contract, combination, or conspiracy in restraint of trade (Sherman Act, Section 1);
  2. To monopolize, attempt to monopolize, or combine or conspire to monopolize trade (Sherman Act, Section 2).
B. In cases where the effect may be substantially to lessen competition or tend to create a monopoly, it is illegal:
  3. To acquire the stock or the assets of competing corporations (Clayton Act, Section 7, as amended by Celler-Kefauver Act);
  4. To enter into exclusive and tying contracts (Clayton Act, Section 3);
  5. To discriminate among purchasers to an extent that cannot be justified by a difference in cost; or as an attempt made, in good faith, to meet the price of a competitor (Clayton Act, Section 2, as amended by Robinson-Patman Act, Section 2a).
C. And, in general, it is also illegal:
  6. To serve as a director of competing corporations (Clayton Act, Section 8);
  7. To use unfair methods of competition (Federal Trade Commission Act, Section 5);
  8. To employ unfair or deceptive acts or practices (Federal Trade Commission Act, Section 5, as amended by Wheeler-Lea Act, Section 3).

thorough than the proceedings in 1890. The aim was to define anticompetitive acts clearly. But agreement could be reached only on four specific acts.[4] These were written into the Clayton Act, and a general clause against "unfair" competition was included in the Federal Trade Commission Act. Both were enacted in 1914. The FTC's powers were slight: it could only tell violators not to repeat.[5] But it was supposed to be expert and independent of politics.

Robinson-Patman. By 1936, small-grocer pressure against the new chain stores had grown strong enough to cause a protective change in the Clayton Act. The aims were *(a)* to eliminate any unfair advantage of the chain stores in buying their goods and *(b)* to restrain their ability to use "predatory" price cutting against their small rivals. The Robinson-Patman Act has had a checkered reputation, but it has limited price discrimination (see Chapter 8).

Celler-Kefauver. The original Section 7 of the Clayton Act was construed by the courts to permit mergers even by direct competitors.[6] From 1920 to the 1950s, this detour around the law was heavily travelled. Concentration

---

[4] The act was much diluted during its passage and was shorn of strict penalties. Few of the powers and resources needed to reduce monopoly were provided for. See Walton Hamilton and Irene Till, *Antitrust in Action,* TNEC Monograph No. 16, U.S. Government Printing Office, 1941, and the references in note 1 above.

[5] For an argument that the Clayton and FTC Acts were part of a conservative move, see Gabriel Kolko, *The Triumph of Conservatism* (Glencoe, Ill.: Free Press, 1963).

[6] *Thatcher Manufacturing Co.* v. *FTC; Swift & Co.* v. *FTC,* 272 U.S. 554 (1926); and *Arrow-Hart & Hegeman Electric Co.* v. *FTC,* 291 U.S. 587 (1934). The decisions turned on a technicality, rather than substance.

was both induced and permitted to rise. Absurd though it clearly was, competitors who could not legally cooperate on prices were free to merge and then fix the prices internally. This loophole was finally closed in 1950 by amending Clayton Section 7 to cover all legal devices of merging. A merger could not "substantially . . . lessen competition or . . . tend to create a monopoly in any line of commerce in any section of the country"; broad language indeed.

B3. Scope and Coverage

The antitrust laws do not reach everywhere, either by letter or by usage. Large parts of the economy have been exempted. A doctrine of moderation has been built in. The resources for enforcement have been scant.

Scope.   The courts have usually tried to give antitrust wide scope.[7] Local industry has often been held to affect interstate trade. The Division will also try to deal with foreign markets if they can be shown to affect domestic markets. A variety of sectors have been expressly included by the Court, such as railroads by an 1897 decision, ocean shipping companies in 1917, milk producers in 1939, and medical groups in 1943.[8] Others have included insurance in 1944, news services in 1945, real estate brokerage in 1950, newspapers in 1951 (but diluted in 1970), building construction in 1954, and all sports except baseball by decisions in 1955–57.[9] The Court continues to draw the antitrust borders widely, when given a chance to do so.

But coverage actually has as many holes as a Swiss cheese. The Court's doctrinal leads often lapse because the agencies do not continue enforcing. And firms often get from Congress the exemption that the courts have denied. That has occurred for many of those markets just listed: for example, railroads, ocean shipping, milk producers, insurance, and newspapers (in part). A summary of literal and de facto exemptions is given in Table 4–3; Chapter 24 presents more details. One cannot measure antitrust coverage exactly, but

---

[7] After a wobbly start in the E. C. Knight case in 1895. This first major Section 2 case was against the American Sugar Refining Company, which controlled 98 percent of the market. The Supreme Court held that the business was exempt, being manufacturing rather than commerce (*U.S.* v. *E. C. Knight Co.,* 156 U.S. 1). This hairsplitting was never repeated, but it did deter antitrust efforts for a decade or more, until after the main trust wave was complete. Therefore it was a crucial decision.

[8] *NLRB* v. *Jones & Laughlin Steel Corp.,* 301 U.S. 1; *U.S.* v. *Trans-Missouri Freight Assn.,* 166 U.S. 290; *Thomsen* v. *Cayser,* 243 U.S. 66; *U.S.* v. *Borden Co.,* 308 U.S. 188; *U.S.* v. *American Medical Assn.,* 317 U.S. 519.

[9] *U.S.* v. *South-Eastern Underwriters Assn.,* 322 U.S. 533; *U.S. Alkali Export Assn.* v. *U.S.,* 325 U.S. 196; *U.S.* v. *Associated Press,* 326 U.S. 1; *U.S.* v. *National Assn. of Real Estate Boards,* 339 U.S. 485; *Lorain Journal Co.* v. *U.S.,* 342 U.S. 143; *U.S.* v. *Employing Plasters' Assn.,* 347 U.S. 186; *Federal Baseball Club of Baltimore* v. *National League,* 259 U.S. 200 (1922); *Toolson* v. *New York Yankees,* 346 U.S. 356 (1953). On the economic and legal issues involved here, see Roger G. Noll, ed., *Government and the Sports Business* (Washington, D.C.: Brookings Institution, 1975), and the cases cited there.

TABLE 4–3
The Main Antitrust Exemptions

	Discussed in
As a Matter of Law	*Chapters*
Agriculture and fishing organizations	24
Milk and certain other farm products	24
Labor unions	24
Most public enterprises	16–19
Regulated industries (in their main activities)	
Public utilities: electric, gas, postal, telephone, railroads	10–15
Others (partial or self-regulation): banks, stock exchanges, insurance, airlines, trucking, ocean shipping, pipelines, broadcasting	20,13,14
Baseball (partly)	24
Newspaper joint operating arrangements	24
Export cartels	4,24
As a Matter of Usage	
Many trades and services (intra-state and larger)	24
Professions (law, medicine, and others)*	24
Urban services (transit, sewage, water)	18
Many health services (hospitals; physicians' services)	
Education	18
Governmental services	16–19,25
Certain national defense suppliers	24
Certain patent-intensive industries (drugs, and so on.)	6,21

* Recent cases have begun to extend antitrust laws to price fixing among lawyers, engineers, and some other professions. But other restrictions are still permitted.

it probably covers less than half of the economy, and this share may be shrinking. Recently the courts have been willing to extend coverage back into parts of certain regulated sectors (bulk electric power, bank mergers, stock exchanges, certain professions, and so on). In short, the lines are often blurred and changing.

Rules of Reason. The Sherman Act is absolute, prohibiting "every" monopoly and trade restraint. At first this seemed to go beyond the common law, which had allowed certain secondary (ancillary) restraints to stand.[10] But in 1911, Chief Justice White read a "rule of reason" into both sections of the Sherman Act, finding Standard Oil and American Tobacco guilty for monopolizing "unreasonably:" for being "bad" trusts, not just for having monopolized.[11] This enervated antitrust for several decades, because it reversed the burden of proof. Agencies now had to prove both *(a)* that a

---

[10] An ancillary restraint is incidental to a legal purpose; it may occur, for instance, when a person selling a business, a partner withdrawing from it, or an employee leaving it undertakes to preserve its value by refraining from competition with its purchaser, a remaining partner, or a former employer. The courts applied a rule of reason, enforcing such restrictions when they were limited in duration and extent, and refusing to do so when they were not.

[11] *Standard Oil Co. of N.J.* v. *U.S.*, 221 U.S. 1; *U.S.* v. *American Tobacco Co.*, 221 U.S. 106.

monopoly or restraint existed, and *(b)* that it had "unreasonable" origins or effects. Further, the Court in 1920 held that later good behavior could exculpate a monopolist. The "rule of reason" held sway for several decades, stopping efforts to restructure several of the original trusts and to apply it to new monopolies and restraints. Despite a bold rejection of the "rule" by Judge Hand in the 1945 *Alcoa* decision, its spirit has continued to govern Section 2 (see Chapter 5).

Some such reasonable evaluation must be made in any case, as Chapter 3 noted. The economy is full of degrees of monopoly and collusion, of probabilities of effect, and of trade-offs among goods and bads. Moreover, agency resources are scarce and cannot cover every slight deviation. So balance is needed. Yet the presence of a "rule" of reason as an effective legal doctrine does give genuine exemption to many firms which hold high degrees of market power.

In short, the U.S. antitrust laws have become a specialized tool for certain sectors. Courts will usually apply them broadly, but Congress grants many legal exemptions, and large *de facto* exemptions also occur. Much depends on the agencies, in mounting broad-scale cases and in asserting their role throughout the economy.

C. ENFORCEMENT

Recall that optimal treatment requires *(a)* that the agency's jurisdiction and tasks be in balance with its powers and resources, and *(b)* that policies be optimal in design as well as extent. In this light, the record of U.S. antitrust enforcement is broadly as follows: *Its jurisdiction is wide and its tasks are difficult, yet its powers are moderate and its resources have been slim. It has become strict in some directions (price fixing, mergers) but gentle in others (especially toward dominance). Its design is often poorly suited to the needed incentives. It is enforced less widely than the letter of its laws.*

C1. Resources

The agencies have been small in comparison to their tasks (see Table 4–4). The total budgets and expert staffs are slender, and much of them are taken up by secondary chores. They contend with private resources which often dwarf them.

Thus the Division's yearly budget is less than the cost of a middle-sized naval cruiser or war plane. It is less than one *week's* profit at stake—and therefore available for resistance efforts—in several major industries. Even if multiplied, as many experts now suggest, antitrust resources would be tiny in a federal government budget of $400 billion and a GNP over $1,700 billion. No economic appraisal guides the setting of these agencies' budgets, even though the marginal yields on antitrust resources may be high. Internal

TABLE 4–4
Budget and Professional Resources in U.S. Antitrust, 1950–1977

Year	Antitrust Division		Federal Trade Commission (all activities)	
	Budget ($ million)	Professional Staff	Budget ($ million)	Professional Staff
1950	$ 3.8	290	$ 3.1	620
1959	$ 4.1	232	$ 6.5	734
1969	$ 8.4	319	$16.9	1,218
1974	$14.8	327	$32.5	1,590
1977	$26.7	459	$54.7	1,792

Sources: Data supplied by the agencies.

budgeting of the resources has improved sharply since 1971. For example, the 1976 budget was over 300 pages long, much of it involving economic analysis.

The resources are thinly spread. On average, there is only the equivalent of two or three full-time lawyers working on each of the five or so largest industries. For the rest—and especially for new industries—there is little or no continuous attention, by lawyers assigned part-time to several industries. A big case—with perhaps five or ten lawyers, two economists, and supporting staff (and perhaps many more, as trial approaches) can take a large portion of agency resources and attention.

Agency lawyers commonly face superior numbers of lawyers on the other side, except when the firm is small or the case is minor. The average quality of antitrust staff also tends—with exceptions—to be lower than their private adversaries. This reflects their far lower pay, and the relative youth and inexperience of much of the staff. Indeed, the agencies are partly a training ground for the private law firms. A year or more in the agencies gives a staff attorney valuable experience for private practice. Many of the present antitrust super-lawyers owe their eminence (and high fees) to such a start. Negotiations, trials, and appeals commonly pit former agency officials against present officials (some of whom will shortly join the private side too!).

There are some offsets to the imbalance of resources. The agencies can invoke broad powers, impose expensive litigation, and call on some outside resources in many cases. On some matters the heads of the agencies need only a little will-power, rather than a large volume of new resources. But there are counter-offsets too, such as the firms' better access to crucial data and their frequent recourse to other public agencies (Congress, White House, the Defense Department, and so forth) for help.

The antitrust agencies are almost surely too small: in technical terms, their resource levels are below the optimum, at which discounted marginal benefits would equal costs.

Francis Miller, Time-Life *Agency*

Officials of du Pont (seated) and their senior attorneys in the du Pont-General Motors case (shown November 1952). Many younger lawyers (not included here) also assisted.

Resources Differ. Such an imbalance is common in antitrust cases involving large firms. (Is the lesson altered by the fact that the du Pont-General Motors case was ultimately decided in favor of the Antitrust Division?)

Francis Miller, Time-Life *Agency*

Antitrust Division attorneys on the du Pont-General Motors Case (shown November 1952).

C2. The Pace of Action

There have been several peaks of enforcement activity, separated by lulls. There is no precise measure of such activity, but the number of cases filed is a popular if rough indicator (see Tables 4–5 and 4–6).[12] There have been two main bursts of activity, during 1904–15 and 1938–52. The rise since 1965 in funds and case activity may eventually rank with the two earlier waves. Distinct low periods were 1890–1904, 1920–38, and 1952–65.

TABLE 4–5
Types of Cases Brought: Antitrust Division

	Period in Which the Case Was Instituted					
	1890 to 1904	1905 to 1919	1920 to 1934	1935 to 1954	1955 to 1969	Total
Horizontal conspiracy	15	119	105	449	301	989
Monopolizing	4	37	24	201	104	370
Acquisitions short of monopoly	1	6	7	13	167	194
Boycott	1	6	35	115	68	245
Resale price maintenance		6	2	5	14	27
Vertical integration		5	4	30	14	53
Tying arrangements		5	2	47	11	65
Exclusive dealing	1	1	4	73	51	140
Territorial and customer limitations				14	65	74
Violence	4	2	21	14	6	47
Price discrimination	2	11	5	70	35	123
Other predatory or unfair conduct	1	8	4	6	19	88
Interlocking directorates			2	10	4	16
Clayton Act, sec. 10				1	2	3
Labor cases	3	8	29	72	13	125
Patent and copyright cases		7	13	106	39	165
Total cases in period	16	173	165	596	605	1551

The table shows the distribution of allegations, not of cases.
Source: Computed from the Bluebook, as reported in Posner, "A Statistical Study of Antitrust Enforcement," *The Journal of Law and Economics,* 365 (1970).

The recent marked rise in private antitrust suits is also shown in Table 4–6. Many of these cases are very small in scope and have no value in defining or enforcing public policy. Yet some are large and precedent-setting, and altogether they are a large mass of case activity.

C3. The Setting

These resources and their uses are influenced by the setting of the agencies, shown in Figure 4–1. It has changed little since the 1920s.

---

[12] Some cases are far more important than others; and some cases (not necessarily the same ones) are much more costly to litigate. Merely counting cases gives them each an equal weight, which may be deceptive.

TABLE 4–6
Antitrust Cases Commenced, Fiscal Years 1960 Through 1976

| Fiscal Year | Total | Government Cases (Antitrust Division and FTC) | | Private Cases | |
		Civil	Criminal	Electrical Equipment Industry	Other
1960	315	60	27	—	228
1961	441	42	21	37	341
1962	2,079	41	33	1,739	266
1963	457	52	25	97	283
1964	446	59	24	46	317
1965	521	38	11	29	443
1966	770	36	12	278	444
1967	598	39	16	7	536
1968	718	48	11	—	659
1969	797	43	14	—	740
1970	933	52	4	—	877
1971	1,515	60	10	—	1,445
1972	1,393	80	14	—	1,299
1973	1,224	54	18	—	1,152
1974	1,294	40	24	—	1,230
1975	1,467	56	36	—	1,375
1976	1,574	51	19	—	1,504

Source: *Trade Regulation Reports,* No. 253, November 1, 1976, p. 7.

Congress.   Budgets are set by Congress, after yearly hearings. Congress also acts on exemptions from antitrust; there are usually a few in the mill. Members of Congress—on behalf of companies and others in their districts— keep up a fair volume of inquiries and gentle persuasion, and sometimes a hard sell. From industry and the public come information, persuasion, and complaints—by customers, competitors, takeover targets, and so on.

Executive Branch.   Other parts of the Executive Branch often influence Antitrust Division moves, though this is usually done discreetly and mainly in acute cases. The White House also sets broad implicit limits, by its general tone toward business and by its appointments to both agencies.

Appointees to head the Antitrust Division are usually of high technical quality, thanks to long traditions set in part by the private Antitrust Bar. By contrast, the FTC has suffered from many mediocre appointments: very junior and very senior politicians, lawyers inexperienced in antitrust issues, and so on.

The agencies have much independence, because they are not within a large business-oriented department, such as Commerce. At the Justice Department, the concern of higher officials is mainly with legal consistency, rather than industrial politics. This independence also keeps antitrust free of adventurous or "radical" actions, which political guidance might cause on occasion.

Judiciary.   The courts are the main arena for the Division, and they can also reverse FTC actions (though recently they have rarely done so). They will usually enforce the agencies' efforts to get evidence and pursue

FIGURE 4–1

The Setting of the U.S. Federal Antitrust Agencies

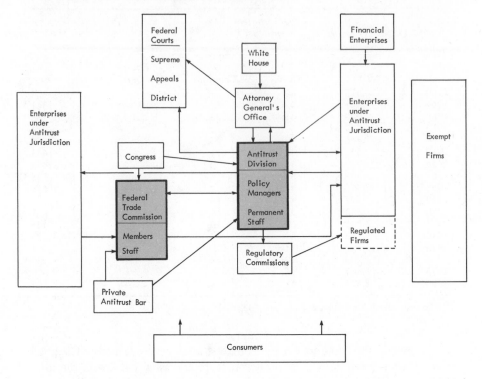

"reasonable" actions. But the courts are usually slow, and they stress legal decisions by the adversary process, rather than neutral economic evaluations.

The private Antitrust Bar is the 10,000 lawyers—in law firms and on corporate and banking staffs—who specialize in antitrust matters. Their pecking order runs from famous older lawyers whose mere presence commands respect, down to small-town attorneys with small-scale clients. Some litigate in open court; others solely advise, prepare strategy, and negotiate. They are an influential and well-paid group, dedicated to the continuation of active antitrust. It is their livelihood, win or lose.

Large firms have their own legal staffs, some with scores of attorneys working on antitrust matters. They advise and warn managers about risky courses of action, handle private and public suits, and negotiate with all parties. "Outside counsel"—from prestige law firms—are often brought in to handle or help with delicate and critical matters. Fees are high, often $100 per hour on up to over $2000 per day for leading lawyers. Fees for larger firms and cases routinely cumulate into millions of dollars. It is a fascinating world, blending diplomacy, a mandarin language and poker-playing strategies, plus plain scrambling and grit—over stakes often reaching into billions of dollars.

The federal courts process and decide that minority of actions issues which become formal cases because they are not resolved by negotiation or pre-avoidance. And filtering into the agencies and courts are new research evidence about the parameters of the problem: economies of scale, monopoly effects, trends, and the like (as summarized in Chapter 2).

C4. Inner Conditions

In short, antitrust is embedded in a setting of influences, traditions, budget limits and mechanisms, which define what it can do—and is expected to do—at each point. What *is* done depends also, in part, on who is running the agencies.

The top decision positions are filled mainly by lawyers: always at the Antitrust Division, mainly so at the FTC. During their brief tenure, these appointees can set a new level of effort, start some new actions, and reach into the pipeline to pull ahead some pending cases.[13] But most basic changes take five years or more to prepare and follow through, and so the degree of strictness tends to vary within a fairly narrow range. The key permanent staff members are also lawyers. They usually mingle an inner hostility toward monopoly with—as they age—a bureaucratic resignation to the likelihood that no large changes will ever be carried through.

The lawyers' job is to advocate and to interpret rules. Most lawyers are untrained in economic analysis, quantitative judgment or, for that matter, basic social issues. Their legal training instills a respect for private property rights and due process. And their efforts on all major cases must proceed through the courts, often at a slow pace.

Therefore staff lawyers tend to go for the cases which *(a)* they can win and/or *(b)* which are (or merely look) active and "tough." The courts—also staffed by lawyers—partly guide the flow of action. But the agencies have a great range of choice and often choose only a narrow set of cases to deal with. In short, the lawyerly control of antitrust yields long-run trends in emphasis, and short-run fluctuations in strictness, which may stray from the optimal patterns.

Since the agencies' resources are scarce, allocation choices are often critical. One result is that large areas of enforcement are routinely neglected; that is, existing powers are not applied. Big cases that are brought are accused—often with some justice—of being too episodic and unexpected, of singling out a few victims rather than treating all offenders evenly.

The agencies' capacity to absorb key information is limited, especially in the Antitrust Division. Because the Census Bureau secretes all data on individual companies, the agencies lack direct and timely information. Repeat: they do *not* have access to secret information in other agencies. They must conduct

---

[13] They are also often amateurs in three key respects. *(a)* They usually know little about managing an agency. *(b)* They are not expert in economic analysis, and *(c)* they usually are not skilled in handling the political pressures which surround them.

their own research, such as it is, from scattered sources including the firms themselves. Even the growing legal and economic staffs are only capable of doing this for, at the most, several large cases at a time. There is still very little chance of mounting thorough, complex research on major industries, on the large scale which the Bureau of Corporations reached during 1906–14.

Therefore the agencies' reach has been turned toward simpler cases.[14] They must usually rely on formal adversary proceedings to bring out full information. This means that for a broad range of major industries, antitrust choices have to be made without thorough information. And the courts often lack means or procedures to carry out well-informed remedies, even when the need for change has been established.

C5. Allocation

In the grip of these pressures, the heads of the agencies divide their resources mainly among:

1. *Policing conduct,* to stop cooperation among firms to fix prices or restrain trade in other ways (Sherman Act, Section 1, and Clayton Act, various sections),
2. *Restoring competitive conditions in established near-monopolies and tight oligopolies* (Sherman Act, Section 2),
3. *Preventing new structural monopoly* via mergers (Clayton Act, Section 7).

The two agencies have to discover these violations, proceed against them, and get convictions in the courts, and then make sure the remedies are adequate. Table 4–4 shows the broad trends in litigation activity among these directions.

Some of these tasks are hard, others quite easy. Restorative cases against existing monopoly are hard; the agencies usually must prove—against severe resistance by the firms—that some new structure would be better than the existing or evolving one. Price-fixing cases are much easier, for the agency lawyers need prove only that an attempt to fix prices was made, not that it was successful or that the industry's conditions need changing.

The bulk of antitrust resources go to *policing* conduct; price fixing, patent restrictions, predatory pricing agreements, and so forth. A recent study suggests that in 1975–77 the Antitrust Division devoted about 65 percent of its staff time to conduct (within that, about 36 percent to horizontal price fixing), 12 percent to Section 2 restorative actions, and 14 percent to mergers.[15]

---

[14] This could conceivably be changing. Also, from 1965 to 1973 there was a yearly appointee as Special Economic Assistant to the Division head (including the present junior author during 1967–68). This provided for close contact and advice on all manner of cases, small and large.

[15] U.S. Senate Subcommittee on Antitrust and Monopoly, *Hearings on Oversight of Antitrust Enforcement,* 95th Cong., 1st sess. (Washington, D.C.: U.S. Government

The FTC's allocation of antitrust resources (which is only half of its total budget) would be roughly the same. Many of these are extremely detailed and complex matters, but most are relatively simple. The number of investigations is of course much higher than the number of cases actually brought, by about 3 to 1. Even the investigations are in total probably only a sample of the actual incidents. Most of the cases are settled informally by consent decree or by a lower court decision. Most are of slight importance; worth doing, but small and not making new law (there is no precedential multiplier).

Certain acts are illegal per se, such as price fixing and market sharing. Conviction requires only a showing that the act occurred or was attempted, not that the result was harmful. Yet such strict rules are not as broad as they seem. Because of the many exemptions of sectors, the per se rules cover only a minority of activity in the economy. And the tight rules induce efforts to attain the same collusive results by other tactics.

Preventive actions are mainly toward mergers. These absorbed a rising share of resources in the 1960s as the merger wave rose and crested. Only a few score mergers at the most, among thousands each year, are intensively studied, and even fewer are eventually opposed. These are usually intended to set precedent in marginal areas. These cases tend also to be quickly dispatched. As the rules against horizontal and vertical mergers have been extended (see Chapter 6), the more subtle issues of conglomerate mergers have come to the fore, especially since 1965. Here, the agencies are entering more marginal issues, different from those in horizontal mergers. Also the Antitrust Division is increasingly involved in treating mergers by regulated firms, such as airlines, electric utilities, banks, and railroads. This often requires arduous efforts to convince the regulatory commissions—and often the courts, on appeal—to disallow or modify merger proposals.

Restorative activities toward existing market power deal with both regulated and unregulated sectors. Antitrust attempts to reduce monopoly and open up entry into regulated markets have grown recently, in such sectors as communications, transportation, and stock exchanges.

In the unregulated sectors, by contrast, restorative policies faded during 1952–1968. In a revival since 1968, changes have been sought in the computer, copying equipment, cereals, oil, and telecommunications industries. Restructuring can occur only in initiating action to prove that monopoly exists and to require remedies. This, we will see in Chapter 5, is usually a difficult and protracted procedure. Yet the near-monopolies are often also quasiregulated informally by the antitrust agencies. Their market positions and profitability are reviewed from time to time as possible triggers for restorative action or other penalties. So the firms may have—or believe they have—incentives to understate their reported profitability, and to moderate their price discrimination.

Printing Office, 1977), pp. 456–62. See also the chapter by Leonard W. Weiss in James A. Dalton and Stanford Levin, eds., *The Antitrust Dilemma* (Lexington, Mass.: Heath-Lexington Books, 1974).

C6. Sanctions and Levers

Certain costs can be inflicted. The agencies' tools are narrow, but they pack various kinds of power. They can penalize past actions, but they can do little to change basic conditions in industry.

1. *Investigation.* The study process can be large, long, and costly to the firm, by choice either of the agencies *or* of the firms themselves.
2. *Suit.* A case inflicts
   a. Direct costs of litigation. These can run very high, as we have seen, and cases usually involve far more legal activity than lay observers realize.
   b. Diversion of executive attention. This indirect burden on management can be extensive.
   c. Bad publicity. This can affect a company's image and goodwill, though it usually has little direct effect on its market position and long-run yields.
3. *Stoppage of company action.* The contested action is often stopped as soon as it is challenged, even if it is eventually exonerated. In merger cases, a stay or preliminary injunction is often obtained to prevent the merger until the case is argued and decided.
4. *Conviction.* This is only a decision on the legal outcome. Its power lies solely in leading to these penalties:
   a. Fines and other civil or criminal penalties, including jail terms.
   b. Remedies, which are of two main sorts: (1) Constraints on behavior ("injunctive relief"), (2) Changes in company structure (the traditional 3Ds: divestiture, divorcement and dissolution).
   c. Private damage suits. (But note that a consent decree or a *nolo contendere* plea, if accepted by the court and agency, does not give a basis for damages.)

It is widely believed that the probability of getting caught is more important than the severity of the resulting penalty. Presently, the chances of getting caught are regarded as low, except for flagrant offenses. The litigation and conviction are themselves often the main penalty.

Fines have been unimportant for most large defendants, even though the ceilings have recently been raised. The $5,000 limit set in the Sherman Act was raised to $50,000 in 1955, but this was a fly-speck for the largest several hundred firms. In December 1974, the ceiling was raised again, to $500,000 for individuals and $1 million for firms.[16] But most judges' actual fines are well below the limits.

Lawyers incessantly figure the odds and values of their clients' alternatives and advise them accordingly. The yield to be gotten *now* from violating

---

[16] For a major analysis of the optimum types and levels of fines, see Kenneth G. Elzinga and William Breit, *The Antitrust Penalties* (New Haven: Yale University Press, 1975).

often well exceeds the discounted present value of a small, distant—and perhaps avoidable—fine. The average fine in price-fixing cases has risen above $100,000 in recent years.[17] Though the impact can be great for small firms, this is peanuts for large companies. Thus the average fine during 1960–69 was only 0.2 percent of the sales of the conspiring firms. Violations can pay handsomely even after deducting the fine.

Criminal penalties have been rarely used, and before 1959 no significant industrialist had spent a day in jail for violating the Sherman Act. Then two cases brought some change. Four officers of hand-tool companies were sentenced to 90 days in jail. And the electrical equipment price-fixing case of 1960 put seven officials in jail for 30 days (see Chapter 7). Jail is now possible. But the sentences are light, and the penalties are used only for occasional brazen cases. Though criminal penalties were stiffened in 1974 for Section 1 offenses, they are still usually applied sparingly.

Private damages can be levied at triple the amount of harm shown to have been caused to an injured party. Therefore a clear agency win can trigger scores of private suits by overcharged customers, excluded competitors, and so forth. This impact often dwarfs all the other penalties, and fear of it often is the real reason for a relentless defense.

Certain market conditions can be changed. *Injunctive reliefs* can stop specific actions, but without penalizing what has been done earlier. They are specific to the firm and action in question: other firms and tactics are not touched. They have recently become effective against certain mergers.

Restorative actions can change existing structure, but they have been sparingly used since 1913 (see Chapter 6). District courts have to settle on the remedies, in the end. These judges have been easily persuaded that "breaking" up companies is hazardous. In any event, they have no resources or expertise to carry out the changes. The courts only decide; the agencies and firms have to agree on remedies. The old maxim is: "The agencies win the decisions but lose the remedies."[18] Though it is quite normal in private affairs, altering business structure has come to be treated by the courts as an exotic act, used only in the last resort.

Consent decrees require a special word. They are a compromise reached in a civil suit; in fact, about nine tenths of the suits are settled in this way. It is possible to arrange at any point, as each side reckons its prospects, comparing one bird in the hand with two in the bush. The agreement is then filed with the court, subject to the judge's approval. It is a flexible,

---

[17] The figure is for the total fine per case, including all defendants; the average fine per firm is closer to $20,000. See James M. Clabault and John F. Burton, Jr., *Sherman Act Indictments, 1955–65* (New York: Federal Legal Publications, 1966), p. 104; and Richard A. Posner, *Antitrust Law* (Chicago: University of Chicago Press, 1976), pp. 32–34.

[18] See Walter Adams, "Dissolution, Divorcement, and Divestiture: The Pyrrhic Victories of Antitrust," *Indiana Law Journal* 27 (Fall 1951), 1–37 and Kenneth G. Elzinga, "The Antimerger Law: Pyrrhic Victories?", *Journal of Law and Economics* 12 (April 1969), 43–78.

FIGURE 4–2

Trends in Antitrust "Wins" and Consent Decrees

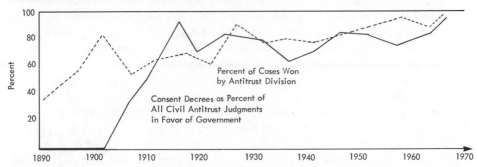

Source: R. A. Posner, "A Statistical Study of Antitrust Enforcement," *Journal of Law and Economics*, 365 (1970), Tables 5 and 11.

cheap, and often sophisticated method, especially attractive to hard-pressed agencies. Often it achieves creative results. And it has been used increasingly, as hinted in Figure 4–2.

Yet there are drawbacks. The settlements are reached in private, with no records. Soft bargains are often struck, or outright retreats. Settlements prevent a clear legal answer. This eliminates any precedential multiplier. It also leaves no basis for damage claims by injured private parties. Economic aspects are regularly neglected as the lawyers bargain. Finally, many decrees are quickly forgotten and unenforced.

Consent decrees were heavily used in the 1950s and extolled as a new approach. But their use is now more sparing and realistic.

In Summary. Some of these tools are potent and can, in extreme cases, exert great power, especially on small firms. The normal steps in using them are shown in Figure 4–3 below. The trail can be a long one, and it can be cut off by a compromise at virtually any point. The agencies also supervise and monitor behavior in continuing ways; and firms can, and do, get agency advice on what to expect if doubtful actions are tried.

The antitrust tools are also narrow, relying on specific processes and penalties. The agencies can threaten and press, but they cannot give positive incentives or rewards.

D. THE ANTITRUST DIVISION

We now look at the two agencies separately. The Antitrust Division is centered in the third floor of the gray Justice Department building at 10th and Constitution Avenue in Washington, D.C. The head offices are elegant, the lesser offices and halls rather bleak. Here one finds lofty power over industry and mind-numbing drudgery; a certain messianic spirit and plodding details.

FIGURE 4–3
The Process of Antitrust Decisions and Litigation

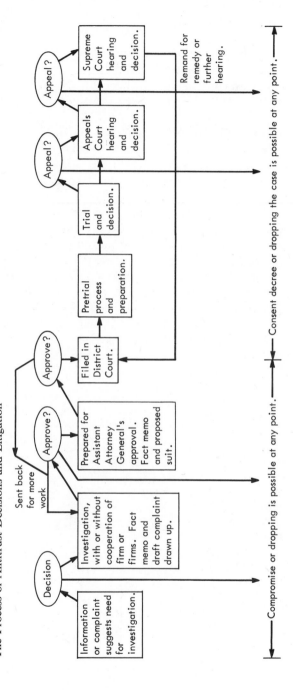

D1. Structure

In the structure of the Division, as shown in Figure 4–4, there are a variety of functional sections, all staffed by *career* lawyers. Above this are the current antitrust chief and his small appointed staff, which the permanent staff more or less fondly call the "front office" or, on occasion, the "Gold Coast."

The staff lawyers develop possible cases which, if eventually approved, are signed and filed in court. Or instead, the suit may be sent back down for further work, or just delayed. There are channels and procedures, but there is also much informal discussion and planning among the levels.

The four trial sections at the center of Figure 4–4 are the core, the draft horses of antitrust. Other sections handle specific tasks. The Appellate Section prepares appeals to higher courts. Public Counsel handles matters relating to other official agencies, such as railway mergers (Department of Transportation) and electric utility mergers (the Federal Power Commission). The Judgments Section polices the old court orders and consent decrees—more or less zealously, often less. The Foreign Section deals with international aspects (the State Department, and so on). And the Economic Policy Office services the lawyer's requests for data, on markets, market shares, and other routine matters (since 1973 it has also begun doing some substantial research).

FIGURE 4–4
Structure of the Antitrust Division

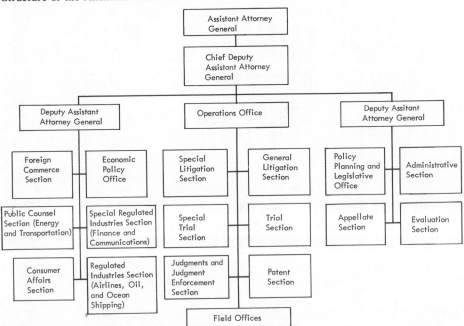

D2. Process

The process by which antitrust decisions are posed and made is fascinating and important to understand.[19] The basic actor is the staff lawyer, specializing in one or several industries. He/she is like a small entrepreneur, seeking to maximize his or her record of successful cases—and to get to be a Section Chief. Large and old industries may be assigned several lawyers, in each agency; small and new ones are often thinly covered or unassigned. The lawyer has latitude to ferret out possible violations, either on his or her own, or on an assigned investigation, or solely in response to a private complaint or tip.

A case or investigation is usually triggered by a complaint or an important change reported in the press. Investigation may also involve staff economists and, on occasion, an outside consultant.[20] The investigation looks mainly for *documents* and also for witnesses. Documents are of all sorts (letters, notes, reports, data), and the critical ones are usually buried in the target company's own files. The agencies must somehow learn or guess where they are, and ask for them. Then the firm's lawyers may produce them *(a)* voluntarily if the firm is cooperating (to show it has nothing to hide), or *(b)* under a court order (a civil investigative demand: CID) if the firm is fighting the action.[21]

The agency must often fish a little, without giving the firm a good chance to criticize it or to "snow" the investigating lawyer with masses of irrelevant materials.[22]

Note that the lawyers learn to rely only on such documents for *proof.* Research findings are usually regarded as too soft for courtroom use, even though they would help to determine the optimum treatment. Judges want to have documentary proof, not theories or probabilities.

The antitrust investigator or group does a research report (a "fact memo") on whether a violation of antitrust law has occurred and a suit against the offender might be justified. The criterion is, of course, legal: can a violation of the law be proven? If the attorney recommends suing, he also draws up

---

[19] This is essential to evaluating the results and the alternative approaches. It is little changed since Walton Hamilton's and Irene Till's superb description of it in their *Antitrust in Action*, pp. 23–100. See also Suzanne Weaver, *Decision to Prosecute: Organization and Public Policy in the Antitrust Division* (Cambridge, Mass.: MIT Press, 1977).

[20] Consultants are often unavailable, especially for large and important cases. Firms often have incentives and ample resources to tie up leading experts as consultants.

[21] CIDs have been available only since 1962. Previously, documents could only be required under subpoena, and subpoenas were available only after suit had been filed or an indictment obtained. So Catch-22: data needed to decide if suit were justified could be gotten only after filing suit. For 60 years this absurdity prevailed and affected antitrust choices.

[22] The firm's lawyers must often sift out and hand over documents which they know to be damning to their client. Why do they do such a tantalizing thing? Because destroying evidence is a felony, leading also to disbarment. Also, the lawyer is only a hired advocate, out to make the best case but not desperate to win at any cost.

a draft complaint. This pair of drafts—the grist of antitrust—then passes up in the mill for discussion, further work, and decision at higher levels.[23] In the Antitrust Division, the Assistant Attorney General for Antitrust decides, usually after more study, whether to approve suit. Then the case is filed. Trial may take three to six years to begin after decision, appeals may take several more years. And in big cases, the Supreme Court may send the case back down for practical remedies, which may take another several years. At the other extreme, actions against planned mergers may have effect in a matter of weeks or even hours. Here time often favors the Division in resisting change, since judges often prevent full consummation of the merger until the basic issues are clarified.

The sides favored by the burden of proof and by having time in one's favor can be summarized roughly as follows:

Subject of Action	The Burden of Proof Favors	Time Delay Favors
Price fixing	Neither side	Neither side
Mergers	Agency	Agency (if injunction is granted)
Restorative	Firm	Firm

These directions of advantage can affect the substance of the outcomes.

D3. Selectivity and "Wins"

In any event, the natural roles are for staff attorneys to make out the best possible case for suit. They will naturally favor small, simple winnable cases which *they* can prepare and carry out themselves. The policy managers then select from the evolving portfolio of possible suits those cases which look best in legal and, perhaps, economic terms. The courts then further select those cases which have merit, with the judicial procedure leaning toward conservative results. The Supreme Court, at the end, can also select the correct margins of policy treatment. In short, a rule of reason can be applied at all levels. But only if the agencies lean on balance toward strictness will the courts have a range for selection.

Therefore a high "batting average" in the Supreme Court is ambiguous. It can show that the Court is quick to back the agencies, even in dubious cases. That is the common view. But instead, it can simply show that the agencies are timid or lax, sending up only the minimum set of safest cases which it can easily win. This deprives the Court of a range of choice and it reflects weak enforcement, not strictness.

---

[23] The firm under study is usually able to keep well-informed of matters as they progress, and commonly its lawyers come in to make frequent efforts to persuade against action.

D4. Problems of Delay

Most Division actions require at least a year or two to run their course, but the variation in times is extreme (see Figure 4–5). Some matters take but a few days: a merger folds when the Division announces it will investigate, price fixers capitulate when caught. But others take years: for example, about 1953 to 1975 for the El Paso Natural Gas case, and 1947 to 1969 for United Shoe Machinery. The average time for completing a litigated antitrust case has been about 5.5 years. This period has stayed relatively constant; the delay factor is *not* rising for the average case.

The delays are partly inherent, since it takes time to investigate, prepare suit, carry out pretrial jockeying, try, appeal, and win a suit, and then apply remedy. Also, time is often needed to let the issues ripen, so that a clear basis for settlement can be agreed. Still, court processes can be maddeningly slow. And often the delay reflects sheer sluggishness or even bungling. Frequently the Division allows itself to be euchred into being snowed with irrelevant documents, which it must then plow patiently through, looking for needles in the haystack.

Where the stakes are high, private parties have managed to stall for years—and reap further monopoly gains—by astute procedural tactics. And justice delayed is justice denied; or rather, policy delayed is policy nullified. The Division can be endlessly patient, but it cannot usually muster large corps of lawyers for major cases. Treatment therefore tends to be labor-saving and time-using. And court resources are treated virtually as a free good.

D5. Hazards of the Legal Process

Litigation poses special problems. In a civil action, guilt must be established by a preponderance of evidence. In a criminal suit, it must be proven beyond a reasonable doubt. The evidence, however, may be largely circumstantial;

FIGURE 4–5
Lengths of Cases

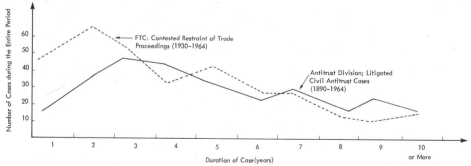

Source: R. A. Posner, "A Statistical Study of Antitrust Enforcement, *Journal of Law and Economics,* 1970, Tables 8 and 10.

documentary proof may be wanting and witnesses reluctant to testify. The complexities of business organization and practice may be difficult for the prosecution to explain and for the jury and the judge to understand. The defendants may be eminently respectable, members of the best clubs, active in charitable enterprises, and pillars of the church. The course of conduct of which they are accused may appear to be quite normal. The jury may hesitate to convict, the judge to provide appropriate remedies.

The matter at stake in a trial is the behavior of an industry in the *future.* The matter discussed is the evidence of its wrongdoing in the *past.* Whatever the issues, the prosecution must seek a conviction, the defense an acquittal. And the process often becomes a ritualized struggle, in which economic issues are neglected.[24] The judge usually faces severe challenges, even though the typical district court judge has little training in economics or antitrust. Moreover, important cases usually pose engineering and accounting problems.[25] In preparing the opinion, the judge makes no separate investigation but chooses among the alternatives presented by counsel for the prosecution and counsel for the defense. The record that must be digested is often voluminous and mind-numbing.[26]

---

[24] "It brings to the settlement of questions of economic order the processes, hazards, confusions, evasions, circumlocutions, delays, of the legal folkways. . . . Persons competent in the habits of industry must give way to those skilled in the techniques of legal combat. . . . The opposing champions are well versed in demurrer, interlocutory motion, the tactics of seeking or avoiding a general engagement. . . . The staging of the question as an adversary proceeding sets lawyer against lawyer. . . . Every move, every witness, every fact, every document becomes a counter in a legal game. "The record" has come to do vicarious duty for an analysis of the industry in operation; and every item, favorable to one side, can win admission only against the heavy cross-fire of the other. Every procedural device which may arrest or speed action, flank or snipe the verbal minions of the enemy, color the conduct on parade with innocence or guilt is called into play. . . . Again and again the attorney and the witness raise their antiphonal voices; the counsel for the adverse party chants the approved formula "incompetent, irrelevant, and immaterial"; the judge from the loft above interjects a responsive "sustained" or "overruled"; and the loser, who intends to fight another day, comes in dramatically with "exception". . . . It takes the final summing up of the lawyers to bring the jury back to the dominant legal issue. And somehow antitrust as an instrument of public policy has gotten lost in the scuffle." (Hamilton and Till, pp. 59–62.)

[25] The judge ". . . is expected to have a critical mastery of corporate finance, marketing practice, industrial structure; to have a sound grasp of physics, chemistry, electrodynamics, in fact the fundamentals of all the mechanical arts. . . . In a word, he must be alike omnicompetent in law and industry—an expert in the multiplex of affairs and disciplines which converge upon the case. . . . In the face of his own ordeal, his tendency is to retire somewhat from the domain of industrial reality and to fortify his judicial performance with a meticulous observance of the technicalities. . . . Even the judge himself becomes an obstacle to bringing into sharp relief the pattern of the industry and its point of restraint." (Ibid, pp. 71–72.) Few judges have had training either in antitrust law or economics.

[26] In the A&P case, the judge was confronted with 45,000 pages of testimony and 7,000 exhibits; in the Aluminum case with 58,000 pages of testimony and 15,000 pages of documents. In the *Sugar Institute* case, the judge spent 14 months writing a 50-page finding of facts and a 178-page opinion. Mark S. Massel, *Competition and Monopoly* (Washington, D.C.: Brookings Institution, 1962), p. 145. The current IBM and AT&T cases may be beyond any judge's capacity to supervise and digest; millions of pages of documents may be involved, with hundreds of expert witnesses.

Culver Pictures

George Wickersham. Taft's Attorney General. A leading private lawyer. Conducted the Standard Oil, American Tobacco and other major cases brilliantly. Returned to private practice.

Thurman W. Arnold. (Left) Born 1891. In office 1938–43. Appointed after writing *The Folklore of Industry,* which said antitrust could do little. Revived antitrust and tried industry-wide studies. Developed or pressed on several Section 2 cases (Alcoa, American Tobacco). Became a federal judge, then returned to private practice.

Culver Pictures

Donald F. Turner. (Right) Born 1922. In office 1965–68. Learned, trained both in law and economics, leading antitrust scholar, a Harvard law professor. Proposed deconcentrating major industries in *Antitrust Policy* (1959). Stressed economic content, raised economists' role. Extended activity to regulated sectors, patents, reviewing old decrees, issuing merger guidelines, prepared big monopoly cases. Did not launch deconcentration program. Returned to Harvard.

Fortune Magazine

Wide World Photos

William Allen, Business Week

Richard W. McLaren. 1918–76. In office 1969–1971. A leading antitrust practitioner from Chicago. Filed major cases against ITT and LTV, the leading conglomerates. Settled both by consent decree before final decision. Moderate in other directions. Became a federal judge in Chicago. Survived the shadow of Nixon scandals.

Thomas E. Kauper. Born 1935. In office 1972–1976. Law professor at University of Michigan. Has pressed actions against conduct and expanded the role of economists. Also, he filed the big AT&T case in 1974, pressed the IBM case, and expanded other Section 2 activity.

An appeal from the decision of a lower court is taken on the basis of error, and error is concerned exclusively with points of law. Here, again, the arcane skills that are brought to bear on questions of economic policy are those not of economic analysis, but of the law.

D6. Trends and Cycles of Division Activity

The rhythm of antitrust has largely been set by the Division. No simple measure can portray the importance of cases, nor the Division's degree of success in the courts. One landmark merger case, for example, can stanch a flood of new mergers. Still, the Division's peak periods of activity were clearly 1904–15 and 1936–52, with a recent rise also visible. The major Section 2 cases were bunched in those periods, and new ground was broken by the courts. During 1952–65 the pace of activity was moderate. Since 1965 there has been a spreading of efforts in several new directions (for example, regulated sectors, foreign aspects).

Before 1901, antitrust activity was minimal. Then Theodore Roosevelt seized the issue, becoming the "Trustbuster." Yet Taft outpaced him. Roosevelt started 44 suits in his two terms: Taft started 90 in one. Wilson also started 90; his beginning was interrupted by World War I. Under Harding, Coolidge, Hoover, and Roosevelt's first term, the Antitrust Division went into hibernation.

In 1938 Roosevelt switched from the NRA detour (see Chapter 24) to a highly publicized campaign against monopoly, under Thurman Arnold until 1943. This continued under Truman, with major cases coming along until 1952. The Eisenhower years of moderation brought a deliberate pullback in restorative actions, especially those toward IBM and AT&T. After several slow years, there was a modest revival after 1958.

The pace continued moderate in the 1960s. Under Donald F. Turner, also a leading antitrust scholar, there was a rise in economic consistency during 1965–68 and new action toward regulated utilities. But the broad attack on tight oligopoly, which Turner had earlier advocated, did not occur. Only a case against IBM was finally filed. And action against the rising tide of conglomerate mergers was studiously moderate.

The Nixon appointee was Richard W. McLaren, an experienced private antitrust lawyer eager to demonstrate strictness. He launched a blitz on conglomerate mergers, but let IBM and other Section 2 matters slide. During 1972–76 Thomas Kauper promoted actions against conduct and raised the economists' role in decisions. He also put large Division resources into the IBM case (see Chapter 5), and in 1974 he filed a major suit against AT&T, which may end up even larger than the IBM case. Donald I. Baker had only 10 months during 1976–77, but he tightened the Division's management and stressed heavier sentences for price fixers.

Antitrust has become bipartisan since 1936, on the whole, but there are distinct swings in emphasis among the three main lines of action. The Supreme Court has led the way, especially during the early 1960s, in tightening merger policy. But on Section 2 it has been given little to work with since 1953.

E. THE FEDERAL TRADE COMMISSION

The FTC's headquarters are in a charming triangular building about halfway between the White House and the Capitol.[27] The main hearing chamber is suitably impressive, but there is also a bureaucratic ambience. The FTC is an independent agency, with its own powers to frame, process, and decide cases. The five commissioners could apply expert judgment, in managing the staff and in briskly settling issues along sound economic lines.

The FTC overlaps with the Division's tasks and tools. It might avoid the Division's problems in the courts and provide better enforcement. In

---

[27] Lesser offices are scattered in six other buildings in downtown Washington, D.C.

practice, these ideals have scarcely been realized. The FTC has two tasks: antitrust and "consumer protection." The latter takes over half the FTC's resources and effort, most of it in small-scale, case-by-case activity.[28] The antitrust resources have frequently been diverted to small, even trivial, cases, rather than grasping the nettle on priority issues.

As with most commissions, the FTC's appointees have mainly been of middling quality. Many of them have scarcely understood the FTC's economic tasks. There has usually been no clear leadership by the chairman, nor a set of economic priorities. Moreover, some of the big cases are appealed to the courts. Though the courts will now reverse the FTC only on issues of law (not of fact), the shadow of appeal leads the agency to be as meticulous and slow about procedures as most district court judges.

The FTC's forms and procedures are summed up in Figures 4–6 and 4–7. The three main parts are the bureaus of Competition, Consumer Protection, and Economics, shown shaded in Figure 4–6. Investigations begin with private complaints, which come in by the thousands, or—the more important cases— by FTC staff initiative. If a formal complaint is lodged, the respondent can reply and settle (as most do), or the issue goes to an FTC "administrative law judge." After judicial-like hearings, the judge either acquits or finds guilt in some degree. Until recently, only a "cease and desist" order could be applied, with no real penalty. The firm or FTC staff can appeal to the whole Commission, which handles the issues and trial record like an appeals court. The FTC's decision is final, unless the firm can persuade the Supreme Court that the FTC erred on the law or in procedure.

The FTC also has developed rule-making powers. It issues rules governing all members of an industry, rather than trying to establish precedents only by individual cases. In 1975 Congress formally backed this practice.[29] In other matters of structure and behavior the remedy is often weak. (The penalty for violating an FTC order is only $5,000.) There is much procedure but often little tight remedy or control.

The FTC's economic yield has been much less than its potential. The Commission comes under intense political pressure when it ventures to be active. Its independent status also leaves it exposed to attack. Congress controls its funds tightly and has reached out to forbid specific actions (such as a study of the largest 1,000 firms in the early 1960s). The FTC therefore

---

[28] In addition to its duties under the Clayton and Trade Commission Acts, the Commission administers the antitrust exemption granted to export trade associations under the Webb-Pomerene Act of 1918; polices the advertising of goods, drugs, and cosmetics under the Wheeler-Lea Act of 1938; and enforces the Wool Products Labeling Act of 1939, the Fur Products Labeling Act of 1951, the Flammable Fabrics Act of 1953, the Textile Fiber Products Identification Act of 1958, the Fair Packaging and Labeling Act of 1966, the Truth-in-Lending Act of 1969, the Fair Credit Reporting Act of 1970, the Fair Credit Billing Act of 1975, and the Equal Credit Opportunity Act of 1975. It has also tested cigarettes for tar and nicotine since 1967.

[29] This was done in the Magnuson-Moss Act. The rules are called "Trade Regulation Rules."

FIGURE 4–6
Basic Structure of the Federal Trade Commission

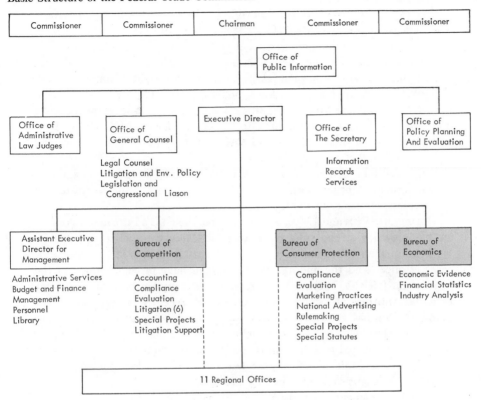

FIGURE 4–7
Steps in FTC Actions

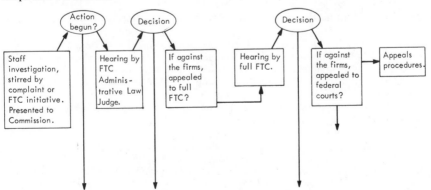

has often bent with political winds and avoided difficult actions, despite its formally independent status.

Swings in FTC zeal have been as wide as those of the Antitrust Division. The high point was roughly 1945 to 1951, when the FTC attacked basing-point pricing, horizontal mergers, and several major oligopolies, all on a shoestring budget. During the 1920s and 1930s, the agency probably did more to promote collusion than resist it. Under Paul Rand Dixon, it decayed in the 1960s so far that abolition was seriously suggested.[30] A revival occurred during 1969–73 under Miles Kirkpatrick, featuring a crack-down on deceptive advertising. Like the anticonglomerate moves by Richard McLaren at Antitrust at the same time, this seemed severe. Yet in fact it skirted the core problems of market power.

Important FTC actions toward cereals firms, Xerox Corporation, and major oil companies began during 1971–72. One can regard the recent degree of strictness as rising but moderate.

During the 1920s and 1940s, and since 1960, the FTC's Bureau of Economics has played a strong role. Its studies are extensive and often valuable. With more than 40 economists, the FTC is able to tackle several major cases at once. And the findings by the Bureau have provided much of the impetus for later FTC actions. This research capacity has been much greater than the Antitrust Division's resources, though recently the Division's economic staffing has grown to be nearly as large. FTC economic studies are published, often with great impact, while economic material at the Division is usually submerged in fact memos and the preparation of individual cases. The FTC's economic effects are far less than the "pitiless publicity" that Woodrow Wilson promised. But they are not trivial.[31]

Dual Enforcement. The two agencies have come to overlap widely in their coverage and basic actions. Mergers, restructuring, collusive and possible predatory devices, all these and more are treated by both agencies over nearly the whole range of industry. This could cause strife and error, and every so often there are proposals to replace them with one super-agency, under an antitrust "czar," in order to coordinate and fortify the treatments.

Yet most experts praise the duality for enabling variety, experimentation, and—yes—competition in carrying out policy.[32] There are few serious dis-

---

[30] American Bar Association, *Report on the Federal Trade Commission,* 1969. The special ABA study committee concluded ". . . if change does not occur, there will be no substantial purpose to be served by its continued existence." See also E. F. Cox, R. C. Fellmeth, and J. E. Schultz, *The Nader Report on the Federal Trade Commission* (New York: R. W. Baron, 1969).

[31] However, the economists' role may be shrinking, with their removal in 1972 from the FTC's main building to an office 18 blocks away.

[32] For two earlier studies commending the dual system, see the Hoover Commission report, Commission on Organization of the Executive Branch of the Government, *Task Force Report on Regulatory Commissions* (Washington, D.C.: U.S. Government Printing Office, 1949), p. 132; and *Report* of the Attorney General's National Committee to Study the Antitrust Laws (Washington, D.C.: U.S. Government Printing Office, 1955), pp. 372–73.

putes over jurisdiction. Budding cases are mostly divided along the heavy-light industry line, but with many sharp exceptions whenever an agency has a special interest. One agency can add its own treatment if it regards the other as too weak; this has happened in several important cases. And a passive—or hyperactive—spell in one agency can be offset by the other. To force them into one meta-agency would invite *monopoly* behavior! Still the issue is an open one, since neither agency is fully responsible for action.

F. PRIVATE ACTIONS, AND ANTITRUST ABROAD

F1. Private Suits

Private parties also use and—indirectly—enforce the antitrust laws. Such cases have mushroomed in recent years from about 300 per year in the 1950s to over 1,000 per year in the 1970s (recall Table 4–6). The stakes are often high, when a plaintiff (a customer, competitor, or other) can assert large losses from an anticompetitive act and claim triple that amount in damages. Frequently the plaintiff has been persuaded to sue by an outside law firm, which handles the case on a "contingency basis" (collecting a fee only if the suit wins). Damages of $100 or $200 million are typically claimed, often in the expectation of reaching a settlement of only $10 or $20 million. Dominant firms normally face a steady drumfire of private cases.

The boom in private cases might affect public action in two ways. It might *pre-empt* policy, taking matters out of the agencies' hands, as when landmark issues are decided in private cases. The private cases may have framed the issues in ways that the agencies do not agree with, and so the precedents are distorted or obscured. Or, instead, private cases might *add* to public efforts, by leading the way into new problems, filling in gaps, or reinforcing the agencies' suits. The whole effect is not yet clear, but it is evident that private cases often fail to crop up where they are most needed and most expected (for example, against dominant firms and price fixers). The agencies still bear the burden of setting mainstream policy.

F2. Foreign experiments

Abroad there has been a growth of antitrust in Britain, Canada, and Australia since 1948 and—even more mildly—in France, Germany, and the Common Market. Of course, all countries take actions affecting competition, often abridging or excluding it. But the more formal policy ventures favoring competition deserve a brief mention here, for comparison with U.S. treatments. (There will be more detail in Chapters 5 through 9.)

Most of the activity is mere formality, studying but not deciding or enforcing. Only in Britain have there been sizable effects.[33] Nearly all formal price

---

[33] See Charles K. Rowley, *The British Monopolies Commission* (London: Allen & Unwin, 1966); and Dennis Swann, Denis P. O'Brien, W. Peter J. Maunder, and W. Stewart Howe, *Competition in British Industry* (London: Allen & Unwin, 1974).

fixing has been ended in Britain since 1956; resale price maintenance was stopped in 1965. The U.K. Monopolies Commission has deflected some mergers and required certain changes. But it has scarcely affected most dominant firms, though it has studied many of them thoroughly. British procedures for treating price fixing and dominance are much more brisk than those in the United States, mainly because lawyers are not given such a crucial role in the hearing process.

Australia has recently enacted antitrust legislation closely patterned on the Sherman Act. Since 1952, Canada's Restrictive Practices Commission has decided against a variety of collusive agreements, but with little penalties. The Bureau of Competition Policy, created in 1960, has a staff of over 200, including 12 economists. Yet both agencies lack powers to compel changes or levy strict fines. Little action has occurred against established market dominance. France's antitrust policies are governed by a commission composed partly of business members. While it has been largely passive, other government officials have directly encouraged mergers and certain other anticompetitive behavior.

In short, the United States is no longer unique in its antitrust strictness, having been joined by Britain. In both countries, antitrust is imperfect. Yet the two countries stand out from the rest.

G. SUMMARY

The economic tasks of antitrust are to stop cooperation and exclusive actions, and to limit dominant positions to the margin where the benefits of competition are balanced by possible economies of scale. The basic laws, the Sherman and Clayton acts, appear to fit these tasks well in concept. They reflect long traditions but a checkered legislative history. There are many exemptions to them, and "reasonable" enforcement of them leaves further gaps.

The two antitrust agencies are small compared to their responsibilities. They are influenced by a variety of public and private groups. They are run by lawyers, concerned to apply rules and win cases. Access to the critical data is limited. Recently, most effort has gone toward collusive conduct and mergers, rather than to remedial actions against dominant firms. The agencies usually penalize the offending firms by onerous proceedings and by reinforcing private damage claims, more than by formal convictions and fines.

The process of study and treatment is often slow and confused by legalisms. Activity has fluctuated sharply, but the long trend is to bear down on medium firms while letting the largest dominant firms stand. The FTC has had a mediocre record. Dual enforcement probably promotes balance and variety, though it avoids direct responsibility. Private suits are booming, but they are not a full substitute for public action. Most antitrust abroad is often mere ritual, even more than in the United States.

The United States experiments in antitrust have had their own peculiar forms, coverage, and incidence. The economic effects are likely to be complex, perhaps with unknown side effects as well. It seems obvious that price fixing is reduced and structure is less tight than if antitrust had not existed. Chapter 9 will consider the effects, after the detailed coverage of Chapters 5 through 8. To whet your thinking now, consider two contrasting hypotheses about the way the parts of antitrust have interacted:

One Hypothesis: Structure Is Hardened. The *Addyston* case in 1899 stirred further trust formation, which the 1904–15 Section 2 actions did not fully reverse. Since 1915, dominant positions have been safe from serious attack. Meanwhile, policies have tightened toward collusion and mergers. The whole effect is to constrain lesser firms more tightly than dominant ones. Lesser firms can neither collude nor merge, while dominant firms can set prices internally and expect to retain their high market shares. This antitrust twist could be optimal *if* high market shares tend to erode rapidly. Otherwise, antitrust tends to *(a)* harden dominant position and *(b)* be unfair, since lesser firms are tightly limited while dominant ones exert market power untouched.

A Second Hypothesis: Competition Is Increased. Antitrust has ensured that oligopoly prevails, rather than monopoly. It prevents collusion among firms, and it only permits dominance when that reflects economies of scale, X-efficiency, or innovation. Potential competition and other market forces therefore drive most markets toward efficient and fair outcomes. Antitrust is effective and fruitful.

Which is it? Or both (in part), or neither? Research so far has not given clear lessons. You must decide for yourself, after learning the main lines and details in the next four chapters.

QUESTIONS FOR REVIEW

1. "The Sherman Act contains an explicit 'rule of reason.' " True?
2. "The Sherman and Clayton Acts merely codified the common law precedent." True?
3. "The Sherman Act did not have a clear legislative intent, either in hearings or floor debate." True?
4. Effective exemption from the antitrust laws includes *(a)* labor unions, *(b)* export cartels, *(c)* intra-state commerce, *(d)* most public enterprises, *(e)* patent-intensive industries. Which?
5. "Because the agencies' lawyers are always outnumbered by the other side, they rarely win." True?
6. "The courts' slowness always makes antitrust actions too slow." True?
7. "Restructuring has been the main line of antitrust since the trustbusting days of Roosevelt and Taft." True?
8. "Since fines are small, the agencies have little leverage on firms." True?
9. The recent rise in antitrust budgets definitely makes them *(a)* about right, *(b)* still too small, *(c)* too large, *(d)* we cannot know. Which?

10. "The average antitrust case takes about 5.5 months, but there is much variation." True?
11. "Legal processes cannot possibly yield good economic solutions for antitrust matters." True?
12. "Overlap between the Antitrust Division and the FTC means that neither—indeed nobody—assumes ultimate responsibility for antitrust policy." True?
13. "British antitrust policies are now roughly equivalent to U.S. policies." True?

APPENDIX:
LEGAL TERMS OFTEN USED IN ANTITRUST

Appeal: request for a reversal of a lower court decision.

Big case: involves a long and complicated trial record; need not involve a "big" company; may take 15 or more years.

Civil Investigative Demand (CID): Antitrust Division request for data, enforced by court order.

Citation: in the title of a case the plaintiff is named first, for example, *Victim* v. *Offender.* Even on appeal, the final decisions are usually cited with the plaintiff named first.

Class action: a suit brought on behalf of a group of victims, claiming damages for all of them. A method of representing the interest of a large number of plaintiffs, each of which has suffered a small or moderate damage.

Consent decree: a formal compromise, filed with a court. The court may require changes in it before accepting it.

Conspiracy: any joint action.

Damages: the alleged value of harm suffered by a party.

Defendant: the alleged offender. In antitrust, usually a firm which holds, or has tried to gain, market power.

Deposition: a method for taking testimony outside the court. The witness is sworn in and "deposed." Strict legal standards apply, but the court's own time is saved. Used extensively to prepare for large cases.

Discovery: the pretrial process of investigation by both sides, to discover *(a)* the arguments to be used by the other side, and *(b)* whatever facts may be thought to be relevant. Discovery is often carried to excess.

Divestiture: separation of part of a firm so as to create more competition. It can be done by selling the part to another firm or by setting the part up as a new enterprise.

Estoppel: prevents retrying of a matter which has already been tried. Once a case is brought and settled, further action is estopped until conditions have changed markedly. Estoppel commonly lasts for 15 to 25 years, but rapid changes can shorten it.

Expert witness: engaged by one side to present a skilled, objective opinion which strengthens that side's claim. In antitrust, often an accountant, engineer, economist, or financial specialist.

Great victory: a dramatic, complete win in court. May involve large economic issues or only a point of law; a large effect or a trivial change.

Guidelines: a public listing by an agency of the conditions or actions which will cause it to sue.

Injunction: a court order stopping a specified act, under possible penalty of contempt of court.

Interrogatories: questions exchanged by parties before trial on matters of fact or anything else germane to the trial. May be brief or extensive.

Nolo contendere: (translation "no contest"), a hybrid plea which does not formally admit guilt but does not attempt to disprove the alleged offense. It cannot be used by other parties as a proof of guilt on which to base their damage claims.

Parens patriae: (translation "the state as guardian"), applies when the government sues on behalf of private victims. Embodied in a 1976 law which empowers state officials to lodge antitrust suits claiming damages for large classes of consumers.

Per se: "as such," without further evidence; for example, price fixing is a per se violation if a mere showing that price fixing existed will always bring a conviction.

Plaintiff: the party bringing the suit (filing the complaint). Commonly a consumer or small competitor.

Precedent: a line drawn in one case which governs decisions in later similar cases. What the line *is* is often intensely debated.

Prima facie: (translation "first made"), a prima facie case is one which appears to succeed on a first showing of the main argument.

Prosecutorial discretion: the latitude which agency managers have to choose specific cases and to interpret "the law."

Reciprocity: an exchange of favors, as when a firm ships its products only via those carriers which have bought their equipment from the first firm.

Record: the printed account of all materials presented at trial and all proceedings of the trial. Appellate decisions cannot go beyond it.

Remedy (or relief): the corrective changes required after decision, in order to stop further violations.

Snow: vernacular for overwhelming an opponent's investigation with a mass of useless, undigested materials. Routinely successful in buying time.

Tender offer: an offer to buy a firm's stock. Used in take-over attempts. The tender offer may specify a simple price or the terms for an exchange of securities.

Treble damages: successful private antitrust actions can claim triple ("treble") the amount of damage suffered.

chapter 5

Monopolization

Where existing structure is tighter than technical economies of scale require, a social loss is likely to occur. If this excess degree of monopoly can be reduced, then economic welfare will increase. Even where economies of scale justify high market shares, the scope and negative effects of the monopoly are to be kept to a minimum.

These economic criteria are clear, the Sherman Act provides a firm legal base, some past actions have been strict, and the candidates for treatment are relatively few and well known. The task seems manageable, and it may be pivotal to the balance of competitive policies.

Yet standard Section 2 treatment has receded recently, touching only a few industries. Policy has heeded the advice of Finley Peter Dunne's old Mr. Dooley: "Th' trusts, says he, 'are heejous monsthers built up be th' enlightened intherprise iv th' men that have done so much to advance progress in our beloved country,' he says. 'On wan hand I wud stamp thim undher fut; on th' other hand not so fast.' "

American treatment is primarily the Section 2 case, alleging monopolization and seeking conviction and a remedy. Its two main parts are proofs that *(a)* monopoly exists (a market share of about 60 percent or more) and that *(b)* the firm sought monopoly deliberately (as shown by acts of various kinds). These proofs have become difficult to establish in the courts. Also, Section 2 has acquired a number of loopholes by usage. The Section 2 route is now long, uncertain, and partly neglected. It is much less strict than the treatments of mergers and price fixing. Why this contrast has occurred, and whether it makes economic sense, is assessed in this chapter.

We begin by defining monopoly and its abuses in some detail. Section B then presents the criteria, candidates, and costs of treatment. The first two series of Section 2 actions are presented in Section C, and then current actions in Section D. Section E evaluates the whole experience and Section F considers whether Section 2 is ineffective. Foreign experiments are noted in Section G, while the alternatives to Section 2 occupy Section H.

A. CONCEPTS

To monopolize is to acquire a monopoly, which is defined by the firm's market share, with attention also to entry barriers. We now review the technical problems of defining the market, market share, entry barriers, and monopolistic abuses.

A1. The Relevant Market

The task is to measure the market share of the firm. That depends on the true extent of the market. Defining the market often determines the treatment.

A market is a grouping of buyers and sellers, communicating quickly and exchanging goods which are substitutable. Perfect markets carry these conditions to extremes: perfect substitution and instant adjustment within the market, but zero substitutability and adjustment across the market's edges. Substitutability in demand is the basic criterion (but substitutability in supply can also be a factor). Substitutability is measured by the cross-elasticity of demand among goods which may be inside or outside the market.[1] In turn, cross-elasticities of demand depend both on the hard physical facts of the product, and on mental images which advertising or other experience may shape. Geography also can enter in, if there are local submarkets within regional and national industries. To define a market, one needs to know *(a)* the nature of the product and its alternatives, *(b)* the consumers' subjective images of the product, and *(c)* geographic limits on interchanging the products.

Many markets have shaded edges, layers of quality levels, and submarkets. Even if there were precise data on these conditions, one would still have elbow room in defining "the" market. In practice, the cross-elasticities, images, and distance factors are hard—even impossible—to measure. In research and in court, many markets can only be roughly estimated, and plausible estimates can differ sharply. The leading firm will try to define the market broadly. Its competitors and public agencies often make it out to be narrow. The extreme positions are: *(a)* that each product competes against everything else for the consumer's dollar, or *(b)* that each firm's products are unique.

Most markets can be reasonably well defined, when a decision must be made. Judgment, comparisons with previous decisions, and research on the main customers, suppliers, and alternative products often suffice. Often, too, the policy criterion asks only if a *substantial* degree of market power, in a

---

[1] Cross-elasticity of demand between goods A and $B = \% \, \Delta \, \text{Quantity}_B \div \% \, \Delta \, \text{Price}_A$. Substitutes have positive cross-elasticities; complements have negative. Close substitutes have high cross-elasticities. For example, if a 10 percent rise in Ford automobile prices raises the quantity of Chrysler cars sold by 25 percent, the cross-elasticity of demand is $+2.5$. But a 10 percent rise in shirt prices would probably cause no appreciable change in the number of Chryslers sold, so shirts and Chryslers are not in the same market. But bicycles? Taxi fares? See any good theory text for more analysis.

significant market, is involved. High precision is often unnecessary. Court decisions have defined markets with some sophistication, though there have been marked shifts and some lapses.

The main legal tests have been the "line of commerce" (roughly, defined by the degree of cross-elasticity of demand) and the "geographic market." The debates in court can be long and involved, with stacks of documents, and with numerous witnesses put under intense cross-examination, often splitting hairs. The choice usually comes down in the end, as it must, to a reasonable but arbitrary guess. Some leading recent court choices are shown in Table 5-1: note how strictness has waxed and waned. Details follow.

Line of Commerce ("reasonable interchangeability of products"). Since the 1940s, the courts have increasingly tried to use cross-elasticity of demand in defining products. But good measures of cross-elasticities have been lacking. The courts have had to rely instead on such rougher criteria as relative price levels and movements, technological factors, production facilities, and common usage.

Early decisions often drew the market too narrowly. Thus sea-green slate, linen rugs, red-cedar shingles produced in the state of Washington, parchment paper, and hydraulic oil well pumps were held to occupy distinct markets, though in each case substitutes were readily available.[2]

The **Alcoa** case (1945) poses with special clarity the problem of defining the product and the market.[3] Judge Hand accepted the Division's view, *excluding* aluminum scrap and *including* not only the ingots Alcoa sold to others, but also the ingots it consumed itself. On this basis Alcoa's share of the market was found to be 90 percent. Scrap competes with ingots but was excluded on the ground that it had been derived from products made from ingots that Alcoa had once produced, though Alcoa did not directly control the scrap supply. Had scrap been included in measuring the market, Alcoa's share would have stood at 60–64 percent. And if Alcoa's consumption of its own ingots had been excluded, its share of the open market would have stood at 33 percent. By adopting the first of these definitions of the market, the court was enabled to make a finding of monopoly. Hand stated that 90 percent clearly was monopoly; 60 percent might be; while 33 percent clearly was not. This *obiter dictum* (or side comment) has become the rule of thumb for all Section 2 cases since then.

In **Times-Picayune,** the Court leaned the other way. It found that the

---

[2] *O'Halloran* v. *American Sea Green Slate Co.,* 207 Fed. 187 (1913); *U.S.* v. *Klearflax Linen Looms,* 63 F. Supp. 32 (1945); *Gibbs* v. *McNeeley,* 118 Fed. 120 (1902); *Story Parchment Co.* v. *Paterson Paper Co.,* 282 U.S. 555 (1931); *Kobe, Inc.* v. *Dempsey Pump Co.,* 198 F. 2d 416 (1952).

[3] The case is *U.S.* v. *Aluminum Co. of America,* 148 F. 2d 416, 424 (1945). Though criticized at the time, Hand's market definition is strongly supported in Darius Gaskins, "Alcoa Revisited: The Welfare Implications of a Secondhand Market," *Journal of Economic Theory* 7 (March 1974), 254–71.

TABLE 5–1
Evolving Ways of Defining the Relevant Market

| Case (year decided) | Relevant Market and the Resulting Share According to the | | | Action Taken |
	1. Defense (percent)	2. Agency or Other Plaintiff (percent)	3. Court in Final Action (percent)	
Alcoa (1945)	All ingot and scrap (33)	Ingot sold (90)	Ingot sold (90)	Alcoa convicted
Times-Picayune (953)	All local advertising (33)	Advertising in morning newspapers (100)	All newspaper advertising	Acquitted
du Pont "Cellophane" (1956)	Flexible packaging (18)	Cellophane (75–100)	Flexible packaging materials (18)	Acquitted
du Pont–General Motors (1957)	Automotive finishes and fabrics (1 to 3)	GM purchases of these items (60 to 100)	GM purchases (60–100)	Convicted
Bethlehem-Youngstown merger (1958)	Structural metals and plastics (1 to 3)	Regional steel markets (25 plus)	Regional steel markets (25 plus)	Merger enjoined
Brown Shoe (1962)	All shoes (5)	Various types of shoes, in various cities (up to 50)	Specific markets (up to 50)	Merger enjoined
Philadelphia National Bank (1963)	National banking (trivial)	Philadelphia banking (36)	Philadelphia banking (36)	Merger enjoined
Rome Cable (1964)	All conductor wire (3)	Bare aluminum conductor (33)	Bare aluminum conductor and others (33)	Merger enjoined
Continental Can and Hazel-Atlas (1964)	Glass and metal containers are separate markets	Containers (25)	Containers (25)	Merger enjoined
Pabst-Blatz (1966)	National beer market (5)	Wisconsin beer market (24)	Wisconsin beer market (24)	Merger enjoined
Von's Grocery (1966)	Los Angeles retail grocery (7.5)	Los Angeles retail grocery (7.5)	Los Angeles retail grocery (7.5)	Merger enjoined
Grinnell	All protective services ("low")	Accredited central station protective services (87)	Accredited central station protective services (87)	Conviction
Telex v. IBM (1975)	All computer equipment (30)	Computer equipment "plug-compatible" with IBM equipment (80+)	All computer equipment (30)	IBM acquitted

Sources: Opinions of the courts in these various cases, as discussed in the text and indexed at the end of the book.

Times-Picayune had no monopoly, having reached this conclusion by defining the market to include all three dailies instead of separating the morning and evening markets and recognizing the *Times-Picayune* monopoly in the morning field.[4]

du Pont Cellophane. A landmark decision involved du Pont, which was charged with monopolizing cellophane during 1924–50. If the market in question were that for cellophane alone, it was clear that the company had a monopoly, since it accounted for 75 percent of the output of the product and, together with its licensee Sylvania, for all of it. But if the market were all flexible packaging materials, including glassine, parchment papers, waxed papers, pliofilm, and aluminum foil, du Pont's share was only 18 percent. The first definition was urged by the government; the second by du Pont. Judge Leahy, in the district court, found for the defense, but cited du Pont's "creative" behavior as much as the definition of the market. The Supreme Court sustained the verdict by 4 to 3, viewing cellophane as "reasonably interchangeable by consumers for the same purposes." The relevant market, therefore, was that for flexible packaging materials.[5]

This was dubious. Cellophane's price had been from two to seven times that of the other materials during 1924 to 1950. And when it had been cut sharply, the price of others held steady or even rose. The Court's minority cited this: "We cannot believe that . . . practical businessmen would have bought cellophane in increasing amounts over a quarter of a century if close substitutes were available at from one seventh to one half cellophane's price. That they did so is testimony to cellophane's distinctiveness." "Reasonable interchangeability" was now very broadly interpreted.

du Pont-General Motors. It was drawn back next year.[6] The defense had urged that du Pont's sales of automobile finishes to GM were only 3.5 percent of all its sales of industrial finishes, and its sales of fabrics to GM only 1.6 percent of all its sales of fabrics. But the Court held that the characteristics of automotive finishes and fabrics were sufficiently peculiar to make them distinct, and that GM in itself constituted a substantial market for these products. The product was defined in terms, not of interchangeability, but of its peculiar characteristics.

In the **Bethlehem Steel** case in 1958 (see Chapter 6), the defendants sought to have their product so defined as to include nonferrous and plastic substitutes, following the precedent established in the *Cellophane* case.[7] Judge Weinfeld refused, holding that the line of commerce involved was a series of products having characteristics sufficiently peculiar to make them distinct, thus following the precedent established in *du Pont-GM*. The key to the

---

[4] *Times-Pacyune Publishing Co.* v. *U.S.*, 345 U.S. 594. See Chapter 8 for more on this case.

[5] *U.S.* v. *du Pont*, 351 U.S. 377 (1956).

[6] *U.S.* v. *du Pont*, 353 U.S. 586 (1957).

[7] *U.S.* v. *Bethlehem Steel Corp.*, 168 F. Supp. 576.

decision, though, was a series of regional markets for specific steel products, where Bethlehem and Youngstown were definitely competitors (see Chapter 6, Section F, below).

In the **Brown Shoe** case in 1962, the Supreme Court recognized three markets: those for men's, women's, and children's shoes. The defense sought recognition for infants' and babies' shoes, misses' and children's shoes, and youths' and boys' shoes and, within the sex and age groups, for medium-priced and low-priced shoes. The Court refused:

> The outer boundaries of a product are determined by the reasonable inter-changeability of use or the cross-elasticity of demand between the product itself and substitutes for it. However, within this broad market, well-defined submarkets may exist which, in themselves, constitute product markets for antitrust purposes. The boundaries of such a submarket may be determined by examining such practical indicia as industry or public recognition of the submarket as a separate economic entry, the product's peculiar characteristics and uses, unique production facilities, distinct customers, distinct prices, sensitivity to price changes, and specialized vendors.[8]

This was nearly a hunting license to find any indicia which could show submarkets.

In the **Rome Cable** case in 1964, the district court had defined the product as including both aluminum and copper conductors. The Supreme Court found that the two types of conductors had different uses, aluminum being used overhead and insulated copper underground. It found, too, that aluminum cable sold at half to two thirds of the price of copper cable and that the cross-elasticity of demand between them was probably low. It therefore reversed the district court, defining the product as aluminum conductor alone.

Continental-Hazel-Atlas.   The government won the Rome Cable case on a narrow definition of the product market. It won the **Continental-Hazel-Atlas** case, decided in the same month, on a broad definition. The metal containers made by Continental and the glass containers made by Hazel-Atlas were found to constitute a single product. "In our view," said the Court, "there is and has been a rather general confrontation between metal and glass containers and competition between them for the same end uses which is insistent, continuous, effective, and quantitywise very substantial.[9] The prices of the two containers differed and the estimated cross-elasticity of demand between them was low. But these facts, while recognized as relevant, were held to be inconclusive, for price is only one factor in the user's choice. Consumer preference (the housewife's preference, for instance, for glass rather than metal in the packaging of baby foods) may lead her to use a container that costs her more. "This may not be price competition," concluded the Court, "but it is nevertheless meaningful competition between interchangeable containers."

---

[8] *Brown Shoe Co.* v. *U.S.,* 370 U.S. 294, 324.

[9] *Continental Can Co.* v. *U.S.,* 378 U.S. 441, 489.

Grinnell. In 1966, the Court decided that "accredited central station protective services" were a market, which Grinnell Corporation had monopolized.[10] This reflected distinct characteristics, compared to watchmen, local alarm systems, proprietary systems and unaccredited central systems. Justice Fortas could dissent that it was Procrustean, tailoring the market to the defendants and ignoring services which were in "realistic rivalry." Either choice was plausible, in fact.

Evidently, "the" market has come to be any product domain within which competition may be appreciably affected. Cross-elasticity can be used as a test, but other indicies are freely used. Indeed, cross-elasticities usually can't be measured accurately, and so one must use other evidence and judgments.

The Section of the Country. The courts have also been willing to regard small geographic areas as markets (or submarkets), even where much larger areas could be accepted. This leaning to the narrower definition became marked in the 1960s.

In a case involving two publishers of farm papers, decided in 1934, a Court of Appeals had found for the defendant on the ground that it did not have a monopoly of the national market for farm advertising. The Supreme Court reversed the decision, holding that the relevant market was confined to the eight states in which the papers of the plaintiff and the defendant had their major circulation.[11] In the **Paramount** case in 1948, where the lower court had found that the five major producers of motion pictures did not have a monopoly of the business of exhibiting pictures, the Supreme Court held that they did have a monopoly of exhibition at the first-run theaters in the 92 largest cities of the country.[12]

Bethlehem-Youngstown. Determination of the relevant geographic markets is equally important under the Celler-Kefauver Act. In defining these markets in the Bethlehem Steel case, Judge Weinfeld listed them as (a) the United States as a whole, (b) the northeast quadrant of the United States, (c) Michigan, Ohio, Pennsylvania, and New York, (d) Michigan and Ohio, (e) Michigan, and (f) Ohio. The projected merger would have lessened competition in Michigan and along the border of Ohio and Pennsylvania, where Bethlehem and Youngstown had both made sales. On this basis, the merger was properly held to be in violation of the law.

In the **Brown Shoe** case, the Supreme Court found different markets to be relevant in considering the probable effects of horizontal combination and vertical integration. The combination of retail outlets, it held, would affect competition in "every city with a population exceeding 10,000 and its immediate contiguous surrounding territory" in which both Brown and Kinney sold shoes at retail through stores they either owned or controlled.[13]

---

[10] *U.S.* v. *Grinnell Corp.,* 384 U.S. 563 (1966).

[11] *Indiana Farmer's Guide* v. *Prairie,* 293 U.S. 268.

[12] *U.S.* v. *Paramount Pictures,* 334 U.S. 141.

[13] *Brown Shoe* v. *U.S.,* 370 U.S. 294, 336.

The integration of manufacturing and distribution would affect competition in the United States as a whole.

A much broader view was taken in a major bank merger case, Continental Illinois National Bank in Chicago in 1962.[14] The bank's national activities were taken as crucial, rather than its post-merger local market share of 40 percent. The merger (one of the last of the big bank mergers: see Chapter 6) was permitted.

Philadelphia National Bank.   But a year later the Court put local banking markets foremost, after all. In the *Philadelphia National Bank* case, the defendants argued that the combined bank would be in a stronger position to compete for business with banks in New York City and asked that the market be defined to include New York. The Court refused:

> The proper question to be asked . . . is not where the parties to the merger do business or even where they compete, but where, within the area of competitive overlap, the effect of the merger on competition will be direct and immediate. . . . In banking . . . convenience of location is essential to effective competition. Individuals and corporations typically confer the bulk of their patronage on banks in their local community; they find it impractical to conduct their banking business at a distance.[15]

On this basis, the Court found the relevant market to consist of the four-county area of metropolitan Philadelphia.

The Court now freely recognizes local markets for closely defined products, but not in every case where it might.[16] The 1960s may have been the peak of such strictness. Cases usually offer many data to justify either narrow or broad market edges. Behind the specific reasons often lurks the judges' real interest in being stricter or more liberal toward monopoly in general.

A2. The Market Share

How much market share makes a "monopoly?" There is no clear economic threshold (recall Figure 2–6). A share of 35 percent or more would normally deserve careful economic study and perhaps treatment, especially if serious entry barriers or other imperfections exist. Market power would clearly be present.

Actual policy has been vague about the concepts, but it also has set quite definite thresholds in practice. The precedents reflect both the Court's decisions and the agencies' choices about what cases to bring. The Court has been willing at times to convict "abusive" combinations with as little as 20 percent and yet to absolve "good" monopolists with as much as 90 percent. The present consensus is that an established market share below 60 percent is safe in the Court, and even 70 to 75 percent may escape (and some 85

---

[14] The merger was eventually approved under the 1966 Merger Act Amendment.

[15] *U.S.* v. *Philadelphia National Bank,* 374 U.S. 321, 409–10.

[16] *U.S.* v. *Pabst Brewing Co.,* 384 U.S. 546.

to 90 percent shares have existed unchallenged for decades).[17] This reflects Judge Hand's *Alcoa* dictum—it was not a true precedent—that 90 percent is monopoly, 60 percent may be, and 33 percent is not.

Yet mergers are usually prevented if they create a market share above 10 percent (see Chapter 6). The resulting gap between 60 and 10 percent is wide. It is a double standard, made possible because no clear economic definition of "monopoly" has been adopted in policy.[18] The problem is market dominance, but Sherman 2 only mentions "monopolizing."

A3. Other Structural Elements

Barriers to Entry. In some recent cases the defendant has argued that a low barrier to new entry should be considered in evaluating the degree of monopoly. If free entry nullifies market power, then even a 100 percent share might be "competitive" and escape treatment. Policy could turn on the height of entry barriers, as well as (or even perhaps instead of) market shares.

Formally, policy has not yet included barriers in the evaluation. This is sensible, for barrier "height" is hard to estimate reliably, much less to measure precisely. Too, the relative weighting between barriers and market share is controversial. Yet informally policy probably does allow for barriers, to a degree. The agencies consider barriers and entry in deciding whether to bring suit, and the courts often note the entry conditions in their opinions. In practice, a low entry barrier can offset at least a few points of market share.

Conversely, the absolute size of the firm or market has come to be treated in some cases as a source of entry barriers. Other than that, the courts have not usually accepted bigness per se as a source of monopoly power.

Vertical Integration. This is the joining of two or more "levels" of production under one firm. It is widespread; even a baker with ovens in the back and display cases in the front is vertically integrated, and some large firms have seven or more stages of production. Integration often provides large technical economies, by reducing risks, by avoiding costly reheating or processing, and by improving the planning of production.

Integration can also affect competition. It takes intra-company sales off the open market, in extreme cases foreclosing market competition altogether. In theory, integrated firms buy and sell as freely as if they were not integrated; but in practice they usually deal with their own branches. Integration can also raise entry barriers by forcing any new entrants to come in at both

---

[17] In Britain, a "monopoly" position is now defined to include shares as low as 25 percent. In other European countries, too, there is little hesitation in recognizing that dominance is the real issue.

[18] In bank mergers, the limit on share is higher, at about 15 to 20 percent. But the safety level for established market shares is also higher, at virtually 100 percent; that is, there is no effort at restructuring banks (see Chapter 20).

levels at once. This takes more capital and increases the risks, so that "capital entry barriers" are higher. Integrated firms may also be able to apply price "squeezes" to their competitors.[19]

The issue is controversial, and the anticompetitive effects are probably softer than those of high market shares.[20] Where true economies of integration are large, they may outweigh the negative effects on competition. But some degree of anticompetitive effect will often exist, especially where a dominant firm is integrated. Court decisions in Section 2 cases have given integration some weight, but usually as a minor element.

A4. Monopolistic Abuses

Apart from its basic economic ill-effects, monopoly may cause—and arise from—specific abuses. These include such practices as maliciously interfering with the production and sale of competitive goods, excluding competitors from access to supplies, obtaining discriminatory prices in purchasing supplies, excluding competitors from access to markets, and other such predatory acts. Such abuses have shaped the present structures, and they continue in many markets.

Several of them need discussion, for they have been important in Section 2 decisions.[21] They are also treated in their own right in Chapter 8.

---

[19] Where an integrated firm is tapered—with a larger share in early stages than in later ones—it will sell to independent firms. To the integrated firm, the prices and margins at successive stages are a matter of convenience, of internal bookkeeping. To its nonintegrated competitors, they are a matter of life and death. Such an integrated concern is thus in a position to squeeze its rivals by raising prices in the markets where they buy and reducing prices in the markets where they sell.

Thus Alcoa, competing with independent companies in the fabrication of aluminum products, was for many years the only source from which these independents could obtain their supply of aluminum ingots and sheets. By raising the price of raw materials and lowering the price of finished products, the company has been said to have made it unprofitable for its rivals to remain in business. A similar squeeze has been experienced by independent refiners of petroleum.

Squeezes occur less often than their victims allege, but they are occasionally quite powerful. The squeeze is difficult for antitrust authorities to attack, since price changes may be adjudged competitive or monopolistic according to their motivation, and motives are difficult to prove.

[20] In perfect market conditions (perfect knowledge, instant adjustment, perfect rationality), vertical integration may not be able to affect competition at all. See Robert H. Bork, "Vertical Integration and the Sherman Act: The Legal History of an Economic Misconception," *University of Chicago Law Review* 22 (Spring 1954), 157–201. The question is how far actual markets depart from these ideal conditions.

[21] Grosser forms of abuse may be fewer now than before, but a classic case of it—*National Cash Register Co.* at the turn of the century—is a good example.

The company set out deliberately to destroy its competitors. It hired their employees away from them. It bribed their employees and the employees of railroads and telephone and telegraph companies to spy on them and disclose their business secrets. It spread false rumors concerning their solvency. It instructed its agents to misrepresent the quality of their goods, interfere with their sales, and damage the mechanism of their machines in establishments where they were in use. It publicly displayed their cash registers under labels which read, "Junk." It made, and sold at less than cost,

130

Exclusion and Discrimination in Buying. A dominant firm often is able to exclude others from access to facilities, credit, equipment, and materials. It may make preemptive purchases, hoarding crucial supplies. It may force suppliers into exclusive contracts, by refusing to buy from those who sell to its competitors. It may also pressure suppliers to give price cuts beyond what costs justify.

Such practices were pervasive in forming the early trusts, and they are still common. Thus, several of the trusts persuaded the railroads to grant them substantial rebates. Standard Oil not only recovered 40–50 percent of the sums which it paid the roads for carrying its own products but also collected a similar share of the rates paid by its rivals! The Aluminum Company of America, enjoying a patent monopoly in its early years, made preemptive purchases of deposits of bauxite and sites for the generation of hydroelectric power, and it bought power elsewhere under contracts which forbade suppliers to sell to other producers of aluminum. In the 1930s producers of the leading brands of cigarettes bought up the stocks of tobacco required for the production of 10-cent brands. And exhibitors of motion pictures prevented other houses from obtaining films by renting more features than they had time to display in their own theaters.

There is also reciprocal buying, where Company A refuses to buy product x from Company B unless Company B will buy product y from Company A. Thus General Motors was charged, in 1963, with telling railroads that if they did not buy GM locomotives, GM would ship freight on other lines. Consolidated Foods was found, in 1965, to have forced its suppliers to buy dried onions and garlic from one of its subsidiaries. U.S. Steel agreed, in 1969, to discontinue the ancient practice of providing its purchasing agents with records of its sales so that they would buy from its customers. This practice is followed by thousands of companies in doing business with one another. When the firm involved controls a small share of the market for the goods it buys and when it invites reciprocal purchases rather than requiring them, any anticompetitive effect will be small. But when the firm is a major buyer and when it uses coercion to force reciprocal purchases, competition may be reduced significantly.

Exclusive Selling. Dominant firms may also impose contracts upon their distributors which forbid them to handle goods produced by other firms. Contracts of this sort have been employed, in the past, in the sale of biscuits and crackers, cameras, dress patterns, canned syrups, petroleum products, and many other goods.

---

inferior machines called "knockers," which it represented to be just as good as theirs. It threatened to bring suit against them and their customers for alleged infringements of patent rights. It induced their customers to cancel their orders and repudiate their contracts. It intimidated prospective investors in competing plants by publishing lists of defunct competitors and by exhibiting in a "grave yard" at its factory samples of the machines which they had formerly made. Such practices, carried on over a period of 20 years, gave the company control of 95 percent of the nation's production of cash registers. Clair Wilcox, *Competition and Monopoly in American Industry,* T.N.E.C. Monograph No. 20, 1940.

Firms also "tie in" their products, requiring the buyer to take A if it wishes to buy B. Shoe machinery, cans, computers, mimeograph machines, and many others have been sold under tying arrangements. Tie-ins by dominant firms can reduce competition.

There has been "full-line forcing," requiring dealers to carry a whole line of products, thus keeping specialized producers off the markets. Farm equipment and movies have been among those involved, and it is present to a degree in many markets.

Discriminatory and Predatory Pricing.   Systematic price discrimination by dominant firms is both *(a)* anticompetitive and *(b)* a main source of monopoly profits (see Chapter 8 for a full treatment of discrimination). It may arise impersonally, or it may be a series of specific predatory incidents. Sharp versions of it helped to build up and maintain the early trusts. Nowadays one finds mainly the impersonal types, with complex systems of discrimination persisting for years, even decades. It is defended as "only rational," as "meeting competition," and as "necessary to build up the market," and to "get funds for innovation." But it is anticompetitive even if—or, perhaps, especially because—it is inherent in the monopoly situation.

These "abuses" surround many dominant positions, helping to create, maintain, and exploit them. They often provide the second leg of Section 2 cases—monopoly *plus* monopolizing behavior—in the United States. Yet they are often hard to discover and interpret, for their intent can often be made out as merely good "vigorous" competition. And, ultimately, they are superfluous in a sound economic appraisal: the degree of monopoly *exists,* apart from these acts.

B. CRITERIA, CANDIDATES, AND COSTS

B1. Criteria for Bringing and Deciding Cases

The basic law is clear enough: every monopoly or attempt to monopolize any part of trade or commerce is illegal. If the agency shows a significant degree of monopoly to exist, the courts presumably would convict. Yet decades of sinuous legal arguments have put large loopholes into Section 2. These tests for conviction are in three classes: formal, informal, and unspoken.

The formal criteria are two. Courts will now normally require proof: *(a)* that monopoly exists (shown mainly by the firm's market share being at least 60 percent), *plus (b)* that it was gained intentionally or abusively. These are the two prime points which the agencies and firms dispute at trial.

Two informal criteria also are invoked by the firm. If it can show that its high market share arises from *(a)* "superior skill, foresight, or industry," or *(b)* economies of scale, then acquittal usually will follow. To convict would be criticized, either as punitive against good performance, or as irrational since no efficient remedy could be devised.

At least four unspoken criteria are also commonly applied. *(a)* The firm and its products must be relatively simple and standard. Otherwise, the courts will be afraid to tamper with complex conditions. *(b)* The firm must be shown to be not innovative. Otherwise, the courts will fear to destroy a progressive enterprise. *(c)* The firm must be shown to be earning high excess profits. Otherwise, it will claim that it has no monopoly power. *(d)* There must be no threat to the price of the company's stock. Otherwise, the courts fear to impoverish thousands of small investors.

These eight substantive criteria reflect the courts' conservatism and the slenderness of their expertise. Dominant firms can usually find one or more of these escape hatches. Even if not, they provide fertile ground for litigation and stalling. In practice, the straightforward study of monopoly at trial is detoured into other complex issues. Anticipating this, the agencies often avoid cases where the secondary criteria will cause trouble. Cases are not prepared even against some firms with market shares of 75 percent and more.

At trial, the debate often proceeds in a strange limbo. The really decisive conditions are scarcely mentioned, while there is pretense that the formal criteria control the decision. The problems of remedy and penalties are allowed to smother the basic question of whether monopoly power does in fact exist.

The upshot is that the true conditions are not investigated in depth, neither by the agencies nor by a process of exposure in a court trial. If Section 2 were applied as it reads, no such paralysis would occur. Monopolists would be simply defined as such. The proper remedies would still pose intricate problems, but the law would apply as it is written.

B2. Candidates for Treatment

The main firms eligible for study and treatment are in two categories: dominant firms and oligopolies. The two groups shade into each other, but they do present distinct problems.

Dominant firms are those with about 50 percent or more of the market. Some leading instances were given in Table 2–5, and their evolution is clarified in Tables 5–2 and 5–3.

In 1910 there was indeed a large core of dominant firms in major industries, including U.S. Steel, Standard Oil, American Tobacco, and others.[22] Most of these were created by the trust movement of 1890–1901. By 1948, as Table 5–2 shows, the cast of characters changed considerably. Automobile, electric, and other companies led the list, but they are scattered further down among the ranks of all firms than the leaders were in 1910. By 1978, Table 2–5 shows that there had been still further changes. But many of the present leaders are familiar from 1948. These include General Motors, IBM, Western Electric, General Electric, Eastman Kodak, Procter & Gamble, and others.

---

[22] John Moody, in *The Truth About the Trusts* (New York: Moody, 1904), gives facts about several score major trusts. Those with lasting power may have been fewer. In any event, dominant firms were a major problem at the time.

TABLE 5–2
Changes in Market Position, Leading Dominant Firms, 1910–1935

Asset Rank among All Industrial Firms in 1910		Estimated Assets, 1909–10* ($ millions)	Estimated Degree of Market Power 1910† (percent)	Estimated Change in Market Power 1910–35 (percent)
1	United States Steel	1,804	22.0	− 5.0
2	Standard Oil (New Jersey)	800	27.0	−11.7
3	American Tobacco	286	27.0	−13.7
6	International Harvester	166	25.5	−10.5
7	Central Leather	138	21.0	−15.0
8	Pullman	131	29.3	− 2.3
10	American Sugar	124	21.0	− 6.3
13	Singer Manufacturing	113	25.7	− 6.0
16	General Electric	102	23.0	− 1.2
19	Corn Products	97	21.0	− 3.7
21	American Can	90	22.0	− 2.3
25	Westinghouse Electric	84	20.5	− 1.2
30	du Pont	75	29.5	−16.0
34	International Paper	71	18.5	− 7.5
37	National Biscuit	65	18.5	− 7.5
55	Western Electric	43	33.0	0
59	United Fruit	41	27.0	0
61	United Shoe Machinery	40	31.7	− 1.2
72	Eastman Kodak	35	29.5	0
‡	Alcoa	35	32.9	− 3.4

* See A. D. H. Kaplan, *Big Enterprise;* Moody's *Industrial Manual;* and G. W. Stocking and W. F. Mueller, "The Cellophane Case and the New Competition," *American Economic Review,* 1955, pp. 29–63.

† Based on estimated market share and entry barriers. It is the rate of profit which the firm's market position would normally be expected to yield. See W. G. Shepherd, *The Treatment of Market Power* (New York: Columbia University Press, 1975).

‡ Not available.

There are probably scores of other near-monopolies, most of them unknown for lack of data.

This core of market power is stable and important. The gains from abating much of it would probably be large. Yet the problem is not metastasizing the way it seemed to be in 1895–1925, and the whole economic loss does not appear to be calamitous or ballooning.

Tight Oligopoly. Some of the main tight oligopolies are listed in Table 5–4, roughly in decreasing order of aggregate market power. Some of these are industries in which antitrust treatments during 1905–20 or 1937–52 were *not* tried or carried out; steel, oil, copper, aluminum, glass, and rubber. Now often permeated with a degree of X-inefficiency and cooperative habits, they are possibly intractable to structural treatment alone, and they do not usually engage in overt price fixing.

Therefore, the discounted policy yields for these candidates seem lower than they are for dominant firms. The probabilities of net benefits are lower,

134

TABLE 5–3
Changes in Market Position, Leading Dominant Firms, 1948–1978

Asset Rank among All Industrial Firms in 1948		Estimated Assets 1948* (est.) ($ million)	Degree of Market Power 1948† (est.) (percent)	Change in Market Power 1948–78 (est.) (percent)
2	General Motors	2,958	22.0	− 0.2
9	General Electric	1,177	20.5	0
20	Western Electric	650	33.0	− 0.4
29	Alcoa	504	28.0	− 1.1
33	Eastman Kodak	412	27.0	0
38	Procter & Gamble	356	19.5	0
47	United Fruit	320	27.0	− 5.0
60	American Can	276	20.0	− 5.2
69	IBM	242	29.5	− 6.0
76	Coca-Cola	222	22.0	− 2.5
‡	Campbell Soup	149	28.2	0
‡	Caterpillar Tractor	147	19.5	0
‡	Kellogg	41	19.5	− 1.2
‡	Gillette	78	24.5	0
‡	Babcock and Wilcox	79	22.0	− 2.5
‡	Hershey	62	25.8	− 2.3
‡	du Pont (cellophane)	(65)	30.5	− 8.5
‡	United Shoe Machinery	(104)	29.2	−10.7

* Based on A. D. H. Kaplan, *Big Enterprise in a Competitive System,* rev. ed. (Washington, D.C.: Brookings Institution, 1965), chapter 7.

† Based on estimated market shares and entry barriers. It is the rate of profit which the firm's market position would normally be expected to yield. See W. G. Shepherd, *The Treatment of Market Power* (New York: Columbia University Press, 1975).

‡ Not available.

TABLE 5–4
Major Tight Oligopolies, U.S. Manufacturing, 1977

Industry Code Number		Value of Shipments ($ million)	Actual Average Concentration (estimated) (percent)	Competition from Imports	Are There Major Geographic Submarkets?
2911	Petroleum refining	22,737	(65)	Slight	Yes
3312	Iron and steel	9,328*	(80)	Moderate	Yes
3211	Flat glass	670	92	Slight	No
3641	Electric lamps	892	92	Slight	No
3522	Farm machinery	4,367	70	Slight	No
3334	Primary aluminum	1,758	90+	Slight	No
3331	Primary copper	673	75	Slight	No
2111	Cigarettes	3,503	84	Slight	No
2026	Fluid milk	8,253	(60)	Slight	Yes

* Value-added is given; value of shipments is not reported.

Source: U.S. Census Bureau, *Value-of-Shipment Concentration Ratios,* Annual Survey of Manufacturers, 1970, M70(AS)-9, U.S. Government Printing Office, 1972; and W. G. Shepherd, *Market Power and Economic Welfare* (New York: Random House, 1970), Appendix Table 8, and various recent data.

especially for technical progress. Restructuring action would embrace several firms, not one, perhaps with higher transition costs. There are few clean cases: most tight oligopolies are now encrusted with special conditions, such as vertical integration, mineral rights, ingrained cooperative behavior, and indirect boardroom interlocks. Moreover, half-loaf antitrust treatments in the past have created estoppel problems for some of them.

B3. Costs of Action

Section 2 cases are usually long and costly. The burden of proof is against the agency, and the firm has time on its side. The firm usually is willing and able to use all tactics in order to escape or at least postpone conviction, at any cost up to the monopoly profits which are at stake (recall Chapter 3). Even small firms can hold out through long and expensive cases. Large dominant firms make for fearsomely big cases, involving hundreds of lawyers, many tons of documents, scores of millions of dollars in expense, and usually up to 20 years. A medium-sized case might cost the Antitrust Division at least ten lawyers and $1 million per year; the defendant normally would multiply those resources by five to 10 times. In 1977 the Antitrust Division chief reckoned that the Division could handle only two important Section 2 cases at a time, given current budget levels.

C. PAST TREATMENTS, 1900 TO 1953

The two big waves of Section 2 action were in 1906–20 and 1938–52. The main cases are summarized in Table 5–5.

The first set of cases started with Roosevelt's trust-busting and flowered under Taft.[23] Then it was stalled and stopped by World War I and its aftermath. Its coverage was remarkably complete, reaching most of the very largest corporations of the time. A few of the cases had sharp effects, but most ended with little or no impact.

The second wave during 1938–52 was confined to firms ranking much lower down in the national lists, but these firms still included nearly all of the major firms with market shares over 50 percent. Several of these cases were successful legally, but others were inconclusive, and the two most important ones—IBM and Western Electric—were abandoned in the 1950s.

Since 1968 a modest revival has occurred, with several sizable actions started. These touch on IBM, cereals firms, Xerox, oil firms, and AT&T. They are assessed below, in Section D.

---

[23] See Simon N. Whitney, *Antitrust Policies*, 2 vols. (New York: Twentieth Century Fund, 1958), for narrative of the main cases.

Roosevelt's actions were moderate, despite his reputation as a trust-buster. Thurman Arnold later described him as the man "with his big stick that never hit anybody." Taft's actions during 1909–13 were much more drastic and effective.

TABLE 5–5
Major Section 2 Cases, 1905 to 1920

	Time between Monopolization and Remedy	
Cases	Years	Interval (years)
1905 to 1920		
American Tobacco	1890–1916	26
Standard Oil	1875–1918+	43+
du Pont (gunpowder)	1902–13	11
Corn Products	1897–1920	23
American Can	1901–	
U.S. Steel	1901–	—
AT&T	1881–	—
Meatpackers, (Armour, Swift, Wilson, Cudahy)	1885	—
American Sugar	1890–	—
United Shoe Machinery	1899–	
International Harvester	1902	
1938 to 1952		
Alcoa	1903–(1953)	(50)
National Broadcasting Company	1926–43	17
Pullman	1899–1947	(65)
Paramount Pictures	1914–48	34
American Can	1901–(1955)	(54)
du Pont (GM holdings)	1918–61	43
United Shoe Machinery	1899–1970	71
United Fruit	1899–1970	71
American Tobacco	(1920)–	—
du Pont (cellophane)	1925–	—
Western Electric	1881–	—
IBM	(1925)–	—
Since 1968		
IBM (1969 case)	(1925)–	—
Cereals (1972 case)	(1950)–	—
Xerox (1973 case)	1961–	14
AT&T (1974 case)	1881–	—

* Based on evidence of the start of official investigation and the end of official action. Parentheses indicate estimates.

Sources: S. N. Whitney, *Antitrust Policies* (New York: Twentieth Century Fund, 1958); M. J. Green et al., *The Closed Enterprise System* (New York: Grossman, 1972); and various other sources.

Time between Beginning and End of Action*		
Years	*Interval (years)*	*Outcome*
1906–12	6	Dissolution into three main firms.
1905–12	7	Dissolution into about a dozen regionally dominant firms.
1906–12	6	Mild dissolution; reversed quickly by effects of World War I.
(1910)–19	(12)	Slight changes from a consent decree.
(1909)–20	(11)	No change.
(1907)–20	(13)	Acquittal. Informal limits on further mergers.
(1909)–13	(4)	Compromise. AT&T retained its position; agreed to interconnect and avoid further mergers.
(1905)–1920	(12)	Compromise. Packers agreed to stay out of adjacent markets and to cease coordination.
1908–14	6	No action. American Sugar's position had slipped already.
(1908)–18	10	USM leasing restrictions were modified.
1906–18	12	Compromise. Trivial divestiture.
1934–50	16	War plants sold to new entrants.
1938–43	5	"Blue Network" divested (became American Broadcasting Corp.).
(1937)–1947	(10)	Divestiture of sleeping car operation. Manufacturing monopoly was not directly changed.
(1935)–1948	(13)	Vertical integration removed.
(1945)–1950	(5)	Compromise: certain restrictive practices stopped, to foster entry.
(1945)–1961	(16)	Divestiture.
(1945)–1969	(61)	Share reduced to 50 percent.
1948–70	22	Moderate divestiture.
1938–46	8	Conviction but no significant remedy.
(1945)–1956	(11)	Acquittal.
1946–56	10	Case effectively abandoned.
1947–56	9	Case effectively abandoned.
1965–	—	Trial begun in 1975.
1970–	—	In process. Hearing began in 1976.
1970–75	6	Compromise. Some opening of access to patents.
1965–	—	In process. Pre-trial

C1. The First Series: "Trust-busting"

The first Section 2 case in 1895 was a fiasco, but renewed action after 1901 led to landmark decisions during 1911–15, some of which had sizable economic effects.

The new Sherman Act was quickly put to the test, in a suit against the recently formed American Sugar Company, which then held a 95 percent market share. The court reached a derisory decision, holding that manufacturing was not interstate commerce and was therefore exempt from the Sherman Act.[24] This narrow view would have nullified the law, but it was soon ignored.

In 1904 Theodore Roosevelt's first "trust-busting" venture, a challenge to J. P. Morgan, resulted in the Northern Securities decision.[25] The Supreme Court dissolved the holding company that controlled the Great Northern and Northern Pacific railroads, parallel competing systems that also competed against other transcontinental lines. Other railroad cases during 1904 to 1922 established that mergers to achieve great market power were illegal, even if the power were not clearly abused.[26] More important, the 1904 case opened the gates to spectacular investigations, trials, and changes in a series of leading industrial firms. The oil, tabacco, sugar, telephone equipment, steel, gunpowder, meat-packing, farm machinery, shoe machinery, and aluminum industries were among those touched. Six of the 10 largest industrial firms were treated. The Bureau of Corporations was formed to do large studies during 1904–15, and the whole series of cases was remarkably thorough and cleanly handled. Several sharp changes in structure resulted, but the majority of the treatments had little or no effect.

The "Bad Trusts." 1911 was the landmark year, with decisions in the Standard Oil and American Tobacco cases. Each had a 90 percent market share, had been ruthless, and had not been especially innovative nor realized large economies of scale. Each produced a simple product, had earned excess profits, and was closely held by a small group of owners. Both put up inept defenses and were the target of a wide groundswell of attacks by citizens, other businesses, and state officials.

Strict though they seemed, the decisions actually clipped Section 2's wings. In a tortuously worded opinion, Chief Justice White inserted a "rule of reason"

---

[24] *U.S.* v. *E. C. Knight Co.,* 156 U.S. 1. Also read Alfred Eichner, *The Origins of Oligopoly* (New York: Columbia University Press, 1971) for an exhaustive account of the trust and its fate.

[25] *Northern Securities Co.* v. *U.S.,* 193 U.S. 197 (1904).

[26] In 1917 the Court found that joint ownership of the Terminal Railroad Association of St. Louis by a number of railroads entering that city was an illegal combination and ordered the Association to admit, on reasonable terms, any other road that might apply (*U.S.* v. *Terminal Railroad Assn.,* 224 U.S. 383). In the same year, the Union Pacific Railroad came before the Court. The Union Pacific's line had stopped at Ogden, Utah. The Company had sought to extend it to the coast by buying stock in the Southern Pacific, which controlled the Central Pacific, which ran from Ogden to San Francisco. The Court held that this acquisition violated the law even though the two lines served different cities and operated between different termini (*U.S.* v. *Union Pacific Railroad Co.,* 226 U.S. 61). In 1922, moreover, the Court held Southern's ownership of stock in Central to be illegal, though they were not competing lines (*U.S.* v. *Southern Pacific Co.,* 259 U.S. 214). Two other cases involved joint ownership of railroads and anthracite coal mines. In 1920 the Court ordered dissolution of the Reading Company, a holding company which controlled the Reading Railroad and mines producing a third of the country's supply of anthracite (*U.S.* v. *Reading Co.,* 253 U.S. 26). In all of these cases, the Court held that the attainment of market power through combination was illegal even though that power was not abused.

as the precedent for future cases. The two firms were convicted because of their abuses, he said, not their monopolies per se. This rule of reason added the "plus" criterion to Section 2, and it placed the burden of proof against the Antitrust Division to prove the abuses.

Standard Oil's history provided a rich variety of abusive practices. It had gained control of all of the important pipelines and 90 percent of refining capacity. It had done so by exacting rebates from the railroads on its own shipments as well as those of its rivals, by selective local price cutting, and by other predatory practices the mere listing of which filled some 57 pages of the trial record. The Court ordered the Standard combine dissolved, and this was quickly done, by 1913.[27] Yet the treatment was scarcely timely or drastic. Standard Oil's market position was already slipping, and the monopoly had existed for nearly 40 years. The holding company was merely removed, leaving the previous series of regional monopolies, still largely under shared ownership. The shareholders realized a 47 percent capital gain during the year after the dissolution. It took some 10 to 20 years for genuine competition to spread in the industry.[28]

American Tobacco, formed around 1890, had also used predatory practices: excluding rivals from sources of supply, buying plants to shut them down, using selective predatory pricing, and selling "fighting brands" at a loss to destroy competitors. This "bad trust," too, was simply separated back into three firms.[29]

The virtual monopoly of du Pont in gunpowder since the 1890s was also ended in 1913.[30] The firm had been less abusive, but its intent to monopolize was clear, its defense was inept, and spinning off some lesser parts was relatively easy. Yet du Pont retained the greater and better parts, and World War I immediately nullified the effects and vastly enriched the firm. The du Pont family then took major holdings in General Motors, U.S. Rubber, and other firms.

The government also threatened action against AT&T for attempting to monopolize both telephone and telegraph services, and for its internal monopoly with Western Electric (recall Chapter 2 and see Chapter 13). Moderate concessions were gained from AT&T in 1913, but it retained its monopoly in telephone production and operation in most cities and all long distance traffic.

Major cases against International Harvester, U.S. Steel, American Sugar, American Can, the four major meatpackers, and Corn Products Co. advanced in the courts, and by 1915 a broad restructuring of industry—reversing much of the trust movement—was in prospect. But then World War I intervened,

---

[27] *Standard Oil. Co. of N.J. v. U.S.*, 221 U.S. 1.

[28] This lag is evaluated in George W. Stocking, *The Oil Industry and the Competitive System* (Boston: Houghton Mifflin, 1925).

[29] *U.S. v. American Tobacco Co.*, 221 U.S. 106.

[30] See Alfred Chandler and Stephen Salsbury, *Pierre S. du Pont and the Making of the Modern Corporation* (New York: Harper & Row, 1971).

the mood changed, the rule of reason began to tell, and the effort collapsed.

The "Good" Trusts.   In 1916, a lower court refused to convict the American Can Company, controlling nine-tenths of the output of tin cans, because the defendant "had done nothing of which any competitor or consumer of cans complains or anything which strikes a disinterested outsider as unfair or unethical."[31] In its decision in the U.S. Steel case in 1920 the Supreme Court revealed a similar complacency. The doctrine contained in this decision granted virtual immunity to monopoly in manufacturing for the next 25 years.

The United States Steel Corporation, created in 1901, was a combination of 12 concerns, themselves resulting from earlier combinations of 180 separate companies, with over 300 plants. It was the largest merger in the nation's history, extending vertically from mining to fabrication and horizontally to all the types of steel mill products, and controlling, at its inception, around two-thirds of the output of the industry. When this colossus came before the Court, it still controlled one half of the supply of steel. But in a 4 to 3 decision, with two of its members abstaining, the Court found that the combination did not violate the law.[32]

The majority eked out its reasons as follows: *(a)* The organizers of the Corporation had intended to monopolize the industry, but they had not succeeded in doing so and, recognizing their failure, had abandoned the attempt. The law was directed, said Justice McKenna, not against an expectation of monopoly but against its realization. Its specific prohibition of attempts to monopolize was thus ignored. *(b)* Admittedly, the Corporation had conspired with other companies, in earlier years, to fix the price of steel. But this only served to prove its lack of monopoly. The practice, moreover, had been abandoned; the evidence showed that the industry was now competitive. Curiously, the important role of the Pittsburgh-plus delivered pricing system was not explained or understood (see Chapter 7 below).

The decision was thus confined to a narrower issue: the legal status of a combination controlling half of an industry. Certainly the Corporation was big and powerful. But, *(c)* said the Court, "the law does not make mere size an offense. It . . . requires overt acts and trusts to its prohibition of them and its power to repress and punish them." *(d)* The question, then, was whether the Corporation had abused its power. Had it acted, by itself, to fix monopolistic prices? Had it excluded others from the market? On the contrary, said the Court, its behavior was exemplary: "It resorted to none of the brutalities or tyrannies that the cases illustrate of other combinations. It did not secure freight rebates; it did not increase its profits by reducing the wages of its employees . . . . , by lowering the quality of its products,

---

[31] *U.S.* v. *American Can Co.,* 230 F. 859, 861 (1961).

[32] *U.S.* v. *U.S. Steel Corp.,* 251 U.S. 417 (1920). For an excellent recent critique of this decision, see Donald O. Parsons and Edward J. Ray, "The United States Steel Consolidation: The Creation of Market Control," *Journal of Law and Economics* 18 (April 1975), 181–220.

nor by creating an artifical scarcity of them; . . . it did not undersell its competitors in some localities by reducing its prices there below those maintained elsewhere . . . ; there was no evidence that it attempted to crush its competitors or drive them from the market." In short, though the corporation was big, it was not bad. The fact of its earlier monopolizing could be forgotten. The law was thus held by the majority of the court, as Justice Day remarked in his dissent, to be "intended merely to suppress unfair practices."

When this decision was announced, the government withdrew its appeals in several pending cases, including the one against American Can.[33] The Court had turned about, and treatment largely ceased. The courts were evidently determined now not to touch dominant firms except in the most extreme cases. Market shares were safe virtually up to 100 percent. The other cases ended in defeat or peripheral consent decrees.[34]

C2. The Second Series

Treatment ceased until 1938, when Alcoa was brought to trial for the monopoly it had held since before 1900. Other cases followed thick and fast under Thurman Arnold and on until 1952. The decisions on Alcoa in 1945 and United Shoe Machinery in 1953 revived Section 2 to a degree; in doctrine, shares of 60 percent could be treated. But in practice, large gaps remained even in this moderate coverage. And after 1952 treatment lapsed once again.

Alcoa had dominated aluminum production under the original Hall and Bradley patents since 1903, realizing very high and steady profit rates. An early Section 2 suit in 1912 was settled with little effect.

The government brought suit again in 1938, charging that Alcoa had monopolized the manufacture of virgin aluminum and the sale of various

---

[33] The issue of size was presented to the Court again in 1927, in a further case against the International Harvester Company. This concern, a combination of five producers of agricultural implements and machinery, controlled 85 percent of the output of such equipment when it was established in 1902, and 64 percent when it was brought before the Court. Its leadership in setting prices was followed by the other members of the industry. These facts, however, did not impress the justices. Six of them, with three abstaining, adhered to the precedent set in the case of U.S. Steel. The law, they said, "does not make the mere size of a corporation, however impressive, or the existence of unexerted power on its part, an offense, when unaccompanied by unlawful conduct in the exercise of its power" (*U.S.* v. *International Harvester Co.,* 274 U.S. 693, 708). Price leadership was rejected as offering evidence of monopoly. In the words of the opinion: "The fact that competitors may see proper, in the exercise of their own judgment, to follow the prices of another manufacturer, does not establish any suppression of competition or show any sinister domination."

[34] The meatpackers decree of 1920 did prevent integration into adjacent markets. Though mild at the time, it came to be challenged vigorously by the firms in 1929 and the 1950s. Denied both times in the courts, the firms finally obtained a revision of the decree in 1976. It permitted the packers, now no longer dominant, to enter a number of concentrated industries which had been off limits.

aluminum products, in violation of Section 2 of the Sherman Act, and asking that it be divided into several parts. A prime charge was vertical price squeezes by Alcoa, involving the price charged for crude aluminum and the prices offered customers for finished goods. After a trial that ran for more than two years the district court found Alcoa not guilty and the government appealed.[35] The final decision was written by Judge Learned Hand in 1945.[36]

The court found that Alcoa manufactured more than nine-tenths of the virgin aluminum ingot used in the United States, the rest coming in from abroad, and concluded that this was "enough to constitute a monopoly."[37] It then considered the argument that the power conferred by this monopoly, though it existed, had not been exercised. This distinction, said the Court,

is . . . purely formal; it would be valid only so long as the monopoly remained wholly inert; it would disappear as soon as the monopoly began to operate; for, when it did—that is, as soon as it began to sell at all—it must sell at some price and the only price at which it could sell is a price which it itself fixed. Thereafter the power and its exercise must needs coalesce.

The doctrine of the Steel and Harvester cases, that the mere existence of unexerted power is no offense, was thus explicitly reversed. Price fixing was found to be inherent in monopoly. The acquisition of market power became the test of illegality. The double standard of interpretation, which condoned the single-firm monopoly while holding agreements among competitors to be unlawful, was rejected as "absurd."

The Court also considered acts which might show intent or abuse (the "plus" factor). It found many, showing that monopoly had not been "thrust upon" Alcoa.

It was not inevitable that it should always anticipate increases in the demand for ingots and be prepared to supply them. Nothing compelled it to keep doubling and redoubling its capacity before others entered the field. It insists that it has never excluded competitors; but we can think of no more effective exclusion than progressively to embrace each new opportunity as it opened, and to face every newcomer with new capacity already geared into a great organization, having the advantage of experience, trade connections, and the elite of personnel. . . . No monopolist monopolizes unconscious of what he is doing. So here, "Alcoa" meant to keep, and did keep, the complete and exclusive hold upon the ingot market with which it started. That was to "monopolize" that market, however innocently it otherwise proceeded.

---

[35] *U.S.* v. *Aluminum Co. of America,* 44 F. Supp. 97 (1942).

[36] *U.S.* v. *Aluminum Co. of America,* 148 F. 2d 416. When the justices who had previously been connected with the prosecution disqualified themselves, however, the Supreme Court could not muster a quorum of six to hear the case. The judicial code was then amended by Congress to enable a Court of Appeals to serve, in such circumstances, as a court of last resort. The case was certified to the Court in the second circuit, and the decision of this Court, having the effect of a Supreme Court ruling, was rendered by Judge Hand.

[37] Ibid., p. 424. This is where Judge Hand added the side comment about 90, 60, and 30 percent.

Learned Hand (1872–1961), a distinguished jurist and senior Judge in the 4th District (Southern New York). His Alcoa decision of 1945 is a modern landmark for Section 2 actions. (He is shown here in 1942.)

Wide World Photo

The defense of good behavior was likewise unavailing. The Court condemned the use of squeeze tactics in the past and enjoined their repetition in the future but made clear that it was holding Alcoa guilty of monopolization "regardless of such practices."

The firm was not found to be abusing its position at the time of the trial, but Congress, said the Court, "did not condone 'good trusts' and condemn 'bad' ones; it forbade all." The antitrust laws were not intended merely to regulate business practices. It was one of their purposes "to perpetuate and preserve for its own sake and in spite of possible costs, an organization of industry into small units which can effectively compete with each other."

Judge Hand's landmark decision made a clean break with the Steel and Harvester precedents. It resurrected Section 2. It required dominant firms to meet a stricter code of competitive fairness than lesser firms must meet. But the sharp reversal in doctrine resulted in very modest economic changes.[38]

---

[38] The case had been remanded for relief to Judge Knox in Chicago. His action in 1950, after five years' wait, exemplifies the way conservative district judges can dilute or reverse a strict decision. He first swamped the competitive standard in other factors:

> In determining the extent of permissible power that is consistent with the antitrust laws in a particular industry, the following factors are relevant: the number and strength of the firms in the market; their effective size from the standpoint of technological development, and from the standpoint of competition with substitute materials and with foreign trade; national security interest in the maintenance of strong productive facilities, and maximum scientific research and development; together with public interest in lowered costs and uninterrupted production.

He then used amateur opinions about business viability to reach the view that Alcoa could not stand to be altered. Aluminum, said Judge Knox, must compete with other materials made by large concerns. Dismemberment of Alcoa's research staff and its managerial personnel would lessen its ability to do so. Success in interproduct competition "can be achieved only by companies that are rich in resources, and which are capable of undertaking extensive scientific and market experimentations. At the present juncture, the weakening of any aluminum producer would lessen the buoyancy of the industry as a whole."

Alcoa's structure was not touched. Instead government aluminum plants built during World War II (and operated by Alcoa) were reserved for new competitors, which turned out to be Reynolds and Kaiser. Alcoa still dominated the new tight oligopoly, being required only to license its patents and cut its ties with Aluminum, Ltd., of Canada.[39] The tight oligopoly has continued with little change into the 1970s.

The Alcoa doctrine was soon extended to the leading three cigarette firms and movie theaters.[40] By 1948 the Court was saying:

It is not always necessary to find a specific intent to restrain trade or build a monopoly . . . It is sufficient that a restraint of trade or monopoly results as the consequence of a defendant's conduct or business arrangements . . . . Monopoly power, whether lawfully or unlawfully acquired, may itself constitute an evil and stand condemned under Section 2 even though it remains unexercised.[41]

Several other cases during the 1940s resulted in modest structural changes, in nonmanufacturing industries. The National Broadcasting Company (NBC) was forced to divest its "Blue" network in 1943; this became the basis for the American Broadcasting Company (ABC). The Pullman Company was required to separate its production and leasing of railway sleeping cars, keeping the part it preferred.[42] In the A&P case, the company was found in 1946 to have gained discriminatory advantages through its wholesale produce subsidiary, the Atlantic Commission Company. A consent decree in 1954 dissolved ACCO.[43] And the Paramount decision in 1948 cut the links between movie producers and theater chains.[44] It also stopped the "block booking" of movies, which had tied the best films to inferior ones (see chapter 8).

---

[39] See M. J. Peck, *Competition in the Aluminum Industry* (Cambridge: Harvard University Press, 1961).

[40] *American Tobacco Co.* v. *U.S.,* 328 U.S. 781, 811; and *U.S.* v. *Griffith,* 334 U.S. 100, 105–7.

[41] *U.S.* v. *Griffith,* 334 U.S. 100, 105–7.

[42] *U.S.* v. *Pullman Co.,* 50 F. Supp. 123 (1943).

[43] *U.S.* v. *Great A.&P. Tea Co.,* 67 F. Supp. 626 (1946); affirmed 173 F. 2d 79 (1949); Civil Action 52–139, District Court of the Southern District of N.Y., Consent Decree, January 19, 1954.

[44] *U.S.* v. *Paramount Pictures,* 334 U.S. 131 (1948). This case involved five of the major producers of motion pictures who also operated first-run theaters in the larger cities and chains of smaller theaters throughout the country. The government charged that these concerns had favored their own houses in supplying films, and had required block booking, minimum admission charges, and protracted intervals between successive showings in leasing films to others, thus making it difficult for independent producers and distributors to compete. It sought the separation of production and exhibition, the elimination of block booking, and the prohibition of other coercive practices. The lower court enjoined the practices complained of, and required that films, instead of being booked in blocks, be leased through competitive bidding. The Supreme Court found this remedy to be inadequate, insisting also that production and exhibition be divorced. The reorganizations were completed by 1952, the five companies being broken into ten: five of them producers and five operating chains of theaters. As a result, markets were opened to independent producers and films made more readily available to independent exhibitors.

American Can.   This suit against the two leading can companies—American and Continental—resulted in a consent decree in 1950.[45] The firms agreed to stop various exclusionary actions, such as refusing to sell can-closing machinery, tying can and machinery contracts, and price discrimination of various sorts. The decree required no divestiture or other structural change. Concentration did decrease by 1955, but the industry remains a tight oligopoly.[46]

Major suits were filed against AT&T (seeking divestiture of Western Electric) in 1949 and IBM in 1951. In 1954 the second United Shoe Machinery case resulted in a landmark conviction but little economic change.

United Shoe Machinery.   The firm had held a virtual monopoly for some 50 years in a rather small market. The decision in 1953 followed an extensive trial.[47] Judge Charles Wyzanski followed the precedent established in the aluminum case, but he also went further. Monopoly, he said, is lawful if it is "thrust upon" the monopolist. Yet a concern's monopoly power is unlawful if that power is the result of barriers erected by its own business methods (even though not predatory, immoral, or restraining trade in violation of Section 1 of the Sherman Act). The firm can still escape if it shows that the barriers are exclusively the result of superior skill, superior products, natural advantages, technological or economic efficiency, scientific research, low margins of profit maintained permanently and without discrimination, legal licenses, or the like.

Systematic price discrimination was the main behavior pattern which, taken with the high market share, violated Section 2 (see Chapter 8 for more detail). United's business practices—such as price discrimination, leasing rather than selling its machines, and making long-term contracts on exclusive terms— were not per se immoral or illegal. But the company had not achieved and maintained its overwhelming strength solely by virtue of its "ability, economies of scale, research, and adaptation to inevitable economic laws." Instead, given its dominant position, its business practices, however legal in themselves, had operated to exclude competitors from the field. Judge Wyzanski, thus, did not find monopolization to be illegal per se. But he imposed on the monopolist a stricter standard of conduct than that applying to competitive concerns. This reaffirmed the tighter standards of behavior set by *Alcoa*.

The Division asked the court to separate United into three competing firms. Judge Wyzanski refused to do so, ordering the company instead to sell as well as lease its machines, shorten its leases, modify their terms, and

---

[45] *U.S.* v. *American Can Co.*, Civil Action 26345-H, District Court, Northern District of California. Final Judgment, June 22, 1950.

[46] For a defense of the decree, see James W. McKie, *Tin Cans and Tin Plate* (Cambridge: Harvard University Press, 1959).

[47] *U.S.* v. *United Shoe Machinery Corp.*, 110 F. Supp. 295. The Supreme Court affirmed in 1954. The firm, originally a combination of three companies with 95 percent of the market, had been sued in 1913 on the same grounds. The Court acquitted in the early case, mainly because the firm had important patent rights. Forty years later the firm still dominated, though by now its market was a rather small one.

grant licenses under its patents to its competitors. During the next decade, United diversified its business, reducing shoe machinery below five percent of its sales and reducing its share of the shoe machinery market to 60 percent. Further action was still required in 1968–69 to get the market share below 50 percent.

The USM victory was largely doctrinal (USM's shoe machinery revenue was in 1968 less than 1/100 the size of IBM), and in fact the doctrine was mild. Conviction required evidence that the high market share did not represent superior performance. A loophole was added and the burden of proof placed against the agencies. And no sharp remedy was granted. To lawyers the Shoe Machinery case is important; to economists it represents a weakening of treatment, in a small market.

du Pont "Cellophane." du Pont had monopolized "cellophane" in the U.S. market from 1923 on, earning high rates of return but preventing the entry of new competitors. The Court chose instead to define the market as all flexible packaging materials (recall Section A). Since du Pont's share of that "market" was only 18 percent, the case stopped there, without reaching the other criteria.

Meanwhile the Eisenhower administration had settled the AT&T and IBM cases during 1955–56 under murky circumstances and with little to show.[48] Section 2 treatment largely ceased until 1969.

D. A THIRD SERIES, STARTING IN 1969?

During 1953–68 structural treatment of the main dominant firms virtually ceased. Eastman Kodak agreed to end its tying of film sales and processing, but its position in film was little changed by the 1970s.[49] United Fruit Co. consented in 1958 to end its old pre-1900 banana monopoly, agreeing to create from its assets a firm capable of handling 35 percent of the market by 1970. Castle & Cook and Del Monte entered the market strongly after 1964. By 1973 United Fruit (now United Brands) no longer led, and it had shifted mainly into other lines. The Division started suits against GM's bus and locomotive monopolies (over 85 percent each), but Turner dropped these by 1966 for lack of foreseeable relief. With only one plant in each case, it was pointless to proceed, he said. Grinnell was convicted in 1966 for monopolizing the market in "accredited central station protective systems," but the

---

[48] On the improprieties in reaching the settlement, see Mark J. Green and others, *The Closed Enterprise System* (New York: Grossman Publishers, 1972), chap. 2.

[49] The Division chose rapid negotiation rather than full trial as a "more efficient" method. But this avoided disclosure of the facts, actions by injured third parties, and, in the event, effective changes. For a defense of the handling, see Theodore P. Kovaleff, "The Antitrust Record of the Eisenhower Administration," *Antitrust Bulletin*, 21 (Winter 1976), 589–610.

market was small and the doctrine was not new.[50] The 1960s brought much study but few cases.[51] Tight oligopoly was not touched.[52]

Since 1968 five significant cases have been started: IBM, cereals, Xerox, AT&T, and major oil firms. There has been much study and increasing grass-roots support for action. Also, new economic factors may be slowly eroding market power in automobiles, computers, and aircraft. But policy is still dormant, and the recent cases now seem unlikely to end with timely and effective relief.

IBM. The firm has held between 60 and 80 percent of the mainframe computer market since 1955. It has not refrained from a wide variety of aggressive actions, which could be predatory.[53] The Division sued IBM under Section 2 in January 1969, after an investigation since 1966 in which IBM formally cooperated.[54] The filing was prompted by private suits against IBM, by the failure of several competitors, and by data showing IBM to have a market share of 70 percent and a thorough pattern of price discrimination. The suit charged that IBM held a monopoly, that the discrimination prevented effective competition by smaller specialized producers, and that the introduc-

---

[50] The relief given in 1967 was easy to arrange and remarkably effective. Grinnell divested American District Telegraph Co. and the restrictive terms were stopped. Firms increased from 40 to 190 by 1969. ADT grew rapidly, became much more efficient, and was soon thriving (see *Forbes* magazine, November 15, 1973, p. 65). The economics of competition under Section 2 operated with high fidelity.

[51] For example, the automobile industry was studied several times, and action was recommended but never quite crystallized under Turner. In 1976–78 it was being "investigated" again. W. S. Comanor researched the role of advertising in the detergent markets for the Division in 1967–68. He established that the predicted relationship between advertising intensity, profitability, and market share did exist. But no action was then taken or even prepared, primarily because no adequate remedy available *under conventional antitrust processes* seemed to exist. Doubts about relief therefore prevented a court evaluation of whether monopoly existed.

[52] In 1967–68, Turner started a study at the Division to identify tight oligopolies which needed treatment under the Kaysen-Turner approach of 1959. The 12 prime candidates (apart from automobiles, which was given separate analysis) appeared to be: electric lamps, tires, flat glass, steel ingots, metal containers, explosives, sulphur, primary batteries, carbon and graphite, cereals, auto rentals. "Marginal" cases were transformers, copper, trucks, and gypsum (see Green, *Closed Enterprise*, pp. 305–7).

But some of these candidates were old and now unprofitable. Others stemmed mainly from patents or advertising, and so remedy would clearly be difficult to bring about. Still others could be argued to face monopsony power; tires, for example. And several were relatively trivial cases. Finally, all of them were less promising legally and economically than such near-monopoly cases as Western Electric and automobiles, which at that time were not being brought. Therefore, there seemed little reason to put scarce resources on these marginal cases, since ones with much higher priority were blocked. That the Kaysen-Turner proposals were not applied therefore had strong practical reasons at the time.

[53] This is shown in Gerald Brock, *The U.S. Computer Industry* (Cambridge: Ballinger Press, 1975). See also the U.S. Senate Subcommittee on Antitrust and Monopoly, Hearings on *The Computer Industry*, 93d Congress, 2d Session (Washington, D.C.: U.S. Government Printing Office, 1974).

[54] *U.S.* v. *International Business Machines Corp.*, 69 CIV 200, So. Dist. of N.Y.

tion of the major 360 line of computers in 1965 was done in ways which eliminated competition. This closely fits the precedents of United Shoe Machinery.

Discrimination has been both *(a)* vertical (among machine types, with higher profit rates on smaller systems, where competition was weaker), and *(b)* horizontal (among the various users of each computer model). Vertical patterns were known from IBM pricing memos about the 360 line of computers about to be introduced in 1964. Further, IBM had used several "fighting ship" computer models (the 360/44 and 360/67) at low or negative profits, to defeat rivals' systems. Horizontal discrimination also occurred, as IBM salesmen promised free programming and other help to secure contracts.[55] Discrimination is systematic and inherent in IBM's position, and it continued into the 1970s (see Chapter 8).

The suit seeks a structural change, not yet determined: possibly a vertical separation between the producing and leasing functions, and possibly horizontally into two or three successor firms. Presently, Burroughs, Control Data, Sperry Rand, and Honeywell are surviving at less than one-seventh of IBM's size.

After six years of poorly handled pre-trial preparation, the trial began on May 18, 1975.[56] On April 26, 1978, the Division finally finished presenting its case, after 473 courtroom days and 51 witnesses. IBM's rebuttal was expected to take even longer. The Division diffused its case to include scores of witnesses' opinions about IBM's conduct and performance. It treated the economic core of the case—the discriminatory pricing which reduced competition—relatively lightly. Accordingly the case ballooned and slowed, partly from IBM's extremely aggressive resistance.

IBM's defense was primarily that: *(a)* its share of the business equipment market is below 40 percent and falling, *(b)* its pricing was competitive, not predatory, *(c)* its market position reflected good performance and economies of scale, *(d)* its products are highly complex, *(e)* it has been innovative, and *(f)* its profit rate has not really been high. Moreover, its shares are widely held by small and large investors, who fear capital losses. IBM's relentless resistance was stiffened by the prospect of billions of dollars in private damage claims should the firm be convicted. Also IBM gained from delay, probably at least $2 million per day.[57]

---

[55] Though IBM unbundled these services in late 1968 in an effort to avert the Division's suit, the unbundling has not been complete.

[56] The economic core of the case was highly compact and complete by mid-1968. The delay in bringing the case to trial has reflected extreme efforts and clever strategy by IBM counsel and, during 1969–72, a lapse in Antitrust Division handling and passive behavior by the court. The Division staff permitted such tactics as extensive tangential interrogatories and snowing by masses of irrelevant documents. Under Kauper after 1972, the case was given far greater resources and was handled more aggressively.

[57] Suppose that about one-fourth of IBM's profits (now running around $1.7 billion yearly) are at stake under Section 2. This is equivalent to $1 million per day, IBM's

A number of private suits also sought damages or restructuring of IBM. Control Data Corp. filed a massive suit in 1968 but settled it in 1973, gaining benefits worth $101 million (including IBM's Service Bureau Corporation).[58] Suits by Greyhound Corp. (1969) and Western Union (1971) were still pending or on appeal in 1978. Telex Corp. sued in 1972, claiming that IBM used predatory pricing to stop its entry into the market for disk and tape drives which were "plug compatible" with IBM equipment. The District Court agreed in 1973 and granted $260 million in damages.[59] But the Appeals Court held instead that *all* peripheral equipment was the relevant market; IBM's share of that was low rather than 80 percent. The Court also declared that IBM's actions had not been abusive, and it granted IBM's counterclaim for $19 million in damages for allegedly stealing IBM trade secrets. Under the threat from IBM's countersuit, Telex did not appeal further. Telex's first victory had stirred a series of similar suits by other firms. Some of these reached trial in 1976–78. They alleged an IBM monopoly in the mainframe systems market (not peripheral equipment), and largely paralleled the Division's case. By 1978 IBM appeared to be winning these cases and settling others for nominal sums.

The whole process has been costly, involving hundreds of lawyers and witnesses, many millions of dollars, millions of pages of documents, and years of court time. It illustrates the weaknesses of the method. IBM is the leading industrial dominant firm, with great profitability and a nearly steady market position. Yet a full treatment of it appears not to be possible, using the traditional approach. If so, IBM will have shifted the margin of treatment, to let dominant firms do with impunity a wide range of aggressive actions. This is a reversal of the *Alcoa* and *United Shoe Machinery* standards of behavior.

Cereals: An Experimental Tight Oligopoly Case.   The FTC charged the major cereal producers—Kellogg, General Mills, General Foods, and Quaker Oats—in 1972 with a shared monopoly. There followed lengthy preparations before a hearing examiner, and the formal hearings began in 1976.[60] The

---

gain from delay. After adjusting for the tax factor (recall equation 7 in Chapter 3), the resources which IBM might rationally devote to delay are about double, or $2 million per day. This dwarfs the resources available to the public agencies and for objective outside study.

[58] Control Data also agreed to destroy in the presence of IBM lawyers a large computerized filing system for trial documents which it had been preparing for use by itself and the Antitrust Division. This destruction added at least a year's delay to the Division's case. Though cited as contempt of court, the action was evidently worth its cost to IBM.

[59] *Telex Corp.* v. *IBM Corp.,* U.S. District Court, N. Dist. of Oklahoma, IPF35-F55 and C10-C14, September 17, 1973. Telex had been nearly bankrupted by IBM's tactics in selling peripheral equipment. The Appeals Court's reversal is *Telex Corp.* v. *IBM,* 510 Fed. Reporter, 2d Series, 894 (1975).

[60] The case had grown large. Hundreds of witnesses were questioned, over 13 FTC lawyers were handling the matter (presumably the companies used scores), and their trial brief in 1976 comprised over 3,700 pages in 12 thick volumes. It alleges

case tries to break new doctrinal ground—citing Clayton Section 5: "unfair" practices—but it relies heavily on arguments that intensive advertising has artificially stifled competition. Even if it is shown that large and unfair advertising has blocked entry, the firms can point to much mutual competition via advertising and other tactics. The leaders have had very high profitability in cereals (around 15 to 20 percent). But the complexity of the issues and the lack of easy remedies suggest that the outcome will not give new precedent or major change. Note that cereals is a relatively low-priority and small candidate among tight oligopolies (recall Table 2–3). If the case were successful, it would open the way to treatment of a range of tight oligopolies.

Xerox. The FTC started action against Xerox in early 1973, alleging a market share of 95 percent in plain paper copiers and 86 percent in the whole office copier market (recall Chapter 2). A series of Xerox's pricing, leasing, and patent acts were said to exclude competition. Many of the conditions and charges closely paralleled *IBM* and *United Shoe Machinery.* Xerox had developed a thorough system of price discrimination, based on numbers of runs, numbers of copies per run, special large user discounts, and still other complicated conditions. By leasing rather than selling its machines, Xerox was able to apply the discrimination fully. Xerox's sales network was a major factor in its dominance. Xerox's nearly 2,000 patents also provided protection against new competition. These acts and conditions were not clearly inherent or necessary. They reflected careful choices and could be enjoined.

The FTC complaint did not ask for restructuring or other drastic changes. Instead, patent licensing, selling of machines, less price discrimination, and severing ties with Rank Xerox (the British affiliate) were sought. Xerox responded by negotiating for a quick settlement. One was reached in late 1974, but competitors pointed out that it accomplished little. A slightly stricter settlement was adopted in July 1975. Certain patents were opened up, and some discriminatory pricing was dropped (but soon replaced by even more complex pricing).[61] Xerox's position was scarcely affected. When new competition arose in 1977 from Savin and Canon (selling Japanese machines), it was not because of the FTC action.[62] The FTC settlement foreclosed a full

---

inter alia that advertising and brand proliferation have crowded out lesser firms' packages from grocers' shelf space and therefore raised entry barriers. Also, the firms allegedly took deliberate steps to avoid price competition and, under a gentlemen's agreement, stopped the use of package premiums for 10 years.

Despite its novelty, the case has a firm economic basis. The top firms may be able to crowd out new entrants by proliferating new brands and variants that fill grocery shelves. See F. M. Scherer, "The Welfare Economics of Product Variety: An Application to the Ready-to-Eat Cereals Industry," and Richard L. Schmalansee, "Entry Deterrence in the Ready-to-Eat Breakfast Cereal Industry," *Bell Journal of Economics* 9 (Autumn 1978), 305–27.

[61] Xerox agreed to license patents at no more than 1.5 percent of sales or rental income, and to supply its technical specifications and "know-how." The prohibition on its "fleet" pricing plan was quickly nullified by an even more complex pricing system, which, however, the FTC ignored. Xerox agreed to put sale prices on all machines; but these were set high enough to induce most users to continue leasing.

[62] In June 1977 a major suit against Xerox by SCM Corp. came to trial. It alleged the full array of Section 2 violations and sought large damages and divestiture. SCM's

airing of the issues and facts, and it estopped further public agency treatment for many years.

Oil Firms. As the "energy crisis" first broke in 1973, the FTC issued a complaint against eight major oil firms for squeezing out independent gasoline sellers. The case was paralleled by actions by many states; this was the first such grass-roots antitrust movement since the early Standard Oil suits in 1906–9. Though some divestiture is requested in the FTC case, the actions did not seriously threaten the basic position of these and other leading oil firms in refining. At best, damages would be levied but little change in market structure seemed likely to occur.[63]

The case was soon in a vast discovery process, and by 1978 the FTC staff were finally being forced to reduce the investigation to manageable size. The state-level cases had mostly run their course, with light penalties at most. The content and outcome of the FTC case were still unsure.

AT&T. After the 1913 agreement and the 1949–55 case, the issue of Western Electric was reopened in 1974 with a new suit by the Division. As a 50-man FCC task force report (of 1,500 pages) had recently recommended, the Division sought to separate Western Electric and possibly divide it into several competing firms within the whole market for telecommunications equipment.[64] The new suit also contemplated separating out the Long Lines Department, "some or all" of the Bell operating companies, and Bell Laboratories. True natural monopoly could remain intact, but the Bell System would be prevented from spreading its monopoly to other, naturally competitive markets. This challenge to the Bell System monopoly was fundamental and sophisticated, and it drew much favorable expert and business comment.[65] The Bell response was adamant, including an effort to get Congress to establish the Bell System monopoly by legislation. The case loomed as the biggest antitrust litigation ever. By 1977, the Supreme Court rejected Bell arguments that only the FCC had jurisdiction. Despite internal dissension in the Division over the content of the case, the laborious process of discovery was under way. Trial was not expected to begin before 1980, and it appeared likely to

---

litigation costs had run $7 million per year in 1976 and 1977. It won a partial victory in 1978, but the decision was appealed. Xerox has settled various lesser suits, for example in 1976 with payments of $8 million to Addressograph Multigraph Corp. and $2 million to Dennison Manufacturing Co.

[63] A staff report underlying the suit did recommend separating out the pipelines and a portion of refining capacity. Bank interlocks among the oil firms are also cited as anticompetitive. But the case was aimed mainly at retail squeezes.

The case for vertical divestiture by the oil firms is summarized in Walter Adams, "Vertical Divestiture of the Petroleum Majors: An Affirmative Case," *Vanderbilt Law Review* 30 (November 1977), 1115–47; see also John M. Blair, *The Control of Oil* (New York: Pantheon Books, 1976).

[64] By comparison, in Canada the parallel firm—Bell Canada—has divested 31 percent of its shares in Northern Electric Co. during 1973–76. Close relations do remain, but the move contrasts with the U.S. Bell System's absolute resistance.

[65] For a lucid statement of the content of the case, see Donald I. Baker, "Competition, Communications and Change," *Antitrust and Trade Regulation Reporter,* No. 698 (January 28, 1975), D1–D6.

dwarf even the current IBM case. The outcome would presumably turn on economies of vertical integration and scale—the bedrock question of where its "natural monopoly" lay. The Bell System's ability to take predatory actions unless its dominance were reduced is also likely to affect the trial and decision. Few observers expect a clear outcome or marked changes.

Parallel to these big cases are certain lesser actions and a flood of private suits. Cross-ownership of TV stations and newspapers has been important in scores of major cities, involving about 100 newspapers. The FCC challenged this in the 1970s, and by 1977 the Court affirmed its power to sever existing links as well as to prevent new ones. Two newspaper chains promptly traded stations in Washington, D.C., and Detroit, so as to avoid further action. Though the Antitrust Division had advocated the ending of cross-ownership, it had not directly brought it about. The whole issue is not expected to be settled before 1983, at the earliest.

Private suits have peppered a number of the larger dominant firms. IBM attracted over 19 during 1965–78, Xerox about 10, and AT&T over 25. Eastman Kodak has been sued in the 1970s by Bell and Howell, Berkey Photo, and GAF Corporation, seeking divestiture and advance notice about product changes. Under this pressure, Kodak agreed to modify its methods of introducing new products.[66] Then, in 1978, Berkey won its case, on the ground that Kodak had gained and held genuine monopoly power. (The trial was short, taking only six months.) Kodak's claims and evidence about its superior performance did not alter the jury's opinion that it had monopolized the market. Damages of at least $81 million were awarded, though they and the verdict were both appealed.

The H. J. Heinz Co. sued Campbell Soup in 1976 for such practices as selective price cutting. Campbell countersued, alleging abuses by Heinz in dominating the pickle market. In 1972 ITT persuaded a district judge in Hawaii to order GT&E to divest all of its operating and manufacturing firms acquired since 1950 (some $3.7 billion of GT&E's $9.0 billion in assets). Though reversed on appeal in 1975, ITT won a retrial in 1978 on the ground that GT&E's in-house purchasing policy for equipment had excluded competition.[67] Hundreds of lesser cases have gone through the mill, often yielding sizable damages to the plaintiff. Many are trivial, but most are a natural result of the existence of market dominance. The routine strategy of the defendant has been to file a countersuit on any possible basis (such

---

[66] Kodak's strategy had been to introduce new cameras, film, and processing chemicals simultaneously, so as to maximize the impact on its competitors. What was permissible, even healthy, among small competitors could be abusive when used with the advantages of a dominant position.

The Berkey-Kodak decision is outlined in *Trade Regulation Reports,* No. 339 (June 26, 1978); D.C. N.Y., ¶62,092.

[67] The appeals court ruled in 1975 that no private case could result in divestiture. The issue could become a critical one. Public cases seem to become comprehensive and get stalled. Perhaps incisive, limited private cases might be able to apply effective relief.

as the stealing of trade secrets or patent abuse) and then use this as a weapon to force a neutral settlement.[68]

Taken altogether, restructuring by public policy has come nearly to a standstill, despite the test-tube perfection of the *Grinnell* outcome and the actions begun since 1968. A Section 2 case may result in some sort of "therapy" which changes the company's practices and eventually, perhaps, the structure of the market. Certain shareholdings or other vertical ties may be cut, as in *du Pont-GM*. But unified, large dominant firms appear to be secure from a major horizontal restructuring. Good or bad, this seems to be a fact of life.

E. RETROSPECT ON THE THREE SERIES

In the larger picture, what have these evolving policies accomplished? The two first waves of cases touched fairly thoroughly on the near-monopolies then existing: in 1910 they were at the corporate pinnacle, in 1948 they were further down. But remedies were mild and cases grew longer. In both periods, tight oligopoly was scarcely touched. Only the meat-packers decree of 1920 and the 1946 tobacco case are exceptions to this, and their effects were slight. Tight oligopoly remained virgin territory. The recent series once again touches the leading cases but seems to lack the briskness of 1904–15.

Severity of Remedies. The severity of remedies was moderate even in the big 1911 cases; it abated sharply after 1911; and it has dwindled further since the 1920s. Relief in the 1911 cases merely undid earlier mergers. Since 1913 there has been little direct restructuring in industry, and the conduct remedies have been moderate. Some current weak-performing firms in basic industry were defendants which escaped treatment in the 1913–35 period: examples are steel, meat packing, and glass. Major wars have played a role in forestalling treatment. World Wars I and II and the Korean War all interrupted the thrust of enforcement waves and softened judicial attitudes toward major firms. In all, the end probability of achieving a full remedy under existing procedures has gone down, probably as far as .1 or .2 and even lower in the biggest cases.

The contrast between formal and actual policy is illustrated in Figure 5–1 (also recall Figure 3–2). For any given market share, a firm is much less likely to be investigated, sued, convicted, or changed than is indicated by formal policy. Even formal policy lets moderate market shares alone. The lines for actual policy have shifted to the right after the two waves of cases. (Locate the current position of the curves in Figure 5–1 according to *your* judgment; and then locate in Figure 5–1 the main dominant firms from Table 2–5. What are their chances for treatment?)

---

[68] Brock analyzes such tactics clearly (in *The U.S. Computer Industry*). The method worked in the Telex case, for example, by turning the tables and making the risk of appeal intolerable.

FIGURE 5–1

Formal and Actual Treatments of Established Monopoly: An Estimate

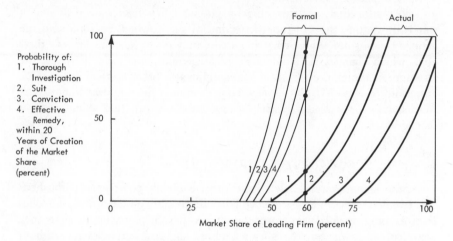

Market Share of Leading Firm (percent)

Despite the lack of formal action, the agencies exert a degree of regulatory constraint on many dominant firms, directly or by anticipation. Since profit rates can tip a Section 2 decision, the firms may moderate them by a variety of actions. Companies must expect their price structures and strategies to be sifted by agency staff and possibly in court. Product strategies also come under scrutiny. This informal regulation may yield benefits at very small costs. Yet it is incomplete and not done publicly. And it is often amateurish, because antitrust agencies lack resources and regulatory expertise.

Duration. The duration of actions—from initial study to remedy—has lengthened, from about six years to about 10 to 15 years. The average interval from the original monopolization to remedy, which was already over 20 years in 1911 (35 to 40 years for Standard Oil), has now grown even longer. In the two major 1911 cases, Standard Oil and American Tobacco, remedy was applied two or more decades after the monopoly was created, and only after the firm's market position was already weakening.

Indeed, restructuring has always lagged at least 20 years behind monopolizing, and the lag is rising. In no case has treatment been applied quickly enough to intercept a rising position of market power. The 1951 IBM case could have turned out to have that effect on the embryonic computer industry. The FTC action toward Xerox in 1973 also was early, by traditional standards. But both cases had little result.

Original Offenders. In no case has the action removed much or most of the capitalized monopoly gain from the original monopolizers. Rockefeller, du Pont, Duke, and other major family wealth was virtually untouched by the early antitrust actions. And the second set of actions was even more remote from the original gains. In effect, a full amnesty for monopolizers has applied. Only the later shareholders have been exposed to antitrust risk.

Conditions for Success. The two pre-conditions for bringing suit were *(a)* a high market share, and *(b)* a high degree of profitability. There were virtually no suits against oligopolists or against firms with average or depressed rates of return. The elements of a legal victory were, in the main: *(a)* A well-conceived and thorough economic case for action, based on extensive research on the critical points. *(b)* Grassroots support, both political and in the form of private and state suits against the target company. *(c)* Brilliant antitrust strategy, particularly to prevent delay. This was helped when *(d)* The private side was caught by surprise, complacent, or inept, and if it had displayed abusive actions and markedly excess profits. *(e)* A specific, feasible basis for remedy had to be available, lest its absence chill the case from the start.

An effective remedy might be ordered, *if: (a)* there were a technical basis for splitting, such as decentralization and an origin in recent mergers, *(b)* the product were relatively simple and standardized, so that innovation or national military involvement were not major questions, *(c)* a moderate weakening in the monopolists' total position were already in progress, so that potential competitors were active and expectations were not sharply reversed by divestiture (but not so severe a weakening as to make action superfluous), and *(d)* the stock were closely held, so that the expected or actual impact was not widespread.

Yields. The net yields of actions appear to have been high, especially for the earlier moves.[69] The results taper down in the more recent actions, mainly because major cases were dropped and relief was slow and slight. The best cases have *(a)* treated large near-monopolies, *(b)* moved quickly after the original monopolization, and *(c)* required major structural change.

F. CAN SECTION 2 BE EFFECTIVE?

F1. Perhaps Not

Traditional policies now seem unable to treat the important cases. Section 2 has been milled away and encrusted with provisos, while the agencies have been left without sufficient resources to prepare cases and to carry

---

[69] A recent estimate of the benefit-cost ratio for major cases gives a rough idea of the probable yields:

Standard Oil	67	Alcoa	19
American Tobacco	21	American Can	7
International Harvester	22	United Shoe Machinery	5
Corn Products	8		

For estimating procedures, see W. G. Shepherd, *The Treatment of Market Power* (New York: Columbia University Press, 1975), chap. 7 and appendix 3. In these and other cases, more thorough and timely treatments could have given larger yields. And the yields foregone from stopping treatment in other cases would presumably be comparable.

out remedies. The very power to damage the defendant—via treble damages which a conviction triggers—ensures total resistance and delay. The agencies lack resources to frame and carry out remedies. And other possible constraints, via other kinds of agencies, are lacking. The United States now has only one main shot in its locker—Section 2—and it does not seem to suit its task. For this reason, and perhaps also because of corporate power, it has come to be disused.

Actual restructuring has been slight; reversing mergers, selling war surplus plants (Alcoa), or detaching subsidiaries (Standard Oil). An aura of untouchability has arisen around more unified conditions, and some firms now centralize their operations in order to immunize against divestiture.

The biases are (a) the scientific basis for estimating costs and benefits has been diluted by the lack of information for research about structure and performance; (b) the agencies have mandates which exceed their resources and powers, either to study, to prosecute, or to carry out remedies; (c) the candidates control most of the germane information, including the costs of remedy; (d) the court process sets the burden of proof and of time against the agencies, rather than evenly; (e) a lack of deadlines further biases the time-structure of decisions against action rather than leaving them neutral; and (f) taxes add to the firms' incentives to resist. The dual-agency system—whatever its other merits may be—means that no one is responsible for a lack of effective restorative action.

The shortness of tenure of the agency heads accentuates the myopia. Section 2 cases are believed in the agencies to have no precedential value. Though this is probably not true, it still influences current policy choices. Meanwhile, candidate firms do routinely resist up to the margin at which the discounted gains equal the costs of resistance. And remedies have to be forced upon defendants: there are no tax or internal incentives for the owners or managers of the firms to comply either after conviction or in anticipation of suit.

Finally, the very infrequency of recent action has made it seem erratic. Defendants can plausibly assert that an action against them is (a) unfair, since like cases are escaping treatment, and (b) injurious to innocent third parties (for example, shareholders), since action is so unpredictable that it creates intolerable risk. These are often persuasive points in court. A thorough and systematic program of treatment would resolve them.

To sum up, large instances of market power remain, even though some instances have been abated, mostly in earlier decades. Apart from mergers by newcomers (see Chapter 6), new instances of monopoly—once established—are free of treatment for at least 15 years, if at all. This probably leads to large economic losses in a range of well-known markets.

F2. Perhaps Treatment Is Effective Enough

Possibly, instead, all dominant firms are fully justified by technical scale economies, and high market shares quickly decline. If so, then Section 2 efforts are superfluous and wasteful.[70] The pause since 1952 would be justified, and the recent cases would be costly mistakes.

In the less doctrinaire version of this view, some monopoly is excessive but the treatments for most monopolies will cost more than the benefits. Only a trickle of cases is needed, and they should pass stringent standards of proof before they are filed.

G. FOREIGN EXPERIMENTS

Other countries face a smaller problem and have been more inventive. Dominance is usually less extensive and durable abroad (recall Chapter 2). It tends to attract imports or new foreign subsidiaries, when profitability is high. American firms especially have added competitive elements in soaps, oil, automobiles, drugs, and tin cans, among many others, in western European countries.

Antitrust strategies are being tried in interesting ways.[71] The new Office of Fair Trading in Britain is surveying the range of dominant firms carefully, looking toward further Monopolies Commission actions in industry and finance. Earlier the Monopolies Commission had issued thorough studies on important dominant positions in industry.[72] Usually, proposed changes were mild and the Board of Trade would not apply them in full.[73] The Office of Fair Trading is expected to have greater power and expertise.

---

[70] For a statement of this view, see John McGee, *In Defense of Industrial Concentration* (New York: Praeger, 1971).

[71] Thus in 1966 the two main U.K. detergent makers, Procter & Gamble and Lever Bros., were required to introduce new brands free of advertising and priced 20 percent below the standard advertised brands. These brands—Tide and Surf—started with about 20 percent of the market, slipped to about 18, and then rose to a steady 23 to 25 percent. Profitability has been significantly reduced, along with consumer prices. The firms are on notice that slippage below 20 percent will land them again in Monopolies Commission action, presumably more drastic.

See various reports of the U.K. Monopolies Commission; and C. K. Rowley, *The British Monopolies Commission* (London: Allen & Unwin, 1966); and W. Pengilley, "Australian Experience of Antitrust Regulation," *Antitrust Bulletin* (Summer 1973), pp. 355–74. In 1973 long efforts to reduce drug prices in Britain finally resulted in a government order to Hoffman-LaRoche to cut prices on its Librium and Valium tranquilizers by half. Roche's British unit was paying its Swiss parent $925 a kilogram for Librium ingredients and $2,300 a kilogram for the Valium ones, when these materials could be bought from Italy at $23 and $50. Hoffman, concerned that other countries might follow suit, fought the action even to the House of Lords and threatened to move research activity out of Britain (*Wall Street Journal,* April 30, 1973, p. 34). Hoffman has sold over $2 billion of the drugs and its prices are actually lower in Britain than in some other countries. Still the profits from British sales were computed at 70 percent of capital, pre-tax.

[72] These included light bulbs (1951), wires and cables (1952), tires (1955), gases (1957), electrical machinery (1957), fertilizers (1958), cigarettes (1961), gasoline (1965), color film (1966), flat glass (1968), beer (1969), tin cans (1970), cereals (1973), and shoe machinery (1973), among others. It also screened mergers (see Chapter 6).

[73] Yet Kodak Ltd. was required to cut the price of color film by 25 percent, and Hoffman-LaRoche was made to reduce the price of Librium by 60 percent and Valium by 70 percent in 1974.

The British Prices and Income Board assessed profits and, on occasion, management performance, while reducing price increases and stopping restrictive practices during its brief 1966–71 life. Public holding companies own part or all of certain leading firms in Italy and several other European countries. Public ownership—partial or complete—gives a degree of public influence in many industries, including steel and coal in Britain and automobiles and aircraft in France (see Chapters 17 and 18).

Public buyers exert monopsony power against leading firms in some other industries, especially via public enterprises and national health programs. In Britain and other European countries, such major industries as electrical equipment, telephone apparatus, drugs, steel rails and rolling stock face such public monopsonies, some of which use their bargaining power actively.

The only important restructuring abroad occurred after World War II, when the victorious Allies sought permanent preventives against fascism in Germany and Japan.

Parallel programs were started in both Germany and Japan in 1945–46 to take apart the combines in heavy industry and finance. This restructuring contained mainly two elements.[74] The first was directed toward the industrial combines themselves. It sought to dissolve the central control of these systems, to create variety and independence out of what had been tightly knit systems. The second dealt with the links between banks and producing enterprises.

The programs were stopped in mid-course by political resistance from the United States, where industrial interests believed that these strict steps might eventually come to be tried also in the United States if they worked well abroad. As a result, both programs were truncated and partial. Within 10 years, in fact, both countries had seen massive waves of reforming most of the original industrial patterns. In Japan, perhaps, coordination within the combines has been looser than it was before 1945.

Two lessons may be drawn from this experience. First, drastic industrial changes are likely to come only in unusual conditions, during which the economic and political status of large industry and finance has been jolted. Second, private enterprise can display enormous resilience in adjusting to and eventually absorbing the effects of major structural changes.

H. ALTERNATIVE TREATMENTS

If Section 2 is in a cleft stick, what alternatives are there to supplement it or take its place? There are several conventional alternatives, which follow. Useful as they may be, they are specialized and have a narrower reach than is often thought. And they are difficult to apply.

---

[74] T. A. Bisson, *Zaibatsu Dissolution in Japan* (Berkeley: University of California Press, 1954). See also Eleanor T. Hadley, *Antitrust in Japan* (Princeton: Princeton University Press, 1971), for a masterly and favorable evaluation of the program, and for other references. Hadley was a leading participant in the restructuring program.

On part of the German program, see Joseph Borkin, *The Crime and Punishment of I. G. Farber* (Glencoe, Ill.: Free Press, 1978).

Reductions in Trade Barriers.   This has been a staple and attractive proposal since Adam Smith's time. Tariffs were integral with the trust issue between 1870 and 1900 in the United States. And in small, trade-oriented economies, these levers already are powerful in many industries.

For the United States there are two main limits. First, it seems impossible to get deliberate, specific cuts in trade barriers in order to apply new competitive forces. The resistance to cuts is focused and effective; either the protected firms are profitable and have a large stake, or they are stagnant and so imports will cause extensive structural changes. There is also a natural unwillingness of any nation to reduce its own trade barriers unilaterally. The political economy, therefore, makes the prospects for using this strategy remote, as is indicated by long experience in the United States and abroad.

Second, the possible scope of tariff cuts would be highly selective, covering a limited range of industries and missing many of the main problem cases.[75] In some instances, the leading U.S. firms are also leading actual or potential importers, and so the effects of tariff-cutting would be diluted. Among the prime examples of this are computers, film, oil, automobiles, copying equipment, soaps, drugs, and toiletries.

Import competition has been powerful in certain cases, particularly steel and automobiles. Yet others—such as computers, copying equipment, soaps, electrical equipment, glass, and telephone equipment—appear to be virtually immune. The causes of immunity vary, ranging from high transport costs for glass, soap, and many other products, over to specific conventions or rules against buying imports (as in most telephone equipment, aircraft, drugs, and electrical equipment). Among the main tight oligopolies, only automobiles, steel, aluminum, and copper appear sensitive to this treatment. And in steel, for one, the recent direction has been toward more protection, not less.[76]

Patents.   Patents have caused dominance and entry barriers in some industries. Shorter patent lives might reduce the monopoly effect while still encouraging technical progress (see Chapter 24). Yet a general shortening of patent lives, even down to five years, would not soon touch the existing problems in these industries. The structure has now hardened sufficiently that, as in many consent decrees which open up patents, little would happen from altering old patents.

---

[75] They include primarily flour, liquor, cigarettes, various chemicals, certain nonferrous metals products, electrical equipment, batteries, ships, films, and specialized instruments. On the measurement of trade barriers—a most difficult subject—see B. N. Vaccara, *Employment and Output in Protected Manufacturing Industries* (Washington, D.C.: Brookings Institution, 1960); and B. Balassa, "Tariff Protection in Industrial Countries: An Evaluation," *Journal of Political Economy,* 1965, pp. 573–94. See also Chapter 24.

[76] An informal international cartel arrangement to limit imports to the United States was created in 1968, with strong State Department efforts. These limits have not stopped import competition, but they have reduced it. In 1978 a set of "reference prices" to force imports to be priced up to near U.S. prices, was applied by the government.

Only in drugs and copying equipment are the gains from altering existing patents likely to be significant. Yet this effect could well take decades. This suggests that *(a)* patent changes can have only a slight effect on existing market power, and *(b)* it is especially important that the patent laws fit preventive goals; that is, they should not create lasting dominance.

Advertising may be an important barrier. Yet the problem is narrowly focused and difficult to treat. The issue is complex. It revolves around the ability of large advertisers to achieve increasing returns in nationwide selling activities. Moreover, advertising is often a weapon for entering a market or establishing a new brand; in short, for *increasing* competition. Therefore, only if *(a)* advertising scale economies were not as genuine as other input economies, and if *(b)* its anticompetitive effects outweigh its procompetitive role, would restrictions on it be efficient.

Even then, designing optimal restrictions would be difficult. A blanket limit on advertising—restricting it, say, to 2 percent of sales—would penalize the *lesser* firms, since the leading firm already has a lower percent because of the scale economies of saturation advertising. Also, many firms would easily adapt by shifting selling expenditures into other forms, such as sales networks and promotional discounts. The current FTC case against leading cereals companies is also facing this dilemma.

Only a handful of rather small industries are strongly influenced by advertising in any event. Even if antitrust doctrine and methods were favorable, abating advertising's effects would have only a limited effect.

Applying Monopsony Power. Public agencies and firms purchase from a wide range of industries. Where they have monopsony power, it could be exercised to constrain market power and to induce a more competitive structure. In the United States this tactic would affect certain problem industries, but only a minority. Abroad, the coverage is more complete.

One candidate is the drug industry, which sells in bulk to large groups (public agencies, nonprofit hospitals, and regulated buyers) at prices far below those to small customers.[77] Unified monopsony purchasing may be the only practical way to abate this market power. It works under some health programs in Western Europe. The present U.S. system of medical insurance—with passive regulated paying groups such as Blue Cross, fragmented among the states—operates almost as if it were designed to *minimize* the effectiveness of such monopsony behavior.

Other sectors are weapons supply and utility equipment. Past treatments have been erratic and often perverse. The tendencies toward passivity and mutual interests in these cases may be inherent in their structure, so that

---

[77] See Senate Committee on Small Business, *Hearings on Drug Industry Prices and Profits* (Washington, D.C.: U.S. Government Printing Office, 1968). In December 1973 it was announced that drugs covered by Medicare and Medicaid would be paid for only at the lowest price for which the drugs are generally available. The effectiveness of such efforts is not known.

other changes may be needed in order to improve performance. Similarly, stockpiling of materials as a constraint device has tended, instead, to be operated so as to minimize the impact on industry pricing.

In short, public monopsony is an unfulfilled possibility, which may need a different setting or incentive structure from what has yet been tried. And its potential reach in the United States is not broad.

Price Controls.   Direct controls on prices have been tried in both war and peace. In principle, this constraint could replace all the other policy tools, by enforcing competitive prices, profits and efficiency. But in fact controls have usually been crude and may have had costly side effects (see also Chapters 11 and 24).

A Reorganization Commission.   A more direct treatment may avoid the present traps for Section 2 action. A special commission, proposed by Senator Philip Hart in a bill in 1972, illustrates the strengths and weaknesses of such an approach. The bill is unlikely to pass, but there have been lengthy hearings and much public debate. It might eventually be enacted in a modified form.

The Industrial Reorganization Act would create a commission, with expert staffing and a large research capacity. Its powers parallel those of the Sherman Act: the commission would determine whether high market power exists, and then remedy it directly or by referral to other agencies. It would avoid judicial delay, and be able to carry out changes directly. The commission would look primarily at seven industries, including many of those in Table 2–8. Once it had treated them—within 10 or 15 years—it would be disbanded.

Even were the commission created, its effectiveness would probably be much less than its stated capacity. In action, the commission would be prone to long research and adversary proceedings. It would *not* be likely to dispatch the major cases directly. Instead, because they are so large and complex, such cases would be referred to Congress for special treatment, to cope with the broader political repercussions. Therefore the commission would probably not solve these problems, but only—at best—expedite some kind of treatment in other forums.

Still, the proposal has interesting possibilities. It might make more progress on the dominance problem than is presently occurring. And, at the least, it might help to bring out the facts on these individual cases.

I. SUMMARY

The treatment of established market power has come to be slow and possibly ineffective. There exists a core of large industries with dominant firms or tight oligopoly. Though markets are often difficult to define, the basic patterns are reasonably clear. Such cases often, but not always, are linked with abusive or systematic monopolizing behavior.

There have been two main series of Section 2 cases, in 1906–20 and 1938–

52. These cases are unwieldy, and they usually occur long after the original monopoly was formed.

Conviction now requires *(a)* a monopoly market share, plus *(b)* monopolizing acts of some kind, plus also *(c)* high profitability and *(d)* clear prospects for relief that will not imperil innovativeness or harm shareholders. The burdens of proof and time are both set against Section 2 treatment, and court processes can be used to get long delays. The agencies must, in practice, establish that a change will be enough superior to the existing structure to justify conviction and the costs of transition.

Despite a wealth of experimentation abroad, there seem to be few chances for revision of U.S. treatments. Freer trade and patenting, abating of advertising, the use of public monopsonies, even a reorganization commission, seem to offer only narrow gains. Therefore, dominant firms are largely immune from treatment for the time being. They can continue to do what lesser firms cannot cooperate to do: to control pricing and behavior over a large share of their markets. This central riddle of antitrust is unsolved.

QUESTIONS FOR REVIEW

1. "Each Section 2 case turns only on abusive behavior 'plus' superior skill, foresight, and industry." True?
2. "Cross-elasticities of demand, if available, would define most markets." True?
3. "The courts have steadily gotten stricter in their judgments about market definitions." True?
4. "A market share of 50 percent will ordinarily trigger a Section 2 case." True?
5. "Entry barriers are not usually a formal criterion in Section 2 cases, but they often enter informally into the outcomes." True?
6. "The first wave of Section 2 actions stopped monopolies less than 15 years after they were formed." True?
7. "Where monopoly exists, antitrust action will remove it even if scale economies justify it." True?
8. "A high market share is necessary but not sufficient for conviction under Section 2." True?
9. "The Alcoa precedent would require a dominant firm to go out of its way to stop new entry, in order to escape conviction." True?
10. "The United Shoe Machinery precedent suggests that enterprising firms can keep their monopolies." True?
11. "Private suits have occasionally stirred the public agencies to file their suits too." True?
12. "Private suits have become an important method for getting divestiture." True?
13. "Western Electric offers great economies of vertical integration, according to Bell System arguments." True?

14. "Section 2 convictions trigger private damage cases, and this ensures cooperation by the dominant firm." True?
15. Was U.S. Steel really a "good" trust?
16. What really causes some Section 2 cases to take so long?
17. Do policies act more slowly than market shares decline?
18. If treble damages were not allowed, might Section 2 work better?

chapter 6

Mergers

Mergers are distinct events, visible and often dramatic. The merger boom of the 1960s has subsided, but there are still over two thousand mergers each year and another wave may begin at any time. Most of these mergers are small and prosaic, and even many large mergers are neutral to competition or have high social value. But others reduce competition without providing economies.

Merger policy is simple in some directions, complex in others. Merger policy also illustrates how the law can grow, with a series of landmark cases marking out new areas. And merger policy tests one's ability to reach good appraisals in the midst of self-serving claims.

U.S. policies now stop nearly all significant horizontal mergers and many vertical mergers. Conglomerate mergers are usually prevented if they involve potential competitors or dominant firms, though the policy lines toward them are still evolving.

This chapter analyses these treatments and their economic sense. First, we consider the reasons why mergers occur and the effects they have. Then we look at the benefit-cost conditions they involve, and at the rhythm of actual merger activity in the past. Then U.S. policies toward horizontal, vertical, and conglomerate mergers are reviewed. Policies abroad are also compared.

A. REASONS FOR MERGERS

A *horizontal* merger unites side-by-side competitors: see Figure 6–1. A *vertical* merger links suppliers and users in the chain of production. A *conglomerate* merger is—in the pure case—anything with no horizontal or vertical element. Conglomerate mergers may link geographic areas (for example, bakeries in two distant towns); these are called market-extension mergers. Or they may add to a product line; these are called product-extension mergers. Most mergers of any significance mix the three elements—horizontal, vertical, and/or conglomerate—but one element is often prominent.

Mergers are only the visible fruit of the endless process of bargaining

FIGURE 6–1
Types of Mergers

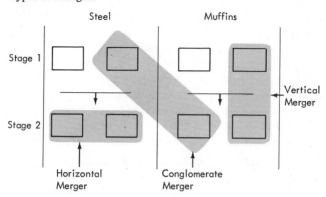

which goes on under the surface in the market for corporate assets. Far more combinations are proposed and negotiated than ever see the light of day. There is a small army of merger promoters at work in investment banking firms in New York and elsewhere. They profile candidates, seek partners, and work out the terms of possible mergers. This functioning of the market for corporate control helps to enforce good performance and accomplish needed change. But the cadre of specialized promoters also helps to raise the volume of merger activity.

Among all possible mergers and quasi-mergers, why do those that occur actually occur? There are three main categories of gains to the firm:

1. Straight Market Power. This in turn provides higher profitability, the basic goal of the firm. The rise in market power can come from a higher market share or higher entry barriers.

2. Technical Economies. A merger may achieve *economies of scale,* as the firm moves down a down-sloping average-cost curve (recall Chapter 2). Or the firm may be able to lower the average-cost curve itself. Vertical mergers may gain *vertical economies* (for example, from avoiding extra handling, uncertainty, re-processing, and so on). More general economies may arise from reducing risks by pooling diverse operations.

3. Pecuniary Economies. All three kinds of mergers may make it possible for the firm to buy its inputs more cheaply. These pecuniary gains (as was noted in Chapters 1 and 2) may affect any input used by the firm. Raw materials, advertising space, managerial talent, capital, and others may be bought more cheaply by the merged firms. Also, mergers often achieve tax benefits, in the pooling of loss-making and profit-making units. These gains are only pecuniary, but they may be powerful.

These more tactical reasons for mergers are also important:

1. Entry to a New Market. Entry is usually easier by merger than by starting afresh. Conglomerate mergers always involve entry of a new outside firm into the market. Such entry does not add new capacity, and so its net competitive benefits are always less than entry by internal growth. Moreover, the new entrant often had already influenced the market as a potential entrant, before the merger.

2. Exit: The "Failing Firm" Case. Many mergers involve the absorption of a firm which is in straits or even, in the extreme, failing. Failure, of course, simply means bankruptcy, which need not cause actual closure and dissipation of the company's activities. Often, indeed, bankruptcy simply leads to a merger. In any case, mergers can salvage failing companies. The difficult policy question often is: how much failure is required for *failure?* Is it a down-turn in sales, the beginning of financial losses, several months or a year or two of red ink, or actual imminence of bankruptcy? Often companies wanting a merger will don sackcloth and ashes, claiming that failure is imminent even though the firm is still strong.

3. Take-Over. Among the many merger types, take-over is the most colorful and, perhaps, socially important. It involves a move by one firm to take over, or seize, another firm against its management's will. In the byzantine world of business, one often has difficulty telling who is taking over whom; whether the take-over is amicable, hostile, or a mixture of the two (perhaps with some board members favoring take-over, and others against). The key element is that management in the target firm comes immediately under different control. The would-be new owners typically make a tender offer to buy a controlling amount of the stock at a price above the current market price (usually 20–40 percent higher). This premium reflects their belief that they can manage the company so much better that profits will rise sharply and the stock price will rise even beyond the take-over price.

A take-over often requires close financial support for the taker, and the resisting management usually appeals for backing from *its* financial allies. So in fact, a genuine take-over is often a struggle among members of the financial sector.[1] Take-overs are often done by corporate outsiders, aiming primarily at sluggish firms with substantial market positions, which have been sitting on unexploited resources and opportunities. In any event, take-overs often differ from the other kinds of routine market mergers.

Mergers often involve selling off parts of a firm to new owners, and so the reasons for disposing of assets also matter. Many firms carry marginal or even heavily-losing branches for decades, either from inertia or as part of larger strategies (for example, to offer a full line of products). Disposal of them may reflect new financial stress or a change in managerial strategy.

In any event, mergers are often difficult to classify and fathom, for they

---

[1] An embattled management often ginns up a friendly alternative merger partner, to forestall the real threat. This complicates the bidding terms and legal footing, so that either time is gained to fight the take-over, or a preferred merger occurs, or the eventual take-over price for shares is enhanced. But few such defensive merger projects actually occur.

can be complex and they often touch raw nerves of corporate and financial power. The stakes are high, and action is swift, and the policy choices are often put under great stress.

B. EFFECTS OF MERGERS

The direct effects of mergers fit in three main categories: *(a)* they may affect competition, *(b)* they may affect performance, and *(c)* they increase global aggregate concentration.

B1. Competition

Horizontal mergers obviously reduce competition. Part of the market process is enclosed under direct internal control. The power to raise price is increased. The larger the increase in combined share, the bigger will be the loss of competition. Though small firms often claim that by merging they can compete better against dominant firms, this point has little merit unless scale economies are present. If *that* is true, then the firm should be able to grow internally, rather than by merger.

Vertical mergers need not alter competition at either level if market conditions are perfect (recall Chapter 5).[2] Yet they will reduce competition if *(a)* the merger raises entry barriers (by making new entrants join both levels at once, thereby raising the level of capital that must be raised on imperfect capital markets), and *(b)* the merger triggers a wave of parallel mergers, which sharply reduce the scope of open-market sales. And if the possibility of price squeezes is increased, the mere threat of this may induce independent firms to behave more passively. *How much* competition is reduced depends on these conditions.

Conglomerate mergers are often—perhaps usually—neutral to competition. But in certain conditions they can reduce or increase it.[3] The new parent company may have better access to capital, advertising, or other resources for competitive strategies. If these are made available to a dominant firm, the effect will usually be to entrench it further. Such an increase in dominance may occur automatically, as lesser competitors acquiesce in their reduced possibilities. Or it may arise from direct tactics by the dominant firm, using its new resources forcefully.[4] In the extreme, a web of conglomerate ties

---

[2] Robert H. Bork, "Vertical Integration and the Sherman Act: The Legal History of an Economic Misconception," *University of Chicago Law Review,* 1954, pp. 157–201. For a counterview, see W. Adams and J. B. Dirlam, "Steel Imports and Vertical Oligopoly Power," *American Economic Review,* 1964, pp. 626–55. See also John S. McGee and Lowell R. Bassett, "Vertical Integration Revisited," *Journal of Law and Economics* 19 (April 1976), 17–38, and the sources cited there.

[3] A full recent discussion is given by Peter O. Steiner, *Mergers: Motives, Effects, and Policies* (Ann Arbor: University of Michigan Press, 1975).

[4] See Harlan M. Blake, "Conglomerate Mergers and the Antitrust Laws," *Columbia Law Review,* March 1973, pp. 555–92, for a thorough review of these factors.

may induce behavior among conglomerates to become diplomatic. Each can retaliate elsewhere against moves in any one market. So competition in the whole range of markets may subside.

Yet competition will probably be increased if the merger takes in a firm with a small share of its market. The new advantages will enlarge its opportunities to take market share away from the leading firms.

One further angle: if the acquirer had been a known, important potential entrant, then the merger may reduce competition by subtracting one firm from the total of all actual plus potential competitors. The net effect on competition will often be slight and obscure, but still real.

B2. Performance

The level of performance may, on balance, rise.[5] *(a)* Economies of scale may be realized by horizontal mergers. *(b)* Economies of integration may arise from vertical mergers. *(c)* A failing firm may be restored. If these gains could be gotten equally well by alternative ways (internal growth, long-term contracts), then the merger yields no net social benefit.

Different from this is *(d)* Greater X-efficiency may be induced by the threat of take-over. This gain can be large, both from the general threat and from specific take-over attempts. To keep the threat credible, take-overs must actually be permitted. They harness private self-interest and skill to the task of discovering inefficiency and correcting it. X-inefficiency in a firm is often tolerated by a passive board of directors. The rules, customs, and power relations in large corporations often make it difficult to apply external pressure on lagging managers and directors. Take-over is an important device for applying such constraints, by threat or deed, from the outside.

Other claimed economies of conglomerate mergers are dubious. "Synergism"—a "dynamic" process in which disparate managerial resources created new learning and skills: "2 plus 2 equals 5"—is mainly a 1960s catchword, with little scientific basis. Capital may be deployed efficiently, even creatively, within a diversified firm.[6] But the net benefit compared to allocation by the capital market may be small or zero.

B3. Global Concentration

A series of large-firm mergers can increase the aggregate concentration of the economy. This can injure local community interests, as absentee man-

---

[5] For one concise analysis of merger effects, see Oliver E. Williamson, "Economies as an Antitrust Defense," *American Economic Review* 58 (March 1968), 18–36, and "Correction and Reply," (December 1968), pp. 1372–76.

[6] For an abstract case that diversified firms are a distinct management form with special efficiency, see O. E. Williamson, *Corporate Organization and the Theory of the Firm* (Englewood Cliffs, N.J.: Prentice-Hall, 1972). See also Steiner, *Mergers,* chaps. 3–5.

agements ignore local conditions and use their power to extract advantages. It can also weaken the political and social fabric, at the expense of individual freedoms and self-determination. Marked rises in global concentration have occurred in the United States and abroad, with a range of negative refects. Even national sovereignty can be reduced by large international mergers; this may on balance cause social loss. These global effects are often diffuse and hard to assess, but in the end they may easily outweigh the specific economic ones.

C. SPECIAL COST-BENEFIT ISSUES FOR POLICY CHOICES

Methods.   To evaluate a merger, one first defines the market (recall Chapter 5) and then measures the increase in market share from the merger. For a conglomerate merger, one appraises the two firms' positions in their markets and any special advantages which they may pool.[7] From these structural facts, one can then roughly estimate the net social benefits and costs of the merger, adjusting the figures for time, probability, and precedent (recall Chapter 3). This is the heart of sound evaluation: simple in concept, possible to do only roughly in practice. Something like it is done in the antitrust agencies, in deciding whether to oppose individual mergers.

Net Gains.   The crucial comparison is between (1) the gains from the merger and (2) those that can be obtained by internal growth or by long-term contracts. *Only the net gains of mergers over the alternatives matter for policy.* Accordingly, the direct social benefits from all three kinds of mergers will usually be quite small and of low probability. Vertical economies from merger will often be larger and more definite than those from horizontal mergers. Yet these too can usually be gotten by building new plants or making long-term contracts for supplies.

Social costs from the loss of competition will usually be relatively large for horizontal mergers and some vertical ones. By comparison, the costs of stopping the merger are relatively small, and any private losses suffered by blocking the merger will be focused on deserving parties (not, as in some Section 2 cases, on third parties who can claim to be innocent). In practice, too, the burden of proof is generally against the merging firms. Time can also be on the agencies' side, because the merger needs to go through on the agreed terms, before conditions change. By contrast to existing structure (recall Chapter 7), merger policy can operate quickly and strictly.

Lessons.   In short, cost-benefit analysis usually favors stopping a wide range of horizontal and vertical mergers. Current antitrust arrangements make that relatively easy and cheap to do. But they also make it easy to stop conglomerate mergers, some of which offer net social benefits. Therefore the optimum social treatment of mergers involves a relatively strict line on

---

[7] The effect on potential competition may also be appraised, but this is usually complex, difficult, and marginal (see Section H).

horizontal and vertical mergers, *and* a relatively open policy on conglomerates.

There is also an additional dimension to the problem in those many markets which have dominant firms. In those markets, a strict line against horizontal mergers, even by small firms, does tend indirectly to defend the dominant firms, by keeping their competitors smaller and more passive (recall Chapter 5). To ban mergers above 10 percent but let 60+ percent firms stand seems patently unfair. It may mean that a strict merger policy is, on balance, insulating the market power of dominant firms.

D. PAST MERGER PATTERNS

There have been three major waves of mergers in the United States. **The first great wave** was in 1897–1904, a period of dramatic industrial turbulence and change.[8] The mergers primarily were horizontal, forming firms with 60 to 90 percent in scores of large and small industries. Much of the activity was strictly promotional, by Morgan, Rockefellers, and other financiers. It was widely believed that these groups would combine their interests on a new plane of financial superpower.[9] This merger wave climaxed in 1901 with the blockbuster U.S. Steel merger. The wave was stopped primarily by changing stock market and economic conditions, plus some effect of Theodore Roosevelt's new use of antitrust in 1902.[10] Many of these mergers were overblown and ill-fated, declining almost as soon as they were formed. But others created dominant firms which remain to this day.

The second merger wave, in the 1920s, swarmed over both industrial firms and utilities. Mainly, they formed oligopolies rather than dominant firms. The industrial mergers tended to form second and third-ranking firms, nearly as large as the existing dominant firms (examples: steel, tin cans, automobiles). This occurred partly because many dominant firms had been put on notice not to make further mergers (recall Chapter 5). In any case, by 1929 the main outlines of industry as we know it were firmly set.

The third merger wave in the 1960s—the great "go-go years"—mainly involved conglomerate mergers (see Figure 6–2). Yet there were also many horizontal and vertical mergers, and many conglomerate mergers had strong horizontal or vertical features. New conglomerates made a series of highly publicized mergers, some of them take-overs. But a wide range of older firms— both unified and diversified—made conglomerate mergers too. Appendix Table 6A–1 gives a selection from this wave.

---

[8] See Ralph L. Nelson, *Merger Movements in American Industry, 1890–1956* (Princeton: Princeton University Press, 1962); and John Moody, *The Truth about the Trusts* (New York: John Moody, 1904).

[9] See Moody, *The Truth about the Trusts;* F. L. Allen, *The Lords of Creation* (New York: Harper Brothers, 1935); and F. L. Allen, *The Great Pierpont Morgan* (New York: Harper and Row, 1949).

[10] For a detailed narrative and analysis, see William Letwin, *Law and Economic Policy in America* (New York: Random House, 1965).

FIGURE 6–2
Trends in U.S. Mergers, by Type

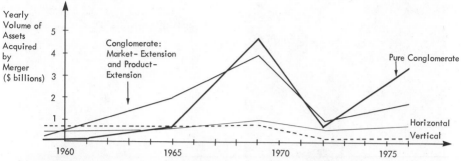

Source: Federal Trade Commission, *Statistical Report on Mergers and Acquisitions* (Washington, D.C.: U.S. Government Printing Office, annual).

Despite some fears that the whole of industry was being transformed, actually structure and global concentration were only slightly altered. The merger boom was punctured by the 1969–70 bear market drop of 40 percent in stock prices, by the antitrust attack on conglomerate mergers during 1969–71 (see below), and by growing disenchantment with the wilder 1960s claims for merger magic. During 1972–77, indeed, many hundreds of the 1960s mergers were being unravelled. Voluntary divestitures became as numerous as new mergers, as firms sifted out their losing operations. In 1975–78, takeovers revived, focused mainly on leading firms in a number of industries. The acquirers now were established firms with large cash reserves, rather than new outsiders with shaky financial backing. A few sectors had many mergers—beer firms, agricultural cooperatives, and, after May 1975, stock brokerage firms—but the lagging stock market and the antitrust limits kept merger activity down during the 1970s.

In other countries mergers continued more strongly during the 1960s and 1970s. Horizontal mergers were important, often giving high market shares. In Western Europe and Japan scores of new dominant firms were formed in the automobile, electrical equipment, steel, computer, aircraft, and other industries.

E. GENERAL FEATURES OF U.S. MERGER POLICIES

Present policies were formed during 1958–66, in a series of landmark decisions. As the law "grew," objective research and new concepts filtered into judicial thinking and took effect.

The Laws.   Section 7 of the Clayton Act is the main merger law. Sherman Section 2's "monopolizing" prohibition was used in early cases to stop railroad mergers but the original Clayton Section 7 of 1914 was soon nullified (recall

Leading Merger Promoters of Two Eras

Culver Pictures

Richard Knapp, *Business Week*

J. Pierpont Morgan (1837–1913) was the leading financier and merger promoter of his time. He was instrumental in forming the U.S. Steel Corporation in 1901, in reshaping the railroad sector, and in a variety of other trust formations. (Shown here about 1900.)

Felix Rohatyn (of the New York investment banking firm, Lazard Freres & Co.), a prolific merger arranger. Born 1929. Involved with at least 43 significant mergers during 1964–77, including such ITT mergers as Airport Parking, Levitt & Sons, Rayonier, Continental Baking, Canteen Corp., Grinnell, Hartford Fire and Casualty Co., and Eurofind. Also RCA's acquisitions of Random House, Hertz, Stamper Foods and Coronet Industries; and McDonnell-Douglas, Owens-Illinois—Lily Tulip, Loew's-Lorillard, Atlantic Richfield-Sinclair Oil, Kinney-Warner Brothers and AMP-Head Ski.

Chapters 4 and 5). The Celler-Kefauver Act amended it in 1950 to preclude mergers which would "substantially . . . lessen competition or . . . tend to create a monopoly in any line of commerce in any section of the country." In 1976 a further amendment required firms to give the agencies advance notice of mergers, so that any policy action could be prepared in time.

Development of Policies. Even well before 1950, some mergers were constrained by antitrust agencies, on an informal basis.[11] Although events aborted the first series of Section 2 actions after 1916, an implicit limit on some mergers remained. Dominant firms in major markets were aware that substantial merger activity on their part would trigger an agency attack. Well before 1950, dominant firms were established in many industries, and many of these firms were also conglomerates (such as General Electric, Westinghouse, chemicals firms, RCA). In the financial sector the two Banking Acts of 1933 and 1935 had neatly fenced off banking from other economic sectors. Accordingly, banks were free from take-over by firms outside their own sector, as also were utilities.

The strict merger treatments since 1950 came upon a scene containing well-established industrial and financial positions of market power. Rather than prevent the growth of incipient monopoly in industry or finance, merger policies could only aspire to avert further rises in market power.

The 1950 amendment to Clayton Act Section 7 made possible, for the first time, a meaningful treatment of mergers. After a pause, the 1950 Act was tested by the *Bethlehem-Youngstown* merger and, in 1958, applied strictly. Successive cases then quickly tightened the law by 1966 to its present limits on horizontal and vertical mergers. Treatment of conglomerate mergers evolved after 1966 as the merger wave peaked and then continued in the 1970s. Even after some wavering by the Supreme Court in the 1970s, the agencies have won nearly every significant case they brought and established a pretty strict set of limits.

Coverage. Virtually all sectors are covered, even the main mass of "regulated" utilities. Often the antitrust agencies have to assert their role vigorously against the regulated firms and even, on occasion, the regulators themselves.[12] A few anticompetitive mergers are still forced through as exceptions. Yet the loopholes are few and the coverage is remarkably broad.

Procedure. Much policy is applied under the surface. Firms often come in ahead of time to urge officials not to oppose a planned merger. Negotiations may grow quite complex, and many times the Division's threat or decision to sue will cause a proposed merger to fold. Mergers are often modified to fit antitrust criteria. Take-over targets often rush in to demand that the agencies stop the merger, "to protect competition" (as well as their own skins). Actual court cases often merely signal that informal bargaining has broken down, or that a new policy line is being set.

The normal regimen is as follows:

1. Firms planning to merge may quietly sound out an agency beforehand, finding out what modifications might be necessary to make it acceptable.

---

[11] See S. N. Whitney, *Antitrust Policies,* 2 vols. (New York: Twentieth Century Fund, 1958), and recall Chapter 5 above.

[12] This has been especially true in banking, insurance, shipping, airlines, railroads, broadcasting, electricity, gas, and telephones.

2. A merger plan is announced by one or both firms, with shareholders to approve in a month or two and the merger to follow shortly after.
3. If the agency suspects or knows that the merger will reduce competition, it asks for delay—usually one to three months—while it studies and decides. During that time, negotiations and advance notice may occur. The agency's decision usually fits within the guidelines given below.
4. If the agency opposes, it files suit and asks the judge for a temporary injunction against the merger until the issues have been aired in trial.
5. At trial, the agency need only show that competition is likely to be reduced. The firm must show the merger to be innocent. If the merger is held to violate Clayton 7, it is permanently enjoined.
6. At any time a consent decree may be reached, whose provisions can reach beyond this merger into other actions by the firms (for example, prohibiting certain other mergers by the firms for a period of years). Or either side may withdraw.

Time and the burden of proof sometimes favor the agencies. Mergers can often be delayed or stopped with minimal effort. Yet judges often deny injunctions and let the mergers occur, instructing the firm to keep the merged parts separate.

Criteria. The lines of policy are set by the Supreme Court, by precedents from their decisions. Table 6–1 codifies these precedents, showing the criteria which the Antitrust Division uses in deciding whether to challenge mergers. The agencies are likely to challenge any significant horizontal merger, especially if the market's concentration is high or rising. Vertical mergers are not quite as strictly limited. Conglomerate mergers must not reduce potential competition or breed reciprocity; and they may give toeholds but not dominant positions. FTC rules are similar but slightly stricter on conglomerates. The agencies will usually not be deterred by claims that the mergers will achieve economies. Rather, they require hard evidence, which would stand up in court, that there are net economies which can only be achieved by a merger.

Beneath these steady policy lines lie a shift in approach by the Supreme Court between the "Warren" Court (1954–68) and the "Burger" Court (since 1969). The "Warren" Court looked ahead at trends and possible competitive harm, and leaned toward protecting competition. Also, it had the task of establishing the first real merger policy. Accordingly, the agencies won all 12 merger decisions during 1958–69. The "Burger" Court has shifted the practical criteria of proof, requiring more evidence of actual anticompetitive effects in the past. This "show me" attitude tends to look backward, and it reverses the presumption of legality. (It can be seen most clearly in the Court's opinions in the *General Dynamics, Fortner* and *GT&E* cases, discussed in Chapters 6–8.) The "Burger" Court has also been more willing to accept the district judges' findings of facts.

F. HORIZONTAL MERGERS

Though mergers often mix horizontal and other elements, the policy lines have developed separately. Treatment of horizontal mergers began with the

TABLE 6–1
Merger Guidelines: Mergers Which Will Probably Be Challenged

Market Definition. There may be several appropriate "markets" in which to test the competitive effects of a merger. Both "product" and "geographic" dimensions are relevant.

Economies will not usually serve to prevent a challenge by the Division, because they are hard to evaluate and are often available by other routes.

---

1. **Horizontal Mergers.** Criteria are mainly market structure.
   a. In highly concentrated markets (over 75% in the four largest firms), these shares will normally not be challenged:

Acquiring firm	Acquired firm
4%	4%
10%	2%
15%	1%

   b. In medium concentrated markets, the limits are looser:

Acquiring firm	Acquired firm
5%	5%
10%	4%
15%	3%
20%	2%

   c. If market concentration has been increasing, all mergers involving over 2% will be challenged.
   d. Also, *any* acquisition of a competitor which is unusually competitive or has unusual competitive advantages.
   e. Failing firms are exempt if they would clearly fail and have tried to make other mergers which fit the guidelines.
2. **Vertical Mergers.** Mergers which foreclose competition and raise entry barriers are to be challenged. Normally,
   a. If a firm that is a customer for a product makes 6% of the purchases and a firm supplying the product makes 10% of the sales, unless their merger raises no significant barrier to entry, or
   b. If a firm that is a customer for a product has 10% of its own market, if the product is essential to its business, and if a firm supplying the product makes 20% of the sales, or
   c. If a customer or a supplier is acquired by a major firm in an industry with a significant trend toward vertical integration, if such a combination would raise barriers to entry, and if it does not promise to cut the costs of production, or
   d. If a customer or a supplier is acquired for the purpose of barring competitors from the market or otherwise putting them at a disadvantage, or
   e. If the acquired firm is not genuinely failing (see above),
   then the merger will be challenged.
3. **Conglomerate Mergers.** Since policy is still formative, at least these categories of merger will normally be challenged:
   a. If a firm that has a large share of a market seeks to acquire a firm that is one of the main potential entrants to the market.
   b. If a merger creates the danger of substantial reciprocal buying.
   c. If the merger creates severe disparity in size between the acquired firm and its competitors, or gives advertising advantages, or otherwise gives leverage to the acquired firm.
   d. (Since 1969.) If any of the largest 200 industrial firms seeks to acquire any significant other firm (roughly, above $100 million in assets).
   e. (Since 1970.) If the acquired firm is much above a 10-percent share of its market.

Source: Based mainly on the Antitrust Division's "Merger Guidelines," issued in 1968.

Bethlehem-Youngstown case of 1958, tightened with *Brown Shoe* in 1962, and *Rome Cable* and *El Paso Natural Gas* in 1964, and reached its present lines with *Von's Grocery* in 1966.[13]

Bethlehem-Youngstown. The first case to be brought before the courts by the government under the new law involved a proposed merger between Bethlehem Steel and Youngstown Sheet & Tube. Bethlehem, the nation's second largest steel producer, had notified the Department of Justice in 1956 that it planned to acquire Youngstown, the sixth largest, thus raising its own share of the nation's output from 15 percent to 20 percent, and the share of U.S. Steel and Bethlehem together from 45 percent to 50 percent. The Department sued to enjoin the merger, and the case went to trial in 1958 under Judge Edward Weinfeld in a federal district court.[14]

The defense argued that the merger would make the industry more competitive, since it would enable Bethlehem to compete more effectively with U.S. Steel. It cited, in particular, the market near Chicago. Here, Bethlehem had no plant and shipped in less than 1 percent of its output. By acquiring and expanding Youngstown's Chicago facilities, it would provide more vigorous competition for U.S. Steel in this area. It declared that it would not otherwise enter the market.

These points were rejected by Judge Weinfeld, who was not persuaded that the merger afforded the only means by which the supply of steel in the Chicago area could be increased. In any case, he said, the argument was irrelevant, since Congress "made no distinction between good mergers and bad mergers. It condemned all which came within the reach of the prohibition of Section 7." The merger was enjoined.[15] Bethlehem did not appeal. In three years it *did* indeed enter the Chicago market by building a large plant at Burns Ditch.

Brown Shoe. The Supreme Court's first decision under the Celler-Kefauver Act was handed down by a unanimous court in the Brown Shoe case in 1962.[16] The Brown Shoe Company, which manufactured 4.0 percent of the nation's output of shoes, had acquired the Kinney Company, which manufactured 0.5 percent. Brown was the third largest distributor of shoes with 1,230 retail stores; Kinney was eighth with 350 stores. In certain local markets for particular types of shoes, the combined share of the two concerns amounted to 20 percent or more (the shares ranged from 5.0 to 57.7 percent).

The Court put less emphasis on the existing structure of the market than on the historical trend toward increasing concentration in the shoe industry.

---

[13] During 1955–56, four merger cases were filed and then negotiated under the new law, without reaching trial. See Theodore P. Kovaleff, "The Antitrust Record of the Eisenhower Administration," *Antitrust Bulletin* 21 (Winter 1976), 603–6.

[14] At first Division officials regarded the merger as immune from suit. But one staff economist, Harrison F. Houghton, persisted in doing a massive study of the industry and these firms. He discovered enough overlaps in submarkets to justify a try in court, which resulted in the conviction after all.

[15] *U.S.* v. *Bethlehem Steel Corp.*, 168 F. Supp. 756.

[16] *Brown Shoe Co.* v. *U.S.*, 370 U.S. 294.

"We cannot avoid the mandate of Congress," it said, "that tendencies toward concentration in industry are to be curbed in their incipiency, particularly when these tendencies are being accelerated through giant steps striding across a hundred cities at a time. In the light of the trends in this industry, we agree . . . that this is an appropriate place at which to call a halt."[17]

The Court observed that Congress did not intend to prevent a merger between two small companies that would enable them to compete better with larger ones or a merger between a corporation which is financially healthy and one that is failing and is thus unable effectively to compete. But it stressed *incipiency* as a criterion, where an important market is rising in concentration.

Philadelphia National Bank.[18] In this important case the Court set two precedents. First, it used a simple clear rule—the market share of the merged firms—as the decision criterion. The earlier decisions had, by contrast, cited many features of the market (for example, number of firms, concentration, growth rates, and so forth) in assessing the effect on competition. Second, this decision extended merger policy to the banking industry.

Alcoa-Rome. The Court went on in 1964 to uphold the application of the law in cases where an acquired firm produced a tiny portion of total output and where the competition of such a firm was only potential. The Aluminum Company of America, producing 27.8 percent of aluminum conductor output, had purchased the Rome Cable Corporation, producing only 1.3 percent. But the Court found that Rome was "an aggressive competitor . . . a pioneer" with "special aptitude and skill . . . and an effective research and sales organization." It was "the prototype of the small independent that Congress aimed to preserve by Section 7."[19]

El Paso. The El Paso Natural Gas Company, the only firm bringing gas into California, had acquired the Pacific Coast Pipeline Company, which operated outside the state. Pacific had attempted to enter the California market without success. But its efforts, said the Court, "had a powerful influence on El Paso's business attitudes."[20] Its actual or potential competition should be preserved. In both *Alcoa-Rome* and *El Paso,* the Court ordered divestiture.

Von's Grocery. This case set the seal on horizontal limits, in 1966. It involved the merger of two retail food chains in Los Angeles. Von's Grocery, the third largest food chain in the area, had acquired Shopping Bag, the sixth largest, thereby moving into second place. But Von's share of the market,

---

[17] Ibid, p. 345. For approval of the decision, see David D. Martin, "The Brown Shoe Case and the New Anti-merger Policy," *American Economic Review* 53 (June 1963), 340–58. For an attack on the decision, see John L. Peterman, "The Brown Shoe Case," *Journal of Law and Economics* 18 (April 1975), 81–146, and "FTC v. Brown Shoe Co.," ibid (October 1975), pp. 361–420.

[18] *U.S.* v. *Philadelphia National Bank,* 374 U.S. 321 (1963). The case is discussed above in Chapter 5.

[19] *U.S.* v. *Aluminum Co. of America,* 377 U.S. 271, 280.

[20] *U.S.* v. *El Paso Natural Gas Co.,* 376 U.S. 651, 659. This remarkable case dragged on for some 16 years, with El Paso using every opportunity for delay.

after the merger, was only 7.5 percent. The share of all the market leaders was declining, and there was no barrier to the entry of new concerns. But the Court noted that the number of stores operated by individual owners had fallen. And it found the merger to be unlawful on the ground that it was the purpose of the law "to prevent concentration in the American economy by keeping a large number of small competitors in business."[21]

General Dynamics. Here a merger among firms producing coal in Illinois and the vicinity raised the concentration of production in that region (in the top four firms from 43 to 63 percent during 1957–67). The Supreme Court's decision in 1973 acquitted, on two grounds.[22] First, the relevant market was held to be much broader than the Division alleged. This loosened the precedent that "any" significant market would show a violation. Second, the Court considered that other facts about the industry must also be considered in judging the competitive effect. The clarity of the 1960s precedents was now diluted with flexibility, and the standard of proof for conviction was raised. The shift in policy was not sharp, since the changes were of degree, not kind.

The strict treatment of horizontal mergers has been perforated by various exceptional cases.[23] Some "failing firm" mergers have also been permitted. RCA and General Electric sold their large computer operations to competitors in 1970–72 without official opposition. In 1976 the Division approved the absorption of "failing" White Motor Corp. by White Consolidated Industries, Inc. In 1975–78 more than ten sizable mergers took place among brokerage firms, directly raising concentration. This reflected the new competition unleashed by the ending of brokerage fee fixing on May 1, 1975 (see Chapter 7). Though many of the firms were not yet strictly failing, the Division permitted the mergers as part of the larger shift to competition. Over 100 viable brokerage firms still remained.

Yet the FTC prevented American Finance System, Inc., from acquiring Beneficial Corp. in 1977.[24] The two consumer finance firms had 442 and 1,780 offices, respectively, and Beneficial had lost $15 million on $106 million revenue in 1976. The FTC regarded these losses as not large or prolonged enough to show complete "failure." In 1978 a merger between LTC Corp. (which owned Jones & Laughlin Steel Corp.) and Lykes Corp. (which owned Youngstown Sheet & Tube Co.) was permitted by Attorney General Griffin Bell, over-riding the Division's decision. The merger created the third largest

---

[21] *U.S.* v. *Von's Grocery Co.*, 384 U.S. 280 (1966). There were sharp minority dissents in both *Brown Shoe* and *Von's Grocery*, arguing that the effect of the mergers would be trivial or procompetitive. The minorities were basically setting a higher burden of proof on the government.

[22] *U.S.* v. *General Dynamics Corp.*, 341 F. Supp. 534 (N. D. Ill. 1972), *affirmed*, 415 U.S. 486 (1973).

[23] These include the merger between the McDonnell and Douglas aircraft firms in 1967 and the Penn-Central merger in 1968.

[24] "In the Matter of American General Insurance Co.," FTC Docket No. 8847, June 28, 1977.

U.S. steel firm, with about 15 to 25 percent shares of various markets. Neither was running losses, but both were in difficulties. Cases like these test the margin of policy in assessing "failure."

Is strictness good economics? Most experts now say yes. In few cases will the policy stop genuine net economies from occurring. The treatment is clean and quick, sparing of public and private resources. Genuine net economies can still be proven by the firms, to the agencies or in court.

G. VERTICAL MERGERS

Vertical merger policy has not had a steady evolution or rich set of precedents. Most cases present unique features, and claimed economies are often provable. The Yellow Cab decision in 1947, Paramount in 1948, and A&P in 1949 had established that vertical integration could not be used to foreclose competition at either level. But specific practices had been adduced in these cases: no general rule against vertical integration per se was applied. Since then the Court has drawn closer limits, nearly accepting that a large rise in vertical integration is per se likely to have the effect of foreclosing competition and raising entry barriers.

du Pont-General Motors. The case was filed in 1949, alleging that du Pont's holding of GM stock gave it preference in the market for automobile fabrics and finishes (recall Chapter 5). The district court acquitted in 1954, saying that a loss of competition had not been proven. On appeal, the Supreme Court reversed by 4 to 2, citing the original Clayton Section 7.[25] The shares were divested, after a special law was passed in 1961 easing the tax burden on du Pont heirs from the forced sale.

Vertical integration had only been partial, and the decision set a moderate limit on the market shares held by the firms. But it did show that markets could be defined closely in vertical merger cases.

Brown Shoe. The Brown case had vertical aspects too. Brown made shoes and Kinney sold shoes. The Court looked less at the small market shares than at Brown's likely policy of requiring Kinney to carry only Brown Shoes. This would foreclose competition in a market which already had rising concentration.

Inco-ESB. In 1974 the International Nickel Co. of Canada acquired ESB, Inc. (the former Electric Storage Battery Company) for $234 million after a bidding war with United Technologies Corp. ESB was the leading U.S. battery maker, with 18 percent of the market. Inco was the dominant supplier of nickel to the battery industry. The Division sued in 1976, arguing that their vertical joinder reduced the competition between the two firms in developing and producing batteries for forklift trucks and mine locomotives. A consent decree in 1977 was designed to prevent the exclusive effects of the vertical merger. Inco promised to give free access to 201 patents on metallic

---

[25] *U.S.* v. *du Pont,* 353, U.S. 586 (1957).

foil batteries and to avoid any merger with other battery makers for ten years.

The economic analysis underlying the problems—and these cases—must be complex and quantitatively imprecise. But the present policy lines do roughly reflect the best judgments about where the limits should be set. There is room for distinct economies to be proven and reasonable exceptions to be made.

H. CONGLOMERATE MERGERS

The backdrop of policy toward conglomerate mergers includes many old blue-ribbon conglomerates, with established major shares many decades old. The new conglomerates have often been corporate raiders (or trivial houses of cards). An efficient policy will reap the efficiency-inducing effects of conglomerate mergers while filtering out the possible reductions in competition.

H1. Conglomerate Firms

The share of new conglomerates in the 1960s wave was large but still less than half. Old conglomerates and unified firms dominated. But the new operators, working as outsiders in a slow-changing industrial scene, drew attention and criticism that were frantic at times. In financial circles and the business press, they were variously said to be wizards, hucksters and destroyers. In Britain, they are often called "asset strippers." They really were part of the normal process of corporate renewal by new blood (recall Chapter 2). Their leaders included:

International Telephone and Telegraph. ITT was before 1960 a foreign twin of AT&T, operating many telephone systems abroad. After 1960 it shifted to take-overs of a string of dominant firms in middle-sized industries.[26] It acted when cost savings of at least 20 percent could be foreseen. It tended more to redirect old managers than sack them. The leading raider of blue-chip firms, it rose to eighth largest industrial firm in 1970. It avoided reliance on weapons sales, and used private antitrust suits to challenge mergers by other firms. It survived a severe antitrust attack in 1969–71. When its political machinations were exposed in 1972–74, the corporate establishment predictably rushed *not* to defend it.

Litton Industries. An early and respectable science-based conglomerate, Litton began in the 1950s. It acquired second-echelon firms and added scientific capabilities. Slightly reliant on military sales, it had severe adjustment problems after 1966 but was still 36th largest in 1970 (69th in 1977).

Ling-Temco-Vought, (LTV), masterminded by James Ling, took over a series of improvable and ever-larger firms during 1960–68, ending with Jones

---

[26] See Anthony Sampson, *The Sovereign State of ITT* (New York: Fawcett, 1975) for a thorough, critical account.

& Laughlin (sixth largest in steel) in 1968. It was the 15th largest industrial firm in 1970. Ling was unique in keeping branches partly separate, with public accounts. Heavily reliant on military sales, LTV was broken after 1968 by a drop in weapons contracts and McLaren's antitrust attack.

Gulf and Western Industries. This grew from auto parts and sugar to a wide variety of products, including movies, paper, and metals. It tried to take over Armour in 1968 and A&P in 1973, among various unconsummated deals. It avoided serious antitrust and management problems but not the general market disillusion with conglomerates. Its actions are highly publicized, though it was only 65th largest in 1970 and 59th largest in 1977.

The new conglomerates are usually built up by one remarkable founder, whose power and genius—and alleged villainy—come to be much exaggerated. Neary all the new conglomerates have been hammered by share-price falls after 1968, caused in some degree by public policy actions.

H2. Policy Criteria

There were sharp turns in policy, as the wave of mergers mounted in the 1960s. One doctrine after another was tried, by the Division and the FTC, all of them speculative. Before 1969, the agencies usually let the burden of proof favor the conglomerates, since direct effects on competition were not provably large. Though Turner was denounced for inaction—both by blue-ribbon corporate interests *and* by critics of big business—his moderate line has been mostly vindicated by events.[27] In 1969, McLaren made a broad-scale attack on conglomerate mergers, with LTV and ITT the main targets. This helped to stop the merger wave, but the attack was compromised before reaching the Supreme Court for a clear decision on the merits.

Therefore, policy remains unclear, a mixture of possible grounds upon which a conglomerate merger might be challenged. The agencies have focused on the danger of reciprocity, on potential entry, on size-disparity and the unfair advantages which a branch might acquire, and on the "toehold" doctrine.

Reciprocity. An early case, decided in 1965, cited reciprocal buying. The *Consolidated Foods Corporation,* operating a nationwide chain of groceries and buying large quantities of processed food, had acquired Gentry, Inc., a small wholesaler making a third of the nation's sales of dehydrated onions and garlic (from such small cases large decisions often sprout!). Consolidated was thus enabled to require the food processors who sold to it to buy their onions and garlic from Gentry, thereby excluding Gentry's competitors from its market for these commodities. The Court held that the reciprocity made possible by the merger was anticompetitive. "We do not say," it went on, "that any acquisition, no matter how small, violates Section 7 if there is a

---

[27] His basic position is given in "Conglomerate Mergers and Section 7 of the Clayton Act," *Harvard Law Review* 78 (May 1965), 1313–95.

probability of reciprocal buying . . . But where, as here, the acquisition is of a company that commands a substantial share of the market, a finding of probability of reciprocal buying by the Commission should be honored."[28] The later big cases in 1969 broadened this, to urge that a giant conglomerate could not escape the likelihood of *some* reciprocity and competitive loss in *some* of its markets.[29]

Reciprocity actually has only shallow roots and effects in most cases (see Chapter 8). Being a tangible act, it carries some weight in court, sufficient to tip some conglomerate merger cases. Yet—another irony—significant reciprocity by older existing conglomerates has rarely stirred court action (instead, it usually occurs in single-industry firms, as in steel).

Loss of a Potential Competitor. Recall that if a potential entrant X comes in by merger, a net loss of competition may result. Practical cases grow complex: was firm X *really* a potential entrant? Was competition reduced by enough to offset other gains?

The *El Paso Gas* case contained elements of potential as well as actual competition. The newcomer, Pacific Northwest Pipeline Corp., was trying to enter the California market for gas when it was bought by El Paso. In the decision in 1964 the Court used the phrase "potential competitor" for the first time.

Penn-Olin. The Court then sent the *Penn-Olin* case back to the district court with instructions to consider potential competition in detail. Pennsalt Chemicals and Olin Mathieson Chemical had formed in 1960 a joint venture, Penn-Olin Chemical, to sell sodium chlorate in the southeastern United States. Since 1951 Pennsalt had considered entering this market; Olin had considered it since 1958. Would the joint venture prevent their entering separately? The district court assessed a variety of subjective evidence from the companies about whether their officers might have chosen to enter the market separately, and decided that they would not have done so. On appeal, the Supreme Court in 1967 let the joint venture stand, by a 4 to 4 vote.[30]

P&G-Clorox. When Procter & Gamble Co. bought Clorox Chemical Co. in 1958, P&G was the largest household products firm and was likely to enter the bleach business in any event. Some of its products were related to bleach, and P&G management had considered direct entry before undertaking to enter by acquiring Clorox. Clorox was the dominant bleach firm, with a long-established 55 percent market share (71 percent in the Mid-Atlantic region), compared to less than 15 percent for Purex, the next largest.

The merger clearly subtracted a leading potential entrant. That alone would disqualify the merger. Yet the FTC (later affirmed by the Supreme Court)

---

[28] *FTC* v. *Consolidated Foods Corporation,* 380 U.S. 592.

[29] That is, LTV owned Braniff Airways. Airplane tail sections contain steel. If LTV owned Jones & Laughlin, it might buy planes only from aircraft companies that bought steel from J&L. This was only one specific charge, but it was alleged and accepted that other reciprocity was inevitable.

[30] *U.S.* v. *Penn-Olin Chemicals Co.,* 389 U.S. 308 (1967).

cited P&G's advertising advantages as the main grounds for preventing the merger (see below).

Ford-Autolite. Electric Autolite Co. was one of only two independent spark plug manufacturers when Ford Motor Co. acquired it in 1961. Various evidence at trial showed Ford to have been a potential entrant, and so the merger was finally reversed in 1972.[31]

As the potential competition doctrine caught on, a number of large mergers were stopped informally by threats to sue on that ground. Among many examples: Bethlehem Steel Company's attempt to buy Cerro (the fifth largest copper firm) for $300 million in 1968 was abandoned. Caterpillar Tractor Company's proposed merger with Chicago Pneumatic Tool Co.—to fill out its product line—was also dropped under threat of suit by the Division.

In the *Kennecott-Peabody* case, a leading copper company bought Peabody Coal Co. (the largest coal producer) in 1967. The FTC found unusually specific memos in Kennecott's files showing an intention to enter the coal business by setting up a new branch of the firm, just before the chance to buy Peabody came up. Kennecott argued that the memos only showed speculation, not plans. The merger was disallowed in 1971, and Peabody was finally sold off in 1977.[32]

Gillette-Braun involved Gillette's purchase in 1967 of Braun, A. G., the third largest European electric shaver company. The Division argued that Gillette did so in order to forestall or mitigate the likely entry of Braun into the U.S. market. Braun had in fact been planning to compete in the United States. In 1975 Gillette consented to restore the pre-merger status. It could keep Braun but, within four years, it had to establish a new firm to sell electric shavers in the United States. Gillette would continue to sell Braun products in the United States and elsewhere.

BIC-American Safety Razor. Also in the razor industry, the French pen company BIC tried in 1976 to buy the American Safety Razor Division of Philip Morris Co. ASR held 11 percent of U.S. razor blade sales in 1976, behind Gillette's 60 percent and Schick's 20 percent. BIC had started trying to sell disposable razors in the United States in 1976, but its ability to stay in the market was still in doubt. The FTC complaint cited it as either an actual or potential entrant (it *was* still partly both), and the merger was stopped.[33] But it was a close case economically. BIC might have needed the ASR base in order to succeed in entering because Gillette was so overwhelmingly dominant.

British Oxygen-Airco. In 1973 the British Oxygen Co. (later BOC) acquired 35 percent of the stock of Airco, Inc. BOC was the dominant British

---

[31] Autolite had held 15 percent of the domestic spark plug market. The case is *Ford Motor Co.* v. *U.S.,* 405 U.S. 562 (1972).

[32] Kennecott staged a remarkable six-year series of delaying tactics, including rehearings and appeals to Congress, before being forced to sell Peabody.

[33] "In the matter of BIC Pen Corporation," FTC Docket No. 9095, February 9, 1977.

firm selling industrial gases, while Airco was a major U.S. seller of gas. In 1974 the FTC objected on grounds that BOC was a leading potential competitor in the United States.[34] BOC officials denied any interest in direct entry, and in 1977 an appeals court validated the quasi-merger. The FTC dropped the matter because the evidence about BOC's intentions was conjectural rather than specific. Eventually Airco's resistance led BOC to drop the merger entirely.

Arco-Anaconda. This case further weakened the potential competition approach. A major oil firm, Atlantic Richfield, proposed in 1976 to buy Anaconda Co. which was the third largest firm in copper mining, fourth largest in refined copper, and a large producer of uranium oxide (the raw source for atomic fuel).[35] The FTC objected, on potential competition grounds, and sought a preliminary injunction to postpone the merger. Arco had long had an interest in entering the copper business. Arco's chairman met with copper merger candidates as far back as 1968. Memoranda showed Arco interest in entering copper by grass-roots exploration, joint ventures, and by buying copper reserves or small firms. The FTC claimed that Arco was one of only a few firms which could meet the high capital cost of direct new entry.

Arco asserted that direct entry was too risky and costly, so that it was not a potential entrant. The appeals court agreed and permitted the merger. "Arco is not poised on the fringe of the copper markets. It has no technological skills readily transferable to the copper markets; it has no channels of distribution which may be utilized to distribute copper." As for the uranium oxide market, Arco had neither the expertise nor reserves to enter it. Direct entry into either copper or uranium would be costly, slow, and risky. The court therefore held in January 1977 that Arco was not a likely potential entrant, and the merger would not reduce competition. Thereupon, the merger occurred and the FTC did not appeal. Whether it was right or wrong in its evaluation, the court had in any event enlarged the variety of evidence for assessing potential entry. By this standard, the Kennecott-Peabody merger would probably have been permitted.

It is now apparent that "potential entry" can be hard to appraise. When evidence is crystal-clear, the courts will use it to stop mergers. But when there is doubt, the evidence is conjectural, the courts will now usually let the merger occur.

"Toe-hold" Mergers and "Entrenchment." Suppose that a merger provides financial, technical, and marketing advantages to the acquired firm.[36]

---

[34] "In the Matter of British Oxygen Company, Ltd., and Airco, Inc.," FTC Docket No. 8955, December 8, 1976.

[35] There had been a "bidding war" with two other firms, Crane and Tenneco, during 1975–76, and Arco had won. The two other suitors were *not* among the likely potential entrants.

[36] On such "conglomerate" effects, see Corwin D. Edwards, "Conglomerate Bigness as a Source of Power," a chapter in George J. Stigler, ed., *Business Concentration and Price Policy* (Princeton: Princeton University Press, 1955).

If that firm is dominant in its market, the merger will entrench it further. But if the merger were instead with a smaller firm in that market—giving the large acquiring firm only a "toe-hold"—then it could heat up competition against the leading firms.

The point is based on valid economics.[37] The importance of the entrenchment and toe-hold features depend on the strength of *(a)* the dominant market positions, and *(b)* the advantages (from finances, advertising, and so forth). The FTC has adopted a 10 percent market share of the acquired firm as a rough dividing line in assessing the effect on competition: below 10 percent is toe-hold; above it is entrenchment. The Division and the courts have also applied entrenchment and toe-hold doctrine where the effects are clearly strong. This approach has mingled with the "potential competition" criterion in several important cases.

In *P&G-Clorox,* the Court went on to stress that P&G would give Clorox overwhelming advantages in advertising and distribution.[38] P&G was the nation's largest advertiser (spending over $175 million in 1967), and its discounts and market power were likely to entrench Clorox further. A toe-hold acquisition would have met this problem. The same reasoning applied in the *General Foods* case.[39] S.O.S., the leading maker of kitchen steel-wool scouring pads, had been acquired by General Foods. To prevent entrenchment, the FTC required divestiture, and in 1968 it was affirmed by the Supreme Court. The *Bendix-Fram* decision in 1970 went further, stating that toe-hold mergers were definitely superior to others.[40] A 17-percent market share (Fram's) could not be bought; a 9.5-percent market share would have been acceptable.

Toe-hold was a part of McLaren's 1969 attack on ITT, LTV, and Northwest Industries, which aimed to get a definitive ruling on conglomerates from the Supreme Court.[41] ITT's control of Canteen Corp., Continental

---

[37] It was advanced by a Presidential Commission on Antitrust in 1968, and in J. S. Campbell and W. G. Shepherd, "Leading-Firm Conglomerate Mergers," *Antitrust Bulletin,* 1968, pp. 1361–82.

[38] *FTC* v. *Procter & Gamble,* 386 U.S. 568 (1967). This effect was affirmed by an episode in Pennsylvania, where P&G had helped Clorox defeat an attempt by Purex to enter the market significantly. For severe criticism of the P&G-Clorox decision, see John L. Peterman, "The *Clorox* Case and the Television Rate Structures," *Journal of Law and Economics* 11 (October 1968), 321–422.

[39] *FTC* v. *General Foods Corp.,* 386 F. 2d 836; 391 U.S. 919 *Certiorari denied.*

[40] "The threat of a toe-hold merger by a powerful firm may often serve as a much greater incentive to competitive performance in the affected market than the prospect of more costly and slower internal, *de novo* expansion." "In the Matter of the Bendix Corporation," Docket No. 8739, 1970.

Fram made automobile filters (oil, fuel, and air), with about 17 percent of the various submarkets. Bendix was a large diversified firm and producer of automotive parts. Bendix bought Fram in 1967 but was required to divest Frame after the FTC's decision was affirmed on appeal in 1971.

[41] The cases cited nearly all of the possible doctrines against conglomerates. This scatter-gun approach was legally untidy, but it would have given the Court a full range of doctrines to choose among in setting the rules on conglomerate mergers. Northwest's inclusion reflected a frantic attempt by Goodrich to avoid take-over by

Baking, Avis, Levitt, Sheraton Hotels, Grinnell, and Hartford Fire Insurance was held likely to entrench these leading firms (though only Canteen, Grinnell, and Hartford were formally challenged). With LTV, the dominance issue was far less clear, since J&L ranked only sixth in steel. As the cases moved along, there was intensive negotiation for compromise. McLaren urged appeals on up to the Supreme Court, to get a decision on the merits. But then compromises were reached, requiring some divestiture and curbs on future mergers.[42] LTV had to sell J&L and was, in any case, so damaged that it soon liquidated most of its holdings.

Budd-Gindy. In 1967 the Budd Company, a leading maker of automobile parts, bought Gindy Manufacturing Corp., a small regional producer of van trailers, containers, and container chassis. The FTC issued a complaint on grounds that Budd was a most likely potential entrant into Gindy's markets. In 1975 the full FTC let the merger stand, because it was a toe-hold merger.[43] Gindy's market shares were in the range of 4 to 8 percent, and Budd was already in the process of building up this small firm to be a national competitor. The loss of potential competitor was outweighed by the rise in actual competition.

The $1.9 billion merger between *General Electric Co.* and *Utah International Inc.* in 1976 also involved entrenchment issues. Utah was a mining and shipping company, while GE mainly produced electrical equipment. Yet Utah mined and sold uranium ore, and this could give advantages to GE, a leader in developing and selling nuclear reactors. To meet objections from the Division about such possible entrenchment, GE agreed to spin off Utah's uranium operations to a new unit, which would be independent until at least the year 2000.

In short, policy does apply the economics of toe-hold and entrenchment effects with reasonable care. The side-effect—of insulating dominant firms from take-overs—is mitigated as much as possible, but it still exists.

Bigness. This was also important in McLaren's attack, and in 1969 it was even announced that *all* significant mergers by any of the 250 largest firms were likely to be challenged. This stretched antitrust doctrine beyond competitive effects into the realm of global concentration and larger social policy. It also gave perfect safety from take-over for these large firms—a very large part of the corporate establishment. This rule has been relaxed moderately since 1969, but bigness is still one element which makes a merger more likely to be challenged.

---

an outside company. Here, and in resisting General Host's take-over of Armour in 1968, the Division was invoked to aid take-over targets, probably *against* the true social interest.

[42] ITT was given a Hobson's choice, between giving up Hartford and giving up Canteen, Levitt, Grinnell, and three other holdings. It chose to keep Hartford, but that too has run afoul of more recent tax rulings and Congressional investigations. See Sampson, *Sovereign State.*

[43] "In the Matter of the Budd Company," Docket No. 8848, September 18, 1975.

To sum it up, a conglomerate merger is vulnerable if it involves *(a)* a potential entrant, *(b)* a dominant and/or large firm, *(c)* a clear probability of entrenchment, or *(d)* a likelihood of reciprocity by leading firms. Existing conglomerates are many, large, and untouched. In part these merger policies fit economic criteria. But they have reduced the influence of take-over threats on the main core of industrial firms. To this extent, the normal market for assets and control has been abridged.

I. OTHER COUNTRIES

Canada has virtually no policy toward mergers.[44] But, as usual, the United Kingdom offers interesting parallels. Mergers have grown since 1960, many of them horizontal ones. During the 1960s some of these were promoted by government departments (the Ministry of Technology, especially). They have helped along a marked increase in concentration since 1958. Since 1965 the Monopolies Commission has formally screened mergers, but only if the Board of Trade (since 1973 the Office of Fair Trading) decides they need screening and "refers" them to the commission.[45] During 1965–77 only 34 mergers out of 1,376 total were referred, though nearly 200 of the mergers would give market shares over 50 percent. Of the 34 mergers studied, 11 were dropped before decision, 11 were opposed, and 12 were found to be "not against the public interest."[46] Mergers are investigated intensively if they involve large size (over $12 million) or market shares (over 25 percent).

Generally, dominant firms cannot make large horizontal mergers, but the limits for smaller firms are not as tight as in the United States. The cult of bigness, which led the government itself to foster large mergers during 1964–69 to meet global competition, has faded. A variety of conditions—size, efficiencies, pricing behavior, exports—are considered in screening mergers, and so no clear guidelines are possible.[47] This contrasts with the main lines of U.S. policy.

On the Continent, most dominant firms informally are aware that large

---

[44] See Charles W. Borgsdorf, "The Virtually Unconstrained Legal Environment for Mergers in Canada," *Antitrust Bulletin* 18 (Winter 1973), 809–25.

[45] J. D. Gribbin, "The Operation of the Mergers Panel since 1965," *Trade and Industry,* Her Majesty's Stationery Office, London, January 17, 1974, pp. 70–73, and D. C. Elliott and J. D. Gribbin, "The Abolition of Cartels and Structural Change in the United Kingdom," in A. P. Jacquemin and H. W. de Jong, eds., *Welfare Aspects of Industrial Markets* (Leiden: Martinus Nijhoff, 1977). The Commission's effect is greater than these numbers show, for many mergers are discussed in advance with the Commission and some are modified or dropped.

[46] Of the 34, some 23 were referred because of the large size of the firms, and 11 because of high market shares. Of the 23, some 15 were mainly horizontal mergers, six conglomerate, and two vertical.

For an excellent appraisal of the decisions about these mergers, see D. W. Colenutt and P. P. O'Donnell, "The Consistency of Monopolies and Merger Commission Merger Reports," *Antitrust Bulletin* 23 (Spring 1978), 51–82.

[47] An attempt at guidelines was made in 1969; see Board of Trade, *Guidelines for Assessing Mergers,* H. M. S. O., 1969.

horizontal mergers may be challenged in some way. But there is little constraint on other mergers, either in individual countries or in the Common Market as a whole. The Common Market Commission's Competition Department challenged Continental Can's merger with a Dutch firm, Thomassen En Drijver, in 1969. Continental dominates cans in the EEC, and Thomassen was one of its few rivals. The EEC court in 1973 let this merger stand, while finding for the Commission "in principle." So far, there is a thin shell of EEC merger policy but no practical content. In France, mergers with large foreign firms are usually resisted or prevented in order to protect their French character.

In Japan, there is scarcely a policy at all, beyond strict prohibitions on foreign take-overs of Japanese firms.[48] A 1972 merger, creating Nippon Steel with a dominant share and second rank among all steel firms in the world, was permitted. Matters are settled by informal negotiations.

In most countries, there is no arm's-length formulation of policy, but rather a complex process of private negotiation, often involving private firms, financial units, and government offices. Commonly, national power and sovereignty become elements in the solution. This makes for murky procedure and criteria.

J. SUMMARY

Since 1960, U.S. merger policy has been extended to nearly all sectors. It has also been made more strict and consistent. The existing structure largely predates this new policy set, and old mergers have not been touched. Therefore the larger effects of merger policy on fairness and efficiency are debatable.

The lines are reasonably clear. Horizontal mergers may not appreciably increase market shares, especially if market concentration has been high or rising. Vertical mergers may not affect large shares or raise entry barriers, or otherwise be likely to reduce competition. Conglomerate mergers usually must not involve potential entrants, nor dominant or large firms, nor make reciprocity likely. Yet there are frequent exceptions, and the mass of smaller and local businesses are exempt in practice.

The policies are mainly rational in the small, constraining market shares and promoting entry. But they have come to exclude the take-over process from the many established leading firms. And they may harden industrial structure, by keeping smaller firms from merging to approach the positions which larger firms already have.

One can regard U.S. treatment as seeming strict but still *(a)* permitting some exceptions and *(b)* tending to shield large and dominant firms. Or one can view it as much the strictest and—case by case—most pro-competitive

---

[48] See Eleanor M. Hadley, *Antitrust in Japan* (Princeton: Princeton University Press, 1970), and various issues of the *Oriental Economist* periodical.

merger policy in the world. Once again, the critical factor is whether high market shares tend to fade away quickly, slowly, or not at all.

In any event, the antitrust agencies and the courts are still groping for the efficient margins and inner balance. A revival of conglomerate mergers could force more testing of their role and treatment. Meanwhile, the horizontal and vertical criteria seem likely to change little. The ultimate effects and wisdom of this remain speculative. You should, of course, draw your own interpretation.

QUESTIONS FOR REVIEW

1. "The gains from mergers are strictly pecuniary, except for vertical mergers." True?
2. "For sound policy choices, one weighs the possible costs from reducing competition against the possible increases in genuine efficiency (economies of scale and integration)." True?
3. "In assessing mergers, it is the net gains (compared to internal growth or long-term contracts) that count." True?
4. "Conglomerate mergers have virtually ceased since 1968." True?
5. "Before 1958 there were no effective formal limits on mergers, and so dominant firms could merge with impunity." True?
6. "Merger policies cover all sectors except utilities and banking, which are exempt under regulation." True?
7. "Policy toward horizontal mergers now rules out almost any merger which appreciably reduces competition." True?
8. "Clear rules toward mergers were set in the *Philadelphia National Bank* case, while *General Dynamics* makes the evaluation more complicated." True?
9. "The 'Warren' Court was usually willing to prevent a merger as long as any significant market was affected. The 'Burger' Court has required clear showings of the 'relevant market' before acting." True?
10. "The criteria for a 'failing firm' exemption from merger policy are not clear or simple." True?
11. "If a conglomerate merger removes the leading potential entrant into an unconcentrated market, it will be prevented." True?
12. "If a large firm buys a firm with 8 percent of a concentrated market, the merger will probably be permitted on toe-hold grounds." True?
13. What social costs does a rule against take-overs of dominant firms have?
14. Should the agencies be able to delay any merger they choose while they study it carefully and decide what to do?
15. Have merger rules channelled merger activity toward conglomerate mergers?
16. How would you revise policy toward conglomerate mergers?

APPENDIX TABLE 6A–1. A Selection of Large U.S. Industrial Mergers, 1952 to 1977

Year and Type	Acquiring Company	Acquired Company	Assets ($ millions)
1952			
PE	Mathieson Chemical	Squibb, E. R. and Sons	106
1953			
H	Kaiser-Frazer (cars)	Willys Overland (cars)	120
1954			
H	Nash Kelvinator Corp. (cars, etc.)	Hudson Motor Car Co.	108
C	Mathieson Chemical	Olin Industries, Inc. (equipment)	232
H	Studebaker Corp.	Packard Motor Car Co.	135
1955			
H	Sunray Oil Co.	Mid-Continent Petroleum Corp.	186
PE	Sperry Corp. (electrical)	Remington Rand, Inc. (office equip.)	207
1956			
H	Gulf Oil Corp.	Warren Petroleum Corp.	163
1958			
C	Socony Mobil Oil	Freeport Sulphur Co.	100
1959			
V	General Telephone & Electronics (telephone systems)	Sylvania Electric Products, Inc.	264
1960			
H	Standard Oil (N.J.)	Monterey Oil Co.	102
1961			
C	Ling-Temco Electronics	Chance Vought Aircraft, Inc.	101
PE, V	Ford Motor Co.	Philco Corp. (appliances, batteries)	242
ME	Standard Oil of Calif.	Standard Oil Co., Kentucky	141
1963			
PE	Eaton Mfg. Co. (auto equipment)	Yale & Towne Mfg. (engineering)	114
1964			
ME	Interlake Iron	Acme Steel	134
1965			
ME	Boise Cascade Corp. (wood products)	Minnesota & Ontario Paper Co.	110
C	Gulf & Western Ind. (conglomerate)	New Jersey Zinc Co.	143
ME	Union Oil California	Pure Oil Co.	766
1966			
PE	Continental Oil Co.	Consolidation Coal Co.	446
H, ME	Atlantic Refining Co.	Richfield Oil Corp.	499
C	American Tobacco Co.	Sunshine Biscuits, Inc.	109
ME	Phillips Petroleum Co.	Tidewater Oil (western manufacturing & marketing properties)	372
1967			
PE	Warner-Lambert Pharm. (drugs)	American Optical Co.	111
PE	Kerr-McGee Corp. (oil)	American Potash & Chemical Corp.	117

APPENDIX TABLE 6A–1 *(continued)*

Year and Type	Acquiring Company	Acquired Company	Assets ($ millions)
PE, V	Glen Alden Corp. (textiles, etc.)	BVD Co., Inc. (clothes)	113
V, PE	U.S. Plywood Corp.	Champion Papers, Inc.	359
H	McDonnell Co. (aircraft)	Douglas Aircraft Co.	850
C	Tenneco Corp. (gas, pipeline, etc.)	Kern County Land (construction equipment)	706
C	Signal Oil & Gas Co.	Mack Trucks Inc.	303
C	Hunt Foods & Industries	McCall Corp. (publishing)	149
PE	North American Aviation	Rockwell-Standard Corp.	454
C	Gulf & Western Ind. (conglomerate)	South Puerto Rico Sugar Co.	122
C	Ling-Temco-Vought, Inc. (conglomerate)	Wilson & Co., Inc. (meat, sports, drugs)	196
C	Studebaker Corp.	Worthington Corp. (engineering products)	296
1968			
PE	Squibb, E. R. & Sons	Beech-Nut Life Savers	172
C	Gulf & Western Ind.	Brown Co. (paper)	196
PE	Hunt Foods & Ind.	Canada Dry Corp. (soft drinks)	105
C	Gulf & Western Ind.	Consolidated Cigar Corp. (largest)	127
C	Montgomery Ward & Co.	Container Corp. of America	397
C	IT&T	Continental Baking Co. (largest)	186
PE	Singer Co.	General Precision Equip. Corp.	322
PE	Occidental Petroleum	Hooker Chemical Corp.	366
PE	Occidental Petroleum	Island Creek Coal Co.	115
C	Ling-Temco-Vought, Inc.	Jones & Laughlin Steel Corp.	1,092
PE	Owens-Illinois, Inc. (bottles)	Lily-Tulip Cup Corp.	108
C	Loew's Theatres, Inc.	Lorillard Corp. (cigarettes)	375
C	Tenneco Corp. (gas pipelines and industrial)	Newport News Shipbuilding & Dry Dock Co.	139
C	Kennescott Copper Corp.	Peabody Coal Co.	315
ME	Northwest Industries	Philadelphia & Reading Corp. (R.R., etc.)	318
H	Wheeling Steel Corp.	Pittsburgh Steel Co.	193
C	IT&T	Rayonier, Inc. (fibers, fabrics)	296
C	Glen Alden Corp. (textiles)	Schenley Industries, Inc. (liquor)	570
ME	Sun Oil Co.	Sunray DX Oil Co.	749
C	American Standard Inc. (plumbing equipment)	Westinghouse Air Brake Co.	302
1969			
C	General Host Corp. (conglomerate)	Armour & Co. (meat)	560
V	Crane Co. (construction equipment)	C.F. & I. Steel Corp.	235
C	IT&T	Grinnell Corp. (alarm systems)	184

APPENDIX TABLE 6A–1 *(continued)*

Year and Type	Acquiring Company	Acquired Company	Assets ($ millions)
ME	Amerada Petroleum	Hess Oil & Chemical	491
C	Norwich Pharmacal	Morton International (salt, etc.)	163
PE	Xerox Corp. (copying equipment)	Scientific Data Systems (computers)	113
H	Atlantic Richfield (oil)	Sinclair Oil Corp.	1,851
1970			
C	Greyhound Corp. (buses, etc.)	Armour	607
ME	Standard Oil of Ohio	British Petrol. Hold/BP Co. Ltd.	627
V	Cleveland-Cliffs Iron (ore)	Detroit Steel Corp.	145
H	Honeywell, Inc. (computers, office equipment)	General Electric Computer Components (from G.E. Co.)	547
PE	American Motors Corp.	Kaiser Jeep Corp. (from Kaiser Industries)	168
PE	Nestle Alimentana	Libby, McNeil & Libby (foods)	267
H	Warner Lambert (drugs)	Parke Davis & Co. (drugs)	399
1971			
H	National Steel Corp.	Granite City Steel Co.	312
1972			
PE	Colgate-Palmolive Co. (toiletries)	Kendall Co. (health products, etc.)	194
C	Illinois Central (railroad)	Midas Intl. (mufflers)	42
PE	Pepsico Inc. (beverages)	Rheingold Corp. (beer)	101
C	CBS	Steinway & Sons (pianos)	18
1973			
C	J. Lyons (U.K.) foods	Baskin-Robbins (ice cream)	14
PE	Colgate-Palmolive (soaps)	Helena Rubenstein (cosmetics)	93
PE	Fruehauf (truck bodies)	Helsey-Hayes (mechanical)	274
PE	North Am. Rockwell	Rockwell Mfg. (machinery)	225
C	Beatrice Foods	Samsonite (luggage)	87
1974			
C	Rockwell Intl.	Admiral Corp. (radio, TV)	276
C	Intl. Nickel (Canada)	ESB Inc. (batteries)	315
C	United Technologies	Essex Intl. (copper)	465
ME	Philips (Netherlands)	Magnavox (TV)	331
	Matsushita (Japan)	Motorola (color TV)	151
1975			
ME	Babcock & Wilcox Ltd. (U.K.)	Am. Chain and Cable	235

APPENDIX TABLE 6A–1 *(concluded)*

Year and Type	Acquiring Company	Acquired Company	Assets ($ millions)
C .... Gulf & Western		Kayser-Roth Corp. (textiles)	402
C .... United Technologies		Otis Elevator	764
C .... Gulf & Western		Simon & Schuster (publishing)	42
C .... Emhart		USM (shoe machinery)	604
1976			
ME .... Marathon Oil		Pan Ocean Oil	265
C .... R. J. Reynolds Ind.		Burmah Oil & Gas	520
C .... General Electric		Utah International (minerals)	2,170
1977			
C .... Atlantic Richfield		Anaconda (copper)	536
PE .... Pepsico		Pizza Hut	313
C .... J. Ray McDermott (diversified)		Babcock & Wilcox (steam generation)	1,124
C .... Kennecott Copper		Carborundum	532

H = horizontal; V = vertical, ME= market extension, PE = product extension, and C = "pure" conglomerate.

Source: Bureau of Economics, Federal Trade Commission, *Statistical Report on Mergers and Acquisitions, November 1977* (Washington, D.C.: U.S. Government Printing Office, 1977).

chapter 7

Restrictive Practices: Collusion

Behavior is, of course, diverse. Much of it is pro-competitive, but some behavior restricts or excludes competition. The effect depends both on *(a)* the act itself and *(b)* the setting (who does it, and to whom?). Policies need to fit these distinctions and—on the whole—they do, as we shall see. Yet some policies are sharply disputed.

Restrictive practices divide into two main classes: *(a)* two or more "competitors" *cooperate* to raise their combined market power and profits, such as by price fixing; or *(b)* one firm *excludes* others from a fair chance to compete, such as by predatory pricing. Generally, cooperation raises the *level* of prices, while exclusionary acts tend to change the *structure* of prices. This chapter covers cooperation, while Chapter 8 treats exclusion.

The economic analysis of collusion is reviewed briefly in Section A. Price fixing—the classic anticompetitive act—occupies Section B. The riddle of tacit collusion by oligopolists comes in Section C. The mixed cases of overlapping directors, joint ventures, and trade associations are reviewed in Section D. Then in Section E we look abroad, to U.S. policies toward international collusion.

The big picture is: U.S. policies are strict against most price fixing, but mixed or lenient toward the other forms of cooperation. The procedures and criteria are roughly optimal. Abroad, Britain has comparable policies, a few other countries set loose limits, and the rest do virtually nothing against collusion.

A. WHY COLLUSION OCCURS

Collusion is endemic in markets ranging from loose oligopoly up to virtual monopoly, roughly from four-firm concentration of 30 percent up to 100 percent.[1] Each firm's incentives are mixed. The firm can gain by colluding

---

[1] See W. G. Shepherd, *The Economics of Industrial Organization* (New York: Prentice-Hall, 1979), chap. 15 and 16. Landmarks in the literature include Edward

FIGURE 7–1

Cost and demand determine the range of oligopoly pricing.

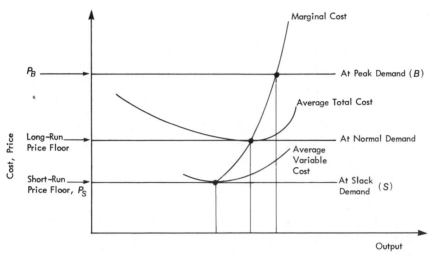

with its fellow oligopolists, but also by "cheating" them and defeating them. Its own best choices will often include a mix of cooperation on some matters and fighting on others. This mix can be unstable and changing, as conditions shift and the rivals try new tactics.

The resulting degree of cooperation is a form of partial monopoly. The colluders get part or perhaps even all of the gains which a direct merger would yield them. Done secretly, the collusion provides market power, and its fruits higher prices and profits, beneath a surface illusion of competition. In the upper ranges of tight oligopoly, collusion can often be tacit, as if the cooperating firms were a "shared monopoly." In the lower range of medium and loose oligopoly, the collusion normally must be explicit, detailed and mutually binding upon the firms, if it is to have much effect. The looser the oligopoly, the more likely is the collusion to fail.

Oligopoly pricing proceeds within a range. The *upper border* for price is the pure monopoly level, reached only if cooperation is perfect and complete. The *lower border* for price is at the level of marginal cost (or "out-of-pocket costs"). Short-run marginal cost will vary more widely than long-run marginal cost. This is illustrated in Figure 7–1. When demand for the typical firm is brisk (demand curve *B*), the firm will seek to have price set at P_B. But when demand is slack (demand curve *S*), the firm will be tempted to cut

H. Chamberlin, *The Theory of Monopolistic Competition*, 8th ed. (Cambridge: Harvard University Press, 1962); William J. Fellner, *Competition among the Few* (New York: Norton, 1949); George J. Stigler, "A Theory of Oligopoly," *Journal of Political Economy* 72 (February 1964), 44–61; and Oliver E. Williamson, "A Dynamic Theory of Interfirm Behavior," *Quartery Journal of Economics* 79 (November 1965), 579–607.

price to P_S. The brisk-demand price P_B gives high profit. Yet the firm would be willing, if it were felt advantageous, to cut price to the bone at P_S. The other firms share this range (although not exactly: their marginal-cost levels might vary). If overhead costs are large, then marginal costs will be low. Accordingly, deep—often called "ruinous" or "destructive"—price cutting may develop, because firms with slack demand will have a low floor for price cuts. Collectively, they gain from keeping prices up toward the monopoly level. Individually, they can gain by cutting or "chiseling," *if* the others don't match the price cuts. This is true only during slack periods; at other times, marginal costs will be higher, as shown in Figure 7–1.

Collusion raises the market price, often providing high profits. Paradoxically, this also rewards price cutting. The firm gains most if *(a)* collusion raises price and *(b)* the firm is outside the cartel, setting a slightly lower price and drawing customers away from the "loyal" cartel members. This temptation is shared by all the colluders, and it eventually erodes many conspiracies.[2] Each firm's cost and size levels will determine its specific mix of pricing incentives.

A1. Conditions Favoring Collusion

These include *(a)* high concentration, *(b)* uniform costs among the firms, *(a)* an entry barrier, *(d)* no powerful buyers able to exert monopsony power, and *(5)* similar attitudes among the oligopolists.

1. When *concentration* is high, the few leading sellers can coordinate more easily. The balance of their interests shifts from competition toward cooperation. Fewness means simplicity of control, and it also means that price cutting can be found and penalized quickly.[3] There is no exact standard for "high" concentration, though a four-firm concentration ratio of 50 percent of the market is a common rule of thumb.[4] Collusion can crystallize at 40 or 60 percent, or break down at 80 percent, depending on the whole situation.

2. When *costs* are similar, agreement on the collusive price is easier.[5] Cost differences undermine collusion. A firm with low costs will naturally prefer a lower price than will its high-cost rivals. In turn, costs can differ because of the sizes of the firms, the ages of the plants, special locations or inputs, or X-inefficiency.

3. A *barrier to entry* will raise the price at which collusion can be effective.

---

[2] In some opinions, all conspiracies can be counted on to crumble soon from chiseling. Only if the conspirators get government support, they claim, can price fixing last. The issue is one for you to judge.

[3] Fellner and Stigler discuss this part especially well. (See note 1 above.)

[4] Joe S. Bain has emphasized this threshhold [see his *Barriers to New Competition* (Cambridge: Harvard University Press, 1956)]; other analysts regard the effect as continuous (or linear), rather than as a distinct step at a specific level of concentration.

[5] This is analysed well by Donald J. Dewey, *Monopoly in Economics and Law* (Chicago: Rand McNally, 1959), chaps. 2 and 3; and F. M. Scherer, *Industrial Market Structure and Economic Performance* (Skokie, Ill.; Rand McNally, 1970), pp. 136–40.

New firms cannot easily enter and thrive. The added security also gives the cartel members a stronger net incentive to stay up at the cartel price level.

4. *Buyers* can neutralize collusion. Powerful buyers can isolate and pressure the sellers into offering special deals.[6] This directly breaks up the cartel's pricing unity. Indirectly, it reduces the mutual trust among the sellers, and so the collusion is less stable even when it does occur. A structure of discriminatory prices is likely to evolve, rather than a single collusive price. Even lacking monopsony power, an alert buyer can sue or seek action under the antitrust laws. When buyers passively accept collusion there is usually some abnormal reason.[7]

5. *Similar attitudes* can cause the firms' interests and expectations to converge. The managers may be from the same background and be long familiar with each other. With practice, they can fine-tune their signals and responses about pricing. The shared expectations can then become self-fulfilling. Such easy co-existence can be upset if one oligopolist changes its attitudes or goals. A new manager, or a take-over by an "outside" group, often injects such shifts. Even just one maverick can be enough to destroy the cooperation.

For lasting success, collusion needs to cover all of the industry. Collusion may be tight and explicit or loose and fluid. A formal cartel will bind its members by various tangible controls. These can include pricing formulas, output quotas, a set of penalties for specific violations, a staff for detecting and punishing the violators, and—in the very tightest of cartels—a direct pooling of profits.

Oligopoly is an arena for recurring strife, where the balance sways between collusion and independence. Because price is only one among many directions for strategy—others include product quality, advertising, and innovation—actual collusion is often as elusive as quicksilver.

The price outcomes vary, as illustrated in Figure 7–2A. As concentration increases, higher prices are more likely. But the other conditions are also at work, and there may be a sequence of collusion and collapses. As concentration rises, the range of variation also increases, as shown in Figure 7–2A. Correspondingly, for each individual firm, the range of its probable outcomes increases as its market share rises (see Figure 7–2B).

A2. Varieties of Collusion

Within these ranges, there is an endless variety of processes and outcomes. Strategies of all kinds are tried, often with bluffing, deceptions, and complex

---

[6] See especially J. K. Galbraith's discussion of "countervailing power," in his *American Capitalism: The Theory of Countervailing Power* (Boston: Houghton Mifflin, 1952); and Scherer's *Industrial Market Structure,* chap. 9.

[7] One cause of passivity is utility regulation. Utility firms under rate-base regulation in the U.S. may lack strong incentives to buy equipment at the lowest possible price. The equipment goes into the firm's rate base, and a higher rate base can give the firm higher profits. See the electrical equipment conspiracy in Section B below for one such instance. See also Chapter 11's analysis of the rate-base effect.

198

FIGURE 7–2
Oligopoly outcomes can diverge from the central patterns.

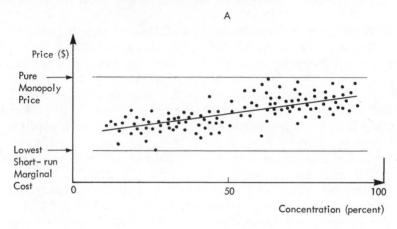

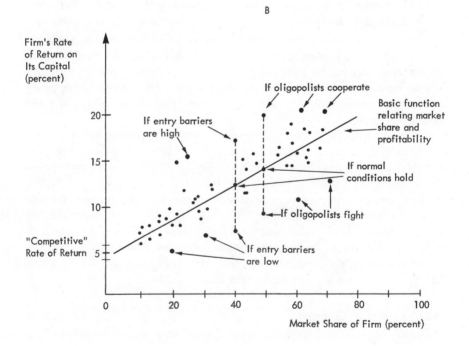

sequences. The theory of games was developed partly to clarify these possibilities.[8] The theory has provided insight, and helped to illustrate some

---

[8] The great landmark study of game theory is John von Neumann and Oskar Morgenstern, *Theory of Games and Economic Behavior* (Princeton: Princeton University Press, 1944), which a few students and faculty can read and understand. An attempt to apply the theory to oligopoly is by Martin Shubik, *Strategy and Market Structure* (New York: Wiley, 1959); the results are interesting but not strong.

of the variety of outcomes. One can analyze simple situations with it. It has shown that tight oligopolies will often converge quickly on tacitly agreed prices. Yet most real markets are too complicated for it to handle in detail.

"Price leadership" often occurs. In the extreme version, the largest firm will select the price which maximizes the joint profits of the group and then impose that price. The other firms then follow this leader. In these markets, long periods of rigid prices are punctuated by brief episodes of collusive, or dominant-firm, price leadership. (They have also been called "administered prices.") In softer versions, the leadership may rotate a bit, or occasionally not be followed rigidly. At the other extreme, this leadership may only be "barometric."[9] The leader merely *finds* the new price level that costs will require; it does not *impose* a higher price. A lock-step pattern of price leadership does not prove that collusion has occurred, though it strongly suggests that it has.

Explicit collusion occurs in loose oligopolies, where there must be tight controls in order to keep mavericks in line. It was long thought that tight oligopolies can rely instead just on tacit collusion. Yet many tight oligopolies do in fact engage deeply in explicit price-fixing schemes.[10] There is often concrete evidence of these schemes, from signed memoranda, notes, charts, and so forth.

Cartels have been common in other countries since 1900, especially in Germany, Sweden and—during 1930–56—in Britain.[11] Some cartels amount virtually to a merger of the members, for their production, pricing, marketing, and profit shares are all centrally handled. Looser cartels take endless varieties of these parts, reflecting both the range of market conditions and the sheer ingenuity of the human mind.

Under U.S. antitrust law, this hard-core collusion is illegal, and so the attempts at it must operate secretly.[12] There are many looser forms of cooperation which, being on the margin of the law, are able to proceed in public: patent pooling and joint ventures are examples. All these gradations of cooperation occur with much variety throughout most of the economy.

A3. The Social Costs and Possible Benefits of Collusion

As a form of monopoly, collusion usually causes social harm, as Chapter 1 noted: inefficiency, lost innovation, inequity, and so on. Colluders often

---

[9] See Jesse W. Markham, "The Nature and Significance of Price Leadership," *American Economic Review,* 41 (December 1951), 891–905; Scherer criticizes the idea in *Industrial Market Structure,* pp. 170–73.

[10] This is shown by George A. Hay and Daniel Kelley, "An Empirical Survey of Price Fixing Conspiracies," *Journal of Law and Economics* 17 (April 1974), 13–38.

[11] George W. Stocking and Myron W. Watkins, *Cartels in Action* (New York: Twentieth Century Fund, 1946), is a massive study of cartels in world markets.

[12] But large sections of the economy are exempt, as Chapter 4 noted; other departures are discussed in detail in Chapter 24.

say that there are offsetting benefits from "orderly marketing," but the claims are always doubtful and often false. The main possible real benefit—economies of scale—is absent, for the firms remain separate as producers. Therefore a clear policy line against price fixing is sound. There might be certain valid defenses; the three most popular ones follow.

Avoiding "Destructive" ("Ruinous," or "Cut-Throat") Competition. The claim is that fluctuations in demand cause price cutting to go too deep, down toward short-run marginal cost (recall Figure 7–1).[13] Meanwhile, since industry demand is inelastic, the physical volume of sales stays nearly the same. The cut in profits causes firms to fail, even though they are able to produce at normal long-run average cost levels. If price fixing could avoid these deep slashes, it is said, the capacity and efficiency of the industry would be greater. "Destructive" competition is most likely to occur when overhead costs are large, so that short-run marginal costs are low. So the research questions are: *are* overhead costs large, *are* price cuts "too deep," and *are* capacity and efficiency reduced?

Research has rarely borne out claims that competition is "destructive." Marginal costs are usually higher than the firms claim, and the causal effects on capacity and efficiency usually cannot be measured, much less proven. Some "predatory" pricing may occur, but that is a separate issue (see Chapter 8). Short-run pricing shifts are not likely to affect long-run performance. Even if they were, price fixing is usually an inferior way to avoid the damage.

Long-term declines in "sick industries" are a separate matter. They induce chronic price cutting below profitable levels. That is the efficient economic process, in order to shrink the excess capacity. Competition may seem to do this too rapidly and cruelly. Yet if a genuine social harm occurs, it usually can be mitigated in ways better than price fixing.

Reducing Risk. Price fixing often stabilizes prices and output, even down to the shares of individual firms. Yet this may not be a social gain. Some degree of risk is a spur for efficiency and innovation. Collusion has often induced slackness and slowness among its participants. For that matter, price fixing might *not* reduce risk. Prices may have sharper fluctuations, as collusion first works, then collapses, then holds again, then collapses, and so on. Such breaks are a common result of attempts to collude. Altogether, risk is not a good justification for price fixing.

Making Other Valuable Actions Possible. The excess profits from collusion might be devoted to better service or innovation, it is said. Colluders might also pool increased resources for large-scale projects (such as mining ventures, development of new technology, and so on). Yet competition is at least as likely to bring about the optimal levels. And the profits might well be siphoned off instead, rather than be used for the praiseworthy purposes. Scarcely any of these claimed needs have ever withstood objective study.

Altogether, there is a compelling social case against explicit collusion, and a strong presumption against most other forms of cooperation. A few

---

[13] For detailed readings, see Scherer, *Industrial Market Structure,* pp. 198–202.

marginal categories of cooperation require a more selective treatment; some, but not all, of them will have minor social effects either way.

B. POLICY TOWARD PRICE FIXING

Recall the basic criterion: the optimum treatment will draw the line at the efficient margin, in light of benefits and costs. The benefits include the economic results of good performance. The costs include the costs of the practice *plus* the costs of the treatment, such as agency costs, courts, and possibly the firms' costs of litigating. A simple rule can save large volumes of policy costs, by avoiding lengthy hearings and claims about the evidence. Generally a clear, definite policy line is better than a complex, uncertain one, as long as it fits the efficient margin reasonably well.

B1. Simple Price Fixing: The Per Se Rule

Simple price fixing is under such a clear rule. It is illegal per se, without any further proof of intent or effect. The prohibition applies also to controls on output, to market sharing agreements, and to cooperative exclusions of competitors by boycotts or other coercive practices. All that an Antitrust Division attorney (or private plaintiff) needs to show at a trial is that competitors actually tried to fix prices or rig the market in some other way. Any evidence of a conspiracy—a scribbled memorandum, an annotated price list, a tape recording of the discussions—is usually enough to convict and invoke penalties. No evidence that prices actually rose, or rose up to some "unreasonable" level, is essential, though that sort of evidence will usually result in stiffer penalties and larger awards for damages.

There are certain marginal issues around this core of clear policy. They will be discussed shortly. First we will review the mainstream cases, which first formed the per se rule in 1899, reaffirmed it in 1927, and set the seal on it in 1940.

Mainstream Cases

The earliest cases involving restrictive agreements among competitors were those of the Trans-Missouri Freight Association in 1897,[14] the Joint Traffic Association in 1898,[15] and the Addyston Pipe & Steel Company in 1899.[16] In *Trans-Missouri* and *Joint Traffic*, groups of railroads had fixed and enforced freight rates. In *Addyston*, six producers of cast iron pipe had assigned certain markets to each of their number and determined the allocation of contracts elsewhere by operating a bidding ring. In all three cases the defendants argued that their restrictions were required to prevent ruinous competition and that

---

[14] *U.S.* v. *Trans-Missouri Freight Assn.*, 166 U.S. 290.

[15] *U.S.* v. *Joint Traffic Assn.*, 171 U.S. 505.

[16] *Addyston Pipe & Steel Co.* v. *U.S.*, 175 U.S. 211.

the resulting rates and prices were reasonable. In each case, the Court rejected this defense, holding the arrangements to be illegal in themselves.

The precedent held for 30 years, decisions being rendered against collusive bidding by purchasers of livestock,[17] exclusion of competing railways from a terminal,[18] the use of patent licenses to fix the price of bathtubs,[19] and the operation of a boycott by retail lumber dealers.[20]

Trenton Potteries renewed the precedent in 1927.[21] Firms producing four-fifths of the domestic output of vitreous enamel bathroom fixtures had agreed to fix prices and to sell exclusively through jobbers. The Court was emphatic in its refusal to accept the reasonableness of the prices fixed as a defense.

The purpose of the law, said the Court, is to protect the public by maintaining competition. Every agreement to fix prices, however reasonable, is therefore condemned.

Doubts about this position were raised by the Court's decision in the *Appalachian Coals* case in 1933.[22] But in the *Socony-Vacuum* case[23] in 1940, the Court reaffirmed the rule of *Trenton Potteries.* This case involved an agreement, under which the major oil companies in ten midwestern states raised and maintained the price of gasoline by purchasing marginal supplies from independent refineries. The Court again rejected the defense that the price established was no more than fair. Said Justice Douglas:

Any combination which tampers with price structures is engaged in an unlawful activity. Even though the members of the price-fixing group were in no position to control the market, to the extent that they raised, lowered, or stabilized prices they would be directly interfering with the free play of market forces. The Act places such schemes beyond the pale. . . . Under the Sherman Act, a combination formed for the purpose and with the effect of raising, depressing, fixing, pegging, or stabilizing the price of a commodity in interstate or foreign commerce is illegal per se. . . . Whatever economic justification particular price-fixing agreements may be thought to have, the

---

[17] *U.S.* v. *Swift & Co.*, 196 U.S. 375 (1906).

[18] *U.S.* v. *Terminal R. R. Assn.*, 224 U.S. 383 (1912).

[19] *U.S.* v. *Standard Sanitary Mfg. Co.*, 226 U.S. 20 (1912).

[20] *U.S.* v. *Eastern States Retail Lumber Assn.*, 234 U.S. 600 (1914). In 1918, in a decision of limited significance, the Court refused to condemn a rule adopted by the Chicago Board of Trade requiring those buying and selling grain outside of trading hours to do so at the price at which the market closed. In 1923 it upheld limits on the output of hand-blown window glass, but only to meet the peculiar problems of a declining trade in a dying industry.

[21] *U.S.* v. *Trenton Potteries Co.*, 273 U.S. 392.

[22] *Appalachian Coals, Inc.* v. *U.S.*, 288 U.S. 344. In this case 137 companies, producing a tenth of the bituminous coal mined east of the Mississippi River and around two thirds of that mined in the Appalachian territory, had set up a joint agency to handle all their sales. The Court recognized that this arrangement established common prices for the firms involved, but it went on to find that the industry was seriously depressed, that competition in the sale of coal had been subject to various abuses, and that the selling agency did not control enough of the supply to enable it to fix the market price. On this basis, the arrangement was allowed to stand.

[23] *U.S.* v. *Socony-Vacuum Oil. Co.*, 310 U.S. 150.

law does not permit an inquiry into their reasonableness. They are banned because of their actual or potential threat to the central nervous system of the economy.[24]

The ruling of the Court could not have been more sweeping; any such agreement, even though affecting a minor portion of the market, was forbidden; any manipulation of prices, whatever its purpose, was against the law.

Biddings rings are one form of conspiracy. Many public purchases and construction projects are set by competitive bidding. Specifications are published, bids are invited and received by a fixed date, the sealed bids are then opened, and the lowest bidder wins. Yet often the bids are rigged beforehand, with the chosen winner low and the others high; the winners rotate among the group, and competition is avoided. Often the others randomize their bids, so as to avoid all evidence of fixing.

These rings too are illegal per se. The biggest one yet caught was the conspiracy among the makers of *heavy electrical equipment,* tried and convicted in 1960. For decades, collusion had been a way of life in seven markets, including transformers, switchgear and generators. Sometimes the collusion came unstuck, but often it put prices up by 20 percent or more and profits up by hundreds of millions of dollars.

The defendants had allocated contracts, selecting the low bidder by drawing names out of a hat, by rotating them in alphabetical order, and by making allotments according to a formula based upon the phases of the moon. The low bidder had then informed the others regarding his bid, and they had adjusted their bids accordingly. The conspirators had met under assumed names in luxury hotels in various cities, in motels, in mountain-top retreats, in cabins in the Canadian woods, and at a Milwaukee bar known as "Dirty Helen's." To maintain secrecy, they had used codes in referring to the companies and their executives, called one another from public telephones, sent letters to their homes rather than their offices, in plain envelopes without return addresses, and destroyed these communications when received.

Twenty-nine companies and 45 of their officers, including General Electric and Westinghouse and 16 of their officials, pleaded guilty or offered no defense in 20 criminal suits. Seven officers spent brief periods in jail. The total fines were only $1.9 million, but 1,900 treble damage suits were filed. One by Consolidated Edison of New York was for $100 million and another by Commonwealth Edison of Chicago was for $75 million. (Note: no private utility had earlier complained of overcharging or helped start the suit. And the damage claims were widely regarded in the trade as soft. Do you understand why these regulated utilities were not aggressive?)[25]

---

[24] Ibid., at pp. 221–26.

[25] See F. M. Westfield, "Regulation and Conspiracy," *American Economic Review,* 1965, pp. 424–43, and Chapter 11 for the reasons for this softness. A lively account of the conspiracy is in R. A. Smith, *Corporations in Crisis* (New York: Doubleday, 1963), pp. 113–66. For an excellent review of the process by which the damages were set, see Charles A. Bane, *The Electrical Equipment Conspiracies* (New York: Federal Legal Publications, 1973).

In the first suit tried, Philadelphia Electric proved damages of $9.6 million and was awarded $28.8 million. The companies then settled the rest privately. The payments ultimately totalled some $405 million, though a special tax ruling—defining these payments as the "normal" costs of doing business and therefore tax-deductible!—reduced the net impact to the firms. The structure of the industry was not changed; indeed Allis-Chalmers, a leading producer, withdrew in the late 1950s. Tacit collusion soon followed in the 1960s (see Section C3 below).

In 1969, 15 of the country's largest manufacturers of plumbing fixtures were found to have met in a hotel room in Chicago to set the prices of bathtubs, toilets, and sinks. And three of the leading pharmaceutical houses were found to have agreed upon the prices to be charged for antibiotic "wonder drugs." Agreements restricting competition in national markets were prosecuted in scores of other cases, ranging from eye-glasses to explosives and including such important products as soap, cheese, watches, electric lamps, typewriters, ball bearings, newsprint paper, stainless steel, fertilizers, and various chemicals.

The flow of cases, large and small, has probably risen in recent years. State antitrust activity against local price-fixing has recently grown to significant levels. The federal agencies also pursue a remarkable variety of small-scale price-fixers.[26] A number of major cases have also occurred in the 1970s. Some of them have altered or refined the law. Several leading cases follow.

Folding-Carton Case. A classic large case caught some 23 major makers of paperboard boxes, who had fixed prices during 1960–74.[27] The boxes were used for foods, drugs, household supplies and textiles. The firms held 70 percent of their market, and some 50 of their officials were also caught. The firms included nearly all the significant sellers, such as Container Corp., Federal Paper Board Co., American Can Corp., International Paper Co., and Weyerhauser Co. The criminal suit resulted in *nolo contendere* pleas by nearly all of the firms and officers. A trial resulted in convictions of the rest. The volume of business was very large, over $1 billion a year, and the Division described the price fixing as being "as egregious as any in the history of the Sherman Act."

The practices were familiar; price information was shared, and winning bids were rotated, while the rest put in deliberately high bids. Also the firms agreed to make uniform price increases to customers they shared. The Division used the case to announce new tough guidelines for price-fixing penalties;

---

[26] For example, during a recent six-month period (in 1975), active cases included the following products, among others: auto body repair, fire extinguishers, Korean wigs, ready mix cement, Hawaii package tours, paper labels, timber, Utah egg dealers, construction firms, gypsum, fertilizer, industrial laundries, bakeries in El Paso, military household storage, school dairy products, travel agents and liquid asphalt. Learn to use the weekly *Antitrust and Trade Regulation Reporter* (ATRR) for details on cases and for judging the whole flow of activity.

[27] See *U.S.* v. *Alton Box Board Co.,* 76 CR 199, N. D. Ill., and *ATRR,* March 22, 1977.

"It so happens, Gregory, that your Grandfather Sloan was de-
tained by an agency of our government over an honest misunder-
standing concerning certain antitrust matters! He was not "busted
by the Feds"!

Drawing by W. Miller; © *1971* The New Yorker Magazine, *Inc.*

an average 18-month jail term, and an average $50,000 fine, plus fines on
the company equalling 10 percent of sales in the product. Adjustments up
or down would depend on the individual circumstances.[28] But the judge in
Chicago refused, setting only light jail sentences on 15 of the 48 managers,
averaging only 10 days, with fines averaging $5,000. Most other judges have
also spared the rod. The new stiff felony penalties for price fixing remain a
plan, not a fact.

Of the two elements of enforcement—probability of getting caught and
severity of penalty—the former remains the main device for deterrence. The
present set of district judges appears to be inclined toward light penalties,
despite the stricter penalties in the 1975 law.

Penalties and Proof.   The recent raising of possible penalties stirred in
1977 a predictable response. Defendants claimed that the increased severity
should nullify the per se basis: the courts should consider how reasonable
the fixed prices were, plus any mitigating conditions. In 1977 a Detroit judge

---

[28] The Division can only recommend sentences. Its purpose is to deter future
violators. The guidelines allow for various factors in individual cases, as follows:
  Prison Terms.   The 18-month benchmark for recommended sentences is only half
the 3-year term permitted by the law. Parole will usually occur after only 6 months.
The recommended sentence will be longer when the conspiracy affects large volumes
of sales; the offender is a high official and/or "linchpin" of the conspiracy, or a

agreed in the *Nu-phonics* case, involving attempts to fix hearing-aid prices.[29] Though price fixing took place, the defendants claimed that it was ineffective and that prices remained "reasonable." If this idea spread, the tougher treatment of price fixing could neutralize itself, undone via district court judges' discretion. (Would this be a proper social approach, balancing greater severity by higher standards of proof?)

Who Can Sue? The Illinois Brick Case. Final consumers of bricks sued to recover damages caused by price fixing by concrete block producers. The Supreme Court held in June 1977 that these consumers were only "indirect" purchasers, who had bought from wholesalers.[30] Only wholesalers, the direct purchasers, could sue, Justice White explained for the 6–3 majority, because otherwise the price fixers would face "multiple liability," and there would be "whole new dimensions of complexity" in settling the correct damages. The issue had important economic content. If wholesalers could pass on the price increases, they would suffer no harm, but the harmed final consumers would be unable to recoup by filing antitrust claims. Unless wholesalers chose to sue—which would be unlikely if their "pass-on" were complete—the final consumers would have no recourse.

The majority opinion hinted that Congressional revision of the 1976 *parens patriae* clause could resolve the issue. Yet the point was more fundamental, and the *Illinois Brick* decision could undercut the force of damage claims in many price-fixing cases. (Should it? How would one divide the damages among the various levels of possible victims?) Conceivably the damages question could raise impossibly complex economic questions about who really suffered the damages. Often direct purchasers are the final purchasers. Yet often the wholesalers do pass on the price effects and will not sue on their own—or their customers'—behalf.

The Uranium Cartel. From 1972 to at least 1975, an international cartel met to raise the price of uranium. Its members were from Australia, Canada, Britain, France, South Africa and the United States. It had support from several governments, including Canada and France. While it existed, the price of uranium rose from $7 per pound to over $42 per pound, an astounding increase. The rise was in increments that paralleled the floor prices set by

---

previous violator; and the conspiracy lasted a long time. Cooperation with the prosecution will mitigate the sentence; remorse and civic virtue will not.

Fines for Individuals are only a "poor substitute" and a "second choice" to prison terms. The same factors as above will alter the $50,000 base fine.

Fines for Companies. These should be severe enough to take the profit out of price fixing and levy a penalty. At 10 percent of the firm's sales in the rigged products during the conspiracy, the standard fine should be big enough. If the profits were larger, or the firm is a repeat offender, the fine is to be raised. A lower fine is proper if the firm cooperated with the prosecutors or if the fine threatened its survival.

The guidelines are given in full in *ATRR*, March 1, 1977, pp. F1 to F6. Are these criteria sound? Are the levels of severity reasonable?

[29] *U.S.* v. *Nu-Phonics, Inc.*, District Court of Michigan, *Trade Regulation Reports*, no. 623, p. 61.

[30] The *Illinois Brick* case; see *The Wall Street Journal*, June 10, 1977.

the cartel. Some 29 defendants (17 U.S. and 12 foreign) were sued in 1976 by Westinghouse Corp., which had contracted to supply large volumes of nuclear fuel, thinking that the old prices would hold.[31] The cartel had met in the United States and elsewhere, and had adopted various tactics to rotate winning bids and raise the price. Meanwhile the Antitrust Division concluded that market forces—including the sharp run-up in oil prices after 1973—were the real cause of the price rise for uranium.

Yet "the club," as its members called it, held protracted negotiations to arrange for price rises. (The meetings were often inept and acrimonious.) These actions would draw a conviction in U.S. courts, but the Division regarded them as beyond reach. The Westinghouse case began trial in September 1977, with an uncertain outlook. It demonstrated that the strict policy against price fixing largely exempts foreign cartels, even if they have U.S. members (in this case, Gulf Oil Corp.) and probably effect prices in the United States.

Oil Industry Cases.   The sharp 1972–73 rise in oil prices provoked a rash of antitrust suits. Several states charged various groups of oil firms with criminal price fixing. In 1973 the Federal Trade Commission staff lodged a major action against eight of the largest oil firms.[32]

The state-level cases were of varying validity, and some were dismissed or dropped. In some cases, the firms claimed that they were simply complying with the federal government's voluntary allocation program after May 1973. Other cases were settled with small penalties.

Federal cases also had little impact. In 1977 five lesser oil firms and a trade association were convicted for price fixing in seven Middle Atlantic states during 1967–74. At the center was an information exchange system. The defendants held only about 20 percent of the market. The conviction (presently on appeal) reflects the long reach of price-fixing policy. The big FTC case charged eight classes of collusive actions at the refining level and three at the retail level. The accusations were vague, and the case relied on a large-scale search of company records. It soon bogged down, both for lack of FTC planning and from resistance by the firms. By 1977 the case appeared to be stalled. During 1978 the case was narrowed, but no early resolution of it seemed likely.

The whole set of oil industry cases showed how a "crisis" can stir antitrust litigation. The need to "do something" about oil prices both *(a)* enlarged the searches for violations and *(b)* made marginal and even dubious cases seem acceptable. Some genuine abuses were found and penalized, but certain cases clearly were not worth their costs.

Sugar.   In 1972–74 sugar prices rose from 10 to 75 cents per pound, and then quickly fell back (in 1977 they were 7 cents per pound). The rise

---

[31] Westinghouse had been sued by 27 utility firms to enforce the contracts to supply uranium.

[32] In the Matter of Exxon Corp., Texaco, Inc., Gulf Oil Corp., Mobil Oil Corp., Standard Oil Co. (Calif.), Standard Oil Co. (Ind.), Shell Oil Corp., and ARCO, Inc., FTC Docket No. 8934, September, 1973.

triggered suits against the leading sugar firms for price fixing, one involving the whole country and another covering the so-called Chicago-West and California-Arizona markets.[33] Price fixing had in fact occurred, accentuating the natural price rise. Most firms pleaded *nolo contendere* and were fined. Scores of damage suits followed and were still being processed in 1978. Their yield will probably be decided so as to hurt but not bankrupt the defendants.

The Professions. In the 1970s there has been growing antitrust pressure against rules preventing competition in certain professions—lawyers, doctors, stock-brokers, accountants, druggists, architects, engineers, and others—which had long been informally accepted. In these "learned professions," one did not even announce one's prices or skills, much less engage in competitive bidding to get contracts. Certain persuasions might be used privately, but the "ethical" codes usually ruled out the explicit information and efforts which effective competition requires. Working quietly, the Antitrust Division had by 1972 prodded the architects', accountants', and engineers' associations to drop rules against bidding.

The biggest single step was a private suit against price restrictions among lawyers. Since 1908, state bar associations have recommended, and the local bar associations have adopted, "suggested minimum fee schedules" for certain standard tasks.[34] Checking the deed for a house buyer is one such task, and the lawyer's fee is usually a fixed percent of the house's value, even though some searches take much more effort than others. In Fairfax County, Virginia, in 1971 the fee was 1 percent ($600 for a $60,000 house) regardless of the actual effort required. Lewis H. Goldfarb, a house buyer, sought out 37 lawyers, none of whom would budge from the fixed fee. His suit against these price fixers succeeded in the district court, lost on appeal, and then won by an 8–1 vote in the Supreme Court in June of 1975.[35] Though the fee schedule was only advisory, the Court noted that it was effective, and that the Virginia Bar Association equated price cutting with misconduct. Also, by state law, title searches could only be done by accredited lawyers, so the house buyer was a captive buyer. The market was not just intrastate, because some buyers' funds come from out of state. Goldfarb did not need to show that the fees were raised; that "the fee schedule fixed fees" was enough to clinch the offense. Virginia had formally delegated some powers to the state Bar Association, but these did not exempt the price fixing from the Sherman Act.

In early 1976 a new legal clinic of two young lawyers, Bates & O'Steen, in Phoenix, Arizona, faced suspension or censure for placing a small factual advertisement of fees for routine services in the Arizona *Republic*. Eventually

---

[33] See *The Wall Street Journal*, May 20, 1977; and the *New York Times*, August 2, 1975 and January 20, 1976.

[34] In 1908 the American Bar Association also banned advertising by lawyers. Down came such prominent signage as the 40-foot-long, 4-foot-high sign a Manhattan office building saying, in large letters, "Howe & Hummel's Law Offices."

[35] *Goldfarb* v. *Virginia State Bar*, Docket No. 74–70, June 16, 1975.

on appeal the Supreme Court, in June 1977, struck down the Arizona prohibitions on advertising.[36] Under Antitrust Division pressure, the American Bar Association moved in 1977 to permit certain factual advertising, amid stated fears of a "cataclysmic flood" of "lying, cheating and swindling" that would "mislead the layman." The flood will probably be only a trickle, but it will assist the new, younger outsider lawyers to get established and give many poor people better access to lawyers.

Fees for some routine services have fallen in some locales after the Goldfarb and Bates & O'Steen cases. By permitting some data about prices and services to be stated publicly, the Court has opened up a degree of new competition in certain small-scale "retail" areas of the law. For example, legal clinics now advertise to do divorces, wills, and house purchases at 20 to 40 percent of the previous prevailing fees. Yet the core of leading firms and major accounts are unlikely to be much affected.

Doctors' restrictions have also been challenged by the Division and the FTC, along the same lines as the actions toward lawyers. Cases against the fee schedules of physicians, radiologists, anesthesiologists, and ophthalmologists have either been filed recently or used to pressure changes.[37] Price advertising by druggists is also being legalized in many states. In the financial sector, the stock exchange's fixing of stock brokers' fees was ended by the Securities and Exchange Commission in May 1975, after seven years of pressure from the Antitrust Division and certain large-scale brokers. Fees dropped by from about 25 to 60 percent and the brokerage business became more efficient.[38] Rate competition spread to the major exchanges.

All of these changes have reduced prices and high returns to some specialists without affecting the quality or integrity of the "professions." Federal and state officials and many private plaintiffs have all helped in the trend. The effort is spreading down to the wide array of licensing barriers in the states (see Chapter 24).

Sports. Each major sport—baseball, football, basketball and hockey— has been run as a form of cartel among the owners of the teams.[39] Each has prevented bidding by the teams for each others' stock of players or for the yearly stream of new players. The owners also rigidly control the number and location of teams. These key controls are surrounded by others. The whole effect has been to keep players' prices below their competitive levels (no pun intended).

Baseball has been formally exempt from antitrust since 1922, for no clear

---

[36] *Bates & O'Steen* v. *Arizona State Bar,* S.C. 76–346 (1977). The American Medical Association and other professional groups had also filed briefs in the case.

[37] One study shows that in 1975 identical eyeglass lenses and frames sold for $18.90 in Texas, where advertising by opticians is permitted, but cost $32 across the Sabine River in Baton Rouge, Louisiana, where it is not permitted.

[38] By 1977 the commissions charged to banks were below the old rates by 43 to 66 percent. More details on this change in policy are given in Chapter 20.

[39] See, among others, Roger C. Noll, ed., *Government and the Sports Business* (Washington, D.C.: Brookings Institution, 1974).

reason. In the other sports, since 1965 various private suits, reinforced by new leagues and other pressures, have weakened the restrictions, and basketball pay in particular has bounced up. Even baseball has been forced by court decisions to permit bidding for "free agents" since 1975. Whether or not some players are now overpaid, there has been a reduction of price fixing in the major sports. Yet the main controls remain. (Should they? Do they protect the integrity and balance of the leagues? Of the sport as a whole?)

Since 1899 the agencies have won many hundreds of standard price—fixing cases, either by trial or by consent decree. There are usually at least 20 or 25 in process at any time, and—except in cases testing marginal issues—the agencies usually win. With good reason, company lawyers tell their executives *never* to discuss prices with competitors. (Why does it occur nonetheless?)

The per se rule is probably an efficient policy. Virtually all price fixing creates social costs and no social benefits. To evaluate the costs and benefits in all cases would be highly confusing and expensive. The cases possibly offering social benefits ("dying" industries?) are few and usually small. Any true social benefits can often be gained by other programs. In fact, many sectors have indeed been exempted or given other special treatments.

So the per se rule is clear and efficient, and its coverage of sectors may be roughly correct. It can be so strict partly *because* there are many exemptions!

In short, action continues against widespread price fixing. The federal and state effort is growing, and the penalties can now be more severe. Section 1 is being extended to professions, stock brokers and sports. Yet actual sentences are little stricter than before. And only "direct" purchasers may be able to sue price fixers.

B2. Repeal of Resale Price Maintenance

Since 1937 certain "fair trade" laws permitted manufacturers to set the *retail* prices for their products. The federal McGuire-Tydings Act authorized states to pass laws which would penalize any firm setting prices below the RPM levels. Some 45 states did enact such laws by 1952, and though enforcement varied, prices on many household items were kept well above competitive levels. This indirect price fixing stirred the rise of discount stores in the 1950s and 1960s, and fair trade did lose force after 1960. By 1975, only 21 states still had fair trade laws, and a federal repeal of RPM in 1975 met little resistance.

Prices did not tumble, though some moved down. Makers can still "suggest" prices, and there are many ways—subtle and direct—of "protecting" these prices from deepcutting. For example, Levi Strauss & Co. used a strenuous program to keep prices on its jeans at suggested levels in 25,000 retail outlets until 1977.[40] The program was attacked by the FTC in 1976 and

---

[40] The company forced dealers to advertise first-line quality products only at the suggested retail price. It monitored the dealers and cut off those who cut prices or even were merely suspected of doing so. *The Wall Street Journal,* May 10, 1976.

modified. In 1977 price cutting of Levi's jeans finally occurred, from $18 toward $12—but only because of RPM's repeal and the FTC's action.

Many producers still print retail prices on their products, ranging from books, bubble gum and clothes over to automobiles, stereo sets and household appliances. This is legal *if* there is no effort to enforce the "suggested" prices. No doubt many efforts to avert price cutting still occur, but they can no longer be enforced by law.

B3. Comparisons Abroad

Until 1955, no country remotely approached the United State's strict treatment of price fixing. Germany permitted cartels, and they could be enforced by the courts. Britain's cartel craze of the 1930s established price fixing in most industries. During 1948–55, Britain had a Monopolies and Restrictive Practices Commission, but it did little more than make studies.[41] Meanwhile, price fixing had spread even further. Then the Conservative government cracked down; the 1956 Restrictive Practices Act required all agreements among competitors to be reported and dropped, unless a positive case for them could persuade the new Restrictive Practices Court to approve them. By 1959 some 2,240 agreements had been filed (up to 2,875 by 1972), from a very wide range of industry and trade. They covered about 55 percent of all industry, a rise from 26 percent in 1935. Some 30 were defended in proceedings during the 1960s, but only 11 have been approved. In about 60 percent of the industries, competitive activity visibly increased, typically with 10 to 20 percent price drops. Although some collusion has merely shifted to informal methods, Britain has—at one stroke—erased many of the old patterns.[42] In 1965 it also banned resale price maintenance, well before the United States did. In 1968 information agreements were also restricted. The British treatments of price fixing are now close to the U.S. per se rule, even though the agencies and procedures differ.

A French law of 1953, modified in 1957, prohibits agreements, but it requires the public agency to prove the harmful effects on prices, costs or innovation.[43] An advisory commission in the Finance Ministry can study

---

[41] See D. C. Elliot and J. D. Gribbin, "The Abolition of Cartels, and Structural Change in the United Kingdom," a chapter in A. P. Jacquemin and H. W. de Jong, eds., *Welfare Aspects of Industrial Markets* (Leiden: Martinus Nijhoff, 1978). This excellent paper surveys the patterns of price fixing and the effects of removing them. See also Dennis Swann, Denis P. O'Brien, W. Peter J. Maunder and W. Stewart Howe, *Competition in British Industry* (London: Allen & Unwin, 1974).

[42] Of course, some agreements were not reported and others no doubt went underground after 1956.

Elliott and Gribbin, among others, believe that stopping price fixing induced many firms to merge, so as to continue the behavior legally within company boundaries. This would parallel the U.S. merger wave of 1897–1901, which partly responded to the then-new ban on price fixing.

[43] See Frederic Jenny and Andre Paul Weber, "French Antitrust Legislation: An Exercise in Futility?" *Antitrust Bulletin,* 20 (Fall 1975), 597–639.

and declare various restrictions illegal.[44] But it usually weighs costs and benefits, and so its policies have not been strict. Repeatedly, mitigating conditions are found. The proceedings are secret, and the conclusions have been lenient. Though the rules seem to prevent price fixing, they are scarcely applied.

In Germany too the burden of proof is on the agency to prove harm. The Common Market has strict formal rules, but enforcement has been slight. In 1974 Australia's weak case-by-case approach was replaced with a virtual per se method, patterned on U.S. law.[45] Its practical force is not yet established. Canada has had a series of cases before its Restrictive Practices Commission, but with little effect.[46] The policy is less strict than the United States and British treatments. Many other countries place little or no systematic limits on price fixing. Some have done the reverse. Japan, for example, has officially supported "depression cartels" to stabilize prices during recessions.[47]

Altogether, there is some spreading of anticollusion policies to other countries, but—curiously—only English-speaking nations seem to put much force into them.

C. TACIT COLLUSION

Informal coordination avoids explicit devices which lawyers can dig out and use for proof. It lies between Sections 1 and 2 of the Sherman Act. Ever since oligopoly became a hot topic in the 1930s, "joint maximizing" in a "shared monopoly" has been a special riddle for antitrust. Several cases during 1939–53 seemed to bring it under Section 1, but no penalties were imposed and action lapsed. Interest revived in the 1960s, followed by several cases in the 1970s. Yet the problem has scarcely been touched; tacit collusion is virtually immune.

C1. The Problem

Some oligopolists collude, some don't. The task is *(a)* to define the harmful cases in objective terms and *(b)* to design effective remedies for these cases.

Tacit collusion has been effective in many industries. High concentration and high entry barriers are the structural basis for it. Mature industries

---

[44] The Commission's members are: six from the civil service, six from the business community, and two economists. This gives little basis for expert, vigorous prosecution.

[45] See Warren Pengilley, "The Australian Trade Practices Act 1974," *Antitrust Bulletin,* 20 (Fall 1975), 589–96.

[46] See David P. Jones, "Trade Regulation," *Ottawa Law Review* 10 (1978), 167–213.

[47] On Japanese efforts, see Eleanor T. Hadley, *Antitrust in Japan* (Princeton: Princeton University Press, 1970), and Michiko Arigo, "Efforts to Revise the Japanese antimonopoly Act," *Antitrust Bulletin* 21 (Winter 1976) 703–26.

often evolve it, as firms learn to coexist and attune their planning to each other. Coordination then crystallizes, but tacitly, in "parallel pricing." These three criteria—concentration, barriers, maturity—plus parallel pricing behavior help identify "shared monopolies" for treatment. But they are not infallible criteria. Some tight oligopolies are highly competitive, at least on occasion. Even for collusive ones hard proof is lacking, and the firms assert they are just responding quickly to each others' moves. The burden of *proof* is against the agency; so is *time,* for the cases are easy to postpone and prolong.

Remedy is even more difficult to arrange. Usually no oligopolist has over 40 percent of the market, and so dividing the firms seems implausible. Economies of scale will be claimed by the firms and must be disproved (if possible). Several firms, not just one dominant firm, must be treated. Against this complexity, the possible gains may seem small and uncertain, compared to dominant-firm cases.

C2. Early Cases

During 1939 to 1953, the economists' new concern over oligopoly was quickly applied by the Supreme Court. Parallel behavior could now be defined and convicted as a Section 1 conspiracy.

In the *Interstate Circuit* case in 1939 the operator of a chain of movie houses in Texas had entered into separate contracts with eight distributors of films, agreeing to show their pictures for an admission charge of 40 cents, on condition they not be rented later to be shown for less than 25 cents or run on a double bill. There was no evidence that the distributors had consulted one another or agreed among themselves. But such evidence, said the Court, "was not a prerequisite to an unlawful conspiracy. It was enough that, knowing that concerted action was contemplated and invited, the distributors gave their adherence to the scheme and participated in it. . . . Acceptance by competitors, without previous agreement, is sufficient to establish an unlawful conspiracy under the Sherman Act." [48] A similar position was taken in the *Masonite* case in 1942. Here, a manufacturer of hardboard had signed an agency agreement with each of his competitors, authorizing them to distribute his product and fixing the prices at which they could sell. And here, again, there was no evidence of agreement among the other companies. But the Court found the plan to be illegal, holding that each of them must have been "aware of the fact that its contract was not an isolated transaction but a part of a larger arrangement."[49]

In these cases there was evidence that plans had been proposed by Interstate and Masonite; the inference of conspiracy among the other companies was drawn from their adherence to these plans. In the second *American Tobacco* case, a criminal suit against the three leading producers of cigarettes, decided

---

[48] *Interstate Circuit Co.* v. *U.S.*, 306 U.S. 208, 226–27.

[49] *U.S.* v. *Masonite Corp.*, 316 U.S. 265, 275.

in 1946, no such proposal was in evidence. Statistics of purchases, sales, and prices were relied upon for proof. In buying tobacco, it was shown, these companies had purchased fixed shares of the supply, each of them paying the same price on the same day. In selling cigarettes, they had adopted identical price lists, changing their prices simultaneously. In other practices, too, there was striking uniformity. "There was not a whit of evidence that a common plan had even been contemplated or proposed. The government's evidence was admittedly wholly circumstantial."[50] But the reliance on inferential evidence did not deter the Court. Conspiracy, it said, "may be found in a course of dealings or other circumstances as well as in an exchange of words."[51] The companies were found to be in violation of the law. The decision, says Nicholls, "brought wholly tacit, nonaggressive oligopoly wholly within the reach of the conspiracy provisions of the Sherman Act."[52]

Conspiracy was also found by the Supreme Court in cases where firms had agreed to identical provisions in the licenses granted them by the owner of a patent[53] and in cases involving delivered pricing systems (discussed shortly). The doctrine was carried furthest in the case of *Milgram* v. *Loew's* in 1950. Here, eight distributors of motion pictures had been sued by a drive-in movie for refusing to supply it with first-run films. A district court found the distributors guilty of conspiracy, holding that their common refusal to supply first runs could not have been due to independent business judgment but was sufficient, in itself, to establish violation of the law. A meeting of minds need not be proven; identity of behavior was all that was required.[54]

But there was a fatal flaw: conviction was not followed by basic remedies. Much of the structure and habits remained. And after 1952 the boldness in inferring conspiracy disappeared both from the FTC and the Court. In decisions involving investment banking (1953), movie distribution (1954), and meat-packing firms (1954), the Court firmly reversed itself and abandoned parallelism—and the broad use of "inferential" evidence—in Section 1 cases.[55]

C3. Recent Issues

The issue persisted. In 1959 Kaysen and Turner urged amending the Sherman Act so that high concentration would be a "rebuttable presumption"

---

[50] William H. Nicholls, "The Tobacco Case of 1946," *American Economic Review* 39, 3 (1949), 284–96, esp. p. 285.

[51] *American Tobacco Co.* v. *U.S.*, 328 U.S. 781, 810.

[52] Nicholls, "The Tobacco Case," p. 285.

[53] *U.S.* v. *Line Material Co.*, 333 U.S. 282 (1948); *U.S.* v. *Gypsum Co.*, 333 U.S. 364 (1949).

[54] *Milgram* v. *Loew's, Inc.*, 94 F. Supp. 416.

[55] *U.S.* v. *Morgan,* Civil No. 43–757, District Court of the U.S., Southern District of New York, October 14, 1953. *U.S.* v. *Armour & Co.,* Civil 48-C-1351, discontinued March, 1954. *Fanchon & Marco* v. *Paramount Pictures,* 100 F. Supp. 84, certiorari denied, 345 U.S. 964. *Theater Enterprises, Inc.* v. *Paramount Film Distributing Corp.,* 346 U.S. 537, 540.

that a shared monopoly exists and violates Section 2.[56] Turner himself was head of the Antitrust Division during 1965–68 but failed to bring any shared-monopoly actions (recall Chapter 5). The "Neal Report" in 1968 reiterated Kaysen and Turner's proposal, but to no effect. The Hart bill of 1972 would create a separate commission to apply the Kaysen and Turner criterion of a rebuttable presumption. About every three years, the agencies announce new investigations into parallel pricing by various industries, usually including steel, automobiles or oil. These proposals and studies have made little difference.

In 1972 the FTC started an experimental "shared-monopoly" case against the leading cereals firms (recall Chapter 5). It dealt mainly with parallel advertising and product policies, rather than with pricing. The only other recent action is the *General Electric-Westinghouse* consent decree of 1976. It stopped a system of tacit collusion which those two leading firms had started right after the great electrical equipment price conspiracies were broken in 1960 (recall Section B above). There was strong price competition in the turbine-generator market from 1960 to 1963. Then in May 1963 General Electric announced a new system of pricing with four parts. *(a)* It greatly simplified the formulas for setting prices and published its method in detail. *(b)* It added a simple multiplier (.76, to be precise) for converting book prices to actual bids. *(c)* A "price protection" clause was to be put in all sales contracts. If GE lowered price for any customer, it was bound to extend the discount—retroactively—to all sales during the preceding six months. This self-penalty assured Westinghouse that GE would not give selective discounts. *(d)* All orders and price offers were to be published, so Westinghouse would not fear secret price cuts.

This ingenious plan surrendered all of the secret methods and strategies of price competition which make oligopoly competition work. Westinghouse immediately copied GE's plan and even the precise numbers in it. Each firm now could coordinate confidently with the other. From 1964 the firms used the same multiplier applied to identical book price levels. There was no price cutting, no flexibility.

The system went beyond simple parallel pricing but stopped a little short of explicit price fixing. GE intended the system to make collusion work, as shown by internal GE documents. Yet the Division ignored it, until an electric utility—American Electric Power—sued both firms in 1971. The Division then developed a strong case, but it was later scared off from filing the suit by Westinghouse's uranium price troubles in 1975–77. It settled for only a consent decree in December 1976.[57] The pricing scheme was withdrawn,

---

[56] Carl Kaysen and Donald F. Turner, *Antitrust Policy* (Cambridge: Harvard University Press, 1959); see also Turner's rethinking of the problem in "The Scope of Antitrust and Other Regulatory Policies," *Harvard Law Review* 82 (1969), 1207–44.

[57] *U.S.* v. *General Electric Co. and Westinghouse Electric Corp.*, D.C. for Eastern District of Penna., Civil No. 28228, December 9, 1976. In 1977 American Electric Power also settled its case, to return to a normal customer relationship with the two suppliers.

but there were no penalties or damages for over eight years of tacit price fixing, nor was the underlying cause—the duopoly structure—changed.

Most tacit collusion has no such complex scheme, plus documentary proof of the intent to collude. Therefore most parallel pricing is unaffected by this interesting case. As of 1978, tacit collusion remains virtually exempt from policy treatment.

C4. Delivered Pricing

Many goods are sold at delivered prices: the nominal factory price plus a shipping markup equals the actual delivered price. The resulting configuration of prices is like a contour map. Competition may obviously be reduced by this, if *(a)* the buyer has no option to buy at the factory instead and ship it himself, and *(b)* several or all firms adopt the same set of delivered prices. Moreover, the location of industry may be distorted.

Such schemes and effects were important from the 1880s to 1949, in the steel, cement, and several other industries. Since 1948 the practice has been diluted and now is of marginal concern. Yet some of its earlier effects live on, and the practice deserves a brief analysis.

Analysis. Delivered pricing matters when output is *(a) uniform* (for example, steel, cement, corn oil), *(b) bulky,* so that transport costs are large, and *(c) centralized* around special inputs (for example, ores, farm products). Consider the simplest system, say a steel industry whose dominant firm is located at Pittsburgh. That firm (call it U.S. Steel) sets prices at $50 per ton at Pittsburgh plus freight (as shown in Figure 7–3) and publishes a detailed price book listing delivered prices for every city in the country. This is a "Pittsburgh-plus" system, with Pittsburgh as the "basing point." All other producers reprint the price-book as *their* price lists. Result: buyers at each location face identical prices. A seller *(a)* whose full cost is below

FIGURE 7–3
Price Contours with a Single Basing Point

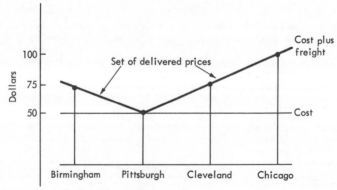

$50, or *(b)* who has idle capacity, or *(c)* who wishes to break in and get new clientele, does not cut price to do so. *First effect:* rigid, identical delivered-pricing schemes prevent competition. The identical prices reflect cooperation, not the free play of market forces.[58] This causes the usual losses in efficiency and equity.

Location of industry is soon affected in two ways. New steel *makers* may locate away from Pittsburgh, selling at "Pittsburgh-plus" and pocketing the plus as "phantom freight." But they may be punished by being made (perhaps temporarily) a basing point themselves. If so, they will choose to locate at Pittsburgh instead. The net effect may go either way, toward overcentralizing or spreading the industry out thinner than the underlying costs prescribe. Only by a fluke will location happen to be efficient. Meanwhile, steel *users* are induced to locate more closely around Pittsburgh than is efficient. *Second effect:* the location of producers and users may be strongly distorted.

Also, buyers have no incentive to minimize transport costs by buying from a nearby producer. *Third effect:* transport resources are wasted.

There may develop several basing points. Then the locational and transport-wasting effects will be less severe, but they will exist. Even if every plant is a basing point, new steel-plant choices may be affected. And even with universal basing points, the collusive role remains.

Actual Systems and Treatments. The practice began in steel in 1880, grew slowly until 1890, and by 1900 embraced nearly every steel firm and product. In 1901 the United States Steel Corporation was organized, and from then on the level of prices was effectively controlled, first through open agreements, then through the Gary dinners, and finally through price leadership. From 1901 to 1903 most steel was sold on a zone price basis. But thereafter all products but rails were priced at Pittsburgh-plus levels.[59]

---

[58] The degree of identity in prices was often astonishing. During the 1930s, when the purchasing agent for the Fort Peck Dam opened ten sealed bids for reinforcing bars, each of them was for $253,633.80. When the Navy Department opened 59 bids for steel pipe, each of them was for $6,001.83. And when the Army Engineers opened 11 bids for cement at Tucumcari, New Mexico, each of them was for $3.286854 a barrel, identity being carried to the sixth decimal place. Again in 1947, when the Illinois Department of Highways asked for bids on cement to be delivered in each of the 102 counties in the state, those submitted by eight companies were identical for each of the 102 deliveries.

On the anticompetitive effects of delivered pricing, see F. A. Fetter, *The Masquerade of Monopoly* (New York: Harcourt, Brace & Co., 1931); "Exit Basing Point Pricing," *American Economic Review* 38 (1948), 815; and Fritz Machlup, *The Basing Point System* (Philadelphia: Blakiston Co., 1949).

Arguments on behalf of delivered pricing include J. M. Clark, "The Law and Economics of Basing Points," *American Economic Review* 39 (1949), 430; and Arthur Smithies, "Aspects of the Basing Point Problem," *American Economic Review* 32 (1942), 705.

[59] The Antitrust Division had filed its Section 2 suit against U.S. Steel in 1910. The firm was acquitted in 1920 (recall Chapter 7). Strangely, the case and pleadings ignored the basing-point system, the Division apparently being unaware of its anticompetitive role. Had that factor been used and tipped the 4–3 vote in 1920, the direction of antitrust and the shape of industry could have been altered.

The system gradually evolved toward multiple basing points after 1920, but by 1946 it still was a device for collusive pricing. The cement industry followed a similar pattern during 1902–1946, under a trade association. After trying since 1924, the FTC finally won Supreme Court decisions in 1948–49 making rigid basing-point pricing illegal.[60]

In *Corn Products,* the Court held collective, systematic discrimination to injure competition.[61] In *Cement Institute,* the Court repeated the holding.[62] And in *Triangle Conduit and Cable,* it broadened the prohibition; basing points as such were condemned, not just the associated acts of agreement.[63] After a congressional exemption of basing-point systems was vetoed by President Truman in 1950, the practice faded. The court victories scarcely led events; trucking was already destroying the rail-freight basis of the systems.

Delivered pricing has persisted in some industries, usually with multiple basing points. An exceptionally strong recent instance is plywood, which before 1963 was produced in the Northwest but then expanded to the South. More than 20 plywood firms kept prices at the old levels of Northwest-plus-freight, as if the southern mills were all in Portland, Oregon! Buyers near the South therefore paid large amounts of "phantom freight" on $600 million per year of southern plywood. Purchasers were prohibited from buying directly from the mill and using their own trucks. The system was rigid, universal and effective.

The effect has lasted from 1963 to the present, despite a tentative FTC ruling against it in 1976. Large private damage suits, filed during 1972–76, have assured that the plywood firms would defend their pricing system fiercely.

D. CONNECTIONS AMONG FIRMS

There is often a "soft" quasi-structure of links among competitors. It can take many forms, and the effects on competition are often debatable. Policy toward them is often indecisive, permitting some versions but leaving others in doubt. Precedents are often unclear. Four main types are included in this section.

D1. Interest Groupings and "Interlocks"

Interest groupings exist quietly in many forms. Large blocks of shares in competing firms are owned by a family group, or a bank trust department, an investment bank, an insurance firm, or pension fund. Similarly, accounting firms, security underwriters, law firms, engineering firms, and others deal intimately with competing firms. This tissue of interests is extensive and

---

[60] Other efforts had been made against basing-point pricing in malt, milk cans, crepe paper, rigid steel conduits and bottle caps, among others.

[61] *Corn Products Refining Co.* v. *FTC,* 324 U.S. 726; *FTC* v. *A. E. Staley Manufacturing Co.,* 324 U.S. 746.

[62] *FTC* v. *Cement Institute,* 333 U.S. 683 (1948).

[63] *Triangle Conduit and Cable Co. FTC,* 168 F. 2d 157 (1949).

intricate in many major industries.[64] It softens independence and inculcates a degree of uniformity.

How deeply this abridges competition nobody can say precisely.[65] Though there is increasing evidence that it influences some industries, it is well short of being a super-web of controls. It is, in any case, beyond the current reach of antitrust policy, or indeed of any policy control now existing. Instead, antitrust deals with the more superficial versions, such as directorates.

Interlocking directorates were common before the Clayton Act, Section 8, made them illegal in 1914. Direct interlocks—one person on the boards of two competing firms—have now mostly disappeared, but marginal cases still occur. Thus in 1968 the Antitrust Division—after much delay and with no penalties—required direct interlocks to be ended between leading automobile firms and oil companies, who compete in selling batteries and other supplies to drivers. There are also direct interlocks between firms and potential entrants. And there are many "indirect interlocks," where two officers of a bank, law firm, and so forth, sit on boards of competing firms. There are other twilight zones, too, where "interlocked" firms are only partly in competition. If two markets converge, the agencies may need to force some board members to resign.

But the degree of overlap is often arguable. Recent FTC cases involved these pairings: commercial banks and savings and loan associations; oil and uranium mining; natural gas and gas pipelines. The division sued in 1970 to stop indirect interlocks by the Cleveland Trust Co., whose officers sit on the boards of 29 machine-tool firms. In 1975 a consent order stopped further such connections, but left the existing ones intact.

In short, the classic interlocks have mostly been gone for several decades. But many quasi-overlaps remain, scarcely touched by policy.[66]

D2. Joint Ventures

A *joint venture* is created by two or more firms, usually for some stated technical purpose (such as to mine ores, do research, or make sales in new foreign markets). When set up by competing firms, they obviously make for common interests and may reduce competition in all the firms' activities. The defense is usually that, instead, they make possible large benefits while

---

[64] U.S. House Subcommittee on Antitrust, *Interlocks in Corporate Management* (Washington, D.C.: U.S. Government Printing Office, 1965); and U.S. House Subcommittee on Domestic Finance, *Commercial Banks and Their Trust Activities* (Washington, D.C.: U.S. Government Printing Office, 1968), 2 volumes.

[65] Only the Securities and Exchange Commission requires some reporting of certain stockholder conditions (holdings above 10 percent). This does not touch the main substance of the problem.

[66] Abroad, the connections are commonly at least as close and even more fully accepted. Family and bank holdings often link firms directly, giving a degree of quasi-merger. Boardroom connections are often close. And in some cases, cooperation and joint control are encouraged by the government. In Britain, Canada, and Australia, direct connections are resisted as a restrictive practice. But indirect connections are untouched.

leaving competition unabated. As in other antitrust issues, one compares the real benefits and costs. The benefits are often quite accessible without the joint venture.

The most pervasive joint ventures are in metal ores, especially steel and copper, where ore supply is vital to competitive strategy. The steel industry is actually three tight interest groups, not a medium-tight oligopoly, because control over ores is tightly shared.[67] Many of the largest copper deposits in the world have been owned and mined jointly by the largest copper firms. They are claimed to be so large that joint financing is needed to raise enough capital. Yet the companies are not so small, nor capital markets so imperfect, that they could not go it alone in most cases.

The leading investment bankers have traditionally used "syndicates" (a form of joint venture) as a cooperative device for joining the underwriting of stocks and bonds. A major antitrust attack on the practice was rejected in 1953; the judge regarded the practice as restrictive but reasonably so, since it was effective in getting securities to the market in an "orderly manner."[68]

In practice, joint ventures are mainly done by large firms, not small ones. Therefore the possible anticompetitive effect is large, while the technical need for the combined ownership is less, perhaps minimal. That many joint ventures do have social costs has been shown by recent research.[69] Generally, the social cost is greater when *(a)* the parent firms have a high share of the market, *(b)* the joint venture is in a highly concentrated market, *(c)* the joint venture's purpose can be met by the firms separately, and *(d)* there are additional restrictions attached to the joint venture.

U.S. policies are roughly in the direction of these economic criteria, but enforcement is limited.[70] Most cases have invoked the Sherman Act, Section 1, against conspiracy. Horizontal joint ventures have been found illegal whenever there is cartel behavior or boycotts and exclusion of competitors. If the result is price fixing—either inherent in the joint venture, or ancillary to it—the joint venture is illegal. Remedy then depends on the market share of the parents of the joint venture. If the shares are large, the joint venture will be dissolved.[71] If the shares are small, the joint venture can continue, *if* it stops the price fixing.[72]

---

[67] Daniel R. Fusfeld, "Joint Subsidiaries in the Iron and Steel Industry," *American Economic Review,* May 1958, pp. 578–87.

[68] The case was *U.S.* v. *Morgan,* 118 F. Supp. 621 (S. D. N. Y. 1953).

[69] See Jeffrey Pfeffer and Philip Nowak, "Patterns of Joint Venture Activity: Implications for Antitrust Policy," *Antitrust Bulletin* 21 (Summer 1976), 315–39.

[70] See Joseph F. Bradley, "The Legal Status of Joint Ventures under the Antitrust Laws: A Summary Assessment," *Antitrust Bulletin* 21 (Fall 1976), 453–84.

[71] Landmark cases in which the joint venture was dissolved include *Lee Line Steamer* v. *Memphis H & R Packet Co.,* 277 F. 5 (6th Circuit, 1922); *U.S.* v. *Imperial Chemical Industries,* 100 F. Supp. 504 (S. D. N. Y., 1951); *U.S.* v. *Paramount Pictures,* 334 U.S. 131 (1948); and *Citizens Publishing Co.* v. *U.S.,* 394 U.S. 131 (1969).

[72] Recent cases of this sort include *U.S.* v. *Sealy, Inc.,* 388 U.S. 350 (1967), and *U.S.* v. *Topco Associates,* 405 U.S. 596 (1972).

Around this core of clear policy are large twilight zones. *(a)* A joint venture formed to enter a new market will be illegal *if* the two parents themselves had been on the verge of entering.[73] Of course, such potential entry is difficult to judge (recall Chapter 6), and so few cases are brought. *(b)* Any explicit geographic limits on competition among the parents or their joint venture will be illegal. But only if their market shares are large will the joint venture be dissolved. *(c)* If the joint venture clearly serves a useful purpose, it will be permitted real latitude in restrictions and behavior. *(d)* If a joint venture controls a natural monopoly, it can stand as long as it offers fair access to all comers.[74] *(e)* Certain vertical joint ventures are proscribed. Until 1948, the main movie makers jointly held many theaters, as part of a massive set of restrictions on movie bookings.[75] The Court dissolved them because they reduced competition among the parents and excluded other theaters from fair access to films. Only if the parents have a small share will their vertical joint venture survive scrutiny.[76] *(f)* Virtually all conglomerate joint ventures—between unrelated firms—are outside any policy constraint.

Most joint ventures come under a balancing (rule of reason) approach, with the burden of proof set against the public agencies. The orbit of firm policy is narrow, and the case activity has been sparse. Most cases have failed to look at the whole structure of the market and the parents' other joint ventures. In oil, chemicals and steel, for example, this larger pattern of linkage and dominance affects the role of the individual joint ventures.

D3. Patent Pooling

Patents are a large subject, which is treated in Chapter 24. Here we consider one corner of the patent problem: how patents may collectively be used so as to reduce competition.

Patents are frequently pooled among firms in an industry. Many arrangements (open access; cross-licensing, with or without royalties; patents on certain products only; older patents only; and so forth) have been used. All of them centralize the control of technology.

Pooling may encourage competition, if it is open and free (as in automobiles

---

[73] Such potential entry situations are exceedingly difficult to evaluate, since nobody can prove how "potential" the entry was. Leading recent cases *U.S.* v. *Marine Bancorporation,* 418 U.S. 602 (1974); *U.S.* v. *Penn-Olin Chemical Corp.,* 378 U.S. 158 (1964); and *U.S.* v. *Falstaff Brewing Corp.,* 410 U.S. 526 (1973). Often the parent firms use the joint venture as a way of entering the market and dividing it; see *U.S.* v. *National Lead,* 63 F. Supp. 513 (S. D. N. Y., 1945), modified and affirmed 332 U.S. 319 (1947); *U.S.* v. *Minnesota Mining and Manufacturing Co.,* 92 F. Supp. 947 (D. Mass., 1950); and *Timken Roller Bearing Co.* v. *U.S.,* 341 U.S. 593 (1951).

[74] The classic case of such bottleneck joint ventures is *U.S.* v. *Terminal Railroad Association,* 224 U.S. 383 (1912). Such situations are rare in practice.

[75] *U.S.* v. *Paramount Pictures,* 334 U.S. 131 (1948).

[76] That was the case in the "Screen Gems" case; *U.S.* v. *Columbia Pictures,* 189 F. Supp. 153 (S. D. N. Y., 1960).

since 1915). But if it restricts access, it may increase monopoly. The terms may be limited, with high royalty rates, and the pool may mobilize large resources in prosecuting patent suits. Policy toward pooling evolved since 1910 to prohibit flagrant restrictions. Yet large areas remain largely free of control.

The leading case on patent pooling, the *Standard Sanitary* case, was decided in 1912.[77] Various patents covering the production of enameled iron bathtubs and other sanitary wares had been pooled with a trade association. Included in licenses issued to firms producing 85 percent of the output of such wares were provisions restricting output, fixing prices and discounts, and controlling channels of trade. These restrictions were held to violate the Sherman Act.

In the *Standard Oil of Indiana* case[78] in 1931, however, a pool controlling patents covering methods of cracking gasoline was allowed to stand. But here the Court was impressed by the fact that many other cracking processes remained outside the pool, that licensees under the pooling arrangement did little more than half of the cracking of gasoline, and that cracking provided only a fourth of the total supply. The pool, thus faced with competition, was found to be powerless to fix prices and was therefore held to be within the law.

In the *Hartford-Empire* case[79] decided in 1945, Hartford had employed the patents in its pool to dominate completely the glass container industry, curtailing output, dividing markets, and fixing prices through restrictive licences; the Court found in Hartford's behavior, as a whole, convincing evidence of unlawful conspiracy.

So, too, with cross-licensing. In the *Line Material* case in 1948, the court was emphatic in its condemnation of a plan that eliminated competition through cross-licensing.[80] Here, each of two small companies producing patented fuse cutouts had licensed the other and fixed the prices it might charge. Their agreement to do so was held to be illegal per se. In the *Besser* case in 1952, the Court held an agreement between two patent holders to refuse licenses to others to be a boycott and, as such, to be illegal per se.[81] And in the *Singer* case in 1963, where Singer had exchanged licenses with Swiss and Italian manufacturers of zigzag sewing machines and then brought infringement suits against importers of Japanese machines, the Court found the three concerns to be conspiring in restraint of trade.[82]

Patent pooling was an issue in another suit which the government brought against the General Electric Company. The basic patents on the electric lamp had expired, and GE had tried to keep its control of the industry by

---

[77] *Standard Sanitary Mfg. Co.* v. *U.S.*, 226 U.S. 20.
[78] *Standard Oil Co. (Indiana)* v. *U.S.*, 283 U.S. 163.
[79] Hartford-Empire Co. v. *U.S.*, 323 U.S. 386.
[80] *U.S.* v. *Line Material Co.*, 333 U.S. 287.
[81] *Besser Mfg. Co.* v. *U.S.*, 343 U.S. 444.
[82] *U.S.* v. *Singer Mfg. Co.*, 374 U.S. 174.

employing later patents on such parts of the lamp as the filament and the frosting on the bulb. It had formed a patent pool with Westinghouse and granted licenses to four other producers, controlling the output and the prices of all six companies. These arrangements were held in 1949 to violate both sections of the Sherman Act. General Electric, said the Court, had conspired with its licensees and had "unlawfully monopolized the incandescent electric lamp industry in the United States."[83]

Among the most important cases involving the operation of a patent pool is that of the Radio Corporation of America. Here, in a civil suit brought in 1954 and a criminal suit brought in 1958, the government charged that RCA had entered into agreements with AT&T, GE, and Westinghouse and with firms in other countries that gave it the exclusive right to grant licenses under more than 10,000 radio-purpose patents in the United States. As a result, other manufacturers of electronic equipment were made to depend upon RCA. In granting licenses, moreover, the company refused to license patents individually, but insisted on licensing all of the patents in a packaged group. RCA pleaded *nolo contendere* in the government's criminal case, paying a fine of $100,000, and accepted a consent decree in the civil suit. Under the terms of this decree, the company agreed to license its existing radio and TV patents royalty-free, to license its new patents at reasonable royalties, and to permit its licensees to obtain patents individually instead of requiring package deals.[84]

D4. Trade Associations

Every trade has its association. Some are solid and powerful, with large budgets, secretariats and influence (for example, druggists, aerospace), while others are just a name, an officer, a secretary and a mailing list. There are thousands of them, promoting their members' interests by economic and political means. Their activities are diverse, some of them neutral to competition, while others reduce it. In the 1930s and earlier, trade associations commonly had negative effects in the United States. And elsewhere, especially in Britain, trade associations were the nucleus for tight new cartels in hundreds of industries.

Recently, trade associations have probably faded in economic importance, thanks partly to antitrust. And their effects tend to be relatively marginal and to occur in lesser industries. Yet they still have a variety of effects, particularly in the more local trades. We consider several of their technical activities.

Typical association activities include industrial research, market surveys, the development of new uses for products, the operation of employment bureaus, collective bargaining with organized labor, mutual insurance, com-

---

[83] *U.S.* v. *General Electric Co.*, 82 F. Supp. 753.
[84] *U.S.* v. *Radio Corp. of America*, 1958 Trade Cases, Par. 69, 164.

mercial arbitration, the publication of trade journals, joint advertising and publicity, and joint representation before legislative and administration agencies. These may serve a trade without disservice to its customers. But they also include the establishment of common cost accounting procedures, the operation of price reporting plans, the collection and dissemination of statistics, the standardization of products and terms of sale, the provision of credit information, the interchange of patent rights, the joint purchasing of supplies, and the promulgation of codes of business ethics. Each of these may operate to restrain competition in quality, service, price, or terms of sale.

Cost accounting may just standardize reports. But it often slips over into describing uniform mark-ups and circulating average-cost data, or even urging members to set prices at the average.

Price-reporting systems are operated by perhaps 15 percent of associations. Through these systems, association members make available to one another, and sometimes to outsiders, information concerning the prices at which products have been, are being, or are to be sold. Such systems, by increasing the amount of knowledge available to traders, might lessen the imperfection of markets and enhance competition.

Price reporting may improve market functioning when the market *(a)* has low concentration and entry barriers, *(b)* homogeneous output, *(c)* elastic demand and *(d)* stable demand. This describes a textbook competitive market. In others, price reporting is likely to support agreement and quicken pressure against price cutters. To help competition, a reporting plan will need to *(a)* be fully available to all sellers *and* buyers, *(b)* not identify traders, *(c)* cover only past sales, not present or planned ones, *(d)* avoid circulating average prices (focal points for new price agreements), and *(e)* be free of any controls or penalties on sellers.

If any one of these conditions—both of industry and plan—are not met, a reporting system is likely to reduce competition.

Other ambiguous activities may also be carried to the point where they restrain competition. Circulating statistics on production, inventories, unfilled orders, idle capacity, sales, and shipments may serve merely to inform traders concerning the state of the market; it may also be used to facilitate a scheme for curtailment of output and sharing of sales. Standardizing products may contribute to convenience and lessen waste; it may also lessen competition in quality and restrict the consumer's range of choice. Standardizing terms of sale may benefit purchasers by saving time, preventing misunderstandings, and affording a common basis for price comparisons; it may also promote collusion by preventing indirect departures from an established price. Providing information on credit risks may increase the safety with which credit may be granted; reporting on customers may also be employed as a means of boycotting those who deal with outsiders or fail to observe a recommended price.

Joint purchasing may increase efficiency in buying; it may be used to establish prices that are unfair to suppliers and to exact concessions that are unfair to competitors. The promulgation of a code of ethics is avowedly designed to raise standards of conduct among the members of a trade, but such codes frequently contain provisions denouncing practices that are found to be offensive merely because they are competitive. Where an association lacks the power of enforcement, these prohibitions are merely persuasive. But where some measure of coercion is at hand, they may be strong.

Cooperation or Conspiracy?   As Adam Smith remarked in 1776: "People of the same trade seldom meet together, even for merriment and diversion, but the conversation ends in a conspiracy against the public or in some contrivance to raise prices."[85] Does this observation apply to the modern trade association? No one knows. There are thousands of trade association offices in the United States. In each of them a staff is working, presumably five days in every week and throughout the year, to administer activities in which competitors do not compete. Upon occasion the Federal Trade Commission or the Department of Justice makes an investigation and certain practices of an association are proscribed by the commission or the courts. But such sporadic action cannot be expected to disclose each of the cases in which competition is restrained.

The lines of policy have come to fit the economic criteria reasonably well. Four seminal cases in the 1920s involved lumber, linseed oil, maple flooring, and cement.[86] The Court held against pervasive reporting schemes which violated the first four conditions just above: access, anonymity, past sales, and no averages. Where an anticompetitive tendency could be seen, the system was rejected. In 1936 an even vaster scheme in the sugar industry was also enjoined from violating the five conditions.[87]

And in 1969 the treatment was confirmed in the major *Container Corp.* case.[88] Cardboard box sellers in one region had a system allowing each seller to call up any other seller and demand the price of that seller's most recent sale. This system was struck down: *(a)* because it would "chill" competition by exposing price cutting more quickly, and *(b)* because buyers did not have equal access to the prices.

In 1975 four leading gypsum companies were convicted of price fixing during 1960–73. They had a "verification" system; each company could call to find out what price the other firm was *currently* offering. This advance notice was needed, the firms said, to protect them from unwittingly violating the Robinson-Patman Act by cutting prices below the competition! The appeals court agreed; Robinson-Patman might be a "controlling circumstance" which justified the slight anticompetitive effect on prices. In 1978 in a Solo-

---

[85] *Wealth of Nations,* book 1, chap. 10, part II.

[86] *American Column and Lumber Co.* v. *U.S.,* 257 U.S. 377 (1921); *U.S.* v. *American Linseed Oil Co.,* 262 U.S. 371 (1923); *Maple Flooring Mfrs. Assn.* v. *U.S.,* 268 U.S. 563 (1925); *Cement Mfrs. Protective Assn.,* v. *U.S.,* 268 U.S. 588 (1925).

[87] *U.S.* v. *Sugar Institute,* 15 F. Supp. 817 (1934); *Sugar Institute* v. *U.S.,* 297 U.S. 553 (1936) 601.

[88] *U.S.* v. *Container Corp. of America,* 393 U.S. 333, 1969.

monic decision, the Supreme Court rejected this rationale but also permitted the defendants a new trial.

E. INTERNATIONAL MARKETS

There are two main parts: *(a)* collusion among U.S. firms as exporters, and *(b)* collusion among foreign firms (and possibly U.S. firms) that affects imports into U.S. markets. Generally U.S. policies apply to actions which clearly affect U.S. markets, no matter where the actions occur. But enforcement is often erratic and unable, in fact, to reach much beyond our borders.

E1. Export Cooperation

For 60 years the Webb-Pomerene Act has permitted "associations entered into for the sole purpose of engaging in export trade." Such associations are not exempt as they may affect domestic trade, but the foreign trade exemption is not trivial. The FTC is given jurisdiction over them, but the supervision has been nominal. There have been only about 30 such associations, which have handled less than 5 percent of the goods exported from the United States. The exemption offers possible public gains; the associations may offset foreign cartels, or achieve economies in the handling of foreign sales. But these and other possible benefits are likely to be relatively small.

E2. Foreign Collusion Affecting U.S. Markets

International markets are often rigged in ways affecting U.S. consumers. After 1901, the world's cigarette markets were divided into three separate preserves, which, though fading, have persisted all the way down to the 1970s.[89] U.S. chemical firms split world markets with British and German firms before World War II. DeBeers Central Selling Organization has long marketed the world's diamonds. Among other current cartels, the OPEC oil cartel stands out for its awesome impact since 1972.

Antitrust's formal coverage of these cartels has had little substance. Especially when foreign governments directly comprise or back the cartel, the problem can be reached only by diplomacy, if at all. Indeed, other U.S. agencies are often busy creating international cartels, rather than breaking them up (see Chapter 24). Certain members of the 1960s quinine cartel were indicted in the United States in 1968, but by 1977 the case had petered

---

[89] American Tobacco invaded British markets in 1901. The U.K. firms then united into Imperial Tobacco. After a price war, the two sides reached a truce. Each firm kept its home market, and a new joint venture—British-American Tobacco ("BAT")—took over their business in the rest of the world. BAT now handles 500 brands, and American brands (such as Luckies) are still made and marketed abroad by BAT. Only in 1973 was BAT's and Imperial's pact concerning Europe detected, and Imperial still owns 16 percent of BAT.

out and the Division was ready to withdraw the suit as being old and impractical to pursue.[90]

Ironically, antitrust does have an influence on many small issues of foreign activity, such as joint ventures, patent restrictions, know-how licenses, and so on. Thus, contracts to exchange know-how between U.S. and foreign firms must avoid any agreements not to compete in each others' areas. International joint ventures come under the same rules as joint ventures in the United States, but the enforcement is even looser abroad. A 1974 case forced certain U.S. and U.K. book publishers to stop agreeing not to sell English-language books in each others' markets.[91] The Division has attacked foreign airline price fixing, in arguments before the CAB. This action has recently had some effect (see Chapter 14), but it is strictly indirect.

In short, antitrust grapples lengthily with certain marginal practices abroad, with some effect. But it has little power over large-scale international collusion.

F. SUMMARY

The long trend has been toward clear lines against price fixing and related kinds of collusion. There remain certain twilight issues and areas, especially the enigma of implicit collusion. Yet the large center of per se policy remains, and it closely fits the economic criteria for efficient policy. For eight decades it has been the U.S.'s most distinctive and successful single policy toward business.

Much collusion still persists, both underground in alternative forms, and in the many exempted sectors (including many local markets). Important international price fixing also affects certain U.S. markets. Policy toward collusion is still largely trench warfare, on many fronts. Progress is often only by inches, and there is a steady stream of new problems to cope with.

QUESTIONS FOR REVIEW

1. Why is short-run cutting likely to be more severe than long-run costs would permit?
2. Do all price conspiracies eventually collapse?
3. What kind of guidelines would you use to point Section 1 investigations at the markets most likely to have price fixing going on?
4. Officers of competitors A through Z meet in a hotel room and agree on a new price schedule. Yet they can't make the new prices stick. Are they guilty? What economic evidence is needed to decide?
5. Do uniform bids prove collusion? If bids aren't uniform, is competition present?

---

[90] Judge David N. Edelstein refused to dismiss the case, noting that many other cases are pursued for much longer periods and that quinine was an important drug. See *ATRR*, November 26, 1974, pp. A6–A9.

[91] *The Wall Street Journal*, July 28, 1976.

6. Will stiff penalties deter price fixers? How stiff should they be?
7. How would you resolve the "indirect purchasers" problem?
8. Which professions and sports should be exempt from antitrust law?
9. What categories of cost and benefit should be used in judging whether the per se treatment of price fixing is wise?
10. Locate five products which carry "suggested prices." Are these prices above the competitive level?
11. Is there presently any policy toward "tacit collusion" or "parallel pricing." What action should there be?
12. Could the GE-Westinghouse tacit collusion method have been modified to make it noncollusive?
13. Does delivered pricing have any *good* effects?
14. How can two firms in the same market create a joint venture without reducing competition in some way?
15. What kinds of price-reporting systems promote competition rather than reduce it?
16. If collusion occurs outside U.S. borders, is it genuinely outside the reach of U.S. antitrust policy?

chapter 8

Restrictive Practices: Price Discrimination and Exclusion

Apart from collusion with others, a firm can reduce competition by two main classes of actions: price discrimination and vertical limits. Each group requires a careful economic analysis, for the issues are often complicated and obscure. Each has had a checkered history of policy actions. Policies toward both groups have continued to evolve during the 1970s, mainly along efficient lines.

A. PRICE DISCRIMINATION

First we analyse price discrimination in Section A1. Then we evaluate policies toward its main forms, in Section A2. Tie-ins are a special type of discrimination; they are reviewed in Section A3.

Price is a sharp weapon, which can be deployed in many ways.[1] Prices can be structured, changed in sequences over time, and used selectively in "predatory" ways—all in combination with other competitive weapons. Price discrimination can be a powerful strategy, but it is only part of the whole spectrum of devices.[2] Other devices include product changes and announcements, predatory spending, advertising blitzes, patent litigation, and many others. Pricing strategies often mingle with these others (for example, a price revision timed with a change in product). One should be alert to these packages of price and non-price strategies, rather than treat prices in isolation.

---

[1] See W. G. Shepherd, *The Economics of Industrial Organization* (New York: Prentice-Hall, 1978), chap. 17, or F. M. Scherer, *Industrial Market Structure and Economic Performance* (Skokie, Ill.: Rand McNally, 1970), chap. 10.

[2] See Basil Yamey, "Predatory Price Cutting: Notes and Comments," *Journal of Law and Economics* 15 (April 1972), 129–42, for a lucid, rounded analysis of the wide range of tactics and weapons.

A1. The Analysis of Price Discrimination

As always, "price" means the "whole" price, allowing for all dimensions of the purchase.[3] This clarifies the many cases where bare price is only part of the terms of the entire transaction.

The core concept is simple: price discrimination is a difference among the price-cost ratios in the selling of like goods to different customers.[4] It occurs when *(a)* buyers have differing demand elasticities, which the seller can discover, *(b)* the seller can fit different prices to these differing elasticities (high prices for inelastic demand, low prices for elastic demand), and *(c)* the buyers cannot re-sell the good to each other. The seller "creams" off the "best" parts of the market—the customers that have little or no choice. In the skim parts of the market, the seller makes do with prices which are down close to cost levels.

In the simplest case, there is one identical good going to two buyers (or groups of buyers). Then

$$\frac{\text{Price to buyer 1}}{\text{Cost}} \neq \frac{\text{Price to buyer 2}}{\text{Cost}}$$

For example, buyer 1 might be retail purchasers of a medical drug (low elasticity of demand), while buyer 2 is a group of large hospitals (high elasticity). Cost might be $1 per bottle. The ratios might then be:

$$\frac{\$10}{\$1} \neq \frac{\$2}{1} \quad \text{so that} \quad \frac{P_1}{P_2} = 5$$

That is fairly steep discrimination. Actual discrimination is usually milder, but it can go even steeper if the conditions are right. (Even small, benign instances of discrimination, such as children's theater or airline tickets, often involve sharp price differences!) The firm gets profits from both parts of the market, but one part is much "creamier" than the other. Consumers pay partly by their ability to pay, rather than by cost levels.

The simple analysis is portrayed in Figure 8–1. There are two contrasting demand curves, but a single, flat cost curve. For each part of the market, the firm sets output where marginal revenue equals marginal cost. The outputs then clear the submarkets at prices 1 and 2.

The sharpness of discrimination depends on the three preconditions: *(a)* the ability to identify differing elasticities; *(b)* the differences among the elasticities; and *(c)* the prevention of reselling by low-price customers to high-price customers. A deficiency in any one of these conditions can limit the total

---

[3] Other dimensions include the quality of output, the terms of payment, time of delivery, degree of security of supply, and so forth.

[4] See also Joan Robinson, *The Economics of Imperfect Competition* (London: Macmillan, 1933) and A. C. Pigou, *The Economics of Welfare* (London: Macmillan, 1920), for early classic discussions, and Alfred E. Kahn, *The Economics of Regulation*, vols. 1 and 2 (New York: Wiley, 1971) for analysis of extensive discrimination in regulated industries.

FIGURE 8–1

The Simplest Case of Price Discrimination: One Good with Uniform Costs, and Two Groups of Buyers

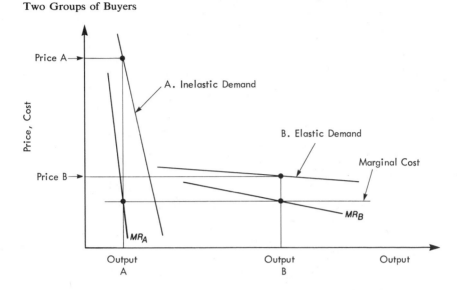

discrimination. Also, obviously, the existence of alternative supplies at low prices also can prevent discrimination. Generally, *the ability to discriminate varies with the firm's market share.* A pure monopolist can discriminate more fully, *ceteris paribus,* than firms with lesser shares. Firms with small shares will scarcely be able to discriminate at all. Competition will press their prices tightly down toward costs.

A perfect monopolist can often discriminate with utmost precision, segregating each customer individually and extracting all consumer surplus. This is called "first degree" discrimination, following Pigou's terms. Third degree discrimination is much cruder. The seller can only arrange two or three large groups, rather than fine-tune the pricing. The simple two-part case in Figure 8–1 is an example of third degree discrimination. The intermediate cases of, say, 10 or 15 groups are "second degree" discrimination. All of these "degrees" fit the same analysis: sellers subdivide the market and their price-cost ratios vary inversely with demand elasticities.

The product need not be precisely uniform. There can be a product line, with a range of products appealing to different "levels" of the market (examples are automobiles, from subcompacts up to luxury limousines; and computers, from small to large systems). Or the same physical product may be sold in regional markets, with varying transport costs. So, as in Figure 8–2, costs—as well as demand elasticities—may differ in the two submarkets. Here again, the price-cost ratios can differ (in this case, the "lower-price" buyer is being discriminated *against,* because its demand is especially inelastic!) If costs vary, then *uniform* prices are discriminatory. In any event, whether

FIGURE 8–2

When costs vary, judging price discrimination is more complex.

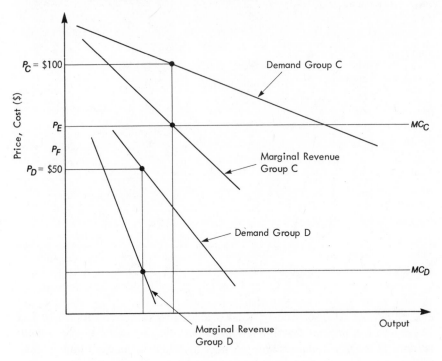

costs vary, or prices vary, or both prices and costs vary, discrimination remains simply a difference in the price-cost ratios among like or related goods. If prices vary in proportion to costs, there is no discrimination. Costs are therefore a key element in judging whether discrimination exists.

Costs may differ because *(a)* There may be economies of scale for the supplier, which permit it to offer price discounts for larger purchases. The question is whether the prices accurately fit the true cost differences; often, instead, the discounts are bigger or smaller than the cost differences. *(b)* The products may differ (for example, some are bigger, or better, or transported further, or supplied with greater security, or supplied at peak or off-peak times, and so on). The task is to measure the cost differences accurately, so that price ratios can be compared. Usually long-run marginal cost is the correct concept of cost. But for time-based products (such as peak-load air fares or new products), short-run marginal cost may instead be the right concept.

Costs are often the very devil to measure, and often they can only be guessed at. Firms rarely measure their marginal costs, and often the precise nature of the good and its costs is debatable. Sellers can often allocate their accounting costs so as to appear to justify a price structure which actually is discriminatory.

If there are large overhead costs in the firm, the discrimination will be even steeper and harder to detect. For then, the marginal costs of each unit will tend to be low, and large floating costs can be assigned among products at the seller's will. In such cases, it may be difficult for outsiders even to discover how steep the discrimination is.

So discrimination is a method for *extracting* excess profit from a market position. If only one price were permitted, profits would be lower (confirm this by trying single prices in Figures 8–1 and 8–2). Discrimination can also serve two other purposes: to help *create* market power and to help *maintain* it. By adroitly manipulating prices in parts of its markets, at different times, a firm can often beat competition. The extreme of this is "predatory" pricing, where the firm selectively cuts prices so as to injure, discipline, threaten, or even drive out a rival firm in part of the market.[5] The firm merely cuts prices deeply where demand is most elastic—in other words, where competition is keenest. It can selectively meet or beat competition, especially if it can draw on its profits from the "creamy" submarkets. There are limits to this: price cuts sacrifice profits, and merger or other techniques may be cheaper and more effective. Yet selective price cutting can often be an efficient way to build up market share.

It can also be used to defend a high share, by keeping new firms out or smaller firms down. The process is not just a balancing of actual prices and costs. The selective pricing is only part of the whole arsenal of tactics, as we noted: non-price tactics are often powerful too. All these tactics can be used to scare off competitors; more precisely, the dominant firm may be able to threaten future losses for rivals, without having actually to cut prices all the way to cause those losses. All it does is change expectations, which then govern behavior. To judge "predatory pricing" therefore often requires sophisticated estimates about a variety of tactics, among which price itself is only part. It is only a special case within the whole domain of discrimination.

Discrimination is not always a unilateral choice by the seller. Much discrimination arises from vertical pressures by buyers. Large buyers may demand special prices and be able to play oligopolist sellers off against each other. Bilateral oligopoly is often suffused with price discrimination, arising from pressures on both sides. Even a virtual monopolist may be under strong buyer pressures. Indeed, discrimination can even occur under coercion by

---

[5] Purists hold that the price must be shown to go below actual costs, in order to prove that a "predatory" effect was present. Others note that price is only one among many weapons for threatening and removing competitors. Even if price does not go below actual average or marginal costs, it may be part of a strategy which "predatorily" eliminates efficient competitors.

Among the recent debaters on the issue, see Scherer, *Industrial Market Structure*, chap. 10; Yamey, "Predatory Price Cutting;" Philip Areeda and Donald F. Turner, "Predatory Pricing and Related Practices under Section 2 of the Sherman Act." *Harvard Law Review* 88 (February 1975), 697–733, and Scherer's rebuttal and further exchange, ibid., 89 (March 1976), 869–903; and Oliver E. Williamson, "Predatory Pricing: A Strategic and Welfare Analysis," *Yale Law Journal* 87 (November 1977), 284–340.

234

FIGURE 8–3
Price discrimination may increase or reduce competition.

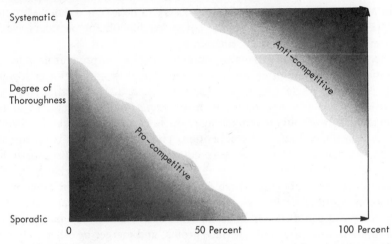

Market Share of the Firm Doing the Discrimination

a third party (see below). So one must be sophisticated in judging the causes and motives in actual cases of price discrimination.

There are two more main economic distinctions to make. One is between the anticompetitive and procompetitive extremes of discrimination. The key criteria are simply two:

1. Market share of the firm. Done by a dominant firm, discrimination usually impedes competition. Done by a small firm, it adds to competition.
2. Systematic or sporadic. Systematic discrimination may reduce competition and prevent entry, while sporadic discrimination usually promotes it and improves the allocative process.[6]

These criteria are summed up in Figure 8–3, in a very rough fashion.

Finally, the competitive effect of discrimination can occur on two different levels, which come up frequently in antitrust cases.

1. "Primary line" effects are at the level of the discriminator and its rivals. (Example: Acme Corp. strengthens its own market share and profitability by discriminating.)
2. "Secondary line" effects are at the next level, among the buyers. (Example: A railroad sets discriminatory rates for oil shipments. The lower rates to Strand Oil Co. enable it to raise its market share at the expense of its rivals.)

---

6 Sporadic discrimination ". . . like a high wind, seizes on small openings and crevices in an orderly price structure and tears it apart;" see Morris A. Adelman, "Effective Competition and the Antitrust Laws," *Harvard Law Review* 61 (1949), 1289–1350, esp. pp. 1331–32.

Discrimination by a dominant firm—even very steep discrimination—can in theory improve the static allocation of resources. It will yield a total output higher than a single-price monopoly output. Yet the output level will be lower than under competition. In certain "natural monopoly" situations, discrimination might be necessary in order to make the firm viable at all. Apart from that exception, discrimination does not improve allocational efficiency.

To a degree, price discrimination tends to be self-correcting. The high price-cost ratios invite other firms (smaller rivals or new entrants) to compete selectively, "cream-skimming," or—to use a British phrase—"picking the eyes out" of the discriminator's market position. This limits the discrimination. The competition may also spread further throughout the price structure. That is precisely what society will gain from. Watch for dominant firms who complain about "cream-skimming." Often they are just trying to protect a discriminatory structure of prices.

A2. Policies toward Discrimination

Several categories of discrimination will usually reduce competition: *(a)* true "predatory" pricing; *(b)* systematic discrimination by dominant firms; and *(c)* tie-ins by dominant firms. U.S. policies have been roughly efficient toward categories *(a)* and *(c)*. Yet most dominant-firm discrimination is scarcely constrained at all.

The basic laws are the Sherman Act, Section 2, against "monopolizing" actions, and the Robinson-Patman Act of 1936, which replaced Clayton Section 2 (recall Chapter 4). Under the first, price discrimination may show a firm's intent to monopolize or stand as an abuse of monopoly power. True "predatory" pricing may be sufficient by itself to convict the firm for monopolizing. This was noted in Chapter 5 and will be enlarged on below. The Robinson-Patman Act places various limits on price discrimination, in order to protect small firms.[7] That Act shifts concern from primary to secondary

---

[7] Good reviews of the Act and its enforcement are in Corwin D. Edwards, *The Price Discrimination Law* (Washington, D.C.: Brookings Institution, 1959); Earl W. Kintner et al., "Reform of the Robinson-Patman Act: A Second Look," *Antitrust Bulletin* 21 (Summer 1976), 203–36; and Edward Wolfe, "Reform or Repeal of the Robinson-Patman Act: Another View," ibid., pp. 237–70.

Sections 2(a) and 2(b) of the Act are its main parts. They are, in full:

ROBINSON-PATMAN ACT

§2(a) That it shall be unlawful for any person engaged in commerce, in the course of such commerce, either directly or indirectly, to discriminate in price between different purchasers of commodities of like grade and quality, where either or any of the purchases involved in such discrimination are in commerce, where such commodities are sold for use, consumption, or resale within the United States or any Territory thereof or the District of Columbia or any insular possession or other place under the jurisdiction of the United States, and where the effect of such discrimination may be substantially to lessen competition or tend to create a monopoly in any line of commerce, or to injure, destroy, or prevent competition with any person who either grants or knowingly receives the benefit of such discrimination, or with customers of either of them: *Provided,* That nothing herein contained shall prevent differentials

line effects, in order to protect small retailers against chain stores which could get supplies at lower prices. Still, the precedents operate at both levels.

A firm accused of price discrimination can first try to show that costs also differed in proportion, or that the goods differed in their grade and quality: hence price differences were not true price discrimination. Beyond that, there are three main economic defenses against a charge of discrimination: that the prices *(a)* only met competitors' prices in good faith, or *(b)* were justified by costs, or *(c)* did not substantially lessen competition. The Act is often blamed for preventing effective competition by limiting price cutting. But in practice, neither its good nor its bad effects are probably very strong. Primary-line effects are the main issue in the following review, though secondary-line effects will get a word at the end.

1. Predatory Pricing and Related Actions. Brazen predatory pricing has long been grounds for a Section 2 conviction. Standard Oil Co. had used predation in at least two ways. One was selective price cutting to force small competitors into more favorable merger terms. The other was Standard's coercion of railroads to give special freight rates, including a rebate to Standard for each barrel of oil shipped for its competitors! The pricing was important to the creation of Standard's monopoly, and it was abusive.[8] For Ameri-

which make only due allowance for differences in the cost of manufacture, sale, or delivery resulting from the differing methods or quantities in which such commodities are to such purchasers sold or delivered: *Provided, however,* That the Federal Trade Commission may, after due investigation and hearing to all interested parties, fix and establish quantity limits, and revise the same as it finds necessary, as to particular commodities or classes of commodities, where it finds that available purchasers in greater quantities are so few as to render differentials on account thereof unjustly discriminatory or promotive of monopoly in any line of commerce; and the foregoing shall then not be construed to permit differentials based on differences in quantities greater than those so fixed and established: And *provided further,* That nothing herein contained shall prevent persons engaged in selling goods, wares, or merchandise in commerce from selecting their own customers in bona fide transactions and not in restraint of trade: And *provided further,* That nothing herein contained shall prevent price changes from time to time where in response to changing conditions affecting the market for or the marketability of the goods concerned, such as but not limited to actual or imminent deterioration of perishable goods, obsolescence of seasonal goods, distress sales under court process, or sales in good faith in discontinuance of business in the goods concerned.

(b) Upon proof being made, at any hearing on a complaint under this section, that there has been discrimination in price or services or facilities furnished, the burden of rebutting the prima-facie case thus made by showing justification shall be upon the person charged with a violation of this section, and unless justification shall be affirmatively shown, the Commission is authorized to issue an order terminating the discrimination: *Provided, however,* That nothing herein contained shall prevent a seller rebutting the prima-facie case thus made by showing that his lower price or the furnishing of services or facilities to any purchaser or purchasers was made in good faith to meet an equally low price of a competitor, or the services or facilities furnished by a competitor.

[8] John J. McGee has suggested that none of Standard Oil's tactics were truly predatory ("Predatory Price Cutting: The Standard Oil (N.J.) Case," *Journal of Law and Economics* 1 (October 1958), 137–69. Predation would have been too costly to Standard Oil to make sense. He searches the trial record in the antitrust case and finds no persuasive instance of predation. Yet his approach is narrow, as Scherer has noted *(Industrial Market Structure,* pp. 275–76). The whole series of Standard's actions may have included predatory actions, of which pricing was only one element.

can Tobacco and the du Pont Gunpowder Trust, too, predatory pricing was a count in the monopoly offense.

From 1914 to 1936, the FTC issued only eight effective orders against price discrimination (four others were appealed and reversed by the Supreme Court). Under Robinson-Patman, the activity multiplied, with 430 cases resulting in 311 cease and desist orders by 1957; of the 23 which were appealed, 19 were upheld.[9] By 1978, the total of orders had gone over 1400, about two thirds of them in food-products markets. The Antitrust Division also brought many actions, over a wider range of markets. Usually the firm offers little defense, preferring merely to change the pricing. The Act specifies five different types of violations, all of which boil down to differences among "whole" prices which are not based on costs, or which show intent to exclude rivals.

Predation has also been alleged in various Sherman Act "monopolizing" cases, brought by private plaintiffs as well as the Antitrust Division. From this welter of case activity and hair-splitting over fine points, a few main lines of precedent stand out.

1.   The agency must show that price discrimination occurred and that it did injure competition.

2.   "Cost" is now usually defined as long-run marginal cost, which includes a normal return on the capital used in producing the good.

3.   A dominant firm cannot cut price below cost, if that reflects an intent—and does have the effect—of increasing its market share. If price covers cost, the firm is innocent, even though other firms are killed off. The firm bears the burden of proving that price did not go below cost, validly measured. The evidence is often murky and inconclusive, since costs can be defined and measured in many ways. Small-share or new firms *can* use such "loss leaders" to build up their positions.

4.   Leading firms can only "meet" competitors' price cuts, not cut below them in a way that increases their market share. As with cost, the defendant bears the burden of proving that it did not go below competitors' prices. Smaller firms can, as before, go below that in order to get established.

5.   Much true predatory pricing slips by unnoticed, for lack of agency action or private complaints.

6.   On the other side, some procompetitive pricing gets incorrectly charged as predatory.

7.   Yet recent court decisions have grown narrow, looking only at price and ignoring the other kinds of predatory actions which can inflict or sharpen a predatory effect.

Points (4) and (6) have stirred much criticism of the Robinson-Patman Act. Yet the harm done is probably slight, and the main-line limits on dominant-firm predation are valuable.

The precedents are not crystal-clear, because the cases often raise confusing evidence and the decisions have often contained economic error. Moreover,

---

[9] Edwards, *The Price Discrimination Law,* chap. 4.

predatory pricing issues are in flux in the 1970s, as IBM, Xerox, AT&T, and other dominant firms have posed the issues with a new urgency and complexity.

Anheuser-Busch is now the leading U.S. brewer, but its industry share in the middle 1950s was only about 7 percent.[10] During 1954–55, A-B cut prices on Budweiser beer in the St. Louis area, but not in other markets, and so there was a price difference not based on costs. A-B had been fourth in St. Louis in 1953 with 12 percent of the market, behind Falstaff, GW and GB. A-B's share rose to 39 percent, but then fell back to 17 percent after the price cutting was over.[11] Despite the discrimination, A-B was exonerated in a court case because *(a)* it had responded to valid causes (sales losses during 1953); *(b)* its prices were not shown to be below costs; *(c)* its competitors in the St. Louis area still made profits; and *(d)* A-B's share slipped back after the price cuts were ended. Note also that A-B was only a poor third in the St. Louis market after the episode.

Utah Pie. In 1957, three national companies—Continental Baking, Pet Milk, and Carnation—shipped in all the frozen pies sold in Salt Lake City, Utah. During 1957–58, a new little local firm named Utah Pie Co. seized 67 percent of this market by cutting prices and saving on transport costs. The three then cut prices below their average total cost levels *and* below Utah's prices, and this dropped Utah's share to 34 percent.[12] Though Utah's share went back up to 45 percent in 1961, and though Utah was able to

---

[10] The case is *FTC* v. *Anheuser-Busch, Inc.,* 363 U.S. 536 (1960), 289 F. 2d 835 (1961).

[11] The actual market shares were:

	December 31, 1953	June 30, 1954	March 1, 1955	July 31, 1955	January 31, 1956
Anheuser-Busch	12	16	39	21	17
GB	14	12	5	7	6
Falstaff	29	32	29	36	43
GW	38	33	23	28	27
All others	5	6	4	7	6

[12] The market shares and prices went as follows:

	Market Shares				Prices (per case)	
	1958	1959	1960	1961	Early 1958	1961
Utah Pie	67	34	46	45	$4.15	$2.75 (August)
Pet	16	36	28	29	4.92	3.46 (April)
Carnation	10	9	12	9	4.82	3.30 (lowest)
Continental	1	3	2	8	5+	2.85 (lowest)
Others	6	19	13	8	n.a.	n.a.

For a full evaluation of the case, see Kenneth G. Elzinga and Thomas F. Hogarty, "*Utah Pie* and the Consequences of Robinson-Patman," *Journal of Law and Economics* 21 (1978).

get and hold its prices below the other firms' prices, the Court inferred a predatory intent from the three big firms' actions. This intent was also shown by other actions, including industrial spying. The Court held that the intent was likely to harm competition if it were permitted to take effect, and so Utah's private suit won.

This decision took the broader view, with prices only part of the whole predatory sequence. It has been sharply criticized by some economists for ignoring the dominance of Utah Pie Co. after 1957. Yet the premise is valid, and in fact Utah did go out of business soon after.

IBM and "Bundling." As the computer industry grew in the 1950s and 1960s, IBM adopted the practice of "bundling" the prices of its machines and software support. Each piece of equipment had a uniform price, but IBM would provide free programming and other assistance to attract or retain customers. Hardware and software were bundled together in one price. This extra spending often was heavy in order to get contracts that IBM wanted badly. Instances of predatory spending had been alleged but not formally proved. In 1968, bundling was part of Control Data Corp.'s suit against IBM, and it loomed as a charge in the Division's case against IBM (recall Chapter 5). IBM thereupon changed policy and ended bundling (or at least some of it).[13] Though no formal legal precedent was set, the episode indicated that sharp—perhaps predatory—price discrimination by a dominant firm could be an antitrust offense.

Telex. In 1975, the limits of dominant-firm pricing were pulled sharply back, and the *Telex* decision was the turning point. On its 360 line of computers, IBM in 1964 set high price-cost ratios on "peripheral equipment," which attaches to the central parts of mainframe computers. This attracted "cream-skimming" by small firms, who copied the IBM peripherals—making them "plug compatible" with IBM computers—and offered them at lower prices. During 1969–70 the newcomers drew away from IBM some 10–30 percent of leasing revenue on these items. To prevent further inroads, IBM in 1970–72 took a series of sharp actions, including cutting price and altering the design of the products to reduce compatibility. By 1972 the newcomers had been sharply set back and one of them, Telex Corp., sued IBM under Sherman Section 2 for predatory actions. Telex won a $329 million decision in District Court in Oklahoma in 1973, lost it on appeal by IBM, and decided at the last moment not to appeal to the Supreme Court.[14]

Among the fairly complex pricing moves, two points emerged: IBM cut prices below Telex's prices, and IBM's internal memos suggested an intent

---

[13] See Gerald W. Brock, *The U.S. Computer Industry* (Cambridge: Ballinger, 1975); and U.S. Senate Subcommittee on Antitrust and Monopoly, *Hearings on the Industrial Reorganization Act, Part 7. The Computer Industry*, 93d Congress, 2d Session (Washington, D.C.: U.S. Government Printing Office, 1974). The unbundling apparently was not complete; it resulted in price changes of only 3 percent.

[14] The first decision is *Telex Corp.* v. *International Business Machines Corp.*, 367 F. Supp. 258 (N. D. Okla. 1973); the appeals court reversal is 510 F. 2d 894 (10th Cir. 1975).

to do away with the newcomers.[15] Whether IBM's prices went below true costs is debatable. They probably went below total average historical costs, but not below short-run or long-run marginal costs. The appeals court accepted IBM's cost defense, holding that IBM had earned at least a 20 percent return on the equipment at all times. Therefore, it said, any intent to exclude was irrelevant.

This erased much of the precedent from *Utah Pie* and earlier cases. IBM did nearly eliminate Telex and others from these new markets, reducing them from vigorous to crippled competitors. Two criteria were at odds in the case—injury to competition and costs—and the appeals court ensconced a narrow concept of cost as being supreme. That altered the *Anheuser-Busch* and *Utah Pie* precedents. Yet bare price and cost may be only part of a course of action, and in *Telex* that was the case.

The 1975 decision in *International Air Industries* accepted the "bare cost" basis even more fully.[16] The small plaintiff Vebco, Inc., had tried to enter the market for "evaporative cooler pads" in the southwestern United States during 1969–71. The dominant firm, American Excelsior Co., had cut prices by as much as 39 percent in that region during the price war in 1971, and there were memos in its files suggesting Amxco's intent to keep Vebco out, or at least "stunted." Vebco sued, claiming that it had suffered a "primary-line" injury from discrimination (Amxco's pad prices stayed up in other regions) but lost both in district court and on appeal.

The decision granted that the "large entrenched . . . dominant . . . firm 'had price discriminated against' a fledgling company attempting to enter the same market." But Amxco's prices during the price war had still brought a 15-cent-per-pad profit to the manufacturing division and a gross margin of 33 percent to its sales division. Generally, the court said, predation occurs only if price goes below average variable cost. And in some cases, a monopolist can even cut price down to short-run marginal cost, even if that is below average variable cost. This criterion greatly widens what a monopolist may do, for new competition often leaves the established firm with excess inventory, which has low marginal cost. Indeed, a rational monopolist could plan always to have over capacity, so that its marginal costs were low, leaving it free to make deep price cuts against any newcomer.[17] The criterion in this case would easily have reversed the *Utah Pie* decision.

---

[15] IBM studied in detail the likely effect on specific competitors from a wide range of possible pricing strategies. In one case the prediction for an action that was later taken was that competitors would be "dying companies." Brock, *The U.S. Computer Industry,* and Senate Subcommittee, *Part 7. The Computer Industry,* at p. 5673.

[16] The narrow price-cost version had been endorsed in Areeda and Turner, "Predatory Pricing," and the judge relied heavily on it in his opinion. So did the opinion in *Hanson* v. *Shell Oil Co.,* 541 S. 2d 1352 (1976), *cert.* denied, 429 U.S. 1074.

[17] As shown in Figure 1–3, average costs decline at output levels below "capacity," and marginal costs are below average costs. That is a prime meaning of having idle capacity: the out-of-pocket costs for additional production are low. See also the exchange between Scherer and Areeda-Turner in the *Harvard Law Review* 89 (March 1976), 869–903.

Therefore *Telex* and *International Air Industries* have given dominant firms a wider range of pricing and other tactics. A plaintiff now must have strong evidence about below-cost pricing and intent to exclude. Other genuinely predatory aspects are likely to be ignored.

2. Systematic, Continuing Discrimination. Toward systematic discrimination—without specific predation—policy has been lenient toward primary-line impacts but strict on secondary-line effects.

The leading primary-line cases involve a few dominant firms whose deep price discrimination has been challenged in a Sherman Section 2 monopolizing suit. The conviction of United Shoe Machinery Corp. in 1956 rested partly on USM's extensive price discrimination, including the bundling of repairs into the machinery price. This discrimination may not have been predatory, but it had reduced competition and reflected USM's intent to do just that, in Judge Wyzanski's opinion.

In the three big Section 2 cases since 1968—IBM, Xerox, and AT&T (recall Chapter 5)—price discrimination is a major element. IBM set price-cost ratios for its various 360-line models which closely fit their varying demand elasticities (that is, the degree of competition). And when rivals' new products soon put the 360/40 and 360/60 models in difficulty, IBM responded with deep price cuts (and, probably, large financial losses) on two "fighting ship" models, the 360/44 and the 360/65.[18] For some individual customers, IBM also provided free programming and other benefits in order to win contracts (as was noted just above). By 1978 the issue was still unresolved, with the case still at trial.

Xerox has refined its discrimination even further, with three-part tariffs, special large-user plans, and frequent revisions to respond to changes in demand (recall Chapter 5). For uniform outputs at uniform costs (such as copies at 1 cent per page), customers are variously charged from 1 to 8 cents, often on millions of copies. Its MUP plan of 1967–75 also involved a form of tie-in.[19] In effect, MUP offered a steep price cut on the small machines (which had come under pressure from coated paper competitors) tied to the use of other Xerox machines by the customer. The FTC complaint in 1973 treated this as a main source of Xerox's continuing high market

---

[18] These were probably good examples of predatory spending, but they have not been singled out for a specific attack. Instead, they have gotten buried in the mass of the Antitrust Division's whole case.

[19] The original "machine utilization plan" (MUP) was in force during 1968–75. Its main features were: *(a)* It was available only to large customers (those with annual copier billings of at least $480,000). There were never more than 184 such customers. *(b)* It was kept secret for over two years and only offered selectively, where necessary to get accounts from competitors. *(c)* All machines used by the customers were put on the same aggregate pricing schedule, including even the smaller 813 and 914 which had higher costs and higher regular prices. *(d)* The uniform price schedule was: 1–20,000 copies on each copier, 2.5 cents per copy; copies 20,001–44,000 on each copier, 1.5 cents per copy; and over 44,001 copies on each copier, .566 cents per copy. Each machine also had a monthly minimum charge (from $40 on the small 813 to $400 on the big 2400 high-speed copier).

Later the threshhold was lowered to $360,000 per year and new machines were added to it. It was effective in reversing the inroads on its faltering smaller machines.

share and profitability. In the 1975 compromise, Xerox dropped the complex MUP pricing plan for large customers. Yet it soon replaced the plan with another even more discriminatory plan, and the main structure of prices remained untouched. Though pricing below cost is unproven so far, the intent and effect to reduce competition appears to have been present.[20] Because of the FTC's gentle handling of pricing in the Xerox case—the one recent settled policy action—the policy limits on dominant-firm price discrimination are now weak. And further basic action on Xerox is estopped by the 1973– 75 case.

AT&T pricing has discriminated, both to promote market penetration and, more recently, to forestall new competition in large-scale data transmission (see Chapter 13 for more detail). The issue is complicated by the fact that the firm's total profits are constrained by regulation.[21] The pricing has been reinforced by refusals to connect, legal tactics, and other nonprice methods for reducing competition. Some AT&T pricing has probably gone below cost, but that is hard to determine, even for the FCC. The very size and complexity of Bell System operations has kept policy from doing more than limiting the most obvious instances. Any antitrust decision on the matter appears to be 10 years away or more.

In short, the policy lines are not settled. Deep price discrimination is presently permitted, even by genuine monopolists. The *USM* precedent is now virtually in suspension. A cost defense is probably sufficient to exonerate, even if competition is intentionally excluded or reduced.

Secondary-Line Effects. Here the treatment is stricter, and the precedents more fully developed. Only the main lines and leading cases are noted here, from the great mass of smaller issues and cases.

A&P. This big case, begun soon after the Robinson-Patman Act was passed, charged A&P with all the counts of discrimination in the Act. The appeals court in 1949 based its conviction mainly on secondary-line effects: that is, A&P *as a buyer* had forced suppliers to discriminate, thereby enabling it to beat out competitors at the retail level. Possibly some of the price differences reflected true efficiencies achieved by A&P, but many did not. The whole judgment in the case was sound (and was not appealed by A&P).[22]

In *Morton Salt* (1948), the price of table salt had varied inversely and

---

[20] A major private suit by SCM Corp. challenged Xerox pricing and other practices. It reached trial in June 1977, and in 1978 it resulted in a conviction on several counts. Xerox appealed.

[21] If a regulated utility needs to depart from cost-based pricing on some of its output, the criteria for the "best" set of departures may be complex. For an advanced discussion, see William J. Baumal and David F. Bradford, "Optimal Departures from Marginal Cost Pricing," *American Economic Review* 60 (June 1970), 265–83.

[22] From the intense debate on the case, see Morris A. Adelman, *A&P: A Study in Price-Cost Behavior and Public Policy* (Cambridge: Harvard University Press, 1959), for criticism of the case, and Joel B. Dirlam and Alfred E. Kahn, "Antitrust Law and the Big Buyer: Another Look at the A&P Case," *Journal of Political Economy* 60 (April 1952), 118–32, and "A Reply," ibid. 61 (October 1953), 441–46, for analysis on the other side.

substantially with the size of orders, over a 15 percent range.[23] The discounts were not "cost justified." Only five large chain stores had ever bought enough salt to get the lowest price. They could resell the salt at prices lower than small grocers could buy it. Evidence showed that the price disparities had caused retail prices to differ. Conviction followed routinely.

In later cases, price ranges as low as 5 percent have been held to be "substantial" enough to reduce competition and violate the law.[24] Cost defenses are, of course, permitted, but they must usually show that prices cover total costs, including a correct portion of overhead costs. Since the defendant bears the burden of proof, and cost disparities must cover *all* of the price differences, the cost defense is often too complex or costly to make in these small-scale cases. The courts are not finicky, and many thousands of price differentials are never brought to trial, so policy does not stamp out the common run of petty price discrimination.

A test case by the FTC in 1977 challenged the *Los Angeles Times's* practice of giving large discounts to its large advertisers.[25] Most newspapers and magazines have long done such discrimination, and so the outcome of the case could have a wide impact. The discounts (some of them 40 percent and more) were said to be much steeper than cost differences could justify. They involve large volumes of money, which could have sizable secondary-line effects among the advertisers.

"Meeting competition in good faith" is the second line of defense. It has prevailed in some cases, and it has an intrinsic validity.[26] Competition requires that firms be able to respond, if not to overreact. Yet "good faith" has been usually too elusive to judge firmly, and so the policy is only a rule of thumb that a larger firm usually cannot slash below a smaller firm's price move in order to chill competition. Generally, the firm bears the burden of proving "good faith."[27] There are no exact rules, and often it is hard to disentangle the exact prices from the sequences, rebates and discounts.

---

[23] *FTC* v. *Morton Salt Co.,* 334 U.S. 37 (1948). The net prices per case of salt were:

Less-than-carload purchases	$1.60
Carload purchases	$1.50
5,000-case purchases in any consecutive 12 months	$1.40
50,000-case purchases in any consecutive 12 months	$1.35

[24] The cases include *American Can Co.* v. *Bruce's Juices* 187 F. 2d 919, 924, modified, 190 F. 2d 73, 74 (5th Cir.), cert. dismissed, 342 U.S. 875 (1951), and *Foremost Dairies, Inc.* v. *FTC,* 348 F. 2d 674 (5th Cir.), cert. denied, 382 U.S. 959 (1965).

[25] See the *Wall Street Journal,* August 18, 1977, p. 4.

[26] The leading case is *Standard Oil Co. (Indiana)* v. *FTC,* 340 U.S. 231 (1951). It abounds in legal fine points. But the main lesson is that the firm can use good faith meeting of competitors' prices as a way of justifying price discrimination.

[27] Yet, note that IBM was able to cut below the PCM firms' prices in 1971–2 and still escape conviction (recall the *Telex* case).

This completes the main body of policy on price discrimination.[28] The treatments have defects, but they follow broadly the efficient lines. Predatory behavior is at least moderately limited, though the recent narrowing toward a bare cost standard tends to neglect other predatory factors. Systematic discrimination is at least indirectly constrained, though in the largest cases it may be too complex to treat. Secondary-line effects are more closely controlled. Firms can usually rely on cost or "meeting-competition" defenses where they are genuinely valid.

The Robinson-Patman Act continues to attract criticism and proposals for repeal. Many of the cases are of little importance or value, whatever their validity may be. The act has bred some uneconomic decisions. Yet its broad role is probably economically sound, or at least not strongly harmful. More urgent than its reform is the need to develop policy toward complex discrimination by leading dominant firms.

A3. Tie-Ins

A tie-in requires you to buy good B, which you don't want, in order to get good A, which you do want. The tying product (good A) is often patented or a popular branded item. The tied item is often a new product, or an inferior one, or simply a complement. The firm holds more market power for good A than for good B. Tying is an ancient custom, though a rather specialized one which crops up only in certain situations. Market processes usually undermine tie-ins, as new firms offer the tied goods separately. While it lasts, tying can: *(a)* extend market power from the tying product into the tied product, and/or *(b)* as a form of price discrimination serve to extract more profit.[29]

Tying by dominant firms (especially those with patents or some other special advantage in good A) can foreclose much or all competition in good B's market. Even if such leverage is not strong, the tie can raise entry barriers, by forcing any new entrants to offer both products, not just one. Some benefits are possible, though less likely. The joint purchase might realize cost savings in ordering, shipping or servicing. Also, tying makes it hard to identify the separate prices of the tied goods. An oligopolist might use tying as a device for quietly offering concealed price cuts.

Policy has treated the social costs of tie-ins as overwhelming, where market

---

[28] There are several lesser clauses in the Robinson-Patman Act, treating *(a)* functional price differences (to differing categories of buyers; for example, jobbers, wholesalers and retailers), *(b)* brokerage fees, *(c)* advertising allowances, and others. They have drawn protracted litigation but they are of secondary importance. For details, see Edwards, *The Price Discrimination Law,* chaps. 5–15.

[29] See Kaysen and Turner, *Antitrust Policy,* and Donald F. Turner, "The Validity of Tying Arrangements Under the Antitrust Laws," *Harvard Law Review* 72 (Nov. 1958), 50–75.

In some views, tying is *only* a device to extract profit: it cannot extend monopoly power from one market to another. See Posner, *Antitrust Law,* pp. 171–84.

shares are large. The per se prohibition (except for small competitors and sporadic ties) was set by the 1930s, but modest exemptions were posed in 1961 and 1977. The leading cases offer fascinating details, as follows.

Tie-ins can violate Sherman 1 (an unreasonable restraint) or Sherman 2 (attempt to monopolize), but it is Clayton 3 which specifically prohibits tie-ins if they "substantially lessen competition." Before 1914, sellers of machines could prevent machine users from using supplies, or other machines, from other sellers.[30] Clayton 3 made most tie-ins illegal, and the *IBM* case in 1936 confirmed the policy. IBM made its customers use only IBM cards, and it had overwhelming dominance (over 90 percent) of both markets. The Court rejected IBM's claim that other cards would jam the machines or cause errors.[31]

International Salt Co. had required users of its patented salt-processing machines to use only its salt in the machines. It claimed that only this could protect the machines from malfunctioning. Though there were competitive machines, and the effect of foreclosure was only "creeping" rather than "at a full gallop," the Court convicted International in 1947 on a per se basis.[32] Block booking of movies had long been a packaging device by which Hollywood studios forced theaters to take inferior films in order to get the best ones. This tie-in was found illegal in the 1948 *Paramount* case, along with other conditions (recall Chapter 5).

American Can required users of its patented can-closing machines to use only its cans in them. When a major monopolization case against it and Continental Can was settled in 1949, a central clause was the prohibition of this tie-in.[33] In 1956 an Antitrust Division action challenging Eastman Kodak's dominance and its tying of film processing to film purchasers was

---

[30] The case of *Henry* v. *A. B. Dick Co.,* 224 U.S. 1 (1912), involved supplies to be used with a potential duplicating machine; see also *Heaton Peninsular Button-Fastener Co.* v. *Eureka Speciality Co.,* 77 F. 288 (1896).

[31] *International Business Machines Corp.* v. *U.S.,* 298 U.S. 131 (1936). By 1956, IBM still had over 90 percent of the card business.

[32] *International Salt Co.* v. *U.S.,* 332 U.S. 392 (1947).

[33] The case is *U.S.* v. *American Can Co.,* 87 F. Supp. 18 (N. D. Cal. 1949); see also James W. McKie, *Tin Cans and Tin Plate* (Cambridge: Harvard University Press, 1959). American and Continental together held 86 percent of both levels (machines and cans).

The *Times-Picayune* case of 1953 involved a more complicated tie-in. The *Times-Picayune*—New Orleans' only morning newspaper—was owned jointly with the afternoon *States,* which competed with the afternoon *Item.* Under the *Times-Picayune* "unit plan," an advertiser could only buy space in both the *T-P* and the *States,* not in either one separately. The restriction did change things; before it, less than half of the morning *T-P* advertisers had also bought space in the afternoon *States.*

By a 5–4 vote, the Court said that the tie would be illegal if the *T-P* had a monopoly. But it grouped all three papers together in "the market" and decided that *T-P*'s resulting 40 percent was not a monopoly. This is scarcely defensible on economic grounds, since there were clearly two separate markets. What really swayed the majority was that *The Item* was thriving, rather than failing. Still, the decision gave a free hand to firms with market shares up to 40 percent. In 1958 the rule was tightened.

settled.[34] The tie was broken, and henceforth film buyers could have a choice of processors. (How wide is your choice presently? Is there more than one alternative processor?)

For many decades, Northern Pacific Railway had sold or leased its land-grant holdings of 40 million acres with "preferential routing" clauses. The land user had to ship all its products over that railway. This clause was struck down in 1958, as a foreclosing device.[35]

The *Jerrold* decision in 1961 held that a supplier of cable TV receiving systems could not prevent users from buying parts of their systems from other firms.[36] Jerrold had pioneered cable TV technology during 1948–55, and its exclusive rule helped it protect quality and grow. But after that initial phase, the "infant company" excuse lost its force, especially because Jerrold now dominated the industry. The effort to sell only complete systems had ceased to be reasonable and was now anticompetitive and therefore illegal. This special "infant company" escape has rarely been used since then.

The *Loew's* decision in 1962 again involved movies.[37] The owners of a large library of old films had required the TV networks to take packages of films rather than let them select among separately priced films. (Thus, for example, "The Man Who Came to Dinner" was tied to "Gorilla Man" and "Tugboat Annie Sails Again.") Loew's claimed that old movies were less than 8 percent of all TV offerings, and therefore a minor competitive factor. The device was primarily aimed to maximize profits rather than extend the firm's market power. Yet it too was held to be illegal per se. Note that Loew's was a large factor in the old movie sector of the entertainment industry.

The most prominent recent decision is *Fortner,* a pint-size case which dragged up and down the courts for 15 years before final decision in 1977. For a time, U.S. Steel made prefabricated houses and also provided generous financing through its U.S. Steel Homes Credit Corp. Some of the houses were poorly built, including 70 erected near Louisville, Ky., for Fortner Enterprises Inc. in 1960. Fortner sued in 1962, charging that U.S. Steel had tried to monopolize the market for prefabs by tying them to its favorable financing deals. U.S. Steel fought hard, more on principle than for the small sums at stake.[38] In 1969, the Supreme Court overturned a summary judgment for U.S. Steel and ordered a full trial, on the ground that financing could

---

[34] A complaint had been prepared in July 1954, whereupon Kodak negotiated to settle the suit before it was filed. The settlement and suit were both filed in December 1954. See *Trade Cases,* para. 67,920.

Kodak had held a complete monopoly of processing of Kodacolor and Kodachrome film, by selling the film only at a price that included the processing charge. This was ended. Kodak also agreed to license its processing patents to others, at reasonable royalties. Within seven years, Kodak promised to divest facilities if its share of processing had not gone below 50 percent (recall Chapter 5).

[35] *Northern Pacific Railway Co.* v. *U.S.,* 356 U.S. 1 (1958).

[36] *U.S.* v. *Jerrold Electronics Corp.,* 187 F. Supp. 545; 365 U.S. (1961).

[37] *U.S.* v. *Loew's, Inc.,* 371 U.S. 38 (1962).

[38] The damages claimed were only $300,000, while the eventual costs of litigation were over $200,000 on the plaintiff's side and at least that much for U.S. Steel.

come under the tying prohibitions as well as do other goods. Since U.S. Steel's share was small, the 1969 decision appeared to widen the reach of the per se rule to nearly all ties. Over 200 other court decisions cited this *Fortner* opinion during 1969–76. But after a full trial and further steps, the Court in 1977 acquitted U.S. Steel. Fortner had not proved that U.S. Steel had been able to use financing as a way of reducing competition in prefabs. Using "cheap financing to sell expensive houses" was harmless to competition. Yet the main body of the per se rule was not eroded, for the case had involved small market shares.

One minor exception is the tie which merely extracts profits, without reducing competition. Such pure cases are few, but professional football tickets are one. In 1974, angry fans filed private suits against six football teams for requiring season ticket buyers to buy pre-season tickets also.[39] The teams were all acquitted, basically on the ground that the tie did not reduce competition in the tied (pre-season) market. Perhaps the small amounts, and the traditional antitrust lenience toward sports, helped in reaching this policy conclusion.

Altogether, the per se rule against virtually all tie-ins by dominant firms is consistent and sound. A rule of reason would—as in price fixing—mire the process in unworkable delays and confusion. There are calls for liberalizing the policy, but any social losses from the present strict line are probably trivial.[40]

B. VERTICAL RESTRICTIONS ON COMPETITION

Among the many kinds of restrictive devices and actions, *vertical* limits on dealers are a large portion. There are two main types. First are limits on what and where the dealers may *sell.* Second are restrictions on what the dealers *buy.* A complicated set of policies toward these practices has evolved, and litigation has recently flourished. To evaluate the policies, one must first understand the peculiar economics of dealerships and franchising.

B1. Analysis

Retailing methods are extremely diverse. At one extreme are discount houses offering a wide variety of products under one roof. At the other extreme, some other products are retailed by the manufacturer itself (such as most computers and copiers). Close to that extreme are chains of specialized franchised dealers, who are quasi owned and controlled by the manufacturer. The degree of control varies, and the supplier or parent firm will often try

---

[39] In addition, the Dallas Cowboys required their season ticket buyers to purchase at least one $250 bond.

[40] Including Posner, *Antitrust Law,* pp. 171–84, and Ward S. Bowman, Jr., "Tying Arrangements and the Leverage Problem," *Yale Law Journal 67* (November 1957), 19–36.

to restrict its retailers' choices. Or the dealers may cooperate horizontally to force the producer to impose, though reluctantly, the vertical restrictions. In either case, competition among dealers may be reduced.

There are many kinds of restrictions: on dealers' selling in each others local areas, on dealers' carrying of other companies' brands, on dealers' pricing actions, and so forth. Many of these are interchangeable, serving much the same purpose. Some of them reduce competition sharply, while others do not.

The restrictions *(a)* reduce *intra-brand* competition in *selling* or the dealers' choice in *buying* their supplies, in order to build up the brand and therefore *(b)* increase *inter-brand* competition and the manufacturer's profits. The policy problem is to identify these effects and weigh them. Only where the loss of *intra-brand* competition is small, while *inter-brand* competition is strongly raised, should the restriction be permitted.

The issue affects many thousands of producers, as they select among many different methods of marketing, and millions of retailing firms, including over 500,000 franchisees. Automobiles, gasoline, flowers, shoes, bicycles, hotels, film developing, machinery, stereo equipment, income tax preparation, and of course fast foods are among the many familiar items so affected.[41] The franchisee or authorized dealer promotes, sells and services the product. For this it gets the franchise and/or other sorts of support from the supplier.

Close vertical relationships arise under certain conditions: *(a)* The product is complex, and so users need assurance of quality. *(b)* The product is important enough to be a major activity of a dealer (for example, there are auto dealers but not safety-pin dealers; shoe dealers but not shoestring dealers). *(c)* The producer has a distinct status, from a patent, brand image or image or simple market share, and dealers can both benefit from this identity and help maintain it. The product or service may gain a higher price when marketed through "high quality" dealers than through mass discounting, and so the maker may take great efforts to keep it out of discounters' hands.

There are inherent conflicts of interest between the maker and the dealers. The maker wants intensive sales coverage; each dealer wants a large exclusive sales area to itself. The maker wants each dealer to focus only on its product; the dealer wants to add new products, even though they would dilute the maker's brand image. The supplier wants the dealer to buy only from itself; the dealers often want a free hand. Yet both sides also gain from mutual support.

The maker generally extracts what monopoly profit it can in its own price and then prefers that the retailing be as wide and cheap—that is, as competi-

---

[41] Recent volumes of sales by franchisers to their franchise holders include the following (for 1974): shoe stores; apparel shops, florists and photography stores, $2.2 billion; automobile accessory stores, repair services, car washes, and tires stores, $1.5 billion; convenience stores, $330 million; fast food restaurants, $325 million; do-it-yourself stores, cleaning services, and repair shops, $90 million (Commerce Department data; see *Business Week,* June 16, 1975, p. 82).

tive—as possible. The maker would restrict this competition only *(a)* during an initial growth and building up phase, *(b)* to foster dealer loyalty and excellence in sales and service, or *(c)* when coerced by dealers to help reduce competition at their level.

Two main kinds of restrictions have drawn the most attention. One is geographic limits on the areas where dealers may *sell* (so-called "territorial restrictions"). These limits *do* cut intra-brand competition among the firm's dealers and *may* raise inter-brand competition by strengthening those dealers. The balance between the two effects depends mainly on the producer's market share. For dominant firms, the loss prevails; for lesser firms, there may be a net rise in competition if the restrictions help them to build up their positions.

The second category is clauses binding the dealers to buy their supplies from the franchiser (so-called "requirements contracts"). They *do* exclude competition from the suppliers' market, but they *may* assure quality at the retail level. So here too the net effect on competition hinges on the producer's market share.

Therefore the broad lines of efficient policy are reasonably clear. Dominant firms would be prohibited from both kinds of restrictions. Dealers would instead have free choice among suppliers and customers. By contrast, producers with small market shares would be largely free to adopt vertical restrictions. There could be exemptions from these broad rules only for exceptional situations.

Private and public suits have proliferated in recent years, many of them marginal and of dubious validity. But the main lines of policy do fit the efficiency criteria fairly well.[42]

B2. Geographic Limits on Sales

The restrictions vary. Starting from the tightest categories there are: territorial restrictions and customer limitations; exclusive franchises and location clauses are of medium force; while "profit passovers" and "areas of primary responsibility" only discourage intra-brand competition rather than prohibit it.[43] Policy has developed toward a per se rule against the first four, but a

---

[42] The mass of legal cases and detail is conveyed by American Bar Association Antitrust Section, *Vertical Restrictions Limiting Intrabrand Competition,* Monograph No. 2 (American Bar Association, 1977), 117 pages.

The economic literature is more compact. See Lee E. Preston, "Restrictive Distribution Arrangements: Economic Analysis and Public Policy Standards," *Law and Contemporary Problems* 30 (Summer 1965), 506–29; William S. Comanor, "Vertical Territorial and Customer Restrictions: White Motor and Its Aftermath," *Harvard Law Review* 81 (May 1968), 1419–38; and Posner, *Antitrust Law,* pp. 159–64.

[43] Definitions of these items are as follows:

A territorial restriction is a pledge by the buyer that it will not resell the goods outside a specified area or to customers who reside or have their place of business outside of that area.

Customer limitations embrace promises by the buyer not to sell to certain customers or classes of customers who are identified other than by their location. Included in this category are promises not to sell to governmental units or to other large customers

1977 decision has limited that coverage to dominant firms with a large economic impact. Meanwhile the remaining two milder restrictions are presumed to be legal under a rule-of-reason approach.

The evolution of the policies has been fairly complex, with several leading cases. In *Bausch & Lomb* in 1944, the Supreme Court held that a vertical territorial restriction which was part of an agreement to fix prices is illegal per se.[44] The Antitrust Division then announced in 1948 a per se basis: it would challenge any vertical restraints which close off intra-brand competition, and for 15 years it got many consent decrees stopping them. Its first litigated case was *White Motor Co.* The District Court held White's restrictions to be illegal per se in 1961, but the Supreme Court reversed in 1963 and remanded for further study and trial.[45] By 1967 both the FTC and the Antitrust Division had drawn back; territorial restraints were only presumptively illegal, not illegal per se. The firm could try to show that on balance the restrictions promoted competition. In *Schwinn* in 1967, the Supreme Court took a tougher line, nearly to a per se basis. In the 1950s, Schwinn had kept its wholesalers from selling to dealers outside their fixed territories or to non-franchised dealers, on threat of termination. The Court held that such restrictions on re-selling the bicycles were illegal, even though Schwinn's market share had by 1960 fallen to 12 percent.[46]

This decision triggered a flood of suits, many strict lower-court opinions, and much criticism. Then in 1977 the Court's decision in the *GT&E* case discarded the per se basis.[47] The intra-brand and inter-brand effects are to

---

whose business is reserved for the manufacturer; promises by wholesalers to sell only to retailers who have been approved by the manufacturer, by retailers to sell only for use and not for further resale, and by consumers not to sell at all; promises not to sell to a particular customer within a specified period of time after another dealer or distributor has made contract with him; and promises to sell only to a certain class of customers—drug stores but not hospitals, for instance.

The exclusive franchise or sole outlet provision denotes a promise by the seller of the goods to the buyer not to sell to other outlets within the buyer's "exclusive territory" and not to sell directly to consumers within that area. A location clause prohibits dealers from opening other outlets, especially in another's exclusive territory, without the approval of the manufacturer. A profit-passover clause requires a dealer who sells in another's territory to pay over to the latter all or some portion of the former's profit on the sale. A primary responsibility clause requires a dealer to concentrate sales effort in a particular territory or at a particular location. For details, see Note, *Restricted Channels of Distribution Under the Sherman Act, Harvard Law Review* 75 (1962); and Martin B. Louis, "Vertical Distributional Restraints Under Schwinn and Sylvania: An Argument for the Continuing Use of a Partial Per Se Approach," *Michigan Law Review* 75 (December 1976), 275–310.

[44] *U.S.* v. *Bausch & Lomb Optical Co.,* 321 U.S. 707 (1944).

[45] *U.S.* v. *White Motor Co.,* 194 F. Supp. 562 (N. D. Ohio 1961), reversed and remanded, 372 U.S. 253 (1963).

[46] *U.S.* v. *Arnold, Schwinn & Co.,* 388 U.S. 365. Perhaps the key passage in Justice Fortas' opinion was: "Once the manufacturer has parted with title and risk . . . his effort thereafter to restrict territory or persons to whom the product may be transferred . . . is a per se violation of Section 1 of the Sherman Act" (at p. 382). The government's brief had explicitly abandoned the contention that the restrictions were illegal per se, asking instead only for a rule-of-season decision.

[47] *Continental TV, Inc.* v. *GTE Sylvania, Inc.,* No. 761–15 (1977). In 1978 the FTC held the exclusive franchise areas in the soda pop bottling industry to be illegal,

be weighed after all. Yet in fact the decision fitted the presumption that restrictions will be prohibited where market shares are sizable. When it enforced geographic restrictions on its deals, GT&E had only a 2 percent market share, which then rose only to 5 percent. Probably, a market share of 12 or 15 percent would have been too high. So the rule of reason will still probably prevent vertical geographic restrictions by any significant firms. The burden of proof is correctly placed. In this area, a "rule of reason" can be applied effectively, if market shares are the key factor. The policy line now appears to be drawn close to the economic optimum. It may take further cases to confirm that precedent in detail.

B3. Restrictions on Purchases, and Related Tie-Ins

Requiring one's dealers to carry only (or mainly) the franchiser's products is an old practice, which has been gradually limited by the courts.[48] Such "exclusive dealing" issues are closely related to "requirements contracts," in which the buyer is forced to buy more of a product, to contract for a longer period, or to buy more related goods, than it wishes. In each case the seller excludes others from competing to supply the goods. The practice involves tying, but here in a special vertical context. The producer may set rigid requirements, or may only try to "persuade." That rigid requirements do have anticompetitive effects is clear, if the supplier/franchiser has a significant market share. Whether "persuasion" for tie-ins reduces competition is debatable. Again the precedents have developed gradually, and the producer's market share has been the key test.[49]

In the *Standard Fashions* and *Butterick* cases in 1922 and 1925, firms making two fifths of the dress patterns sold at retail excluded their competitors from the best stores in the cities and from the only outlets available in many smaller towns.[50] In the *Eastman Kodak* case in 1927, a firm producing more than nine tenths of the motion picture film made in the United States entered into an agreement with its customers, through an association of laboratories making motion picture prints, forbidding them to purchase film imported from abroad.[51]

In the *Carter Carburetor* case in 1940, the principal manufacturer of carburetors gave discounts to dealers who bought exclusively from it and denied them to those who bought from its competitors.[52] In the case of the *Fashion*

---

in cases affecting Coca-Cola and Pepsico (FTC Dockets 8855 and 8856). The outcome of the companies' appeal was unsure.

[48] Familiar examples are the franchised gas station which is required to carry certain brands of tires or accessories, and "fast food" shops which must buy their meats or containers from the franchiser.

[49] *FTC* v. *Sinclair Refining Co.,* 261 U.S. 463; and *Pike Mfg. Co.* v. *General Motors Corp.,* 299 U.S. 5 (1936).

[50] *Standard Fashion Co.* v. *Magrane-Houston Co.,* 258 U.S. 346; *Butterick Co.* v. *FTC,* 4 F. 2d 910, cert. denied, 267 U.S. 602.

[51] *FTC* v. *Eastman Kodak Co.,* 247 U.S. 619.

[52] *FTC* v. *Carter Carburetor Corp.,* 112 F. 2d 722.

Originators' Guild in 1941, an association of dress manufacturers, whose 176 members made three-fifths of the dresses sold at retail for $10.75 and up, sought to prevent "design piracy" by signing contracts with 12,000 retailers forbidding them to buy from imitators.[53]

In all of these cases, exclusive dealing was enjoined on the ground that its use by a dominant seller had substantially lessened competition and tended toward monopoly. In later cases, a less rigid criterion was employed.

In the *International Salt* case, where a contract tying the sale of salt to the lease of a patented salt dispenser was found to be illegal in 1947, the Supreme Court went on to say that ". . . it is unreasonable per se, to foreclose competitors from any substantial market. . . ."[54] This reasoning was applied to exclusive dealerships in the *Standard Oil of California* case in 1949.[55] Standard Oil, producing 23 percent of the gasoline sold in seven western states, contracted with some 6,000 independent dealers, handling less than 7 percent of the gasoline sold in the area, to fill all of their requirements for petroleum products and, in some cases, for tires, tubes, batteries, and other accessories. The lower court held Standard's contracts to be illegal on the ground that competition is substantially lessened when competitors are excluded from "a substantial number of outlets."[56] Standard appealed and the Supreme Court, in a 5 to 4 decision, affirmed the lower court's decree. It is enough, said Justice Frankfurter, to prove "that competition has been foreclosed in a substantial share of the line of commerce affected." Standard's contracts created "a potential clog on competition."

This precedent was followed in the *Richfield Oil* case in 1951. Richfield's exclusive contracts with filling stations on the Pacific Coast accounted for but 3 percent of the gasoline sold in the area, but the rule of quantitative substantiality was applied and the contracts condemned.[57] In the light of these decisions it appeared that exclusive arrangements were to be outlawed per se. But later developments point the other way.

During the 1950s, the FTC declined to proceed against exclusive arrangements that appeared to be harmless, confining its orders to cases in which the probability of actual injury to competition could be shown. Then, in 1961, in the case of *Tampa Electric Co.* v. *Nashville Coal Co.,*[58] the Supreme Court modified its earlier position. Tampa had contracted to purchase from Nasvhille, for 20 years, all of the coal required for one of its generating stations. Since this affected only 1 percent of the Nashville area coal market, and did give both partners a degree of security, it was let stand. In *Loew's*

---

[53] *Fashion Originators' Guild* v. *FTC,* 312 U.S. 457.

[54] *International Salt Co.* v. *U.S.,* 332 U.S. 392, 396.

[55] *Standard Oil Co. of California* v. *U.S.,* 337 U.S. 293.

[56] *U.S.* v. *Standard Oil Co. of California,* 78 F. Supp. 850, 857.

[57] *U.S.* v. *Richfield Oil Corp.,* 99 F. Supp. 280 (1951), sustained per curiam 343 U.S. 922 (1952).

[58] 16/365 U.S. 320.

(1962) and *Perma Life Muffler* (1968), the Court rejected rigid tie-ins, but said that the suppliers could use "persuasion."[59]

In the 1970s, several decisions further defined the range of permitted vertical tie-ins. Chicken Delight, Inc., had required its franchisees to take its chickens and supplies, even at prices above alternative suppliers. These were only a few essential items, which helped to make the retail food distinct. Though Chicken Delight had no large market share, the appeals court held in 1972 that it was distinct in the market, and that trade had been restrained.[60] In 1973, the FTC's *Chock Full O'Nuts* decision affirmed that the franchiser of chains can't make franchisees buy from itself or from designated suppliers. Yet the franchiser could try to show that the tie-in is needed to ensure quality.[61]

By 1975, Dunkin' Donuts was appealing an adverse decision on a further fine point; it had only used persuasion, but its offers were "package deals" (that is, tied combinations).[62] Such cases might refine precedent within a narrow area, where persuasion shades over into packages and rigid tie-ins. But no final answers are likely, since the devices and pressures can vary so subtly and widely.

C. SUMMARY

The behavior to be "controlled" comes in many forms and shadings, often raising complex points of economics and law. The agencies have probably been hyperactive on Robinson-Patman and vertical restriction issues. Meanwhile, price discrimination by dominant firms has only recently begun to get the attention it deserves.

Since the 1950s, precedents have jelled, some of them along roughly the efficient lines. Consistently, rules are stricter against dominant firms than their lesser competitors (the principle of "quantitative substantiality"). Selective pricing below cost is effectively banned, except for firms with small shares. Tie-ins are illegal, except for small share firms. Likewise, vertical restraints on sales and purchases also are under a correctly tilted rule, which is stricter on firms with larger market shares. These rules are not only in the right direction but are applied strictly. After a flurry of case activity in the 1960s, policy seems to have stabilized and streamlined.

The gap in policy is exclusionary actions by dominant firms. Recent decisions have permitted dominant firms to price-discriminate sharply, even to

---

[59] *U.S.* v. *Loew's, Inc.*, 371 U.S. 38 (1962), and *Perma Life Mufflers, Inc.*, v. *International Parts Corp.*, 392 U.S. 134 (1968).

[60] *Siegel* v. *Chicken Delight, Inc.*, 448 F. 2d 43 (9 Cir. 1971), cert. denied, 405 U.S. 955 (1972).

[61] The FTC did accept Chock Full O'Nuts' argument for coffee and baked goods, which were more important for the brand image of the chain (634 ATRR, A-22).

[62] *Ungar* v. *Dunkin' Donuts of America, Inc.*, No. 75–1625, CA3, appellants' brief filed 7/23/75.

the point of killing off rivals, as long as their prices did not go below costs. This neglects the fact that bare pricing is only part of a larger range of strategies which can exclude competition. Several large cases now in progress may eventually clarify or tighten the policies. Meanwhile policies in this area depart from the strictness and balance shown by the others.

QUESTIONS FOR REVIEW

1. "Price discrimination arises simply from differences in prices." True?
2. "Price discrimination can help create and maintain market power, as well as help to extract maximum profits." True?
3. "Price discrimination is pro-competitive when it is done systematically by a dominant firm." True?
4. "A pricing move can be predatory in effect if it causes a firm to expect losses and therefore go out of business, even if price does not actually go below marginal cost." True?
5. "A firm can defend its pricing with a "cost" defense of "good faith" defense. The FTC usually accepts these at face value." True?
6. "Pro-competitive price discrimination by firms with small market shares will usually be innocent under the Robinson-Patman Act." True?
7. "In the 1970s, dominant firms have been given wider latitude in using pricing tactics against small or new rivals." True?
8. "The A&P case dealt mainly with secondary-line effects. A&P won because its price differences were cost justified." True?
9. "Tie-ins are harmful to competition only where the tied product has a high market share." True?
10. "By preventing intra-brand competition among its dealers, a producer may be able to increase inter-brand competition in the market as a whole." True?
11. "Territorial restrictions seemed to be illegal per se after Schwinn, but now a rule-of-reason basis applies." True?
12. "A franchiser can try to 'persuade' its franchisees to buy supplies from it but cannot require them to, if the franchiser has a substantial share of the market." True?
13. Is present policy too strict on price discrimination by small firms? By dominant firms?
14. If you are a dominant firm wishing to drive out a small rival who has lower costs than yours, what devices can you use—including pricing—and still escape an antitrust challenge?
15. Are vertical restriction cases by public agencies likely to be both numerous and of little net social value, as is often said? What criteria should be used by the agencies in deciding whether to bring such cases?
16. Draw up a balanced critique of the Robinson-Patman Act, including its main probable costs and benefits. What reforms might be warranted?

chapter 9

Antitrust Appraised

Antitrust policy is a strong and growing activity in the United States, as both the agencies and the private side continue to expand. You are now equipped to form judgments about "optimal" antitrust policy and to compare them with what has actually occurred and seems likely to happen in the future. This chapter offers a brief guide for such an appraisal. No definitive lessons can be drawn, but the economic effects have grown clearer in recent years. After 80 years of experience, U.S. antitrust may be ripe for revision. But in which ways, and how?

We review first its tasks and then its effects. This brings out the main causes of its difficulties. Possible "reforms" are then passed in review. The chapter considers finally the practical prospects for change.

A. THE CONDITIONS BEING TREATED

Recall that there are sizable net yields from preventing or reducing market power in a wide range of markets. Loose oligopoly is the optimum market structure, except for the unusual cases with steep economies of scale. Yet much tight oligopoly and near-monopoly exists, and still more would arise if antitrust policy were withdrawn. The core of high market power in major industries has become increasingly stable in recent decades. Some of these dominant firms appear to have averted the normal erosion of high market shares. In these cases, and in oligopoly generally, the rate of decline of market power now seems to be low.

Many of these market shares have little scientific social justification from economies of scale. In some regulated sectors also, natural monopoly conditions are receding, so that there is an increasing scope for competition.

The social costs of excess market power are not small. Prices and profits are increased. Efficiency is reduced. The fertility of invention and innovation usually declines. The degree of inequality of wealth, income, and opportunities is increased. Altogether, the economy and society bear avoidable burdens and stress.

An optimal set of policies would not press to the extreme of the pure competitive ideal, but it would seek to reduce market power in many markets. It would also contain a good balance among the several parts of antitrust.

B. EFFECTS OF ANTITRUST

Evidently, antitrust in the United States has not been optimal. Yet it may have had some strong effects and come close to the optimum in certain directions. One cannot be sure about such judgments, for research on antitrust's economic effects has barely begun.[1] But some specific influences—and their composite effect on the whole structure of industry—are reasonably clear.

Price fixing and related cooperation have been reduced and altered. Formal cartel agreements have mostly been eliminated (except for certain exempt sectors). Price fixing is still frequent, or even epidemic, in some sectors. Yet antitrust has made it covert and more fragile. A degree of "fair trade" price setting also remains, plus specific common practices in certain industries which avert price cutting (for example, brand-name prescribing in drugs). Parallel pricing in shared monopolies has not been treated directly. Large areas of the economy (regulated, local, exempted) are formally free of constraint, and other large areas are informally exempted by custom or lack of staff. The strict line against cooperation appears to be close to the optimal *where* it applies. But that is probably less than one half of all market activity.

Mergers among direct competitors have been tightly constrained since about 1962. Previously, mergers had been encouraged by the strict policy against cooperation. By the 1960s, the main levels and lines of industrial concentration had been settled for decades. If the close limits on mergers remain, concentration may eventually be eroded. Viewed in the small, horizontal and vertical merger limits now seem to fit efficient criteria reasonably well. The burden of proof and time are roughly in line with the economic factors.

Conglomerate merger policy is less efficient. Decisions based on potential entry and toe-hold effects have been roughly correct. But take-overs have probably been too broadly resisted. This may avert some entrenching effects from mergers among leading firms in different markets. And the rate of

---

[1] Earlier scholars looked only at legal results. The few studies of practical effects have had to be speculative. The most detailed is S. N. Whitney, *Antitrust Policies* (New York: Twentieth Century Fund, 1958), 2 vols. Yet his appraisal predates the Section 2 moratorium and the new merger strictness. Legal studies praising Americn antitrust are typified by two from the 1950s: U.S. Attorney General's Committee to Study the Antitrust Laws, *Report* (Washington, D.C.: U.S. Government Printing Office, 1955); and A.D. Neale, *The Antitrust Laws of the United States* (Cambridge: Cambridge University Press, 1959, rev. ed., 1970). Neale, a Briton, aims only to summarize U.S. antitrust, and he relies heavily on the Attorney General's Committee Report (which in turn reflects the views of its instigator, S.C. Oppenheim).

There exists no recent, full, analytical appraisal of antitrust's effects. The Nader group study (Mark J. Green and others, *The Closed Enterprise System* (New York: Grossman Publishers, 1972) is flawed and not analytical, but it has voluminous detail and its conclusions—that antitrust needs greater resources, powers, and economic consistency—may be valid.

rise in global concentration may have been slightly abated. But the loss in efficiency from shielding firms against take-overs may have been appreciable. An efficient treatment would stop anticompetitive mergers but retain more of the pure conglomerate take-over process.

Established market power has been largely untouched for 25 years. Indeed, one could say it has scarcely been treated for 65 years. Certain leading cases were addressed and moderately revised during the first wave of Section 2 action (1906–20). The second wave recovered some of the doctrinal ground lost by the "rule of reason," but it had even slighter practical effects. Since 1952 treatment has been nearly suspended, and the post-1968 actions have so far yielded mainly pretrial litigation, not clear evidence or well-designed economic effects. This virtual moratorium arises from several causes. It reflects rational choices by political appointees coping with biases in the system, and by managers of firms. The result: Section 2 cases likely to pose remedy problems are not even prepared or filed, in order to give the courts a chance to air the issues and set the margins of policy. Earlier, courts did define some monopolies and shared-monopolies as such, even if remedies did not ensue. Presently, even the process of evaluation—of thinking about what exists and how it might need change—has ground nearly to a halt. Even the several post-1968 suits face the same procedural blocks that have inhibited earlier treatments.

Policy now seems slower than market forces in reducing monopoly power. Yet those forces are probably too slow in many cases. This retardation of Section 2 is not really recent. Even the earlier actions came long after the original monopolization and scarcely touched the monopolizers' gains. The present acquiescence tends neatly to regularize and legitimize market structure. Moreover, action which might touch the deeper financial structure surrounding these industries is simply beyond the reach of antitrust. Antitrust has itself become part of the industrial fabric, tending to preserve the existing industrial order and to limit change.

There are positive effects. If there were no antitrust, then collusion and concentration would probably be greater. the deterrent effect may have been strong. Recently, antitrust has been moving to reduce monopoly in regulated and exempt sectors. The effectiveness of the Division and the FTC ranks above some regulatory and other agencies to be seen in later pages of this book. Yet the main lines of U.S. antitrust now appear to be off the optimum. There is need for a better balance among activities, a fuller use of antitrust powers, and a leaner use of agency resources. New tools and agencies may also be in order. Presently, antitrust relies on a narrow set of tools and procedures which may be incapable of treating some of the core problems.

C. CAUSES OF DIFFICULTY

At least five causes may be at work, especially in the Section 2 area.

Procedure.   The judicial process of "perfect justice" is slow and contains several important biases. Legal issues and evaluations supplant economic ones. Long, lucrative delay can be spun out, often precisely where the social interests are largest. Weaknesses in judicial skills can be exploited by fears and illusions.

Agency Resources and Powers. These may be far too small to treat the breadth and severity of problems within the agencies' jurisdiction. These tasks are increasing in size and complexity, while the agencies' real resources have grown moderately. Research is often inadequate for lack of staff and access of information. Attorneys are routinely outmanned whenever treating major cases (pursuing small defendants is much easier). Fines are often trifling and uncertain for the most important cases. And the agencies lack resources to carry out remedies efficiently, even if they were ordered. Pyrrhic victories are all too common, because *(a)* legal victories are about all the agencies have the resources to attain, and *(b)* the firms retain the power and information to control remedies. "The agencies win the decisions; the defendants win the remedies."[2]

Laws. The antitrust laws are broad and often vague. Parts of them are too comprehensive to be applied flatly (for example, "every monopoly" in Section 2). Informal loopholes have been read into them by 80 years of varying court opinions. There is much room for hair-splitting and mendacity.

Expertise. Many agency officials lack skill in the issues of economics, finance, engineering, accounting, and so on, which are the substance of the problem. As they pass through the revolving door of public office, they can hope only to learn the ropes and to pull along a few pending actions. Basic changes are usually beyond their understanding or reach. Career staff members, on their part, are mainly lawyers attuned to courtroom standards, working to legal definitions rather than economic criteria.

Mistakes and Waste. Agency officials are quite human (some of them more so!) and so they often make errors and tolerate varying degrees of inefficiency. Most are not trained administrators, and their decisions are often made under extreme pressure. There are factions among parts of the agencies and often real deadwood among the staff and/or political appointees. Resources are often lavished on trivial activities, either by choice or in tasks imposed from outside. Powers are sometimes let rust, even those which could operate with few resources (Section 2 is one example). The FTC has been the more wasteful, but the Division has had errors and inefficiencies too.

Political Economy. Perhaps after all the root cause is the political economy surrounding antitrust. Power and interests play upon and around the agencies, using them and molding them as well as seeking redress in other forums. If so, the specific defects—procedural biases, scanty resources, inexpert officials, and errors—could merely be *effects* of the deeper real forces which distort antitrust and block *any* optimum solutions. Perhaps the bedrock

---

[2] See Walter Adams, "Dissolution, Divorcement, and Divestiture: The Pyhrric Victories of Antitrust," *Indiana Law Journal* 27 (Fall 1951); and Kenneth G. Elzinga, "The Antimerger Law: Pyrrhic Victories?" *Journal of Law and Economics* 12 (April 1969), 43–57.

of social and economic power is firmly set against what economists would call optimal antitrust policy. This fits the view of, among others, both the libertarians and the radical left, as well as skeptical observers of moderate persuasion. *Classical liberal:* Given the cruel world as it is, one cannot expect policy to be more effective than what the markets give. The less of this maladroit interference there is, the better. *Radical left:* Finance capitalism underlies monopoly power and it controls the political process. It has seen to it, and will continue to see to it, that antitrust serves—even expresses—corporate power rather than controls it. In the middle, some leading "moderate" scholars, too, are skeptical and have only modest hopes for antitrust.

Each reader must judge *(a)* how far antitrust departs from optimality, and in which directions, and *(b)* what the causes are, specific or deep. American antitrust may be remarkably effective, even increasingly so. Or at the other extreme, it may be a pawn, controlled rather than controlling. The appraisal is determined by one's view of: *(a)* the economic conditions needing treatment, *(b)* the real effects of policies, and *(c)* the *realpolitik* surrounding policy. And these trace back, once again, to the natural rate at which market power diminishes.

Yet there is agreement that the procedures are slow and contain bias; that the agencies are bantams compared to their formal tasks; that officials often lack expertise; and that mistakes and waste occur. It is also agreed that antitrust is likely to continue largely as is, a system in political and economic equilibrium. There are few powerful groups seeking change. Most industrial interests who might be deeply hurt by antitrust have been exempted, formally or de facto. Nearly all sides engaged in the antitrust process find something to gain from it—some very much indeed. Even the dominant firms that face Section 2 treatment gain legitimacy by the existence of agencies which might be able to treat them but don't. Otherwise, the citizenry might demand something more effective.

By comparison, a few antitrust policies abroad have had real substance and variety. Britain's agencies now have powers and resources comparable to those in the United States. Certain British treatments—especially of resale price maintenance and formal agreements—are probably as strict as in the United States. Procedures are more brisk. Fact-gathering resources are also at least as adequate, compared to the apparent problems. In the United Kingdom and elsewhere, there is more use of supplementary treatments for the core cases. Such alternatives include public monopsony buying, price-screening bodies, and public enterprises of several sorts.

D. POSSIBLE REFORMS

U.S. antitrust has deep roots and great inertia, though its present twist has arisen mainly since 1952. A wide variety of reforms have been proposed, directed mainly at curing the problems in the Section 2 area.

Four main directions for improving U.S. antitrust may be appropriate.

D1. Enrich and Enlarge

The agencies could be given more and better resources. Larger budgets, with less external control on their use, would give a freer hand for treating the core problems more thoroughly. Appointees, especially those to the FTC, could be more broadly skilled and have longer tenure. Powers to get information and bring about basic changes could be added. In short, policy resources could be brought up toward parity with the problems to be treated.

This is a standard proposal, and it has merit. Actually, the budgets have grown more rapidly since 1968, at about 10 percent per year. Reallocation within the agencies and a more intensive use of existing powers would also increase effective resources.[3] And getting large increases would require a major shift in the budgetary process as it is now handled both in the Executive offices and in Congress. As for officials, there seems little prospect of easing the grip of traditional lawyers upon the top positions.

D2. Use Incentives More Effectively

Several experiments could bring policy more into line with real incentives, power, and access to information. Amending the antitrust laws is a hazardous process, for it could easily be diverted into gutting them. But there is merit in these proposals:

1. Using fines more precisely. The use of economic penalties is now crude and haphazard. The economic objective is to set penalties and probabilities of conviction just high enough to induce optimal choices of behavior and structure by the firms. Optimal fines therefore can be lower if enforcement is more thorough. And for some offenses by small firms, fines are already steep enough. But for major offenses by very large firms, fines are presently too small. Even if used imaginatively by judges (for example, X thousand dollars *per day* and per individual offense), they often leave even a convicted offender with large monopoly gains for every day the infraction lasted. The correct solution is to base fines on the degree of harm caused and/or the firm's ability to pay. This could be a percent of the monopoly profits, or of all profits, of the firm.[4] At present, fines are too small to be efficient in treating many problems. And their incidence—hitting smaller firms harder—often is quite unfair.

2. Change the rules about treble damages. The Sherman Act's provision for treble damages for private victims has its merits, but it does accentuate the problems of Section 2 action. By opening up vast damage claims, it encourages fanatical efforts to resist, and that has helped to cause the current

---

[3] Also, the Division's sections might be realigned on a functional basis, with one specializing on price fixing, another on Section 2 cases, etc. Or, the trial lawyers could be used just as barristers, to try the cases, rather than as investigators and evaluators.

[4] See Kenneth G. Elzinga and William Breit, *The Antitrust Penalties* (New Haven: Yale University Press, 1976).

problems.[5] There are several possible revisions, but none is clearly best. The trebling feature could be revised downward (but how far?). The groups eligible to collect damages could be narrowed. Criteria for calculating damages could be limited. Such revisions would need great care, for the damages provide a splendid mechanism for compensating victims and inducing self-corrective action against monopoly.

3. Positive incentives for reducing market dominance. Section 2 treatment presently runs against the grain of corporate power, incentives, and information. Both managers and shareholders, and often workers too, believe that treatment would hurt their interests, even though in many cases it would actually benefit them. They are well set to resist study, trial, and effective remedy, as we have seen. If incentives could be reversed, so that corporate interests benefited by reducing dominance, the problem might become self-correcting. Various incentives could include:

a. Tax liability. Suppose that dominant firms were defined as such and given a deadline for reducing market power, and that share-price effects were given favorable treatment only if the deadline were met. Stockholders would then bring pressure on the managers to *achieve* the change, rather than serve as an excuse *not* to make it.

b. Graduated tax on size or market share. A gently graduated progressive tax could tip managements toward reducing their market positions.[6] The ideal version would be a tax on firms' market shares in their main industries. This would apply steady rewards for actions to reduce those shares, possibly by spinning off new firms. Where technical scale economies exist, their benefits would partly be realized by the public, rather than kept by the firm. Practical problems of defining markets and applying optimal tax rates would be serious, but they might be less than with present policies.

A general progressive tax on firm size would be cruder but much simpler to apply.[7] It would presumably be scaled with a gentle gradation, just enough to achieve the social benefits.

Other ways to align private and social incentives might be devised. None is perfect, and the most effective ones may be the most difficult ones to enact. But they might be less out of alignment with corporate interests and power than Section 2 enforcement presently is.

D3. A New Agency?

The Antitrust Division carries the main burden of treating dominance, and yet its reliance on court procedures makes it vulnerable to delay. If

---

[5] Ibid.

[6] See W. G. Shepherd, *The Treatment of Market Power* (New York: Columbia University Press, 1975), chap. 7.

[7] The subject has not been adequately researched as yet. See the discussion by Julian L. Simon, "Graduate the Corporate Income Tax to Abate Bigness Efficiently," *Challenge* Magazine (November 1977)

dominance and tight oligopoly are of large dimensions, a new agency with brisk procedures may be the only effective way to treat them. In 1959 Kaysen and Turner proposed amending Section 2 to make high concentration "presumptively illegal."[8] That would reverse the burden of proof and narrow the many informal loopholes (recall Chapter 5). The proposal was endorsed by a Presidential task force in 1968 (the "Neal Report"). Yet it has had little political support so far.

A new agency was proposed by Senator Philip Hart in 1972, as noted in Chapter 5. The Industrial Reorganization Commission would deal with seven major industries, and it could provide an amnesty on past offenses (thereby avoiding treble damage claims). It would have powers to proceed effectively in studying the markets, defining the needed changes, and helping to carry them out. Its actual role could not be predicted, for it might move timidly and rely on Congress to apply remedies. Though it is unlikely to pass in its present form, the Commission proposal is a good model of what might be needed. In fact, Congress has been getting drawn into possible actions on some of the seven industry candidates. Proposals for restructuring the oil industry have nearly passed the Senate. The surrounding debate has been lively but little practical effect seems likely. The telephone sector has also been involved, with the Bell System's bill to extend its monopoly and other efforts to affect FCC policies.

D4. Private Suits

Private suits offer an important force against monopoly power. The boom in private litigation since 1960 is an experiment in the effectiveness of the approach. Repeatedly, private actions have been prepared earlier, filed sooner, and litigated more effectively than agency actions. In some areas, private actions have been really "making the law," by posing new claims and evoking landmark decisions. To some observers, this may go too far, by-passing the official agencies in forming the ruling precedents of "public" policy.

Yet small plaintiffs are still often brushed off by the massed legal resources of dominant firms. Private suits are either lacking or unsuccessful against the leading dominant firms, as well as many lesser ones. "Class-action" suits offer a way to mobilize the interests of numerous victims who have suffered small individual losses. They are brought by one victim on behalf of the others, seeking penalties which can justify the cost of the action. The courts have resisted class-action suits, but perhaps legislation authorizing them would be appropriate.[9]

---

[8] Carl Kaysen and Donald F. Turner, *Antitrust Policy* (Cambridge: Harvard University Press, 1959).

[9] The 1976 antitrust amendments included a so-called *parens patriae* provision. It empowers state attorneys general to lodge antitrust actions on behalf of state citizens who have suffered monopoly damages. This gives some of the effect of class-action suits. But it leaves the initiative to state prosecutors, and it divides the class-action classes into state-size bits rather than permit nationwide suits. The results remain to be seen.

D5. Dubious "Reforms"

Several other ways to supplement antitrust have been noted, especially in Chapters 5 and 6. Trade barriers could be cut. This would affect several industries, but it is not a promising or general solution. Patents could be revised. This would affect a rather wide set of industries, but prospects for it are even less favorable. Nor would it abate the cases of settled market structure already created under patents.

Finally, there are several "reforms" which seem more likely to be *harmful* than efficient.

Abolition.   This is occasionally suggested, on grounds that antitrust is *(a)* too powerful and harmful, or *(b)* a tool of corporate power. Sheer abolition, with no alternative, would surely lead to far more collusion and concentration, plus possibly rather more flexibility in structure. Until other alternatives have been more fully tried, simple abolition seems extreme and crude.

Performance Criteria.   It is urged occasionally that antitrust act only where performance is poor, rather than treat behavior and structure directly. Thus price fixing and monopoly would be treated only if performance could be shown to have been hurt. Chapter 3 helps us see that this proposal simply shifts the burden of proof and alters its content. Since performance data are hard to interpret and are controlled by the firms themselves, this proposal would bring antitrust nearly to a standstill and increase the load on the judiciary. In fact, it is precisely because performance questions have seeped into Section 2 actions that they have slowed to a crawl and become nearly unmanageable in court. To increase their role would paralyze antitrust policy behind a facade of economic rationality. Performance is already influential in policy, perhaps *too* influential.

More Consent Decrees.   Compromises do get half-loaves of remedy while sparing agency resources for other uses. Greater use of them could spread antitrust treatments further. Yet consent decrees have drawbacks (noted in Chapter 4) which caution against a shift toward them. *First,* they are often ineffective. They are routinely ignored after a few years, by the firm, courts, and the agencies themselves. Soon after a case is settled, the staff experts on it are gone or preoccupied elsewhere, so that a threat to reopen the case is often empty. Practices change to soften the decree's limits.

Second, they stifle private treble damage suits. No conviction is obtained, so private suits must start from scratch. They are also hobbled by the fact that the agency has not pressed for a conviction. Therefore a decree often throws away the one tool for treating the problem. *Third,* a decree immunizes. It legitimizes the situation, so that further action is presumed to be inappropriate for at least a number of years or decades. *Fourth,* it leaves policy unresolved (as in conglomerate mergers in 1971). Precedential multipliers are not applied.

One Big Agency.   Unifying antitrust under one agency is a perennial proposal. This would avoid overlaps and gaps. Responsibility would be focused and more accountable. Yet the change could be merely cosmetic, unless real resources and powers were changed. It would cause a seismic upheaval in treatment. And it could merely breed bureaucracy and political pressure, rather than efficiency. Only if the unified agency had increased powers to withstand the more focused interest groups might it be able to improve the actual treatment. Most experts prefer to retain two rival agencies—partly competing and emulating—in place of a monopoly agency.

Antitrust reform is a popular pastime, but it contains more quirks and illusions than is usually realized. Some reforms are clearly unwise, no matter how one appraises the present effectiveness of antitrust. Others are surely needed but are unlikely to occur. Still others are untried and speculative. Devising optimal antitrust is a test of analytical skill, ingenuity, and sophistication. One can expect the topic to persist unresolved for the next several decades, at least.

QUESTIONS FOR REVIEW

1. "Antitrust only hardens dominant positions. Therefore it should be abolished." True?
2. "The effects of U.S. antitrust policy have long been pretty well known." True?
3. "The agencies win the remedies, while the firms win the decisions." True?
4. "British antitrust policies are similar to U.S. policies in kind but far weaker in degree." True?
5. "An Industrial Reorganization Commission could escape some of the present difficulties of antitrust, but others would remain." True?
6. "Private antitrust suits have not appreciably affected many of the leading dominant firms." True?
7. What degree or direction of twist do you think that U.S. antitrust policies cause?
8. What incentives of Section 2 policy most need correcting? How could it be done?
9. Define the scope and procedures of an appropriate Industrial Reorganization Commission. Is one needed?

Part III

REGULATION

10.
Tasks and Forms of Regulation

11.
Price Level, Price Structure, and Efficiency

12.
Regulation of Electricity and Gas

13.
Regulation of Communications

14.
Regulation of Transportation

15.
Regulation Appraised

REGULATION

Regulation—optimism's form;
Small craft sent out to bind and bend the storm,

Yet roughly tossed. Survival is their hope;
By trimming sail and lying low, they cope.

Conceived in compromise, it's oddly made,
Beset by trivia and hopes betrayed,

Yet tries to fit the public interest;
The bender bent, not worst but scarcely best.

chapter 10

Tasks and Forms of Regulation

Regulation is what regulators do. It is an American experiment, reflecting a confidence in independent authority and skill, and a faith in private ownership. Utility regulation is one special hybrid among the possible varieties of "regulation."[1]

To "regulate" has at least three definitions. One is tough and unilateral: "to govern or direct according to rule." Another refers to compromise and smoothing over: "to reduce to order . . . to regularize." And another is superficial, perhaps empty: "to make regulations." Actual regulation varies among these, sometimes strict, sometimes trivial or even a tool of corporate interests.

Ideal. The ideal image of regulation fits the first definition, as follows. A utility sector is a natural monopoly, and so its firms are given exclusive franchises to supply their areas and are put under a regulatory commission. This commission has full information on the utility and great skill in analyzing it. The commission sets "fair" ceilings on the utility's prices and profit rates, and ensures that the utility price structure is "just and reasonable." The commission monitors service quality and makes sure that the utility operates efficiently.

Ideal regulation therefore ratifies monopoly where—and only where—it is necessary in the public interest, prevents exploitation by the producer while reaping economies of scale, and yet avoids using public capital, subsidies, or guarantees against risk.[2] The result: maximum public control with minimum public resources.

---

[1] The best treatises on it include A. E. Kahn, *The Economics of Regulation,* 2 vols. (New York: Wiley, 1970, 1971); Charles F. Phillips, Jr., *The Economics of Regulation: Theory and Practice in the Transportation and Public Utility Industries,* rev. ed. (Homewood, Ill.: Irwin, 1969); and J. C. Bonbright, *Principles of Public Utility Rates* (New York: Columbia University Press, 1961). These are heavy books; one might best look into them *after* reading Chapters 10 and 11 here.

[2] Regulation is also appropriate for *public* firms (see Part IV). The economic criteria are the same for both public and private enterprises, in utility sectors and elsewhere. But in the United States it is often (incorrectly) regarded as "an alternative to" public enterprise.

Courtesy of Cornell University

Courtesy of MIT

Courtesy of Michigan State University

Alfred E. Kahn (born 1917) of Cornell University, a leading scholar of regulation, has urged that regulation, though imperfect, is workable and often effective. He was chairman of the New York State Public Service Commission during 1974–77 and of the Civil Aeronautics Board during 1977–78. He led the CAB's deregulation of prices and routes. (Shown here in 1955.)

Paul MacAvoy (born 1934) of Yale University suggests from his research that the regulation of natural gas, railroads, and electricity has been unnecessary and costly. While on the Council of Economic Advisers in 1974–76 he promoted the efforts to deregulate transportation and natural gas.

Walter Adams (born 1922) has stressed that regulated firms are often given too much monopoly. A leading scholar of industrial competition and antitrust, he has also critically analysed military purchasing policies. He is at Michigan State University.

Such ideal regulation is rare on this earth. It might, even if it were perfect, have costly side effects, as we will see. Our job is to learn how actual regulation differs from the ideal, why it differs, and what effects it has had.

Hazards.   There are hazards in regulation. *(a)* It is part of a larger social contract which grants a real monopoly in exchange for a possibility of regulating it. *(b)* Technology and demand change as the years go by, but the regulatory treatment may not adjust. *(c)* Since regulation deals with large and tightly focused interests (the utility firms and their main customers), they may cause regulation to be weak or biased (recall Chapter 3). And *(d)*, regulation relies on personal judgments about complex issues, rather than on clear laws or economic criteria.

So one approaches regulation hoping for the best but braced for the worst. Regulation's true character and effects are warmly disputed. Some think it awful; others see it as the best possible approach in this rugged world; most think it a mixed blessing.[3] Your tasks are to understand its economic effects and to judge it fairly.

Format. The topic requires a thorough coverage in this book because regulated industries are important, and because it is such a complex, thriving, and spreading phenomenon. This chapter sets the stage by presenting regulation's nature and forms. The next chapter sets forth the basic economic tasks: to control the *level* of prices and profits and the *structure* of prices for regulated services. Then we take up—in separate chapters—the power sector, communications, and transport. These include the core, standard utility sectors under regulation. The larger lessons from the regulatory experiment are drawn in Chapter 15.

Here in Chapter 10 we will first define the criteria for what should be regulated, and then review which sectors are regulated. Then come the economic tasks of regulation, in Section D. The evolution of utilities and regulation is analyzed in Section E, and a brief history is given in Section F.

A. WHAT SHOULD BE REGULATED?

"Natural monopoly" is the basic criterion for applying regulation. But there are others, too, and in actual cases the choices can be difficult. The criteria often conflict, and actual conditions are usually debatable.[4]

1. Declining costs. Monopoly is "natural" when economies of scale are steep and extend out to the size of the whole market. Monopoly is then inevitable, and it provides average costs lower than competition can. Figure 10–1 illustrates a case where monopoly costs are one half those of a three-firm oligopoly; more competition means higher cost. Ideally regulation identifies such clear cases, gives a franchise to one firm, and then limits price to P_N rather than the monopoly price P_M.

Such simple cases are rare. Usually the utility produces many distinct outputs from its basic capacity and sells them to many customer groups.[5]

---

[3] Consider this sample of expert opinions. Henry Simons (1936): "Unregulated, extralegal monopolies are tolerable evils; but private monopolies with the blessing of regulation and the support of law are malignant cancers in the system." Walter Adams and Horace Gray (1955): "Among all the devices used by government to promote monopoly, public utility, or public interest, regulation is in some respects perhaps the worst." Donald Dewey (1974): "I put it to you that as citizens we wish the regulatory agency to serve as a forum for group therapy, a better business bureau, a check on bureaucracy, and a brake on economic and social change." Richard A. Posner (1969): "Public utility regulation is probably not a useful exertion of governmental powers." Ben W. Lewis (1966): "Public-utility regulation has not lived up to its early 20th-century promise." Roger Cramton (1964): "Much regulatory activity has little economic significance." John Bauer (1950): "Under the conditions that have existed, the wonder is that regulation has worked as well as it has."

[4] Good analyses are given in Kahn, *The Economics of Regulation,* vol. 1, chap. 1, and Bonbright, *Principles,* chapters 1 and 2.

[5] Utility capacity often involves heavy capital investment (such as in railroad trackage and electricity plant). High capital intensity is often said to be a reason for regulating an industry. Yet it is neither necessary nor sufficient. High capital intensity is simply a frequent side effect of the other basic conditions.

FIGURE 10–1
Simple natural monopoly

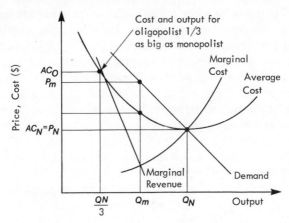

Still the basic lesson holds. Extreme economies of scale (in one direction or many) call for monopoly and some sort of public regulation. Good examples are local electricity and telephone service. With one set of wires down the streets and to users, costs are at $P_N = AC_N$; with three sets of wires, costs would be at AC_O.

This clear criterion is often diluted in practice by three kinds of difficulties:

1. "Natural monopoly" conditions often exist only in part of the "utility" sector.[6] Moreover, this mixture often changes over time, as technology evolves. Fitting the utility franchise only to the true natural monopoly parts becomes a ticklish job. Telephones, electric power, and railroads pose this problem especially.

2. Scale economies vary in steepness, so that the "natural monopoly" is not distinct. Where scale economies are slight, natural monopoly is marginal, as illustrated in Figure 10–2. Whether to regulate at all, rather than rely on antitrust, is then a close question. For example, computers and canned soup may be closer to natural monopoly than parts of the railroad and telephone sectors. The postman on the daily round is a basis for the postal utility; why not milk delivery?

3. Actual cost conditions are often hard to measure. This is acute where the utility produces outputs from a central capacity or network. Determining true costs is then a prime regulatory task.

---

6 Thus local telephone and electricity services seem clearly to be natural monopolies, for duplication of the systems of wires would be technically odd. Yet other parts of these systems—such as intercity business data transmission, and wholesale electric power—may easily support several or many competitors. Or, some railroads (and some parts within railroads) are natural monopolies, while others are not. For good analysis of such conditions, see Almarin Phillips, ed., *Promoting Competition in Regulated Markets* (Washington, D.C.: Brookings Institution, 1974).

FIGURE 10–2
Marginal conditions of natural monopoly

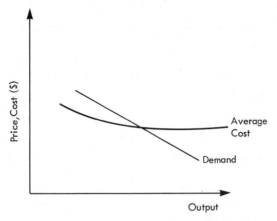

2. **A "Necessity."**   Some goods seem to be especially "necessary" or "vital" to their users. In economic terms, demand is highly inelastic, at least
for the minimum necessary level of use. This gives rise to two strands of
the social interest. *(a)* A loss of supply can wreak havoc with users, causing
wider social disruption (for example, a power failure in New York). *(b)*
The supplier could overcharge the users unmercifully. Where the "necessity"
is universally used, but supplied by only one firm, regulation naturally follows.
Even if only a small fraction of the populace uses the "necessity," regulation
may occur if that group is regarded as needing protection.[7]

Yet many "necessities" need no regulation: foods, housing, clothing, for
example. The key reason is that there are many sources of supply, so that
the users do not have inelastic demand *for any one supplier.*

3. **Demand Elasticities Vary.**   This permits price discrimination, which
can go to extremes (recall Chapter 8). Inelastic demand creates "creamy"
markets, where high excess profits can be earned. Elastic demand makes
for "skim" markets, where the efficiency benefits of competition occur. Discrimination is especially likely where a common service is sold to greatly
varying customer groups. Some discrimination may be proper, but a full
monopoly is likely to carry it too far.

4. **Output Fluctuates Sharply and Regularly.**   The system faces pulses
of high "peak" demands and low off-peak demands, by hours, days of the
week, and seasons. Examples are rush-hour bus loads, electricity loads, and
telephone traffic during business hours *vs.* 1 to 5 A.M. This makes cost and
demand conditions very complicated, raising the need to supervise the firm's
pricing choices.

---

[7] For example, cable TV or bus service may be used by only a minority of the
population. Should they be regulated?

5. Physical Connections. Users may be directly hooked up to the supply system, by wires, pipes, access roads, or other means.[8] Users therefore cannot change suppliers easily, nor can they resell the utility output among each other. This enhances the supplier's ability to price discriminate.

6. Uniform Product. Regulation is facilitated if the utility product is uniform and slowly changing. Uniformity does not call for regulation, but it is nearly essential for regulation to work. Otherwise, the seller can manipulate the nature and quality of the product.

These criteria boil down mainly to *scale economies plus the danger of too much price discrimination.* They make a single producer "natural," and this increases the power to victimize some or all users. The outcome would be both inefficient and unfair (recall Chapter 1).

The criteria do not neatly mark off a clear set of utilities for regulating. The criteria often conflict mutually. Often their conditions are only weak and marginal. The conditions usually evolve as time passes (see Section E below). The conditions can be misrepresented, either to fend off regulation or to extend it too far. Setting the lines of regulation is an intensely controversial activity. The economic criteria do not provide crystal-clear answers.[9]

Yet the real conditions do exist, regardless of the difficulties in discovering them. At each point of time, there is an array of sectors; some strongly need regulation, while at the other end many other sectors have no "regulatable" features at all. This array evolves over time, as technology changes, and so regulation needs to be added to some sectors and withdrawn from others.[10] The set of industries needing regulation in 1980 differs from those of 1900, and those of the year 2050 will probably differ too.

B. WHAT IS REGULATED?

Regulation now extends to any sector which the legislature votes as being "affected with the public interest" and sets up a commission to regulate. The rugged political process, not refined criteria, is what creates regulation.

Sectors. In fact, there are four broad classes of "regulated utilities": in the energy sector, communications, transport, and urban services. In each

[8] Examples include wires for electricity, telephones, and cable TV, and pipes for water and gas.

[9] Harold Demsetz has suggested that utilities not be regulated at all. Rather their franchises would be auctioned off at the outset for the maximum price, which would give to the public in advance all of the monopoly rent. Later monopoly exploitation by the utility would not be truly harmful since the overpricing would already be neutralized by the purchase price of the franchise. See his "Why Regulation Utilities?" *Journal of Law and Economics,* 11 (April 1968), 55–65. The proposal has fatal defects, which are reviewed in Lester G. Telser, "On the Regulation of Industry: A Note," *Journal of Political Economy,* 77 (November/December 1969), 937–52, and Oliver E. Williamson, "Franchise Bidding for Natural Monopolies—In General and With Respect to CATV," *Bell Journal of Economics* 7 (Spring 1976), 73–104.

[10] Currently, the marginal cases include some, such as cable TV and hospitals, where regulation seems to be spreading in. Others, such as railroads, airlines, trucking, and natural gas production, are presently regulated but may need to be deregulated.

TABLE 10–1
Present "Utility Sectors" under Some Degree of Regulation

Primarily Monopolies	Partially or Primarily Competitive
Telephone service	Railroads
Electric power	Waterways
Natural gas	Pipelines
Postal services	Airlines
Cable television	Broadcasting
Urban transit	Hospitals
Water and sewage	Trucking
Ports	

sector, only part should clearly be regulated, while the rest could nearly or definitely be competitive. There is intense debate over which parts are which. Tables 10–1 and 10–2 outline the sectors and parts. Figure 10–3 illustrates how actual regulation may stray from the formal and appropriate areas. Western railroads, telephones, electric power, and gas have been the classic cases of needed and actual regulation. Some sectors are under public ownership (for example, some urban systems and postal service); their regulatory issues are treated in Chapter 18.

The sectors generate about 8 percent of national income. Since they are capital-intensive, their share of national investment is about 17 percent (the share of all business investment is even higher, at 36 percent). This share is probably growing gradually, for telephone and urban investment have risen especially rapidly in recent years. By contrast, their share of all civilian employment is only 4.7 percent.

Commissions. There is a patchwork of federal and state commissions "covering" these sectors. In some parts they overlap, while in others they

TABLE 10–2
The Scope of Certain U.S. "Utility" Sectors, 1977

	National Income Originating in These Sectors (%)	Share of These Sectors in:	
		Total Fixed Investment (%)	Total Industrial New Plant and Equipment (%)
Electric, gas, and sanitary services	1.9	9.3	19.1
Communications: telephone and telegraph	2.2	5.6	11.4
Transportation	3.6		
Railroad		1.0	2.1
Other		1.5	3.1
Total	7.7	17.4	35.7

Source: *Survey of Current Business,* May 1978.

274

FIGURE 10–3
Actual regulatory coverage may differ
from formal coverage—and from "natural
monopoly" areas.

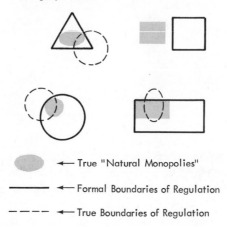

True "Natural Monopolies"

Formal Boundaries of Regulation

True Boundaries of Regulation

leave gaps. Table 10–3 shows the main federal commissions and a selection of state commissions. Federal commissions have jurisdiction only over *interstate* operations. The line between these and *intrastate* operations is often obscure, for much of a utility system's plant may be involved in both operations. State and federal commissions have been struggling over jurisdiction for more than 60 years.[11] Also there is feuding among federal agencies for control over some utility sectors. Altogether, the coverage of utility sectors is as much a crazy quilt as it is a "system of regulation."

C. THE ECONOMIC TASKS

Regulation involves complex—often delicate—relationships and tasks. As always, the aim is to attain maximum efficiency, fairness, and social contribution (recall Chapter 1). With regulation, these boil down to several specific practical matters (Chapter 11 gives more detail). Regulated firms have *rights* and *duties,* usually as follows:

Rights. *(a)* They are entitled to "reasonable" prices and profits. *(b)* They are given complete or partial protection from competition (via a franchise). *(c)* They can exercise eminent domain in acquiring property, even by coercion. *(d)* Rules governing them must be reasonable.

Duties. *(a)* Prices and profits are to be no more than "reasonable." *(b)* At those prices, all demand must be met, even at peak times. Service must

---

[11] For example, the National Association of Regulatory Utility Commissioners (NARUC), whose members are state commissioners, has lobbied strongly for decades to keep federal regulation out of its members' jurisdictions.

TABLE 10–3

The Main Federal Commissions and Selected State Commissions

Commission (and the year it was formally established)	Number of Members	Number of Staff Members	Expenditures Fiscal Year 1979 ($ million)	Jurisdiction
Interstate Commerce Commission (1887)	5	2,200	69	Railroads; motor carriers; water shipping; oil pipelines; express companies, etc.
Federal Energy Regulatory Commission (1934)	5	1,550	56	Electric power; gas and pipelines; water-power sites
Federal Communications Commission (1934)	7	2,200	67	Telephone; television; cable TV, radio, telegraph
Civil Aeronautics Board (1938)	5	850	27	Airlines (passenger and cargo)
Postal Rate Commission (1971)	5	150	8	Postal service
Alabama (1919)	3	79	2	Electric, gas, telephone, railroads, buses, trucking, taxis, water
California (1912)	5	980	28	Electric, gas, telephone, railroads, buses, trucking, water shipping, pipelines, water, warehouses, cable TV
Illinois (1913)	5	253	7	Electric, gas, telephone, railroads, buses, trucking, water shipping, pipelines, water, cable TV
Iowa (1963)	3	127	2	Electric, gas, telephone, railroads, buses, trucking, warehouses
Massachusetts (1885)	3	147	3	Electric, gas, telephone, railroads, buses, trucking, taxis, water
Michigan (1919)	3	325	9	Electric, gas, telephone, railroads, buses, trucking, water carriers, pipelines
Montana (1913)	5	39	2	Electric, gas, telephone, railroads, buses, trucking, taxis, pipelines, water, cable TV
New Mexico (1941)	3	108	2	Electric, gas, water
South Carolina (1912)	7	155	2	Electric, gas, telephone, railroads, buses, trucking, taxis, water, sewage
Wisconsin (1907)	3	174	7	Electric, gas, telephone, railroads, buses, trucking, water, sewage

Sources: U.S. Government, *Budget, Fiscal 1979* (Washington, D.C.: U.S. Government Printing Office, 1978), Appendix volume: National Association of Regulatory Utility Commissioners, *Annual Report on Utility and Carrier Regulation, 1976* (Washington, D.C.: 1102 Interstate Commerce Commission Bldg., 1977), various tables; and various state commission reports.

be adequate in quantity and quality. *(c)* All changes in services (adding *or* dropping them) must be approved in advance. *(d)* The safety of the public is to be protected.

The firm is given a franchise (often an exclusive monopoly), but it is still a private firm with shareholders. There is no direct control over the selection of directors or managers of the firm. Therefore the firm naturally strives to maximize its profits, by actions both in the market and toward the regulators.

The franchise enlarges and hardens whatever "natural" monopoly there may be, and it excludes entry. The firm is shielded from actual *and* potential competition. The franchise raises the value of the enterprise, but the commission strives to keep the value from containing large monopoly rents.

In this situation, the regulators have three main tasks: to restrain price and profit *levels,* to get an efficient and fair *structure* of prices, and to get efficient internal management and correct input combinations.

C1. The Level of Prices and Profits

The big effort of regulation has been to restrain total profits to some efficient—the usual term is "fair"—rate of return on the utility's investment. The basic choice is in these terms:

$$\text{Rate of return} = \frac{\text{Total revenue} - \text{Total cost}}{\text{Capital}}$$

Capital is supposed to include all fixed assets actually used—and necessary to use—in supplying the utility service. The rate of return includes the return to all investors, in both equity and debt. The firm's costs and capital are to be kept to the minimum, for each level of output.

The regulators then try to set the firm's prices just high enough to yield total revenues which will provide the "right" rate of return on the capital. Usually the fair return (after tax) is somewhere between 6 and 12 percent, or about two points above the rate on "riskless" Treasury securities (see Table 11–1). A "fair" return would just cover the cost of the capital used. Typically the commission estimates the "cost of capital" and then sets the "fair" rate of return just above that level.[12] The process of decision is usually just a compromise between proposals by the company and the commission's staff.

The precise optimal rate of return cannot be known definitively, of course. But it is almost sure to be within the 6 to 12 percent range, and so the commission's decision cannot be very far wrong. And seriously wrong decisions are soon shown by events to need correction. Therefore the process is usually reasonably successful.

---

[12] The methods and rationales are often obscure and dubious, as Chapter 11 will note. Usually the firm and the commission staff put in contrasting estimates of the "fair return;" the firm around perhaps 10 to 15 percent, the staff about 6 to 8 percent.

C2. The Structure of Prices

The second task is to get an efficient structure of prices. Utilities supply many different consumers, in residences, shops, industry, offices, and so on. The outputs also vary, in times, amounts, and terms of supply, but they are usually supplied via direct physical connections to the users. The utility usually has a lot of elbow room to price discriminate; that is, to set prices in line with demand elasticities.

The regulators' task is therefore to prevent discrimination, except where it may be justified. This usually means setting prices in line with the true costs of service; *that is what efficient allocation means* (recall Chapter 1).[13] These real costs, properly defined, are marginal costs (which may be hard to measure in practice. Chapter 11 analyses marginal cost in some detail).

The broad objective is to set each

$$\text{Price} = k \text{ (Marginal cost)}$$

where k is some ratio which is similar among outputs and which is as close to 1 as possible. The utility wishes k to vary, setting it highest where demand is most inelastic, so as to maximize its profit and avert new competition. Various customer groups will press at rate hearings for lower rates. Caught between consumers and the utility managers, who know their own cost and demand conditions best (though not always very well), the regulators usually settle on compromises which reflect both cost and demand conditions. Or they may just leave these complex issues to the utility to decide, acquiescing in most or all of the proposed rates.

C3. Internal Efficiency

This task requires care and thoroughness. X-inefficiency is likely to occur, because *(a)* the firm's monopoly power insulates it from market discipline, and *(b)* the regulatory constraints themselves may cause inefficiency (see Chapter 11). Regulators need to define the efficient cost levels and factor combinations and then see that the firms attain them. Instead, regulators have done little to monitor or enforce efficiency.

D. COMMISSIONS AND THE REGULATORY PROCESS

D1. Structure and Staffing

The standard commission has *(a)* members (usually three to seven), *(b)* a staff with various skills and tasks, *(c)* a budget, and *(d)* various legal powers. Structures of two "typical" commissions are shown in Figures 10–4 and 10–5.

---

[13] One exception is where a single price would not attain enough revenue to cover total costs. There are others, too, and so a fair amount of price discrimination may be appropriate in regulated firms with many products. The issue is treated in Chapter 11.

FIGURE 10–4

The Federal Communications Commission in 1977

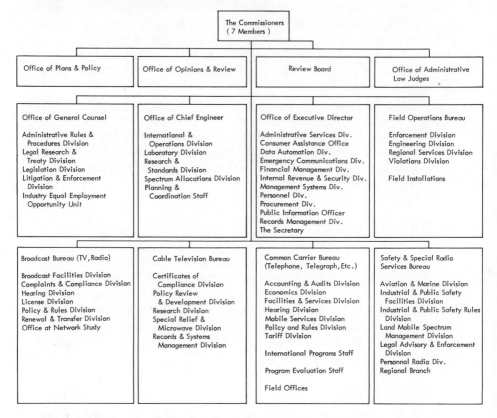

FIGURE 10–5

Format of a Sample State Commission (the Michigan Public Service Commission)

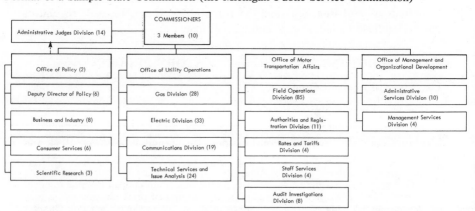

Employees in each part are given in parentheses.

FIGURE 10–6
The Typical Setting of Regulatory Commissions

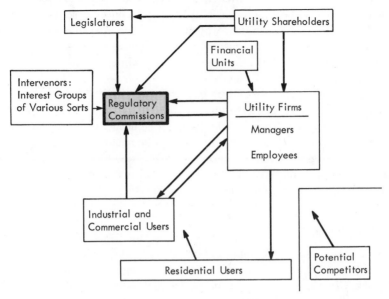

The relation of commissions to their interest groups is outlined in Figure 10–6. Commissions are the focus of many interests and pressures. The commissioners are appointed by an executive (President, governor, or mayor) while the budget is screened by the executive offices and (usually) voted by the legislature. Commission effort goes outside, to advocating better laws and testifying about current issues, as well as into the internal process of hearing and deciding cases. To a large extent, the business of regulation is to compromise among these interests.

Commission resources are often absorbed mainly by secondary duties and housekeeping chores (monitoring service, inspecting railroad crossings, answering complaints, and so forth).[14] Most commissions are underfunded, but a few manage to dissipate ample budgets. The staffs often include brigades of clerks and accountants but scarcely any well-trained economists.

As in antitrust, the top officials come and go, often rapidly, while the career staff work on along conventional lines.[15] Also, as in antitrust, the

---

[14] For example, the FCC's core task is to regulate the telephone system (see Chapter 13). Yet only about one tenth of its budget actually goes to that purpose (in 1977, about $4 million out of $42 million). Such things as ham operators, aviation and police services, radio licenses, and inspections take up the rest. To test this point, look carefully through the latest annual reports of the FCC, ICC, FERC, and other commissions.

[15] As elsewhere, the better people tend to be lured away by outside offers, while the others stay on. The few really long-time commissioners (some stay 15 or 20 years) therefore are often the least qualified and innovative.

private side's resources routinely dwarf those of the agencies. The agency people are lower paid and often less skilled. Commissioners have usually been politicians, either young ones using regulation as a stepping stone to higher office, or old ones on their way out to pasture. Recently a few minority members, economists, and consumer activists have been appointed to the better commissions. Yet the standard type is a white, male, politically motivated lawyer of no great distinction.

Generally, the structure and budget of a commission are not decisive to its performance. What matters most are the skill and zeal of the commissioners, and their support from outside groups. The needed skills include: understanding the economic issues, administering the agency, organizing the support of interest groups, and mastering publicity to win general support. Such combinations of skills are rare. Many appointees are, instead, mediocrities or amateurs. Therefore, commissions rarely perform up to their potential.[16]

D2. Procedures

Commissions act by hearings and decisions. Usually, the hearings are precipitated by the utility, requesting a price change or a change in service offerings. Occasionally, a crescendo of complaints by the public stirs action. The typical sequence is summarized in Figure 10–7. It involves *(a)* open hearings, offering opposing rationales for a decision, *(b)* setting the range of possible compromise, and then *(c)* picking the compromise and explaining it by one or more rationales. Like most social decisions, regulatory actions start off with a range of choice, and all that follows is simply a roundabout way to pin down and explain the exact splitting of the difference. In some cases, the hearings become a mere ritual, often long and dreary. In others, they are head-on collisions among the parties, with great drama and suspense about the outcome. But the normal process is simply to find the range of reasonable compromise, split it (often right down the middle), and then justify that split to interested parties.

The hearing process is an adversary proceeding, conducted by lawyers following legal rules. Economists are used only in preparing some features of the staff proposal; some may also be used as expert witnesses by the companies to defend their side. Since there are economists of all persuasions to choose among for expert witnesses, even the economic input tends to become ritualized and wooden.

Also, much is done informally between commissions and firms, in negotiating small (and even large) issues of pricing and service. This can be quicker and smoother than full-dress public cases. But the process is covert, and the issues are not openly raised and settled. There is no record of facts and opinion. Outsiders—including *consumers*—are left out of the process. There

---

[16] For a lively account of the foibles of actual officials and agencies, see Louis M. Kohlmeier, Jr., *The Regulators* (New York: Harper & Row, 1969).

FIGURE 10–7
The Conventional Process of Regulation

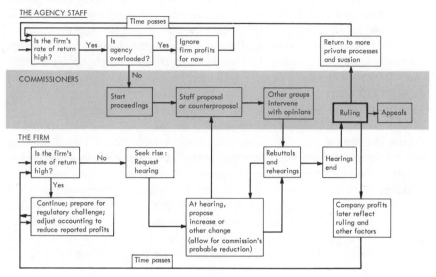

is little "public responsibility," which is what regulation is supposed to provide.[17]

The process is partly diplomatic in nature. It breeds overstatement in the firms' rate requests, as the firms anticipate the cuts which "tough" regulators need to make. The firm asks for what it would like, the commissioners usually cut it by about half, and so the firm ends up with what will suffice (and what it probably expected).[18] The managers complain about the unrealistic commission, while the commissioners appear strict. Customers may feel that their interests have been protected. Occasionally the commission does seriously stray from the range of expected choice, but normally there is little real surprise (nor much economic meaning) in the process.

In a related vein, the process often expands to fill the time available. Before 1970 rate cases were often long, leisurely affairs, taking up to a year or two from request to decision. Under special forces of rising costs during 1970–75, the process was often telescoped into a few months, without losing much in quality. As pressures ease, the duration of cases can be expected to lengthen again.

---

[17] For one extreme instance, the FCC chose to regulate the telephone industry informally—by so-called continuous serveillance—from 1938 to 1965. Some state commissions in the 1950s and 1960s went for five to eight years without a formal hearing.

[18] For an analysis of the conditions which trigger rate cases, and of the outcomes, see Paul L. Joskow, "The Determination of the Allowed Rate of Return in a Formal Regulatory Hearing," *Bell Journal of Economics* 3 (Autumn 1972), 632–44, and "Pricing Decisions of Regulated Firms: A Behavioral Approach," ibid. 4 (Spring 1973), 118–40.

Altogether, the process inserts a degree of delay and uncertainty into the utility firm's pricing and profits. The economic effect differs sharply between inflationary and other times. During *inflation,* delay squeezes the utility's profits, as price increases lag behind cost increases. This gives the commission great power. By contrast, if costs are falling, the firm can sit pretty, earning excess profits while the commission tries to catch up by starting cases to cut the prices. Roughly speaking, the process involved falling costs during 1930–65 but then reversed to rising costs after 1965 for most utilities. This dramatically raised the power of the commissions over the firms.

The process can include an appeal by the firm to the courts, trying to reverse the commission's decision. Such litigation can be protracted, in some cases beyond 10 years (see for example the TELPAK case in Chapter 13). Utilities often turn to legislatures to reverse commissions by new laws. Commissions often act to counter such moves, by their own lobbying, testifying, or use of publicity. Usually the commissions are outclassed in this kind of struggle. Their basic protection is that courts are reluctant to reverse commissions except on points of law or procedure. Most commission decisions are upheld on appeal unless there has been some sort of gross error in handling.

D3. Motives

Regulators are "normal" people, working within a specific set of pressures and rewards. Their success comes from continuing in office or moving to higher positions. This they achieve by avoiding two things: *(a)* appearing too lenient toward the firms, and *(b)* breakdown of supply (for example, blackouts, stoppages). Their motivation is defensive, to avoid trouble, to pacify.[19] To this end, they will seek larger budgets, for fuller staffing. They will also encourage the utility to have higher degrees of reserve capacity, so as to avoid service breakdowns. They may also become absorbed in small issues, leaving the divisive ones to the firm to settle as quietly as possible.

Utility managers face unusual constraints and rewards. Their monopoly is strong but may contain marginal areas of competition. The firm's profits are regulated, but not tightly. Profits can be raised by manipulating the commission as well as by actions in the market.

The prime objectives of utility officers are three. *One* is to raise the permitted profit ceiling. Such rises can have potent effects on shareholder capital, since a "mere" one point rise in the rate of return—say, from 8 to 9 percent—can add 10 or 20 percent to the price of the company's stock. A *second* motive is to set low prices where there is actual or potential competition,

---

[19] Since 1965 there have been interesting efforts to frame the regulators' motives in general "theories of regulation." Yet they have not added much predictive power. See George J. Stigler, "The Theory of Economic Regulation," *Bell Journal of Economies* 2 (Spring 1971), 3–21; Richard A. Posner, "Theories of Economic Regulation," ibid. 4 (Autumn 1974), 335–58; and Sam Peltzman, "Toward a More General Theory of Regulation," *Journal of Law and Economics* 19 (Autumn 1976), 211–40.

FIGURE 10–8
Commissions may control, negotiate, or acquiesce.

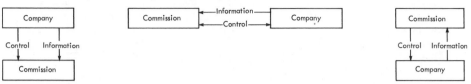

covering the balance of costs from its more captive markets, where demand elasticity is low. This minimizes long-run risk and enlarges the rate base upon which profits can be earned (Chapter 11 discusses this further). The *third* motive is to avoid, at almost any cost, a service failure (for example, a blackout), for that stirs public resentment and endangers—more than any other event—the utility's privileged status.

Several traits of behavior are likely to follow. First, the managers are likely to self-select into a group of relatively conservative, risk-avoiding people. The premium is on avoiding trouble, rather than aggressive innovation. Second, they will be preoccupied with reinforcing their monopoly position, by choices about price structures, technology, and other issues. Third, like the regulators, they will prefer to have high degrees of reserve capacity, in order to avoid service breakdowns. In short, the special conditions may affect economic structure and efficiency.

Both groups share the motive of making regulation seem to work. Otherwise, their security is removed. This joint motivation underlies all of their surface arguments. It unites them against most outside efforts to change or replace regulation.

D4. Outcomes

The natural outcomes are for commissions to vary widely in their quality and strictness. Some commissions will exert great power, others will negotiate, and others will rubber-stamp the companies' decisions (as illustrated in Figure 10–8). Some fluctuate between the extremes. Few commissions will apply economic analysis thoroughly. Most will slide over difficult problems by compromise.

The ultimate responsibility for performance will be shared by the commissions and the firms. Each will publicize and take credit for success. Each will understate the failures and blame them on the other. Certain economic effects toward inefficiency will tend to occur: Chapter 11 analyses these.

E. THE EVOLUTION OF UTILITIES AND OF THEIR REGULATION

Most utilities pass through a life cycle, during which regulation is added and evolves. Regulation is a "social contract": a monopoly is granted in

TABLE 10–4
Stages of Utility Life Cycles: Approximate Intervals

	Stage 1	Stage 2	Stage 3	Stage 4
Manufactured gas	1800–1820	1820–1880	1880–1920	1920–1950
Natural gas	1900–1930	1930–1950	1950–	
Telegraph	1840–1850	1850–1916	1916–1930	1930–
Railways:				
All	1820–1835	1835–1910		
Passenger			1910–1935	1935–
Freight			1910–1960	1960–
Electricity	1870–1885	1885–1960	1960–	
Street railways	1870–1885	1885–1912	1912–1922	1922–
Telephone	1875–1880	1880–1947	1947–	
Airlines	1920–1925	1925–1965	1965–	
Television	1935–1947	1947–1965	1965–	
Cable TV	1950–1955	1955–		

exchange for a degree of public control. But the conditions change. By seeing commissions in this light, you can evaluate their behavior more fairly. There are nine points.[20]

1. Utility sectors commonly proceed through four stages. In *Stage 1* the system is invented, often leading to control by patents. This period is usually brief but decisive for the future form of the system.

In *Stage 2* the system is created and grows, often displacing a prior utility (for example, buses replace trolleys, telephone displaces telegraph). Cross-subsidies among users, and a separation of creamy and skim markets, become embedded in the price structure. The new service *seeks to get itself regulated,* in order to achieve permanence, legitimacy, and market control. The new regulators act as promoters, doing what they can to make the service available to all households.

In *Stage 3* the system becomes complete as a matter of technology and market saturation. It now shifts from an offensive to a defensive stance. Competing new technologies arise beyond the utility's control to substitute for it in its basic and peripheral markets. Its physical layout and pricing structure increasingly are out of fit with evolving city patterns. The utility finds itself increasingly trying to obstruct new technology or to warp it to fit its own private interests.

Finally, in *Stage 4,* the system is ready to revert back—no longer a utility—to conventional competitive processes. Or, in certain cases where externalities, equity, or other social effects are peculiarly important, a degree of public ownership may be adopted.

Table 10–4 estimates very roughly the stages for a number of present and past utilities. During these stages, the basic technology prescribes *different* optimum structures and policy treatments.

---

[20] This discussion draws on W. G. Shepherd, *The Treatment of Market Power* (New York: Columbia University Press, 1975), Chapter 9.

2. Regulation usually starts in Stage 2, in harmony with the pre-existing interests of the utility and its larger industrial customers. The structure of mutual interest, the profit expectations, and the basic terms of exchange (especially the supplier's rate level and structure) therefore *precede* regulation. Thus placed atop the pre-existing situation, regulation naturally tends to legitimize, reinforce, and smooth these interest-group compromises—recall the middle definition of regulation: ". . . to regularize." Rate structure is not thoroughly assessed and changed. *Regulators operate within the "contract."* They cannot really change it (for example, rescind the franchise or cut rates sharply), though some observers wrongly think they can.

3. Regulation has (barring the odd exception) inadequate funds and medio-cre talent for its true economic tasks. So those at its center usually have little motivation, or even understanding, to change the basic "contract" and the process.

4. The "contract" excludes seller competition from the service area, in ex-change for a review process. The efficacy of the review tends to atrophy, from lack of funds, expertise, and powers. The exclusions spread and become absolute. The franchise and regulatory process themselves become manipu-lated by the managers as part of their whole efforts to maximize the utility's value and minimize the risk and uncertainty of their positions. And since the utility's share prices capitalize the value of the franchise, any threat to their value—such as by unilateral new entry—is regarded as "confiscation," *ergo* intolerable to the *regulators* as well as the utility.

So regulation is not neutral toward new competition: the bias arises from the very contract itself, and it is accentuated by the profit constraints. So regulation tends to prevent the natural evolution of new competition. That might be appropriate for Stage 2, but it is not for Stages 3 and 4.

5. The "contract" turns out in practice to allot responsibility and service liability increasingly to the commission. Penalties and rewards are not ap-plied—either in general or specific directions—to the utility's performance. Instead of asserting or imposing the public interest, the commission often ends up accepting responsibility for service, good or bad.[21]

6. So the "contract" hyper-excludes, in at least six ways.

a. It excludes seller entry from primary markets and often even from second-ary and tertiary ones.

b. It excludes inter-area competition by the utility firms for each others' major customers.

---

[21] Under it, too—and this is perhaps the crowning oddity—there are few practical, specific penalties which can be applied to the utility for specific lapses (for example, brownouts, crossed wires, late planes or trains) or for general failures of management. The regulatory contract lacks explicit performance standards, and it lacks mechanisms for enforcing good performance. The only penalties which can really be applied to a utility are political ones—for example, open criticism—and these usually hurt the regulators as much as the utilities. The utility's and commission's objective therefore becomes simply to minimize political repercussions, to avoid facing basic issues, to gloss over. The strangeness of the managers' role is matched by that of the regulators'.

c. It excludes take-over or lesser changes in managerial and financial control, either by private interests or ultimately by the commission itself or other public groups.

d. It excludes service-liability claims by legitimate plaintiffs.

e. It excludes rivalrous innovation, of Schumpeterian or other types.

f. It excludes regulatory choices which would cause significant reductions in utility share prices.

Taken together, these exclusions are often large and long lasting.

7. *In short, there is a reversed evolution of regulation, in the opposite direction from what utility evolution calls for.* Regulation comes to shield firms, rather than permit the proper degree of competition.[22]

8. *This contract and regulatory process tend to induce inefficiencies of several sorts* (to be seen in Chapter 11). They are likely to include *(a)* internal inefficiency, because of the lack of financial or regulatory constraints, *(b)* the design of utility technology is made more exclusive to the established utility, and *(c)* excess peak demand and capacity is induced by inefficient price structures.

These costs are likely to increase during Stage 3. The normal constraints on management are reduced or absent. And the utility's incentives are to tighten the exclusions further.

9. *The exclusions tend to be stable and self-perpetuating.* Entry by new sellers is difficult to force unilaterally upon a utility. Any severe such depressant on utility stock prices is asserted to be confiscatory. Large firms are commonly reluctant to enter, partly because their other profit opportunities exceed those which regulation formally permits. Small entrants are vulnerable and usually of trivial effect. "Better" regulation of rates—by hiring more brilliant commissioners or staffs, giving them bigger budgets, and so on—does not correct the basic contract, the structural conditions, nor the inefficiencies.

The upshot can be anti-Darwinian with a vengeance: regulation is often ill-fitted from the start, evolves the wrong way to fit its proper economic function, and survives only too well. Abolition is usually too simple and abrupt an answer, except for some Stage 4 cases. What is needed now is regulation which *(a)* lasts only as long as is appropriate, *(b)* contains inducements for its own termination, and *(c)* while it lasts, induces optimal choices by those in the regulated firm.

F. A BRIEF HISTORY OF REGULATION

Regulation has developed slowly and fitfully—and often stormily—during the last 100 years.

---

[22] For alternative statements of this basic conclusion, see the classic article by Horace M. Gray, "The Passing of the Public Utility Concept," *Journal of Land and Public Utility Economics* 16 (February 1940), 8–20; and Marver H. Bernstein, *Regulating Business by Independent Commission* (Princeton: Princeton University Press, 1955).

Early Origins.   Variants of regulation—giving favor to an enterprise and setting limits on it—trace back into prehistory. Then during 1400–1700 monopoly grants by the sovereign came to carry varying rights and duties. The great laissez-faire rollback of many of these interferences during 1750–1850 cleared away many quasi-regulatory devices.

The legal origin of modern regulation traces back to 1670, when Lord Chief Justice Hale in Britain summarized the law of businesses "affected with a publick interest."[23] Speaking of ferry boats, as well as port facilities, he noted that they were not merely private, because—as monopolies—they had public effects and public duties. This concept of *public interest* has been the pivot upon which all later setting of *public* constraints upon *private* capital have turned.

During 1820–70, there was much local experience in America with rate regulation: for example, private wharves, chimney sweeping, bread, and horse-drawn transportation, in Washington, D.C., and in other cities.[24] By 1860, five eastern states had tried advisory commissions for regulating railroads: they relied on competition plus supervision. By 1870, a variety of small-scale utilities—gas works, water works, railroads, and so on—existed and were being loosely treated in many ways. Competition was still commonly part of the approach.

Modern Regulation Begins.   It was railroads and the newer utilities—electricity, telephones, and city transit—which crystallized the modern regulatory method during 1880–1920. Transcontinental railroads evolved during 1850–70. They had great bargaining power in the Midwest, dealing with individual farmers. In contrast to many Eastern lines, where a degree of competition was possible, farmers out on the plains usually had no alternative ways to get their products to market. Grain elevators also exercised monopoly power, often tied directly in with the railroads. Therefore, by the mid-1870s, a deep-going set of discriminatory practices had been developed by the railroads, to charge all that the traffic would bear (see Chapters 14 and 17). The resulting wave of opposition took form as the Granger movement, and was the origin of what we now recall as "prairie populism."

By 1874, many Midwest states had created regulatory commissions to control railroad rates. Most of them quickly became passive, for railroad power was really a regional problem. The landmark *Munn* v. *Illinois* case in 1877 established that states could assert regulatory authority over trades (in this case grain elevators) "affected with the public interest."[25] The criteria

---

[23] Sir Matthew Hale, *De Portibus Maris* and *De Jure Maris,* London, 1670.

[24] See C. L. King, ed., *The Regulation of Municipal Utilities* (New York: Appleton, 1912), and M. H. Hunter, "Early Regulation of Public Service Corporations," *American Economic Review* 7 (September 1917), 569–81.

[25] In *Munn* v. *Illinois* (94 U.S. 113), the Court approved a law, enacted by the state of Illinois, controlling the charges made by grain elevators and warehouses. In the words of its opinion: "Property does become clothed with a public interest when used in a manner to make it of public consequence, and affect the community at large. When, therefore, one devotes his property to a use in which the public

of "public interest" were: *(a) necessity* of the service, and *(b) monopoly.* The decision set the general precedent that regulation can be applied wherever a public interest can be perceived. Yet it fatefully set *monopoly* as the prime target of regulation, and that still persists in the orthodox image.

By 1887 pressure had risen to redress the monopoly power of Midwestern railroads. This meshed neatly with the Eastern railroads' wish to create a cartel device to prevent periodic bouts of price competition among them.[26] The result was the Interstate Commerce Commission, created in 1887. Despite its apparent position of control, the fledgling ICC was blocked by the courts from settling effective rate ceilings until about 1910 (see Chapter 14). By the 1920s the railroads were already under heavy new competition from road carriers. The ICC therefore failed to regulate when it was appropriate and then did regulate after it became largely unnecessary.

Regulation Spreads. By 1900 electric and telephone utilities were already well advanced and evolving toward regional and national scope. Initially, open franchising had been the rule, with cities often having several or more little "utility" systems. But then the doctrine of natural monopoly took hold. During the watershed period of 1907–30, most states created public service commissions to franchise and regulate these private firms.[27] In many cases the firms lobbied hard to create regulation, as preferable to public ownership

---

has an interest, he, in effect, grants to the public an interest in that use, and must submit to be controlled by the public for the common good. . . ." The elevators along the Chicago waterfront were found to stand "in the very gateway of commerce, and take toll from all who pass." It was permissible, therefore, that they be regulated, so that they might "take but reasonable toll."

This concept was subsequently employed in approving public regulation of such industries as the railroads, and water, gas, electric, and telephone companies. It was called upon in 1914 in upholding a Kansas law providing for the regulation of fire insurance rates (*German Alliance Insurance Co.* v. *Kansas,* 233 U.S. 289). But it was used for a decade to invalidate laws extending public controls to other fields. In 1923 the Court rejected a Kansas law providing for compulsory arbitration of labor disputes in basic industries (*Wolff Packing Co.* v. *Court of Industrial Relations,* 262 U.S. 522); in 1927, a New York law fixing the markup of theater ticket agencies (*Tyson* v. *Banton,* 273 U.S. 418); in 1928, a New Jersey law regulating the fees of employment agencies (*Ribnik* v. *McBride,* 277 U.S. 350); in the same year, a Tennessee law controlling the price of gasoline (*Williams* v. *Standard Oil Co.,* 278 U.S. 235); and in 1932, an Oklahoma law restricting entry into the ice business (*New State Ice Co.* v. *Liebmann,* 282 U.S. 262). In each of these cases, the Court, usually speaking through Justice Sutherland, held that the business concerned was not affected with a public interest. But no standards of judgment were consistently applied. Whether an industry could be regulated depended on no objective criteria, but upon the undisclosed predispositions of the members of the Court.

[26] See Gabriel Kolko, *Railroads and Regulation, 1877–1916* (Princeton: Princeton University Press, 1965), and Paul W. MacAvoy, *The Economic Effects of Regulation* (Cambridge: MIT Press, 1965).

[27] There was also much experimenting with hybrid forms of franchises, incentives, sliding scales, and other regulatory devices. See King, *Regulation;* Martin G. Glaeser, *Outlines of Public Utility Economics* (New York: Macmillan, 1927); I. Bussing, *Public Utility Regulation and the So-Called Sliding Scale* (New York: Columbia University Press, 1936); and John Bauer, *The Public Utility Franchise* (Chicago: Public Administration Service, 1946).

or federal regulation. Most state commissions had little leverage until the 1930s. Powers and resources were lacking, and/or firms created long, sterile controversy over the proper rate base, and these staved off action during the 1920s (see Chapter 11).

Federal regulation of electric power and telephones was formally established only in the 1930s, in reaction to severe scandals from utility stock manipulations during the 1920s stock market craze. In 1934 the Supreme Court opened the criteria for regulated industries to include any industry the public wished to regulate.[28] The federal commissions have had perpetual conflict with state agencies over who controls? From the start, state commissions have sided with the firms, against what is seen as the common threat of the (marginally) stricter federal commissions. State regulation has also been used openly as a haven from federal regulation in insurance (the McCarran Act of 1945) and other trades.

In short, the concept and legal basis for effective regulation ripened in good time—in 1877, before electric, telephone, and other modern utilities emerged. But actual regulation has lagged behind by decades. As noted, it has been set atop existing structures of firms and interests. Actual regulation has been tried, under adverse conditions and only in scattered areas, only for several decades. From the start, most commissions have had scant resources. Also, the utilities have gained by using obtuse doctrines and procedural tactics to congest and fend off regulatory efforts. In the early 1920–35 period, this led to a morass of stupefyingly complex debates over reproduction cost as the value of the rate base. The whole effect of it has made much regulation into arid ritual.

Still, an image of adequate regulation persisted after 1940. New sectors evolved (natural gas, airlines, TV, cable TV, etc.), each with mixed motives

---

[28] The concept of a peculiar category of industries affected with a public interest was abandoned in 1934 when the Court handed down its decision in the Nebbia case (*Nebbia* v. *New York,* 291 U.S. 502). The state of New York had set up a milk control board and empowered it to fix the retail price of milk. The board had fixed the price at nine cents per quart. Nebbia, a grocer in Rochester, had sold two quarts for 18 cents and thrown in a loaf of bread. When sued for violating the law, he argued that the milk business was competitive rather than monopolistic, having none of the characteristics of a public utility, and that the state was therefore powerless to regulate the prices that it charged. The Court, in a 5 to 4 decision, rejected this defense.

Having thus broken with the past, the Court went on, in the next few years, to uphold a state law fixing the charges of tobacco warehouses (*Townsend* v. *Yeomans,* 301 U.S. 441 (1937)), federal laws requiring inspection of tobacco (*Currin* v. *Wallace,* 306 U.S. 1 (1939)), restricting the quantities of tobacco that could be marketed (*Mulford* v. *Smith,* 307 U.S. 38 (1939)), providing for the establishment of minimum prices for milk (*U.S.* v. *Rock Royal Cooperative,* 307 U.S. 533 (1939)), and providing— a second time—for minimum prices for bituminous coal (*Sunshine Anthracite Coal Co.* v. *Adkins,* 310 U.S. 381 (1940)), and a state law curtailing the output of petroleum (*R. R. Commission* v. *Rowan & Nichols Oil Co.,* 310 U.S. 573 (1940)). This legislation, arising largely from conditions of business depression, carried state and federal governments into new regions of control. Its approval by the Court removed a major barrier to the further extension of regulatory activity.

toward being regulated. Slight as its known effectiveness was, regulation was extended to new areas. By the 1950s it covered—formally—nearly the whole of the economic infrastructure of the U.S. economy. This was probably the peak coverage of conventional regulation, and many observers assumed—from optimism or ignorance—that it actually did *regulate*.

Yet by the 1950s no one could say in any detail or depth what the effects of regulation had been and how well they conformed to the public interests. Research on regulation had nearly ceased. During the 1960s, the more searching economic questions about regulation began to be asked again: What, if anything, should be regulated? What are its effects? What levels and patterns should it follow? The possibility that regulation was a charade, a cloak for utility interests, or itself a source of unnecessary monopoly, came to the fore.

The Stresses of 1965–75. The 1940–65 "golden age" was marked by downward-drifting relative costs in electricity and telephones. Problems became routine and benign. Then several new problems converged with a jolt. Inflation forced up costs, and fuel prices jumped in 1973–74. Ecological problems came to the fore, preventing the use of choice power station sites and slowing the use of nuclear energy. Poor planning caused the first serious breakdowns ever in Bell System service during 1969–71 in New York City and elsewhere. The whole promotional ethic of utility managers ran head-on after 1965 against the new scarcities of urban and national life.

New research after 1960 has shown that regulation may have weak "good" effects and important costly side effects on efficiency (see Chapter 11).[29] This stirred political efforts to deregulate, especially in airlines, railroads, trucking, and natural gas. The fight over deregulating natural gas was a heated Congressional issue in 1977 and 1978, for example. And deregulation of the airlines made remarkable progress in 1976–78. Yet deregulation was turning out to be complex, both in economics and politics. And regulation was being extended to some new sectors, such as hospitals.

Therefore, from many directions, the institution of regulation and the activity of the regulated companies have come under severe new doubts and stresses.[30] And still regulation seems to flourish and spread! The 1970s may be a genuine watershed for the further fate of regulation. Yet, even if any sharp changes in it do occur, they are likely to fit within the process of evolution outlined earlier.

---

[29] Some of the research is in a series of studies inspired by George J. Stigler at the University of Chicago to prove that regulation is ineffective or harmful. Most of these papers have come out in the *Journal of Law and Economics.* The student should browse among these and form a judgment about their individual validity and their whole import for the value of regulation. For an unsparing critique of them, see Harry M. Trebing, "The Chicago School Versus Public Utility Regulation," *Journal of Economic Issues,* 10 (March 1976), 97–126.

[30] There is also much intriguing folklore about regulation. For example, only a handful of utility regulators stand out as being effective and forceful, from among the vast numbers of those which have held office down the years. Among state commis-

QUESTIONS FOR REVIEW

1. "Natural monopolies are defined by economies of scale. Therefore regulation is found where, and only where, there are great economies of scale." True?

2. "Utility sectors change, making it hard to keep regulation in line with the ideal coverage." True?

3. "Green vegetables and good music are necessities, vital for a healthy life. Therefore they should be, and are, regulated." True?

4. "A physical connection between utility and customer increases the scope for price discrimination." True?

5. "Regulation is well planned, so that the federal and state commissions neatly divide the regulated sectors between them." True?

6. "Regulation is often merely a forum for hammering out compromises among the interested groups." True?

7. "Since the 'correct' rate of return is usually in the 15 to 20 percent range, regulation can't really go seriously wrong in setting profit levels." True?

8. "Regulation is mostly done by skilled experts, representing a cross-section of consumers and the populace." True?

9. "Utility firms are tempted to enlarge their rate requests, knowing that the commissions will cut them back." True?

10. "Inflation gives the utilities great power, while deflation transfers power to the commissions." True?

11. "Regulation induces cautious behavior and a desire for excess reserve capacity, both among regulators and utility officials." True?

12. "It usually is hard to assign credit and blame for performance between the regulators and the firm." True?

13. "As the utility and regulation evolve, the commission tends increasingly to exclude competition." True?

14. "Regulation has existed since 1888 at least, but it has been forcefully applied only for a few decades." True?

15. Which criteria ought to govern in deciding what to regulate?

16. If regulation is merely a form of compromise rather than clear direction, is it then useless?

17. What old utilities need to be deregulated? What new sectors need to be put under regulation?

---

sions, a few are known to be strict or at least creditable. Meanwhile, there is a rich folklore about utility performance and management. For example, electric power managers since the 1930s are agreed to have been relatively stodgy and insular; hence their severe difficulties in meeting the new problems since 1965 (see Chapter 12). Bell System management is widely regarded as thorough, conservative, and tenacious in its defense of the Bell System's monopoly. During the 1920s there were widespread efforts by utilities to influence academic and public discussion of utility interests. In some cases this reached the level of open scandal. Since then, utilities have been more careful to avoid even the appearance of trying to twist debate their way. Nonetheless, utilities are also anxious to have a favorable image, and the Bell System in particular cultivates academic and public approval in a wide variety of ways. The persuasive and social power of these large, settled enterprises can be great.

APPENDIX: A GLOSSARY OF REGULATORY TERMS

Affected with the public interest. Defined by the legislature as being eligible for public regulation. The grounds for inclusion are almost limitless.

Common carrier: A franchised utility required to serve all customers at the regulated prices.

Cream-skimming: Entering the most lucrative part of the market. Alleged by the utility against newcomers.

"Fair" rate of return: The criterion the regulators are supposed to meet: avoids confiscation of owner's value while not gouging consumers.

Franchise: Legal difinition of a common carrier's market position. It usually excludes some or all competitors and is enforced by public agencies.

"Just and reasonable" rates: The ideal price structure; blending several considerations.

Marginal-cost pricing: Setting price strictly in line with specific marginal costs (not in line with demand differences). "Peak-load pricing" is one variant.

Natural monopoly: In concept, a case in which average costs decline over such a wide range of output that only one firm will survive.

Original cost: The value of utility investment when first installed. (Now commonly used instead of reproduction and historical cost.)

Price discrimination: Prices set in line with demand. Often called "value of service pricing."

Public utility. Vernacular phrase for a common carrier. May be privately or publicly owned.

Rate base: The asset value which the commission accepts as the utility firm's investment, for rate-setting purposes.

Tariff: The published set of regulated prices charged by the firm (also called prices or rates).

chapter 11

Price Level, Price Structure, and Efficiency

Regulation is costly, both in the resources it uses and in possible bad side effects it may have. Yet it may also yield large benefits for the public. "Optimal" regulation will seek to keep the costs low and the benefits high.

In practice, the regulators apply two criteria: profits and price levels are to be "fair," and the price structure is to be "just and reasonable."[1] In other markets, competition is expected to give these happy outcomes. Here it is to be done by scrutiny and price ceilings. If things go well, there will result (a) precisely the efficient level of capacity and output in each part of the utility and in its total, (b) no X-inefficiency, (c) the optimal rate of innovation, no more, no less, and (d) a fair division of burdens and rewards among investors, consumers, managers, and others.

Commissions must try to do most of this indirectly via rate cases about price levels and structures. These may bring about the good economic results. But this is not assured; mistakes may occur, the indirect influence may not be tight enough, or the regulatory process itself may insert new biases. And one goal may conflict with another; for example, prices which maximize *efficiency* need not be *fair*.

So we consider controls on price levels and structures in this chapter. In both parts we first define the optimum constraint and then compare with what is actually done. Then in Section E we look at the problem of inefficiency and how it might be solved. Section F considers the special problems of regulating oligopoly rather than monopoly. Thus equipped, the student can then take up the specific sectors of electricity and gas (Chapter 12), communications (Chapter 13), and transport (Chapter 14).

---

[1] For more advanced analysis of these core economic issues, see Alfred E. Kahn, *The Economics of Regulation* (New York: Wiley, 1971), especially vol. 1; James C. Bonbright, *Principles of Public Utility Rates* (New York: Columbia University Press, 1962).

A. SETTING PRICE AND PROFIT LEVELS: ECONOMIC CRITERIA

A1. The Problem

Assume first that the utility's price *structure* is correct. At what *level* should that whole structure be set, so that the total profit rate is consistent with efficient allocation? Recall from Chapter 2 that net profit is

$$\text{Net profit} = \text{Total revenue} - \text{Total cost}$$

$$\text{Net profit} = \left(\begin{matrix} \text{Output} \\ \text{prices} \end{matrix} \times \begin{matrix} \text{Output} \\ \text{quantities} \end{matrix}\right)$$

$$- \left[\left(\begin{matrix} \text{Input} \\ \text{prices} \end{matrix} \times \begin{matrix} \text{Input} \\ \text{quantities} \end{matrix}\right) + \begin{matrix} \text{Annual} \\ \text{depreciation} \end{matrix} + \text{Taxes}\right]$$

$$\text{Net Profit} = \Sigma(P_i \cdot Q_i) - [\Sigma(p_j \cdot q_j) + d + T] \tag{1}$$

where each i is an output and each j is an input (other than capital inputs). The profit *rate* π on investment is

$$\pi = \frac{\text{Total revenue} - \text{Total cost}}{\text{Rate base}}$$

$$\pi = \frac{TR - TC}{\begin{matrix} \text{Original value} \\ \text{of investment} \end{matrix} - \begin{matrix} \text{Accrued} \\ \text{depreciation} \end{matrix}}$$

$$\pi = \frac{\Sigma(P_i \cdot Q_i) - \Sigma(p_j \cdot q_j) - d - T}{\Sigma(p_k \cdot q_k) - \Sigma dt} \tag{2}$$

where each k is a piece of investment installed at some previous time and Σdt is the sum of past depreciation over the years. Don't be daunted by the full equation (2). It merely sums up some simple accounting categories of revenue, cost, and investment. (For more complex versions, read recent issues of the *Bell Journal of Economics*.)

The commission decides the P_i at the end of the rate case. This is supposed to combine with the other elements to permit the firm only a "fair" rate of profit π on its rate base. The commission can try to scrutinize each of the other items in the full equation (2), by looking through the utility's records and quizzing the managers during the hearings. It can try to judge whether the amounts of inputs (q_j) used by the utility, or the prices paid for them (p_j) are too high. If they are, there is X-inefficiency. The same goes for p_k and q_k in the rate base. If they are too high, the rate base is inflated. The commissioners can also debate and decide whether the firm's chosen rate of depreciation (d) is too low or too high. If so, that would affect both the yearly profits and the rate base itself. The commissioners can also adopt a different basis for figuring the rate base. For example, they may use a "present value" (based on "reproduction cost" or "replacement cost") instead of the original prices paid (p_k).

At any rate, this is "rate base regulation."[2] The standard rate case and decision focus only on the prices, P_i. They are evidently just one element in a complex set of variables. The key choice is usually about π_f, the "fair" rate of return which will be set. How high should this profit-rate ceiling be set? The firm cares intensely about this. The market value of the firm (that is, the price of its stock) will rise if the profit rate (π) can be raised, even by just a little.[3] If large capital gains are at stake, the utility will be willing to use large resources—and virtually any line of argument—to persuade the commission to raise the ceiling on π. There is a range within which reasonable π could fall: 6 to 12 percent is a good estimate.

The main issue resolves down to two simple diagrams. Figure 11–1 shows the simplest utility case, with one output and economies of scale large enough to make a "natural monopoly." The firm prefers point Q_A with its restricted output and maximized profits. The social optimum is at a higher output level, at or near point Q_B. The recurring struggle—repeated in scores of commissions year by year—is over the size of that sliver of price which goes to profit.

Criteria for the Rate of Return.   What *should* π be? Answer: it should be at the level which attracts the efficient rate of new investment into the firm. This depends on the marginal productivity of capital, both in this firm and in the rest of the economy. The decision looks ahead to new investment, not to past investments. The basic choice is shown in Figure 11–2. There is a range of future projects to invest in (plants, networks, offices, and so forth) with varying returns. Funds for them can be acquired at a cost shown by CK (for cost of capital).[4] The regulator's job is to set the profit rate ceiling just above the cost of capital, so that investment occurs at just the efficient level. If that ceiling is too high, the supply of capital will be too large and actual investment will be too small. And vice versa; if π is too low—so that the utility's prices are all too low—then demand for services

---

[2] This is because the rate base is a pivotal part of the regulatory equation, and expanding the rate base may become a means for the firm to raise its profit (see Sections B and E below). It is also "cost-plus" regulation. The firm can set prices at "cost plus a profit margin," and so costs too may come to be overexpanded.

[3] Example: a utility with $2 billion in total asset value and a π of 10 percent (there are more than 50 larger than this). Leverage is 50 percent (half equity, half debt), and the current market value of the stock is $1 billion, or 8.3 times the net income flow of $120 million per year (that is, a price-earnings ratio of 8.3: quite normal). Interest on bonds is at 8 percent, and the estimated cost of equity is 12 percent.

Now suppose the commission raises the permitted rate of return on all assets to 11 percent, up a mere one point. Net income will rise by $20 million per year (1 percent of $2 billion). This will capitalize at a price earnings ratio of 8.3 into a stockholder gain of $166 million, or 16.6 percent. The leverage of a small change in profit rate can be strong.

[4] Though shown here as flat, the cost of capital curve will often be upward-sloping. This standard fact of corporate finance does not change the lessons about regulation.

FIGURE 11–1

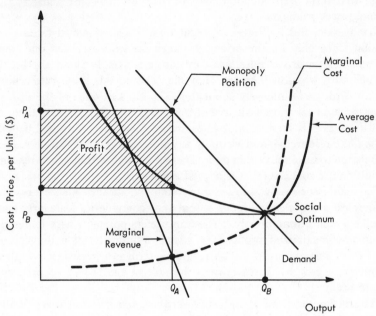

FIGURE 11–2

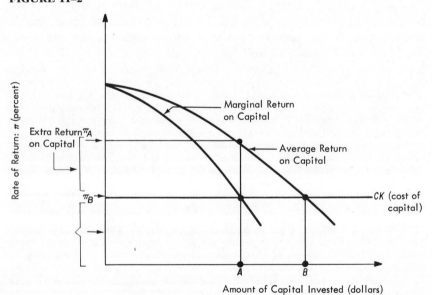

will be too high and capacity will have to be larger than the supply of capital permits.

Note where the strain arises: the utility firm prefers point A, where its monopoly profit is maximized and it makes excess profits of $\pi_A - \pi_B$. The competitive—generally, the optimal—result is point B. These points correspond to points Q_A and Q_B in Figure 11-1. The commission endeavors to press π (and prices) down to costs (barebones costs, minimum costs, or by any other name) but not below. The firm tries to show that costs are really much higher, especially when the true costs of capital are allowed for.

The efficient level of price is roughly in line with competitive levels, but not rigidly.[5] The utility's profit rate is to be fitted within the efficient allocation among all markets. Profit and risk conditions elsewhere influence the correct answers here. If profit rates elsewhere are high, even for secure firms, then this regulated firm's π should perhaps be put up a little. Otherwise it will go begging for funds and will soon be below its optimal capacity. Thus arises the conventional regulatory concern about the cost of capital and capital-attraction; company lawyers try to scare the commission with forecasts that capacity will lag and breakdowns will occur if π is set below the cost of capital.

A related criterion is "comparable earnings." It may be fair and efficient to let utility A earn a profit rate equal to those earned by comparable firms elsewhere; comparable in risk, technology, size, growth prospects, and so on. Ultimately this boils down to the capital-attraction premise: "comparable" earnings will bring about the right allocation of capital between utility A and all other firms.

Specific criteria therefore include:

1. *The cost of capital.* The measured average cost of acquiring investment funds to make necessary investment in the system.
2. *Capital-attraction.* Returns on capital high enough to induce capital markets to supply at least the efficient level of new capital.
3. *Comparable earnings.* Returns on capital commensurate with returns in other enterprises having comparable risks.

These seem sensible and mutually consistent. But they present some tricky theoretical and practical problems. They are circular and perhaps empty, though commissions regularly seek to apply them.

A2. Defects of the Criteria

Circularity. The criteria are circular because the commission cannot hope to "find" the economic conditions and then fit π to them. Instead, the commis-

---

[5] To be precise, the regulated levels should also allow for deviations from competitive results elsewhere. These are called "second-best" criteria. See Kahn, *Economics,* and the sources cited there at I, 195–99.

298

sion itself sets much of the utility's risk and performance conditions. The commission can force low profits, onerous service burdens, and even new competition on the utility. Such risks may greatly exceed the "innate economic risks" of the firm. Commissions cannot *find* the profit-risk conditions: *they make them.* By ignoring this, the standard rate-of-return criteria involve pretense.

Impracticality. The criteria don't yield easy, clear answers in practice. The cost of *new* capital is difficult to measure. The cost of *existing* capital is easier to pin down but it is not the correct basis to use (though commissions do use it; see below). "Capital attraction" implies a specific correct level of investment, but there are no precise ways to measure that level. "Comparable" risks are also a vague concept which is almost impossible to apply in practice. Indeed, the existence of a risk-return relationship is debatable.

Depletion or Growth? The correct growth rate for a utility may be high, low, or negative, depending on its life cycle stage. Capital may need to be depleted or held constant, rather than attracted. This in turn may prescribe negative or low profit rates for the shrinkage of "over-built" utilities (as shown in Figure 11–3). Or there may need to be extremely high profit rates for excess demand or super-rapid growth (see point B in Figure 11–3). Only for a "normal" growing utility—with capacity in line with demand—will capital attraction require a profit rate in the normal range of 6 to 12 percent (see point C in Figure 11–3). The extreme profit rates may be correct, but they will usually be regarded as unacceptable.

Profits Are Given, not Earned. The earnings of the firm should come from relative efficiency, not from a guaranteed rate of return. Instead, the three criteria give the profits as a right, regardless of efficiency or innovation. That has been one great fallacy of regulation; that by making the profit results *look* like competition, the other results of competition—efficiency,

FIGURE 11–3
Efficient prices depend on the relation of demand to marginal cost.

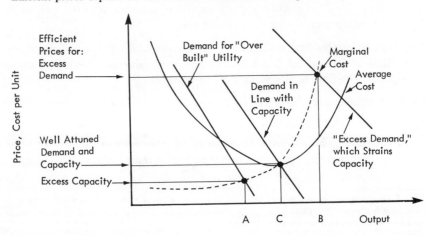

equity, innovation, and so on–could be guaranteed. A truly economic criterion would vary with performance. (In fact, regulatory lag can give that effect: see below.) But to that extent, the formal criteria for rate of return are empty and irrelevant.

In light of all this, the intelligent commission will treat various sophistries about criteria with good-humored skepticism. Normally the rate of return should fall somewhere in the 6 to 12 percent range. The reasonable commission will consider the following, without pretending to have a rigid formula or crystal ball:

1. The general financial condition of the utility.
2. The recent trend of the utility's stock price.
3. How well the utility has been performing (a composite of many things: service complaints, adequacy of capacity and expansion plans, trade commentary on managerial and service quality, and so forth).
4. General price and wage trends, by comparison with the utility.
5. The degree of strictness of *other* commissions in setting π, rate base, allowable costs and—in general—price levels for their utilities.
6. The intensity of pressures and of expected criticisms.

Single criteria can give some guidance and clarity. But good decisions also draw on a variety of present and future conditions, weighed carefully but informally. The 6 to 12 percent rage is a battleground which matters keenly to the firm but not much to allocation. If π is really too low, it will quickly be seen. Otherwise, the decision largely reflects the regulators' liberality to investors and their prudence in leaving a margin for safety.

B. SETTING PRICE AND PROFIT LEVELS: ACTUAL METHODS

How do commissions set rate levels? They make three main evaluations: costs, rate base, and the fair rate of profit.[6] The firm urges a high π, on one criterion or several. The staff rebuts, favoring a low π. The commission listens, questions, adjourns, and then later announces some π, almost always less than the firm's request.

B1. Setting Allowed Costs

Under regulation, the firm can gain by padding its costs: *(a)* by *accounting methods* which make utility costs look bigger than they are. Accounting methods leave much room for choice. *(b)* by *transferring nonutility costs*

---

[6] Full information is necessary (if not sufficient) for a good regulatory decision. Yet early regulators lacked good data for decades (for example, the ICC for 20 years). Even now, accounts are often deficient and good figures on critical costs are often unavailable. Regulation does force much vital data out into public view. But the effort to get full information is a continuing one.

onto the accounts of the utility operations. This can be done outright or, more subtly, when the firm's overhead costs include both utility and nonutility items. The transfers may be made among existing operations or by adding new nonutility services to the pre-existing utility operations and labelling them part of "the utility." *(c)* by *actual waste* [raising the levels of q_j in equation (2)]. Waste can arise in many forms, since utility managers have wide discretion over technology and operations. Costs of any or all types (workers, capital items, purchased inputs, and so on) may not be minimized. And specific types—managers' rewards and perquisites, benefits for favored groups, propaganda activities—may be enlarged.

In the "typical" utility, expenses divide roughly as follows, as percents of revenue: labor costs, 25 percent; purchased materials and services, 25 percent; depreciation, 20 percent; and taxes, 10 percent. It is these groups which may be altered.

Operating Costs. The problem has been recognized at least since 1892.[7] A few commissions scrutinize costs and disallow inflated or unnecessary items. Usually the burden of proof is borne by the commission, to show that managers' choices are wrong or abusive.[8] Most commissions accept (that is, validate or rubber-stamp) most utility expenses as valid.

Depreciation offers much discretion to managers in setting their accounting levels of cost. Assets decline in value as time passes, mainly from *(a)* wear and tear (physical depreciation), and *(b)* obsolescence (functional depreciation), as innovations render old plant inferior and, therefore, destroy their value. Yearly depreciation is a valid cost of business. It is entered as a cost. Its summed totals appear in the balance sheets, where total fixed assets minus accrued depreciation reflects the *net* value of assets actually in use.

Key point: the level of *costs* is thus connected to the rate base via depreciation. A high rate of depreciation (for example, writing off an investment in five years rather than 20) will *increase* the current cash flow—permitted profit plus yearly depreciation. *But* it will also keep the rate base *lower* in later years. The utility naturally optimizes by choosing a depreciation method which attunes present cash flows versus its future rate base, in line with the firm's motivation.[9] The standard method of "rate-base" regulation favors a high rate base, and so slow depreciation—with long assumed asset lives and small yearly depreciation—is common. It may go to excess.

Depreciation involves *(a)* salvage value, *(b)* asset life, and *(c)* the method

---

[7] In the decision *Chicago & Grand Trunk Railway Co.* v. *Wellman,* 143 U.S. 339 (1892).

[8] That precedent was established in *West Ohio Gas Co.* v. *Public Utilities Commission of Ohio,* 294 U.S. 63 (1935), and *Acker* v. *U.S.,* 298 U.S. 426 (1936).

[9] The balance of incentives for the utility—between high present cash flow vs. a large rate base in the future—can grow quite complex. For rigorous treatment, see such accounting textbooks as Sidney Davidson, James S. Schindler, and Roman L. Weil, *Fundamentals of Accounting,* 5th ed. (Hinsdale, Ill.: Dryden Press, 1975), and Walter B. Meigs, A. M. Monich, and E. John Larsen, *Modern Advanced Accounting* (New York: McGraw-Hill, 1975).

of write-off during the life. A short life with no assumed salvage value will give large present write-offs. A long life with high salvage value gives small yearly write-offs. Accounting methods—straight-line, declining-balance, and sum-of-the-years' digit are three common ones—give further choice. Figure 11–4 illustrates the discretion. After eight years a piece of capital might be worth anywhere between $1.2 million or $9.5 million, depending on the method of depreciation.

These sharp differences do not exaggerate the real cases. Plausible estimates of service life and salvage value can differ by multiples. Most utility accounting ignores obsolescence. Yet it may actually be rapid, and a major innovation can quickly render valueless much of a utility's entire investment. (That, indeed, is precisely what can and does happen in Stages 3 and 4: for example, trolleys, manufactured gas.)

Therefore, despite its seeming dullness and obscurity, depreciation is intensely controversial and keenly argued. It is mostly guesswork, put into "objective" formulas. Engineers can try to measure the useful physical life on a piece of equipment (20, 30, even 40 years), but these are really only rough estimates. And innovation can falsify them quickly; so can changes in demand and in official requirements.

In practice, utilities are usually permitted to choose their preferred depreciation method, which they must then stick with. After long debate, the *original* cost of assets is almost universal as the required basis. But any reasonable

FIGURE 11–4
The choice of depreciation method can sharply affect the accounting value of capital: an illustration.

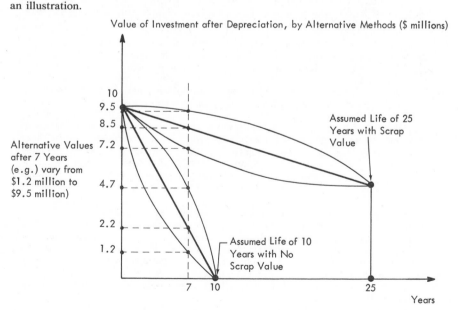

Value of Investment after Depreciation, by Alternative Methods ($ millions)

Alternative Values after 7 Years (e.g.) vary from $1.2 million to $9.5 million)

Assumed Life of 25 Years with Scrap Value

Assumed Life of 10 Years with No Scrap Value

Years

service lives and depreciation techniques are permitted. And if unexpected changes arise, commissions usually permit utilities to handle them as they wish.

Taxes are treated as a cost. They are not an important economic issue.[10]

B2. The Rate Base Problem

The utility is permitted to earn profits (at π) on the full value of the rate base. Regulators need to prevent it from being padded or overstated: to limit it strictly to "prudent investment" actually needed for utility service.

The rate base can be enlarged in three ways, similar to those affecting costs: *(a)* accounting devices which overstate its value, *(b)* assigning nonutility assets to the utility services, and *(c)* actual expansion of real investment.

Accounting valuation is, again, partly a matter of optimum depreciation strategy by the utility. It was also—during 1898 to about 1940—a morass of empty dispute about reproduction versus original cost of assets. The Supreme Court opened the floodgates in the landmark *Smyth* v. *Ames* case in 1898.[11]

The decision was a meaningless fruitcake, containing indefinable and conflicting principles.[12] During 1920–40 it was cited to justify long and tortured

---

[10] A special problem since 1954 has stirred sharp debate. Accelerated depreciation (under a special tax rule of 1954) permits faster writeoffs and shifting of taxes over time. Utilities could either pass these benefits on immediately, or normalize them over time. A complex debate has ensued. Immediate *flow-through* of the benefits is possible, but it might negate the stimulus to investment. *Normalization* would preserve that incentive but also permit higher real profits and neglect a chance to cut prices to consumers. The state and federal commissions have divided about evenly on the issue: the FPC, ICC, and 23 state commissions require or favor flow-through.

[11] 169 U.S. 466. Rejecting a Nebraska attempt to regulate railroad rates (William Jennings Bryan argued for the state), the Court added a dictum on valuation:

We hold . . . that the basis of all calculations as to the reasonableness of rates to be charged by a corporation . . . must be the fair value of the property being used by it for the convenience of the public. And, in order to ascertain that value, the original cost of construction, the amount expended in permanent improvements, the amount and market value of its bonds and stocks, the present as compared with the original cost of construction, the probable earnings capacity of the property under particular rates prescribed by statute, and the sum required to meet operating expenses, are all matters for consideration, and are to be given such weight as may be just and right in each case. We do not say that there may not be other matters to be regarded in estimating the value of the property. What the company is entitled to ask is a fair return upon the value of that which it employs for the public convenience. On the other hand, what the public is entitled to demand is that no more be exacted from it . . . than the services rendered . . . are reasonably worth.

[12] Actually, *(a)* operating expenses are irrelevant, having nothing to do with the determination of the rate base; *(b)* earnings capacity and *(c)* the market value of stocks and bonds are logical absurdities, since these depend upon the rates that are being fixed; *(d)* original cost and *(e)* present cost, while relevant and logical, are inconsistent, since the values to which they lead are far apart. What is fair value: original cost or present cost or some compromise between the two? The Court does not say. Both must be considered, and each must be given "such weight as may be just and right. . . ."

arguments against the *original cost* rate base approach, which is palpably the only workable method.[13] Not until 1944 did the *Hope Natural Gas* case lay it firmly to rest.[14] The rate base could at last be settled, and attention could rightly center on the rate of return.[15]

This detour is now mostly closed (though about half of the states profess to consider reproduction cost). It did deep damage to regulation while it lasted. And it ensured that regulation had little effect on railroads, telephones, electric and gas utilities until well into Stage 2 or even Stage 3.

Intangibles were another bogus tactic used to inflate the rate base. Intangibles have been claimed to include good will, franchise value, water rights, leaseholds, and value as a going concern. All of these—and especially good will and going concern value—are inappropriate, for they are not productive assets, and their value depends—circularity again!—on the commission's own decisions. Yet these values were solemnly asserted during 1898–1935 to be valid parts of the rate base.

Actual investment may also exceed efficient levels, either by mistake, design, or as a natural response to regulatory incentives. Justice Brandeis urged during the 1920s that only "prudent investment" be allowed, excluding unwise, extravagant, or fraudulent investment. Some commissions do examine utility investments for prudence, though exclusions are rare. But the problem is now recognized to be more subtle and, probably, insoluble.

Managers usually have a wide degree of choice in designing their systems and in innovating new technology. *Rate-base regulation routinely induces these choices to favor higher capital-intensity.*[16] The effect operates quietly, and pervasively, to shift the margin of choice toward capital-intensive plant (see Figure 11–5). By making capital cheaper, in effect, regulation may induce some extra use of it, large or small.

---

[13] Reproduction cost appears to fit economic analysis, since it seems to reflect what the assets are *now* worth. Yet it ignores the bedrock fact that the regulators *make* the value of the assets by their own decision. And reproduction cost invites endless differing estimates. The assets can't actually be sold to anybody (perhaps regulators *should* permit such bidding and take-overs: but regulatory policy would still influence value). And estimates of cost can be made in at least four different major ways, which give varying values. That the Supreme Court was willing even to entertain the sophistry of reproduction cost during 1920–40 was inexcusably bad economics.

[14] *FPC* v. *Hope Natural Gas Co.,* 320 U.S. 591 (1944).

[15] Still, some state commissions are willing to use reproduction cost. But many of them compensate by setting lower profit-rate ceilings.

[16] The landmark analysis of this is H. Averch and L. L. Johnson, "Behavior of the Firm under Regulatory Constraint," *American Economic Review* 53 (December 1963), 1052–69. A stream of later articles has left its main point intact and given it empirical support. See E. E. Zajac, "A Geometric Treatment of Averch-Johnson's Behavior of the Firm Model," *American Economic Review* 60 (March 1970), 117–25; Elizabeth E. Bailey, *Economic Theory of Regulatory Constraint* (Lexington: Lexington Books, 1973); and Robert M. Spann, "Rate of Return Regulation and Efficiency in Production: An Empirical Test of the Averch-Johnson Thesis," *Bell Journal of Economics* 5 (Spring 1974), 38–52.

This rate-base effect is ingrained in the situation and unarticulated by the managers—most of whom stoutly deny that it could even exist, though common sense plainly says otherwise. It is scarcely recognized by regulators as a natural effect of their efforts, and it would be virtually impossible to factor out from actual investments. Therefore, it remains largely untouched by regulatory discussions and actions.

The Separations Problem. Separating the rate base between state and federal jurisdictions is a necessary and hugely complex operation for telephone, electric, railroad, and certain other utilities. (Costs and revenues must be allocated, also.) Further, utilities which operate in several states must divide their assets, costs, and revenues among those states.

The task is an economist's nightmare, for large volumes of true overhead and joint costs have to be arbitrarily sliced up into economically dubious

TABLE 11–1

Rates of Return Granted by Selected Federal and State Commissions, 1976 (in the most recent case)

Commission or State	Electricity Firms: Rate of Return on		Telephone Firms: Rate of Return on	
	Assets	Equity	Assets	Equity
Federal Energy Regulatory Commission	8.90	12.50	—	—
Federal Communications Commission	—	—	9.5	12.0
Alabama	7.33	14.24	8.5	12.5
Arkansas	9.48	13.5	8.45	11.5
California	9.20	12.83	—	—
Connecticut	8.66	12.45	—	—
Florida	—	—	9.10	11.28
Georgia	—	—	9.38	12.0
Hawaii	9.33	13.0	—	—
Illinois	7.83	—	8.5	—
Iowa	8.68	12.75	9.2	12.25
Massachusetts	8.13	12.00	—	—
Michigan	9.38	13.50	8.34	10.19
Minnesota	9.16	13.28	—	—
Mississippi	—	—	9.48	12.8
Montana	7.71	11.25	—	—
New Hampshire	—	—	10.01	12.5
New Jersey	9.88	13.0	—	—
New York	9.35	13.50	9.24	12.0
Ohio	9.56	—	8.29	—
Pennsylvania	6.80	10.54	8.99	12.21
South Carolina	9.38	13.5	9.86	12.5
Tennessee	—	—	9.1	11.47
Texas	—	—	8.37	11.42
Vermont	—	—	9.28	—
Virginia	9.3	13.0	9.20	12.5
Washington	8.57	12.75	9.50	12.0
Wisconsin	8.91	11.50	—	—

Source: National Association of Regulatory Utility Commissioners, *Annual Report on Utility and Carrier Regulation,* 1976 (Washington, D.C.: 1102 Interstate Commerce Commission Bldg., 1977), Part II, pp. 296–335.

FIGURE 11–5
Regulation can alter the rate of return and the level of investment.

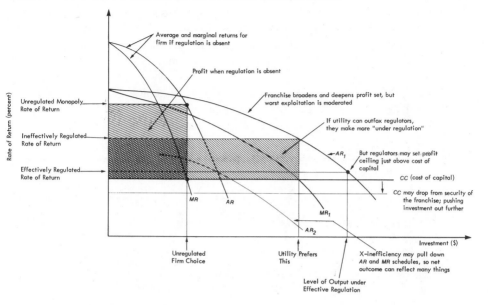

portions. The firms try to maximize the share assigned to the states (and, among states, to the more liberal states). The resulting allocations may bear some relation to economic categories, but the whole process is suspect and probably routinely biased against federal coverage.[17]

B3. Setting the Fair Rate of Return

The correct π is never clear. It needs to be above the rate on riskless assets (for example, the Treasury prime rate), for utilities have some risk (depending on their life cycle stage and regulatory treatment). But how much higher? The *Bluefield* decision early cited several possible criteria.[18] But like

---

[17] An excellent analysis of the problems in one industry is given in Richard Gabel, *Development of Separations Principles in the Telephone Industry* (East Lansing, Mich.: Institute of Public Utilities, Michigan State University, 1967).

[18] *Bluefield Waterworks and Improvement Co.* v. *Public Service Commission,* 262 U.S. 679 (1923).

"The rate of return . . . must be determined by the exercise of a fair and enlightened judgment, having regard to all relevant facts. A public utility is entitled to such rates as will permit it to earn a return . . . equal to that generally being made at the same time and in the same general part of the country on investments in other business undertakings which are attended by corresponding risks and uncertainties; but it has no constitutional rights to profits such as are realized or anticipated in highly profitable enterprises or speculative ventures. The return should be reasonably sufficient to assure confidence in the financial soundness of the utility and should be adequate, under efficient and economical management, to maintain and support its credit and enable it to raise the money necessary for the proper

Smyth v. *Ames,* it left priority and weightings among the criteria unresolved. In practice, **comparable earnings** has not controlled. Competitive industries have *lower* profits and *higher* risks. As Chapter 2 noted, a general positive relation between risk and return has not yet been scientifically shown. Instead high profits appear to relate mainly to market power or—in some cases— economies of scale. And practical measures of comparable risk are difficult to prepare.

Commissions instead usually look to the **cost of capital.** Estimates of the cost of past capital are prepared.[19] They are also guesses about the cost of new capital. And the commission usually adds a safety margin. The resulting figure, artificial and inelegant as it is, does give a safe and sane approximation roughly in line with reasonable judgments.

The resulting estimates of fair return lack clear guidance.[20] The rates

---

discharge of its public duties. A rate of return may be reasonable at one time, and become too high or too low by changes affecting opportunities for investment, the money market, and business conditions generally.

[19] The method uses weighted averages of the cost of debt and equity capital. The process can grow arcane, with formulae for finding the cost of equity capital, in light of dividend pay-out ratios, growth rates, and so forth. But it all boils down to reasonable guesses within the traditional range. For more details, see Charles F. Phillips, Jr., *The Economics of Regulation,* rev. ed. (Homewood, Ill.: Irwin, 1969), chap. 9.

Leverage is often part of the measurement of cost of capital. Leverage (or "capital structure") is the ratio of debt to total capital; a "highly levered" firm has a lot of debt (say, over 50 percent) in its liabilities. The cost of debt is taken to be the interest rate paid, usually about six to nine percent. The cost of equity is usually reckoned at least four points higher. Therefore, the orthodoxy has it, high leverage gives cheaper capital. And each firm has an ideal capital structure for its risk situation.

Yet the capital structure is probably broadly irrelevant. The true economic cost of capital is mainly determined by the firm's basic risk conditions. A leading statement of this point is F. Modigliani and M. H. Miller, "The Cost of Capital, Corporate Finance, and the Theory of Investment," *American Economic Review* 48 (1958), 261. See also the accounting textbooks in note 9 above. The issue is complex, but the nub is that higher leverage—because it increases risk—tends to *increase* the cost of both equity and debt, rather than just substitute cheap borrowing for expensive equity.

Normally, risky utilities should have lower leverage. Electric firms have had high leverage, too high for the new uncertain times since 1965. And Bell System leverage was moved up at regulatory insistence after the 1950s, on the ground that the firm's risk was relatively low. Put generally, leverage should peak in early Stage 3 and then move down as normal risks arise.

[20] One example shows how the estimates can vary. In a 1968 telephone rate case in New Hampshire, five witnesses gave these estimates:

	Debt Ratio	Cost of Equity	Cost of Capital
McIninch	—	9.5–10%	—
Conrad	35%	10–11	8.0%
Barker	35	10	7.75–8.5
Lowell	35–40	10–11	8.0
Kosh	45–50	6.95–8	5.5–6.05
Commission decision	45	7.75	6.11

Re *New England Telephone & Telegraph Co.,* 42 PUR 3d 57, 60–61 (N. H., 1961), summarized in Phillips, *Economics,* p. 288.

actually allowed by the commissions and the courts have usually been conventional or arbitrary. They have usually been based on expert testimony and rules of thumb, with little pretense of economic analysis. There has been no real study of the conditions governing investment decisions, the character of alternative investment opportunities, or the expectations that must be satisfied if new investments are to be made. Bankers and brokers appearing for the companies give their opinion that future risks are likely to be great and that earnings, consequently, must be high if securities are to be sold. Witnesses for the public point out that risks, in the past, have been small.

The commissions and the courts have exercised judgments as best they can, coming up with a figure that can rarely be proven to be correct. Usually this figure has fallen somewhere between 6 and 10 percent. The allowed return differs from state to state and from industry to industry, and it varies over time.

The use of judgment is not per se incorrect, for differing complex conditions cannot efficiently be settled by crude uniform rules. Rather, it is the seeming shallowness of the exercise which is disturbing. Perhaps nothing better could be expected, even from Solomon: the political pressures are great, the facts are obscure, and the principles clash. Fortunately, the precise choices do not appear to have strong effects. The actual levels often stray from the ceiling, and a strict decision often merely provokes a quicker return for the next rate request.

B4. Results

Averages and Dispersions.   Regulated profits often seem to reflect a degree of restraint, but there is naturally much variety. Table 11–1 gives recent formal ceilings for rates of return set by some federal and state commissions. During 1945–58, utility rates of return on equity hovered around 8 to 11 percent, while industrial firms' returns averaged about 15 percent. Since 1959, returns have been about equal, in the range of 10 to 15 percent.

Actual rates of return do not follow the ceilings rigidly; some of them shift or stay above, while others move below. Figure 11–6 shows the spread among about 190 private electric firms in recent years. Most utility firms actually get returns on equity in the range of 11 to 15 percent.

The spread reflects utility life cycles and relative efficiency (see below) as well as regulatory limits. Broadly, the mainline utilities have had returns surprisingly close to the average for all large firms, and some have done even better. Others have done poorly—eastern railroads, Consolidated Edison during 1965–75, and so on—not only from known blunders but also because of underlying life cycle determinants.

Regulatory Lag.   During about 1945–65, average costs in some utilities (for example, telephones, electricity, airlines) were stable or declining, as scale economies were explored (see Chapters 12–14). This was a golden age of regulation: few rate hearings, steady or falling utility prices, good service quality, simple issues, and handsome profits.

FIGURE 11–6
Rates of Return in Private Electric Utilities, 1971

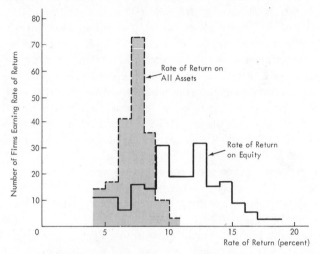

Source: Federal Power Commission, *Statistics of Privately-owned Electrical Companies* (Washington, D.C.: Government Printing Office, 1972).

FIGURE 11–7
Movements of Utility Stock Prices since 1950

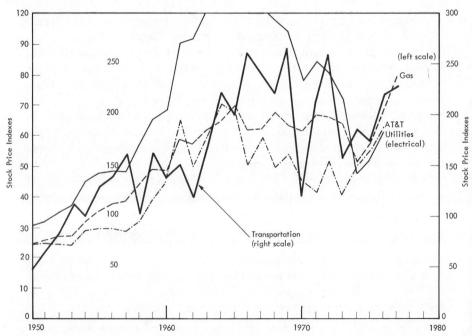

Regulatory lag favored the firms, and the excess profits were not recaptured. But it seemed not to matter, for utility finance, performance, and price trends all seemed favorable. There was even a boom in AT&T stock and many other utility stocks during the 1950s.

Since 1965—and especially during 1971–75—regulatory lag has crimped the firms. For several years, utility earnings were hurt by the delays. The pressure of events has forced a drastic shortening of the old regimen of rate hearings. Even so, commissions have been quite able to force out decisions on large increases in a small fraction of the time formerly needed to decide small changes. Regulation still lags, but it has adjusted to avoid hurting utility profits. This shift is reflected in the trends in utility stock prices, shown in Figure 11–7.

The probable effects of rate-level regulation on efficiency are noted below in Section F.

C. RATE STRUCTURE: ECONOMIC CRITERIA

We now turn to the inner structure of prices. The problem is important and complex. The utility—private or public—usually has much latitude in designing its prices. A great variety of price structures will be consistent with any single global objective (profit rate, efficiency, innovation). Some of these structures are socially "best;" others can be grossly unfair and inefficient.

C1. Cost as the Basis for Prices

As usual, there is a core of relatively simple concepts, which can be refined down to the point of hair-splitting. The basic objective is clear: *individual prices should normally be as close to marginal cost as is reasonably possible.* This harmonizes with the basic criteria of efficiency and fairness. In Chapter 10's simple equation,

$$\text{Price} = k \text{ (Marginal cost)}$$

k is to be at or close to 1. The k ratio will not, in any case, vary sharply among the utility's outputs and customers. Though marginal costs are often hard to define and measure, they are the correct basis.

Yet the firm invariably wishes to *to discriminate in prices,* varying k inversely with demand elasticity on each output (recall Chapter 8). It calls it "value-of-service pricing," or "ability-to-pay" pricing, or some other nice name, but it is still discrimination. "Creamy" markets are those where the users have strong minimum needs for the output and where there are no alternative sources of supply. "Skim" markets have less urgent users' needs and/or rivalry among suppliers. Being a utility, the firm can discriminate extensively. Doing so will maximize its profits while minimizing its long-run risks from new competition.

The two sides are at loggerheads: the commission's objective is to line

FIGURE 11–8A.
Marginal-cost pricing and discriminatory pricing may converge.

FIGURE 11–8B.
Marginal-cost pricing and discriminatory pricing may diverge.

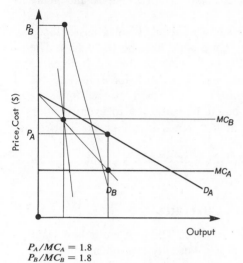

$P_A/MC_A = 1.8$
$P_B/MC_B = 1.8$

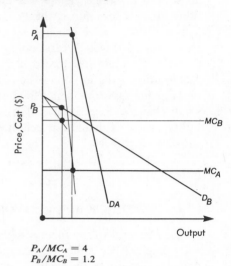

$P_A/MC_A = 4$
$P_B/MC_B = 1.2$

up prices with marginal *costs,* while the firm wants to fit prices to *demand* conditions. In some parts of the utility, costs and demand conditions are parallel, so that marginal-cost pricing and discrimination are also parallel.[21] Figure 11–8A shows such a case. Efficient pricing then may occur voluntarily though supervision is still needed. Occasionally, too, some price discrimination is socially valid (see Section C4 below). But elsewhere the two criteria are in conflict.

Regulation has often been created in reaction to brazen price discrimination. So commission decisions on price structure can be an acid test of their effectiveness. Yet until 1960 or so rate level questions largely crowded out rate structure from regulatory attention. The 1960s reawakened interest, and the 1970s have thrust price structure to center stage in electricity, telephones, and other sectors.

Marginal cost is the key concept.[22] It is the true cost of supplying the additional (or "incremental") unit, at a given level of output. *Long-run mar-*

---

[21] Thus, long-distance telephone rates clearly reflect the structure of costs, both by distances and by time of day (for example, low night and weekend rates). Airlines offer discounts for late-night travel and stand-by service, where costs are lower.

[22] For more advanced discussion of marginal costs, see Kahn, *Economics,* 1, chapters 3–5; Bonbright, *Principles,* chapters 4, 16, 17, and 20; James R. Nelson, ed., *Marginal Cost Pricing in Practice* (New York: Prentice-Hall, 1964); and Harry M. Trebing, *New Dimensions in Public Utility Pricing* (East Lansing, Mich.: Institute of Public Utilities, Michigan State University, 1976). One wrinkle is that the "producer's unit" for marginal cost may differ from the "consumer's unit." For example, an airline's marginal unit may be a whole airplane flight, while the customer's marginal unit is a single seat on the flight. Such differences can make it difficult to define "the" marginal cost.

FIGURE 11–9
Efficient pricing often can smooth loads and reduce needed capacity (*A, B, C,* and *D* correspond to the same letters in Figure 11–10).

FIGURE 11–10
Efficient price structure: prices are in line with marginal costs at *B* and *C.*

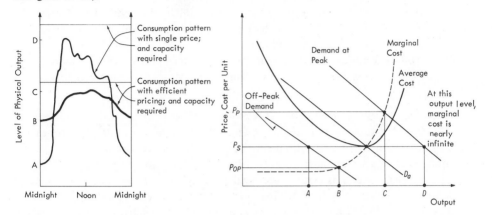

ginal cost is defined for the future, letting all inputs vary (including fixed capital). *Short-run marginal cost* assumes some costs as given (usually fixed capacity costs, or "overhead" costs), and therefore includes only those costs which can be changed (roughly, "out-of-pocket" costs). The ideal criterion is long-run marginal cost, since it reflects the basic pattern of future resource choices. Also, regulators try to fix prices for a period of years, rather than have them jump about. Yet the long run is a series of short runs, and so pricing often needs to fit short-run variations in cost.

Marginal costs vary in two broad categories: (1) by *output types,* and (2) by *time.*

1.   Outputs vary in physical type, location, and other conditions of service. (Examples: electricity at high and low voltages; local vs. long-distance telephone calls; and mailing a 1-ounce letter versus a 20-pound package.) The costs vary because of identifiable differences in the resources used. Overhead costs may blur the measurements, but the concept of differing outputs is clear. They are reflected by the cost levels in Figure 11–8A and 11–8B. Obviously, users of *B* should pay higher prices than users of *A.*

2.   Outputs vary by time of use; by time of day, day of the week, and season of the year. When output cannot be stored, peak-load costs may differ sharply from off-peak costs.

Figures 11–9 and 11–10 sum up the key points. Use fluctuates, and so costs vary. Figure 11–11 simplifies down to two periods, such as peak and off-peak. Demand for each period is in a different range of marginal costs. These correspond to peak conditions commonly found in the electricity, transit, telephone, and other sectors.

How can marginal costs vary so sharply among periods? There are three main causes:

1. The last margin of capacity is used only at peak, and so the total costs of installing, depreciating, and maintaining it year-round are focused on just a few units of use. This cost properly falls on peak-load use, which is responsible for requiring the capacity.[23]

2. Utilities use their best capacity for base load, holding their worst units (for example, old buses, inefficient generators) for use only at peak times. Their variable costs may be high.

3. At off-peak times, fixed (capacity) costs are zero and variable costs may be low (for example, slight costs from using an idle telephone exchange or line).

These factors can set peak costs at a multiple of off-peak costs. A telephone call, an extra subway ride, a light switched on, or a letter: at peak times they are much more costly than off the peak. Moreover, external costs are often much higher at peak periods. (Examples: old smoky generators, old fume-emitting and noisy buses are used only at peak times. They increase pollution disproportionately.) Therefore, social costs would be shown by curves above those in Figure 11–10, tipping up extra sharply at the right-hand end.

These short-run cost differences are parallel to long-run costs, for a succession of capacity-straining peaks ultimately means that peak costs are high in the long run.

If a utility is on an efficient growth path, it will usually have peak and off-peak conditions similar to Figure 11–10. Its aggregate revenues from all periods will balance out to cover total costs. Marginal-cost pricing will not cause chronic deficits or surpluses unless the utility gets seriously overbuilt or short of capacity. *Normally, marginal-cost pricing is fully compatible with private ownership and fair rates of return.*[24]

For efficient allocation, price should be in line with marginal cost for each individual class of output. This results in a peak level price at P_p which is much higher than the off-peak price P_{op}. When costs differ, prices should differ in line with them. If demands are at all elastic, efficient pricing will smooth fluctuations and raise the load factor (as in both Figures 11–9 and 11–10). If D_a represents some kind of average demand conditions and the commission required a single price to be set at P_s, the resulting levels of output demanded would diverge sharply and perhaps disastrously from the efficient levels, as shown in Figure 11–10. Peak level demand would be far

---

[23] Peak-load "responsibility" is a complex issue; see Kahn, *Economics*, 1, 87–103. Generally, predictions of future peak use have caused the capacity to be installed, and so peak use ought to cover all or most of the cost of capacity used at peak. Responsibility may need to be shared in some degree. Yet the general lesson holds: that peak use should bear a high proportion of capacity costs.

[24] It is not tied to socialist firms or company-wide financial deficits, despite a common impression to the contrary. That arose from the belief—traceable back to Alfred Marshall—that all "utilities" have decreasing costs and from the 1930s literature on pricing in public enterprise. As we will see, U.S. private utilities do a great deal of marginal-cost pricing, call it what they may.

to the right, straining capacity so severely that true marginal costs would be almost infinitely high. In practical terms, the utility would be short of capacity and some demand would *not* be met. Meanwhile off-peak usage would be less than optimal.

Evidently, marginal-cost pricing can be of critical importance, for it may avoid gross and chronic overload on the system. Before 1970 this point often fell on deaf ears; the new scarcities have at last driven it home. Without it, the inherent tendencies of regulated utilities to overinvest will be aggravated. Therefore peak-load pricing is an essential offset to the other distortions which regulation may induce.

Marginal-cost pricing in practice faces difficult problems in defining peak-load responsibility and cost. In some cases, peak-load costs are relatively easy to determine, while in others they are virtually beyond measurement. Still, the principle is the same: during peak-load periods pricing should be up in line with costs, while off-peak prices should be relatively low.

C2. The Case for Discrimination

A social rationale for discrimination is that, in certain conditions, it is the only way to cover total costs. Normally, as we have seen, a properly designed utility recovers enough revenue from all prices to cover its costs and stay in business. Two exceptional cases are *(a)* very high overhead costs in the whole system, so that the identifiable marginal costs of individual outputs are all low, and *(b)* excess capacity, for the system as a whole (recall Figure 11–3).

The excess-capacity case is transitional, while the utility is being trimmed back; during that period there ought to be financial losses to reflect the retirement of valueless capital. The overhead-cost situation is more difficult. A standard proposal is to cover the overhead costs by charging more than marginal costs (that is, putting k above 1), but varying the differences inversely with the elasticities of demand.[25] Letting discrimination thus dilute marginal-cost pricing would, it is said, minimize the inefficiency, while making the utility viable. The logic is valid, but the practical impact may be minor. Most utility costs can be allocated fairly reliably, and so discrimination will be justified only in a narrow range, if at all. The firms will, by contrast, claim a need for wide price discrimination, and so the correct allocation of costs can be decisive to the outcome.[26]

---

[25] See Kahn, *Economics*, I, chap. 5, and William J. Baumol and David F. Bradford, "Optimal Departures from Marginal Cost Pricing," *American Economic Review* 60 (June 1970), 265–83.

[26] Price discrimination is partly self correcting, if new competitors are permitted to enter (recall Chapter 8). The entrants will be attracted to the "creamy" markets first, and so they will cut back the discrimination. Once established, they may spread to other submarkets, and so the whole discriminatory structure will be undermined. This occurs, though, only if the regulators permit it. And they must be careful that the new competition does not attack the viability of the whole utility system.

In short, optimum price structure sticks close to marginal costs, with deviations only under unusual conditions. The pressure for such deviation will be intense and widespread. But unless they hew to the unified principle of marginal-cost pricing, regulators will give free play to the utilities' ability to charge what the traffic will bear.

D. REGULATORY ACTIONS TOWARD PRICE STRUCTURES

Commissions have rarely tackled rate structures thoroughly. In a standard rate-level case, prices have usually been increased equally across the board. Only when new services are offered, or a specific price is challenged, have commissions tried to allocate costs in setting a price. Yet such treatment is piecemeal and infrequent. Commissions have mainly avoided the divisive issues of price structure by accepting what the firms propose.

Yet regulation's broad effect has been to reduce price discrimination. The pricing for broad customer groups—such as residential, commercial, and large industry—often is less discriminatory than it would be if left free. But much discrimination remains, particularly in railroad pricing.

Until about 1965 there was little careful action. Pricing had come to be mainly *promotional,* with volume discounts for higher use (so-called "declining block" and two-part tariffs: see Chapters 12–14). This promoted use and growth, but it probably overstimulated peak-load use and involved widespread discrimination. Many utilities have voluntarily used marginal-cost pricing for some services.[27]

Since about 1970 major efforts have begun toward time-of-use rate restructuring, especially in electricity and telephones. Federal commissions and the better state commissions have had hearings and some experiments. This has been reinforced by the utilities' own interests in avoiding excess investment and peak-load breakdowns. Yet action so far has been only a beginning. Concepts and methods are still formative. Peak-load use is still underpriced in most utility systems. And price discrimination among customer groups continues largely unchanged.

E. PROBABLE EFFECTS ON EFFICIENCY

Regulatory treatments are a crazy quilt of action, inaction, partial controls, and fallible choices, with much slippage between the formal and the real. Several main effects on performance are likely to occur from all this.[28]

Recall that utility managers routinely lack pressures and incentives for efficiency. During Stages 1–3 the degree of internal efficiency is partly a

[27] See William G. Shepherd, "Marginal Cost Pricing in American Utilities," *Southern Economic Journal* 33 (July 1966), 58–70.

[28] For more detailed discussion, see Kahn, *Economics,* II, and Almarin Phillips, ed., *Promoting Competititon in Regulated Markets* (Washington, D.C.: Brookings Institution, 1975).

matter of choice. Only if the regulators somehow manage to maintain the possibilities of take-over or of other close outside supervision (either by themselves or by other private entities) will there be a normal kind of efficiency constraint. In fact, they do not, as we have seen. Therefore, the cost curves illustrated in Figure 11–2 and 11–10 may not be as low as possible. If they are shifted upward by a margin of inefficiency, then prices will be higher and output levels will be lower.

Bear in mind also that the firms usually benefit from having an extra margin of capacity and quality, to avoid breakdowns and to present an image of high-grade service. Regulators often share this preference, and so they are not diligent in estimating this margin and trying to keep it from being wasteful.

In short, serious questions about efficiency and investment arise under regulation and seem to have no easy solution. Regulation might even hit the efficient overall profit levels right on the button, while still fostering thick layers of inefficiency, excess capacity, and unfairness.

Types of Loss. There are five main probable effects. *First,* the process tends to extend and harden the degree of monopoly held by the utility during Stages 2 and 3, and even Stage 4. The commissions come to defend the companies against potential competition. The natural effects of monpoly on efficiency are therefore reinforced.

Second, the process encourages inefficiency, by applying a "cost-plus" incentive system (the firm charges cost plus a profit margin). The managers are remarkably free of constraints, and so the resulting degree of inefficiency is likely to be significant. These tendencies can affect all inputs, labor, capital, materials, and services.

The *third* effect stems from the special focus of regulation upon the rate of return on *capital.* This causes two special effects. *One is that the firm prefers a higher level of capital than it otherwise would.* This effect may increase the utilities' capital-intensity by a great amount or perhaps by a fairly slight margin. But the direction is clear: toward higher levels of investment.

A related impulse is toward capturing adjacent markets at below-cost prices. Recall that most utilities operate across a variety of markets, some of which are core natural monopolies, others which are partly natural monopolies, and still others which are related but could be quite competitive. Because of the rate-base effect, utilities will have a steady incentive to reach out into the further markets as long as the capital for the production can be included in the rate base.

The *fourth* probable side effect of regulation is upon innovation.[29] Where the utility also makes its own capital equipment (as does the Bell System), it will have incentives which are different from those operating when supply is open and competitive. The integrated system will tend to increase the

---

[29] See William G. Shepherd, "The Margin of Competition in Communications," chapter in William M. Capron, ed., *Technological Change in Regulated Industries* (Washington, D.C.: Brookings Institution, 1971).

316

total expenditure on invention, but also to inhibit the application of these results. The system also applies incentives to arrange innovation so as to keep out competitors. The result will probably be a different and nonoptimal pattern of innovation.

Fifth, capacity and peak use are enlarged where peak-load pricing ignores true marginal costs.

These effects of regulation depart from the optimum. Yet one can instead take a more optimistic perspective on the rate-base effect, suggesting that even if it does occur it may promote long-run efficiency rather than retard it. Kahn has argued that the rate-base effect will tend more to promote long-run innovation than to waste capital, as long as innovation requires new investment.[30] The monopoly conditions tend to encourage utilities to restrict, while the rate-base effect induces them to overexpand. To that extent, the rate-base effect may be a productive—though unintended and poorly understood—side effect of the regulatory process.

How severe are these social costs? They are subtle and usually hard to measure, because they are woven into the fabric of operations. Commissioners and firms usually deny them. There have been few scientific studies of their extent. Still they have probably been sizable, as Chapters 12–14 will suggest, possibly enough to outweigh regulation's benefits in some cases.

Possible Cures. The efficiency problem has long been recognized by experts, though regulators and firms prefer to ignore it. There are frequent calls for incentive regulation to correct the biases, but it is not clear that any practical relief can be expected. Several treatments to avert the possible inefficiency have been aired or tried, as follows.

The *first* one is incentive regulation. In one version, regulators would determine which utilities are the more efficient and then reward them by letting them have a higher profit rate. This might restore incentives for efficiency. The treatment would have two parts: *(a)* a method for making objective estimates of efficiency, and *(b)* a method of applying rewards and penalties. So far both parts have proven impractical to arrange. Another version is simply regulatory lag. If utilities have a period to gain from better efficiency, then slow regulation may neatly promote efficiency!

A *second* tactic is to order direct audits of managerial performance, to fill the void of control. These outside audits would be a basis for specific changes in the firm's form, staffing, and activities. They would also give the regulators and directors a basis for differential rewards.

Managerial evaluation is a well-developed professional field, with a great variety of unbiased assessors to choose among. The problem requires expert, sophisticated judgment. Yet the mere possibility of undergoing an audit may inject strong incentives for minimizing costs and searching out new technologies. It would clarify the regulatory role too, by fixing responsibility for performance. These points hold equally for private, public, or mixed owner-

---

[30] Kahn, *Economics,* II, 49–59.

ship. So far audits have only been tried once or twice with no reinforcement. If the practice became routine, its effects could be thorough.

The *third* strategy is to permit entry; that is, to relax regulatory bars to entry by new sellers, competing against the utilities. It is optimal and natural to do this in Stages 3 and 4, and recently it (and its extreme form, deregulation) has been seen as a main route for regulatory reform. Actually, there are three forms of "entry:" by new firms against old utility sellers, by the old sellers against each other, and by new ownership over the old sellers themselves. Recent commentary has favored the first, but the second and third may be more promising in a wider range of utilities.

F. REGULATING OLIGOPOLY

When regulation is applied to several firms rather than just one (airlines are one example), some of the main problems and results change. There is some degree of natural monopoly, but not enough to prescribe just one utility firm. If overhead costs are high enough, then there may be a tendency toward "destructive" and "unstable" competition. That is the reason for which such companies usually try to get regulated. In general, the conditions are those like Stage 4 in which the utility would—if unshielded—become competitive.

In this setting regulation tends to apply price floors as well as price celings, as part of the effort to stop or contain price competition. Usually the regulation of oligopoly applies little or no ceiling to the rate of return.

The main features and effects of such regulation are four, as follows.

Cartel Support.   Regulation becomes a support for cartel price fixing and the prevention of new entry. Prices tend to be higher than they otherwise would, because regulation sets minimum prices in order to avert "ruinous" competition. Strict bars to entry are set up, and routes and market divisions are set officially. In some cases, ceiling prices are also set. These then tend to become a *floor* price. The effects on price levels are roughly the same as under private cartels, though the official support makes the cartel tighter.

The Shift to Nonprice Competition.   Competition naturally turns to the nonprice features of the service or product, which are often quite numerous. They include the reliability of service, quality, frequency, and still other features: airlines and broadcasting exemplify these varieties. In airlines, service is made more reliable and convenient. It is made fancier with such things as meals, personal service, and decor. Service is also made more frequent, as airlines add flights at small intervals throughout the day in order to match each others' takeoff times.

However, this does not guarantee that service diversity will be optimal, or even very large at all. Rather, the diversity of offerings tends to be less under regulated oligopoly than under either monopoly or unregulated oligopoly. This is because regulation reduces uncertainty and makes experimentation more difficult. The well-known tendency for oligopolists to match each others' offerings—rather than to explore the demands of minority customers—

is sharpened.[31] The result is clear, for example, in the case of television (see Chapter 13). The breadth of offerings tends to be narrowed by the effects of regulation.

Price Discrimination. Even if profits are constrained by the regulators, a degree of price discrimination usually continues. This is because the regulated oligopolists still have strong incentives to exploit differences in demand elasticities among the consumers. Because the sellers are multiple rather than single, regulators may have even more difficulty securing valid data on costs. Therefore, even if regulatory strictness is great, price discrimination is likely to occur.

Regulatory Inertia. The extent of regulatory control against competition will tend to exceed what is optimal, especially as the technological need for regulation fades away in Stage 4. Such regulation is too valuable to the firms to be let go. Regulators will think of their controls as being coexistent with the public interest rather than against it. Therefore they will defend their partitioning of the market strongly, permitting new entry and the loosening of control only reluctantly. Especially because the companies are not monopolies, the commission will take an avuncular interest in keeping them secure. Therefore the tendency toward excessive regulation may be as strong as under the regulation of single-firm utilities.

In short, regulation of several firms tends to be excessive, anticompetitive, conducive to excess service quality, and skimpy or negative in net public benefits. Some of the direct effects differ from those which the regulation of monopoly yields.

G. SUMMARY

We have now reviewed the basic conditions and effects of regulation as it is normally done in the United States. We now turn to specific regulatory commissions and industries. We will look especially at:

1. Actual levels of profit rates and prices permitted under regulation.
2. Evidence about price-cost structures.
3. Control against entry by new competitors.
4. Incentives toward efficiency or inefficiency.
5. Indications of possible excess service quality.
6. Possible excess capacity or other rate-base effects.
7. Anticompetitive regulation of oligopoly cases.

If we see regulation clearly and honestly, without illusion, we can then perceive its true effects and effectiveness. We will bear in mind that the

---

[31] H. Hotelling, "Stability in Competition," *Economic Journal* 39 (1929), 41–57; Arthur Smithies, "Optimum Location in Spatial Competition," *Journal of Political Economy* 49 (1941), 423–39; and P. O. Steiner, "Program Patterns and Preferences, and the Workability of Competition in Radio Broadcasting," *Quarterly Journal of Economics* 66 (1952), 194–223. Recall also the analysis at the beginning of Chapter 7.

alternatives may be less satisfactory, but at the least we will see what is really there. And in some cases we may be pleasantly surprised.

QUESTIONS FOR REVIEW

1. "The prices of outputs are only one part of the whole regulatory equation." True?
2. "Commissions need to check on the correctness of the p_j and q_j choices, but they usually do not do so." True?
3. "In some cases a regulated firm should not attract capital for investment." True?
4. "A comparable earnings criterion would simply set utility profits at the level of the highest monopoly profits in other sectors." True?
5. "One can easily prepare figures for the cost of capital, but the true cost of capital is difficult to define and measure." True?
6. "If regulation were efficient, the utility would have to earn its rate of return rather than be given it as a right." True?
7. "Cost-plus regulation will always induce great X-efficiency." True?
8. "A high depreciation rate gives low cash flow now, but it pays off by providing a higher rate base in later years." True?
9. "Rate-base regulation tends to encourage inflation of the firm's real and accounting capital." True?
10. "Most utility firms' actual profit rates on equity are not far below those realized in nonutility sectors." True?
11. "The correct basis for rate structure is marginal cost, perhaps with some price discrimination for special conditions." True?
12. "Cost and demand conditions sometimes give parallel results for price structures." True?
13. "Correct peak-load pricing can help to avoid overexpansion of the rate base." True?
14. "Price discrimination is lessened by regulation, but much of it remains." True?
15. "Regulation tends to induce several kinds of inefficiency." True?
16. "Regulatory lag can restore incentives for efficiency." True?
17. "Regulation of oligopoly is usually a strong device for preventing cartel results." True?
18. Explain why the regulators' search for "the" fair rate of return is circular.
19. Regulation often tries to enforce a competitive-looking outcome (low profit, prices near costs). Explain why such a simulation does not guarantee efficiency and fairness, the ultimate economic objectives.
20. What are the main costs of regulation? The main benefits?
21. Should regulation deliberately provide regulatory lag?
22. List as many instances of marginal-cost pricing of utility services as you can.

chapter 12

Regulation of Electricity and Gas

Electricity is a highly typical regulated industry. It is conventional in its origins, regulatory status, profit rates, and price structures. And it is an old case. Yet it also has new problems of scarcity, an ill-fitting price structure, and potential competition in wholesale markets.

Gas regulation is conventional at two of its levels: pipelines and local selling. But it is caught in unique problems at the wellhead where gas is fed into the pipelines.

Electricity and gas compete against each other for many customers. And both have been deeply affected by the "energy crisis" since 1968. With this set of basic conditions and a degree of change, they present many of the standard issues of regulation.

A. ELECTRICITY

A1. Structure

Levels. Electricity is a three-stage sector.[1] The first stage is *generation,* the production of electricity by rotating large electric motors backwards. The driving force may come from conventional sources of heat, such as coal, oil, and gas, or from water power. Recently nuclear energy has begun to be a significant generation source. By now most of the good hydroelectric sites are occupied, and the future sources of power lie mainly between coal and nuclear energy—with possibly fusion and solar heat further ahead.

Transmission is the bulk carriage of electricity from generating sites to final-use areas. The pylons and huge towers which march across the country-side carry these high voltage power lines. Figure 12–1 suggests how large

---

[1] For good summaries of the sector see Russell E. Caywood, *Electric Utility Rate Economics* (New York: McGraw-Hill Book Co., 1956); Edwin Vennard, *The Electric Power Business* (New York: McGraw-Hill Book Co., 1962); and Federal Power Commission, *National Power Survey* (Washington, D.C.: U.S. Government Printing Office, 1970), 4 vols.

FIGURE 12–1
Electric Supply Facilities in One Region of the United States

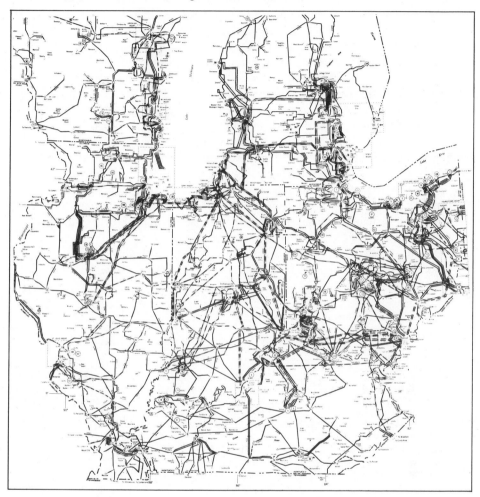

and complicated the lines are, by showing them in one sector of the United States. As transmission scale has increased, the country (and certain sources in Canada) has become partly interconnected. But these are a series of separately owned systems, coordinated to a degree but owned mainly by about 170 private companies.

The *distribution* systems are local: from the substation to the final users. This involves wires to a great variety of users, including residential, commercial, industrial, and public agencies. These are the end points of electricity supply, which require much servicing and change, as customers and uses shift.

Ownership. In addition to this technical structure of electricity, the ownership structure is important. About three-quarters of the industry is privately owned in the United States, in about 170 firms; leading ones are given in Table 12–1 and Figure 12–2. The conventional pattern is for all three levels of operation to be integrated vertically within the same firm. This condition has been common since the reorganization of the industry during 1935–50.

During the 1930–60 the publicly owned share of the industry rose, but now it is stable. It exists *(a)* in hundreds of small local municipal systems, *(b)* in one statewide public power system (Nebraska), *(c)* in hundreds of Rural Electric Cooperative systems, and *(d)* in the bulk generation and transmission of power by the federal government, mainly from hydroelectric sources, and primarily in the Tennessee Valley and in the Northwest and Southwest of the country. This parallel role for public and private power is in contrast to the conventional situation in other countries. There public ownership is virtually complete, and it is unified in one fully planned and controlled system. In some countries, the primacy of public ownership dates from generations ago, but in several main European countries it has existed only since 1945–50 (see Chapters 16 and 18). The United States is unique among advanced economies in having mainly *(a)* private ownership and *(b)*

TABLE 12–1
Leading Electric Utility Firms, 1977

	Firm	Main Area Served	Also a Large Gas Supplier?	Revenue ($ million)
1	Pacific Gas and Electric	North and Central California	Yes	3,506
2	Consolidated Edison	New York City	Yes	3,023
3	Southern Company	Ala., Georgia, Miss., Fla.	No	2,661
4	Commonwealth Edison	Northern Illinois	No	2,095
5	Southern California Edison . .	California	No	2,065
6	Public Service Electric and Gas	New Jersey	Yes	2,033
7	American Electric Power	Ohio, W. Virginia, Indiana, etc.	No	2,031
8	Consumers Power	Michigan	No	1,637
9	Florida Power and Light	Florida	No	1,465
10	Detroit Edison	Southeast Michigan	No	1,451
11	Middle South Utilities	Ark., Miss., Louisiana	No	1,443
12	Philadelphia Electric	Philadelphia	No	1,395
13	Texas Utilities	Central Texas	No	1,368
14	Virginia Electric & Power . . .	Eastern Virginia	No	1,359
15	Duke Power	Western N. and S. Carolina	No	1,267
16	General Public Utilities	N.J., Pennsylvania	No	1,252
17	Niagara Mohawk Power	Upper New York State	Yes	1,226
18	Central & Southwest	Texas and Oklahoma	No	1,167
19	Northern States Power	Wisconsin, Minn., S. Dak.	Yes	882
20	Long Island Lighting	Long Island	Yes	824
21	Carolina Power & Light	N. and S. Carolina	No	808

Source: Annual *Reports* of the firms; and Moody's *Handbook of Common Stocks* (New York: Moody's Investors Service, Inc., quarterly).

FIGURE 12–2
Service Areas of the Largest Private Electric Utilities

Adapted from map supplied by *Electric Light and Power,* Cahners Publishing Co., Boston. Numbers are keyed to the firms in Table 12–1.

fragmentation in a patchwork of geographically separate operations. Dotted among the private systems are over a thousand public and rural systems, most of them small, and the occasional large federal system. There is no overall control over the coordination of the system, by contrast with the unified electricity supply in most other countries. There is a degree of coordination among neighboring electric firms, in order to pool capacity and supply for peak loads. The trend toward coordination is strong and rising, but the suppliers are still separate.

A2. Technology

There are relatively slight economies of vertical integration. More important are the economies of scale at each level. At both the generation and transmission levels the scale economies have been large, favoring an increasingly large size of apparatus during the last several decades. Yet it is *distribution* at the local level where natural monopoly most clearly exists. There the inefficiency of duplicating the network of wires seems to be clear and compelling. Distribution is *the* core of natural monopoly in electricity supply.

In *generation,* the last four decades have seen a rise in size of units and a reduction of average costs. This was not strictly a technological advance, but rather the realization of pre-existing economies of scale. In the last decade, it has become apparent that the limits of scale economies are being reached.[2] Therefore generation is characterized by economies of scale which are definite but limited. In the future the size of new plants will probably grow slowly rather than rapidly.

Transmission has been at increasing scales also, and further economies seem to be large. Large-scale transmission offers major new opportunities for carrying bulk supply over long distances and in high volume. This could lead either to new competition in wholesale electricity, or to more unification in a "national grid." Transmission is therefore the most sensitive area for future adjustments in the scope of local monopoly and regulation.

On the whole, the technology is evolving so as to permit realignments of the old service areas and competitive strategies.[3] The core of natural monopoly at the distribution level will continue, but the pressures for detaching it from the rest of the sector—so that new structures can evolve—are growing. Electricity is currently at a watershed, from which new structures and regulatory treatments could evolve. Therefore the conventional regulation which held from about 1935 to 1970 is likely to change appreciably, because new technology is offering wider choices.

A3. Historical Background

The sector originated in the 1870s, when the basic technology of generating and illuminating was invented and applied. During 1890–1920 electricity evolved from a luxury of the rich into a more broadly used service. It also developed from a small local service to intercity and statewide systems. But this evolution was not easy or quick. Among the early leaders of the industry, Samuel Insull pushed his colleagues toward a wider supply system and a promotional pricing system to stimulate demand.[4] The result was growth and falling costs. By 1910 the basic groundwork of the industry was in place, with suppliers in most areas already in being and fully related to their main customers.

There followed a further growth and unification of the industry among cities, and then the great rise, peak, and crash of holding companies in 1920–33. The great stock market boom which ended in 1929 was fed in large part by intricate schemes to pyramid control and profits from the base of ordinary electric companies. The resulting abuses of utility holding companies

---

[2] Federal Power Commission, *National Power Survey,* 1970, vol. I; and M. Galatin, *Economies of Scale and Technological Change in Thermal Generation* (Amsterdam: North Holland Press, 1968).

[3] See especially Leonard W. Weiss, "Antitrust in the Electric Power Industry," in Almarin Phillips, ed., *Promoting Competition in Regulated Markets* (Washington, D.C.: Brookings Institution, 1975).

[4] Forrest McDonald, *Insull* (Chicago: University of Chicago Press, 1962).

were fully exposed in the early 1930s, after the stocks had plummeted. Ironically, Insull was pilloried as the symbol of the manipulator. But the trickery had been much more widespread and cynical than his, and the whole scandal and its effects led to drastic reorganization of the industry.

Holding company abuses were severe. Control could be pyramided over several levels, with a small stake at the top giving control over vastly larger investments. There were as many as 12 layers, and one Insull operating company was controlled by an investment of 1/200 of 1 percent. Profits were correspondingly pyramided, often over 100 percent of the top-level investment.[5] But pyramiding was also risky, for a small dip in operating profits could plunge the holding company into bankruptcy. The holding company operators thus took control of an industry that was guaranteed a legal monopoly of a necessary service and turned it into a highly speculative enterprise. From the soundest investment in the market, they converted utility shares, at the upper levels, into counters in a game of chance.

In 1928 the Federal Trade Commission had been directed by Congress to investigate electric and gas utilities. In 1935 it published its final report, summarizing more than 70 volumes of hearings and exhibits. Many holding company abuses were thus brought into glaring light. Meanwhile the largest holding company systems—Associated Gas and Electric, Insull, and Foshay in Minneapolis—had come down in ruins, scores of others were bankrupt, in receivership, or in default, and hundreds of thousands of investors had seen their savings disappear. The sector was overripe for reform.

The Public Utility Act of 1935 had two parts. Title II for the first time gave jurisdiction over interstate transmission of electricity to the FPC. Title I was the Public Utility Holding Company Act. This was the most stringent corrective measure ever applied to American business. It required the reorganization of corporate structures and forced divestment of property. It made the Securities and Exchange Commission a potent regulator of electric and gas holding companies. Wherever abuses had been disclosed, it provided powers of control.

The Commission approached its task with caution. It was not until 1940 that voluntary distintegration plans were submitted and formal proceedings begun. By 1951 the commissions had undertaken the reformation of corporate structures including more than 200 holding companies and nearly 2,000 other companies. By 1952 the job was largely done.

The Commission was strict in its enforcement of the principle of integration. It favored a compact system, confined to a single area, its facilities interconnected or capable of interconnection, its operations coordinated, and its management unified. It opposed the common control of electricity and gas, and the operation of companies providing other services, unless they could be shown to bear a functional relationship to the provision of electricty or gas.

---

[5] Federal Trade Commission, *Control of Power Companies* (Senate Doc. 213, 69th Cong. 2d. Sess.) (Washington, D.C.: U.S. Government Printing Office, 1927).

In this way the many-tiered holding company systems with widely scattered properties were eliminated and the simpler, closely integrated systems were preserved. There are about 20 regional holding company systems remaining under Commission control.

This sweeping reorganization of the electric and gas utility industries was a significant accomplishment. It did not in itself make the regulation of rates and services effective. But it removed a major obstacle to control.

This decentralization of financial control assured a continuing decentralization of operations, despite a series of mergers since the 1950s. It also assured a trauma in management and ownership during the 1930s and 1940s from which the industry is only now emerging. The senior management in electric utilities during the 1950s and 1960s had started out during 1930–50, when the industry was in shock. It is not surprising that the relatively simple and undemanding decisions required of electric utilities between World War II and 1965 fitted well the urge for managerial security. From 1930 on, the industry engaged primarily in a push for growth by means of promotional pricing and the realization of scale economies. It was a rather easy ride during that period, with all growth signs upward and a downward trend in costs.

This golden era came to a rude halt in the late 1960s, as scarcity and complexity suddenly arose. There were several special problems. One was the narrowing leeway in picking sites for generation and in setting transmission lines. Urban problems and concern about pollution made the siting problem critical in the largest utilities. As nuclear power came on in a rush after 1963, it too encountered a rash of unexpected problems, of *(a)* delay in completing plants, and of *(b)* public resistance to possible dangers from nuclear plants. Moreover, the growth of electricity demand was higher than had been expected, and this accentuated the capacity crisis in which many utilities suddenly found themselves by 1970. The old push for sheer growth was no longer appropriate or indeed possible. The old promotional schemes now could be shown to be inefficient and inequitable. And to top it all off, the prices of fuels surged upward, especially from the OPEC oil price jump of 1973–74.

The whole effect was to plunge a mature and settled growth sector into new cross-currents, which required not only a new delicacy and sophistication in handling but also fundamental changes in the old ways of doing business. The crisis has already had marked effects. It has arisen under regulation, in ways which—if one understands what regulation has and has not been doing—are predictable. Regulation has fitted conventionally into Stages 2 and 3 of the industry's growth. From the start it has served the companies as well as—in part—constraining them.

A4. Profits under Regulation

Regulation was first developed on the state level, with some commissions becoming fairly effective by the middle 1930s. A federal regulating group was created in 1920 but it dealt only with hydroelectric projects and had little regulatory content. The FPC did gain power in 1935 to regulate interstate transmission, but for three decades it did little more than develop a uniform system of accounts.

The FPC was revived after 1960 by Joseph C. Swidler (Chairman 1961–66). Rate hearings became markedly more thorough, meaningful, and strict. And a massive *National Power Survey* was made, with industry cooperation. Published in 1964, the *Survey* showed that large savings were to be had from fuller pooling and coordination. The *Survey* was sophisticated and foresighted; a second *Survey* was finished in 1970. By tackling both rates and technology, the FPC at long last began to achieve the modest targets that were possible. In 1977 the FPC became the Federal Energy Regulatory Commission (FERC), associated with the new federal Department of Energy. Most of the independence and tasks remained about the same as before.

The companies still strive to keep as much of their operations as possible under state regulation, because it usually is more liberal. In some cases, company activities and pooling have been confined within state borders, despite the gains from connecting across state lines.

The leading electric companies summarized in Table 12–1 and Figure 12–2 therefore reflect certain dramatic episodes and moderate regulatory efforts. These firms differ. Some are tied to old, slow-growth areas (New England, for example), while others are in booming regions (Florida, the Southwest). Some have been growing by mergers, while most have not. Some are known to have first-class managerial quality, while others have been mediocre or worse.

Profits. Rates of profits are in the "normal" range, as was indicated in Table 11–1 and Figure 11–6 above. Only since the 1930s has regulation had much influence on them. Differences among company profits arise both from regulation and from underlying economic conditions.

During the 1920s and 1930s the reproduction-cost controversy and the holding company phase effectively deprived regulation of any real profits control. By the 1960s the FPC and some state commissions had put a degree of constraint on some company profit rates. But the constraint was not tight, and it was made more tolerable before 1965 by the natural decline in relative electricity costs over the years.

But after 1965 there was a massive shift toward rate increases. There is some tendency for commissions which are strict on rate base concepts to be relatively liberal in setting rates of return. Therefore the overall differences in the bite of regulation on profitability are not very great among the states. One could fairly conclude that state regulation has little effect at all in most states, and that federal regulation has applied only a mild constraint.

A5. Price Structures under Regulation

These have evolved toward a standardized pattern, in which users pay either according to declining-block or two-part tariffs (and some tariffs com-

TABLE 12–2
Illustrations of Electric Rates

Declining Block—for Residential Customers
1. Monthly customer charge: $1
2. Energy charge per kwh.
   7.85¢ for the first 50 kwh.
   4.29¢ for next 100
   1.95¢ for next 200
   1.67¢ for next 500
   1.50¢ for all additional kwh.

Two-Part Tariff—for Industrial Customers (at 4,800 to 120,000 volts)
1. Demand Charge per kw.
   $8.00 per kw. for the first 200 kw.
   $6.50 for next 800
   $5.50 for next 500
   $5.00 for all additional kw. of demand.
   (Demand measured by the maximum load of the customer at any time during the previous month.)
2. Energy Charge: 1.5¢ per kwh. plus fuel adjustment per kwh.

---

bine both). Generally, residential and small users are given declining-block tariffs, while large users are given two-part tariffs (with a monthly "demand" charge and a flat "energy" charge per kilowatt-hour).[6] Table 12–2 and Figure 12–3 illustrate them. The key *promotional* feature is that the effective price declines as usage rises, in the familiar pattern of bulk discounts. This may reflect some degree of cost difference, as the user takes more units via a constant set of supplying apparatus. This classic promotional price structure evolved over decades of many years of effort, debate, and intense controversy during 1900–1940. It means that large users get electricity cheaper than small users. The differences can be sharp, up to a multiple of three or four. As for the comparisons among different user classes, large-scale industry and commerce will obviously get electricity more cheaply than do small residential users. Typically, the residential user pays about 1.5 to 2 times the price charged to large industrial users. The fundamental question is whether this fits true cost differences or instead is simply price discrimination.

Consider Costs, First. An electricity system has large overhead costs in supplying a great variety of users. There are wide fluctuations in daily and seasonal loads (see Figures 12–4 and 12–5). Actual costs can vary sharply, by time and other conditions of supply.

The accountants divide costs into three categories: output costs, customer costs, and demand costs. *Output costs* are those incurred in the operation of a plant; the costs of labor, fuel, materials, and supplies. They vary with the volume of production, but not very sharply. *Customer costs* are those

---

[6] See Ralph K. Davidson, *Price Discrimination in Selling Gas and Electricity* (Baltimore: Johns Hopkins Press, 1955); and Charles J. Cicchetti and John Jurewitz, eds., *Studies in Electric Utility Regulation* (Cambridge: Ballinger, 1975); and Caywood, *Electric Utility Rate Economics.*

FIGURE 12–3

An Illustration of a Declining-Block Tariff for Electricity

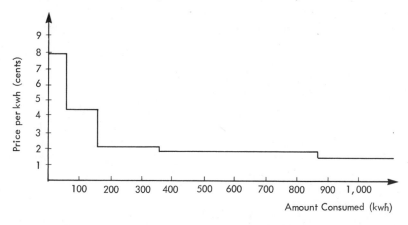

incurred in reading meters, sending and collecting bills, keeping accounts, and the like. They vary with the number of customers. *Demand costs* are also known as "readiness-to-serve" costs. They are the overhead costs of capital and management involved in providing a plant that is large enough to meet the peak demand that may be made on it at any day and hour. They are thus a function of capacity.

FIGURE 12–4

Typical Daily Load Patterns

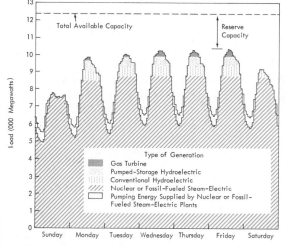

Source: Federal Power Commission, *National Power Survey, 1970,* p. I–7–5.

FIGURE 12–5

Estimated 1970 Monthly Peak Demands

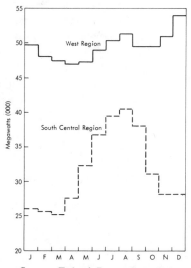

Source: Federal Power Commission, *National Power Survey, 1970,* p. I–3–3.

It is in demand costs that the explanation for differences in cost per kilo-watt-hour is mainly to be found. Investment in electric plants is heavy, and so overhead costs are high. The investment required depends upon the peak demand. A kilowatt-hour taken at the peak adds to the overhead; one taken at another time does not. The cost of the first, therefore, is higher than that of the second, often by a multiple.

Load and Diversity Factors. Utility accountants, in their analysis of costs, speak of the load factor of a utility system, the load factor of an individual customer, and the diversity factor of the system as a whole. The *system's load factor* is its average load expressed as a percentage of its capacity. Thus, if the average load over a period is 6,000 kw. and the available capacity is 9,000, the load factor is 66⅔ percent. The *customer's load factor* is its average consumption expressed as a percentage of its maximum consumption.

The *system's diversity factor* is determined by adding up the maximum demands of all of its customers, whenever they occur, and dividing this sum by the maximum demand made on the system as a whole at any one time. Thus, customer A may take 1 kw. at 8 A.M., customer B 2 kw. at noon, and customer C 3 kw. at 4 P.M., a total of 6 kw. Yet the maximum demand made on the system at any hour may be only 3 kw., and so the diversity factor is 2.

The average cost per kilowatt-hour will be reduced if the system's load factor can be raised. This may be accomplished in two ways: by improving the load factor of each customer, or by raising the diversity factor. The customer's load factor may be improved by encouraging it to increase consumption at off-peak hours. The diversity factor may be raised by attracting groups of customers whose maximum demands will be scattered, also coming at off-peak hours.

The system peak usually falls during week-day business hours—8 A.M. to 5 P.M.—during December–January in northern states and July–August in southern states. At peak, costs are often five, ten, or more times higher than at off-peak times.[7] This was illustrated in Figure 11–10.

Ideal rates would overlay any block and two-part features with time differentials, as illustrated in Table 12–3.[8] Instead most declining-block rates ignore the time of day, week, or season. The last low-price block is available for

---

[7] A. E. Kahn, *The Economics of Regulation* (New York: Wiley, 1971), vol. I; and Charles R. Scherer, "Estimating Peak and Off-peak Marginal Costs for an Electric Power System: An *Ex Ante* Approach," *Bell Journal of Economics* 7 (Autumn 1976), 575–601.

[8] Whether the underlying rates continued to have volume discounts or not is a separate question.

After 1973 there was consumerist pressure for "lifeline" rates, with a first low-price block for minimum household needs, and then a higher standard rate for all other power. Thus a household might pay 2 cents per kwh for the first 200 kwh per month and then 4 cents per kwh for all additional use. Such rates could benefit the poor, but they could also benefit rich people with small electricity usage. The idea was applied in several states, after much agitation. It bore little relation to efficient rates, though it might promote fairness.

TABLE 12–3
Illustrations of Time-of-Use Electric Prices

Residential Rate
Customer charge per month $2.75
Meter charge per month (for a time-of-day meter) $2.50/meter
Water heating credit (applicable in all months)............. $1.50/month

Energy charge (high use hours: 7 A.M. to 7 P.M. Monday–Friday, inclusive)

	Billing Periods*		
	Summer July– September	Winter January– March	Base All Other Months
First 500 kwh/month	7.69¢/kwh	5.10¢/kwh	3.71¢/kwh
Over 500 kwh/month	7.69¢/kwh	4.50¢/kwh	3.41¢/kwh
Energy charge (low use hours: all other hours)			
All months...................	0.94¢/kwh		

Large Commercial and Industrial Rate (for customers contracting for three-phase, 60 hertz power service and using over 80,000 kwh per month)
Customer charge per month $15
Demand charge per month

	Billing Periods†		
	Summer July– September	Winter January– March	Base All Other Months
All kw/month	$5.10/kw	$1.70/kw	$1.20/kw

Energy Charge (high use hours: 7 A.M. to 7 P.M. Monday–Friday, inclusive)

	All Seasons
0–50,000 kwh	2.44¢/kwh
Next 450,000 kwh	2.24¢/kwh
Over 500,000 kwh	1.74¢/kwh
Energy Charge (low use hours: all other hours)	
Off-peak	0.84¢/kwh

* Subject to adjustment for cost of fossil production.
† Billed demand under this rate will be the customers' 15-minute maximum demand between 7 A.M and 7 P.M. Monday–Friday, inclusive.

extra use at 1 cent or 2 cents per kwh even during deepest winter or hottest summer, when the true cost may be 5 cent, 10 cent, or even 15 per kwh. Two-part tariffs for large users are also largely time-blind. The demand charge is set by the user's maximum load in the previous month, regardless of whether it came during the system peak or off-peak. The energy charge per kilowatt-hour is usually constant all day and all year round.

The rub is that rates should reflect the *system's simultaneous peak* load, whenever that peak occurs. High peak prices would encourage shifting to low-cost off-peak consumption.

Electric rates are imperfect because they evolved from simple beginnings through a promotional period, with no comprehensive revaluation. In the early years, electricity was sold at a uniform rate per kilowatt-hour. Then as producers sought to extend their operations, they began to discriminate. In order to sell to groups who were unable or unwilling to buy at the established rate, they classified their customers, fixing a lower rate for the new customers, maintaining the higher rates for the older ones. And in order to encourage greater consumption by present customers, they fixed lower rates for larger quantities, maintaining the higher rate for smaller ones.

Electricity rates became a patchwork of special deals; some customers squeezed better terms from the utility, while other customer groups became "creamy" markets. Regulation came after these deals took form and has tended only to ratify them. The process continues: rates are adjusted to meet competition (for example, against gas for new apartment blocks or industrial users) and to gain preferred customers.

The structure of electric rates has long been highly differentiated. Different classes were established for residential use, commercial light and power, industrial power, etc. The typical utility now has 6 to 12 rate categories, each with different prices.

Demand conditions encourage sharp discrimination. Elasticities vary, with businesses generally having higher elasticity of demand than residences. Electricity is essential for lighting—that is, demand is inelastic—so all households need some electricity. For appliances (stoves, water heaters, air conditioners), demand for electricity is fairly elastic. The key fact is that businesses can often generate their own power or substitute other fuels for power in their industrial processes. Therefore, business and residential demands correspond roughly to those in Figure 11–8B. Discrimination would prescribe the basic pattern of rates which has evolved: higher prices for residences, declining blocks to induce the use of electric household appliances, and demand charges which ignore system peaks.

Are rates cost-based or discriminatory? The answer is both, and there are three reasons. First, broad cost patterns (in the regional price of fuel, in obvious customer costs, and so forth) are bound to show through in rates. Thus, the sharp state differences in typical utility bills (shown in Figure 12–6) mainly reflect such cost differences. Second, cost and demand conditions are parallel in some areas: for example, most households cost more per kwh to supply than most businesses. Third, regulation has had some effect, but nobody can be sure how much. The role of costs as a price criterion is probably increasing, as the new scarcities since 1965 have forced both firms and regulators to design more efficient rates. Some European systems developed marginal-cost pricing in the 1950s and 1960s.[9] France was the leader, but Sweden, Germany, and Britain have also gone beyond what U.S. utilities are now beginning to adopt. Private ownership in the United States apparently

---

[9] See James R. Nelson, ed., *Marginal Cost Pricing in Practice* (Englewood Cliffs: Prentice-Hall, 1964); and various papers and citations in Harry M. Trebing, ed., *New Dimensions in Public Utility Pricing* (East Lansing: Institute of Public Utilities, Michigan State University, 1976).

FIGURE 12–6
Monthly Bill for Residences Taking 750 kwh per month

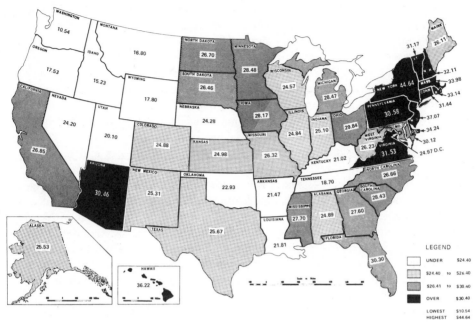

Source: Federal Power Commission, *Typical Electric Bills* (Washington, D.C.: U.S. Government Printing Office, 1977).

leads to a higher degree of price discrimination than public firms usually practice.

A5. Main Current Issues

From this background emerge four main questions about regulation of electricity. They all relate to the performance of utilities under regulation, and therefore they help us form an impression of the role of regulation itself.

Performance.   A main dimension of performance in electricity supply is the trend in costs over time. This was downward relative to prices in the whole economy until 1965, before the energy crisis, and so regulation may share the credit for this gain. We will talk about it on two planes. Both of them suggest that regulation may not promote efficiency.

The decline in relative costs of electricity was marked, but it arose mainly from the inherent scale economies embodied in new equipment, as larger scale frontiers were explored. Therefore, the long-run trend in costs cannot be clearly credited to utilities, regulators, nor perhaps even to the equipment makers.

Differences in real efficiency can also be compared among the individual utilities. This has been done in several cross-section studies, which factor out some of the basic economic determinants of cost, leaving the rest to be "explained" by real differences in managerial skill.[10] During the 1950s and 1960s there were sharp contrasts among private utilities on this basis, some showing remarkable efficiency while others were notorious for inefficiency.

Regulation has induced costs and rate-base levels to be marginally higher.[11] But the effect is not uniform. The cases of gross inefficiency have usually come to be corrected by natural market forces or changes in the management, rather than by any direct regulatory effort. So the effects of regulation on utility efficiency are marginally negative, but not conclusively known.

Marginal-Cost Pricing. Some promotional features were reversed after 1965. Firms began to preach energy-saving and dropped "all-electric" rates (an extra volume discount for users who would abjure gas and oil). But they continued the basic price structure even after a few state commissions began acting after 1974. These new actions focused on peak-load pricing, rather than a revision of other basic features (customer groupings, cost allocations, replacement of two-part tariffs, and so forth). Wisconsin led with the tariffs given in Table 12–3, but New York, Massachusetts, and California followed during 1976–78. In each case, the firms' cooperation was critical, for their control over cost data permitted them to stall rate revisions if they wished. Though Congress in 1977 rejected a proposal to require peak-load pricing, a grass-roots move toward some time features had begun.[12]

Competition in Bulk Supply. The bulk supply of electricity has now reached the end of Stage 3 (thanks to growing scale economies) and is now technologically capable of effective competition in many areas. This is raising—in practical *and* theoretical form—the prospects for a major change

---

[10] See William Iulo, *Electric Utilities—Costs and Performance* (Pullman: Washington State University Press, 1961), for the pioneering study of this kind.

[11] Recent studies affirming these costs include R. M. Spann, "Rate of Return Regulation and Efficiency in Production: An Empirical Test of the Averch-Johnson Thesis," and L. Courville, "Regulation and Efficiency in the Electric Utility Industry," both in the *Bell Journal of Economics,* 5 (Spring 1974), 38–74; and H. Craig Petersen, "An Empirical Test of Regulatory Effects," *Bell Journal of Economics,* 6 (Spring 1975), 111–26.

After 1972, the rise of fuel prices forced electric firms to make a rapid-fire series of rate increases. The "fuel adjustment clause" was devised to pass on automatically—without regulatory review—the "unavoidable" rises in fuel costs. The clauses took several forms, all of them exempting fuel costs from close review. They have two main defects. *(a)* They remove pressure on the utility to seek the lowest possible price for fuel. *(b)* They encourage technological choices which are fuel-intensive. Though these faults have become widely known, fuel adjustment clauses are still common.

[12] "Load management" is an important supplement to pricing. It involves ways of encouraging users to adjust the load to off-peak times, and mechanisms for cutting individual users' load at key times. Thus a central microwave control has been developed to switch off users' air conditioners. Special low rates can then be offered to users, on condition that they let their air conditioners be switched off selectively for five minutes per half hour. This permits reducing the system's peak loads more sharply than pricing alone could do. There are other techniques in load management as well.

in regulatory standing.[13] Many utilities could compete, and would compete, vigorously among themselves for at least their major customers. Each utility would gain by raiding its neighbors' main clients. Many cities have at least two or three alternative suppliers. Therefore the technical basis for competition now exists in bulk electricity. It could evolve away from the traditional tight vertical integration of the three levels within each geographic monopoly. This would simply restore normal economic behavior. The gains from this change could be large. Inefficiency would be under direct constraint. Service standards and cheapness would both be used to gain customers, as they should be; this would ease the possible present bias toward excessive service quality. Utilities would be induced to develop and use the technology of large-scale supply more fully, in order to penetrate each other's markets for bulk electricity.[14]

Environmental Problems. Until the 1960s the main problem of environment—or amenity, as it was called—was the location of the high voltage lines in the countryside. These questions involved a small drumfire of debate and social pressure, but on a minor scale. Since 1965 there have arisen major problems with the siting of utility plants, the use of nuclear fuel, and the pollution from old plants. These have run straight against the industry's old habit of solving problems by ample investment. On the contrary, the investments themselves have become the problem.

The basic problem arose when environmental groups discovered the ease with which the regulatory process could be used to block investment projects by the utility companies. Here again, the critical importance of the burden of proof and the advantage of time worked in favor of one side, in this case the environmentalists. By 1974 a whole range of investments in conventional and nuclear plans have been slowed or stopped, by a skillful use of regulatory delay. The blockage continued into the late 1970s.

The problem was further compounded by the technical delays in completing many nuclear projects, often years beyond the original target date. These could be blamed on the handful of equipment suppliers (mainly General Electric, Westinghouse, and Combustion Engineering). Caught in the middle were the electricity firms, stopped in front by the environmentalists in regulatory proceedings, and undercut from behind by the equipment suppliers. To some, it seemed that regulation now stood squarely and awkwardly in the path of necessary utility expansion. The delay has continued, as new doubts about the economic and social costs of nuclear power have emerged.

---

[13] James E. Meeks, "Concentration in the Electric Power Industry: The Impact of Antitrust Policy," *Columbia Law Review* 72 (1972), 64–130. A thorough economic analysis is by Leonard W. Weiss, "Antitrust in the Electric Power Industry."

[14] Alternatively, a publicly owned national grid may be the better direction to move. It might offer 10 percent lower costs than the present fragmented series of individual pooling arrangements. See FPC, *National Power Survey,* 1970, and Stephen G. Breyer and Paul W. MacAvoy, *Energy Regulation by the Federal Power Commission* (Washington, D.C.: Brookings Institution, 1974), chap. 4.

A6. Effects of Regulation

Standing back from the whole sector, what lessons are there about the regulation of electricity? *First,* even here where it is most likely to be possible, measuring regulation's effects is virtually impossible. The whole apparatus of regulation in this sector has operated and grown for six decades. Yet nobody can say with much precision what its results have been (although some inefficiency has been estimated).

Second, a few possible effects can be discerned. One is the tendency toward excess capacity and peak use. Another is the tendency to hold off new competition in the major old markets which are nearly in Stage 4. Indeed, regulation may now stand in the way both of *(a)* the formation of an efficient national grid for bulk supply which technology may now justify, and *(b)* a competitive bulk supply market. *Third,* regulation has proven brittle and unable to cope smoothly with large new problems.

All of this reflects regulation's peculiar origins and biases. It is tracing the conventional evolution of regulation; late and weak in starting, it is strong in resisting its own withdrawal.

B. THE SUPPLY OF GAS

The gas industry has three levels: production in the oil fields, transmission by long-distance pipelines, and distribution in cities and towns.

Production. Natural gas is obtained as a by-product with oil, in the fields shown in Figure 12–7. Before the 1930s it had little use. Then new pipeline technology made it economic to send the gas to distant cities. Natural gas quickly displaced manufactured gas (from coal), which had been used from the early 1800s. Natural gas now supplies about one-third of the nation's energy. Its share and per capita use peaked during 1971–74 and are expected to decline slowly from now on. About one third of the gas supply goes to 40 million residential customers.

Gas is produced by a variety of oil and gas companies, ranging from giants down to small independents. There is a degree of competition "at the wellhead," but there are ties among the larger producers, and some pipeline firms. Some say the market is effectively competitive, while others appraise it as a tight oligopoly, with much collusion. Gas production has been regulated by the FPC (now FERC) since 1954. Yet the need for any regulation at all is an open question, which has stirred intense controversy and high political drama (see Section B3 below).

Transportation. There are now many pipelines, in many routes. Some are owned by producers, some by distributors. There are some scale economies in pipelines, but not enough for natural monopoly along the major routes. The great majority of the lines cross interstate boundaries and so they are regulated by the Federal Energy Regulatory Commission.

Distribution is within parts of states by local utility firms, under conditions of natural monopoly. Of the three stages, distribution involves the largest

FIGURE 12–7
Major National Gas Fields and Pipelines

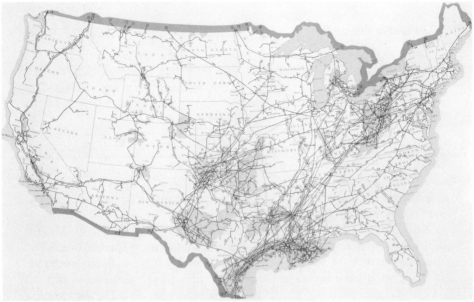

Source: Based on maps and reports filed with the Federal Power Commission; U.S. Government Printing Office, 1971.

costs (in the local pipeline network), transport far less, and production of the gas itself least of all. Distribution has been regulated for decades, mainly by the state commissions but in some cases by city governments.

B1. State-Commission Regulation of Distribution

Regulatory treatment follows the standard regimen and criteria, and it is no different in strictness. The pattern of gas rates is similar to that of electric rates. Customers are classified and rates are varied in accordance with differences in the elasticity of demand. Lower rates are charged, for instance, for industrial than for domestic use, and for space heating and air conditioning than for cooking and water heating where competition is not so stiff. Overhead is allocated on the basis of noncoincident demands. Consumption is measured by meters, and rates usually are of the declining-block type. Many sellers have a general service tariff for most or all customers.

But the pattern is simpler than with electricity, and the differentials involved are not as great. This may be attributed, in part, to an important difference in the character of two services. Electricity must be produced as it is used; gas can be manufactured or imported and kept in storage. With gas, therefore, operations can be carried on with greater regularity. The load factor is less important, and there is less need to improve it by manipulating rates. Yet gas faces stronger and wider competition than electricity, and so the degree of discrimination remains high.

B2. Federal Regulation

Until 1938 state and local authorities were powerless to control the price that distributors paid for imported gas. Interstate pipelines, the Supreme Court held, were beyond their reach. As a result, they were confined to regulating distribution charges. Controlled gas rates floated on top of the uncontrolled prices charged at the city gates.

The Natural Gas Act of 1938 brought the interstate transmission of natural gas and its sale for resale under the control of the FPC. It established the usual pattern of rate control, requiring the pipelines companies to publish and adhere to their charges and give prior notice of prospective changes. It empowered the Commission to suspend such changes, to fix "just and reasonable" rates, and to eliminate "undue" preferences.

Regulation of Pipeline Rates. It is in the regulation of over 220,000 miles of gas pipelines that the FPC has done its most important work. The commission, over the years, has made substantial reductions in pipeline rates. In doing so, it has adhered to the principle of making valuations at original cost. It was the commissions's defense of this principle that led to the decisions of the Supreme Court in the *Natural Gas Pipeline* case in 1942 and the *Hope Natural Gas* case in 1944, repudiating the "fair value" doctrine of *Smyth* v. *Ames* and breaking its hold on the regulation of gas and other utilities. In 1961 the FPC also forbade all indefinite escalation clauses in future contracts save those providing for renegotiation of prices at five-year intervals.[15]

Setting pipeline prices raises the old state-federal problem, and so complex allocations of pipeline costs have to be made. The standard method is the so-called "Seaboard formula," which has five steps.[16] There are various adjust-

---

[15] Before money can be raised to build a pipeline or permission obtained from the FPC for its construction, the pipeline company must be assured a lasting supply of gas. To this end, it enters into contracts with producers for periods running as long as 20 years. Since market conditions for such a period cannot be foreseen, these contracts contain clauses providing for escalation of producer prices. Some of the escalation clauses are definite, requiring specific price increases on specific dates or reimbursement for larger taxes on production. Others are indefinite, requiring price increases whenever the contracting pipeline or another pipeline pays more to another producer or collects more from a distributor. Some provision for price adjustment is necessary in contracts running as long as 20 years. But indefinite escalation makes for spiraling inflation. See Breyer and MacAvoy, *Energy Regulation,* chap. 2, and Charles R. Phillips, Jr., *The Economics of Regulation,* rev. ed. (Homewood, Ill.: Irwin, 1969), chap. 16.

[16] The steps are:

1. Costs are placed in main categories; production, transmission, and so forth.
2. These are further subdivided into fixed and variable costs.
3. These are then reclassified as "commodity costs" (variable costs plus half the fixed costs) and "demand costs" (the other 50 percent of fixed costs).
4. Demand and commodity costs are assigned between state and interstate. Demand

ments to it in practice, but its basic form is common. It does tend to assign too few actual peak costs to peak sales, and so it encourages excess peak use and capacity.[17] Once again, the rate-base effect is reinforced by imperfect price structures.

Practical rate cases get into mind-numbing detail, as sellers optimize their private gains by complex discrimination and the wholesale buyers press their claims. The FPC (now the FERC) hears a spectrum of intervenors—each with its special interest—and then usually strikes a compromise giving something to all sides: that is, letting much discrimination occur. The resulting rates reflect costs (from different fields and differing pipeline conditions) only partly.

The net effect of regulation on gas prices and pipelines profit rates has probably been "either very low or zero."[18] Despite the formal trappings and extended cases, the Commission has done little more than arbitrate among the interested parties.

B3. Regulating the Field Price of Gas

Regulation of price at the wellhead has stirred a hornet's nest of debate. The FPC was reluctant to try it, and acted only after the Supreme Court gave it jurisdiction in 1954.[19] By 1960 some 2,900 applications were pending, and the FPC was forced to improvise a method to set "area prices." That method and its effects on gas exploration were the focus of sharp attack.[20]

Conventional regulation presumes that there are definite costs of service and that regulation is necessary to hold prices down to those costs. In gas, by contrast, costs may not be definite or simple, and regulation may be

---

costs are related to peak volumes; commodity costs are related instead to annual volumes.

5.   Finally, demand and commodity costs are similarly allotted among market areas, again in line with peak and annual volumes, respectively.

The basic method arose in *Re Atlantic Seaboard Corp.* et al., 43 PUR (NS) 235 (FPC, 1952).

[17] The tendency is lucidly analyzed in S. H. Wellicz, "Regulation of Natural Gas Pipeline Companies: An Economic Analysis," 71 *Journal of Political Economy* 30 (1963), 30–43.

[18] Breyer and MacAvoy, *Energy Regulation,* reach that estimate by several types of tests (p. 54).

[19] In the Phillips case: *Phillips Petroleum Co.* v. *Wisconsin,* 347 U.S. 672 (1954). Phillips was the largest of the independent producers of gas. The company raised its price and was brought before the FPC upon complaint by the state of Wisconsin and the municipalities of Milwaukee, Kansas City, and Detroit. The Commission decided that it lacked the power to act.

The plaintiffs appealed, and in 1954 the Supreme Court found Phillips to be a natural gas concern within the meaning of the Natural Gas Act, holding that exemption of the functions of production and gathering did not involve exemption of subsequent sales. It was therefore the Commission's duty to determine whether the prices charged by Phillips were just and reasonable.

[20] Among the criticisms, see Paul W. MacAvoy, *Price Formation in Natural Gas Fields* (New Haven: Yale University Press, 1962); and Breyer and MacAvoy, *Energy Regulation,* chap. 3.

unnecessary. The key economic conditions are *costs* and *market structure.*

Cost. Gas is a *joint product* in an *extractive industry.* Both features make cost indefinite. As for jointness, gas and oil usually appear together. Gas wells do exist, but they are usually a byproduct of the search for oil. Of the costs incurred in exploration, all are joint; of those incurred in development and production, as much as half are joint; of the total costs of such an operation, less than a third are clearly separable and more than two-thirds are joint. The cost determined for gas is thus dependent upon the method chosen for use in allocating joint costs. Yet all of the methods used are largely arbitrary, rather than economic.[21]

Like other extractive industries, gas varies in its quality and cost from field to field, from well to well, and even among levels within the same well. There is no single cost, but only a spectrum of costs, low at the "best" wells and ranging up to high at the "worst." A market-clearing price gives economic rents—not profits—earned on all gas whose costs are below the going price. If the price rises, those rents rise *and* the asset value of all the remaining gas rises. Yet such rents are mainly windfalls, not necessary to induce supply. Liberal regulation, or the removal of regulation, can give enormous capital gains to the owners of gas reserves, at the expense of consumers. In fact, avoidance of such windfall gains is perhaps the main motive in keeping regulation on.

The producers urge, instead, that low prices choke off exploration for new gas, and that this has caused gas reserves to decline in recent years. Only deregulation, they say, will stimulate the discovery and supply of adequate gas in the future. Gas prices must be permitted to rise to the market-clearing levels of long-run cost. In fact, no such unique price standard exists, but prices would be increased in any event.

In this fluid setting, a conventional regulatory attempt to fix a value for the rate base and find an appropriate rate of return for each well (or each company's set of wells) would be absurd.

Market Structure. It would also be unworkable and unnecessary. The series of regional gas markets have high numbers of producers and may be effectively competitive. The four-firm concentration ratios are mainly in the range of 20 to 40 percent—roughly, loose oligopoly.[22] Pipeline buyers are more concentrated and may, in any event, exert countervailing power on the producers. Competition may therefore control prices effectively.

Yet on the contrary, there may be high monopoly power. Submarkets are dominated by the leading oil companies, who engage in a web of joint

---

[21] Under one method, annual costs are allocated in proportion to the respective revenues received from sales of oil and gas, and fixed costs according to the respective values of reserves remaining in the ground. Under a second, joint costs are allocated in proportion to the British thermal unit content of these products. Under a third, they are divided in proportion to the respective costs of producing gas and oil from wells where they are produced alone.

[22] MacAvoy, *Price Formation,* and James W. McKie, "Market Structure and Uncertainty in Oil and Gas Exploration," *Quarterly Journal of Economics* 74 (November 1960), 543–71.

ventures and collusive actions.[23] The markets may therefore behave like very tight oligopolies. Further, the ties between some oil firms and pipeline companies may supplant the possible countervailing power with, instead, a greater ability to raise prices.

These brief points are only the nub of a large, complicated controversy. Both sides can offer persuasive facts and arguments. Even if monopoly power is high, however, conventional regulation would not work. There are too many sellers, and one cannot specify meaningful costs and rate bases.

The Method Used.   The FPC was forced to improvise a system of "area prices," which were first announced in 1965.[24] It defined about 20 relatively homogeneous gas fields or "areas," mainly around Texas. Then it set two ceiling prices for each area. One price was for "old" gas, from existing wells, or gas jointly produced with oil. The "old" gas price ceiling was based on the average costs and investment as of 1960 in each field. The "new" gas price was based on industry-wide estimates of the costs of producing new gas. Starting with the Permian Basin area in 1965, the FPC then set prices for the other areas. The method was rather crude, but it did cut through the indeterminacy and complexity of conditions. It gave price ceilings that were workable and not clearly unreasonable.[25] The system of prices was adjusted upward as scarcity increased. By the early 1970s, uniform national prices were adopted instead, differentiating only between "new" and "old" gas. By 1978 the average price of interstate gas had multiplied from about 15 cents per mcf to 50 cents to 80 cents per mcf on "old" gas and $1.45 per mcf on "new" gas. Yet it was still below the market-clearing price of about $2 to $2.25 per mcf.[26]

The Gas "Shortage."   The FPC's move did stabilize the price for gas in the 1960s, after a long period of sharp rises, and the prices since 1970 have been well below the free-market levels. By restraining gas prices, regulation has benefited present customers. But it may have put the incentive to explore for gas below the efficient long-run level. The slippage in gas reserves and the need to limit supplies to certain customers in the 1970s has been said to show a "regulation-induced shortage of natural gas."[27]

---

[23] For example, see David A. Schwartz and John W. Wilson, statements to the Senate Antitrust and Monopoly Subcommittee, *Hearings* on the Natural Gas Industry, June 27, 1973 (Washington, D.C.: U.S. Government Printing Office, 1974). They show four-firm concentration at each gas field to be above 60 percent, and averaging over 80 percent. They also show a variety of connections among the major producers and between them and pipeline companies.

[24] *Permian Basin Area Rate Cases,* 390 U.S. 747.

[25] The FPC also soon permitted a degree of negotiation between producers and transporters in setting prices.

[26] This was reflected by the diversion of much gas into *intrastate* sales (in Texas, Oklahoma, and so on), where prices were unregulated and higher. This diversion partly accounted for the shortages of gas that appeared in other states during 1975–77.

[27] Paul W. MacAvoy, "The Regulation-Induced Shortage of Natural Gas," *Journal of Law and Economics* 14 (April 1971, 167–99; and MacAvoy and Robert S. Pindyck, "Alternative Regulatory Policies for Dealing with the Natural Gas Shortage," *Bell Journal of Economics* 4 (Autumn 1973), 454–98.

On the other side, it was argued that the prospect of a price rise was inducing suppliers to hold back new finds until the new higher prices were set. Therefore the case for higher gas prices was alleged to be quite circular, hanging by its own bootstraps (that is from expectations), as well as perhaps from a degree of collusion among the major gas owners. If price rises were explicitly renounced, the holdback would cease and gas supplies might well turn out to be adequate.

Furthermore, the price rises would confer a large windfall capital gain to the holders of gas reserves, not only of the new reserves but also all old reserves. The gas price rise would therefore have a large redistributive effect on wealth, perhaps shifting several tens of billions of dollars in a sharply disequalizing direction. The basic case against a major rise in the price of gas was that much of the "regulation-induced shortage of natural gas" was in fact a self-fulfilling mirage, based on expectations and some market power. A rise would be neither efficient nor equitable.

In the event, the political pressure for gas supplies and the industry pressure for specific gains proved more than the FPC could resist, and nearly a doubling of the price of gas was permitted during 1973–74. Deregulation of gas became a leading battle in Congress in 1977–78, but much of the rise in gas prices to "free market" levels had already occurred. Four basic prices of gas applied in 1978, ranging from 52 cents per mcf on the gas from very old wells to $1.50 per mcf for new gas from wells drilled in 1975 and 1976.

Under the 1978 law, price controls would be removed January 1, 1985, from newly-discovered interstate and intrastate gas. Also freed then would be hard-to-get gas from wells over 5,000 ft. deep that were drilled after 1976. During 1985–88, controls could be reimposed by the President or both houses of Congress, if gas prices were thought to be rising too quickly. Otherwise, all controls would end by 1989.

With the new law, the ceiling price of new gas rose from $1.50 to $2.09 per mcf. It is to rise by the general rate of inflation plus 3.7 percent until 1981; thereafter, by the inflation rate plus 4.2 percent, until 1989. If inflation averages 6 percent per year, gas will be about $3.70 per mcf in 1985.

During 1978–89, the controls on old gas are made more complicated, with some 17 to 25 categories based on the wells' histories and geological characteristics. The result is expected to be confusion and litigation, beyond what the regulators can handle.

The law also has a complicated plan for incremental pricing, designed to make large industrial users bear most of the burden of higher prices during 1978–89. It would benefit homes and public units, while inducing industry to shift to other fuels. The FERC is to designate those firms and industries which will pay the higher prices.

In short, deregulation of natural gas is a complex, difficult process, which may take more regulatory effort—not less—during the transition. If, instead, a fair method of taxing the windfall gains to gas owners had been applied, the whole process would probably have been smooth and swift.

One gains perspective on this by looking at the supply of natural gas abroad. There the system is almost universally under public ownership on a national scale. The systems operate as self-suppliers or as monopsonists in buying supplies. Therefore, they are able to drive a hard bargain and acquire gas at virtually the lowest possible economic cost. This has shifted much of the rents, which producers might have gathered, to consumers. To this extent, public monopsony has substituted much more effectively for the FPC effort to establish and retain direct regulation. And it has prevented expectations from forcing—by circular processes—a rise in price and in producer surplus.

C. SUMMARY

The energy sector illustrates the problems arising when regulation occurs on several levels and by overlapping agencies. The regulated firms have sought out the line of least resistance, and they have exerted a wide degree of choice in their own internal management and performance. Regulation has protected the producers while giving perhaps moderate benefits to consumers. It is virtually impossible to factor out the effects—and often even the content— of regulation in this sector.[28] The main virtue may be that large errors are, on the whole, probably avoided because of the fragmented variety of decisions. Moreover, it is conceivable, though not likely, that the rate-base inducements toward extra investment have speeded along the progress of technology in the sector, rather than caused a degree of waste.

Nonetheless, regulation has not made full use of its opportunities either for *(a)* control, or for *(b)* reintroducing competition. At present, it tends to block a number of processes which would improve both structure and performance in the sector. In short, it has evolved in the standard directions and had checkered performance, much as would be expected.

QUESTIONS FOR REVIEW

1. "All three stages of electricity supply have ceased to be natural monopolies." True?
2. "Full vertical integration in the electricity industry was not established until after the 1930s." True?
3. "The FPC lost its main powers when it became FERC in 1977." True?
4. "Peak-load costs of electricity may be five or 10 times as high as off-peak costs." True?
5. "Block and two-part tariffs have been offered strong volume discounts during 1900–1970. This is often called promotional pricing." True?
6. "Electricity prices do fit cost patterns in some respects." True?
7. "In some areas, the bulk supply of electricity is no longer a *natural* monopoly." True?

---

[28] Breyer and MacAvoy, *Energy Regulation,* find the net benefits of FPC regulation to be small; others, such as Kahn *(Economics),* find a much higher net social value.

8. "Gas is both an extractive product and a joint product. This makes its cost patterns elusive." True?

9. "Gas pipelines are natural monopolies, especially on the major interstate routes." True?

10. "The 'Seaboard formula' tends to encourage excess investment in gas production, by misallocating the costs of capacity." True?

11. "If gas prices are restrained, the exploration for new gas will be encouraged." True?

12. "That there are thousands of gas producers means that regulation is necessary, in order to restrain destructive competition." True?

13. "The FPC's gas pricing system, whatever its other faults, at least sets a different price of gas for each region." True?

14. Try to outline an efficient time-based pricing system for electricity. Would it still include declining blocks and two-part tariffs?

15. If gas is a uniform product, isn't a two-price system irrational?

16. Should the field price of gas be deregulated?

chapter 13

Regulation of Communications

The communications sector has three distinct parts: telephones, broadcasting, and postal services. The first two both involve instant telecommunications but they are quite different: telephone is point-to-point, while broadcasting is from one point to many. The two are treated in this chapter. Postal systems are normally public enterprises and are reserved for Chapter 18.

The main actors in U.S. telecommunications are familiar: AT&T, the television networks, and the FCC. But there are many other important firms, and the sector is suffused with actual and potential competition. Many classic points of pricing and investment policy do crop up on the telephone side. But the hardest regulatory choices in both telephones and broadcasting lie in setting the correct margin of competition.

A. TELEPHONES: POINT-TO-POINT TELECOMMUNICATIONS

A1. The Sector

The core natural monopoly is local telephone service, familiar to everyone.[1] The other, newer parts—such as long-distance traffic and large-scale business services—are growing faster. U.S. telephone capacity is more advanced than most other countries, both in the coverage of households and in the quality of service provided.

---

[1] There is no single best reference on the telephone sector and its regulation. Important references include John Brooks, *Telephone: The First Hundred Years* (New York: Harper & Row, 1976), an AT&T-sponsored corporate history; Federal Communications Commission, *Investigation of Telephone Industry* (Washington, D.C.: U.S. Government Printing Office, 1939); U.S. Senate Subcommittee on Antitrust and Monopoly, Hearings on *The Telecommunications Industry,* 93d Cong., 1st Sess. (Washington, D.C.: U.S. Government Printing Office, 1973); Manley R. Irwin, *Telecommunications Policy: Integration vs. Competition* (New York: Praeger, 1970); and William G. Shepherd, "The Margin of Competition in Telecommunications," chapter in William M. Capron, ed., *Technological Change in Regulated Industries* (Washington, D.C.: Brookings Institution, 1971).

Courtesy James Flora and *Fortune*

Up, Up and Away, the FCC regulates the unruly communications sector in this 1967 view. The problems and interests have gained even more stress since then.

The telephone system—primarily under AT&T is actually just part of a wider set of telecommunications markets, as illustrated in Figure 13–1. There are two main levels: *(a)* the *production* of equipment, and *(b)* the *operation* of equipment. AT&T combines both levels, in a virtually closed, vertically integrated system. Its Western Electric Co. supplies nearly all of the important equipment to its 23 operating companies (see Figure 13–2). But in the whole sector—and even in parts of the AT&T domain—there is competition and choice.

FIGURE 13–1
The Complex Communications Sector

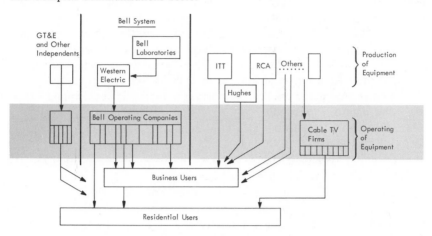

Production of Equipment.   These producers can be divided into two categories: *(a)* those owned by regulated carriers, such as AT&T and General Telephone and Electronics: and *(b)* all other equipment-making firms, large and small. Group *(b)* firms generally innovate and market their equipment under competitive, or at least rivalrous, conditions, although there are tenden-

FIGURE 13–2
The Bell Telephone Companies

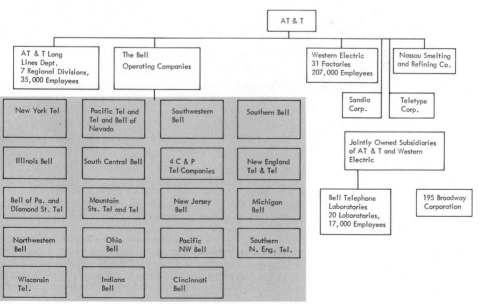

cies toward tight rather than loose oligopoly. Western Electric does not compete in these markets. There are many buyers of broadcasting equipment (networks and individual stations), even though one buyer is owned by a major producer (Radio Corporation of America owns the National Broadcasting Company). Since the networks' earnings are not regulated, rate-base preference is not a factor in their purchasing policies. Some items are affected by competition from European and Japanese firms. Market structure is particularly competitive in the smaller, peripheral products, such as terminal attachments for data transmission.

In short, AT&T sticks out as a large zone of monopoly in a competitive sector. AT&T (and GT&E) are in fact the main vertically integrated utilities in the country (compare electricity, gas, railroads, airlines, cable TV, the postal service, and various urban services).[2]

Operations. Telephone operations involve three main parts. *(1)* The core is the *local system* of lines and a central switching office. This core natural monopoly would be more costly if duplicated by competitive systems. Switching is done by electrical or, more recently, electronic equipment. (Try to locate the central switching office in your town.)

(2) Transmission among cities involves a network of long-distance facilities, including complex routing equipment. Signals travel by several modes, such as cable, land-based microwave, terrestrial satellites. Messages include both voice and data, each requiring specific levels of quality transmission. In Figure 13–2, some intercity transmission is done within the 23 operating systems (for example, from Albany to New York City within New York Bell). Traffic among these systems—and among all other independent systems—is handled by the AT&T Long Lines Department.

Transmission may be a natural monopoly, but that has not been independently established.[3] Whether the Long Lines Department could be operated efficiently as a separate unit is also an open question.

(3) Terminal equipment is what the user has on its premises, such as a telephone set or two in the home or store, a private exchange system of 50 telephones in a business or college, feed-ins for data, printing devices, display units and so forth. From the old uniform black telephone of 1900 to the 1950s, these proliferated in the 1970s to a great variety. They have little or no natural monopoly conditions.

The local service monopoly has been apparent from the industry's start about a century ago. It is the nub of the basis for regulation. The other two parts have been added as parts of AT&T's actual monopoly. Yet terminal

---

[2] Bell Canada is the only other telephone firm in the world that owns its equipment supplier (Northern Telecom), which it has partially divested since 1975 (recall Chapter 5).

[3] See the analysis of scale economies in Leonard Waverman, "The Regulation of Intercity Telecommunications," chapter in Almarin Phillips, ed., *Promoting Competition in Regulated Markets* (Washington, D.C.: Brookings Institution, 1975).

equipment is separable and naturally competitive. Transmission may also be separable. The scope of natural monopoly in the sector is limited and debatable.

Technology.   A telephone system does need to function well as a whole. Reliability may be enhanced by having the equipment produced by a branch of the system itself. Yet full monopoly is not preordained, and indeed the "system" has many separable parts. The key word is *choice:* choice in the technical design of the system itself and choice about the scope and form of the company.[4]

Telephone technology offers much room for choice in designing equipment and coordinating it throughout the system. Even before 1920 there was variety in switching equipment handsets, office exchanges, and so forth. Since then the range of choice has widened sharply. Long-distance cables were supplemented by microwave towers after 1945, and then satellites, while cable capacity itself was being vastly improved and increased. Further alternatives— wave-guides, lasers, and so on—are in prospect. Local switching by electro- mechanical devices has gradually been replaced by electronic, computer-based switching since 1965. Local lines and long-distance lines, now all of metal, are likely to be displaced by optical fibers during the 1980s. And terminal equipment has developed since the 1960s into a profusion of alternatives.

The shape of the system is not predestined. There must be adequate quality, of course, but even the standard of quality is a matter of choice. Probably a variety of quality levels (reliability, fidelity, and accessibility) should be offered. A monopoly system has scope for selecting a technology which maxi- mizes its own interests. Its preferred system may diverge from the socially best system. The technological trade-offs are known most intimately by the system's managers, but they are interested parties rather than dispassionate observers. Their interest is in designing the system, and describing the choices, so as to enlarge the scope of their monopoly. Such slogans as "The system is the solution" simply assert that the trade-offs favor a complete monopoly system. Instead, the system is the *question:* what are the vertical economies, the scale economies, the possibilities for arm's-length coordination, and the likelihoods of X-inefficiency under monopoly? In what parts might the benefits of competition outweigh the gains from monopoly?

Many technical choices are neutral to possible monopoly. Probably the broad flow of technical choices in American telephony have been sound, and the whole set of systems has developed well. Yet several present choices can be critical for the proper scope of monopoly, especially satellites, fiber optics, and the role of computers in switching. During the 1970s and 1980s these choices are interacting with regulation to modify what has, until recently, been a uniquely large and tight two-layered monopoly.

---

[4] See Shepherd, "The Margin of Competition," and Irwin, *Telecommunications Policy.*

A2. The Bell System

AT&T dominance and the role of regulation can be understood best by looking at its origins. The company had stormy beginnings during 1876–1920, settled into a long golden period during 1920–65, and then was struck by new stresses.[5] It has changed during the 1970s toward a more market-oriented, cost-conscious enterprise. The severity of the changes and of their effects are still to be seen.

Early Years. Telegraphy was the first breakthrough to modern communications. Western Union, a combination, controlled it after 1856, when it was formed by merger. The company remained a powerful, lucrative firm until the 1920s.

Telephony was probably first invented in 1875–76 by Alexander Graham Bell. His patent application was filed only a few hours before Elisha Gray's, but six years after Daniel Drawbaugh invented a telephonic device. The infant Bell interests then launched into intensive patent litigation with Western Union and Drawbaugh backers. In 1879 Western Union and AT&T divided up the sector, with Bell taking all voice communications. Bell added Western Electric in 1881, and then began to drive out hundreds of small local firms.[6] By 1900 some 1,002 of 1,051 U.S. towns over 4,000 population had telephone service; 414 Bell, 137 independent, and 451 both. Under Morgan interests after 1905, it continued its drive toward national dominance, mainly by absorbing rivals and refusing long-distance interconnection to others.[7] By 1906 the Bell System was notorious, the corporation counsel of Chicago, for example, describing it as "a ruthless, grinding, oppressive monopoly." During 1909–11 AT&T took over Western Union as well, and it achieved clear dominance in telephony. In 1913, under rising antitrust pressure, AT&T drew back. In the "Kingsbury Commitment" it agreed to divest Western Union, stop taking over telephone companies, and to interconnect with independent systems.[8] Thus was set the basic structure that continues to the present.

---

[5] Historical reviews are given by Brooks, *Telephone;* the FCC *Report* of 1939; Irwin, *Telecommunications Policy;* and Charles F. Phillips, Jr., *The Economics of Regulation,* rev. ed. (Homewood, Ill.: Irwin, 1969), chap. 17.

[6] It did not win out over Drawbaugh until 1888, and then only by a 4 to 3 vote in the Supreme Court. Bell's methods of eliminating competition were pitiless, comparable to Standard Oil's at the time. Up to 1898 it brought infringement suits against 600 small local companies, converting the losers into licensees. It refused to sell telephonic equipment manufactured by Western Electric to independent companies, refused to connect them to its long-distance lines, and drove them out of business by undercutting their rates. Bell bought the shares of its licensees and those of independent companies. Where no such companies existed, it encouraged local promoters to establish them, assisted their development, and then acquired control. Proceeding ruthlessly over the years, it virtually monopolized the business of telephony.

[7] The refusal to interconnect was crucial, for it cut off the independents from all other cities. Interconnection has remained crucial down to the present day, as a Bell System means of preventing competition.

[8] The compromise was formalized in a letter by Nathan C. Kingsbury, an AT&T vice president.

TABLE 13–1
Milestones in Point-to-Point Telecommunications

1875	Alexander G. Bell invents the telephone.
1876–94	Basic Bell patents apply.
1879	Western Union and Bell interests agree to stay out of each other's area.
1881	Western Electric Manufacturing Co. partially merged into AT&T.
1881–85	Early growth and consolidation.
1890s	Rapid growth of the Bell system.
1885–87, 1907–19	Theodore Vail in charge of Bell policies.
1900–1907	Independent systems grow rapidly.
1907	Bell gains control of Western Union.
1907–1913	Rapid Bell acquisitions of independents.
1913	Kingsbury Commitment.
1921	Bell System resumes merging of small systems.
1924	Bell Laboratories established.
1930s	FCC and state regulation acquires standing.
1948–50	Bell System secures control of microwave transmission.
1949	Antitrust suit filed seeking divestiture of Western Electric.
1951	General Telephone acquires suppliers.
1956	Western Electric case settled.
1959	"Over 890" decision by FCC reduces Bell microwave monopoly.
1961–1974	Telpak issue drags on.
1962–1974	Capabilities for domestic satellite exist, but are not implemented.
1965–77	First formal hearings on rates of return, rate structure, and the role of Western Electric.
1965–67	New Western Electric suit prepared; not filed.
1967	First electronic switching station.
1968–69	MCI and Carterfone decisions by FCC, contested further by AT&T.
1972	GT&E ordered by District Court to divest its suppliers and all operating systems acquired since 1950s.
1974	Major Section 2 case filed against AT&T. Begins pre-trial activity.
1975	GT&E decision reversed, new trial ordered.
1976–78	Bell seeks full monopoly by the "Bell bill." Also, it shifts toward better marketing and a more competitive approach.
1978	GT&E is convicted again, and appeals. A drastic revision in regulating communications is proposed in a major Congressional bill.

Golden Years, 1920–1960s. In the 1920s AT&T promptly resumed its old campaign toward "universality" by moving into radio, motion-picture sound, and foreign telephone operations.[9] It also resumed taking over rival

---

[9] By 1925 some 60 percent of all radio sets in the United States were served by radio stations which Bell either owned or licensed. As before and later, AT&T used its control over intercity lines to exclude other firms. After 1925 Bell's radio business was sold off to avoid intense patent litigation (see below). Under antitrust threats,

phone firms, ignoring its 1913 promise, and by 1940 it controlled over 85 percent of the nation's telephones. It formed Bell Laboratories in 1925, and survived a critical examination by the new FCC in 1935–41 with little change. The 2,000 remaining independents stabilized their position after 1940, but they have been passive to AT&T policies (echoing Bell rate patterns and defending Bell interests).[10]

In 1948–50 Bell reached out to monopolize the new microwave technology (those towers at 30-mile intervals which carry television plus other signals). A 1949 antitrust effort to divide Western Electric out was abandoned in 1956 (recall Chapter 5). The 1960s brought major new issues of competition, on trunk routes and in the supply of terminal apparatus. New technology also seemed fruitful, in satellites, optical fibers and lasers, electronic switching, and other directions. But some expected breakthroughs—such as "Picture-phone"—turned out to be slow and slight. Instead, the pedestrian problem of service quality became acute in several areas in the late 1960s (especially New York). Large parts of the system were in classic late Stage 3 conditions: new competition, changing city patterns, capital scarcities, pressure on the rate structure.

Changes in the 1970s. The Bell System was ill-prepared for the new stresses. It clung to its monopoly, it offered reliable but uniform services on a cost-plus basis, and it was slow to innovate.[11] The firm's costing of operations was poor, and it had been insensitive to the diversity of customer needs. Pressures rose to force more competition in terminal equipment and

---

its foreign telephone systems were sold to the new ITT firm. An electrical equipment firm, Graybar, was also sold in 1928.

The motion picture sound business was kept, and it is still the leader in its field. AT&T's other ancillary activities later came to include Sandia Corp. (maker of all U.S. nuclear weapons), Teletype Corp., Nassau Smelting and Refining Co. (wire and related products), and Western Electric's variety of military operations, including the old Nike system, the Distant Early Warning system, the Minuteman system, and others totalling over $1 billion annually in the 1970s.

[10] Indeed, General Telephone and Electronics (GT&E), second largest with about 10 percent of U.S. telephones, copied the Bell System structure by acquiring two equipment companies in 1950, from which it purchases all its equipment. The next two firms—United Telecommunications, Inc., and Continental Telephone Corp.—also have their own integrated suppliers!

[11] See John B. Sheahan, "Integration and Exclusion in the Telephone Equipment Industry," *Quarterly Journal of Economics* 70 (May 1956), 249–69; the 1939 FCC *Report;* the Senate Subcommittee Hearings on *The Telecommunications Industry* in 1973; and Irwin, *Telecommunications Policy.* More specifically, the inefficiencies included: (1) obsolete forms of organization, (2) little marketing staff or effort, (3) product design that fitted technical factors rather than customers' needs, (4) a focus on dominating regulation rather than developing market variety, (5) cross-subsidizing among services, such as a $3 billion transfer from long-lines profits to deficits on local operations, (6) poor costing of operations, (7) slow innovation, such as being "years behind" in private switchboards, teletype equipment and telephone sets, and (8) keeping obsolete, undepreciated equipment (as of 1978, only $20 billion of the system's $102 billion assets were depreciated). See "Behind AT&T's Change at the Top," *Business Week* (November 6, 1978), 114–39, for a lucid discussion of these problems.

long-distance transmission.[12] AT&T fought back, seeking in 1976–78 to get Congress to legislate a complete monopoly for it in the telecommunications sector. Instead, a complex 200-page bill was worked out to revise drastically the structure and regulation of the whole sector. It would promote competition in the telephone sector and broadcasting. The Bell System's integration would be separated (much as in the Antitrust Division's suit), but the System would be given a freer reign to compete.

Internally, the Bell System changed to a vigorous competitive stance. In some instances it used predatory types of actions against new competition. These turned aside some of the new competition. More positively, AT&T began developing a more responsive marketing ability, and it began to fit its pricing of services more closely to cost patterns.

Innovation.   The Bell System has stressed *reliability* of service and ample capacity. It has also promoted *uniformity* of service and equipment. This has increased the compatibility of parts and may have achieved economies of scale in production. Yet it has meant a narrow range of consumer choice until the 1970s.[13]

AT&T has also adopted an "evolutionary" rate of innovation, fitting new methods into the old ones. For example, it was slow to bring in dialing, and by 1977 it had converted only 20 percent of its local operations to electronic (computer) switching. This approach may not be adequate for fast-changing areas of technology.

Pricing has been guided by "value of service," an AT&T phrase for price discrimination. Such promotional pricing helped spread the use of telephones to most households and businesses by 1950.[14] Since the 1960s, though, new scarcities have forced the system to fit prices somewhat more closely to costs (with so-called "usage-based" pricing). This shift has partly been forced on the system from outside, even though it has improved AT&T finances rather than eroded them. Much discrimination remains, in any event.

The Problem of Social Power.   As the country's biggest, most complete monopoly, the Bell System has inevitably posed problems of social power. Its one million employees are spread into nearly every city and town, and they are urged to promote the system's interests in a variety of ways.[15]

---

[12] See the President's Task Force on Communications Policy, *Final Report,* December 7, 1968; the Senate Subcommittee Hearings on *The Telecommunications Industry;* and, most thorough and devastating, the massive three-volume study by the FCC's own Task Force, *Proposed Findings of Fact and Conclusions of the Common Carrier Bureau's Trial Staff,* Docket No. 19129 (Phase II), (Federal Communications Commission, February 2, 1976), totaling 1,227 pages.

[13] Until about 1960 Bell customers could get only one style of telephone set and only in one color—black. In contrast, the choice of equipment is now wide and changing (see A5 below).

[14] Also, setting residence rates below business rates was an effective way to gain popular approval of the company.

[15] For example: "A carefully groomed cadre of Bell employees cultivates political and government officials. Schools use AT&T-designed courses and textbooks and AT&T-trained and selected teachers. Federal, state, and local governments 'borrow'

The political power is large, especially at the grass-roots levels. Problems of corruption and improper political activities surfaced in some parts of the system (especially Southwestern Bell) in the 1970s. The system also seeks support from the academic community in a variety of ways; and of course there are 2.9 million shareholders. The FCC and state commissions lack the resources and will to contain their power in a strict sense.

The potential for economic and social abuses is not small, but the record so far is relatively clean. Some economic actions have been predatory, but few major social abuses are known.

A3. Regulation

The ICC was given some authority over telephone service in 1910 but did next to nothing. Some of the new state commissions were capable of regulating intrastate telephony by 1930 but they too were mainly passive. The FCC merely studied the Bell System in the 1930s, and its report largely ratified the whole structure of the industry.[16] The FCC did act formally

---

phone company experts for special projects. . . . The Bell System's boosterism is unique in its scope and degree of penetration into nearly every nook and cranny of American life. . . .

"When needed, AT&T can muster local government relations people from 48 states—troop strength that few businesses can deploy. Little of this is suggested by the modest sums AT&T and its subsidiaries report for lobbying expenses. . . . But membership dues in influential business and community organizations is another matter. Southwestern Bell Telephone Co. alone shells out over $500,000 yearly to keep some 1,600 employees in various clubs. . . .

"AT&T employees attend Rotary and Kiwanis meetings for more than the creamed peas and fruit cocktail. Continual company 'training' sessions ensure that employees are well-versed in AT&T's official posture on such matters as competition, community service, and antitrust. The company's community-relations manual advises employees to arrive at club meetings early and leave late, in order to have ample time to talk up the company and to deal with any phone service complaints. Above all, they are told to report back to management on anything they hear that might affect the company . . . Sanford L. Jacobs, "On the Job or Off, AT&T People Polish the Company Image," *The Wall Street Journal,* April 16, 1975, p. 1, 21.

AT&T units also pay large amounts to universities and their faculty members for consulting, for running on-campus seminars, and for testifying on AT&T's behalf in rate cases.

16 The FCC study was large. Some 300 lawyers, accountants, and engineers were engaged in the work over a period of four years. The basic record included 8,500 pages of testimony, 2,000 exhibits, and 77 staff studies. The Commission's final report was published in 1939. It disclosed no such financial scandals as those found by the Federal Trade Commission in the electrical industry. But there were real problems. AT&T had taken advantage of its opportunity to increase profits at the expense of the consumer, by padding the operating expenses and the property valuations of the associated companies.

AT&T was found to have issued instructions which compelled the associated companies to purchase practically all of their apparatus, equipment, and plant materials from Western Electric. Since Western obtained its orders without competitive bidding, it was not forced to sell at a competitive price.

The company's cost accounts did not afford an authentic basis for testing the reasonableness of the prices which it set upon specific products. Its prices, moreover,

on certain competitive issues during 1940–65, but it dealt with rates and profits only informally, if at all. The Commission was, in any case, overburdened with other tasks.[17]

Issues during 1934–70. Telephone *price levels* trended downward. This largely flowed from the natural technology and growth of the system, not strictness by the FCC or the state commissions.[18] The informal FCC "surveillance" sacrificed the leverage of open hearings, and it hid the FCC's actions and their possible effects. *Price structure* was left almost entirely to the suppliers to decide.

Western Electric's profits came to be indirectly "regulated;" each year AT&T reports the results under several functional headings. The reported profits are usually about 9 to 12 percent on assets. If they are valid, they suggest that the Bell System rate base is not padded by overpriced equipment. The FCC, state regulators, and the companies also developed a massive "separations" system for allocating costs and rate base between intrastate and interstate activities.[19]

Until 1965 there had been no public FCC review at all of the profit criteria, the price and cost structure, the equipment purchasing policies, and the interconnection and terminal equipment policies of the telephone industry. Since 1965 there has been some review of some of these, but the FCC's posture is still basically passive.

Since 1948, and especially since 1960, the FCC has been forced to review prickly issues affecting the structure of communications markets. These include particularly spectrum allocation, microwave access and interconnection,

---

bore no apparent relation to its own statement of costs. Both costs and prices for many items were above those reported by independent firms. Western Electric profits had never been subject to any sort of public control.

From 1882 to 1936 the company realized a net income on its paid-in capital that exceeded 20 percent in 41 years, 50 percent in 25 years, and 100 percent in six years. To the extent that Western's charges were excessive, the excess entered into the property valuations and operating expenses of the associated companies and thus compelled the state commissions to fix rates that yielded more than a fair return.

[17] The overwhelming burden of tasks has continued. For a graphic description of how the commissioners must pass on hundreds of matters, with inadequate preparation, see Nicholas Johnson and John J. Dystel, "A Day in the Life of The Federal Communications Commission," *Yale Law Journal* 82 (July 1973), 1575–1634.

[18] The United States has offered exceptionally favorable conditions for innovation in communications. Its great size, scattered large cities, and extensive commercial use of telecommunications have all favored the creation of high-density trunk routes that can exploit the major potential advances in transmission technology. These have been the main cost-reducing innovations in the last 40 years. Also, at least a large portion of demand is probably income-elastic. Rising incomes have brought about high and rising levels of demand for basic and optional services, so that many other innovations have been relatively easy to prepare, test, and carry out.

For an evaluation of the effect of state regulation, see C. Emery Troxel, "Telephone Regulation in Michigan," chapter in William G. Shepherd and Thomas G. Gies, eds., *Utility Regulation* (New York: Random House, 1966).

[19] See Richard Gabel, *Development of Separations Principles for the Telephone Industry* (East Lansing: Institute of Public Utilities, Michigan State University, 1967).

the division of data transmission between Western Union and the Bell System, foreign attachments, and satellite transmission. Until 1959 the FCC usually let AT&T extend its control in these cases. Since then it has gradually changed to promote a modest degree of competition. But AT&T has been able to slow and soften these actions. The Bell System holds and controls the information about key variables, with the FCC striving to get an adequate, neutral picture of its choices.

State regulation is more passive. Commission resources in telephone matters are slender (except for New York and California, which have begun to regulate fairly effectively). States can aspire to regulate no more than a small piece of the entire system, in which great volumes of overhead costs can be allocated arbitrarily. Worse, 36 states, with about half of all Bell telephones, are served by *multistate* Bell operating firms (such as Southwestern Bell Telephone, which provides service in Missouri, Kansas, Arkansas, Oklahoma, and Texas, a total of 40 million telephones). The scope for effective state regulation has been reduced as the distinction between interstate and intrastate operations has become increasingly blurred.

The states are more passive on profit rates, rate structure, and market control. The carriers find it natural to try to regain at the state level what the FCC may have denied them.

On the whole, the regulation of telecommunications came late, has not been very effective, is caught among powerful interests, and has only begun to make adjustments which may be needed in Stage 3.

Abroad, telephony is publicly owned (except in some Canadian provinces). Most systems display the same tendency to monopolize as the U.S. systems do, but none is vertically integrated. Many of them have innovated more rapidly than AT&T, and nearly all developed more efficient cost-based price structures decades before the 1970s. The Canadian regulatory commission has been about as active as the average U.S. state commission.

A4. Current Issues of Prices and Profits

In 1965 the FCC started a series of full-dress hearings on rate of return, rate structure, and competitive issues, in that order.[20] The rate-of-return hearings led in 1967 to a seven to 7.5 percent rate-of-return target, raised to 8.5 to 9 percent in the 1970s. The rate structure hearings then ran for several years, with much complex debate over concepts but no major result.

Profits. The FCC's rate-of-return ceiling is in the reasonable range of 8 to 9 percent. The Commission has resisted AT&T claims that "comparable earnings" standards reflecting the risks of new competition require much higher returns.

---

[20] As for X-efficiency, that remains hard to evaluate in such a large organization. Yet there are indications of much room for improvement: see Jack Ross and Michael Kami, *Corporate Management in Crisis* (Englewood Cliffs, N.J.: Prentice-Hall, 1974); the FCC Task Force *Statement and Recommendations,* 1976; and the candid appraisal in "Behind AT&T's Change at the Top," *Business Week.*

State regulation of Bell System profit rates has a certain surreal quality. The operating companies are only parts of a larger system, and so their risk and performance are virtually impossible to assess. Only AT&T stock is on the market, and so state regulators have little to compare their own appraisals with and no direct way to test the financial effects of their actions.

Rate Structure. Bell officials have pressed for value-of-service pricing. Since 1970 they have also used marginal-cost pricing arguments for some prices. This partly reflects a genuine shift toward more efficient pricing. But in other areas, this is just another way of rationalizing price discrimination to head off new competition.[21] Certain new Bell services have been provoked by new entry and then priced low so as to prevent the entry. The FCC and some state commissions have, instead, leaned toward "fully distributed costs" as the basis for prices. This rough method would prevent predatory discrimination, though it might also miss some of the valid patterns of marginal cost. Since Bell costs have been so slippery and easily manipulated, it is not clear which criterion is best for practical uses.

Local pricing has mainly followed conventional lines. This pricing—your phone bill—has mostly been promotional, with a flat monthly fee and a *zero* price for each call. This has induced extra use, including added peak load and indifference to the length of the call. Figure 13–3 illustrates the inefficiency of such pricing. This also erodes revenues, by reducing the average revenue per unit as growth occurs. The degree of inefficiency depends mainly on the elasticity of demand and on the cost gradients.

Since 1965 the burden of this has gradually been recognized, and message-unit pricing has spread from business use and large cities down to residence use in medium-sized cities. With smaller monthly fees and roughly a five cent charge per call, the rates now fit cost conditions more closely. But they still usually ignore the timing and length of calls, so that peak use is still enhanced. In 1978 the most advanced rates were those in New York, with time of day differentials and other refinements.

In most European systems, pricing has long been more rational. Metering is usually precise, so that prices can be closely fitted to the true costs of peak and off-peak use.[22] Only now are U.S. metering equipment and pricing beginning to move toward the sophistication which has long existed abroad.

In the U.S. prices also vary between business and residence users (business rentals are higher) and among basic and optional services.[23] Discrimination

---

[21] This point is made in William H. Melody, "Interservice Subsidy: Regulatory Standards and Applied Economics," Chapter in Harry M. Trebing, ed., *Essays on Public Utility Pricing and Regulation* (East Lansing: Institute for Public Utilities, Michigan State University, 1971), pp. 167–211.

[22] See W. G. Shepherd, "Residence Expansion in the British Telephone System," *Journal of Industrial Economics,* 1966, pp. 263–74.

[23] Also, rates have long been higher for cities than towns, with steep gradients across the range of sizes. This made good political sense, but it did not fit cost patterns. Recently, these differences have been narrowed, but small town users still typically pay only about 75 percent of big city rates.

FIGURE 13–3
Illustration of Local-Service Telephone Pricing

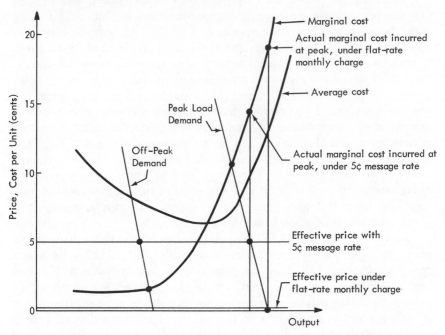

is common. The monthly rentals charged for added equipment, for instance, ($1 to $1.25 for a "Princess" phone, $0.90 for an extension phone, and $0.35 for an extension cord) are based, not on costs ($4.20 a year yields an astronomical return on the company's investment of a few pennies in a length of wire), but on the subscriber's docility. Business users are charged more than domestic users because they find the service indispensable. Domestic users are charged more for single party lines mainly because they are willing to pay for added convenience. Recent revisions of rates have made them more— often bewilderingly—complex. The remaining degree of discrimination is hard to appraise, but it is not small.

Long-distant rates seem to fit costs more closely. Here marginal-cost pricing appears to have been traditional and voluntary, with lower evening and weekend prices. Yet cost patterns might differ even more sharply than the rates. The whole issue is open.

Special rates for large customers since 1960 have posed acute problems for the FCC. The main case involved TELPAK and WATS (wide area telephone service). TELPAK provided during 1960–77 price cuts of 51 to 85 percent for customers who leased bundles of 60 or 240 lines. WATS provides telephone customers with long-distance service to specified areas for a flat charge, and therefore a zero price per call. (An 800 number is a WATS service.)

TELPAK was a response in 1960–61 to new private microwave competition in the upper radio spectrum, above 890 megacycles.[24] The TELPAK price cuts hurt Western Union, and on its complaint the FCC required AT&T to justify the rates with cost data. AT&T's report in 1965 showed TELPAK to be earning only a 0.3 percent return on assets, well below the 10 percent return on assets from telephone operations. The FCC ordered TELPAK prices to be raised, but the several hundred major TELPAK users applied strong pressure to keep it. After numerous FCC decisions, AT&T appeals, rehearings, and other delays, AT&T finally moved to discontinue TELPAK in 1977. The reason: customers could share or resell their lines, under a 1976 FCC order. That opening to new competition was regarded by AT&T as more of a threat than the loss of TELPAK's potential profits.

WATS service caters to a variety of users which need large-volume but geographically focused long-distance service. Without WATS they would seek other means, which would involve new competition. Therefore WATS involves a competitive response to potential competition, by means mainly of discriminatory pricing. It is not clearly predatory, and so the FCC has treated it more gently than TELPAK, asking for cost justifications but not ordering changes.

In both cases the services probably can be done at low marginal costs, as an add-on to the whole complex operations of the system. Yet this would give AT&T the classic ability to prevent all new competition by price cutting, while recouping profits in the creamy markets. The FCC has adopted reasonable—if often inexact—policies to avoid such an inefficient outcome.

A5. The Margin of Competition

The regulators have also had to deal more directly with issues of natural monopoly and the margin of competition. Recall that competition can be good but should not make the whole firm unviable. There are three main issues: Western Electric, trunk-route competition, and terminal equipment.

Western Electric. This is a very old issue, posed in 1911–13, in the 1949 case, and then again in the 1974 Antitrust Division suit (recall Chapter 5). An antitrust solution was begun in 1949 and then aborted. In the 1956 decree, no way was provided for outside suppliers to compete in the sale of equipment to Bell operating companies, and little was done in this direction until 1977. At the same time, Western Electric agreed to produce only telephone equipment, for sale largely in the Bell System and to government agencies.

Thus the consent decree of 1956 operates as a detente, which neatly eliminates two possibilities for new competition. It leaves intact what is probably the country's largest industrial monopoly (in Bell System supplies, over $7

---

[24] The "Above 890" decision was: *Allocation of Microwave Frequencies Above 890 Megacycles,* 27 FCC 359 (1959).

billion in 1977). It also excludes Western Electric from competing in other communications and electronic equipment markets, many of them substantial.[25] Despite a thorough Task Force Report in 1974 recommending divestiture, the FCC chose in 1977 not to act. AT&T regards retention of Western Electric as supremely important, and it has the proven skill and resources to get its way. At the most, some modifications toward outside purchasing might gradually be required. The FCC required more open purchasing in a 1977 decision, but the results are unsure.

The new Antitrust Division suit filed in 1974 opens up the issue for an airing at trial and possibly a real change (recall Chapter 5). The process seems likely to be long and intense, lasting 15 years or more, unless cut short by compromise.

Parallel Systems on Main Routes. The Bell trunk lines have always been paralleled by a variety of private specialized operators (railroads, certain large firms), but Bell has always refused to let them interconnect. Yet—as technology ripens and Stage 3 continues—the basis for connected and competing systems has evolved. This is already true of the main intercity routes (for example, New York–Chicago), and it appears to be evolving with cable TV in the cities. The FCC first permitted the Bell System to capture microwave in 1948–50, then decided in 1969 to let some competition in. AT&T officials criticize the newcomers for "cream-skimming," which threatens the finances of the whole system.

Microwave during 1946–69. Microwave technology dates back to 1915, and a variety of public and private groups—American and British—participated in its development during the 1930s and World War II. By 1945 microwave had emerged as the obvious technique for carrying the new television traffic. By 1946 several firms had created or planned microwave capacity between major eastern cities and had applied for an FCC franchise, with further expansion in prospect.[26] The Bell System recognized the advantages it could gain in displacing these independent systems, and it proceeded to do so.

It mounted a large, rapid two-stage innovation effort between 1946 and 1950 to create a nationwide microwave relay system—called the TD2—to preempt the microwave field. This involved a crash program to catch up with the others. By this quick, costly stroke, the Bell System had acted quickly enough to take over virtually the entire domestic microwave carrier field.

---

[25] One result of this exclusion is that discoveries by Bell Laboratories may fail to be applied. Thus, the Nobel Prize-winning discovery of the transistor occurred in 1948 but was kept internal while Bell sought higher reliability. Only when some scientists left Bell in 1951–52 and formed new firms to make transistorized products did the innovation occur. See also Shepherd, "The Margin of Competition."

[26] Donald C. Beelar, "Cables in the Sky and the Struggle for Their Control," *Federal Communications Bar Journal* 21 (January 1967), 26–41; and A. C. Dickieson, "The TD2 Story: Changing for the Future," *Bell Laboratories Record* 45 (December 1967), 357–63.

AT&T then refused to interconnect with rival microwave systems. By 1949–50 the Bell System had succeeded in maneuvering the FCC into converting the microwave field—with much potential for fruitful competition—into a monopoly, not only of transmission operations but also of equipment manufacturing. The FCC excluded all private microwave until 1959. Only when the FCC's "Above 890" decision removed that exclusion did the Bell System respond with the TELPAK offering and related data-transmission services. Until 1969 renewed efforts to open trunk-route microwave transmission were deflected by the FCC's reluctance to order the Bell System to interconnect with independent systems.

MCI and Competition since 1969. By the middle 1960s mainline data traffic had grown so large that new competition was quite feasible. The Bell System resisted, charging that parallel systems would merely skim off these markets the cream which was needed to support the whole system. When a small firm—Microwave Communications, Inc. (MCI)—applied for FCC approval, Bell refused to let MCI interconnect. MCI sought to provide cheaper economy-grade service for a range of users who did not need high fidelity "voice-grade" transmission. This challenged both the pricing and the quality criteria of long-standing Bell System practice.

In 1969 the FCC approved MCI's entry, creating a category of "specialized common carriers" on an experimental basis.[27] Further delay ensued as the Bell System exhausted its tactical opportunities for rearguing and appeals, but MCI eventually began carrying signals. By 1977 MCI was struggling along, but several other entrants had gone bankrupt. AT&T could still say that entry posed a threat to its main trunk routes, but it could set rates for connecting with MCI which left MCI little or no room for survival.[28] By 1978, it was not clear that important long-run entry had actually occurred.

Satellites. Deeper changes may be brought by satellites. By 1969 seven *international* satellites were in orbit, tied in with 40 ground stations in 25 countries. Much larger new ones have been added more recently.

Yet their use over the United States waited for more than 10 years, as the many interests contended and regrouped. Against the natural Bell System interest in adding this to their system, there are such others as Western

---

[27] The decision was *In the Matter of Microwave Communications, Inc.,* 18 FCC 953. The general doctrine of specialized common carriers was established by the FCC in 1971, *First Report and Order,* Docket 18920 (May 1971). It was fought by state commissions and NARUC, but finally upheld by the Supreme Court in 1976. The alliance of state commissions and NARUC with Bell interests reflects the underlying conditions (recall Chapter 10).

[28] Thus in 1978 the Supreme Court affirmed, after lengthy appeals, that AT&T must provide more local telephone connections for long distance service provided by MCI and other specialized carriers. This would permit MCI's "Execunet" service to expand from 18 to 30 cities. AT&T then promptly filed tariffs for this service which would probably—though they are too complicated to assess easily—double the prices being charged. AT&T acknowledged that the rates were designed to inhibit the new inter-city competition. MCI's appeal of the prices to the FCC would probably take years to settle.

Union, Comsat (which operates international satellites), the TV networks, various electronics firms, IBM, public broadcasting, the Ford Foundation, etc.[29]

The problem was, in fact, too big for the FCC to decide—or even arbitrate—and in 1970 a remarkable White House initiative set an open-access policy for domestic satellites. All qualified applicants can send up and operate satellites. By 1974 several had gained approval, and by 1978 several satellites were actually up. Though the Bell System still held the trump card of interconnection, new technology was reducing its power. In any event, the Bell System will be only one among several operators, by contrast with the earlier microwave outcome.

In short, the Bell System's grip on mainline transmission is no longer fully exclusive, though the inroads are only marginal so far and can still be closely influenced by the Bell System. Despite Bell alarums, the impact on the whole system seems likely to be modest, partly because Bell still controls the technology. Also, the FCC is ready to avert any harmful effects, if they should emerge.

Terminal Equipment.   Until 1969 the Bell System forbade its subscribers to attach to their phones—by *any* means, electrical, inductive, or acoustical— any equipment not provided by Bell, contending that such attachments might impair the quality of its service. The company thus attempted to prevent the use of one-piece Swedish handsets, of antique handsets, and even of simple "Hush-a-phone" mouthpieces that enabled users to converse without being heard by other persons in the room. Such restrictions curbed the growth of independent phone systems and helped AT&T to maintain its monopolies of the long-distance telephone and television transmission markets.

Bell's rule was challenged in the 1960s by the Carterfone Company, a tiny Texas firm making a coupling device that plugged two-way mobile radio communications systems into subscribers' telephone lines, so that any phone could be used to communicate with radio-dispatched vehicles. AT&T had put Carter out of business by harassing its customers. Carter brought suit under the antitrust laws and the courts referred the question to the FCC. In 1968 the Commission outlawed Bell's ancient attachment rule, holding it to be unreasonable and discriminatory.[30] The telephone subscriber, said the Commission, has the right to attach any device that serves its convenience without detriment to others.

This decision made possible the use of a variety of devices which serve customer uses but which AT&T had not chosen to develop. The decision appeared to open the way to competitive development.

---

[29] Comsat is a mixed private corporation, created in 1962 after efforts to try a public enterprise form were defeated in Congress. It has a franchised monopoly, is under FCC regulation, and does earn a profit. It has tried and partially succeeded in capturing the U.S. domestic satellite market. It competes with transoceanic cable (owned by the Bell System) and has had excess capacity for most of its life so far.

[30] *In the Matter of Carterfone,* 13 FCC 420 (1968).

AT&T delayed the effect of the order for several years, but in 1977 the Supreme Court finally cleared the way for the FCC's policy. Bell officials had warned that systemic integrity would be harmed by permitting "foreign attachments," as it called them. Instead, no severe effects have occurred, and the financial impact on the Bell System has been slight (at less than five percent of Bell equipment expenditures). Innovation and choice in the apparatus market have been greatly stimulated. Bell companies, as well as others, now offer a remarkable variety of handsets, in contrast to the earlier stock uniformity.

The new variety in handsets and business equipment that users have enjoyed since 1970 is the result of long, hard battles to open up AT&T policies. It is a test-tube demonstration of the value of competition.

Bell resistance to competitors' attachments is still strong, often leading to sharp tactics and pressures upon customers to reject non-Bell equipment.[31] This helped stir the Division's 1974 suit, which seeks to end such abuses. For this, too, separating Western Electric from AT&T would probably be necessary.

Data Processing.   There is an overlap between the transmitting of business data and processing the data by computer. AT&T would like to add data processing to its activities. As the main transmitter of data, and as a large owner of computer facilities, it would be able to set prices and terms which could quickly monopolize this large, growing, and lucrative market. Eventually, the computer companies' interests (especially IBM's) may clash directly with AT&T's in this area.

During 1971–78, the FCC permitted the Bell System to transmit data but not to process it. This was meant to promote growth and variety. By 1978, the Commission was shifting toward letting Bell compete in this area, in part to foster the emerging competition with IBM.

A6. Summary

Regulation has begun to reverse its long passivity to the carriers' policies on pricing, profits, and market control. The new scarcities of the 1970s are also inducing the carriers to revise pricing more in line with costs. Discrimination is at last coming under analysis. And the margin of competition is being drawn more carefully and tightly than before.

The FCC's awakening has, however, yielded only marginal changes so far. It has not been matched at the state level. This may reflect that the basic problems are beyond their scope. But it also reflects the limitations of state regulation, in resources and perspective, as it is forced to deal with small parts of national problems.

---

[31] Some of these actions are described vividly in the Senate Subcommittee Hearings on *Telecommunications.*

B. BROADCASTING

Regulation of broadcastng is a hybrid.[32] There are several suppliers, not one. Regulation deals with market control and, obliquely, program content, not with profit and price constraints. It reviews and renews franchises, rather than leaving them frozen as in other utilities. Part of its sector—radio—has been in Stage 4 since 1960 or so. Regulation is strictly at the federal level. It is entangled in the stressful introduction of new forms (cable TV, pay TV, public broadcasting) which touch on deep vested interests.

In all this the FCC has been mainly a vehicle of compromise, not an expert group applying clear criteria to functional economic problems. The basic economics of broadcasting in this affluent country would support a great degree of diversity, among modes and within each mode. Yet the FCC has consistently reduced that diversity—first in radio and then in television—and helped to retard the use of new technology. The FCC was added on after the basic structure was set, and it has protected narrow interests rather than promoted diversity.

The social goals are of two kinds:

1. *Economic efficiency,* in meeting consumer preferences.
2. *Good program content,* especially local interest, diversity, and culture.

These further divide into *(a) localism,* fitting local interests, *(b) diversity,* servicing the whole range of social and cultural interests, and *(c) minimum quality,* avoiding harmful effects, such as inculcating violence or exploiting ignorance in children. The main reason for regulation would be a divergence between efficiency and good content, and indeed the FCC *has* tried to influence content. The whole social impact of this regulation could—in a society where people watch television some three to four hours *per day* on average—surpass any regulatory benefits in other sectors. The actual impact is obscure and possibly even negative.

First we need to understand the economics of the sector. Then the nature and effects of regulation can be assessed.

B1. The Sector

The basic tension is between the economies of scale from mass exposure on the networks and the diversity of local and group interests. U.S. broadcasting is unique in the world for being mainly private, based on advertising. Elsewhere it is mainly public, with some private role. Whether the U.S. system is an aberration or the best model is a prime question.

Broadcasting is mainly television, both by size and by public impact (see Table 13–2). Television is primarily the three private VHF frequency networks

---

[32] A good general source on the subject is Roger G. Noll, Merton J. Peck, and John H. McGowan, *Economic Aspects of Television Regulation.* (Washington, D.C.: Brookings Institution, 1973).

TABLE 13–2
U.S. Broadcasting Data, 1975

Media	Number	Revenues ($ million)
Commercial TV stations	693	4,094
3 networks	15	2,069
Other stations	678	2,025
Commercial radio stations	5,535	1,725
AM and FM (related)	4,832	1,582
FM independents	703	143
Cable TV systems	3,366	(300)*

* Estimate.
Source: U.S. Federal Communications Commission, *TV Broadcast Financial Data*, and *AM-FM Broadcast Financial Data*, annual.

(ABC, CBS, NBC), plus some 438 affiliated stations. UHF stations have also grown since 1960 in some areas, but VHF dominates. Revenues are primarily from advertising; exceptions are cable TV (mainly subscriptions) and public broadcasting (public and foundation funds). Advertisers, in turn, choose freely among all types of media (newspapers, magazines, TV, radio, and so forth), and other selling devices such as sales networks and discounts. Therefore the demand for broadcast advertising is often highly elastic. Moreover, television especially attracts mass advertising, because the other media and devices are more attunable to specific groups.

Broadcasting mingles urban and national markets. Viewership in a city appears to be roughly constant, regardless of the number of stations. Profits therefore depend critically on the number of stations in each market and on the ability to stretch overhead costs. The present structure—with three dominant networks and a relatively few stations even in the largest cities— reflects the pressure to achieve scale economies and to limit competition. Technology is not close to natural monopoly, and program content is more responsive when there are at least three sources. But more stations would be viable in most of the larger markets than are now permitted.

Radio.   The present TV structure grew directly from the early radio patterns of the 1920s. The first public broadcast in this country, using the method of amplitude modulation (AM), occurred in 1920 when Westinghouse station KDKA in Pittsburgh announced the election of Warren G. Harding. Other stations were soon established by Westinghouse, General Electric, and AT&T. It was assumed, at this time, that broadcasting was to be financed by manufacturers of receiving sets and, perhaps, by educational institutions and city governments. Then, in 1922, commercial broadcasting was inaugurated by the AT&T station, WEAF in New York, and radio soon became an advertising medium. The first network was set up by AT&T in 1923. Then, following an agreement with GE, Westinghouse, and their patent-holding company, RCA, in 1926, AT&T withdrew from the field, its network being taken over by an RCA subsidiary, the National Broadcasting Company. The Columbia

Broadcasting System was set up in the following year. Network domination of the broadcasting business dates from this time. Frequency modulation (FM) broadcasting, on a commercial basis, was authorized in 1940, television in 1941, and color television in 1951. The business has grown phenomenally. There were 7,500 broadcasting stations in the United States in 1978 and receiving sets in more than 60 million homes. Radio and television programs were reaching almost all of the country's population. Cable TV also grew after 1950, and it became widely established in the 1970s.

Early radio had no fixed frequencies for stations, until in 1927 regulation was imposed to allocate the radio spectrum. The new Federal Radio Commission accepted and favored the commercial network structure; it had few powers and slight resources. R. A. Coase has noted that this spectrum allocation was inappropriate, since spectrum was not in fact scarce and the net effect was to create unjustified monopoly.[33] By the time the FCC was assigned broadcasting regulation in 1934, the situation was the conventional one: regulation was added after the industry was formed, increasing the degree of monopoly.

Television. Radio's heyday was 1925–50. Its rigid structure dissolved during 1950–65 back toward effective competition. The radio networks predictably influenced the FCC to extend their dominance into television, when it arose after 1945. At first the FCC allotted to television only the very high frequency band (VHF) of 54 to 216 megacycles per second, which has room for only 12 stations in any area. (In practice no more than six stations can operate well, because of mutual interference.) Television was structured around these few channels. Though 70 ultra-high frequency (UHF) channels were later authorized (1952), it was only in 1962 that the FCC began requiring new sets to have UHF tuning. VHF stations, dominated by the networks, have therefore dominated commercial broadcasting. Network and VHF station profits fully reflect this market position (see Table 13–3). The really big profits (including most of the networks' profits) are creamed off in the few very largest cities: rates of return there are probably over 200 percent yearly.

Cable TV began in 1950, simply to help small town viewers pull in distant signals. It grew and by 1960 was ready to offer better pictures and newer services in major cities. But the FCC blocked it entirely from the 100 largest cities until 1972, primarily in order to protect TV broadcasters' interests, though assertedly to protect the more vulnerable UHF stations. Though cable TV could greatly enrich intracity communication—and offer local and national programming now neglected by broadcasters—it has been crippled by FCC restriction and fell on hard times in the 1970s. About 10 million households now have cable TV service, some 300,000 also having a pay-TV basis for special programs. Eventually, cable TV may develop complex

---

[33] R. A. Coase, "The Federal Communications Commission," *Journal of Law and Economics* 2 (October 1959), 1–40.

TABLE 13–3
Profitability in U.S. Broadcasting, 1974 (dollar amounts in millions)

	Number of Stations	Broad-cast Reve-nues	Broad-cast Ex-penses	Net Profits before Tax	Net Tangible Invest-ment	Profit Rate on Net Invest-ment (percent)
Television						
Three networks and their 15 stations ...	15	$1,921	$1,590	$331	$140	236
Other VHF stations ..	479	1,627	1,216	411	523	78
UHF stations	175	228	233	−5	114	−4
Radio						
AM,AM–FM stations (partly network related)...........	6,314	1,410	1,315	95	434	22
Independent FM	637	193	204	−11	38	−29

Source: Federal Communications Commission, *Annual Report,* 1975 (Washington, D.C.: U.S. Government Printing Office, 1977), pp. 105, 117, 125, 126.

two-way communications, a variety of pay TV offerings, and social programming.

Television and radio broadcasting creates consumer benefits greater than their costs of *(a)* production and of *(b)* consumption (sets, electricity, and so forth).[34] Yet it operates below its social potential. Its technology is too narrow, and its offerings are also culturally narrow, neglecting a variety of viewing interests.

One basic reason for this lies in advertising as the source of TV revenues. TV offerings are a side effect of—or a vehicle for—advertising messages. These messages, in turn, are most efficiently delivered to mass audiences on a nationwide basis. It is well known that oligopolists will cluster at the center of a market (for example, the middle of a town), and so TV advertising and programming tends toward identity at the *cultural* mean reflecting the most viewers' *tastes.*[35] These tastes are, in turn, subject to molding by the media and advertisers. The outcome tends toward standard light fare. And networking, with its ability to spread costs over a large audience, has crowded out most local content.[36]

---

[34] Noll, Peck, and McGowan, *Economic Aspects,* pp. 20–26.

[35] See P. O. Steiner, "Program Patterns and Preferences, and the Workability of Competition in Radio Broadcasting," *Quarterly Journal of Economics* 66 (May 1952), 194–223. Also, recall the analysis of oligopoly at the beginning of Chapter 7.

[36] Extensive studies of Oklahoma, New York, the District of Columbia, Maryland, Virginia, and West Virginia were made by FCC members Kenneth Cox and Nicholas Johnson during 1969–72. They showed "local" programming to be less than 20 percent, often much less, and to be mainly weather, sports, and news. Noll, Peck, and McGowan, *Economic Aspects,* pp. 108–16.

In fact, nearly all TV writing and program production originates in Los Angeles,

The fewness of networks adds to the narrowness. If there were five or six networks—or more—rather than three, their willingness to cater to specialized audiences would be much greater.[37] Oddly, at the other extreme, collusion or outright monopoly would probably *increase* the variety of content, compared to the three-network competition for the center of the mass market. Generally, a 3-firm oligopoly is the situation that most nearly minimizes diversity in programming.

The "freeness" of advertising-based broadcasting further cuts down on diversity. Viewers cannot directly respond to existing programs. Rating services do reflect viewing, and purchases may vaguely respond to the program content as well as the advertisement. But intensively felt preferences go unrecognized. And one—or a group—has no direct way to foster programs that are not offered. Some device for pay TV therefore is needed to supplement the present system.[38]

Further, the social impacts of TV content are simply irrelevant to advertising-financed choices. External costs may occur and external benefits be ignored, even though they are likely to be large in our television-oriented culture.

In short, the present network structure and financing basis may be close to the least favorable economic setting for program diversity. In this country, where the citizens' interests are astonishingly diverse, that could cause large social losses.

B2. Policies

FCC "policies" have caused—or at least facilitated—much of this narrowness. The FCC has tried to promote a balanced degree of competition and innovation, while encouraging localism. Nobody's appraisal is definitive, but it seems probable that the FCC has maintained too much market control, retarded innovation, and achieved little local content.

Allocating Spectrum. From the start in 1927, the FCC's spectrum allocation has been crucial. In TV the primacy of the scarce VHF channels is an FCC artifact, which has consigned the great mass of UHF slots to limbo. And within VHF the scarcity operates to create especially large economic rents for stations in the largest cities (see Table 13–4). The 15 next largest cities have the highest profit margins—around 30 percent. This reflects their fewer stations: 4.3 on average. But the return on capital is highest in the largest cities.[39] These profits have naturally been capitalized: probably half

---

California. This alone sets peculiarly narrow limits on its social outlook and cultural level.

[37] Noll, Peck, and McGowan, *Economic Aspects,* pp. 49–54, and Rolla E. Park, "New Television Networks," *Bell Journal of Economics* 6 (Autumn 1975), 607–20.

[38] There is of course an extensive process by which network personnel try to predict viewers' interests, select programs, and then interact with station managers in trying to sell them. That such a massive process *still* gives forth bland, narrow content suggests that the basic incentives are defective.

[39] See Harvey J. Levin, "Economic Effects of Broadcast Licensing," *Journal of Political Economy* 72 (April 1964), 151–62.

TABLE 13–4
Broadcasting in the Largest U.S. Cities, 1975 (dollar amounts in millions)

| | Number of Stations per City | Sales of Time | | Total Broadcast Revenues | Profit before Tax | Profit as a Percent of Broadcast Revenue (percent) |
		Total	Local Only			
New York	10	$ 207	$ 50	$ 177	$ 36	20
Los Angeles	12	166	60	142	28	20
Chicago	7	136	37	111	30	27
Philadelphia	6	80	27	68	17	25
San Francisco	7	80	32	67	18	27
Boston	5	74	22	62	16	26
Detroit	5	65	20	55	20	36
These 7 TV markets .	7	806	248	682	164	24
All other TV stations (687)	4.3	1,751	731	1,548	348	23

Source: Federal Communications Commission, *Annual Report,* 1975 (U.S. Government Printing Office, 1977, pp. 118–20.

of the asset value of stations is the value of the franchise itself. The FCC's contrived scarcity created the value as a gift to the lucky ones who got franchises. And the FCC has no powers to limit the resulting profits or pricing behavior.

It is widely agreed that some version of an auction system for franchises would be more efficient and fair, with proceeds going to the public purse or to enriching the content of broadcasting. Yet the past excess profits are effectively out of reach, being part of present value. And the FCC has not responded to the many authoritative and sophisticated proposals for auctions or other ways of skimming off the excess profits it has created. The alternatives are noted in Table 13–5.[40]

Meanwhile UHF continues unprofitable. Its development is one prime way to increase diversity. The other main way is cable TV.

Cable TV. The FCC prevented the growth of cable TV in the major city markets during the 1960s. Yet the economies of cable offer decreasing costs and an escape from the scarcity of channels. The cost function for over-the-air service rises, because UHF channels are more costly and less efficient than VHF. But cable costs per channel fall, because the marginal cost of added channels on an existing system is virtually zero. Cable can replace the high economic rents created by over-the-air TV with low cost and a technologically richer service. Cable TV offers special possibilities for *local* service. Ultimately, systems with refined two-way signalling, information and entertainment banks, free public access, news, and other local services— may result. Indeed, as cable technology matures using optical fibers, *it may*

---

[40] See Harvey J. Levin, "Spectrum Allocation without Markets," *American Economic Review* 60 (May 1970), 208–18; and sources cited there for a full discussion of the alternatives.

370

TABLE 13–5

Alternatives to the Current System of Spectrum Allocation

A. Freely-transferable Rights.
   1. Rights created in the courts under tort law, through inclusion and exclusion, with spectrum bought and sold outright, like land.
   2. Federal designation of rights, leaving them freely-transferable after their subsequent sale outright.
   3. Federal designation of rights, periodic competitive leasing for limited periods, with lessees substantially free to transfer at will.
B. Auctions of Federally-Designated Radiation Rights.
   1. Interband contests to determine reallocation as between different services, in addition to intraband contests limited to like users within the same service.
   2. Interband contests to ration grants among like users, within different services competing for the same spectrum, with managers free to utilize the resultant values in further reallocation of spectrum between the two services.
   3. Intraband contests within a single service to ration rights there, with results used to set user charges elsewhere too.
C. User Charges.
   Applied on occupied three-dimensional spectrum as measured by some index of physical usage.
   1. Per unit rates derived from intraband auction values.
   2. Per unit rate derived from estimated shadow prices.
   3. Per unit rates set at some arbitrary flat dollar rate.
D. Shadow Prices.
   Derived from maximum sums that current spectrum users and systems designers would be willing to pay rather than do without some small amount of spectrum.
E. New Administrative Techniques.
   Greater role for frequency clearance,* secondary rights,† and a heavier burden of proof on spectrum managers where they deliberately override economic considerations.

* The requirement that federal government users secure prior authorization to use particular frequencies (from the Director of Telecommunications Management) before disbursing funds to develop or build any communications system.

† Rights to share or borrow frequencies contingent on noninterference with rights of the primary user.

Source: Harvey J. Levin, "Spectrum Allocation without Markets," *American Economic Review* 60 (May 1970), 209–18.

converge with local telephone technology. In the 1980s, an eventual fusion of cable TV and telephone systems may be a major policy issue: who will own it, what content and access will it provide, and how might it be regulated?

Meanwhile the FCC impeded cable TV growth until 1972, to protect "free" TV.[41] This protective policy changed partway in 1972. Cable TV can at last import signals, originate multiple programs, and operate multiple channels. But a host of restrictions remained, to protect the older TV interests. Indeed, the 1972 rules were mainly a compromise struck between the old

---

[41] In 1962, 1963, and 1965 it forbade importing programs for use on cable. In 1966 it affirmed that cable TV was to be supplementary and proposed prohibiting cable systems from originating programs. In 1966 and 1968 the FCC virtually prohibited cable systems in the largest 100 cities, and it limited the cable firm's own program orientation to just one channel.

and new interests and stamped "Approved" by the FCC.[42] Regulation is still extensive and protective, though a complete FCC withdrawal from regulating cable TV would make economic sense.[43]

Cable TV is not thriving in the larger cities. During 1970–76 cable TV firms had hard financial times, and perhaps only in the 1980s will the technology ripen, as subscription TV, specialities, and two-way capabilities are developed. Networking of cable systems may develop, mingling national with local programming. Open public use of several channels offers external benefits: it gives free access to media for all shades of local social and political opinion. Cable may supply much of the balance to network TV by adding pay cable TV, which provides content in direct response to viewers' preferences.[44] This plus the developing public network might eventually provide an approximation of efficient broadcasting performance.

Cross-Media Ownership.   The FCC has permitted a byzantine and monopolistic world of combined newspaper and TV ownership to evolve. By 1971, 231 daily newspapers were jointly owned by broadcast licenses in the same city. In many cities the one radio or TV station is owned by the one newspaper. In most major cities there is an important degree of joint ownership. This clearly creates monopoly in the local markets for advertising,

---

[42] Thus, the FCC has

1. limited CATV imports of commercial station signals to two in the 100 largest markets; and in smaller markets which are served by three networks and one independent station, denied commercial station imports altogether;
2. required that the two imported signals, where authorized, be from nearby cities;
3. imposed program exclusivity protection for local stations, whereby CATV may not duplicate local station programs for a year or two, and must black out such programs on imported signals;
4. imposed strong blackout restrictions on CATV importation or carriage of sports programs;
5. denied carriage by CATV of the signals which can, in fact, be received over-the-air from nearby "overlapping" markets;
6. emasculated cable pay TV by prohibiting programs which TV stations or networks usually buy. Thus FCC denies to cable pay TV the showing of films between two and ten years old; sports programs which are less than two years old; or any series programs with interconnected plots or using the same cast of principal characters. And it further constrains pay TV by not permitting revenue advertisements before or after, as well as during programs;
7. required concurrence by the local ETV station and educational authorities before permitting importation of outside ETV signals; recommended and endorsed provisions for the new copyright statutes which greatly extend protection of stations, networks, and copyright.

[43] The Sloan Commission on Communications, *On the Cable* (New York: McGraw-Hill, 1972); and Harold J. Barnett, "Perspectives on Cable TV Regulation," a chapter in W. G. Shepherd and T. G. Gies, *Regulation in Further Perspective: The Little Engine that Might* (Cambridge, Mass.: Ballinger, 1974). An important Cabinet Committee *Report on Cable TV* (January 1974) urged freeing cable TV from virtually all restrictions (reprinted in *Television Digest,* Vol. 14, January 21, 1974).

[44] For analysis of cable TV economics, see R. W. Crandall and L. L. Fray, "A Reexamination of the Prophecy of Doom for Cable Television," *Bell Journal of Economics,* 5 (Spring 1974), 264–89 and the other research which they cite.

news, and entertainment. This in turn has monopoly effects in these markets.[45] The FCC has preferred to let this structure stand, but it may be changed by court actions (recall Chapter 5).

License Renewals. The FCC hands out and renews valuable prizes which its own market controls have created. Grants have been a highly charged and—in the 1950s—partly corrupt process. Renewals have been mostly automatic; yet they offer an unorthodox regulatory opportunity to enforce "good" performance. The criteria officially include residence, experience, the nature of proposed programs, and past performance. But the choices, even at best, are subjective and speculative, often involving grandiose claims, counterclaims, and promises.

In practice it has been a murky business, with little content or consistency. Despite efforts since 1960 to block renewals of stations with "poor" social performance, only six TV renewals were denied during 1960–72, none of them because of citizen protests about performance. Most of them were in small towns. Burdened by the hundreds of renewals it must decide (plus all its other tasks), and beset by political and special interest pressures, the FCC scarcely uses its renewal powers at all.

B3. Summary

Broadcast regulation fits the standard patterns both for *(a)* regulatory evolution and protection, and *(b)* multiple-firm regulation. Regulation has consistently limited competition too tightly. The FCC has created (or arranged, by compromise; or largely acquiesced in) a structure which does provide a degree of competition, diversity, and localism. Yet the system and its financing tend to minimize diversity and local service. New technology has been retarded. Large excess profits have been made and become fixed in property rights. Antisocial effects of programming have gone uncorrected.

This outcome has been predictable, since the FCC has been quite out of its depth from the start. It will presumably continue more to arbitrate interest group conflicts—and protest the established interests—than to put broadcasting firmly on optimal lines. Given its modest powers, resources, and bargaining position, that is about all it can do.

QUESTIONS FOR REVIEW

1. "The U.S. telephone sector is practically alone in the world in being *(a)* privately owned and *(b)* vertically integrated." True?
2. "The core natural monopoly in the telephone sector is in terminal devices. Intercity transmission is an in-between case." True?
3. "There has been, and still is, a wide range of choice in designing the technology of the entire telephone system." True?

---

[45] Advertising prices are probably 10 percent higher, at least: see B. M. Owen, "Newspaper and Television Station Joint Ownership," *Antitrust Bulletin,* 18, 4 (Winter 1973), 787–807.

4. "Telephone thrust aside an earlier monopoly, namely the telegraph." True?

5. "The refusal to interconnect has been a key AT&T method of excluding competition." True?

6. "The FCC was passive to AT&T on competitive issues during 1940–59, but it did clarify rate issues by public hearings and extensive opinions." True?

7. "A flat monthly rate for local service is economically irrational, for at least some calls incur significant costs." True?

8. "TELPAK is certainly a valid pricing system, for it cuts price to the consumer." True?

9. "The FCC is often doing the right thing when it prevents AT&T from cutting prices on some services." True?

10. "The Bell System has never presented full, concise data on the economies of integration which it gains by having Western Electric as part of the Bell family." True?

11. "The Caterfone decision was especially valuable in opening up trunk-route competition, for economies of scale there no longer preclude competition." True?

12. "Broadcast licenses have become valuable because the FCC keeps them scarce." True?

13. "Radio has slipped over into stage 4 and is workably competitive." True?

14. "The FCC has protected network interests, for instance by restricting the growth of cable TV." True?

15. Which telephone rates reflect value of service, and which ones reflect cost of service?

16. How can state regulation of rates of return of Bell companies make sense if only the parent firm raises the capital?

17. What elements of cost and benefit would need to be appraised in judging the Bell System's vertical integration?

18. What better policy should the FCC adopt toward licensing TV stations in major cities?

chapter 14

Regulation of Transportation

Transportation is a patchwork of a sector, combining railroads, road traffic, waterways, pipelines, and airways. It mingles competition and monopoly in its various parts, and the mix changes as technology advances.

Its main regulatory agency, the ICC, has come to seem a model of regulatory failure. The rise of competition has, belatedly, brought moves to deregulate some parts of the sector in the 1970s. Setting the correct margin of regulation in this unruly sector is unusually difficult, and it stirs sharp debates.

This chapter therefore appraises the need for regulation as well as the content of regulatory actions.[1] First, basic economic issues of transportation are presented in Section A. Next, Section B summarizes the regulatory agencies. Then Sections C through F review policies toward railroads, trucking, waterways, and airlines, in that order.[2]

A. BASIC ECONOMIC ISSUES

All transport involves a *route* (or roadbed) between two or more points and *vehicles* to move goods or people along the routes. There are several *modes* of transport, with varying roadbeds and vehicles: for example, roads used by trucks, buses, and automobiles; and railroad tracks used by engines and cars. The roadbeds and vehicles can be owned and operated under varying arrangements, ranging from exclusion to open access. The vehicles may be purely private or "common carriers."

---

[1] Good sources on the economic issues include John R. Meyer, Merton J. Peck, John Stenason, and Charles Zwick, *The Economics of Competition in the Transportation Industries* (Cambridge: Harvard University Press, 1959); National Bureau of Economic Research, *Transportation Economics* (New York: Columbia University Press, 1965); chapters 2–4 in Almarin Phillips, ed., *Promoting Competition in Regulated Markets* (Washington, D.C.: Brookings Institution, 1975); Ann F. Friedlaender, *The Dilemma of Freight Transport Regulation* (Washington, D.C.: Brookings Institution, 1969); George W. Douglas and James C. Miller, *Economic Regulation of Domestic Air Transport: Theory and Policy* (Washington, D.C.: Brookings Institution, 1974); and James T. Kneafsey, *Transportation Economic Analysis* (Cambridge: Ballinger, 1975).

[2] Urban transit and foreign railroads (under public enterprise) are treated in Chapter 18.

Each mode will have a network of routes among many points, as illustrated for U.S. railroads and airlines in Figure 14–1. Traffic will include goods and passengers, taking infinite varieties of trips under varying conditions of speed, size of load, safety, and so forth. As markets shift and technology alters, the networks and their traffic will evolve. Such great variety and change underlie the gross totals for the main U.S. transport modes shown in Table 14–1. From the old canals, rivers, and highways of 1800–40, through the Railway Age of 1840–90, to the mixed sector of the present day, there have been major shifts with large impacts on the country. The social objective is the optimal mix and format of transport at each point of time. There are many markets for transport within the national borders. They are often difficult to define, and so the degree of competition in them is often a matter of sharp debate.

The social objective might be achieved by open competition, as in other "normal" sectors. Or instead, competition may be unstable and confusing, so that regulation must intercede to guide pricing and allocation. The basic question is: how different is transportation? We now consider five economic issues.

A1. Natural Monopoly

There are many pockets of natural monopoly and areas of "natural oligopoly," but most of the sector is naturally competitive. Competition can occur between modes (for example, trucks competing against railroads, and airlines against buses), as well as among firms within each mode. The main natural-monopoly parts are in some Western railroads in handling certain commodities. In these cases there is only one railroad, and trucks cannot match the costs of large volume rail loads. Otherwise there are several or more direct competitors in almost all transport submarkets. This degree of effective competition has increased markedly since the heyday of the railroads, and it is still increasing. Reinforcing it is the ability of most shippers and passengers to use private trucks or cars of their own, in a form of potential competition.

Costs differ among the modes, because technology differs. Railroads have large costs for fixed patterns of roadbed. Trucks have larger elements of variable costs, with great flexibility in routes. Air travel involves costs for airports and flight routes, while the aircraft themselves can often be leased rather than owned. Cost structures are hard to unravel, but the basic patterns fit common sense. Costs for freight favor trains for high-bulk, large-scale, long-haul cargo going more than 200 miles at intermediate speeds. Trucks do best at moving high-value goods in small quantities for short hauls with diverse destinations. Water carriers are superior for slow, large-scale, high-bulk items along certain routes. Airline costs favor rapid, long-distance carriage of high-value goods to diverse destinations. In many cases, a shipment

FIGURE 14–1
Principal U.S. Railroad Routes

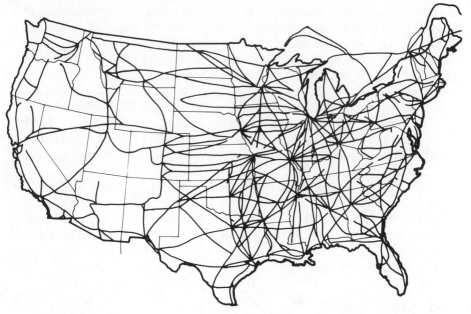

Airline Routes

Source: Civil Aeronautics Board, Office of Facilities and Operations.

TABLE 14–1
Trends in U.S. Transportation 1940–1975

	Rail	Truck	Bus	Auto	Water	Air	Pipe-line
Revenues ($ billion)							
1940	4.7	0.9	0.2	—	0.1	0.1	0.2
1950	10.2	3.7	0.5	—	0.3	0.6	0.4
1960	10.2	7.2	0.7	—	0.4	2.1	0.8
1970	12.8	14.6	1.1	—	0.5	7.1	1.2
1975	17.7	21.0	1.4	—	0.9	11.9	1.9
Ton-miles ($ billion)							
1940	412	62	—	—	118	0.01	59
1950	628	173	—	—	163	0.3	129
1960	595	285	—	—	220	0.8	229
1970	771	412	—	—	319	3.3	431
1975	757	488	—	—	343	3.7	488
Passenger-miles ($ billion)							
1940	50	—			—	2	—
1950	32	—	26	438	1	10	—
1960	22	—	19	706	3	34	—
1970	11	—	25	1,026	4	119	—
1975	10	—	28	1,143	4	146	—
Number of companies (1975)	350	16,005	950	—	320	30	105
Number of employees (1,000) (1976)	528	1,097	40	—	197	370	17

Source: U.S. Census Bureau, *U.S. Statistical Abstract* (Washington, D.C.: U.S. Government Printing Office, 1978), Section 22.

needs to go by more than one mode (such as rail cargo which is delivered by truck to the final destination).

Each mode is superior for certain conditions of trip length, speed, type of cargo, and geography. The optimal transport mix will fit these advantages. It will usually involve a division of traffic among modes and many firms, rather than a natural monopoly of one firm in one mode.

A2. Price Discrimination

Some degree of price discrimination is common in the sector, for three main reasons. First, shippers vary in demand elasticities. Second, some modes have high overhead costs, which leave room for variety in cost allocation. Railroad track costs have been the prime example of this, for the same track will carry both freight and passenger trains under differing degrees of congestion. The true cost of "track service" for a freight or passenger car is often obscure, and prices will often be fitted to the users' demand elasticity instead.

Third, there are networks, with shared costs among many routes. This leaves still more room for price discrimination. (For example, trucks running one way may easily add loads for a longer trip or a round-about return trip. If marginal cost is low, then discriminatory pricing to get the load is likely.

In railroads during 1850–1920, the scope for such discrimination was very large on many routes. The rise of trucks, buses, and airlines has greatly reduced it. Competition would now permit only moderate price discrimination in most parts of the transport sector. The discrimination would mostly be of Type A in Figure 8–3: procompetitive because it is shifting and done by many lesser firms in the same market. Many rail, truck, and airline firms assert instead that price discrimination would be deep and harmful, of Type B in Figure 8–3. Large shippers would extract favored rates, as did Standard Oil during 1880–1900 (recall Chapter 8). This would promote monopoly both among transport firms and among the shippers.

The issue hinges on cost patterns and market structure. Among objective observers, the consensus is that most price discrimination in transport would be moderate and procompetitive. The exceptions would be relatively easy to spot (mainly in certain railroad and airline routes) and could be dealt with specifically.

A3. Regional Pricing

Transport prices can influence the location of industry, trade, and population among regions. They can encourage development of new regions or help retain industry in old ones. They can tip the balance of location between cities and the countryside. These effects in turn can change social patterns.

Some such external effects of transport pricing are big and clear. Others are small or subtle, or counterbalancing. Normally the prices might be ignored or treated as valid economic signals for allocation. Yet they often become politically charged in inter-regional struggles. Some transport prices have been thoroughly altered by special tax devices or subsidies. Also much regulation is said to be designed to assure balance or "parity" among regions. Yet what balance or "parity" ought to be is often quite obscure.

A4. Unequal Subsidies

If the net subsidies are unequal among modes, then prices based on the private costs will bias traffic choices away from the unsubsidized mode. That has been the railroad's complaint since the 1920s: that the other modes get subsidies and tax privileges. Table 14–2 gives details of the railroads' view on relative subsidies and freedom of choice. There are investment and operating subsidies for some modes more than for others. Truckers reply that fuel taxes and other charges offset their seeming advantages.

If users paid the same proportion of cost on all modes, then transport choices and allocation could be efficient. Certain steep subsidies do stick out: free provision of the waterways (locks, channels, dams, and so on); free provision of much airport capacity and in-flight guidance; and low charges on heavy trucks compared to the damage they do to highways.

Since 1970 the balance may be becoming more equal. Federal subsidies

TABLE 14–2
Desparities among Modes of Domestic Transportation

Item	Railroad	Highway Freight	Air	Water
Right-of-way:				
Financed and built by ...	Railroads	Government	Government	Government
Maintained by	Railroads	Government	Government	Government
Investment cost paid by ..	Railroads	Government	Government	Government
Property taxes paid by ...	Railroads	Tax free	Tax free	Tax free
Traffic control provided by .	Railroads	Government	Government	Government
Terminals:				
Financed and built by ...	Railroads	Truckers (some by government)	Government	Water carriers (some by government)
Maintained by	Railroads	Truckers	Government	Water carriers
Investment cost paid by ..	Railroads	Truckers	Government	Water carriers
Property taxes paid by ...	Railroads	Truckers (some tax free)	Tax free	Water carriers (some tax free)
Cash subsidy paid by government	None	None	Some airlines	None
Rates regulated	Yes	About one-third of truckers	Yes	10 percent
Payment for facilities used .	100 percent	Partial	Only nominal	Small

Source: *Problems of the Railroads* (Hearings before the Subcommittee on Surface Transportation of the Committee on Interstate and Foreign Commerce, Senate, 85th Cong., 2d sess.) (Washington, D.C.: U.S. Government Printing Office, 1958), Part 1, p. 297, with later adjustments.

to railroads have risen as part of the salvaging of bankrupt eastern and midwestern railroads. Some sunk capital costs have been written off, operating subsidies to Amtrak and Conrail have been large, and low-cost funds have begun to be given for equipment purchases. Bus firms began to complain that rail tickets were subsidized unfairly against them. In 1978 the first users' charges were about to be imposed on waterways firms.[3]

Subsidies are now less tilted against railroads than before, but the whole sector is still honeycombed with subsidies that affect allocation.

A5. Shrinkage

Railways have had to cope with shrinking demand since the 1930s in the eastern part of the country. Their excess capacity left them in the situation illustrated by point A in Figure 11–3. The problem was caused by a combination of natural limits on the rate of depletion of railway capital, external limits on the railroads' efforts to drop services and close down routes, and

---

[3] Previously the waterways—including over $4 billion in locks and improvements—had been provided free. The new 1978 charges were only a start, at below 10 percent of these costs.

poor management. During the shrinkage to an efficient network, financial deficits are appropriate. They have in fact occurred, putting many eastern and midwestern railroads into bankruptcy, and they continue under the new Amtrak and Conrail systems. The policies are hotly debated, for the large subsidies may weaken the incentives to restructure the systems. The ICC's pricing policies during 1930–70 probably worsened the economic problem. The ICC permitted the railroads to set higher, discriminatory rates. This improved the finances but made the declines in traffic even sharper. Then it stopped railroads from cutting specific prices in order to fit marginal costs and to promote innovation.

In short, railroad shrinkage has been a severe problem, which was poorly handled for decades. Policies toward it are still highly controversial.

Altogether, the economic tasks for policy are difficult. Competition and stability are to be correctly balanced in scores of differing submarkets. Structural change is to be promoted. Subsidies and controls are to be applied and adjusted sensitively. Amid all this variety, policies are somehow to be standardized and fair. Nobody would expect perfect policies. Perhaps some of them have been reasonably efficient.

B. REGULATORY AGENCIES

Policies are applied mainly by the ICC, the CAB, and the Department of Transportation. State commissions have little role in the main economic issues.

B1. The ICC

Early railroad growth in the United States during 1830–1880 was by private ventures, with little planning and much turbulence. By 1887 railroads were the dominant mode of haulage in large parts of the country. In the West, there was much monopoly along major lines; in the East, powerful competition was common among two or more roads along most routes. Possibilities for abuse and price fixing were large and routinely exploited. Price discrimination was set deep in the system, promoting monopoly in the oil industry and other sectors.

As the network grew toward maturity in the 1880s, the ICC was established to "regulate" it. Several forces created the ICC. One was Granger resistance to western railroad monopoly. Another was the desire of eastern railroads to stop mutual rate-cutting competition.[4] Another was a complex of financial interests seeking to merge railroads further but often engaging in spectacular battles. The ICC was thus born of uncertain parentage, in a new form recently made possible by the 1876 *Munn* v. *Illinois* decision. It could be expected

---

[4] See P. W. MacAvoy, *The Economic Effects of Regulation: The Trunk-Line Railroad Cartels and the Interstate Commerce Commission before 1900* (Cambridge: MIT Press, 1965); and Gabriel Kolko, *Railroads and Regulation* (Princeton, N.J.: Princeton University Press, 1965).

to have, on balance, light effects in limiting railroad monopoly but strong effects in stopping price cutting.

This in fact occurred. The Supreme Court soon emasculated the ICC's powers to put ceilings on rates.[5] More than 20 years passed by before Congress gave the ICC authority to get data and to set effective ceilings on prices. During this interval the ICC did help to keep rates up against railroad price cutters. But not before 1906–10 did the ICC possess more than shadow powers to *reduce* railroad rates. Therefore, when railroads were most powerful, regulation was a mere pretense or even a prop for railroad cartels. When the need for strict regulation had passed by the 1920s, it began.

Strengthening the ICC 1906–10. The Hepburn Act of 1906 undid some of the damage that had been done by the courts. *(a)* It authorized the Commission, when rates were found to be unreasonable, to specify the legal maxima. *(b)* It contained many provisions designed to prevent personal discrimination. It increased the liability of recipients of rebates and the criminal penalties that could be imposed. *(c)* The law forbade railroads to haul (except for their own use) goods they had themselves produced. This "commodities clause" was designed to remove the advantage in car service and rates enjoyed by railroad-owned anthracite mines over their independent competitors. *(d)* The law strengthened the ICC in other ways. It required that all accounts be kept in such forms as the Commission might prescribe. It provided heavy penalties for delay and falsification in the submission of reports.

The Mann-Elkins Act of 1910 made other significant changes in the law. *(a)* Under the Act of 1887, the ICC had been unable to pass upon a rate until after it had been put into effect. The new Act gave the Commission power to suspend proposed increases, for a stated period, while it considered their legality. The burden of justifying higher rates was put on the carriers.

(b) When one rate was cut, under the original Act, the railroads could compensate for the reduction by raising another. Now the Commission was empowered, on its own motion, to consider the schedule of rates as a whole. *(c)* The Commission was also authorized to control the system used in classifying freight.

The new laws rehabilitated the Commission. Its orders, in general, came to be accepted by the courts.

World War I brought a strange interval of government operation of the railroads.[6] The railway regulation was drastically tightened with the Trans-

---

[5] The main cases were *Counselman* v. *Hitchcock,* 142 U.S. 547 (1892), *ICC* v. *Cincinnati, New Orleans and Texas Pacific Railway Co.,* 167 U.S. 547 (1897); and *ICC* v. *Alabama Midland Railway Co.,* 168 U.S. 144 (1897).

[6] The strains of war transport overloaded the existing system, and so the government had to take them over in order to apportion capacity and unify operations. The U.S. Railroad Administration took over the railroads in December 1917 and operated them until March 1920. The government paid rental for the use of properties, while actual management of operations was left to the officials of the roads. Only the larger allocation of railroad resources was controlled by the government. The experiment was costly to the public purse, but this loss occurred because railway rates were held down despite the rise of costs.

TABLE 14–3
Milestones of Transportation

1840–60	Several states build railroads (Pennsylvania, Illinois, Indiana, Michigan, Georgia, and others).
1870s	Granger Laws passed.
1887	Interstate Commerce Commission created.
1888–1906	ICC powers are gutted by the Supreme Court.
1906–10	Hepburn and Mann-Elkins Acts give powers to ICC.
1917–20	Railroads are taken over for war operation by the U.S. Railroad Administration.
1920	Transportation Act sets ICC powers and criteria still used now.
1935	Regulation is extended to motor trucking.
1938	Civil Aeronautics Board is created to regulate airlines.
1940	Reed-Bullwinkle Act legalizes railroad cartels.
1958	Transportation Act modifies regulation.
1966	Department of Transportation is created to "coordinate" policy.
1970	Amtrak is formed to operate passenger service or railroads.
1975–78	The CAB promotes competition in pricing and routes. Deficits of Amtrak and Conrail deepen.
1976	The "4-R Act" salvages bankrupt railroads and encourages flexible pricing; "Conrail" is formed.

portation Act of 1920. This act gave new authority to the Commission over service, securities, and rates. The Commission could establish minimum as well as maximum rates. Its powers to control prices and operations were firmed at the level at which they have remained ever since. The Act empowered the Commission to look into the honesty, efficiency, and economy with which the railroads were managed. It also set the "fair" rate of return at six percent.

Weaker railroads were to be assisted. They were now encouraged to pool their resources or even merge. During 1921–29 the ICC prepared a comprehensive plan for consolidating stronger and weaker railroads in a system of about 20 competing railroads. But the stronger systems, instead, merged with the better of the weak systems, leaving the main problem unsolved.

The Depression. The Great Depression hit the railroads hard. Car loadings fell off; from 1929 to 1932 gross revenues were cut in half. If the railroads had been less highly levered financially, they would have been in a better position to sustain this loss. But 56 percent of their capitalization in 1932 was in bonds, bearing an average interest charge of 4.6 percent. In many cases, though operating costs were covered, interest could not be paid. By 1938, 111 railroads, with more than 30 percent of the country's mileage, had become insolvent and were in receivership. Railway bonds had been conservative investments, held by institutional investors. The railway problem became, not that of protecting the shippers against the railroads, but that of protecting the holders of railroad securities against financial loss.

In 1932 the Hoover administration set up the Reconstruction Finance Corporation and empowered it to make loans to the railroads, among others (see Chapter 17). In the next 10 years such loans reached a total of $850 million, enabling many roads to stave off bankruptcy.

World War II restored traffic for a while. But the long-term malaise persisted, and the new interstate highway system—mostly complete by 1965—plus the spread of airline travel, further eroded the position of most eastern railroads.

The railroad problem partly reflected special subsidies to the competing modes, and the ICC also repeatedly blocked the railroad's efforts to compete by price cutting. Yet there were also efforts to use regulation to help the railroads.

Regulation was extended in 1935 to trucking, airlines, and waterways. The methods were conventional. But the motivation was different: to contain competition, not constrain monopoly. Also the rate bureaus, which had long served as private railroad cartels, were legalized in 1948 by the Reed-Bullwinkle Act.[7] Rate bureaus are regional cartels run by the railroads and their larger customers. Any proposals to change railroad rates go through a process of consensus in these bureaus. The bureaus' recommended rates are mostly rubber-stamped by the ICC, in practice.[8] Truckers, airlines, and water carriers also operate by this process. The rate bureau cartels usually keep rates more stable and higher than they would be under competition. They also embody a vast amount of price discrimination among types of goods.

After a World War II boom, the "railroad problem" worsened during 1945–70, as trucking and airlines grew rapidly. The ICC was slow to let beleaguered railroads cut prices toward marginal cost, in order to meet competition. The discriminatory sets of price structures were continued by the ICC. A new law in 1958 permitted railroads to undercut the prices set by truckers and waterways. But the ICC resisted such price cutting on into the 1970s (see Section C below).

By 1959 it was clear that deregulation of railroad prices was in order for much or all of the railroad sector. Yet the ICC has resisted such a change, backed by other interested parties. The ICC shifted its policies toward mergers after 1958, to permit almost all railroad mergers. It ignored Antitrust Division arguments about their possible anticompetitive effects. The 1958 law also permitted railroads to cut services more freely, and by 1968 passenger services had been deeply reduced.

By the 1970s the ICC had proven incapable of applying an efficient set

---

[7] In 1944 the Department of Justice brought a suit against the Western Association of Railway Executives, the American Association of Railroads, and a number of western roads, charging that the establishment of rates through bureaus was a violation of the Sherman Act; and the state of Georgia brought another suit in which the legality of such activities was attacked. In the light of existing precedents, there was little doubt that the bureaus would be held to violate the law. The railroads therefore turned to Congress for exemption. The Reed-Bullwinkle Act, granting their request, was passed over the veto of President Truman in 1948.

[8] Formally, there are chances for complaints and differences. But normally the bureaus' rates stand.

of controls. It had blocked competitive pricing but permitted a number of anticompetitive mergers. Its controls were slightly loosened after 1975, but the ICC's main role of trying to protect the existing set of interests has continued.[9]

The ICC has internal problems of management. It has large resources, but it is bureaucratic. Much of its budget goes for unimportant housekeeping tasks. The commissioners have been strong on political connections but weak on other skills.[10] Members and staff officials are intimately involved with the industries they regulate, often changing jobs as by a revolving door.[11] They supervise a mountainous array of rates: for example, some 270,000 new rates were filed in 1969. Only one percent of its actions involve rule making; some 70 percent involve protection of modes against each other.

The ICC is variously described as bloated, rigid, senile, and the worst of all major commissions.[12] Even its defenders admit the need for improvements. Yet major changes are not now in prospect, even after more than two decades of intensive deregulation efforts. This is because the ICC is the focus of strong interests, including truckers, the Teamsters union, certain favored shippers, and others.

The ICC costs about $69 million per year in direct expenses. It also imposes

---

[9] The 4-R Act of 1976 encouraged more flexible pricing in several ways. The "Railroad Revitalization and Regulatory Reform Act" had several purposes, including

the implementation of the USRA Final System Plan, the continuation of local rail service, the Northeast Corridor Project, railroad mergers and consolidations, rehabilitation and improvement financing, and ICC reform and revision of rail ratemaking (section 202). . . . Section 202 amends Part I of the Interstate Commerce Act to provide.for greater ratemaking flexibility. It establishes new standards for determining when the justness and reasonableness of a rate may be questioned. Under these new standards, no proposed railroad rate can be found to be too low if it does not violate any other section of the Act. In addition, no rate can be found to be unjustly or unreasonably high unless the Commission finds that the proponent carrier has market dominance over the service involved; market dominance means the absence of effective competition for the traffic or movement to which the rate applies. Unless the Commission finds market dominance to exist, the Commission has no power to suspend any rate on the ground that it may be unjustly or unreasonably high. These changes are intended to encourage more competitive pricing in rail transportation. . . . For a protested rate to be suspended, the protestant must show that if the challenged rate were to go into effect the failure to suspend would cause substantial injury to the protestant.

A large share of rail transport could benefit from this new flexibility, according to a detailed ICC report, *The Impact of the 4-R Act: Railroad Ratemaking Provisions* (Washington, D.C.: Interstate Commerce Commission, October 5, 1977). Yet the railroads were slow to act and the Act is expected to have little effect.

[10] "ICC appointees are cleared with railroad officials, and usually truckers too." Louis M. Kohlmeier, Jr., *The Regulators* (New York: Harper & Row, 1969), p. 48.

[11] Of 11 commissioners leaving the ICC in the 1960s, all took jobs with railroads, or specialized in legal practice before the ICC or, in one case, became the president of the National Association of Motor Bus Operators. See Robert C. Fellmeth, *The Interstate Commerce Omission* (New York: Grossman, 1970).

[12] For the ICC's view, see successive issues of its *Annual Report*, which provide extensive detail on developments in surface transport.

TABLE 14–4
Alternate Estimates of the Loss Caused by ICC Regulation of U.S. Railroads

Author	Estimate Relates to	Estimated Welfare Loss (current $)	Welfare Loss as a Percent of Freight Revenue
Harbeson	1963	1.1 to .9 billion	12 to 32
Friedlaender	1969	2.7 to 4.2 billion	24 to 36
Boyer	1963	125 million	1.37
Levin	1972	53 to 135 million	0.3 to 0.8

Sources: Kenneth D Boyer, "Minimum Rate Regulation, Modal Split Sensitivities, and the Railroad Problem," *Journal of Political Economy* 85 (June 1977), 493–512; Anne F. Friedlaender, "The Social Costs of Regulating the Railroads," *American Economic Review* 61 (May 1971), 226–34; Robert W. Harbeson, "Towards Better Resource Allocation in Transport." *Journal of Law and Economics* 12 (October 1969) 321–38; and Richard C. Levin, "Allocation in Surface Freight Transportation: Does Rate Regulation Matter? *Bell Journal of Economics* (Spring 1978), 18–45.

various economic costs of inefficiency in transportation. Excess railroad trackage is kept on and traffic flows are distorted. Estimates of this burden are summarized in Table 14–4. They range from negligible to about $5 billion per year. Appraising these estimates is an excellent term-paper project.

B2. The CAB

Air transport developed during 1920–38 to embrace 16 airlines, operating a variety of routes. There was much competition and change during 1933–38. Government mail contracts were used as a form of regulatory control and reward, in promoting growth and new services. In 1938 the CAB was created to stabilize the sector.[13] It certified the existing carriers and reorganized route structures so that 90 percent of city-pair markets (with 59 percent of all passenger miles) were monopolies. As air service mushroomed after 1945, the CAB developed two lines of policy. *(a)* It controlled entry into the main routes and freight services. While keeping out newcomers, it extended existing firms' routes until by 1970 nearly all routes had two or three airlines. *(b)* It supervised air fares, nominally at first and then with some force after 1970. Meanwhile, it permitted entry into local and feeder services. It channelled subsidies to the main airlines until 1957, and to lesser air services from 1938 to the 1970s. Soon after 1950, it was recognized by critics that CAB regulation had diverted competition toward increased flights and amenities, thereby reducing efficiency and raising prices. Table 14–5 summarizes several recent estimates of the losses caused by CAB regulation. After 1975,

---

[13] See R. E. Caves, *Air Transport and Its Regulators: An Industry Study* (Cambridge: Harvard University Press, 1962); George Eads, *The Local Service Airline Experiment* (Washington, D.C.: Brookings Institution, 1972); W. A. Jordan, *Airline Regulation in America: Effects and Imperfections* (Baltimore: Johns Hopkins Press, 1970); and Douglas and Miller, *Economic Regulation.*

TABLE 14-5
Estimates of the Economic Impact of Civil Aeronautics Board Regulation

Author	Estimate Relates to	Estimated Effect of Regulation on Prices	Estimated Welfare Loss from Regulation	
			Total	As a Percent of Revenue
Jordan	1960s	30% higher	$1.5 billion	20
Douglas and Miller	1969	4% to 6% higher	$0.3 billion	4
Keeler	1974	30% to 50% higher	$1 billion to $3 billion	10 to 30

Sources: William A. Jordan, *Airline Regulation in America: Effects and Imperfections* (Baltimore: John Hopkins Press, 1970); George Douglas and James C. Miller III, *Economic Regulation of Domestic Air Transport* (Washington, D.C.: Brookings Institution, 1974); and Theodore E. Keeler, *Domestic Trunk Airline Regulation: An Economic Evaluation*, part of *A Framework for Regulation*, U.S. Senate Government Operations Committee (Washington, D.C.: U.S. Government Printing Office, 1978).

the CAB reversed course and began removing its controls over fares and routes.

The CAB is a smallish federal commission, with a fairly limited, simple set of tasks. The Federal Aviation Authority handles many of the technical chores for the sector.[14] CAB commissioners have mainly been industry-oriented, but Chairmen John Robson (1974–77) and Alfred E. Kahn (1977–78) shifted the Board sharply toward dismantling regulatory protections. By 1978 the CAB had become an effective agency for research and control, and was engaged in withdrawing its main controls. This reversed the usual evolution of regulation (recall Chapter 10).

B3. The Department of Transportation

The Department of Transportation was created in 1966. It handles transport planning and subsidies. It intervenes in some ICC and CAB matters, but its main role has been in funding highways and urban transit and in salvaging the bankrupt railroads. With a large budget and extensive powers, it is deeply involved in the issue of balance among regions and modes.

C. RAILROAD REGULATION

Here we appraise the ICC's main regulatory activities.

---

[14] The FAA employs 45,000, including 15,000 traffic controllers at over 300 airports and a score of control centers. FAA services are not priced—peak, off-peak, or otherwise—and so the efficiency of their allocation and use cannot be appraised. They simply attempt to cope with whatever traffic burdens are placed on them. This fits the "passive" model of public firms (see Chapter 16 below).

C1. Rate Structure

Generally, rates may be justified either by costs or by the value of the service to the shippers.[15] The basic rule is that no rate may be less than "out-of-pocket" costs, which is close to a short-run marginal-cost floor under prices. Yet in key cases the ICC leans instead toward "fully allocated" cost; out-of-pocket costs plus a share of capital costs. Prices can go down only to the cost levels that reflect each carrier's "inherent advantage." The firm cannot cut prices to "noncompensatory" levels, which merely reflect predatory motives. But in all cases the true levels of cost are debatable. So both the definition and the details of cost become controversial, and the ICC must occasionally make rough, politically charged decisions.

Above the cost floor, rates may discriminate, and they do. Carriers may meet each other's competitive rates and otherwise fit demand elasticities. But a rate may be protested by any party for discriminating unfairly. Both first- and second-level damages (recall Chapter 8) may be used to protest a rate. Each mode complains vigorously about price cutting by the other modes below the level of its own "inherent advantage." Yet most rates go through routinely. And the basic discriminatory structure of freight rates was firmly in place even before the ICC existed. There are millions of rates, some of which are themselves hundreds of pages long. Most rates are simply filed away by the ICC rather than scrutinized or even critically appraised.

In several key cases after 1958, the railroads tried to compete more effectively but were resisted by the ICC. In 1963 the Supreme Court set aside the Commission's rejection of a cut made by the New Haven Railroad, saying, "If a carrier is prohibited from establishing a reduced rate that is not detrimental to its own revenue requirements merely because the rate will divert traffic from others, then the carrier is thwarted from asserting its own inherent advantages of cost and service."[16] But the Court did not say how inherent advantages were to be measured, whether by average total costs or by out-of-pocket costs, including no charge for overhead.

Big John Hopper. The next case to come before the Court involved the rates set by the Southern Railroad for carrying grain. Most of this traffic had been handled by trucks and by barges that were exempt from rate control.

---

[15] The Interstate Commerce Act contains a number of provisions with respect to the structure of rates. Section 1 requires that the rates charged on particular goods and between particular points be "just and reasonable," and that the systems used in classifying goods be "just and reasonable." Section 2 prohibits discrimination between persons. Section 3 covers other forms of discrimination, making it illegal for a carrier to give any "undue or unreasonable preference or advantage" or to impose any "undue or unreasonable prejudice or disadvantage." Section 4 applies to a particular form of discrimination between places, forbidding a carrier, without express permission of the ICC, to charge more "for a shorter than for a longer distance over the same line, in the same direction, the shorter being included within the longer distance." Section 6 requires that rates be published and adhered to and forbids changes in rates without prior notice.

[16] *ICC* v. *New York, New Haven & Hartford R. R. Co.*, 372 U.S. 744, 759.

In an effort to compete for the business, the railroad designed a new hopper car, known as the Big John. Made of aluminum, it had twice the capacity and half the weight of the old box car and could be loaded and unloaded more easily and at lower cost. In 1961 the Southern proposed to cut its rates on movements of grain in trains of such cars by as much as 66 percent. Its proposal was fought by southern elevators and millers who saw grain moving more cheaply to the East, by the truckers and the barge lines, and, on behalf of the barge lines, by the TVA. The issue was disputed before the ICC and the courts for the next four years. In 1963 the Commission disapproved Southern's rates, holding them to be insufficiently compensatory. In 1965 a district court rejected this decision, finding the evidence on which the Commission based its action to be inadequate. The Supreme Court agreed, returning the case to the ICC for further consideration.[17] And finally, the Commission reversed itself, deciding that the rates were legal after all. They were thus allowed to take effect.

Ingot Molds. But a defeat for the railroads soon followed. Ingot molds had been moved from Pittsburgh to Steelton, Kentucky, by barge and truck for a charge of $5.11 per ton. In 1963 the Pennsylvania and the Louisville and Nashville Railroads cut their joint rate on this shipment form $11.86 to $5.11. The barge and truck lines complained, contending that the railroads' move violated national transportation policy by depriving them of their inherent advantage. The ICC found that the railroads' out-of-pocket costs on the shipment were $4.49; their fully allocated costs $7.59. It rejected their argument that rates were legal if they covered out-of-pocket costs, holding that they must cover fully allocated costs. The Commission was reversed by a district court that found its choice of fully allocated costs to have inadequate support. But it was finally upheld, in 1968, by the Supreme Court, which ruled that the selection of a method of costing whereby to determine inherent advantage was within the authority of the ICC.[18] The ICC did loosen its controls after 1968, but it still leans toward a "fully-allocated cost" rule, which impedes the railroads' efforts to compete by price. The 4-R Act of 1976 has not altered this basic policy.

C2. Rate Levels and Rate Bureaus

By permitting rate bureaus to "recommend" transport prices collusively, the ICC has helped to raise the price level. After 1930 this did not help the eastern railroads plagued by falling demand. But many lines still hold enough market power to benefit from the collusion. Such collusion, accentuated by the ICC's enforcement of discrimination, enables some railroads to draw excess profits. For these parts, deregulation would give positive social benefits.

[17] *Arrow Transportation Co.* v. *Cincinnati, New Orleans and Texas Pacific Ry. Co.,* 379 U.S. 642 (1965).

[18] *American Commercial Lines* v. *Louisville & Nashville Ry. Co.,* 392 U.S. 571.

The 1976 Act permits regulation only where railroads have "market dominance." By narrow market definitions (recall Chapter 5), the ICC has found such dominance in over 50 percent of railroad operations. Therefore its controls have remained extensive.

C3. Merger Policies

Each decade or so the idea of consolidating the railways into five, or eight, or 15 "major" systems is revived, and a wave of merger proposals arises. There is also a stream of merger proposals, some involving financially troubled railroads. The ICC has usually approved such mergers, with little regard to their reduction of competition. In fact, the ICC's approval usually cites the intense competition which railroads are said to face.[19] The mergers often fail to yield the benefits claimed in the hearings: of streamlining, coordination, enlarging services, and—of course—eliminating "useless duplication." The X-efficiency and innovation which competition stimulates are ignored. The Penn-Central fiasco of 1970 is the biggest such failure of ICC judgment, but other mergers too have been permitted even though they would reduce competition and efficiency. At no time has the ICC had a long-run plan for railroads to use in appraising mergers.

C4. Economic Effects

ICC policies have probably caused *(a)* excess trackage east of the Mississippi River, *(b)* too much loss of rail traffic to other modes, *(c)* too much concentration among railroads, and *(d)* too little innovation by railroads. The first three points are summed up in the estimates of Table 14–4. The effect on innovation is even harder to judge. Several cases of retardation are well known, such as the *Big John Hopper* and *Ingot Molds* cases.[20] There may be social benefits from the ICC's encouragement of stability. But the total net costs of ICC regulation of railroads may still be above $2 billion per year.

Altogether, regulation by the ICC has impeded the railroads' natural shift toward competition in their Stage 4. Monopoly tendencies in pricing have been reinforced, without either *(a)* effective controls to give competitive performance, or *(b)* guidance toward an optimal restructuring. Though careful removal of much ICC regulation is widely agreed to be needed, vested interests seem likely to keep the ICC in business largely as is for decades more.

---

[19] If competition were in fact so completely effective, then the ICC's other regulatory actions would be irrelevant. The ICC has not admitted the force of this paradox.

For a critical appraisal of railroad mergers since 1900, see Richard Saunders, *The Railroad Mergers and the Coming of Conrail* (Columbia: University of South Carolina Press, 1978).

[20] See Paul W. MacAvoy and James Sloss, *Regulation of Transport Innovation: The ICC and Unit Coal Trains to the East Coast* (New York: Random House, 1967), and Phillips, *Promoting Competition.*

D. TRUCKING REGULATION

ICC regulation of trucking since 1935 has paralleled the treatment of railroads. There are three classes of truckers: common carriers, contract carriers, and private carriers. The 16,000 common carriers do over 90 percent of the interstate trucking business. Like railroads, they price through rate bureaus, and they face similar ICC criteria about reasonable rates.

Without regulation trucking would be highly competitive and efficient. There are virtually none of the standard "utility" features (recall Chapter 10), nor any real likelihood of chronic destructive competition.

Regulation in this situation has been weak, restrictive, and a morass of bureaucracy. It was imposed in 1935 partly in order to benefit the railroads by restricting their competitors. It has been largely functionless and obscure, but burdensome and rigid.

There are various insurance, accounting, and merger rules under the Motor Carrier Act of 1935. The main controls are on entry and rates. In both areas they tend to reduce competition and increase prices. And their slowness further stifles normal market forces. Altogether, trucking regulation flouts nearly every criterion of optimality.

Entry. In controlling entry the Commission is restrictive. Applicants for new operating authority, for alternate routes, and for extensions of existing routes are required to prove that the proposed service is really needed, that the services already available are inadequate, and that adequate service cannot be provided by carriers already in the field. They are asked to justify their applications in detail: to defend the financing they propose, the equipment they intend to use, and the schedule they plan to follow. For small concerns, the obstacles created by this procedure are almost insurmountable. Decisions may be delayed for months or years. Certificates may then be refused on the ground that adequate service can be rendered by established truckers, or even that rail service is available.

Where operating rights *are* granted, they are strictly limited. Operators are often confined to hauling particular goods between particular points. They may be required to follow circuitous routes, forbidden to serve intermediate points, and denied the right to carry cargo on the return haul.[21] They are thus prevented from reducing costs by filling empty space. By cutting operating rights into bits and pieces, the ICC condemns the carriers to inefficiency. In considering whether to issue a certificate of public convenience and necessity, the Commission directs its attention only to "necessity," ignoring convenience. This leads to a waste of resources.

Pricing. With regard to rates, too, the Commission has made the industry less competitive. Changes in motor carrier rates, as with the railroads, are

---

[21] In one instance, a carrier operating between New York and Montreal had to detour 200 miles via Reading, Pennsylvania; a carrier operating between the Pacific Northwest and Salt Lake City could carry cargo eastward but not westward. Walter Adams, "The Role of Competition in the Regulated Industries," *American Economic Review* 48, 2 (1958), 527–43 at p. 531.

agreed upon in rate bureaus before being proposed to the ICC. Here, the burden of proof is on the carrier who proposes to cut a rate. The Commission concerns itself, as in the case of the railroads, not with the individual companies, but with the carriers as a whole. But it does not judge the rate level by measuring the return upon the carriers' investment, since investment in the industry is so small in relation to revenue that rates calculated to yield a fixed return might not suffice to cover costs. Instead, it seeks to insure an operating ratio that will afford a safe margin of revenues over costs, generally holding a ratio of 95 (costs being 95 percent of revenue) to be reasonable.

In acting on particular rates, the Commission employs the same principles, in the main, that it does with the railroads: it is more concerned with fixing minima than maxima, as noted in Section B above.

The need to deregulate trucking entry and rates is now almost universally agreed among economists and others who do not have vested interests in it. Yet it has easily withstood growing efforts since the 1950s to restore competition.

E. WATER CARRIERS

There are some 1,500 waterways firms, the great majority of them unregulated. There is little concentration. Most of the U.S. traffic is in the Great Lakes and Mississippi River systems, mainly bulk cargoes on an unregulated basis. The cargo is mostly minerals and grain, high-bulk goods with little need for speed. Less than 25 percent of waterborne traffic is on a common carrier basis and therefore actually regulated by the ICC. The level and mix of water traffic often shift strongly, as trade patterns change. The basic routes and terminals are mostly provided by public resources. Since the shippers provide little more than the boats themselves, they can therefore adjust rapidly, even shifting into foreign operations.

Regulation here suffers from the same flaws as it does in trucking. Entry control is unnecessary and biased to protect older firms. Price regulation is passive. The water carriers—acting together in rate conferences—set their rates at a fixed differential—often about 20 percent—below those charged on competing hauls by rail. This saving keeps shippers from asking that rates be lowered; rail competition prevents the carriers from asking that they be raised. The Commission (as we saw above) has tended to prevent cuts in rail rates in order to keep competing water carriers in business. Here again, ICC regulation appears to be socially useless and costly, on balance.

F. REGULATION OF AIR TRANSPORT

There are 11 trunk airline firms, operating in a maze of routes between U.S. cities. Regulation of this complex oligopoly has probably had several predictable effects: (a) concentration on the main routes has been higher than it would have been if entry were free, *(b)* price fixing has been supported, *(c)* costs of service have risen above efficient levels, because of the diversion to non-price competition.

F1. Special Economic Conditions

Differential Traffic. Routes between cities differ sharply in their traffic density, as Table 14–6 shows. The main routes between the biggest cities

TABLE 14–6
1972 Fares and Costs for One-Way Trips on Major U.S. Routes

Route (and number of airlines on that route)	Number of Passengers Carried, 1975	Estimated Long-run Marginal Cost 1972	Actual Fare 1972	Percent Markup
Boston–New York (3)	1,685	$14.31	$ 22.22	55.3%
Chicago–New York (4)	1,598	35.66	54.63	53.2
New York–Washington (4)	1,569	15.96	24.07	50.8
Miami–New York (3)	1,448	41.76	76.85	84.0
Los Angeles–New York (3)	1,169	90.21	150.93	67.3
Los Angeles–San Francisco (7)*	919	15.70	15.28	−2.7
New York–San Francisco (3)	822	93.49	150.93	61.4
Chicago–Los Angeles (4)	694	64.34	101.85	58.3
Detroit–New York (3)	655	25.56	41.67	63.0
Las Vegas-Los Angeles (4)	636	13.83	25.00	80.8
Boston-Washington (4)	559	22.93	35.18	53.4
Atlanta-New York (3)	552	36.37	56.45	55.2
Chicago-Washington (4)	472	30.97	47.22	52.5
Chicago–St. Louis (3)	441	17.36	25.93	49.6
Chicago–Miami (3)	385	44.73	84.42	84.3
Chicago–San Francisco (3)	397	67.38	113.88	69.0
Dallas–Houston (2)*	387	15.41	18.52	20.2
Boston–Chicago (3)	569	40.54	62.96	55.3

* Intrastate routes not under CAB regulation.
Source: *Official Airline Guide,* periodical; T. E. Keeler, "Airline Regulation and Market Performance," *Bell Journal of Economics* 3 (Autumn 1972), 399–424; and Civil Aeronautics Board, *Handbook of Airline Statistics,* annual.

are busy, while peripheral routes have light traffic. The main routes are lucrative and could support many competitors. The lesser routes offer lower profits (though some are very profitable), but they may provide external benefits to the towns.

Economies of scale are limited.[22] There is no cost superiority in large airlines. The business is very personal and customer-oriented. Bigness breeds impersonality and X-inefficiency, while not providing scale economies. The

---

[22] See Caves, *Air Transport;* Douglas and Miller, *Economic Regulation;* Jordan, *Airline Regulation;* and Theodore E. Keeler, *Domestic Trunk Airline Regulation: An Economic Evaluation,* report in U.S. Senate Government Operations Committee, *A Framework for Regulation* (Washington, D.C.: U.S. Government Printing Office, 1977).

industry is definitely not a natural monopoly; most of it is "naturally competitive."

Demand elasticities vary, and so price discrimination can be sharp. Most passengers are businessmen on expense accounts, who are often indifferent to fares. Many others are infrequent travelers who have no close substitute, and so their demand is also inelastic. Yet many users are price conscious, for they can go instead by automobile.

Short-run marginal costs are low except for peak periods, for it costs almost nothing to fill an empty seat. The average load factor has been 50 to 55 percent (before the recent loosening of controls). That is, planes have flown about half empty, on average. Pricing could reflect such low marginal costs, but only since 1976 have they begun to do so. The optimal load factor, meanwhile, is about 70 to 80 percent.[23]

Public provision of airports and air traffic control guidance has relieved the airlines of some portion of costs. Their costs are primarily in aircraft and personnel, which are relatively variable. The airlines could be highly flexible in their routes and scheduling. "Destructive competition" would not be likely to occur.

These economic conditions would make for an effectively competitive industry, which prevented systematic price discrimination. If instead competition were abridged, then discrimination would be sharp and performance would decline. That is what regulation has brought about.

F2. Regulation's Effects

Before 1978, the CAB has let only four lines at most into the densest routes, and only two or three on the others. This has kept competition well below its potential levels. The airlines claim that the "cream" from these routes has enabled them to maintain unprofitable services on the lesser routes. Yet such network balance is debatable. Service on lesser routes could often be fully provided by small lines, flying small planes. As it is, some lines holding monopolies of lesser routes have charged their *highest* price-cost margins on those lesser routes and made large profits from them.

Before 1976, fares were mainly set collusively, as in the railroad and trucking sector, in order to assure uniform prices. The CAB had altered the proposed rate levels on occasion, but it enforced the uniform basis of the fares. The diversion of competition to service tended to induce rises in costs. Planes flew more frequently, half empty, and with fancier services. Careful studies have suggested that costs were raised some 30 to 40 percent as a result. Unregulated *intrastate* airlines in Texas and California, by contrast, had costs and fares that are much lower.[24] Table 14–6 draws the contrast sharply.

---

[23] See George C. Ead's chapter in Phillips, *Promoting Competition;* and Douglas and Miller, *Economic Regulation,* chapter 5.

[24] See also Jordan, *Airline Regulation;* Keller, *Domestic Trunk Airline Regulation;* and Douglas and Miller, *Economic Regulation.*

During 1965–75 there were small experiments at price flexibility, in the form of youth fares, stand-by fares, late-night fares, and family fares. Also, the CAB permitted new competition from "charter" lines in parts of the market, and this grew during the 1960s on the longer routes. At first charters were strictly limited to "affinity" groups, and so forth. In the 1970s the rules were liberalized, but charters still scarely affected the mainstream of traffic throughout the country. Concurrently, the CAB finally developed cost studies and principles so that fares could be aligned more closely with costs.[25] For example, it moved in 1974 to raise first-class fares toward their true costs, and this virtually dried up first-class ticket sales. The mileage-based tapering of fares was also moved more closely toward actual costs.

Deregulation Begins. Then in 1976 the CAB began shifting to permit some price competition. Some airlines promptly responded, with "no-frills," "super-saver," "travel-anywhere," and other discounts. On the international scene, the newly permitted Laker "Sky-train" fares on the New York–London route in September 1977 drew heavy publicity, and "stand-by" fares at half the regular fares spread to other cities.

Yet the CAB was guiding the process carefully. It prevented or modified some discounts, which it felt were a predatory effort to kill off the new price-cutting entrants.[26] It acted briskly so as to let market forces work. By 1978 the new price cuts had proliferated in many forms and had begun to affect traffic on the major U.S. routes. The new competition was fairly selective, and many routes were little affected at first. The CAB also began shifting in 1978 to a "permissive" policy toward new entry on specific routes. For example, it simplified its criteria to permit relatively free entry into Oakland, California, and Midway Airport in Chicago, both little used.

The CAB moved quickly, and it pressed through Congress a 1978 law which would end all price and route controls by 1983 and abolish the CAB itself in 1985. The airlines could cut fares 50 percent or raise them 5 percent, without seeking CAB approval.

The shift toward competition was real, with a strong economic impact.[27] It was also important on a symbolic level. The CAB had broken the usual

---

[25] Douglas and Miller, *Economic Regulation,* summarize this new analysis well.

[26] The Laker innovation also stimulated sharp price cuts by the established airlines. The CAB held that these price cuts were predatory and would drive Laker out, so that high fares could be enforced once again. The CAB permitted smaller price cuts, in order to let the experiment develop. Instead of matching Laker's $236 round-trip New York-to-London fare, the carriers were permitted to cut stand-by fares only as low as $256.

There are sharp differences between the international and internal-U.S. policy situations. The CAB had moderate leverage in the first area, but complete authority over the second.

[27] The likely effects are appraised in Paul W. MacAvoy and John W. Snow, *Regulation of Passenger Fares and Competition Among the Airlines* (Washington, D.C.: American Enterprise Institute, 1977).

Air freight was deregulated in 1977, under CAB pressure. Yet existing carriers were given one year free of new entry. They used this time to expand so as to fend off new competition. Consequently the gains from deregulation have been slight.

pattern of protectionism and rigidity, in order to guide its sector back onto a competitive basis. It showed that deregulation in transport could be started, though the process still needed careful guidance, step by step.

G. SUMMARY

In such a complex sector, regulation has had mixed effects. The ICC has probably impeded the adjustment to an efficient long-run balance between railroad, highway and water transport. Its control on free movement of goods may cause waste, and the limits on flexible pricing have prevented healthy competition. Yet little shift toward more efficient policies seems to be in prospect.

Airline regulation, by contrast, began moving after 1975 toward a more efficient basis. Pricing was freed up and entry barriers began to be loosened, under careful guidance. The process seems likely to go much further.

QUESTIONS FOR REVIEW

1. "The transportation market in the United States is simply the area within the national borders." True?
2. "An optimal allocation in transport involves some specializing by modes but also a lot of overlap (that is, competition) among them." True?
3. "Price discrimination of various kinds is widespread in transportation." True?
4. "The railroad problem of the 1930–60 period was simply one of poor management." True?
5. "The ICC had strong power at first but then became passive as railroads entered Stage 4." True?
6. "Rate bureaus are essentially cartels, supported by the ICC." True?
7. "The ICC has limited railroad price cutting by stressing short-run marginal cost as the floor." True?
8. "Trucking is a natural monopoly, for only the large fleets can provide full service." True?
9. "Free waterways have helped the water carriers to have an "inherent advantage" in light, diversified cargo." True?
10. "Costs and prices on intrastate airlines are generally 30 to 40 percent lower than those for interstate airlines on comparable flights. This suggests that the CAB's past regulation has raised airline prices." True?
11. In what ways does the transport sector genuinely differ from normal competitive conditions, so that regulation is needed?
12. Under what conditions might it be wise for social policy to prevent truckers from taking freight on their return trips?
13. Do lower intrastate air fares *prove* that the CAB has raised airline costs?
14. Has the CAB's policy shift toward competition since 1975 brought on "destructive" competition?

chapter 15

Regulation Appraised

A definitive appraisal of regulation is not really possible. Regulation's real content and effects are not yet known, beyond rough estimates. It may scarcely ever have been tried properly, or with the force which it nominally has. Perhaps it never will be fully applied. Regulation *as it is* must be compared with practical alternatives, not just judged as regulation, *Si* or *Non*. It may be a doubtful device, but the alternatives may be less attractive.

A. REGULATION: IDEAL AND ACTUAL

Regulation has been tried *(a)* formally since 1870, *(b)* in some practical degree since the 1930s, and *(c)* under reasonably favorable conditions since the 1950s. Its lessons are mixed.

It usually conforms to the evolutionary process outlined in Chapter 10. Most "utilities" go through life cycles with four phases. Commissions are often added late, and they often retard the natural evolution of their utilities back toward normal conditions.

Actual regulation has passed through distinct periods. During 1888–1910 the ICC demonstrated that regulation could have little effect. During the 1920s and 1930s the valuation controversy stalled much regulation still further. The 1950s passed with only moderate regulatory actions. A partial revival in the 1960s coincided with rising doubts about regulation's economic effects. The new stresses since 1965—scarcity, ecology, competition, high interest rates, inflation—have placed regulation in a difficult, perhaps a watershed, situation.

There have also been constants since 1870. Regulation has often been passive, overloaded with tasks, and weak in treating the really critical matters. State commissions have frequently fought federal regulators. Actual regulation serves to mediate in political compromises rather than to apply lucid economic criteria. Yet regulation thrives on adversity: even when its flaws are known, it seems to grow and spread.

Ideally it applies expert, independent judgment, briskly, with clear principles. It induces progress and clarity. In practice:

1. **Expertness** has been the exception among commissioners, while political loyalty has been the rule. Turnover is high, so that most commissioners barely learn the industry and the issues before they move on. For some decisions, political skills are helpful; but for the most important ones, one needs to grasp the deeper issues before tempering them with political "realities."

2. **Independence** is diluted. Commissions are often influenced by legislatures and executives, on the issues that really matter. And the really big issues are often taken from the commissions for settling elsewhere. The commissions frequently become industry-minded and protective. Pure independence may exclude some suitable political influences and—in any event—be impossible to get. But many commissions serve mainly as compromisers or industry promoters, and increasingly so as the industry and the commission age.

3. **Briskness** is hard to attain. Procedures are often and easily manipulated. Regulation often delays changes for years or even decades.

4. **Principles** are often fudged and obscured. Even when sound criteria do have an influence, they are frequently diluted with fine points and mistakes of judgment.

5. **Technological progress** is often retarded. In some cases regulation not only impedes innovation but also inhibits the evolution of new suppliers and services.

These departures are serious defects of regulation, to be weighed against its benefits.

B. PROBABLE EFFECTS: GAINS AND LOSSES

Nobody knows, beyond reasonably good guesses, what effects regulation has actually had. The likely effects can be summarized, with *good* and *bad* effects in that order. Many of the analytical predictions about regulation's direct and side effects (in Chapters 10 and 11) have been borne out in practice.

At the least, regulation is likely to give the following **benefits:**

1. It is a safety valve, which lets all parties have the impression—sometimes, perhaps, only an illusion—that their interests and reasons have been heard and considered in the official decisions. It also provides a continuing forum for returning with further complaints.

2. It brings about compromises among the parties at issue. This smooths the adjustment process, perhaps as efficiently as is possible. Also, it eliminates many of the gross abuses which could occur under unfettered monopoly conditions.

3. It is occasionally quite strict and in line with optimum criteria—in some periods and on some issues.

4. Where it is ineffective or slow, the resulting lag may supply good incentives for efficiency, in line with effective market processes. This is part of

the "regulatory-lag" hypothesis, by which regulation does **best** for efficiency when it is doing **least.**

5. And finally, the rate-base effect toward greater investment may promote technical progress in these capital-intensive sectors, offsetting the restrictive tendencies which would otherwise prevail.

These benefits would not be trivial, especially by the realistic standards which we have learned to apply in this book. In some cases, they could easily justify the costs of regulation, as they are ordinarily measured. Indeed, the best commissions during their best periods are excellent indeed. If public ownership were the only alternative, regulation's uncanny ability to conserve on public capital and direct subsidies might put it ahead in most cases.

But there are **costs:**

1. The first cost is the frequent grant of monopoly greater than would be necessary or natural in the absence of the franchise. This is a loss in itself and a cause of many other costs.

2. The direct costs of managing the regulatory process, and of private efforts to resist and twist it, are not small. Nor are these costs closely correlated with effective regulation: some of the largest commissions are among the least effective.

3. The firms' inefficiency which arises under the regulatory franchise and process may be large. This has proven difficult to assess, but the likelihood of its occurring is great, and there is growing evidence that it is significant. It varies from case to case, but it is a normal part of the regulatory outcome.

4. The rate-base effects, in enlarged capital investment, are probably of medium but real scale. They relate to the lack of marginal-cost pricing. Together, these two influences induce excess peak load and capacity and other directions of extra investment.

5. The level of service quality probably tends to be higher than is efficient. It also tends to be less diverse, offering a narrowed range of consumer choice in most regulated sectors (especially communications and transport). This reflects both the shared anxiety of regulators and firms to avoid service break-downs, and the inherent tendencies of monopolies and oligopolies to converge on a narrow set of offerings.

6. And finally, where the supply of equipment is vertically integrated with the utility operating level, the rate and direction of innovation may be altered from the optimal.

These are tendencies which appear to be borne out objectively in practice, in a variety of utility sectors. They have not been proven conclusively, but logic and the burden of proof are in their direction.

C. ALTERNATIVE IMAGES OF REGULATION

There is a wide range of plausible images about regulation's nature and effects. The choices include at least the following:

Success. Regulation is the best possible treatment, in the world as it is. The monopoly is inevitable, at least at the start, and it disappears over time; and the regulatory controls do have some good effects. It is cheap, effective enough, and foolproof, because even—or especially—where it is loose and lagged, it is a tonic for efficiency.

Defective. It needs reform or at least more vigilance. Regulation works from time to time, especially when appointees are excellent and staff resources are abundant. But it requires vigilance plus a high order of political support and resources. Various minor and major reforms are needed, including a strong expansion of regulatory budgets. Generally, economists should replace lawyers as key operators of regulation.

Irrelevant. Regulation is unnecessary and of little consequence in either direction. It does not alter the basic economic outcomes. Instead, it simply provides a series of rituals, at which solemn dignitaries pretend to be deciding issues which, in fact, they neither understand nor control.

Ineffective. Regulation usually gets diverted and mired down in side issues, while the main economic conditions go untouched. The side effects are costly, even when regulation is performing as advertised. On balance its costs exceed its benefits, save in the rare cases of early and inspired regulatory leadership.

A Fraud. Finally, regulation may be a sham, invoked by firms, their investors and main customers, in order to enlarge their ability to exploit. Not only does regulation further disequalize wealth, income, and opportunity, by serving as a tool of the private interests. It also stands in the way of other, more effective treatments.

There are still other images, which the reader may explore now or which may arise in the future. But these six images do include the main current interpretations of regulation. They are all plausible, and evidence can be adduced for each of them.

Despite this wide range of images, there is a narrower set of technical features which regulation does seem to display consistently. It does seem to evolve perversely, during the broad utility evolution from Stage 1 to 4. It does seem to induce large costs of resistance or evasion by the private firms. And it does induce a variety of side effects, which alter the levels of resource use. And finally, it often creates an impression of effective public action when, in fact, there is little—or even antipublic—action.

D. ALTERNATIVES TO STANDARD REGULATION

A number of alternatives or supplements to regulation have long been considered or are live possibilities for the future. Their urgency varies inversely with one's image of regulation's success. We will consider several of these now in turn. The possible changes come under three main headings: more and better regulation, deregulation, and new hybrids of regulation.

More and Better Regulation. One step would be to shift most regulatory attention from profit rates to price structure. Some of this is already occurring, by necessity. Also, more attention is needed on market structure and the possibilities of new competition. State regulation has been barren ground for this improvement, though federal commissions are now more receptive. The FCC and CAB are already shifting, and the FPC and ICC may adjust further.

Next, more resources are needed for most commissions. At the state level, this is often a multiple of the present levels. But where are such resources to come from? From the legislatures? There the utilities themselves will resist strongly. One method is to draw extra resources from the utilities themselves, as is being done in several states.

Further, better commissioners and staffs may be sought. One proposal is to replace lawyers with economists. But, good as this idea is in principle, it suffers from the thinness of the ranks of available economists. Other experts are also in short supply. The political economy of the sector assures that state regulation will continue to be managed by lawyers and politicians.

As long as regulation is as extensive and unsure as it is, calls for better quality and talent are in order and may lead to marginal gains. But major improvements are unlikely.

Deregulation. Regulation could be withdrawn, either partially or entirely. Partial deregulation, down to a core of regulatory activities, is a realistic goal. Indeed it is the proper sequence for regulation to follow during Stages 3 and 4. In most sectors, the core of natural-monopoly activities can be defined relatively clearly as it evolves over time, and regulatory constraints could be adjusted to those without major legislative effort. The result would be closer attention to the key utility problems, and a gradual withdrawal from irrelevant and harmful activities. But this too is caught in the crosscurrents of utility and large-customer interests. It would take resolute, clear-minded and powerful commissions—with supportive legislatures and executives—to follow this route. The CAB has had precisely this combination during 1976–78. Others have not.

Complete deregulation is another matter. It requires a legislative act withdrawing both the constraints and the monopoly franchise. Consider the legislative sequence. Some party must introduce legislation and get it a fair hearing on its economic merits, despite its threat to powerful and focused utility interests. By Stage 4, the commission is a protector, not a limiter. Therefore support must be rallied from a wide range of potential gainers against the strong interests of the central parties. These parties include the regulators themselves, as a threatened group, who will naturally resist. Therefore the phasing out of regulation will usually be arduous and confused. In principle, abolition of regulation is clean and efficient. In practice, it is usually the opposite. Again, the CAB is an outstanding exception.

Recall from Chapter 11 that there are several kinds of new entry which can be fostered as part of deregulation. Those include new entry by sellers, take-over, revision of the present structure, and new inter-utility competition. A skillful commission might anticipate the needed changes and foster them. But most commissions can be expected to resist and divert them, as they have in the past.

New Hybrids. Supplements to regulation can be of several sorts. One is to review the franchises, in contrast to the present *de facto* perpetual grant of monopoly. Actually an old idea, this device would provide incentives for efficiency, if renewal required a showing of good performance.[1]

Second, profit constraints may be tied directly to performance. Rate increases can be made conditional on specific actions or results. This avoids the difficulties of estimating total performance (recall Chapter 10). It would face the disincentive problem and apply clear incentives.

Third, direct audits of utility performance could be ordered (recall Chapters 10 and 11). These could appraise general management performance or specific actions. Experiments with this device in the 1970s have been inconclusive. Such studies—whether published or not—could help fill the partial vacuum now surrounding managerial behavior.

Other supplements can be devised and tried. Presently regulation is settled in conventional lines. It attempts to do more than is possible, in ways which often lack feedback from performance and which stir strong company resistance. Reforming regulation by increasing its quality and quantity is not enough. The incentive structure also needs changing, including ways to induce regulators to withdraw from Stage-4 former "utilities."

Reformed or not, regulation will continue and probably spread, and it is needed for public as well as private utilities. Your image of the optimal design of regulation—as a device or package of devices—depends on your image of the actual effects of regulation. These effects may include a wide array of positive and negative influences.

It also depends on your image of the changing group of utilities. One can view them as brief departures from normal markets, requiring little unusual treatment. Or the distinction between utilities and other industries may seem sharp and permanent. Whatever images you form, they will govern your policy judgments. In all the utility sectors, these questions are intensely debated, for the stakes are high and the policy issues continue to be open. Form your own images and policy lessons carefully *and* independently.

---

[1] On early renewal experiments, see Martin G. Glaeser, *Public Utilities in American Capitalism* (New York: Macmillan, 1957); Emery Troxel, *Economics of Public Utilities* (New York: Rinehart & Co., 1947); and Paul J. Garfield and Wallace F. Lovejoy, *Public Utility Economics* (Englewood Cliffs, N.J.: Prentice-Hall, 1964).

Part IV

PUBLIC ENTERPRISE

16.
Fields and Forms
of Public Enterprise

17.
Public Enterprise in Finance and Industry

18.
Public Enterprise in Utility, Urban, and
Social Sectors

19.
Public Enterprise Appraised

chapter 16

Fields and Forms
of Public Enterprise

More than most students realize, public enterprises are integral and important in the U.S. economy. Their role varies from country to country, and the firms come in many forms and varieties. There are gradations of public ownership, of public financing, of market positions, pricing policies, and internal management. They provide a rich set of experiments in many sectors.

The United States has long had thousands of public enterprises, many of them as familiar and American as apple pie. The private-enterprise ideology of the country causes them to be ignored and belittled, and indeed some public enterprises do perform badly. Yet many are efficient and innovative. Their scope and variety are expanding, at any rate, and so the wise student will try to understand them. Increasing social complexity is likely to enlarge their role further, both in the United States and abroad. Public enterprise is more common and varied in other countries, and so these four chapters will use international comparisons freely. The aim is merely to clarify public enterprise, not to praise or blame it.[1]

---

[1] There is no comprehensive treatment of the economics of public enterprise. Good sources include W. G. Shepherd and Associates, *Public Enterprise: Economic Analysis of Theory and Practice* (Lexington, Mass.: Lexington Books, 1976); W. G. Shepherd, *Economic Performance under Public Ownership* (New Haven: Yale University Press, 1965); R. Pryke, *Public Enterprise in Practice* (New York: St. Martin's Press, 1972); R. L. Pryor, *Property and Industrial Organization in Communist and Capitalist Nations* (Bloomington, Ind.: Indiana University Press, 1974); and M. Einaudi, M. Bye, and E. Rossi, *Nationalization in France and Italy* (Ithaca: Cornell University Press, 1955).

For lucid treatment of certain economic issues, see W. A. Lewis, *Overhead Costs* (London: Allen & Unwin, 1949); W. A. Lewis, *Principles of Economic Planning* (London: Allen & Unwin, 1950); Ralph Turvey, *Economic Analysis and Public Enterprises* (London: Allen & Unwin, 1971); and Christopher D. Foster, *Politics, Finance, and the Role of Economics: An Essay on the Control of Public Enterprise* (London: Allen & Unwin, 1971).

For a survey of U.S. public firms, see Annmarie Hauck Walsh, *The Public's Business: The Politics and Practices of Government Corporations* (Cambridge, Mass.: MIT Press, 1978).

A. BASIC TYPES OF PUBLIC ENTERPRISE

A1. Publicness

There are three main economic dimensions to the "publicness" of public enterprise. One is **ownership,** the traditional criterion. Public firms may be totally publicly owned, and many are. Yet the public can hold only part of the ownership, in all gradations from 0 to 100 percent. So ownership is not the only criterion.

Second, the public may **subsidize** the public enterprise, in some degree. The firm may show financial losses on its operations, which are covered by payments of public funds. Put the other way round, the firm may charge prices which cover none, some, all, or even more than all of its operating costs. The firm's capital needs may also be met by the government. A public firm whose operations and investment are heavily subsidized is more "public" than one which earns a profit and raises its own investment funds.

Third, the closeness of public **control** over the firm affects its publicness. This control can range from tight down to nil. Some so-called public firms are quite independent of outside guidance. At the other extreme, some units are parts of the government itself, closely involved with the "state." Note the basic point: a public enterprise is not necessarily controlled by the government.

The variety of subsidy and control are illustrated in Table 16–1 with a selection of U.S. public enterprises. The other dimension—the degree of ownership—cannot be shown easily in two dimensions, but it too can vary, as we shall see. Whenever studying a public enterprise, *first try to appraise where it fits in these three dimensions.* Generally, cases to the upper right of Table 16–1 are socially preferable to those in the lower left. Public subsidy without public control is the worst of both worlds.

A2. Active versus Passive

Then try to judge whether the enterprise is "active" or "passive." An **active** firm makes structural changes, in order to accomplish definite objectives. These aims can be social, economic, or both. The firm changes its environment and content. A **passive** firm, by contrast, merely adjusts to standard commercial or budgetary rules. It does not explore new conditions of demand or technology.

Most public firms are active at first but then evolve toward passivity, as Chapters 17 and 18 will show. Passive firms usually imitate private firms (in profit targets, pricing, labor policy, and so on), and so their value as public firms becomes doubtful. The conditions may depend on the life cycle of the industry itself. It is easier to be an active firm in Stages 1 and 2, with growth and change.

TABLE 16–1
Selected Public-Enterprise Activities in the United States, by Approximate Degree of Control and Subsidy

Degree of Effective Public Control

	Slight Control	*Partial Control*	*Full Control*
No Subsidy	Port of New York Authority	State liquor stores	Municipal utilities (water, sewage)
	Federal Reserve Board	National land management	
	FHA housing program	Amtrak	AEC enrichment plants
	Tennessee Valley Authority	SBA programs (including minority support)	U.S. Government Printing Office
	Performing arts centers	FAA programs	
	Sports stadiums	Airports	Social Security
	Public housing	Highway construction and maintenance	Municipal parking facilities
	Medicare	State courts	Municipal transit
	Medicaid	Local courts	Federal courts
	Public universities	Federal maritime program	Public law
	SST program	Mental hospitals	Child-care programs
	Military R&D contracting	State and local law enforcement agencies	Primary education
	Vetrans Administration hospitals	Prisons	
	Weapons purchasing and management	Corps of Engineers	
		Census Bureau	
Full Subsidy			

(left axis: Degree of Public Sponsorship)

A3. Commercial versus Social

The firm's activities may be strictly commercial (for example, producing electricity, or airplanes, or tools) and/or social. The social part may be dominant, and the output or service may be provided free (those along the bottom of Table 16–1 are of this type). If the commercial part dominates, then prices covering much or all (or more than all!) of the costs may be charged.

Most public enterprises have both commercial and social activities. For clarity, these need to be disentangled. Ideally, the social part is subsidized directly by the public, while the commercial part is paid for by the customers, through prices which cover costs. In practice the two parts are hard to keep clear, and much controversy over public enterprise turns precisely on the questions of its true social activities.

Still, the student should look closely at this whenever studying a public firm.

A4. Three Basic Types

Among all this variety there are three main familiar types of public enterprise, as follows.

The Classic Public Utility Form. This is the public corporation. Furthest developed in Britain, it is found in utility sectors throughout Western Europe and, less frequently, North America. It is commonly—but wrongly—regarded as *the* alternative to the regulated *private* utility.

This type of public enterprise: *(a)* is wholly publicly owned, *(b)* is in a "utility" sector, *(c)* is a monopoly in its market, *(d)* gets all its capital from the Treasury or under a public guarantee, *(e)* is not regulated, but supervised by a government department, *(f)* is required to meet commercial profit targets. As illustrated in Figure 16–1, the firm is embedded in both economic and political interest groups. Though formally "autonomous," the firm is supervised and given various "social" objectives to meet. It sells its output and is supposed to avoid financial losses. Yet the social and commercial activities often become entangled.

The firm's board members are public appointees, but they are often virtually identical to their counterparts in private firms. A minority of managers are also like private managers, drawn from the same pool of talent, and moving between public and private positions. Such officials naturally lean toward commercial policies. Even the lifetime public-firm managers often follow policies that are largely commercial.

The classic public firm often unifies—that is, monopolizes—its industry, perhaps backed by franchise and entry protections as strict as those of private firms under regulation. Its target or *minimum* rates of profit are set in the same range (6 to 10 percent) as regulatory *ceilings* on the rates of return

FIGURE 16–1
The Setting of a Typical Public Enterprise

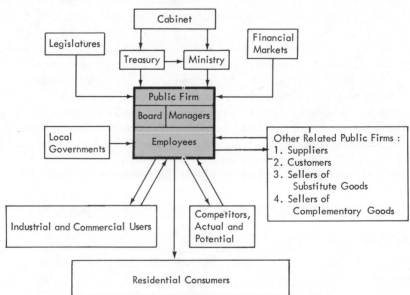

of private utilities in the United States. This often leaves the price structure questions at least as indeterminate as they are in private firms under regulation.

This classic form tends to enlarge the public's commitment of capital and to limit its control over what the enterprise does. Even so, the public subsidy element may be small compared to the firm's total revenues. This type is discussed in Chapters 17 and 18.

Public Investment Banks. This is a variety of bank or holding company which exerts control through its holdings of manufacturing firms. It may have no subsidy element at all. The objectives are often strictly economic: to allocate investment and control so as to improve performance in industrial firms.[2] Public banks take partial or complete holdings in companies where profitable changes can be made, often where private finance is not enforcing efficient management or requiring needed restructuring. Such banks may play a strong take-over role. They work best when not overloaded with ailing industries which have large social burdens. They work mainly through competitive capital market processes, as discussed in Chapter 17. (An example is Britain's National Enterprise Board, with its holdings in British Leyland, British Aerospace, and a variety of smaller companies.)

Social Enterprises. These have a specific purpose (for example, education, social insurance, health care) and are usually subsidized. They are enterprises, producing services, and so they need to be managed well just like any other firm. They operate under budget constraints, but their managers lack the strict guidance of the profit motive. They may hold monopoly power and develop X-inefficiency, just as private firms with ample profits may do. They are discussed in Chapter 18.

These three types of public enterprise (and others) are merely variants of the more conventional forms of behavior which antitrust and regulation deal with. Their responses and yields may differ slightly, but they need social scrutiny and constraints. As a first approximation, most public-firm managers behave similarly to private managers. The constraints may differ, but they usually involve (a) budgetary limits on costs and revenues, (b) a definite profit target, and (c) a degree of financial supervision akin to what actually occurs in large private firms. It is the outside constraints and support for the firm which may cause it to give distinctive results.

Our proper objective is not to reach some grand Teutonic judgment between public and private enterprise. Rather, it is to analyze the variety in public enterprise, to identify the more efficient types, and to learn how to combine them with other strategies. Evidently, "nationalization" and "public ownership," in the classic British and TVA style, are special cases, not representative of the whole. There exists no nationalization in any Western economy which is comparable in scale to "nationalization" in the giant U.S. economy. Abroad, even the largest public firms are only on a regional and local scale

---

[2] They are discussed enthusiastically in Stuart Holland, ed., *The State as Entrepreneur* (White Plains, N.Y.: International Arts and Sciences Press, 1973).

by U.S. standards. And public *ownership* is only one choice within the whole public enterprise toolkit.

B. ACTUAL PATTERNS OF PUBLIC ENTERPRISE

The present scope of public enterprise in the United States was noted in Table 1–2. Some international differences are illustrated in Table 16–2. There is much variation, and yet the large role of public enterprise is clear enough. Its extent is almost certainly increasing, in a wide range of countries.

In nearly all countries, the central banks are owned by governments; in some countries, other banks and insurance companies are public enterprises. Almost all of the railroads outside of the United States are public enterprises. Commercial airlines are usually government-owned. Telephone and telegraph services, too, are usually public firms. Radio and television broadcasting is mainly a public enterprise in most countries. Urban transit and electricity are usually provided by governments. Rental housing, in cities, is mainly public. There are important industrial firms too; some 15 of the largest 200 manufacturing firms outside the United States are public enterprises, in a wide range of industries (see Table 17–4).

Competition between public and private firms is found in many industries, and its extent is growing. It occurs in Canada in railways, airlines, steel,

TABLE 16–2
Share of Public Ownership in Selected Sectors in Selected Countries, 1978

Industrial Section

(Privately Owned: ○   Publicly Owned: ◔ 25%   ◑ 50%   ◕ 75%   ● All or Nearly All)

Country	Posts	Tele-communications	Electricity	Gas	Railways	Coal	Airlines	Motor Industry	Steel	Ship-building	Country
Austria	●	●	●	●	●	●	●	●	◕	na	Austria
Belgium	●	●	◔	◔	●	○	●	○	○	○	Belgium
Britain	●	●	●	●	●	●	◕	◑	◕	●	Britain
France	●	●	●	●	●	●	◕	◑	○	○	France
W Germany	●	●	◕	◑	●	◑	●	◔	◔	◔	W Germany
Holland	●	●	◕	●	●	na	◕	○	◔	○	Holland
Italy	●	●	◕	●	●	na	●	◑	◑	◕	Italy
Spain	●	◔	○	◕	●	◑	●	○	◔	◕	Spain
Sweden	●	●	◑	●	●	na	◑	○	◔	◕	Sweden
Switzerland	●	●	●	●	●	na	○	○	○	na	Switzerland
United States	●	○	◔	○	◔	○	○	○	○	○	United States
Yugoslavia	●	●	●	●	●	●	●	●	●	●	Yugoslavia

Note: The proportions shown are often approximate.
Source: Adapted from *The Economist*, March 4, 1978, p. 93.

broadcasting, linerboard, pulp and paper, and others. In Britain, such competition occurs in the steel, automobile, trucking, broadcasting, sugar, shipbuilding, aircraft and airlines industries. In Italy, it is even more widespread.

The United States differs from other western economies chiefly in the low share of public enterprise in its utilities, industry, and finance. Otherwise U.S. patterns are not peculiar. The typical pattern in Western economies is *(a) utilities,* entirely or mainly publicly owned, *(b) finance,* one or several public banks, *(c) insurance,* large social insurance programs, *(d) industry,* several major industries under partial public ownership, *(e) social services,* mainly under public ownership, and *(f) distribution,* with little public enterprise.

Public enterprise exists in many parts of the U.S. economy. There is a great variety of forms and behavior, as suggested by Table 16–3. It ranges from conventional utility cases, such as TVA, to industrial and service areas, over into certain subsidy programs, and into important *social* enterprises such as public schools and universities, mental hospitals, the courts, and prisons. Yet these public enterprises tend to be a phantom presence in the United States, not recognized for what they really are.

There is much debate and change in public enterprise. Table 16–4 gives a selection of such changes during 1970–78. Chapters 17 and 18 will give more detail on some of these firms. Individual changes go both ways, but the whole scope of public enterprise appears to be increasing.

C. REASONS FOR PUBLIC ENTERPRISE

Public enterprise is merely a set of devices which can be used for a number of social and economic purposes. They include:

1. Social Preference. A society (city, state, or country) may simply prefer public to private control, especially for certain prominent sectors. Such cultural preferences seem to explain much of the great variation in Table 16–2.

2. Inadequate Private Supply. A new industry or project may seem too large and risky for private firms to invest in. They will demand government guarantees or grants, and possibly other subsidies. It may seem wiser to put the public cost under direct public ownership. Such cases are often controversial. A backlog of them is usually on tap at any time, each with its backers and beneficiaries. Only a few will justify public support.

3. Salvaging Firms. The public often "rescues" failing firms by buying out their capital and supporting their rehabilitation. There are always new candidates for such residuary treatment. Some are valid. But they tend to burden the public with sick industries which absorb large subsidies.

4. Exerting Competition. One firm in an oligopoly may be made a public enterprise and then run aggressively as a "pace setter." This can reduce prices, improve efficiency, and stir innovation. Alternatively, the public firm may provide indirect "yardstick" competition in utility sectors. For example,

TABLE 16–3
Local, State, and Federal Public Enterprises in the United States

1. **Local**	**Extent of Public Enterprise**
Utilities	
Transit (bus, subway, trolley commuter lines)	Most large cities
Water and sewage	Virtually all large cities
Garbage disposal	Most cities
Electricity	Many smaller cities, several large cities
Ports	Most port cities
Airports	All large cities
Social Units	
Schools	All cities and towns
Libraries	Virtually all cities and towns
Parks, golf courses, pools	Virtually all cities and towns
Sports stadiums	Many cities
Museums	Many cities
Zoos	Some large cities
Cemeteries	Most cities and towns
2. **State**	
Prison facilities	All states
Insurance services	Unemployment: all states
	Workman's Compensation: 18 states
Parks	Most states
Liquor retailing	16 states
Electricity	All Nebraska, a large share of New York
Ports	Port of New York Authority (transport and urban facilities); New Orleans; other ocean ports
Toll roads, bridges and tunnels	29 states
Health care	Mental and old age institutions
3. **Federal**	*(Expenditures in 1978–79)*
Electricity	Corps of Engineers, $1,420 million; Bureau of Reclamation, $618 million; Tennessee Valley Authority, others
Postal service	$17,700 expenditures; $784 subsidy (millions)
Lands	Forest Service, $834 million; National Park Service, $364 million
Commodities stockpiles	Value, about $700 million
Transport	Alaska and Panama Canal railroads; Military air and sea transport services; St. Lawrence Seaway
Loans and guarantees	About 100 agencies, includes housing, farming, rural electricity and telephones, Export-Import Bank, Small Business Administration
Insurance	Many agencies: banks, housing, crops, shipping, foreign investment, stock markets, veterans life and annuity insurance, old age pensions (see Table 17–3)
Health care	Medicare, Medicaid, veterans hospitals
Industry	Various: Government Printing Office, Military production, etc. (World War II aluminum, steel, rubber and other plants)

Sources: For figures, U.S. Government, *Budget, Fiscal Year* 1979 (Washington D.C.: U.S. Government Printing Office, 1978), Appendix volume.

TABLE 16–4
Selected Events Involving Public Enterprise, 1970–1978

United States

Finance .... Federal National Mortgage Assoc. ("Fannie Mae") converts to semi-private status, grows rapidly. Government National Mortgage Assn. ("Ginnie Mae") and Federal Home Loan Mortgage Corp. ("Freddie Mac") also grow rapidly, and assist mortgage financing.

Utility .... U.S. Postal Service becomes a public corporation in 1971: losses deepen 1974–78. Competition from private carriers rises. "Amtrak" begins in 1970; its deficit also grows during 1974–78. "Conrail" is created in 1975 to absorb bankrupt eastern railroads. City transit systems become nearly all publicly owned by 1977 (including all 117 largest cities). Puerto Rico buys the local ITT telephone system. State universities increase their share of students by undercutting private tuition rates. TVA's management shifts toward progressive aims in 1978. Public television expands its network and programming, and is put on a firmer financial basis during 1975–77. National Park Service revises policies for its 286 units during 1975–78.

Other .... Uranium enrichment is retained in federal ownership. State lotteries develop and flourish in 13 states. New York's Offtrack Betting Corp. grows to 144 offices. Panama Canal faces growing financial problems. Prison factory operations take form in federal and some state prisons. Smithsonian Institution grows to 14 major museums and galleries.

Canada .... Canadian Development Corp. is created to take industrial holdings to protect national interests. British Columbia extends public ownership 1973–76, then retracts. Alberta takes over the province's main airline, but Air Canada is shifted to a commercial basis in 1978. A national health system is extended and refined. Railroad passenger service is put in a public firm.

Britain .... Public-firm prices are tightly controlled 1970–73, then permitted to rise. Rolls-Royce aerospace capacity is nationalized following bankruptcy; car operations are left private. A 1970–73 attempt to "hive off" secondary activities of public firms is abortive. British Leyland and British Ship-building take over private operations. National Enterprise Board created in 1975, takes numerous holdings (Ferranti, Ltd.; ICL, Ltd. (computers); etc.). British National Oil Co. is created to control and share in profits from North Sea oil. British Airways is created to unify most airline capacity. Private broadcasters are permitted in radio. British Steel Corp. runs growing deficits 1975–78.

France .... Public tobacco monopoly sets fees for all cigarette sales. Renault takes leadership in auto production. Credit Lyonnaise incurs $36 million loss in 1974. Private TV commercials are permitted.

Italy .... Price controls cause large deficits in scores of public firms after 1972. Montedison slips toward greater state ownership and control.

Oil countries .... Public ownership is extended to most oil operations, but slowly and with compensation.

Brazil .... Develops weapons production, oil monopoly (Petrobras), electricity and other capacity under new public firms.

Other LDCs .... Indonesia's Pertamina (oil monopoly) falters in 1976, is reorganized. Pakistan, India, Algeria, Zambia, Mali and other African states extend public ownership to major sectors. Public-private joint ventures spread in many industries.

a public electricity system may achieve lower costs than private firms, thereby putting pressure on the private firms to do better.

5. Inner Nature of the Firm. Public firms may modify the power structure and working conditions of private management. Such changes may be significant even if they do not magically transform the social content of the firm as much as the workers had hoped.

6. External Impacts. Public firms may allow for outside social harms or benefits which private firms ignore. There may be a structural disequilibrium (for example, shrinking railroads) with transitional social impacts, or a continuing social benefit that justifies continuing subsidy. In the extreme, the service may be a *pure public good* calling for a full subsidy.

7. Sovereignty. A country may take over the local branches of large international firms in order to neutralize their power. When the country is small and the private firm is big, the action may be necessary for the country's political stability.

8. Incomplete Supply to Needy Users. Universal coverage of some services (for example, good housing, primary education, health care) is often regarded as part of a "good" society. Private firms may supply only the more lucrative groups of customers, leaving needy groups unprovided. Public programs may be the most efficient way to give complete coverage on a fair and decent basis.

These and other conditions for public enterprise are often valid. But they are often misrepresented and usually controversial. Even where an external effect exists, it can often be treated more efficiently by incentive devices, partial public control or ownership, direct public programs, or other packages, rather than a conventional fully public firm.

Viewed broadly, public enterprises are best fitted for sectors where *(a)* goals are multiple, hard to measure, transcend efficiency, and pose hard choices of equity, and *(b)* pricing choices are discretionary and have a large effect on equity. So public enterprise suits complex and socially important sectors, much more varied than just the "utility" sectors. This fits its richness of forms and tactics.

D. ECONOMIC ISSUES

The criteria for guiding and evaluating a public firm's performance are the same as before (recall Chapters 1 through 3). Ideally the firm operates at quantity and quality levels which bring marginal social benefit into line with marginal social cost. Its investment policies also fit such efficient lines. Equity, progress, and other criteria are included in the appraisal. In conventional public firms, commercial criteria will usually suffice, with only small adjustments for social-private divergences. In wholly social firms, social benefit-cost analysis should apply to the core decisions.

The more detailed issues divide into four categories.

D1. Origins of the Enterprise

The extent of ownership should fit the extent of public interest in the industry. A small or moderate public interest calls for only a partial public holding, just enough to achieve the specific aim.[3] Only if the special public-interest element is large will total public ownership be necessary. So defining the social element clearly is important right at the start.

The take-over price can be crucial. If the private owners are paid off too handsomely, it may be both unfair and inefficient. Unfair because the funds flow to a few. Inefficient because the now-public firm will be saddled with too-high costs of capital. This will sacrifice the social benefits in advance and force the firm to set its output prices too high.

The "correct" price for acquiring the assets is usually their market value, even if that is below what the private owners originally paid. The government must be very strict in this matter. Otherwise they will simply be exploited to enrich investors. The price usually governs the ideological fight over creation of the public enterprise. The resistance will be inversely related to the price offered. The government must resist the pressure to overcompensate the private owners.

Real change for the better? The social aim is to change the management, performance, and content of the firm. Yet, instead, things may go on as before, with the public now sheltering the interests of the managers and suppliers. Indeed, public firms can be a device for corruption and sloth. Therefore one needs to look closely at their changes from the start.

D2. Market Structure

Size and Economies of Scale. The public firm should be large enough to achieve technical economies of scale and economies of integration. It should not go much beyond minimum efficient scale. In fact, many public firms are monopolies, when scale economies require only a moderate share of the market. The familiar effects of excess monopoly power then occur (recall Chapter 1).

Natural monopoly conditions may exist, especially in "utility" sectors (recall Chapter 10). Or, the social purpose may require a single system in the market or submarket, which deals equally with all (for example, a public school system, or courts of justice). Such natural monopoly conditions need to be defined carefully and then weighed against the normal costs of monopoly.

Choice and Change. The public firm can be confined to one product or market, but that is often unwise. Healthy enterprises usually need to evolve from older, shrinking activities into newer, growing ones. Such diversification can go too far, but some degree of it usually gives an efficient redeployment

---

[3] See William C. Merrill and Norman Schneider, "Government Firms in Oligopoly Industries," *Quarterly Journal of Economics* 80 (August 1966), 400–12.

of capital. Only if there are clear social reasons should the public firm be confined to just one area.

D3. Operations

Efficiency. The public firm should of course avoid X-inefficiency. The problem can become severe when the social element is large. It eats into the usual commercial tests (see below). Moreover, the social objectives themselves may be complicated and hard to evaluate.

There should be the "correct" amount of subsidy for the social element of operations. Also, that subsidy should be designed so that it does not become a prop or an excuse for slacking off on the commercial part. Often, instead, the public firm comes to count on the subsidy as a way of covering any inefficiency it has.

Pricing. The basic criterion for prices is still long-run marginal cost.[4] Users should pay the true cost of what they consume. Of course this is to be adjusted for *(a)* external effects, and/or *(b)* needy users who are to be deliberately subsidized. But these are only specific departures from the fundamental rule.

The price structure should avoid harmful discrimination, which public firms may be tempted to do, just like private firms. Only "socially valid" discrimination is to occur, in line with the firm's special objectives. "Cross-subsidizing" is to be avoided where possible: it is the covering of losses in some parts of the firm by high profits in other parts. If subsidies of some parts are needed, they should be defined openly and subsidized directly by the public.

(During the 1930s to 1950s, some analysts argued that public firms would always need to run deficits because they were in decreasing-cost industries.[5] In such cases marginal costs are below average costs. Marginal-cost pricing became identified with heavy subsidies to public firms. Instead, *(a)* marginal-cost pricing is valid under any variety of ownership. *(b)* Public firms spread into many sectors other than utilities. And *(c)* even in utilities, efficient pricing will not usually require financial deficits at all (recall Chapter 11). Therefore, efficient pricing in line with marginal cost is a perfectly valid and practical rule for public firms.)

Profit Objectives. Capital has an opportunity cost which is usually in the range of 6 to 10 percent. Public firms need to fit within that range, except where there are strong social reasons for a departure. The costs of

---

[4] The criteria for pricing have been developed extensively in Britain since 1960. See especially the U.K. government's White Paper on *The Nationalized Industries* (London: Her Majesty's Stationery Office, 1978), which codifies the basic rules.

[5] For the flavor of this debate see Abba P. Lerner, *The Economics of Control* (London: Macmillan, 1944), and Nancy Ruggles, "The Welfare Basis of the Marginal Cost Pricing Principle," *Review of Economic Studies,* 17 (1949), 29–46, and "Recent Developments in the Theory of Marginal Cost Pricing," ibid. (1950), 107–26.

straying very far from the 6 to 10 percent range are two. First, there will probably be a misallocation of capital. Low rates of return may induce too much output and capacity; and vice versa for too-high profits. Second, X-efficiency can be hurt. Big financial deficits often demoralize the managers and workers, breeding a sense that normal efficiency is hopeless. Conversely, high profits breed complacency and slack.

Usually, the public firm is set a profit *floor* (such as a rate of return of *at least* 8 percent). This contrasts with the profit *ceilings* placed on private utilities under regulation (such as *no more than* 8 percent). Both targets are in the same range, but they are in different directions. They may have contrasting effects, even though in practice they are not air-tight.

Since the pure public firm issues no voting stock, it poses a special problem for setting the correct profit target. Some of its capital comes from bonds, and the rest—perhaps the majority—may eventually come from reinvested earnings. The interest payment on the loans is the correct payment for that part of the capital. But for the reinvested earnings (which in a private firm are part of stockholders' equity, and which draw dividends), what is the right rate of profit to be earned?

It might be the same as the "cost of equity" in comparable private firms, usually in the range of 10 to 15 percent. This reflects the inherent "business risk" in that industry. Or instead, the government guarantee of the firm might reduce its risk so much that the right profit rate would be a low-risk 6 to 8 percent.

There is no clear guideline for picking the "right" rate within this wide range, from roughly 6 to 15 percent. Such undeterminacy is not a bad thing, for it leaves room for the government to align the profit policy with its social objectives. But it can lead to debate and misunderstandings. A low profit rate will anger any private competitors of the public firm. A high profit rate will seem unfair to the public firm's customers.

So the profit policy for public firms can be intensely debated and will often lack a unique guideline. Your evaluation of any specific public firm should include a careful analysis of its capital and of the firm's "true" risks.

Investment.   The familiar investment criteria apply to public firms too: invest up to the point where marginal expected returns are equal to the cost of capital. Often public enterprises have avoided such a rate-of-return "screen." Yet informal rules or informal judgment can come close to the same results. The "social" factor also needs to be included, and it may not be so easily calculated. Indeed, even the "commercial" screening of investment often involves sheer guesswork underneath the neat, precise figures. Investment choices, therefore, are a complex area where one only expects reasonably balanced evaluations.

Public firms are often accused of investing too much, because they get capital "too cheaply." Sometimes the government provides investment funds directly, at low interest rates. Or the public firm may float bonds, but with a government guarantee which reduces the interest rate it has to pay. Such "cheap" capital might then induce the public firm to invest more than it would if the price were correct (Chapter 18 will consider this). Note that this corresponds to the "rate-base effect," which induces regulated *private* firms to invest too much (recall Chapter 11)! Still, the overinvestment by public firms may be limited. The lower interest costs may scarcely affect the choices. And the government often controls the investment funds directly, thereby perhaps keeping wasteful tendencies in check. Overinvestment might occur, but one needs to appraise it case by case.

D4. Performance

The familiar performance criteria apply, plus whatever specific social objectives are to be met. Of course, the rate of profit is to be considered, but it is only one part of the whole evaluation. Popular debate will usually overstress the profit outcome, while ignoring other elements, such as efficiency, pricing, innovativeness, and social values.

Success can only be appraised in light of the external support and burdens of the firm. If the social tasks are costly but no subsidy is provided, then firm's most nearly "correct" choices may involve cross-subsidies and financial losses. Such outcomes may be socially better than a rigidly commercial profit-making result. High profits may merely reflect monopoly and a lack of social effort. Of course, low profits or deficits may also reflect mistaken policies. So it depends. One must make a rounded judgment both of the firm *and* of the treatment which it gets from the government.

Comparisons with private firms are useful but always hazardous. In most cases one cannot find really "comparable" units. This is especially so when one tries to compare *(a)* across national lines, such as between American private telephone firms and foreign public ones, or *(b)* among sectors, such as between private electricity firms and public railroads in the United States. Also, performance is hard to measure. The quality of service is often a complex, subjective matter, involving 10, 20, or 50 aspects of the service. Prices can be compared, but they too usually have many parts and special influences. Costs too are complicated. And innovation can be interpreted many ways. Above all, the performance within the public firm may be shaped by forces and assistance from outside it. Therefore, the wise student avoids rash, simple-minded comparisons between public and private enterprises.

D5. Policy Constraints

Public firms do not automatically find and fit the public interest. They need the right balance of pressure, guidance, and support. Antitrust policy and/or regulation should usually apply to them, depending on their market positions. In practice, some are under these healthy policy constraints, while others aren't. Generally, creating a public firm is easier than applying the right balance of outside control to it.

E. HISTORICAL ROOTS

The history of public enterprise is checkered. One line is autocratic, from ancient statecraft through to the Organic State of Italy, Soviet-type economies, and other nondemocratic political systems. Another is sentimental British and Continental socialism, which is embodied in national firms in certain utility and sick-industry cases. Still another line is the pragmatic city utility, common throughout history and increasingly widespread in the United States.

Early Origins. From the earliest tribal days, there have been tools and productive units which were held and operated in common. No society has been devoid of them, though few have relied wholly on public units.

In ancient days, many varieties occurred. Athens' theaters were the city's, but many plays were sponsored by wealthy citizens.[6] The mines were state-owned and profitable. Some naval expeditions were sponsored collectively; in others, private sponsorship was central. Public entities were numerous and important; their atrophy coincides with the postclassical decline of Athens. In dynastic Egypt, the state dominated, partly by religious power. Production was organized about the great collective resource—the Nile—and the common system of irrigation. In the code of Hammurabi and the Old Testament alike are references to various communal workings. But the ancient lines are often blurred and not easily translated into the modern forms.

The Roman empire at its peak had a variety of "public enterprises."[7] Armaments and defense arrangements were one part. Another was the provision of public facilities for trade, shipping, religion, water and bathing and—of course—popular games and circuses. Land was the prime element of official control, often to be disposed of or controlled by the current authority. As always, coinage and weapons were primarily under direct control.

The descent into the Dark Ages was sped by the disintegration of the great public works and enterprises—port, aquaducts, courts, markets—which had given order and support to the flow of trade and the fabric of society. Only local seigniorage and almonry remained, together with the growing church ownership of lands, and simple production and basic services. Under feudal hereditary rights or church control, land remained a staple quasi-public factor in the medieval economy.

Later, European cities rose and thrived with a variety of public entities and related forms. As the power and scope of hereditary aristocracy and monarchs then grew, the church receded into a rentier role, owning but not operating. By the 16th Century, kingship had prevailed in much of Europe, and the regional scope of much trade and production was ripe for efforts to induce development.

Mercantilist policy came to stress manufacture and trade, including a range of devices to stimulate new (if primitive) industries. Along with patents,

---

[6] See A. Boeckh, *The Public Economy of Athens* (London: John Murray, 1828).

[7] Edmond Gibbon, *The History of the Decline and Fall of the Roman Empire,* 5 vols., 1776–1788.

a common device was the state-sponsored work.[8] The State also commonly made at least some of its own weapons and monopolized trade in such items as salt and tobacco. At the local level, public works and enterprises in the growing infrastructure—ports, highroads, water and sewage, courts, and so forth—helped to induce the rise of early mining and manufacture.

Modern Patterns. As the Industrial Revolution (1770–1850 in Britain) advanced, the relative scope of private enterprise naturally rose. But a variety of new public enterprises also evolved in Europe and the United States. Finance and industry were primarily private—with attendant consequences both in growth and in social impacts—while much infrastructure was public.[9] The post, the mint, and the arsenal were alike public.

As new utilities evolved during 1830–1900, the European and American choices began to diverge. But in railroads, canals, and then electricity, telephone, and city transit, America went largely private, while Europe went mainly public. This reflected partly the low state of American political management at all levels during about 1870–1900, in which public enterprises were liable to deep abuse. But larger traditions were also at work: collective experience, the free run of private greed, and differing standards of amenity.

The contrast is only partial. The full scope of western European public ownership was only reached as late as 1945–50, and much public enterprise has existed all along in the United States. But there were real differences, especially after the United States veered sharply toward regulation of private utilities from 1900 onward. In social infrastructure too, Europe developed earlier than the U.S.: public schools (after 1870 in Britain), social insurance, health care, public housing, museums, and so forth.

By 1930, public enterprise was extensive. It has continued and spread since then. To summarize:

For more than a century governments have monopolized certain industries, operating them as sources of public revenue. From 10 to 20 countries, in each case, have thus monopolized tobacco, matches, alcoholic beverages, and salt. In Europe, Australia, various states of the U.S., and elsewhere, governments finance themselves in part by conducting public lotteries.

Other long-established fields of public enterprise include transport and communication. Highways and port facilities have been publicly provided

---

[8] C. W. Cole, *Colbert and a Century of French Mercantilism* (New York: Columbia University Press, 1939).

[9] One example, among many, of important state-owned railroads is detailed in Robert J. Parks, *Democracy's Railroads: Public Enterprise in Jacksonian Michigan* (Kennikat, 1972). The courts have not barred public enterprise. The Supreme Court of the United States upheld the establishment of a municipal fuel yard by the city of Portland, Maine, in 1917, socialization of banking, grain storing, milling, and other enterprises by the state of North Dakota in 1920, initiation of a wholesale and retail gasoline business by the city of Lincoln, Nebraska, in 1927, and the right of the federal government to engage in the business of generating, transmitting, and distributing hydroelectric power in 1936. See *Jones* v. *City of Portland,* 245 U.S. 217; *Green* v. *Frazier,* 253 U.S. 233; *Standard Oil Co.* v. *City of Lincoln,* 275 U.S. 504; and *Ashwander* v. *TVA,* 297 U.S. 288.

nearly everywhere. The railroads of Belgium, Italy, Germany, and Switzerland were taken over by governments in the latter years of the 19th Century. All those of France were taken over by 1937. The railroads of more than 50 countries, including all the major powers but Britain and the United States, were nationalized before World War II. Urban transit systems have been public undertakings; the telegraph systems, in most countries, have been developed by the postal authorities. In Germany the telephone service was developed by the state telegraph system. Elsewhere in Europe the telephones were public operations by the turn of the century.

Public utilities, throughout the world, have long been owned by governments. Water supply, in nearly all large cities, is a public responsibility. Gas and electricity were publicly provided in more than three-fourths of the cities of Germany and in more than half of those in Great Britain before 1930. Regional systems for the generation and transmission of electricity were operated by governments in Canada, New Zealand, and South Africa. The Central Electricity Board, in Great Britain, was given a monopoly of transmission lines by a Conservative government in 1926.

Housing has been supplied by governments for longer periods and in greater quantities in Europe than in the United States. In England public housing was first permitted by law in 1851. In Germany and the Netherlands, it dates from 1901. Elsewhere it has its origin in the shortages that followed World War I. In some cases—notably in the city of Vienna—housing was built and operated by the governments themselves. In Great Britain, between the two world wars, a fourth of the new housing, including virtually all of the rental housing, was constructed by local authorities. The public share has since increased further.

Since 1930, four main further increases in public enterprise have occurred. *(a)* Whole economies were shifted, as in China and eastern Europe after 1948, and Yugoslavia developed a hybrid set of "worker-managed" enterprises. *(b)* A nationalization wave in western Europe rose during the 1930s and crested during 1945–52, touching mainly utility sectors. *(c)* Rising urban and "post-industrial" problems in the United States have bred a series of pragmatic new public enterprises (mostly in utilities and social sectors). And *(d)* Many less-developed countries have tried new public enterprise for sovereignty, infant-industry, and other reasons.

In Italy, industries were made public less by design than by default.[10] An Institute for Industrial Reconstruction was set up during the depression of the 1930s to manage the assets of scores of failed banks. This agency, with its subsidiaries, came to hold the shares of many Italian companies. These holdings, moreover, were continued and increased during and after the war. As a result, IRI controls a substantial part of Italian industry, owning nearly all of the stock in shipbuilding, most of that in iron and

---

[10] See Holland, and M. V. Posner and S. J. Woolf, *Italian Public Enterprise* (London: Duckworth, 1967).

steel, and a large part of that in the manufacture of transport equipment, electrical equipment, tractors, and machine tools.

In addition, the government owns the country's five largest banks, the railroads and the airlines, the telephone, telegraph, radio, and television systems, the motion picture studios, the coal mines, and the petroleum industry. Public enterprise, though adopted without reference to any logical pattern, is thus as extensive in Italy as it is in Britain or in France.

The nationalization program of the Labor Party in Great Britain, effected through measures adopted in 1946–50, included finance (the Bank of England), Commonwealth communications (civil aviation, cables, and radio), public utilities (gas and electricity), transport (carriers by rail, by water, and by road), a depressed industry (coal), and another industry that fell into none of these categories (iron and steel).

In France the postwar nationalizations included the Bank of France and the four largest commercial banks, the 34 largest insurance companies, as much of the coal, gas, and electrical industries as still remained in private hands, the Renault automobile works, and a firm making engines for airplanes. In addition, the government extended its participation in mixed companies in a number of different fields: aviation, shipping, motion pictures, broadcasting, news service, chemicals, and petroleum. Public enterprise was to promote economic reconstruction, transfer economic power from the capitalists to the workers, and in some cases, such as the Renault works and the airplane engine company, it was to punish collaborators.

Elsewhere in Western Europe, public enterprise was also expanded in utility areas before 1955. Then patterns stabilized. More recent shifts have been instead toward public banking and social enterprises. Among industries, only sick firms (for example, aircraft, shipbuilding) have drawn much new public ownership.

In the 1970s, inflation brought a form of crisis for public firms in some western European countries. Governments required the public firms to restrain their price increases, even though their costs were rising. This caused large financial losses, especially for public firms in Britain and Italy. In turn the governments were forced to provide large subsidies, while the firms' investment levels were cut back. These pressures threatened cut-backs in jobs, and so the firms' workers became more militant and productivity suffered. Altogether the price restraints were futile and destructive.

The main lessons of history appear to be:

1. Virtually all types and extents of public enterprise have occurred within our cultural mainstreams.

2. The specific set of enterprises is largely a cultural matter, varying widely in line with social traditions and preferences.

3. Many public enterprises are residuary, filling gaps or assuming responsibilities unmet by private interests. This often includes only the burdens and poor risks left after private groups have skimmed the cream off the market. There is strong, continuing pressure on public resources to sponsor or protect private interests via forms of public enterprise.

4. Few public enterprises are created rationally and carefully. Usually public enterprises spring from some kind of crisis, which tips the old balance of interests. A major war almost always increases public enterprise, often permanently. Depressions create corporate orphans requiring support (for example, by the Italian IRI and the American RFC).

5. Resistance to public takeover is mainly a matter of the price offered for the private firm. Almost every private enterprise will agree to becoming publicly owned if the terms are favorable enough. *Ideological* battles against public enterprise are often merely a tactic in the underlying *economic* contest over the price to be paid.

6. The greatest yields arise in firms which take an *active* role in changing structural conditions and their own content. Thin or negative yields are common when the public firm merely tries to mirror commercial behavior.

7. The benefits of any public enterprise will normally tend to become *less progressive* over time. The public firm is, like any other social device, a target for interest groups to use their advantage. Large firms and affluent citizens will normally be able to adjust more fully, to reap the benefits of public enterprises (for example, low-price outputs). Over time this means that the benefits will shift toward less needy groups.

8. The economic purposes and operations of public enterprises are highly varied, from high profits to high subsidies and from narrow financial targets to broad social effects.

9. The operating policies and external support of a public firm—*not* its public ownership per se—largely determine its performance.

10. Comparisons of performance between public and private firms are usually difficult and inconclusive.

F. SUMMARY

Public enterprise is varied and integral in the modern economy. It takes many forms and roles, ranging from commercial-like to social. It ranges also from partial to complete public ownership, and in other dimensions too.

It has deep historical roots, which reflect pragmatic social needs as well as cultural preferences. Abroad, it occurs in utility, finance, and social sectors, with scatterings in industry and trade. There is less of it in U.S. finance, utilities, and industry, but versions of it are more widespread than is usually recognized. It is tending to spread and evolve in new directions.

It has certain economic properties, which can be clinically analyzed. The conventional form is the public corporation in a utility sector, under pressure to mirror commercial behavior. Improvement of content, equity, and other social objectives have been increasingly neglected in practice and the literature. Yet the potential of public enterprise is broader and richer. New public banking and social enterprises are exploring new ways to yield social benefits while easing the drain on public resources.

Social criteria for public enterprises are the usual ones. Antitrust, regulation and other treatments are as suitable for public firms as for private ones. Managers of public firms usually have problems and criteria essentially similar to those in private firms, and bureaucracy has common properties in both. The origins, constraints, and criteria usually define the economic performance which public firms will show. Several low and high yield types of public enterprises can be identified.

These economic properties of public enterprise can be tested and evaluated in practice. We now look at several groups of public firms, in finance and industry, and in utilities and social sectors.

QUESTIONS FOR REVIEW

1. "There are at least three elements to public enterprise: control, subsidy, and ownership." True?
2. "As time passes, most public firms go from passive to active." True?
3. "The classic form of public enterprise is the utility monopoly getting its capital from the Treasury and trying to meet commercial profit targets." True?
4. "Some public enterprises give their outputs or services away." True?
5. "Public enterprise is rare in the United States." True?
6. "Societies avoid all public enterprise except to rescue failed private firms." True?
7. "The resistance to becoming a public firm varies inversely with the price offered to the existing owners." True?
8. "Public firms often have too much monopoly power, just like some private firms." True?
9. "The mingling of commercial and social elements may encourage X-inefficiency." True?
10. "The basic economic criteria for public firms are the same as those for private firms, plus specific social aims." True?
11. "Public firms are specifically designed to run best when incurring large deficits or achieving large profits." True?
12. "Public firms may overinvest, just as private regulated firms are likely to do." True?
13. "A public firm may be a success while incurring a deficit but a failure when achieving profits." True?
14. "Public enterprises have proliferated for at least 3,000 years and they are still spreading." True?
15. "Most public firms were carefully planned at the outset, but they are led astray by too-generous subsidies." True?
16. Are there natural areas of the economy where public firms are appropriate? How do you define these?
17. Identify five public firms which you deal with routinely. Are they performing well? By what criteria?
18. What are the main risks for society in using public enterprises?
19. Why is public enterprise likely to grow in scope and variety in the next century?

chapter 17

Public Enterprise
in Finance and Industry

In these sectors the United States has less public enterprise than is common in other Western economies. Still there is much variety of form and experience. This chapter surveys this variety and gives a number of case studies.

A. FINANCE

There are three basic financial functions to be performed: commercial banking, investment banking, and insurance (Chapter 20 gives more details). Public enterprises have been growing in all three categories. Some of the main cases in Western economies are shown in Table 17–1, while others are presented later in the chapter.

A1. Commercial Banking

Whether they are private or public, commercial banks have three main activities: clearing checks, making loans and holding savings, and counselling and supporting their main business clients (see also Chapter 20 for more details on this). Much of this is done by public banks in Europe: in France and Italy, for example, the four largest banks are public (see Table 17–1).[1] Central banks of course, are publicly owned nearly everywhere in the world, except the United States where the Federal Reserve Board is quasi-private.

The public banks' clearing, lending, and counselling roles are largely routine and passive. The banks usually avoid price competition as carefully as private bankers do, rather than acting aggressively as "pace setters." They

---

[1] Surveys are in R. L. Sayers, ed., *Banking in Western Europe* (London: Macmillan, 1962); D. Alhadeff, *Competition and Controls in Banking: A Study of the Regulation of Bank Competition in Italy, France, and England* (Berkeley: University of California Press, 1968); and W. G. Shepherd and Associates, *Public Enterprise: Economic Analysis of Theory and Practice* (Lexington, Mass.: Lexington Books, 1976), chap. 8.

TABLE 17–1
Selected Public Enterprises in Financial Markets

Country and Entity	Conditions
Belgium	
Post Office checking system (giro)	The main clearing system.
Savings Bank (Caisse Generale d'Epargne et de Retraite)	Nearly half of all deposits, operates like a deposit bank.
Specialized lending banks (Credit Communal for local authorities: Societe Nationale de Credit a l'Industria for industry; Boerenbond for agriculture)	These perform a variety of functions, working closely with their clients.
Canada	
Canadian Development Corporation	New, small and specialized (see Table 17–2).
France	
The four largest deposit banks, including	Assets, 1977 ($ billion):
Banque Nationale de Paris	54
Credit Lyonnais	48
Societe Generale	47
	They follow conventional lines.
Industrial development bank (Institut pour le Developpement Industrial)	Established 1970, to deal with telecommunications, motorways and multinational firms.
Italy	
Istituto per la Ricostruzione Industriale (IRI)	Large holding company with diverse, complex interests (see Table 17–2).
Large banks (primarily held by IRI): including	Acquired 1933; operated along conventional lines Assets, 1976 ($ billion):
Banco Nazionale del Lavoro	28
Banco Commerciale Italiana	24
Banco di Roma	19
Credito Italiano	14
Various insurance units: Istituto Nazionale Assicurazioni Le Assicurazioni d'Italia	Cover a large share of national markets.
Sweden	
Post-Giro (checking system)	Over half of all checking deposits
Post Office Savings Bank	About 20 percent of savings
Sveriges Kreditbank	Created 1950, handles state accounts, third largest bank
Statsforetag (holding company)	Created 1970 with about 30 state firms, the 7th largest corporate group in Sweden.
United States	
Federal Deposit Insurance Corp.	
Overseas Private Investment Corp.	
Export-Import Bank	
Federal National Mortgage Assn.	Partially public
Small Business Administration	Makes many small-size loans to trade and industry
Federal Housing Administration	Insures mortgages
Agricultural banking includes Banks for Cooperatives	There are many such units, in addition to these.

TABLE 17–1 *(continued)*

Country and Entity	Conditions
Federal Land Banks	
Federal Intermediate Credit Banks	
Federal Employees Life Insurance	Over $40 billion coverage
Social Security system	$50 billion yearly in payments
West Germany	
VIAG (United Industrial Companies)	Holdings in electricity, aluminum
VEBA	Oil, chemicals, glass, shipping
Salzgitter Group	Steel, shipbuilding, trucks
IVG	Motor vehicles
Saarbergwerke	Mining, petrochemicals
DIAG	Machine tools
Provincial checking (giro)	
banks, including	Assets, 1977 ($ billion):
Westdeutsche Landesbank	39
Bayerische Landesbank	28
Hessische Landesbank	21
Nord-deutsche Landesbank	14

Source: W. G. Shepherd and Associates, *Public Enterprise: Economic Analysis of Theory and Practice* (Lexington, Mass.: Lexington Books, 1976), pp. 197–98, and *Fortune* magazine, *Directory of the 500 Largest Industrial Corporations Outside the U.S.,* August 28, 1978.

aim for profits and security, much as private bankers do. The public banks rarely require subsidies. But their distinctive public contribution is hard to discover.

A2. Public Investment Banks

These units take a more direct role toward company management, mingling long-term loans and financial support with a degree of supervision and control.[2] Their economic potential is great. They can fit their holdings in private firms to the social need and change these holdings freely. They can focus on small growth companies as well as on established firms. Since they are a roving presence, their threat or promise of action can often have effects beyond their actual holdings. They can support takeovers, in which investment banks operate upon, rather than with, established firms. They can seek capital gains as well as dividend income.

In short, investment banks can directly alter structure and change management behavior, while also drawing earnings. Public benefits arise especially where *(a)* private banks are not adequately supervising or constraining industrial management, and *(b)* where financial markets create or maintain inequitable distributions of wealth.

---

[2] See Stuart Holland, *The State as Entrepreneur* (White Plains, N.Y.: International Arts and Sciences Press, 1973), and the sources he cites; and John Sheahan, "Experience with Public Enterprise in France and Italy," in Shepherd and Associates, *Public Enterprise,* chap. 7.

TABLE 17–2
Selected Investment Banks

Country and Bank	Years	Purpose	Size (assets, at peak)	Nature of Holdings
Italy				
Instituto per la Ricostruzione Industriale (IRI)	1933–present	Rehabilitation, growth, regional balance	~9 billion lire	Wide range of industrial and utility firms
United States				
Reconstruction Finance Corporation (RFC)	1932–1953	Avert failures during the depression	Over $10 billion	Wide range of industrial firms, utilities, banks, farms, etc.
United Kingdom				
Industrial Reorganization Corporation (IRC)	1965–70	Restructure industries	£150 million	Temporary holdings in smaller firms
National Enterprise Board (NEB)	1974–present	Supervise and reorganize industries	£2 billion	British Leyland, aircraft, shipbuilding, others
Canada				
Canadian Development Corporation (CDC)	1971–present	Assert Canadian control	$ 150 million	Selective; natural resources, others

Several public investment banks are summarized in Table 17–2. Each has had a distinctive role and result.

The IRI. The Italian IRI acted as a type of corporate and banking receiver after 1933 for three major banks. Through their stock holdings, IRI was given full or partial control of half the Italian steel industry, two-thirds of telephone service, 80 percent of shipbuilding, one-third of electricity supply, and lesser shares in several other engineering industries.[3] Specialized holding companies for each industry were created within IRI, and the holdings were aligned. After severe wartime damage and postwar reorganization, IRI has stabilized and its holdings have gradually grown.

It has mainly followed commercial forms and criteria, with modifications. Standard management and profit guidelines are adjusted to fit such social criteria as *(a)* regional balance (especially improving southern Italy) and *(b)* easing the social impact of closures. Capital is raised mostly from private sources (60 percent during 1958–69), and company securities are traded in private markets. This applies a degree of external supervision. Investments

---

[3] Holland, *The State as Entrepreneur;* and M. V. Posner and S. J. Woolf, *Italian Public Enterprise* (London: Duckworth, 1967).

mostly undergo a conventional screening for yields. There is both growth and reorganization among the constituent companies.

Some mistakes and distortions have occurred. There was delay in reorganizing engineering and shipbuilding after 1945. Regional development has only been modestly promoted. Vague public-interest notions have induced (or excused) some wastes of investment and current resources.

Yet the whole record is remarkably good. IRI has been flexible and responsive to the main criteria of performance. It has fostered change and growth, while easing certain social costs. Much IRI success derives from a handful of gifted officials. But the main lines of reasonably efficient policy now appear to be firmly set. It may be "a machine without a driver," lacking tight social direction.[4] Still, it has become an important innovation in public enterprise.

The RFC.   In the United States the Reconstruction Finance Corporation was created in 1932 by Herbert Hoover to supply credit to distressed firms during the Depression. It became the country's largest single source of industrial credit. It did not assert management control, though it did act to some degree as a financial adviser to some firms. For 20 years the Reconstruction Finance Corporation was the largest lender in the United States.[5] Its original purpose was to check financial disaster by extending emergency aid to such enterprises as railroads, banks, and insurance companies. But its life was repeatedly extended and its powers enlarged. During the 1930s it was employed to finance relief and recovery programs; during the war, to finance the procurement of strategic materials and the construction of industrial facilities.

Throughout it was conservative and business-oriented, supporting large firms rather than small ones. The Democrats moved in 1948 to widen its powers and interests, but in 1953 the Republicans terminated it. In 20 years the RFC had made 640,000 loans and lent or spent $48,740 million. It had suffered defaults on only 1 percent of its loans, and had paid more than a billion dollars into the Treasury; its remaining assets were valued at $700 million. On the whole, it had been a passive public enterprise.

Two agencies still make business loans. The Export-Import Bank lends to American traders and their foreign customers. The Small Business Administration lends to meet the capital needs of small concerns. Here, as with the loans to farmers, there is an element of subsidy.

Others.   Since 1965 several experiments along IRI lines have been started in other countries. They are small and mostly began without a large prior portfolio of holdings. Britain's Industrial Reorganization Corporation (1966–71) was to use its £150 million to arrange mergers to improve international competitiveness. It marginally encouraged a series of mergers, but it did not exert control. Since 1972 the National Enterprise Board has followed

---

[4] Posner and Woolf, *Italian Public Enterprise,* p. 128.

[5] See the entertaining description of the RFC by its conservative chief officer, Jesse H. Jones, *Fifty Billion Dollars* (New York: Macmillan, 1951).

IRI's model, taking positions in a variety of firms. Though saddled with several large money-losing firms, it is trying to induce better management and operate flexibly.[6] The Canadian Development Corporation, by contrast, was created in 1970 with several holdings and is adding others. It aims to assert Canadian control in key resources and "science-based" industries, following the IRI pattern. Sweden created in 1970 a larger IRI-type firm, the Statsforetag, with 22 holdings from preexisting public firms. In all of these newer cases, the utilities and social enterprises are left outside the holding company, in separate firms supervised by the government.

The public holding company is still experimental, its potential not yet tested. It has not had a free run for control and takeover. Rather, it has been assigned specific functions: reorganizing, asserting sovereignty, regional development, encouraging mergers, and so forth. Still, it has shown that effective control can be exerted with minimal burdens on public resources. High commercial skill can be combined with a concern for social aims. The United States is conspicuous among industrial countries for lacking any such public entity. Various subsidies (especially to weapons and ship producers: see Chapter 24) have not been linked with public controls.

A3. Insurance and Risk-Absorption

Public insurance enterprises divide into two broad groups: those providing services directly to persons, and those insuring other enterprises. The distinction is not an absolute one, for some personal insurance is done by programs which operate by insuring private firms; and vice versa.[7] Table 17–3 shows the main such units that now operate in the United States: there are also many other small ones. They are a remarkable array, ranging from services for the poorest citizens to coverage for powerful corporations. The effects on equity also differ widely. Some have a broadly equalizing effect (although even these usually contain some regressive elements). Others disequalize.

Their scope is wide. The familiar social security and housing insurance units are only the core of a large and diverse group. Their scope has been growing and their operations are increasingly varied. Some are quasi-public. Most cover their direct costs with revenues, on standard insurance principles. A few of them are partially subsidized. Yet even where there are no direct subsidies, there is a cost to the public from absorbing private risks. This cost can be large, though it is hidden.

The performance of these units varies widely. In the narrow sense of

---

[6] NEB's main holdings are British Leyland Ltd. (the auto and bus producer), Rolls-Royce Ltd. (aerospace), ICL Ltd. (the main U.K. computer firm), and Ferranti Ltd. (electronics). It also has interests in nearly a score of small firms in a variety of sectors. The main task has been to get British Leyland profitable, despite a heritage of inefficiency and strikes.

[7] For example, the Federal Deposit Insurance Corp. in the United States insures *personal* accounts, but this indirectly stabilizes the commercial banks' own positions.

TABLE 17–3
Leading U.S. Federal Insurance Entities

	Indicators of Size, 1978–79 ($ billion)	Dimension
Personal Security		
Old Age and Survivors Insurance (Social Security)	104.1	Benefits paid
Federal Disability Insurance Trust Fund	15.1	Benefits paid
Federal Unemployment Insurance	17.4	Benefits paid
Federal Employees Life Insurance	64.8	Insurance in force
Federal Hospital Trust Fund	20.6	Payments
Federal Supplementary Medical Insurance Trust Fund	8.4	Payments
Housing		
Federal National Mortgage Association	64.9	Loans insured
Federal Home Loan Bank Board	25.7	Loans insured
Federal Housing Administration	101.5	Mortgages insured
Veterans Administration	87.4	Mortgages insured
Finance		
Federal Deposit Insurance Corporation	100.0	Expenses
Federal Savings and Loan Insurance Corporation	110.3	Expenses
Securities Investors Protection Corporation		Authorized capital
Export-Import Bank	12.5	Loans insured
Agriculture		
Banks for Cooperatives	7.3	Assets
Federal Intermediate Credit Banks	18.0	Assets
Federal Land Banks	29.3	Assets
Federal Crop Insurance Corporation	2.3	Insurance in force
Other		
Student Loan Insurance Fund	.3	Costs

Source: U.S. Government, *Budget, Fiscal Year 1979* (Washington, D.C.: U.S. Government Printing Office, 1978), Appendix volume.

administrative efficiency, most of them have done well for several decades. There is little evidence of X-inefficiency in their operations. But in allocational efficiency, their effects are less clear. The programs have increased the level of risk taking, perhaps beyond optimal levels. For example, in house buying and farming, the levels induced by mortgage and other guarantees may be above the social optimum. Investor protection by the Securities Investor Protection Corporation since 1971 is likely to be either inefficient (by overinducing small traders to take risks) or inequitable (protecting only larger investors); or possibly both.

The *equity* benefits are doubtful. Social Security is largely *regressive* because of the way it is financed. The federal government insures the risks of a large range of commercial operations in this country and abroad. There may be some benefits for all from abating these risks. But the direct benefits focus tightly among upper economic groups.

On the whole, public insurance enterprises are strongest by narrow performance criteria (for example, X-efficiency) and weakest by the major social criteria. Their administrative costs are usually a much smaller share of insured value than is true for private insurance. Reforms in this sector should mainly be directed not at the inner functioning of these agencies but rather at their size, their incidence, and—in some cases—their very existence. The negative effects—especially on equity—could be altered if the charges for these services were set differently. These are set by the political process, not by the public enterprises themselves. Once again (as with antitrust and regulation), the main defects lie in the setting within which the policy tools operate.

B. INDUSTRY AND SERVICES

The sprinkling of public firms in American industry, trade, and services was shown in Table 16–3. Large public firms in other countries are given in Table 17–4. The U.S. cases lie outside the core industries, especially those with market power. Elsewhere, public firms hold large shares in a number of major industries, and the role of public enterprise is increasing.[8] Elsewhere, too, there is much variety in mixed private-public firms, while nearly all U.S. public firms are wholly public.

Some of these firms are monopolies, while others are under stiff competition. Some are old, some new. Here we start with several broad points and then review a few U.S. and foreign examples.

B1. Basic Points

These points will emerge from the following details.

1. The firms have no systematic economic origins. They are *not* carefully pre-planned and made public.
2. They do not cover the core problem industries (recall Chapter 2) in Western economies—and least of all in the United States.
3. There is no broad tendency to inefficiency among them. Managerial performance varies more by nation and sector than by the type of firm.
4. There is also no clear equity gain from them.
5. Their source of investment funds does seem to influence their performance. A degree of funding from private markets induces the firm to behave more commercially and responsively to the market.
6. The firm's success depends closely on its individual leaders, and outside support, at least as much as on analytical conditions and criteria.

---

[8] For example, in Britain since 1965 the new public units include the British Steel Corporation, British Leyland, British Aerospace, National Shipbuilding, Rolls Royce, British National Oil Co., and National Car Parks, each with a leading or monopoly position in its industry.

TABLE 17–4
Large Public Firms in Industry, Outside the United States

Rank (by Sales) among Large Industrial Firms Outside U.S.	Company	Country	Main Industries	Sales, 1977 ($ million)	Employees 1977 (1,000)
2	National Iranian Oil	Iran	Petroleum	22,315	66
3	British Petroleum	Britain	Petroleum	20,940	81
9	ENI	Italy	Petroleum, gas	10,367	103
11	Renault	France	Motor vehicles	10,018	45
12	Petroleos de Venequala	Venezuela	Petroleum	9,628	25
21	Petrobras	Brazil	Petroleum	8,284	58
25	Elf-Aquitaine	France	Petroleum	7,754	37
34	British Steel	Britain	Iron and Steel	5,304	208
43	British Leyland	Britain	Motor vehicles	4,541	195
51	National Coal Board	Britain	Coal mining	4,207	307
54	DSM	Netherlands	Chemicals	4,131	33
73	Pemex	Mexico	Petroleum	3,394	105
90	VOEST-Alpine	Austria	Iron and steel	2,731	80
91	Salzgitter	Germany	Iron and steel, shipbuilding	2,710	52
100	Italsider	Italy	Iron and steel	2,539	53
103	Charbonnages de France	France	Coal mining, chemicals	2,391	92
106	Indian Oil	India	Petroleum	2,315	18
107	ENPETROL	Spain	Petroleum	2,303	9
121	Statsforetag Group	Sweden	Diversified	2,079	43

Source: *Fortune, Directory of the 500 Largest Industrial Corporations Outside the United States,* August, 1978.

B2. Case Studies in the United States

Uranium Enrichment Plants. The Atomic Energy Commission was created to promote and control the development of nuclear power. A public monopoly, it has relied on incentives and subsidies to private contractors. It has restricted activities to a relatively few established firms (especially General Electric and Westinghouse), and so the new nuclear power equipment industry is matching the tight oligopoly structure of the older electrical equipment industry. Development lagged well behind United Kingdom and other advances. Then in 1963 the seeming success of a test plant at Peach Bottom, New Jersey, triggered a rush of private-utility orders for nuclear plants. Major hitches have plagued this expansion, and the future role of nuclear power is quite uncertain.

After selling off most of its facilities in this area, the Department of Energy now retains only its research facilities plus three plants which enrich uranium.

These plants bridge all three main policy contexts: antitrust, regulation, and public enterprise. They pose the economic choices about public enterprise with remarkable clarity.

The three plants are at Oak Ridge, Tennessee; Portsmouth, Ohio; and Paducah, Kentucky. Using electric power in large quantities (partly from TVA), these plants raise the uranium content of ore from less than 1 percent to about 3 percent, using the "gaseous diffusion" process. The plants cost about $2.6 billion when built in the 1940s. Having armed a vast stockpile of nuclear bombs for military use during the 1950s, the plants now provide uranium for atomic power plants. They are the only source of commercial enrichment services in the United States and, until recently, in the world. These plants illustrate how the desirability of public ownership depends closely upon the operating and pricing policies adopted.

The plants' services have been sold at prices well below their true cost. Only in the 1970s has the price been raised—from $26 per kilogram toward $90 per kilogram enriched—to meet the real costs of operations and capacity. After 1963, as orders for reactors suddenly blossomed, the interest of private groups in taking over these plants also bloomed. Concurrently, the Budget Bureau grew restive at providing over $500 million to build a fourth plant. Why not, it asked, sell them all to private firms?

The decisions about the ownership of these plants—and of additional future plants—has been a vector of all the lessons about public policy choice we have been exploring. The management of the plants and of innovation in the sector has been efficient.

The question of transferring ownership related directly to the pricing policy for enrichment services. A private-market price would have been higher, but how much? If a new monopoly or tight oligopoly under private control were created, would not the price be excessive? Could it be regulated? If a transfer were approved, who should be permitted to own the plants, and by what criteria should the choice be made? The basic question is whether any transfer at all can be designed which is better than the existing ownership *plus* an optimal pricing policy. If a high price were to be charged by the AEC for enrichment services, that would favor keeping the plants in public hands.

Among the potential bidders for the plants are the private operators—Union Carbide and Goodyear—plus other firms already in the nuclear power sector, such as General Electric, Westinghouse, and uranium ore firms. The latter group would gain from vertical integration, but this might also increase their market power, which already is substantial. If the two operating firms acquired the plants, then the entry of other firms would be less probable. Yet these two groups of firms would be likely to offer the highest bids for the plants, precisely because they would reap special advantages!

The contradiction is inherent: those with most to gain in public expense would be willing to offer the most to get it. Therefore a delicate choice would have to be made, in which the highest bids would probably be denied in place of lower ones. That optimal choice might not be possible in practice. Also, some regulation would be necessary if the plants were highly monopolistic; yet Chapters 10–15 have shown the hazards of that treatment. The question also turns on the pricing policy to be followed. On balance, the optimum treatment is to keep the plants public and to set the price at least as high as the true cost. Since 1970 the plants have been run as separate public unit, and the price has been raised toward true cost levels.

This and the current price closely fit the optimum treatment for the time being. In 1976–77, private firms showed some interest in building the fourth plant which rising demand may make necessary. This could fit the optimum, for it would mean that private funds would bear the risk inherent in the marginal plant. That this was induced by existing price umbrella is both natural and acceptable. Yet the private firms demanded costly public guarantees, which were wisely not offered. The issue is likely to recur. The future price and investment strategies will adjust as events mature and centrifuge technology is developed further.

Government Printing Office.   The Government Printing Office is the largest printing plant on earth, doing over $450 million of business each year. By common agreement, its production operation is run efficiently, and it covers costs with revenues. Its content is unusual, including both the Congressional Record and other high-speed operations, and the vast outpouring of government publications, across a wide spectrum. Some of its publications are of limited interest and have little sale or circulation. Unlike private printing houses, the GPO does not select its own titles; instead it passively produces what is required by other agencies.

Still, it somehow manages to surmount its vast publishing tasks with reasonable efficiency. Sales are made by the Superintendant of Documents, which buys documents at cost and resells at a markup of about 50 percent. This operation currently turns a $20 million profit for the Treasury. Despite its core of specialized publishing, the GPO has a variety of offerings which do overlap with private issues. Here the quality is at least comparable to that available elsewhere, and the management of inventory and product strategy is also comparable. In this sense, the GPO is an efficient public enterprise which meets the standard commercial tests of performance. It also is a conduit for social benefits from some of the publications it produces.

The Post Exchange System.   As all ex-GIs know, the PX system markets an immense array of goods at military bases throughout the world. The PX system is in fact one of the largest retail systems operating anywhere in the world. It sells at a discount, it buys in very large volumes, and it covers direct costs with revenues. PX privileges are eagerly sought, for the PX sets low prices.

Its main economic advantage is volume buying, by which it obtains discounts on many of its purchases. But there are also other elements at work. These include the avoidance of certain taxes and the use of military base and warehousing facilities (this is a prickly problem in allocating joint costs; the true costs and subsidy elements are not clear). PX discounts therefore are partly an illusion, resting also on indirect subsidies from the taxpayer though the military budget. Still, the PX system is a notably aggressive and successful marketer. Its purchasing is at least as effective as large private chains, and its inventory and retailing operations are widely considered to be efficient. Its flexibility in setting its composition of shelf items is also high.

In short, the PX system is a skillful, aggressive, and efficient marketing organization, the opposite of the classic image of public-enterprise distributors as slow and rigid. The benefits of its operations do not offer large equity gains. Rather, they are merely a supplement within the whole strategy of military pay and hiring policy. The PX system is a well-performing operation as a public enterprise, though its setting does not permit it to generate large equity gains.

State Lotteries and Liquor Marketing.   State and national lotteries were popular before 1890, but scandals then caused them to be shunned for some 70 years. Since 1963 state-run lotteries have spread, grown, and thrived again. They are designed to earn a profit for the state, on the order of 45 percent of revenue (which is an astronomically high return on the tiny amount of investment). Essentially a retailing operation, the lotteries operate through existing retail outlets. They have proliferated their brands (for example, into Instant and Million-Dollar offerings) and perfected their marketing skills, as in televised drawings. They have been a solid financial success, though the social contribution—of stimulating gambling against unfavorable odds, much of it by low-income people—is doubtful.

The pari-mutuel systems for race track gambling in many states are another set of profitable public enterprises. The Off-Track Betting Corp. in New York City has scores of offices and profits of 20 percent of revenue. Each state's gambling operation has a tidy geographic monopoly. Yet each claims to be in competition with illegal gambling.

Liquor retailing has been done by sixteen states for many decades. These are large businesses, several with scores of stores and more than $500 million in annual sales. They usually have a statewide monopoly of all sales of liquor by the bottle. They have combined to extract lower wholesale prices from national liquor suppliers. Their profits go to the state treasuries. All are profitable, some of them highly so.

Their retail prices are lower than those of private retailers in other states.[9] This reflects their lower wholesale prices, efficiency, and pricing policies, in varying degree. State revenues are much larger through the state stores than from taxes in other states. These public enterprises therefore perform well, on the whole.

B3. Several Case Studies Abroad

Renault.   Before 1945, the Renault company was one of the three largest automobile makers in France, well established for many decades. Its owners chose to collaborate with the Germans in World War II. In retaliation it

---

[9] See the excellent analysis by Julian L. Simon, "The Economic Effects of State Monopoly of Packaged Liquor Retailing," *Journal of Political Economy* 74 (April 1966), 188–94.

was expropriated in 1945, and it has continued under public ownership to the present.[10] It had been one of the leaders in the French market, specializing in medium-range cars. Its competitors included Citröen (which has models both in the luxury class and the utility level) and Peugeot. Renault under public enterprise continued to get its funds primarily from the private market.

Its operations have been efficient and competitive, by wide agreement. During the 1950s its behavior was distinctive in several ways which reflect its public-enterprise status.

The social objective for French industry during 1945–55 was to recover and grow rapidly. Therefore Renault was especially under encouragement to expand. It responded, and by 1955 it was the largest in the industry. This it did both by normal competitive growth and by a deliberate attempt to develop a small economy car for lower-income buyers. This conscious effort partly reflected social criteria, as well as private returns to the firm. More recently, increasing competition from German and Italian cars has confined Renault's ability to modify commercial objectives, and it has evolved towards a standard commercial approach. Though its labor relations are unusually good, this is not a drastic difference and is in line with simple good management.

Renault therefore is one of those public enterprise which have, at least for a period, adapted to distinctive social criteria which were also consistent with commercial guidelines. This fits the general pattern that social criteria are usually followed only temporarily by public enterprises, especially if they are under competitive pressure. In any event, Renault shows that a public firm can perform well in a major, changing, and competitive industry.

The National Coal Board.   In Britain coal mining supported much of the nation's industrial development, but after World War II the demand for coal began a long decline. Shrinkage was badly handled by the private owners during 1920–40, and World War II worsened the problems. Since the 1890s nationalizing the mines had been a central aim of labor unions. In 1945 it was finally done, uniting the 800 significant collieries under the new National Coal Board. The NCB's performance has been widely debated as a test case of all British public enterprises.

That performance has been pretty good.[11] Until 1956 the NCB was forced by the government to maximize coal output at virtually any cost. In the period of coal surplus that followed during 1957–73, the NCB quickly applied a balanced plan to streamline production in bigger, modern mines. From 710,000 workers in 825 mines in 1957, the NCB trimmed down to 263,000 workers at less than 200 mines. This severe cutback was well managed and peaceful, far more so than private firms would have managed to achieve.

---

10 See Sheahan's chapter in Shepherd and Associates, *Public Enterprise;* and John R. Sheahan, *Promotion and Control of Industry in Postwar France* (Cambridge: Harvard University Press, 1963).

11 See W. G. Shepherd, *Economic Performance under Public Ownership* (New Haven: Yale University Press, 1965), and Richard Pryke, *Public Enterprise in Practice* (New York: St. Martin's Press, 1971), and the references cited in these two books.

Social impacts on the coal regions were kept small, while productivity was sharply raised. There was some cross-subsidizing between the best and worst pits. Yet this was not permitted to distort the basic price structure nor the long-term investment plan for reshaping of the industry. Throughout, the NCB urged that coal output not be cut too deeply, for capacity would be needed in the longer run. The energy crisis since 1973 has affirmed that judgment and led to a growth of production once again.

The whole experiment was probably 40 years overdue and was begun under severe adversities. It has been adequately financed, and of course the NCB has made some mistakes. On balance it has been successful in solving very hard social and economic problems.

The British Steel Corporation. Among all public enterprises abroad, you are mostly likely to have heard of the British Steel Corporation. Created in 1967, it manages over half of the British steel industry and is the fourth largest steel firm in the world. Its origins are intensively controversial. The industry stagnated during 1920–40 and was a leading instance in Britain's 1930s cartel craze.[12] Its labor relations were poor, and so nationalizing it was formally proposed as early as 1920. It was the only deeply divisive case in the postwar British nationalizations, and it was only barely voted in in 1951. The new Conservative administration in 1953 put most of it back under private ownership, under a supervisory Iron and Steel Board. It is a marginal candidate for public enterprise, a mingling of industrial power, industrial dislocation, and social burdens; a small dose of public ownership might suffice. Instead, Labour returned about two thirds of the industry to public ownership in 1967, under the single BSC. This basis now appears permanent.

During 1953–67, the Iron and Steel Board's activities had boiled down to setting maximum prices which, in practice, soon became minimum prices. Therefore it operated with the frequent regulatory effect of stabilizing cartel prices. It also presided over industry that was moderately progressive but too fragmented to achieve major economies of scale and slow to close down its obsolete plants. In 1965–67, Labour government officials may have erred on the other side; they probably overstressed a "need" for coordination and rationalizing. This led them to create one wholly public dominant firm, rather than several competitive ones or a mixed firm.

The BSC emerged in 1967 looking remarkably like the U.S. Steel Corporation at *its* creation in 1901. It had about two-thirds of the basic capacity of the industry, but by no means a complete monopoly. It centered in the older and less lucrative basic steels rather than in the newer, specialized, and more profitable submarkets of the industry.[13] Moreover, it includes disparate units,

---

[12] D. L. Burn, *The Economic History of Steelmaking, 1867–1939* (Cambridge: Cambridge University Press, 1940); and *The Economic History of Steelmaking, 1940–1956* (Cambridge: Cambridge University Press, 1957).

[13] BCS's shares ranged from over 90 percent in tinplate, plates, blooms, billets, and slabs, 83 percent in hot rolled strip, and 57 percent in wire rods, down to 27 percent in alloy tubes and pipes, 11 percent in high speed steel, and five percent in

many of them obviously facing closure. Therefore, like U.S. Steel, it seemed fated for a long period of indifferent financial results, arduous structural change, and a steady decline in its market position.

BSC quickly evolved a reasonably sound plan for streamlining the industry, and it aimed to reach commercial profit targets. Its pricing and management policies have both followed standard commercial lines. There is some price discrimination among major users, in order to provide a profit base. Costing of operations is reasonably good. The commercial core of the business has not been undermined by the social problems.

Yet the social problems have delayed the BSC's reorganization plan. To consolidate in efficient plants would require closing some older factories. These are in militant labor regions, such as South Wales, and so the pressure to avoid closures has been intense. Strikes have forced the BSC to retain some important losing operations, at large financial costs. A full solution would require the government to give more direct aid and to induce other firms to locate in those regions. Instead, the BSC has had to carry most of this burden internally. Its losses have been increased by the 1975–78 slump in world steel demand.

Despite the large financial losses, BSC's whole performance has been creditable. A different treatment—with three or four competitive public firms, or with several joint ventures—might provide comparably good results. Simple re-privatizing is not now a viable choice, at least until the main changes have been made. A private steel industry would really provoke labor turbulence and resistance. Moreover, some degree of quasi-regulation or antitrust limits still would be needed, and this would have its own costs. Presently, there are controls and pressures on BSC's use of investment resources as it strives to maintain its market positions. That market position may well dwindle naturally, perhaps over the next decade or two.

Therefore, BSC is a good example of a tightly constrained public corporation facing major economic and social dislocations. Accordingly, its performance has been mixed.

Yugoslav Enterprises.   Midway between East and West, and yet with its own peculiar brand of public enterprise, the Yugoslav economy offers a distinctive set of lessons about the structure and uses of public enterprise. There are some 22,000 such self-managed firms, in all parts of the economy. We will consider the general forms of Yugoslav enterprise, rather than specific branches of it.[14]

On the surface, many Yugoslav firms are much like any private firm, and some of them are highly sophisticated, diversified, advanced-technology industrial enterprises. Yet there are several distinctive features.

---

castings. BSC, *Annual Report and Accounts, 1967–68* (London: Her Majesty's Stationery Office, 1969), pp. 40–41. The new firm also found itself owner of such other stray holdings as a football club, a wire company and £60 million in overseas assets.

[14] See Jaroslav Vanek, *General Theory of Labor-Managed Market Economies* (Ithaca: Cornell University Press, 1966); and Joel B. Dirlam and James Plummer, *An Introduction to the Yugoslav Economy* (Columbus, Ohio: C. E. Merrill, 1973).

1. Enterprises are owned variously by the central and regional governments.
2. Many firms hold great monopoly power in regional or national markets.
3. They are funded in part by banking and fiscal resources, and by retained earnings.
4. Management is both by professional managers and, in part, by workers. Although the degree of worker participation varies from case to case, it is not merely formal.
5. It governs certain key economic choices about wages, finance, and investment. The net surplus of the enterprise for each period is divided among those participating in the firm, particularly the workers. This is like a year-end bonus in some private firms, which the participants will naturally wish to maximize.

There may be a doubly restrictive effect from this method of deciding the worker's share of the profits. Workers will prefer that new revenue be maximized. And they will prefer to have it shared out rather than be reinvested. Accordingly, the enterprise will tend to have smaller capacity and smaller output levels in the future. Since this occurs across a wide range of Yugoslav enterprises, the national levels of growth and investment may be reduced. This poses intriguing parallels to private monopoly in Western economies.

The degree of monopoly held by most Yugoslav enterprises is not small. Most of them operate in regional submarkets or with substantial market power in the national markets. The central authorities take a passive role toward the monopoly power of most firms, and so many Yugoslav markets are correctly seen as a series of tight oligopolies or near-monopolies. This shows once again that public ownership need not reach the underlying economic problems, nor substitute for antitrust, regulation or still other treatments. Still, the Yugoslav economy has performed well. This may show that the grass-roots initiative and control is neatly balanced by key centralized policy levers, especially constraints on investment budgeting and prices.

In any event, Yugoslav public enterprise is quite distinctive. As before the mere fact of public ownership may matter much less than the forms and policies which are used. And even Yugoslav firms only begin to explore the variety which public enterprises may follow.

C. SUMMARY

Despite the great diversity of actual public enterprises in finance and industry, there are large areas of experimentation yet untouched. Even if the scope of public enterprise in these sectors does not grow in the future, there are likely to be more trials of hybrids and new forms. More likely, the scope of public enterprise will continue to rise in these sectors, although only gradually and under close constraints and burdens. In this process of learning by doing, old methods are tried and often discarded in favor of new ones.

Since there is only modest impetus in the U.S. for enlarging the role of public enterprise in industry and trade, new experiments are likely to be *ad hoc* and for special purposes. For these, we have seen that public enterprise offers flexibility and variety and—in some cases—quite good performance. One can also learn from the negative cases. At any rate, there is no scientific general case against public enterprise in finance and industry. As industrial conditions continue evolving, public enterprise offers many ways to treat a variety of problems.

QUESTIONS FOR REVIEW

1. "Public commercial banks have largely fitted private patterns of behavior." True?
2. "By avoiding diversification, the Italian IRI has managed to maintain profitability and efficiency." True?
3. "The RFC in the U.S. displayed largely 'passive' behavior in its lending operations." True?
4. "Public units providing insurance in the United States are confined mainly to agriculture." True?
5. "If the uranium enrichment plants were in private hands, close regulation or antitrust supervision would be needed." True?
6. "State lotteries are excellent ventures, as proven by their high profitability." True?
7. "Renault has met commercial tests well, while also risking some social contributions." True?
8. "The NCB and BSC show that deficit-ridden public firms do not serve social objectives." True?
9. Might a public investment bank be useful in the United States? Where might its operations focus?
10. If you were going to develop public enterprise in U.S. manufacturing industries, what data would you use to guide your selection of actual cases?

chapter 18

Public Enterprise in Utility, Urban, and Social Sectors

By tradition, public enterprise clusters most closely in utility and social sectors (that is, sectors which leave large external effects). This chapter will summarize the broader patterns and then touch on several utility sectors (electricity, railroads, and communications) and then several social sectors (schools, courts, and housing).

A. UTILITY SECTORS

A1. General Features

Utilities are commonly under public ownership elsewhere—but with exceptions (see Table 18–1). These details reflect oddities of historical chance and cultural traditions, rather than tight economic laws. Some economic determinants do exist. Being capital-intensive infrastructure, utilities have often been created publicly as a means of guiding development and stabilizing total investment levels. Public ownership gives more direct control over these "natural monopolies." Further, failing private utilities in Stages 3 and 4 are often salvaged under public ownership (for example, U.K. railroads, eastern U.S. railroads). The United States stands out with its low share of public enterprise, but the share is rising. If the rise continues, it will probably reflect impersonal chance and policy cross-currents, rather than a clear design.

The main lessons can be put briefly:

1. Public enterprise is extensive in utility sectors.
2. It tends to be in the conventional form of the public firm, with full public ownership, risk-absorption by the public, and a natural monopoly.
3. The costs in capital, managerial talent, and policy supervision—and subsidy, in some cases—are often high.
4. The net social benefits—compared to the best alternatives—are usually real but rather small. They arise mainly from unification, from better content and work relations, and from stricter economizing on capital and service quality than in regulated private firms.

5. Profit rates and price structure closely resemble those of private regulated utility firms.
6. These public firms yield little of the deep social gains which some of their creators hoped for. Most are simply large, investment-absorbing public firms doing highly technical, narrow functions.
7. The benefits become more regressively distributed as time passes. The net gain in equity is, at best, modest.

A2. Electricity

U.S. experience is in' *(a)* TVA and other federal power programs, *(b)* New York and Nebraska, and *(c)* the many local electric systems scattered around the country (see Figure 18–1). Tables 18–2 and 18–3 add detail on them.

Abroad, public enterprise arose first at the local level, during 1890–1930. As national systems matured, national grids became publicly owned. Gas and electricity were publicly provided in more than three-fourths of the cities of Germany and in more than half of those in Great Britain before 1930. Regional systems for the generation and transmission of electricity were operated by governments in Canada, New Zealand, and South Africa. The Central Electricity Board, in Great Britain, was given a monopoly of transmission lines by a Conservative government in 1926. The present patterns were firmly set by 1950 (recall Chapter 16). The structure of these units, and their policies on profit rates, price structure, and investment, have stabilized along lines closely akin to those in private U.S. utilities.

In the U.S. thousands of city power systems evolved from the start, followed—mainly in the 1930s—by federal and state agencies. The Tennessee Valley Authority is the leading case of federal power.

TVA. The Tennessee River's large potential for water power was first tapped in World War I at Muscle Shoals. After much sharp controversy, the TVA was created in 1933 to *(a)* control floods, *(b)* assist navigation, *(c)* generate electric power, and *(d)* promote regional growth. TVA was made a semi-autonomous agency, free of Civil Service regulations but financed with Treasury help. It is largely free of regulation or other controls.

It has developed a large power system, based on its dams and on fuel-fired electricity plants (see the map). Where possible it sells its power to public and cooperative nonprofit distributors. After struggles with private utilities, it gained sole rights to generate power in the Tennessee Valley. Though it has built over 20 dams, it now gets over three-fourths of its power from steam generators. The TVA sells 22 percent of its output to other federal agencies, the most important being the Atomic Energy Commission, 23 percent of it to private industries, and 55 percent to distributors, 157 in number, 102 of them municipalities, 53 rural cooperatives and two small private companies.

TABLE 18-1

Public Firms in Utility Sectors, 1976 (Figures indicate share of the sector publicly held, a█ employees. Some figures are estimates.)

	United States	United Kingdom
Energy		
Electricity	Various Federal, state, and local units. 25% of supply; 90,000 employees	Electricity authorities. 100% of sales; 158,000█ employees
Gas	None	British Gas Corporation 100%; 94,000 employe█
Transport		
Railroad	Amtrak, Alaska, Panama, eastern railroads	British Rail 100%; 240,000 employ█
Airline	Military (large operations)	British Airways 100%; 25,000 employe█
Intercity	None	National Bus Corporatior 100%; 58,000 employe█
Transit	Most large cities have complete systems; also many other cities. 70–90%; 163,000 employees	City systems. 100%
Waterways	New York State and certain others	British Waterways Board 100%; 3,000 employees
Ports	Port of New York and certain others	Various city ports; 100%
Communications		
Postal	U.S. Postal Service. 100%; 679,000 employees	Post Office 100%; 165,000 employe█
Telephone, telegraph	Defense system	Post Office 100%; 260,000 employe█
Broadcasting	Public broadcasting network; educational stations, 5%	British Broadcasting Cor█ ration TV 50%; Radio 90%

Sources: European Center for Public Enterprise, *The Evolution of Public Enterprises in the Comm█ Market Countries* (Brussells: May 1973); Stuart Holland, *The State as Entrepreneur,* (White Plains, N.█ International Arts and Sciences Press, 1973); annual *Reports* of public firms; and various other sourc█

Pricing. In fixing its initial rates, the TVA sought to promote expansion in the use of power, assuming demand to be elastic and setting its charges at a level designed to create a market that would enable it to produce at full capacity. In regulating the rates of its distributors, too, it required that they be set at levels designed, not to yield a profit that would finance the other activities of local governments and reduce their taxes, but to increase the use of power and contribute to the valley's economic development. At the time, such low-cost promotional pricing was novel. It fitted the TVA's objectives to help small customers.

This low-rate policy has continued. Residential customers in TVA's area pay about one-half the average U.S. price for electricity (Figure 12–6 above reflects this difference). The policy has been successful. From 1933 to 1972, in the region, the number of farms electrified rose from 3 percent to more than 99 percent. The use of domestic power, per customer per annum, rose

France	Germany	Italy
ench Electricity 00%; 94,000 employees	A large number of separate and combined systems, under varying controls 80%; 88,000 employees	ENEL 100%; 106,000 employees
ench Gas 00%; 26,000 employees	Systems under varying controls 80%; 85,000 employees	Various gas units 100%; 10,000 employees
ench Railways 00%; 254,000 employees	German Railways 100%; 360,000 employees	State Railways 75%; 156,000 employees
r France 00%; 28,000 employees rious public systems	Lufthansa 100%; 23,000 employees	Alitalia 100%; 14,000 employees Various systems
ris and other cities 00%; 80,000 employees	Various city systems 100%; 110,000 employees	Various city systems 100%; 115,000 employees
rious maritime units 00%; 7,000 employees rious ports 00%; 3,000 employees	Various waterway units 100% Bremen and others 100%,	Various maritime units 100%; 11,000 employees Venice, Naples, Genoa and others, 100%; 8,000 employees
stal and Telegraph 00%	German Post Office 100%; 430,000 employees	Postal and Telegraph 100%; 142,000 employees State Telephone System 100%; 60,000 employees
diodiffusion-Television Francaise. 100%	A Federal System and a set of provincial systems	Radiotelevisione Italiana 100%; 11,000 employees

from an average of 600 kilowatt-hours to 14,040, a figure more than twice as high as that for the nation as a whole. The total consumption of power rose from 1.5 billion kilowatt-hours to 91 billion.

Subsidies are small. It is often charged that the customers of TVA are subsidized, because *(a)* the authority does not pay taxes, *(b)* it does not pay a proper share of the joint cost of the multipurpose facilities or charge to power a proper share of joint administrative costs, and *(c)* it does not pay the market rate of interest on capital provided by the government. Each of these points requires examination.

The TVA itself pays to state and local governments, in lieu of taxes, 5 percent of the revenue it collects from customers other than the federal government. Its distributors make such payments as the laws of their states require. In 1972 these payments, taken together, amounted to more then $53 million, some 8.3 percent of total revenue. The taxes paid by neighboring private

FIGURE 18–1

Non-federal Publicly Owned Systems (municipal, state, county, and power districts)

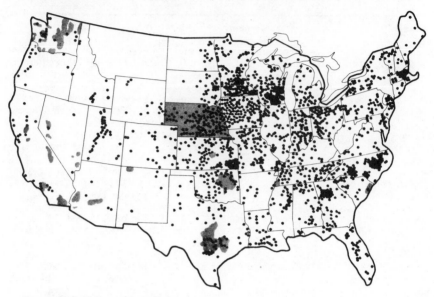

Source: Federal Power Commission.

TABLE 18–2

Selected Data on Public Power Systems in the United States, 1975

| | Assets (net utility plant) ($ million) | Kwh Sold: (billion kw hours) | | Residence Revenues as a Percent of Total |
		To Final Users	For Resale	
Tennessee Valley Authority	5,499	42	64	0%
New York Power Authority	2,184	5	20	0
Los Angeles	1,996	22	3	35
Nebraska (total)	986	6	1	41
All public systems	(274)	225	212	39
All federal systems	(11.0)	71	145	0.01
All municipal systems	17.4	183	67	43

(Estimate)

Source: Federal Power Commission, *Statistics of Publicly Owned Electric Utilities in the U.S.* (Washington, D.C.: U.S. Government Printing Office, 1977).

TABLE 18–3
Rates of Return on Net Utility Plant in Selected Public Power Systems, 1975

	Assets ($ million)	Net Income as a Percent of Assets
Ames, Iowa	16	1
Eugene, Oregon	208	1
Jacksonville, Florida	452	2
Knoxville, Tennessee	101	2
Lansing, Michigan	148	3
Los Angeles, California	1,996	5
Omaha, Nebraska	661	5
Pasadena, California	61	7
Sacramento, California	807	4
Salt River, Arizona	879	1
San Antonio, Texas	527	6
Seattle, Washington	455	0
South Carolina Public Service	460	1

Source: Federal Power Commission, *Statistics of Publicly Owned Electric Utilities in the U.S.* (Washington D.C.: U.S. Government Printing Office, 1977).

FIGURE 18–2
Extent and Complexity of the TVA System

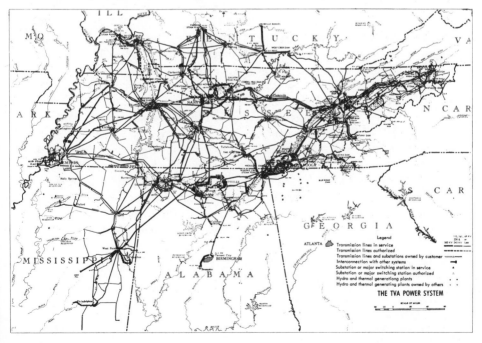

utilities ranged from 4 to 10 percent of revenue. The TVA does not pay the federal tax on corporate net income, which is a tax on private profit rather than a cost. But it is repaying the government's investment in its plant, a charge the private companies are not required to meet.

TVA rates have covered the costs of building and operating the facilities that are used exclusively in producing power. This includes the steam plants that turn out three fourths of the power, the hydroelectric plants, and the transmission lines. The only question that can be raised is whether the Authority is paying its proper share of the cost of the multipurpose dams and charging enough of the cost of general administration to power. In fact it allots 27 percent of the cost of the dams to navigation, 31 percent to flood control, and 42 percent to power. Correspondingly, it charges 30 percent of the cost of general administration to navigation, 30 percent to flood control, and 40 percent to power. Whether this is the proper allocation is a matter of opinion. Since this issue is now relevant only to a minor part of the cost of a minor part of the supply of TVA power, it has lost whatever importance it may once have had.

As for **the cost of capital,** there is probably no major difference. TVA gets rather lower interest rates, but private utilities get accelerated amortization which is at least as valuable. Moreover, as noted, the TVA has had to start paying off its $1 billion in debt, something that no private firm would have to do.

Long-time friends of TVA complain that its character has changed, going from active to passive. It is now more interested in the production of electricity, they say, than in the other purposes for which it was originally created. There is some basis for this criticism. But it should be noted that many of the social activities initiated by the Authority have been taken over by the region's state and local governments. The environment in which the agency now operates differs markedly from the one into which it was born in 1933.[1] Over half of TVA power now goes ultimately to private industry. Its rural development aims have been met, and it is now much like any other large power system. Its rate structure has had little peak-load pricing features.[2]

In 1977–78, new board members began shifting TVA sharply toward clearer social concerns, such as ecology, pricing structure, and social impacts. If the change lasts, TVA would return to the original type of priorities.

City Power Systems. These systems have been under pressure, for power technology has shifted sharply to curtail their discretion. Most systems are now small dependent clients of large private suppliers, merely managing local distribution. In certain cases—especially in New England and the Eastern

---

[1] See G. R. Clapp, *The TVA: An Approach to the Development of a Region* (Chicago: University of Chicago Press, 1955); J. R. Moore, ed., *The Economic Impact of TVA* (Knoxville: University of Tennessee Press, 1967); and Richard Hellman, *Government Competition in the Electric Utility Industry: A Theoretical and Empirical Study* (New York: Praeger Publishers, 1972).

[2] See W. G. Shepherd, "Marginal Cost Pricing in American Utilities," *Southern Economic Journal* 23 (July 1966), 58–70.

seaboard—large private joint projects for generating plants have tried to exclude them. This would cause their prices to be higher, and so the private systems could buy them out at lower prices. Public systems have therefore been embedded increasingly in hostile and powerful arrangements. The *Otter Tail* and other court decisions have backed up the public systems' access to cheap power on fair terms. But the trends remain.

Meanwhile, the city systems are diverse, a few skimming off high profits for the city treasury, most supplying strictly at cost, as Table 18–3 shows. There is no hard evidence about their efficiency compared to private systems.[3] The continuing inducements to sell off to private utilities applies a steady pressure toward efficiency on many city systems. In many cities the public power system is active, efficient, and innovative.

Public Power Systems Abroad.   These are also diverse but show generally good performance.[4] In France, Sweden, and Britain, marginal-cost pricing is advanced and sophisticated both in bulk and retail supply. This reflects both the greater scarcity of capital and the presence of several gifted economic analysts in the systems (especially Marcel Boiteaux in France and Ralph Turvey during 1963–67 in Britain). Also, the objective cost-based price structure is a valuable device to deflect political pressures for special rate cuts to backward regions, powerful customers, and other claimants.

Coordination is effective, and there appears to be no strong tendency toward excess capital-intensity (compare Chapters 11 and 12). Pooling of capacity is thorough. The forecasting of demand has been no better than average, and they too have exaggerated the gains which nuclear power might offer.

The siting and safety of nuclear plants have not posed a crisis such as the United States has had. This reflects the closer supervision which the systems get. Amenity, too—the routing of transmission lines, and pollution of air and streams—has been better handled than by the American commissions, preoccupied as they are with rate of return, rate base, and price questions. Therefore, in those social-economic issues which have recently plagued American utilities, public systems abroad have routinely shown superior performance.

---

[3] Interesting analysis is given by Louis DeAlessi, "An Economic Analysis of Government Ownership and Regulation: Theory and the Evidence from the Electric Power Industry," *Public Choice* 19 (Fall 1974), 1–42; and Sam Peltzman, "Pricing in Public and Private Enterprises: Electric Utilities in the United States," *Journal of Law and Economics* 14 (April 1971), 109–147.

[4] See Richard Pryke, *Public Enterprise in Practice* (New York: St. Martin's Press, 1971); W. G. Shepherd, *Economic Performance Under Public Ownership* (New Haven: Yale University Press, 1975); James R. Nelson, ed., *Marginal Cost Pricing in Practice* (Englewood Cliffs, N.J.: Prentice-Hall, 1964); and John Sheahan's chapter 7 in W. G. Shepherd and Associates, *Public Enterprise: Economic Analysis of Theory and Practice* (Lexington, Mass.: Lexington Books, 1976).

Both Britain and France apply marginal-cost pricing in bulk and retail markets: in France, it is the green tariff, in Britain, the White Meter tariff. See Nelson, *Marginal Cost Pricing;* Ralph Turvey, *Optimal Pricing and Investment in Electricity Supply* (London: Allen & Unwin, 1968); and *Annual Reports and Accounts* of the U.K. Electricity Council.

A3. Transport

Railroads. Railroad systems abroad are nearly uniform in two surface respects: they are mostly public, and they run large financial losses. But the more basic economic lessons are more diverse.

First, most of the systems are national monopolies, which combine commuter, intercity passenger, and a variety of freight operations. Most of these countries suffer serious problems of urban congestion and amenity which road transport burdens aggravate. Also, rail passenger service is optimal for runs below 200 miles. Therefore, the economic case for a railroad system as an important mode in these countries is strong.

The common pattern of these systems is

1. An overhang during 1945–55 of excess capacity, especially in nontrunk parts, which has required trimming of trackage, rolling stock, and work force.
2. A concurrent effort to "modernize" via high-speed trains, containerization, and other engineering devices. This effort often approaches messianic levels, both as an engineering challenge and as a diversion from more pedestrian financial problems.

The systems commonly have had very low short-run marginal costs, much like certain eastern U.S. railroads. Therefore, even if operations were conducted with internal efficiency—as, on the whole, they are—the correct pricing basis is to set rates at levels below average costs and thus incur a deficit.

Moreover, pruning the system involves closures, some of which impose serious social costs. The socially optimum rate of shrinkage is therefore below what profits alone would dictate. In fact, closures are required to pass governmental screenings, which are usually slow. Meanwhile, the railroads themselves have no choice but to maintain loss-making operations which enlarge their deficits.

Finally, there is the basic issue of road-bed subsidy. The large carriers in other modes tend to be subsidized via road, airport, and other programs, while railroads must finance their own tracks (recall Chapter 14). The true comparative costs are usually unclear, but the railroads usually carry some degree of net burden (though they are often permitted to write off part of their capital, to ease their interest payments).

These factors together explain on economic grounds at least part—and perhaps all or more—of the losses run by most public railroad systems, especially on passenger services. The deficits are endemic partly because they *do* fit optimal criteria. This does not excuse the occasional inefficiency in pricing and/or investment.[5] But on the whole, performance compares well with U.S. railroads during recent decades.

---

[5] The 1956 British Railways modernization plan, for example, contained certain economically irrational parts which can best be explained by the lingering attachment to the 19th century "iron horse" image of railroads. See Select Committee on the Nationalised Industries, *Report on British Railways*, H. of C. 254 (London: H. M. S. O., 1960) for a searching appraisal; see also Pryke, *Public Enterprise*

Meanwhile, the efficiency and innovativeness of these systems has not been deficient (with exceptions). There may even have been too rapid a shift to new traction, containerizing, and similar engineering improvements (which some U.S. railroads, under regulation, have tended to slight). But the upshot has probably been reasonably close to the long-run optimal pattern of innovation, in many cases.

The rate structure of these public systems tends to avoid clear inefficiencies. The degree of discrimination is probably less than in private systems. On the whole, public systems have developed price systems more rational than those common in regulated private railroads.

Airlines. Public airlines are nearly universal elsewhere. These entities, many of them quite large indeed, are also stand-by military carriers for their governments. But they follow commercial policies and join fully in the international price cartel. This involves extensive price discrimination and pricing against marginal-cost criteria.

All face international competition (though not in fares) but hold important monopoly positions on their home routes. They have adhered to the international airline rate cartel, even in the face of recent pressure toward competitive pricing.[6] Britain since 1971 has deliberately added a degree of competition, but this is exceptional.[7] The lines appear to be comparable in total efficiency (X-efficiency, pricing, and innovation in planes and ticketing systems) to private airlines.

A4. Communications

We will consider—briefly—postal, telephone, and broadcasting activities.

Postal Service. The basic postal system is everywhere a public enterprise. It is the most familiar and criticized of all public enterprises. The postal service, wrote Adam Smith in 1776, "is perhaps the only mercantile project which has been successfully managed by, I believe, every sort of government. The capital to be advanced is not very considerable. There is no mystery in the business. The returns are not only certain, but immediate."[8] Under the Constitution, a postal system, including 74 post offices, was established by the first Congress in 1789. The system was originally set up as a separate agency under the President. In 1829 the Postmaster General was admitted to the Cabinet. And in 1872 the Post Office was made a department of the

---

[6] See M. Straszheim, *The International Airline Industry* (Washington, D.C.: Brookings Institution, 1969) for a thorough analysis.

[7] See the "Edwards Report," *British Air Transport in the Seventies,* Committee of Inquiry into Civil Air Transport, Cmnd. 4018 (London: H. M. S. O., 1969).

[8] *The Wealth of Nations,* book 5, chap. 2, part 1. Smith was still correct in the 1970s. Postal costs are 85 percent labor. By contrast, labor costs are only 20 percent in electricity, 18 percent in gas, 54 percent in railroads, 43 percent in airlines, and 47 percent in telephones.

On the monopoly character of the system, see George L. Priest, "History of the Postal Monopoly in the United States," *Journal of Law Economics* 18 (April 1975), 33–80.

Costumes and architecture change, but the basic postal operation of sorting is much the same as in the 1840s at the British main Post Office in London, seen at the time when Rowland Hill was establishing the "penny post" uniform letter charge. This principle continues even now.

government. In 1971 it was revised into a semi-autonomous public corporation, under the Postal Rate Commission. In the early days of the republic, the postal service had a vital function to fulfill. In the absence of modern means of communication, it afforded the only tie that bound the country together, uniting the wilderness with the capital, scattered settlements with centers of trade and finance. It contributed to a sense of national identity, to economic and political unity. It was a basic instrument of public policy.

Today the Post Office is one of many media of communication. It is big business with 30,000 offices, over 670,000 employees, and a budget of $16 billion a year. It delivers mail each weekday to nearly every business and household in the land, handling 90 billion pieces each year. Only 14 percent of this is personal correspondence. A tenth is newspapers or magazines. More than a fourth is advertising matter. Over half involves business transactions: orders, invoices, bills, checks, and the like. The volume of such materials is twice as great today as it was 20 years ago. It is likely to keep growing.

In the United States and Britain, it has recently been converted from department status into a public corporation. The common pattern abroad is for postal services to be combined with telecommunications (the French PPT, the British Post Office, and so forth). This corresponds to combining the Bell system and other telephone independents with the Postal Service and telegraph service—*but* also splitting it into five small regional systems. Since these foreign systems are all less than one-fifth as large as the U.S. system, the total monopoly effect is rather less than it might seem. Also, the services are usually operated, accounted, and evaluated separately.

In the United States, as elsewhere, the postal service is among the country's largest employers. In fact, the postman (or woman) on the daily round is part of a network which constitutes the core of natural-monopoly conditions in this industry. Repeat: the local delivery and pick-up system is the one clear element of natural monopoly. Of course, there are the sorting and bulk shipping parts of postal service. But these are more separable and less marked by decreasing costs.[9]

Deficits. Postal services commonly run a financial deficit. This stems from a variety of political and social factors, possibly related to external benefits which postal services may provide. An informed and well-communicating populace is an important precondition for healthy democracy. First-rate postal service may contribute to this, and therefore its value may ultimately be greater than the individual users may be willing to pay. That is the rationale behind the subsidies which have been extended traditionally to such postal users as magazines, newspapers, and senders of educational materials.

Yet postal services are overwhelmingly *business* services: 70 percent of all mail is business mail (bills, ads, reports, and so forth). The system routinely subsidizes the circulation of advertising and other strictly commercial items. Therefore, one needs to learn the marginal costs of the different kinds of service, and whether social effects justify subsidies to cover these marginal costs.

Cost Structure. The structure of costs arises from the special rhythm of postal activities, primarily in the sorting facilities and the delivery networks.

In every post office there is a morning and evening peak of activity; these fit the standard analysis of peak-load costs.[10] These peaks are similar to those of other utility services. They cause sharp variations in real marginal costs; peak costs are sharply above off-peak costs. The common schedule of postal rates reflects this, though perhaps not precisely. First-class mail is presumably handled at the peak and is charged a high price—perhaps in line with its true marginal costs—while other types of mail may be set aside for handling during the low-cost, off-peak periods. If postal operations were

---

[9] President's Commission on Postal Organization, *Towards Postal Excellence* (Washington, D.C.: U.S. Government Printing Office, 1968); and Morton Baratz, *The Economics of the Postal Service* (Washington, D.C.: Public Affairs Press, 1955).

[10] Post offices are merely arenas within which mail is handled. In the early morning hours, the mail comes in from other cities. There follows a rush of handlings: emptying of bags, sorting of mail, and packaging for the deliverers to take out in the early morning. Next there follows a slack period during the middle of the day. Then comes the late afternoon rush, during which the mail sent by people in the city piles up and is sorted and packaged for sending outward. These rush periods commonly strain the capacity of the post office and its employees.

in fact closely costed, the proper peak level and off-peak cost (that is, basically, first-versus second- and third-class rates) could be ascertained within reasonable boundaries. But this is not regularly done, and the cost allocations are debatable.

Price Structure. Instead, the tradition of uniform geographic postal rates still governs postal pricing. Designed under Rowland Hill in the early 19th century to foster circulation of messages within the British Isles, the standard "penny post" rate has been extended into the present on the philosophy that all mail should share in covering the costs of the system. Therefore, most postal rates are averaged among users rather than fitted directly to the real costs involved. The structure of rates among the classes of mail is shown in Table 18–4.

Do first-, second-, and third-class postal rates fit the true costs involved? In all probability they tend to overcharge first-class mail and to undercharge the lower groups. These prices reflect both actual costs and the political power of these groups which have been able to gain preferential postal rates.

TABLE 18–4
Rates and Revenues by Postal Classes

	Rates ($ per piece)		Revenues Mix, by Class of Mail, Fiscal 1976	
	Fiscal Year 1971	Fiscal Year 1976	Revenue ($ million)	Percent of Total Revenue (%)
First-class mail				
letter	6.00	13.00	$ 7,228	64.9%
Second-class mail			267	2.4
News magazine	1.98	9.35		
General interest magazine	2.23	10.20		
Rural newspaper	0.66	4.73		
Veterans' magazine (nonprofit) ..	0.78	6.77		
Third-class mail			1,522	13.7
Bulk-rate advertisement	4.00	7.70		
Advertising catalog	8.00	15.00		
Fund-raising letter (nonprofit) ...	1.60	3.70		
Controlled circulation				
Trade journal	5.60	9.60		
Special-rate fourth-class mail			680	6.1
Book parcel	30.00	82.00		
Encyclopedia set	204.00	332.00		
Cassette parcel................	12.00	40.00		
Fourth-class mail				
Five-pound parcel	90.00	119.00		
Government...................			577	5.2
International			447	4.0
Special services			378	3.4
Other			41	0.4
Total...................			$11,140	100.0%

Source: *Report of the Commission on Postal Service, April 1977* (Washington, D.C.: U.S. Postal Service, 1977), pp. 671 and 683.

The "true" cost patterns are endlessly debated. Good postal price structures could be decisive to the financial health of the postal systems, both in the United States and abroad. Most of the postal deficits arise from handling of high-weight, low-class mail. If there are external benefits from advertisements, they must be very large to justify the subsidy which has been given in the past.

Management. Postal management has faced severe problems under the old departmental basis. Critical decisions were limited from outside. This external control also bred excessive internal caution, and decisions were over-centralized in a rigid process. Key personnel had to be selected on political grounds. Worker morale was low.

These problems reached crisis proportions in late 1966, when the Chicago post office—the largest in the world—was virtually paralyzed for three weeks. Several factors caused the breakdown: a rise in bulk mailings, equipment failures, labor problems, and the like. But the problems were recurring and cumulating elsewhere too, under the old rules.

To free the postal service from the paralysis and rising deficits, a special commission in 1968 recommended turning it into an independent postal corporation. It would have normal personnel policies, thorough cost accounting, and the ability to set postal rates (under regulatory—not Congressional—constraint). It would draw capital by selling bonds in private markets. This was done in 1971, paralleling a similar change in Britain in 1969. The new Postal Service is supposed to be self-supporting within 15 years, as management and pricing are reformed.

Yet the deficits have continued, despite sharp cuts in staff. The main cause is the highly labor-intensive nature of postal service, as wage levels have risen. Management since 1971 is agreed to have been efficient and aggressive, but the outside pressures have been too strong.

The new Postal Rate Commission, on its part, has had little effect, except for delaying increases in postal rates. The members are inexpert, and staff efforts to raise key economic issues have been brushed aside. The Commission has done little more than mediate on secondary issues.

Competition. To some extent, the postal system is under stress from growing competition with telecommunications and package delivery systems.

The handling of parcels is partly a joint product of the main sorting and shipping operations. It can be coordinated with off-peak operations at low cost. But even so it does not really share in the core natural monopoly of the system—the final delivery and pick-up network. Therefore it is arguably eligible for an open competitive approach. In fact, United Parcel Service Co. has already built up a private near-monopoly of its own in small, high-value, high-speed parcels. Its high profitability fully reflects its market position. Various air delivery firms also compete for parts of this market. In this and other areas, the post office "monopoly" is actually under close constraints.

A fair evaluation would be that U.S. postal managers are slowly emerging from a politicized managerial situation, and that many of their more lucrative markets are being skimmed. Beset by inherited deficits and traditions, they are not doing poorly. The moves toward rational pricing—both in the United States and abroad—have to overcome strong pressures.

Point-to-Point Telecommunications. This is the provision of telephone service plus the growing new role of data transmission. Abroad, this is commonly combined with postal services. There the degree of monopoly is great (compare Chapter 16). Yet the supply of telephonic equipment is nowhere fully integrated with the operating system, as it is in the Bell and GT&E systems.

The extent of penetration of residential and business markets is usually lower abroad than in the United States, because the standards of income and consumption are lower. Moreover, the quality of service is also usually lower than in the United States, as indeed are the standards of other consumption items. In many European countries and elsewhere, the home telephone is still largely an upper-class device. Yet normative lessons from this are slippery.

One can make useful policy comparisons between Britain and the United States. The U.K. system aims broadly at a rate of profit comparable to that in the U.S. under regulation. The price structures have differed but are converging slowly. British pricing has long been more closely cost-based.[11] Business rentals are only slightly above residential rentals. The metering of local telephone usage is far more thorough in Britain than in the U.S. Usage is charged by units of time—often with peak–off-peak differentials—so that prices quite closely fit the costs of service. Moreover, in long distance usage the degree of fineness in pricing has been greater than the United States. As U.S. pricing is improved, these differences are receding. But British pricing has set the norm for efficient pricing. A prime reason is that capital has been scarcer and rate-base effects have been absent under public ownership.

On the whole, public telephone systems in western Europe have not been inferior in internal efficiency or innovative ability. Though not as promotional in marketing, they have been experimental and quick to try new technology, leading the U.S. systems in many innovations.[12] Their local-service price systems have been more refined and efficient than those in the United States, although this gap is closing under the new financial and urban pressures on the Bell System. Service quality is marginally lower abroad, but the normative lessons from that are not clear.

Broadcasting. The main comparison is between the state-owned television systems which are common elsewhere and the private broadcasting networks in the United States. The issues are complex, turning in large part on program

[11] See W. G. Shepherd, "Residence Expansion in the British Telephone System," *Journal of Industrial Economics* 16 (July 1966), 263–74.

[12] During 1920–55 they tended more to lead than lag in new technology and service offerings. See John Sheahan, "Integration and Exclusion in the Telephone Equipment Industry," *Quarterly Journal of Economics* 70 (May 1956), 249–69.

content and local service, rather than on narrow economic criteria. Even so, certain comparisons can be ventured.

There have been three main distinctive features in most other systems: (a) public ownership, (b) monopoly, often in a single entity, and (c) financing by a television tax plus a degree of direct subsidy, rather than advertising. These differences have helped cause the clear differences between United States and other television fare. Abroad, broadcasting hours are much shorter. There are only one to three channels to choose among. Program content is of higher quality: less light material and violence, more culture and local-interest programming. Instead of the oligopoly convergence on mass appeal (recall Chapter 13), the offerings cover the spectrum of special interests more fully. Advertising is either absent or, where it is presented, it is spaced and presented less obtrusively. News coverage, however, is usually less complete and independent than U.S. news broadcasting has become since 1960.

These basic differences of ownership, form, and finance have receded since 1955 (see Table 18–5). Britain and Canada have private broadcasting systems. Some state networks carry a small amount of advertising. Public entities now usually offer two or three channels, with differences in emphasis and level. The United States now has a small public broadcasting system. Yet where the public system is larger and well financed, the basic contrasts in programming remain.

The economic lessons are predictable. In both systems, the viewer—once the set, antenna, and any TV taxes are paid—receives programs at virtually zero prices, which is roughly in line with the marginal cost of the broadcaster. When separate systems compete, they are mutually induced toward mass programming, whether they are public or private. Thus when new commercial TV in Britain in the 1950s forced BBC toward lower program quality, this reflected more than just the invasion of U.S.-style "wasteland" fare. It also forced BBC to compete for maximum viewership, rather than focus on "elevating" taste and culture. Differences do remain: BBC and other public networks deliberately offer better and more varied content, while commercial TV inevitably maximizes its audience exposure to advertising messages.

On the other side, U.S. private networks benefit from having a minor public network to cater to specialized interests. This leaves them politically freer to program for maximum private returns. Private networking and large-city franchises are highly profitable abroad, just as they are in the United States. But stricter franchise-renewal criteria have induced them to maintain program content above the U.S. levels.

The steady revenues for public systems permit them to treat programming in larger and longer perspective. This has fostered a series of major high-quality serials (The Forsyte Saga, Shakespearean plays, etc.) which U.S. networks find profitable to show but do not finance or produce.

The public and mixed conditions abroad do unquestionably yield more varied and especially responsive program content (except, in many cases, for news coverage). The optimal situation appears to include a strong public

TABLE 18–5
Television Broadcasting in Selected Countries

	Type	Regional Units	Regulated	Advertising Revenues, Share of Support
Canada				
Canadian Broadcasting Corp.	Public	Yes	Indirectly	25%
Canadian Television	Private	Yes	Yes	100%
UK				
British Broadcasting Corp.				
(2 channels)...............	Public	Yes	No	0
Independent Television	Private	Yes	Franchise renewals hinge on program "performance"	100%
Sweden				
Swedish Broadcasting Corp.	Public	Yes	Yes	Part
France				
Radiodiffusion-Television Francaise (3 channels)	Public	Yes	Indirectly	Small
Italy				
Radiotelevisione Italiana (2 channels)...............	Public	No	Indirectly	Part
Germany				
Federal Network	Public	No	Indirectly	0
Nine regional systems (which also pool programs)	Public	Yes	Indirectly	Part
Australia				
Australian Broadcasting Commission	Public	Yes	Indirectly	0
Private stations	Private	Yes	Lightly	100%
Japan				
Noncommercial, nongovernment system (based on subscription fees)	Semi-public	No	Indirectly	0
Commercial	Private	Yes	Indirectly	100%

Sources: World Television *Fact Book*, periodical; and Walter B. Emery, *National and International Systems of Broadcasting* (East Lansing: Michigan State University Press, 1969).

system with two or more channels, genuine competition with one or more private networks, and reasonably strict criteria for franchise renewal.

A5. Summary

Evidently, public enterprise in utility sectors is firmly fixed abroad and has established a performance record that is, in some respects, superior to that of regulated private utilities. Yet the cost of these units (especially in electricity, railroads, and telephones) is not small—in public capital, risk-absorption, managerial talent, and subsidies in some cases. They are usually small firms by comparison with the national counterparts in the entire U.S. Moreover, there are other national differences in culture and public traditions which may affect their performance. And finally, their performance is often affected by a degree of competition. Therefore, public enterprise is often less important than its setting, criteria, and constraints. Public firms in utility sectors often perform better when they *depart* from the conventional model, rather than fit it closely.

B. URBAN AND SOCIAL SECTORS

B1. General Lessons

Enterprises in these sectors have six common features:

1. They are diverse and integral in modern life.

2. As city size and density increase, the role of public enterprise in urban services also increases. This is because natural monopoly and social elements deepen. Their role has therefore grown naturally, as urban size and density have risen.

3. These units offer economic and social yields which may rival or exceed those which antitrust and regulation offer in the standard industrial and utility sectors.

4. Their economic conditions vary. Some of them yield mainly private benefits, but under natural monopoly conditions (subways, water, sewage, garbage disposal). Some also offer large benefits from externalities and improved equity (for example, parks, libraries). Some involve subsidies which may be highly regressive (frequently: airports, theaters, sports stadiums).

5. Their pricing and investment policies vary. The degree of subsidy ranges from total down to zero (even to negative, in some profit-earning units). Some price structures are simple, some sophisticated; and some have quite irrational parts. The cost of capital is treated variously, in some cases scarcely being considered at all.

6. The *nature* of service itself is often the main problem. What coverage, frequency, and reliability should bus and subway service have? What kinds of parks and libraries should there be, and where located? Often services become narrow and rigid. Operations may be profit-earning, or internally efficient, but not fully optimal.[13]

We will look first at the core urban services, which are now mostly under public enterprise. Then we turn to several major social enterprises: schools, courts, and public housing.

B2. Urban Enterprises

These units range from subways and water systems to zoos, parks, and libraries. Many of them are quite necessary and utilitarian—and as *dull* as only sewage, garbage disposal, and cemeteries can seem. But others pose

[13] See the excellent volume by S. J. Mushkin, ed., *Public Prices for Public Products* (Washington, D.C.: Urban Institute, 1972) for basic discussion and applications in several areas.

wider choices and raise hot controversies: airports, for example, enclosed sports stadiums, and hospitals. Here we will briefly consider transit, water, garbage, and libraries.

Transport. This includes a variety of operations, from cross-town transit (bus, subway, and so on), bridges and parking, to commuter lines, ports, and airports. Despite their range, the key feature is their mutual dependency. They interrelate, both as *alternatives* (buses versus subways; commuter lines versus bridges and tunnels for private traffic) and as *supplements,* which feed into each other. This mutual externality—the need to "integrate" them technically and economically—makes them both difficult to optimize and also natural for a public treatment. Conceivably one could keep them as private firms and use pricing rules, taxes, and subsidies to coordinate them and minimize their external costs. But that is usually not practical. Instead the choices need to be applied directly via public enterprise and combined treatments. Accordingly, nearly all cities now have public systems.

Public systems often follow deviant policies, but they possess the preconditions for perceiving and applying an efficient treatment. They can see interactions among the parts of the urban transit system (for example, how parking fees relate to subway fares and bridge tolls) and set the prices in line with that—*and* arrange the necessary subsidies of some units. Their broader social effects (for example, service to ghetto areas; and easing noise and air pollution) can be fitted into other criteria for decent city life.

The main allocation issues concern pricing and subsidizing of the various modes. These also tie in with equity questions, for the subsidies are often big.

The basic fact is the daily rush-hours, coming in during 7 to 9 and going out during 4 to 6. This causes the true costs of road use, buses, and other modes to be very high at those peaks, but close to zero at off-peak times. The private car usually averages 1.3 riders, at costs far above those of public transport. Added social costs of car use (from congestion, pollution, and paving of city areas) are often large.

If transit capacity is optimal, then the efficient level of subway fares is (at long-run marginal cost) much lower than private costs. It would eventually induce travelers to shift to public transport. Conversely, car drivers should be set a high effective price; but how can this be applied? Bridge and tunnel tolls, and parking fees by curbside meters and at parking lots and structures, are the main practical hope. Total "road pricing" is not feasible and perhaps never will be, but the other devices can give a rough approximation. These extra revenues would be pooled against the financial deficits which efficient pricing prescribes for some of the mass transit units.

Practical methods are not so well refined, but most cities provide fairly good public systems. Few are able to come close to efficient pricing of travel by car. That remains the unsolved problem of urban transit.

Water and Sewage. These systems have become key urban problems, as many cities reach ecological limits for clear water and sewage disposal.

They are public enterprises (indeed, city departments) almost everywhere, and they often (with major exceptions) set prices somewhere near their average operating costs. Price structure and ecology are the main economic problems.

The technology virtually requires public ownership. Here is a rare permanent natural monopoly (not a life cycle: recall Chapter 10). It is closely related to public health, and there are deep possibilities for price discrimination. For decades, water and sewer systems were scarcely recognized as an economic problem. They have simply been built big enough to allow growth and then priced with utmost simplicity. Water metering has been strictly at fixed prices, and in many cities the final user pays no price per unit at all. Thus, most New York users pay fees unrelated to the amounts used, and in all cities many apartment dwellers pay no individual price at all. Such zero pricing induces use out to levels of zero marginal utility, even though water is often urgently scarce.[14]

City growth often causes the long-run marginal costs for these systems to be well above true average and short-run marginal costs. New suburbs and major apartment buildings are routinely planned, approved, and supplied with water and sewage service at going rates (often zero unit prices), even though these additions impose new capacity and service costs at levels sharply above the average costs of the existing system. Such pricing accentuates urban sprawl and burdens the finances of central city areas.

Ecological problems often require regional solutions, which in turn involve struggles among public units at various levels up to federal agencies. Public ownership is virtually a necessary (not sufficient) condition for internalizing these effects.

On the whole, these systems operate with tolerable internal efficiency, avoid conscious price discrimination, and are part of a system for solving the larger problems of supply. But they often need sharp revisions in price levels and structures, to align them with true scarcity levels.

Garbage Disposal.   This humble operation also has encountered new problems. Recently relabelled as "solid waste disposal," it now faces a growing avalanche of solid wastes, for which the dumping places are getting few and costly. Moreover, newer packaging materials (plastics, metals, nonreturnable bottles, and so forth) add to the difficulty.

Once again, the old ways—primarily, a unit price of zero—worsen the problem. Though operating costs and scarcities of dumping space make long-run marginal costs high and probably rising, the service is usually given away, even to many heavy users. The obvious answer is to set prices at costs, based on volume, frequency, and other conditions of service. Where private service remains, it at least charges a price in line with private cost (though the use of public dumping space is often under-priced).

Public management is necessary in most cases to provide a pick-up network plus adequate dumping capacity. But the design of capacity, service provision,

---

[14] See Mushkin, *Public Prices,* chapters 6 and 12 for analysis and actual patterns.

and prices needs revision in many cities.[15] Few cases show so clearly how the efficiency of public enterprise depends on how it is designed and priced. Since other specialized private haulers operate alongside the regular service, the basic problem—and opportunity—is to optimize the basic system while also applying some degree of competition from alternative haulers for the high-cost, commercial loads. The inefficient treatment is to make disposal free, with a service design which overloads large high-cost users on to the basic system.

Libraries and Museums. These are public enterprises with cultural effects. They also have permanent natural-monopoly conditions, and demand is probably elastic at any significant price level.

Libraries are funded directly, rather than by user charges. There are occasional entrance fees to museums. Where they are only nominal, such entrance fees and library fines still leave the basic social function nearly intact: to make knowledge and culture available widely. If charges are also adjusted to ability to pay, then virtually everyone is able to share at low or zero prices.

But even here there are intriguing issues of design and equity. First, design. Libraries are necessarily in few locations, not equally near to all. Moreover, their open hours often penalize those not able to come in during standard working hours. Recent cut-backs under budget pressure have borne most heavily on weekend and evenings hours.

Second, the equity benefits of libraries and museums are relatively narrow. Use is mostly by middle and upper groups, according to income and education. This is less broadly based than the city tax revenues which pay for them. Therefore, even in these exemplary units—and even assuming they are internally quite efficient and yield large total social benefits—there may be a negative net effect on equity.

Summary. We have accentuated the negative about urban enterprises, to show where the main problems of structure and pricing lie. If they were designed and priced as public enterprises, in line with basic policy analysis, they would be more efficient and equitable.

But these criticisms do not challenge their being *public* enterprises. In these cases, public enterprise is appropriate and, probably, necessary. It is mainly their pricing and coordination that need review and revision.

C. SOCIAL ENTERPRISES

Social enterprises are familiar as government or public-agency operations, and some are very large. Their central operations and problems are often

---

[15] Also, equity is often at issue. Thus, high-income households may have four or more times as much garbage as poor households and less accessible houses, thereby imposing more costs than they pay in taxes or fees. See S. J. Mushkin, *Public Prices,* chapters 8 and 9.

closely related to industrial organization. When they deviate from efficient and fair patterns, it is often from a neglect of these attributes and an isolation from market processes. These enterprises usually have a degree of competition and complex pricing and allocation choices. They are suited to a variety of market tests.

Here we briefly consider three of them: schools, courts, and public housing. First, their common features need to be noted. How do these activities differ from, say, selling cabbage or pencils?

1. They are subsidized to users, entirely or in part.
2. They are designed to provide comprehensive coverage, so that no group is excluded by inability to pay.
3. The user often is compelled to participate, as part of the social purpose of the operation.
4. Equity is a central objective, as well as social externalities.
5. Yet many of their functions can be, and are, provided by private units selling under market process.

Therefore, one needs to ask of all of them: Is an alternative structure more efficient? Should their capacity be at different levels and forms? Are their prices optimal? Is more competition appropriate? In this light, these agencies have different character and results than the old government-agency image implies.

C1. Education

Schools are a form of enterprise, producing a service. The student learns, under supervision, in a process using costly resources. The "industry" has a large number of enterprises operating in thousands of local submarkets (see Table 18–6). Most schools for grades 1 through 12 are public. Their operations are often the biggest single public activity in town. They are also controversial, for they affect whole lifetimes of opportunity.

TABLE 18–6
Educational Operations, 1976

	Number of Units (1,000)	Expenditure ($ billion)	Number of Students (million)
Primary and Secondary Schools			
Public	88	73	45
Private	18	9	5
Higher Education			
Public	1	34	8
Private	2	16	2

Source: *U.S. Statistical Abstract,* 1978, Section 5.

Problems of Choice and Supply. The consumer—the student—is changed by the process, rather than having well-formed, independent demand.[16] The conditions for choice are unusual, because:

1. Important choices are made at early, immature stages of life, under conditions of ignorance and short-sightedness.
2. These decisions are largely irreversible.
3. The higher ranges of career opportunity require, for those not advantaged by family support and/or wealth, a virtually complete avoidance of incorrect decisions.

Youthful choices can keep upper opportunities open, or close them off. But the student is least competent to make decisions precisely during those early years when the choices are critical and largely irreversible. Schooling can tend to offset the advantages of birth—to "equalize" opportunity—or instead to reinforce them. An ideal, fair school system will impart skills and provide equal access. It will cater to alternative interests and skills (intellectual, vocational, arts, industrial, financial, and so on) and personality types (aggressive, selfless, artistic, miserly, and so forth). And further, it will also provide fresh chances for those who temporarily waver.

Large public resources are provided for education, and a large share of the political process is devoted to supervising these public units.

Conditions. The basic structure of the system is familiar to most readers, so that only certain special features need to be reviewed.

Monopoly is the prevailing condition of supply. Public schooling in grades 1 through 12 is provided by one system in each locale. Further, the "neighborhood school" basis is prevalent, leaving users no choice, even among schools within the system. Access to private schools is directly related to family wealth and income, so that the poor face the highest degree of monopoly in educational supply. To some extent, moving one's residence can give one a choice among schools, but this element of choice is also directly related to economic (and racial) status.[17]

Quality of supply is also related to income. Commonly, better neighborhoods have better schools; better in plant, teachers, equipment, location, amenity, etc. Despite frequent proposals for inverting the pattern, so that schools in deprived areas will be "models," the pattern remains strong and deeply rooted.

---

[16] On the special economies of education and learning, see G. S. Becker, *Human Capital* (New York: Columbia University Press, 1964); the reprint volumes by M. Blaug, *The Economics of Education,* vols. 1 and 2 (London: Penguin Books, 1968–69); C. Jencks et al., *Inequality: A Reassessment of the Effect of Family and Schooling in America* (New York: Basic Books, 1972); K. J. Arrow, "Higher Education as a Filter," *Journal of Public Choice* (July 1973), pp. 193–216; and B. S. Bloom, *Stability and Change in Human Characteristics* (New York: Wiley, 1964).

[17] Even where one may choose among schools in one's city (as is true in Britain), the practical degree of choice is limited by such other factors as income, transportation, and overcrowding in some schools.

Tracking within each school system begins early and takes hold with enough force to determine the future field of opportunity for most children. It commonly reflects the inequalities in family support which the child brings to school. There are exceptional teachers and children who offset this pressure or who get re-tracked at later stages. And the degree of tracking in U.S. schools probably is less than it is in other western countries. Still, a degree of tracking is the normal effect of public school operations.

A high degree of public subsidy is the common basis for financing education. In grades 1–12 and in correctional facilities, the subsidy is virtually total. For higher education, the subsidies to public universities are large. The net incidence of such college subsidies is regressive, because college students are drawn primarily from upper economic groups.[18]

Effects.   The natural outcome is a loss of equity and efficiency. Opportunity is not equalized; rather, the schools tend on the whole to reflect and, in part, to reinforce the original disparities. Monopoly and rigidity are particularly present in the early years (grades 1–12), where children's choices are the least informed and reversible.

Efficiency is lost in the failure of talents to develop. If innate talent is randomly distributed, this loss would be very large. And there is X-inefficiency in many school systems, encouraged by the high degree of monopoly.

Possible Revisions.   The most sensible revisions would increase choice and competition in certain directions, and to adjust these public enterprises in line with the more general lessons we have drawn. A common proposal is to give students free choice and full support for going to any school they wish. This "voucher" device would provide a degree of choice for users and of competition among schools...

But it does not obviate (though it mitigates) the need for reversing the relationship between neighborhood income and school quality. Also, travel to school would need to be provided at zero price, lest that continue to limit educational choice (and even so it imposes unequal burdens in loss of time and content). Nor does it remedy the problem of tracking. All this is clear from Britain, where a large degree of choice among schools *is* provided along lines sought by the voucher proposal, and yet the basic problems remain.

The voucher proposal does include private schools. This would induce valuable competition—on an equal footing—from outside the public system. And the location and variety of private schools could possibly tend toward optimal patterns, after a period of adjustment and growth. But the technology is lumpy and slow-adjusting, so that large deviations would remain. For example, few private schools comparable to those of the highest quality would soon locate in the many inner-city areas of low-income suburbs.

---

[18] See W. L. Hanson and B. A. Weisbrod, *Benefits, Costs, and Finance of Public Higher Education* (New York: Markham Publishing, 1969). Also, E. Dennison, "An Aspect of Inequality of Opportunity," *Journal of Political Economy,* 78 (September/October 1970), 1195–1202.

C2. Courts

Basic Conditions. The courts are a set of devices, or arenas, for social decision and compromise. They are merely the visible tip of the whole process of private negotiations, which settle conflicts and reach specific decisions about individual rights and property.[19] Cases that reach the courts are often the toughest ones, which have resisted any other means of resolution (or in which one party is able to pursue its interests without limit). This is the "justice" system, which resolves issues short of violence.

The system has many separate parts and layers, from federal down to state and local courts. This patchwork of public forums may provide justice. It may also be regarded as a system, or perhaps *the* system, by which those with advantages perpetuate them. Therefore the functioning of the courts— as simply another, but important, public enterprise system—needs a skeptical appraisal.

Courts are a series of related public enterprises in which inputs are used to generate outputs. The output is the decision reached, at least in some cases. But in many cases the trial activity simply speeds or crystallizes the settlement among disputing private interests. Where the range of negotiation between the parties was clear, the court's service as an arena or mere mediator is of little social value. It can even be a social burden, when resort to the courts in a litigious strategy is used to prevent a "fair" outcome. The court system in fact is often used or abused as a free good, in order to gain advantage in private conflicts.

The inputs of the enterprise are several: the court resources themselves (judges, recorders, clerks, and personnel, space, utilities, archives, and so on), lawyers, witnesses, other sources of information to be used in the case, and of course the laws themselves which are written by legislatures and modified by court decisions. These inputs are combined within a formal procedure and structure, which affect the speed and often the content of the outcome. This structure includes burdens of proof in civil and criminal cases, advantages of time for one side against the other, rules of evidence, standards of precedent, rules of pretrial discovery and conduct at trial, and other features which were noted in Chapters 3 and 4.

The social aim is to minimize the costs of both *(a)* operating the systems, and *(b)* erroneous decisions. Cases actually reach trial—rather than get settled privately—for four sets of reasons. (1) The two sides may differ in expectations, risk preferences, or access to legal resources. (2) One side may be so desperate that trial offers at least a hope (or valuable delay). (3) Court services are usually provided at zero price, which increases the level of usage. (4) The larger the stakes, the more likely trial is to be used.

As enterprises, the courts raise the two standard economic questions, about

---

[19] For example, less than 5 percent of automobile injury cases reach a court hearing. See Richard A. Posner, *Economic Analysis of Law* (Boston: Little, Brown, 1972), p. 337.

their efficiency and equity. The first is about the funding and supply of resources to the court system, and how its services are priced. This also includes
optimizing the total size of court resources and the selection of matters which
take up court time. The second concerns how closely its results fit either
the status quo or even greater inequality, on one hand, or the strict equality
of legal rights.

Efficiency. A primary fact is the congestion of court dockets. This is
most acute at the upper levels, where the most important decisions are reached.
Delays of years in beginning trial—much less reaching a final resolution—
are common. These intervals cause uncertainty and, in most cases, losses
for one side or both. Some degree of delay is optimal, to allow pretrial preparations and possible settlement. But present delays clearly exceed the optimum
for large categories of suits.

Some, perhaps much, of the congestion occurs because the courts are
provided free. In most cases both sides can treat the courts as a strictly
free good, even though the direct social costs of them are high and the
indirect costs from delaying other cases may be a multiple of that.[20] The
delays often generate large losses and inequities. Some citizens, for example,
are routinely imprisoned while awaiting trial, for periods which are regarded
as intolerable for people of means and "good" social standing. One solution
is to enlarge the resources; but as with highway expansion at zero user charges,
this tends only to stimulate more demand so that congestion continues.

An efficient solution includes several parts. *One* is to price court services
at costs, including external costs of delay and congestion.[21] This would raise
the cost of bringing suit and serve as a normal indicator of true scarcity.
(But it might violate the objective of equal access, favoring richer litigants.)
A *second* is to improve the internal management of courts. Especially in
handling jury sources, there is much room for using resources more efficiently.
But the major scope for change is, *third,* in removing or excluding from
courtroom handling whole ranges of cases which presently congest the courts.
These include the wide variety of private compromises which could as well

---

[20] Direct social costs of a typical federal district court can be estimated as follows.
Personnel include judge, clerk, transcriber, bailiff, secretary, jury selection officers,
etc. These total at least $100,000 per year. Each trial day involves at least another
day of meetings in chamber, preparation of opinion, and so on. At 130 trial days
per year, this is $760 per trial day. The premises costs include space rental for the
courtroom, offices, jury rooms, jury selection offices, library, and so forth; fittings,
equipment, references; upkeep; air conditioning, other building services, and so on.
These would easily be $3,000/month, or $300 per trial day. A jury adds perhaps
$1,350/day (19 juror equivalents, allowing also for nonselected jurors, at an average
value of $75 per day). Estimated trial cost is at least $1,000 per day; with jury,
about $2,500 per day. See also W. M. Landes, "An Economic Analysis of the Courts,"
Journal of Law and Economics 13 (1971); and D. L. Martin, "The Economics of
Jury Conscription," *Journal of Political Economy,* vol. 80 (1972). This does not include
private costs, with lawyers and expert witnesses commonly at $300 to $800 each
per day, and often much higher.

[21] This is complex, for pricing must avoid excluding poorer claimants. Some degree
of price discrimination, with a sliding scale based on income, might be optimal.

be handled by professional private mediators and arbitrators.[22] By contrast, many courts are mired in trivial private-party tactics.[23] The low social benefits, compared to the true costs, reflect gross waste and inequity.

Equity. The basic fact is that access to legal counsel and information about the use of court resources are not equal but, rather, highly correlated with wealth. The system favors those who can afford the best counsel and who are most aware of their legal rights and strategies.[24] A partial solution is to make legal aid universally available at zero costs.[25] Yet even if such free legal aid were supplied (as small programs have recently been made for certain categories), it will presumably be of an inferior quality. Moreover, it will not overcome the inhibitions which most citizens feel about asserting their legal rights. At present, federal legal aid programs are adopting the form of a public enterprise. But they will be a small factor against the whole bias of the system. More promising is the rapid growth of legal clinics and of bargain-priced services, as competition among lawyers has sprouted since 1975 (recall Chapter 7).

The efficiency and equity of the judicial system as a whole are shaped by forces outside it, which limit its resources, procedures, and pricing. The courts are also a complex of public enterprises which are managed by officials untrained to optimize their operations. The larger effects are predictable and well known. Changes are in order, and the directions for improvement are fairly clear. They need to fit the nature of courts as specialized public enterprises.

C3. Public Housing

The United States, like virtually all societies, provides some publicly owned housing at subsidized rents. The stock of public housing is large, though it

[22] This sector of activity is already well developed, in handling labor disputes and settling claims. In fact, a wide range of disputes are resolved among lawyers, acting in quasi-judicial fashion. But there is much room for expanding it. Probably half or two thirds of courtroom activity could thus be excised, leaving the remaining cases for brisker treatment.

[23] This is accentuated by the judicial custom of exhaustive procedures. See M. Fleming, *The Price of Perfect Justice* (New York: Basic Books, 1973).

[24] There are several levels to this problem. First, most citizens are unaware of their full legal rights and/or too awed by the court system to seek them out. Second, among those who are aware, most are unable to afford counsel to represent their interest fully. Third, there are vast differences among lawyers in quality and standing, with the best talent being priced so high that the mass of citizens are left only with the lower levels of legal talent. Consequently, the legal scales are often tipped by the quality, use, or even the presence of superior advocates.

[25] This would run the risk of wasting legal resources, since they would be used up to their level of zero marginal productivity rather than up to the level at which their true cost was in line with their marginal productivity. Yet the gain in equality by underpricing in this way might justify the marginal misallocation, at least for some categories. For many wealthy or powerful corporate interests, legal talent is virtually used as a free good, up to the point where the marginal benefit from litigation is reached.

is less than two percent of all urban dwellings. These programs generate problems and performance which are matters of dispute. *Private* home ownership is also subsidized publicly, via the insuring agencies noted in Chapter 17. The direct public housing programs are only a part of the whole public subsidy of housing.

Starting in 1933, public housing has grown to large size. There were 1,180,000 dwellings under public management in 1970. Relatively, public housing is of small significance, accounting for only 2 percent of the stock of urban dwellings and sheltering little more than 1 percent of the families in the country as a whole.

The supply of public housing falls far short of the demand. It could be rationed by raising the rents, but this would defeat the purpose of providing low-rent housing for the poor. The rationing is therefore done administratively. Entry is limited to families whose incomes are less than five times the rents, preference being given to applicants of good character in accordance with the urgency of their needs. Continued occupancy is limited to families whose incomes, following entry, do not increase by more than 25 percent. The median income of public housing tenants is less than $4,000 a year. Many are broken families. A quarter are over 65 years of age. A quarter are on relief. The average cost of providing a unit of public housing is about twice the rent charged. The housing is provided as a form of public charity.

Housing actually is on the margin of "social" activities. The great mass of housing choices are strictly private matters, properly decided in private markets. Public housing is a residuary, passive public enterprise. By definition, public housing absorbs those who cannot meet market tests either for housing prices or for keeping their houses in shape. There are long waiting lists for public housing at the subsidized rent levels. This may indicate large social benefits from public housing. Or it may be that rents are set too low and that social benefits are small.

In any event, public housing tends to be funded, designed, and operated differently and separately from private housing markets.[26] Many economists suggest that public housing should be merged with the private housing sector by simply subsidizing rents of deserving citizens, rather than directly providing housing units.

The actual performance of public housing units can be evaluated in terms of public enterprise. There are familiar conditions of old-style public firms: public ownership is complete, it is directly subsidized by public funds and guarantees, it is assigned customers which private markets do not supply, and it is insulated from various market tests of efficiency. In addition, it must operate through the local political process, which tends to minimize the political power of the poor. Therefore, it is likely to exhibit the classic

---

[26] On U.S. patterns, see Henry J. Aaron, *Shelter and Subsidies: Who Benefits from Federal Housing Policies?* (Washington, D.C.: Brookings Institution, 1972) and references cited there. On British and other national patterns, see David V. Donnison, *The Government of Housing* (London: Penguin Books, 1967).

symptoms of costly public enterprises. In addition, U.S. programs have developed corruption and abuses which have actually destroyed significant amounts of the housing stock since 1968.

The result often has been a series of large and poorly designed public housing projects, which often become expensive instant slums. The inevitable emphasis on minimum cost per unit results in defective design, despite decades of experience. The preferences of users for specific housing attributes are virtually ignored.

In short, much—possibly most—public housing shows an excess of public cost over probable benefits. This arises both in the total level of activities and in the way the programs are designed and priced. These programs appear to be part of a stable equilibrium, which persists because it nicely suboptimizes among a special set of private interests.

C4. Summary

This selection of urban and social enterprises provides some lessons about good structure and operations. Many of them are reasonably efficient but most could be improved by closer use of the standard criteria for public enterprise. Often competition is excluded or biased too much. Some efficiency criteria are scarcely considered. Pricing could especially be improved. These urban and social enterprises may be the richest frontier for study and revisions in industrial organization, offering even more than antitrust and regulation in conventional sectors.

QUESTIONS FOR REVIEW

1. "The TVA is heavily subsidized, and so it gives unfair competition to private power systems." True?
2. "As scale economies have increased, small city power systems have grown obsolete. They cannot give economic benefits and should all be absorbed into private systems." True?
3. "Deficits in public railroad systems may be consistent with efficient operations." True?
4. "Being a capital-intensive utility, postal service needs only to get cheap capital in order to solve its basic problem." True?
5. "If first-class mail is sorted at peak times, then it should be charged more than lower-class mail." True?
6. "Public telephone systems abroad have developed cost-based pricing more thoroughly than U.S. private systems." True?
7. "Efficient urban transit pricing may involve bus fares *and* prices for private-car commuters." True?
8. "An X-efficient library may still be 'unfair' if it is located in an isolated, wealthy section of town." True?
9. "Give every child a free ticket to any school of his or her choice, anywhere in the country, and equal opportunity through education will still not be achieved." True?

10. "Courts need to be priced efficiently, as well as managed efficiently." True?
11. "The long waiting lists for public housing show that it is performing well." True?
12. Which public enterprises in utility and social sectors are performing pretty well? Why do they do well, while others don't?
13. What main revisions or "reforms" are needed in the U.S. Postal Service?

chapter 19

Public Enterprise Appraised

Public enterprise needs a careful evaluation, which recognizes its variety and complexity. It is evolving and assuming new forms, well beyond its old-fashioned roles. Its experience is growing, but it has been little researched.

Still, certain basic attributes do recur. We will review them and then consider the further evolution of public enterprise.

A. BASIC PROPERTIES

1. Public enterprise can be suitable for a wide range of markets and social sectors, not just for utilities.

2. It is not a substitute for regulation or antitrust. Rather it needs to be combined with them (and with other policy devices) in balanced policy packages.

3. Public enterprise can assume a variety of forms, market positions, financial constraints, and economic criteria. These include varying degrees of public ownership and public operation: they range from government departments to public corporations and to partial public holdings and investment banks. A public enterprise can be largely private in secondary features, but quite public in essentials. There is also a wide range of pricing and investment policies which public enterprises can follow.

4. A broad shift is occurring from older totally public firms toward the more mixed and flexible varieties of public enterprise.

5. The publicness by itself does not transform the enterprise. But it does alter some basic relationships and make large changes in behavior and performance possible.

6. The forms, market position, and criteria of public enterprises will often govern their performance more closely than the mere fact that they are publicly owned.

7. Public enterprise is not generally inferior to private enterprise by any of the main criteria of economic and social performance. One must look at it case by case.

8. Some categories of public enterprise levy predictable costs. These tend to be *passive* enterprises: high degrees of subsidy and low degrees of public control, combined with monopoly and overcentralization. The costly results are primarily matters of form and criteria, not simply of publicness itself.

9. Conversely, certain types of *active* public enterprise, under certain conditions and policies, tend to yield high benefits. How well they work depends partly on the sector involved and the specific social objectives at stake.

10. The main benefits come from *(a)* making large changes which have social impacts, *(b)* improving the inner content of the enterprises (for example, sharing of power within the firm, and labor relations), and *(c)* avoiding windfall capital gains from monopoly positions or other special advantages. These benefits are, however, rarely achieved fully in practice.

11. Public enterprises tend to grow more regressive over time, although of course with exceptions. Avoidance of the regressive shift often requires a finite life for the public enterprise in its original sector and purpose. Ideally, the whole group of public enterprises would usually shift as decades pass, some units being phased out, others being added.

12. Public enterprises are often overloaded with economic and social targets, compared to their resources. This is the normal policy condition, in which the device is created, designed, and funded on a basis which is inadequate to its formal social task. (Parts II and III noted that much the same is true of antitrust and regulation as well.)

13. Usually the financial status of the enterprise is set by conditions and decisions outside its own control. These may cripple the enterprise from the outset. Yet a moderate degree of guidance from outside—by invited and uninvited criticism, and by official pressures—is beneficial. Without clear analytical criteria, a public enterprise is often prey to outside pressures for special favors. At the least, the correct economic guidance for pricing and investment decisions can help public enterprises to fend off special pleading by vested interests.

14. Generally, public enterprises need a continuing skeptical evaluation. There usually is a need to consider increasing competition, to constrain the use of public resources, and to improve the efficiency and equity impacts. The distributional effects, in particular, need to be analyzed critically, because of their regressive tendency.

More broadly, the need to *experiment* with new forms and sectors for public enterprise is a continuing one. There is no final form or sectoral pattern for public enterprises to reach. On the contrary, public enterprises—singly and collectively—need to evolve and to cope with new changes so that forms and resources do not become frozen.

B. FURTHER CHANGES

Several lines of future evolution of public firms can be predicted from recent trends. Abroad, there will be more experimenting with public firms and holding companies in industry and finance. There will be fewer sharp changes, even though "socialist" parties in each country have evolved long lists of industries "to be nationalized."

The gradual spread will enrich our knowledge about the performance of public enterprise, and their treatment will continue to become more sophisticated. This will come especially from financial public firms, operating both as competitors to private units and as supervisors of public and quasi-public firms in other sectors. Yet these changes will probably be slow and have large exceptions. One should not expect dramatic new forms or lessons. Nor is there likely to be a large shift of public firms toward private status.

In the United States, discussion and action will probably continue to be biased against objective uses of public enterprises—though perhaps the bias will diminish. In *practice,* public enterprise will still be used freely where powerful interests can gain from it.

There will probably be further instances of the more negative, passive types of public enterprises. These will rightly warrant criticism, though they will be primarily the outcome of their setting.

Across the range of public firms in the U.S. economy, one may expect some improvements toward more efficient forms and criteria, especially in urban and social enterprises. There will be less than an efficient degree of experimenting with public enterprise in industry, finance, and especially utility sectors. Of these, the greater loss will be from the financial sector, where unrealized social gains now appear to be appreciable. It is precisely because effective public enterprises in finance would impinge on deeply set private interests that the prospects for them now seem limited.

To anticipate the evolution of public enterprise in U.S. and elsewhere, one must understand both *(a)* the inner forms and criteria, and *(b)* the surrounding political economy. Public enterprises and their determinants continue to operate in the context of private interests whose ingenuity and flexibility are great. Actual benefits are often absorbed by non-deserving groups. Defects—real or imagined—are exaggerated. And objective analysis is not encouraged.

Ultimately, the prospects for public enterprise are comparable to those of antitrust and regulation. There is potential for inefficiency and abuse, but also for excellent performance. Many of the hazards are predictable, and most of the essential issues can be cast in a sensible cost-benefit form. *No rational analyst will be either for or against public enterprise on the whole, except for personal interests or purely ideological reasons.* The economic task is to identify what is happening in the existing public enterprises, to define the directions for at least the most obvious corrections, and then to derive the optimum conditions under which new enterprises might be tried.

Part V

SPECIAL CASES

chapter 20

Financial Markets

Financial markets are a network of economic control in the modern economy.[1] They stand above industrial, utility and trading firms, supervising and influencing their actions. They allocate capital among enterprises in all sectors. They appraise performance and risk, and they fund new ventures and innovation.

Directly and indirectly, they influence managers, owners, consumers, and the other economic actors. They also shape the gaining and holding (and losing) of personal wealth. They can pool risks to insure against severe losses. Their degree of competition affects competitiveness in other markets. In short, they influence efficiency and equity throughout the economy.

Policies toward these markets have been distinctive, with strong effects. There is much self-regulation, a degree of public regulation, and recently a marginal but growing role for antitrust. Public enterprises also are important in parts of the sector (see Chapter 17).

The financial sector is complex and diverse. This chapter outlines it and its analytical properties (structure, costs, links with other enterprises, and so forth). The focus is on banking, investment finance, and insurance, which tie most closely to structure and performance in other markets. The policies toward these three areas of finance are also treated in the separate sections.

---

[1] Good basic works on financial markets are Gerald Fischer, *American Banking Structure* (New York: Columbia University Press, 1968); David Alhadeff, *Monopoly and Competition in Banking* (Berkeley: University of California Press, 1954); and Irwin Friend et al., *Investment Banking and the New Issues Market* (Cleveland: World Publishing, 1967). An excellent survey is given by the set of reports by the Commission on Money and Credit, especially *Private Financial Institutions* (Englewood Cliffs, N.J.: Prentice-Hall, 1963); for a racy but sound introduction to stock market realities, see Adam Smith, *The Money Game* (New York: Random House, 1967). See also the chapters by Phillips and H. M. Mann in Almarin Phillips, ed., *Promoting Competition in Regulated Markets* (Washington, D.C.: Brookings Institution, 1975). Extensive surveys of the stock market are given in Securities and Exchange Commission, *The Structure, Organization, and Regulation of the Securities Market* (Washington, D.C.: U.S. Government Printing Office, 1971); and Senate Subcommittee on Securities, *Securities Industry Study,* 93d Cong., 1st Sess. (Washington, D.C.: U.S. Government Printing Office, 1973).

Finance is highly sophisticated and flexible, often as elusive as quicksilver. It contains some of the country's most talented and intensely motivated commercial specialists, playing for the highest stakes of wealth and economic power. One must approach the issues with care, not expecting clear lines, full data, or optimal policies.

A. COMMERCIAL BANKING

The basic system of banks and their regulators is shown in Figure 20–1. The main lines of banks and their operations are shown in Table 20–1.

A1. Basic Conditions

Banking is what bankers do. The cashier's window handles only a small and peripheral part of the main business. As part of the financial sector, banking specializes in making loans, money transfers, and supervision—in a mnemonic phrase: *credit, clearing,* and *counseling.* It coexists and partly overlaps with investment banking, insurance, savings and loans, and other financial "industries," but commercial banking is much larger than the others. All of these sections provide capital in some form.

The heart of banking is loans to business, and at the core of these are the banking relationships. These relationships are stable and intimate: the

FIGURE 20–1
The Banking "System"

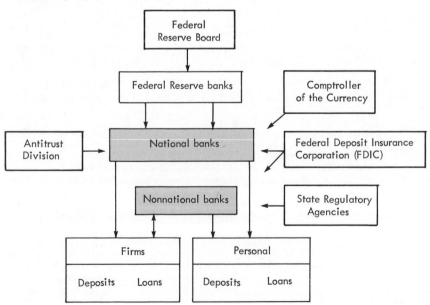

TABLE 20–1
Evolution of Commercial Banking: Selected Data, 1870–1976

	1870	1920	1935	1950	1965	1976
National banks						
Number	1,612	8,024	5,425	4,971	4,707	4,735
Assets ($ billions)	1.6	23.3	26.0	89.7	264.9	583.3
Nonnational banks						
Number	325	22,885	10,622	9,705	9,298	9,937
Assets ($ billions)	0.2	29.8	33.9	89.5	189.2	447.5
Branch banks and offices as a percent of all bank offices	1.0	5.7	21.3	31.6	63.6	(81)†
New banks and de novo branches (previous 5 years)	—*	—	—	1,238	5,953	11,277
Bank suspensions	3	168	32	5	6	1
FDIC insured deposits, as a percent of all deposits	0	0	37	47	58	(64)†

* —indicates data not available.
† () indicates estimate.
Source: U.S. Department of Commerce, *Historical Statistics* (Washington, D.C.: U.S. Government Printing Office, 1957), and *Statistical Abstract* (Washington, D.C.: U.S. Government Printing Office, annual).

bank comes to know all about any firm that relies on it for much capital. Prudent bankers must know their risks, and so bank and company officials operate on long-standing terms of mutual trust and familiarity. In some cases bankers are directors of their client firms, but that is only a surface sign of the real relationships behind the scenes.

Banks acquire funds from depositors of various kinds (checking deposits, savings, certificates of deposit, commercial accounts, and so on). They dispose of funds chiefly by loans and lines of credit, but also, increasingly, in a range of other debt forms. Before 1960 bank loans to companies were mainly short-term credit, to finance routine cash needs of firms (for example, seasonal inventory shifts and payrolls). Recently there has been a strong shift into long-term loans, for nonrecurring basic corporate projects. Short-term loans are covered primarily by collateral. Long-term loans are "covered" by pre-dicted cash flows, a much riskier matter; and large firms have become sharply more reliant on debt (that is, their capital structure has become more highly *levered*) since 1960. This has drawn banks ever deeper into the whole of corporate planning and risk sharing. The banks' own risks have risen. The banking relationship now involves real—often great—mutual risk and dependence.

So private commercial banks nurse along their core of prime clients as their central concern. They also perform small-scale "retailing" functions, of the kinds that you can observe (checking, savings deposits, safety boxes, and mortgages). In seeking to maximize their profits, consistent with some degree of prudence, they basically manage a set of assets and liabilities (recently "liability management" has become about as important as "asset management").

Structure. Banking markets are at local, regional, national, and international levels.[2] Market edges are often blurred and controversial, but most of them can be defined reasonably well. Some seven large urban banking centers do 35 percent of the volume of all U.S. banking, but the mass of medium and small firms deal in genuinely local banking markets.

The larger markets are moderate to tight oligopolies (see Table 20–2), while the smaller city markets run toward tighter structure. Yet some small cities have surprisingly low concentration. Structure has been stable for decades, despite a modest degree of shifting and perhaps a very slow receding of the average degree of concentration. On the whole, banking structure is tighter than is usually found in other markets.

The total share of the largest banks has been high and steady; the largest 20 banks have held about 29 percent of all bank assets since 1960. Mergers and differing regional growth rates have bred most of the changes in the large-bank list. The 1950s merger wave strongly increased the degree of monopoly, creating anew the largest bank in Chicago and other large cities. In the 1960s, scores of one-bank holding companies were created, to permit banks to engage in related financial activities.

Scale Economies. Scale economies in banking could arise in any of the banking functions (loans, deposits, and so on), and so they are difficult to measure precisely. The best evidence suggests that average costs decline at small sizes but then are relatively flat over medium and large sizes.[3] This is reinforced by the low concentration in many small banking markets. One large loan can be made more cheaply than many small ones, because there is less processing and (probably) less risk. But this advantage is offset by various scale diseconomies, so that banking efficiency could be reached with a degree of concentration much lower than exists in most banking markets.

Formal banking structure is embedded in strong cartel restrictions and bankers' codes of behavior. These limit price competition and various other kinds of destabilizing behavior within the banking fraternity. They also tightly control new entry and other natural forms of corporate change, by making

---

[2] See the Commission on Money and Credit, *Private Financial Institutions* (Englewood Cliffs, N.J.: Prentice-Hall, 1963); J. M. Guttentag and E. S. Herman, *Banking Structure and Performance* (New York: New York University Press, 1967); Fischer, *American Banking Structure;* and David Leinsdorf and Donald Etra, *Citibank* (New York: Grossman, 1973).

About 78 percent of U.S. banking markets are "effectively monopolized," according to Arnold A. Heggestad and J. J. Mingo, "The Competitive Condition of U.S. Banking Markets and the Impact of Structural Reform," *Journal of Finance* 32 (June 1977), 649–61.

[3] See Guttentag and Herman, *Banking Structure;* A. Phillips' chapter on banking in his *Promoting Competition in Regulated Markets;* and D. Jacobs, *Business Loan Costs and Bank Market Structure* (New York: National Bureau of Economic Research, 1971).

TABLE 20–2
Banking Concentration in Selected U.S. Cities, 1975

Metropolitan Area	Total Deposits ($ billion)	Percent Held by the:	
		Largest Bank (%)	Largest Three Banks (%)
Largest Seven			
New York	112	16	46
Chicago	45	20	46
Los Angeles...................	28	31	66
San Francisco	26	44	80
Detroit	17	29	59
Philadelphia...................	17	20	46
Boston	10	32	53
Others			
Phoenix, Arizona	4	43	87
Portland, Oregon	3	34	74
Columbus, Ohio	3	35	78
Hartford, Conn.	2	47	86
Nashville, Tennessee	3	30	76
Jacksonville, Florida	2	16	42
Albany, Georgia	2	27	62
Lowell, Massachusetts	1	54	86
South Bend, Indiana	1	23	55
Galveston, Texas	1	21	53

Source: Federal Deposit Insurance Corporation, *Summary of Accounts and Deposits in All Commercial Banks,* (Washington, D.C.: U.S. Government Printing Office, 1976).

official bank charters difficult to get. Whether or not these restrictions are optimal, they do make the degree of monopoly greater than formal concentration suggests.

Until 1970, banking had become very secure. Since 1935 the rate of bank failures has dropped nearly to zero, and it has remained low even during the stressful 1969–78 period. This is far below the business risks in any other major sector. This reflects deliberate policy, including the restrictions on competition, the insuring of deposits, and Federal Reserve policies.

Bank-Firm Ties. Banking relationships—between banks and their main client firms—are hard to discover, being highly sensitive facts which are not collected or published by any official agency. Patterns of banker directorships reflect some of the underlying tissue of connections.[4] Together with financial folklore, they indicate that there are strong and stable ties among leading banks and firms. Within the whole array, there are definite clusters around certain bank groups, especially the descendants of the original Rocke-

[4] See U.S. House Subcommittee on Antitrust, *Interlocks in Corporate Management,* 89th Congress, First Session (Washington, D.C.: U.S. Government Printing Office, 1965).

feller and Morgan interests.[5] The few extra-large international firms may relate to several or more major banks, partly for local connections and partly to play the banks off against each other. But for the greater mass of firms, a single strong banking relationship—reflecting the firm's own status—is normal.

Each bank can be regarded as relying primarily on a relatively few direct relationships with its major clients. It nurses these along, providing a variety of services and expertise, plus whatever insider and privileged information it can supply from any of the sources it can develop. These ties are not formal, but they are often exceedingly strong. It is common knowledge, for example, that banks do not normally try to compete away each others' main clients. It is simply not done (with few exceptions), and in any event the ties resist most price-cutting inducements.[6] The key is the whole package of mutual trust and support which the banking relationship involves.

In short, banking tends toward very tight formal and informal market structure, much more than efficiency requires. In addition, its relationship to producing enterprises involves a degree of quasi-vertical integration and shared access, both to favorable credit terms and to higher-quality inside advice and information. Therefore, banking touches on both the efficiency of its own allocation and of its allocation of capital among other producing units.

Banking behavior and performance fits these structural patterns. There has been little direct price competition among banks. A degree of competition does occur on quality and fringe service features, much as it does among regulated airlines (recall Chapter 14). But behavior reflects the market structure and informal restrictions among banks. It has also been stodgy and sluggish—especially during 1935–65—but partly for historical reasons.[7]

---

[5] See the excellent summary by James C. Knowles, "The Rockefeller Financial Group," in Ralph L. Andreano, ed., *Superconcentration/Supercorporation* (Andover, Mass.: Warner Modular Publications, 1973). Also see U.S. House Committee on Banking and Currency, *Commercial Banks and Their Trust Activities,* 2 vols., 90th Cong., 2d Sess. (Washington, D.C.: U.S. Government Printing Office, 1968), for a massive body of evidence. As for underwriters, the clustering is also strong. Thus Morgan Stanley & Co.—successor to part of the old Morgan group—has as clients six of the 10 largest U.S. industrial firms and 13 of the 25 largest, including auto, computer, electrical equipment, steel, chemical, photographic, and farm equipment firms.

[6] Thus, the failure of Franklin National Bank in 1974 traced back partly to its efforts to enter New York City banking in the 1960s. It could not hope to attract major new clients away from other banks. Only inferior lending activities were accessible, and so it was kept on the higher-risk fringe of the market from the start. This is the normal experience for new entrants. See Sanford Rose, "What Really Went Wrong at Franklin National," *Fortune* magazine, October 1974, pp. 118–21 and 220–27. The negative effects of structure on performance are lucidly reviewed in Arnold A. Heggestad's survey chapter in Franklin R. Edwards, ed., *Financial Regulation* (New York: McGraw-Hill, 1978).

[7] "Banking was a dead, dreary business in the days after World War II. Bankers were first stunned by the debacle of the 1930s and then dulled by years of doing little more than financing the massive U.S. war debt. A full generation of talented

Behavior. Banks have earned stable and rather high rates of return. Taking the top two banks in the 10 largest banking centers, the average return on equity for these 20 banks during 1970–76 was 14 percent. There was little variation (either among the group or from year to year), reflecting a low degree of risk.

Interest rates differ by the size, market position, and banking relationship of the borrower. Large dominant-firm clients usually pay lower interest rates, often by several percentage points. Interest paid on private deposits also varies, with larger depositors getting better terms.[8] Also, bank trust departments have usually catered mainly to large clients, such as with portfolios above $100,000. The best of the trust departments deal only in larger accounts, starting at $500,000 or more.

A2. Evolution of Banking and Policies

American banking first grew slowly and locally, but it changed rapidly after the Civil War. It matured during 1890–1930 in several directions, but the bankers' traumas of the Great Crash of 1929–1933 brought on a strong preference—among bankers and public officials—with security, to be reinforced by rigid divisions and regulations. Since about 1960 banking has increasingly bent and flowed around these constraints, with rapid changes by some larger banks since 1965.

The main lines of evolution in banking in the United States are given in Table 20–3. The origins were local, in supplying credit and quasi-moneys to oil the wheels of nascent commerce.[9] The First and Second National banks (1787–1836) stirred a variety of local and political resistance, so that subsequent banking in the United States remained mainly a localized operation. By 1900 a range of *(a)* state and national, *(b)* branch and single-unit, and *(c)* grass-roots and Wall Street banks had evolved.

Charters were given liberally in most areas, to help foster development. Bankers' activities spread into many lines, just as they still do in most other industrial economies. Banks were variously engaged in investing, factoring, brokering, merger-promoting, underwriting, and other "financial" operations—and in directing many industrial companies—as well as in the traditional deposit banking. By 1900 unit banking prevailed, but branch banking then spread, and by 1935 held more than half of banking assets. Now it

---

college graduates went into almost every business except banking." (*Business Week,* "The New Banking," September 15, 1973, pp. 88–92.) Some change came during the 1960s, toward the degree of entrepreneurship common in other sectors.

[8] The official ceilings set by the Federal Reserve on interest rates for savings deposits were at four percent up to 1970, and not above 5.5 percent during 1970–74; yet a variety of Treasury bills, short-term bonds, and other certificates commonly used by the wealthy were paying as high as 10 percent.

[9] See Fischer, *American Banking Structure,* and for more details, Davis R. Dewey, *Financial History of the United States* (New York: Longmans, 1911).

TABLE 20–3
Milestones in Banking and Public Policy

1782–1840	Early banks form (Bank of North America, 1782; 28 state-chartered banks by 1800; Bank of United States, 1791–1811; Second Bank of United States, 1816–32; 901 banks by 1840).
1864–1865	The National Bank Act (amended) sets conditions for charters, favors unit banking, covers most state banks (1556 banks in existence).
1865–1900	Growth and turbulence. Unit banks become prevalent, policies shift to limit branching (4338 banks in 1886 to 29,151 in 1910).
1907	Panic threatens the entire banking system, once again.
1914	The Federal Reserve System is created.
1920–1935	Turmoil, then collapse; 15,000 bank suspensions (9000 in 1930–33 alone) and 7000 mergers. Federal Reserve fails to support the system during 1929–33. Half the states prohibit branching by 1930, and most others limit it.
1933–1935	Bank Acts fix banking rules, define limits. The Reconstruction Finance Corp. (RFC) created in 1932, continues until 1952. The Federal Deposit Insurance Corp. (FDIC) is created in 1933–34.
1930s	Many Federal credit agencies are started (farming, housing, etc.).
1930s–1950s	Bank cooperation is approved and reinforced. Bank of America (San Francisco) leads in branching, becomes the largest bank.
1950s	The banking share in the financial sector begins to slip by 1950s.
1951–1963	A bank merger wave; many major horizontal mergers.
1956	The Bank Holding Company Act legitimizes, but limits, bank holding companies.
1960	The Bank Merger Act. Moderate; it tries to define criteria and assign agency jurisdiction.
1960s	Term loans assume greater importance. One-bank holding companies spread.
1961–1964	Several Antitrust Division cases attack bank cooperation. James Saxon, Comptroller of the Currency, opens up entry and chartering policies.
1963	The *Philadelphia National Bank* case stops a major merger. Later cases further tighten limits on horizontal mergers.
1965–1974	"Performance banking" spreads, led by First National City Bank of New York.
1970	The Bank Holding Company Act is amended to permit (and limit) holding companies.
1970–1975	A rise in holding companies, to include nearly all large banks. Bank failures increase to significant levels. FDIC and comptroller arduously arrange absorptions of several tottering banks.
1974	The Federal Reserve intervenes to influence bank support on real estate and other loans.
1974–1978	The period of high-risk exposure passes, with only a few bank failures.

handles the great majority of all banking activities. Yet antibranching restrictions have remained tight in many states, as local banks resisted the incursions—and new competition—of big-city money.

Instability has been a chronic problem in a local banking system, for panic runs on banks could arise at any time, spread, and cause the widespread destruction of deposits as well as of the banks themselves. This occurred in the 1870s, 1890s, 1907–8, and of course in 1929–1933 (see Figure 20–2).

FIGURE 20–2
Bank Suspensions since 1890

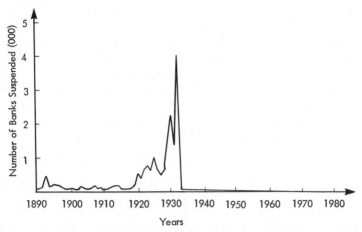

Source: *Historical Statistics of the United States,* 1957, and the *U.S. Statistical Abstract, Annual*

By 1930 the new Federal Reserve Board had powers to avert many failures, but by a great error of omission they did not use these powers. The 1929–32 trauma led to a six-part set of policies to assure "sound" banking:

1. The FDIC was to guarantee most deposits, by insurance and inspection.
2. Banks were sealed off from all other activities.
3. The Federal Reserve System was to stand ready to keep the whole system liquid enough so that failures could not spread.
4. New entry was tightly restricted, to avert the "unstable" effects of competition (branching was also more tightly limited).
5. Examiners of the FDIC, Federal Reserve, Comptroller of the Currency, and state agencies were to scrutinize banks' operations, to prevent risky loans and other actions.
6. Price competition among banks (for example, by offering interest on deposits) was officially restricted in various ways.

Some of these new policies merely reflected the internecine struggles among banking interest groups. Others helped all banks at the expense of banking customers. And some policies genuinely reflected "the public interest." Altogether, they more than doubled the policy safeguards that were needed in order to assure an optimum degree of stability.

At any rate, banking became tightly restricted in the 1930s, and during 1930–60 it was managed by officials whose main objective was security. There were exceptions, as the Bank of America and others sought ways around some of the limits. By the 1950s the pressures and experiments were rising, but only after 1965 did the main lines come under strong pressure. By 1975 the changes included:

1. A shift (perhaps to be reversed soon) from prudence to "performance" as the aim of the larger banks.
2. A shift from safe, secured short-term loans to riskier—even speculative—long-term loans and debt instruments.
3. Increased speed and flexibility in portfolio-type operations, including those in the Euro-dollar market, real estate, railroads, and so on.
4. A massive shift to one-bank holding companies during 1965–70, which entered a range of adjacent financial markets (factoring, credit cards, and so on).
5. Increased entry during 1961–65 and then more slowly, both by new banks and by more branching.

Underlying these changes were technological gains in data processing, which were evolving toward giant capacities to hold deposits and clear transactions quickly. Some physical trappings of banking operations (checks, cashiers, bonds, and the like) are now superfluous, for a unified giro type of clearing system can do virtually all of it by computer. Some of the operations and technology of banking, therefore, continue as a form of cultural lag, which might be improved by more competition, wise regulation or public banking units, or by some mixture of the three.

A3. Forms of Regulation

The whole set of public regulations and agencies is a "crazy quilt," as the Federal Reserve termed it as long ago as 1938. The overlapping activities of federal and state regulations are summarized in Table 20–4. These formal lines do not show the full range of activities and conflicts. Thus, the Federal Reserve was active during 1974–75 in getting banks to renew support for real estate trusts and other shaky firms; that goes well beyond its traditional role of general support. The Antitrust Division has entered deeply into—even dominated—the screening of mergers since 1961, pushing aside the other agencies in many respects. The then Comptroller of the Currency, James J. Saxon, during 1961–65 adopted a permissive policy toward new entry.

Still, Table 20–4 faithfully conveys the degree to which "regulation" is mixed and, therefore, *full responsibility is not borne by any single unit.* Note also that regulation touches only on security, market presence, and minimum prices. There is no economic regulation of the classic, complete sort: of maximum prices and permitted profits. Therefore, banking regulation can verge on self-regulation, which—when it reduces competition among oligopolists—is often the least satisfactory type of regulation.

B. CURRENT POLICY ISSUES

The basic lesson is that banking has been more restricted than is needed to meet the aim of secure deposits. The FDIC and Federal Reserve's support

TABLE 20–4
Regulatory Coverage in Banking, 1976

Number	Assets ($ billions)		Comptroller of the Currency	Federal Reserve	FDIC	State Agencies
4735	583	**National Banks**				
		Chartered by	✓			
		Examined by	✓	✓	✓	
		Reserves required by	✓	✓	✓	
		Subject to regulations of	✓	✓	✓	
		Mergers and branches limited by	✓	✓		
1023	190	**State Member Banks**				
		Chartered by				✓
		Examined by		✓	✓	
		Reserves required by		✓		
		Subject to regulations of	✓	✓	✓	✓
		Mergers and branches limited by		✓		✓
8639	231	**Insured Non-member Banks**				
		Chartered by				✓
		Examined by			✓	✓
		Reserves required by				✓
		Subject to regulations of		✓	✓	✓
		Mergers and branches limited by			✓	✓

functions appear to avert any serious hazards. To this extent, the rest of the policy apparatus is superfluous and costly.

Restrictive Practices. These remain pervasive with official backing, and so banking competition is usually reduced and confined to peripheral service items. Large clients get more flexible treatment, via full-service banking. But the pricing within these banking relationships is obscure, and competing for major clients is largely against the bankers' traditional code of behavior. The limits vary from state to state, but the effects are similar. The restrictions often just formalize an underlying cooperation within the banking fraternity.

These roles do not erase all competition. The larger firms often play banks off against each other. Even under free competition, interest rates would vary among customers. But they would be more flexible and open to innovation and change.

Structural Controls. There are four main parts:

1. Entry into banking markets can occur only with official approval, which is influenced by the interests of established banks.
2. Banks cannot be taken over by nonbanking enterprises.
3. Mergers among banks now are limited to relatively small market shares, after a period when many large-share mergers were freely permitted.
4. In many states, banks' ability to set up multiple branches in different cities is limited or prohibited.

Entry control has been at the heart of banking policy for 40 years. The decisions to permit entry are made by the Comptroller, the Federal Reserve, and various state banking regulators. An aspiring entrant must prepare a case which proves a concrete need for additional banking services, beyond what is already being supplied by banks or is likely to be supplied in the future. The burden of proof is mainly against the entrant (recall Chapter 3). Proof is usually difficult. The criteria for showing an "unmet banking need" are subjective, involve debatable predictions, and can always be disputed.

Entry was more liberally permitted during 1961–65, but the net effects were modest. Entry was mainly into the smallest city markets, but even so the degree of concentration remained high. In the larger cities, new banks had a negligible impact.[10]

The controls reduce new entry *and* the formation of new banks by experts presently working in the established banks. This second effect probably is the more important. Upper bank officials might otherwise tend to move freely to form new banks, taking the better corporate clients with them. Banking economics would yield a fluid banking structure, more efficient and adaptable. By comparison, entry by small, inexperienced outsiders is likely to be peripheral.

The 1930s rules ended certain abuses by sealing off banking from nonfinancial activities. But this also immunized banks against take-over from outside. Since banking and regulatory motives strongly favor security, the lack both of take-over discipline and of competition would naturally foster inefficiency. The degree of inefficiency has probably not been small. The recent rise of one-bank holding companies does not correct this, because the really powerful nonfinancial groups are excluded. The barrier between banking and other markets is still intact.

Mergers have been a prominent issue but are of moderate importance. The 1950–63 wave was stimulated partly by the hope of getting in under

---

[10] D. A. Alhadeff and C. P. Alhadeff, "Bank Entry and Bank Concentration," *Antitrust Bulletin* (Spring 1975). New banks (all those entering during 1948–66) had in 1970 only about 2 percent of deposits in the large-city markets.

the wire before the Celler-Kefauver Act could be tightly applied. This worked, in fact, and so the 1963 *Philadelphia* case and its aftermath (recall Chapter 6) has had the same effect as merger policy in industry: it tends to ratify and harden a tighter structure. In 1973–74 the Supreme Court at last found against the Antitrust Division in two small bank merger cases. Yet these were marginal cases, involving small market shares and merely potential competition from banks presently in separate cities. "Competitive effect" has now become the ruling criterion for bank mergers (superseding various banking factors cited in earlier agency approvals). But the net effect of the whole tilt and timing of policies has been to ratify tight structure in many banking markets.

Branching is a natural form of banking, with local units spread out within cities and among towns. Yet it remains prohibited or closely limited in many states. The main valid reason for these restrictions is to foster local interest and support by banks. This could be important on Jeffersonian grounds, if absentee-owned banks did systematically ignore local clients in favor of large impersonal firms. Yet some of the local banks, thus shielded, tend to be inefficient and restrictive, so that the net effects of branching rules may well be negative.

Branching appears to improve bank performance, if the branching does not involve increased local market shares. These two elements are separable. In nonbranch states, old banks in the smaller cities often live cloistered lives and their client have restricted choices. The loss is: *(a)* allocative inefficiency, for rates are not competed down and service expanded, and *(b)* X-inefficiency, for the banks are often isolated from modern management techniques and portfolio criteria.

The old branching prohibitions are eroding, but they are still extensive. Moreover, branching among states is also outlawed, and this limits competition even more severely. Still further, banks and quasi-banks—savings and loan societies, credit unions, and so forth—have not been permitted to compete directly, under official policies. These policies add up to a balkanization of markets similar to franchised utilities, with the predictable negative effects. Though eroding, these barriers are still important.

Banking Relationships.   Policy toward banking relationships scarcely exists. There is no policy or means for disclosure of them. Little is done to offset the advantages which they give to established firms against small and potential entrants. No agency presently has the resources or political standing to press the issue.

Summary.   The main effect of banking policies appears to be toward rigidity, inefficiency, and a retardation of progress. Many of the restrictions could be removed (perhaps gradually) without reducing the security of deposits and of banks. Rather, the change would improve banking performance in several directions. "Banking reform" has been brewing actively in Congress during the 1970s, but it has succumbed to lobbying by the banking community.[11] This is understandable, given the structure of the interests. But the economic case for more competition is clear. Some increase in competition has been occurring, in spite of official policies. How much further it should go is the question.

C. SECURITIES MARKETS

C1. Basic Conditions

Stocks are only one among the many kinds of asset values that are traded: there are also bonds, commodities, futures, options, warrants, discounted paper, debentures, rights, etc. But the stock market is crucial for corporate evaluation and control.[12] There are two levels to analyze. One is the narrow brokerage function: handling stock transactions for a fee. The other is the substance of trading, information, and control over firms: the market for corporate control.

---

[11] As one eminent bank lobbyist put it, "The bank lobby can almost certainly stop anything it does not want in Congress." In addition, "the power of the banks rests on an intricate political and financial structure that has many elements. Among them are political contributions, the power to make loans, a highly sophisticated lobbying effort, a close similarity of interests with such powerful groups as the Chamber of Commerce and, perhaps most telling, unsurpassed social and economic leverage in almost every town and city in the United States.

"Another distinct advantage enjoyed by financial institutions is that in virtually every town, city, and state, bankers are among the most powerful and influential citizens. In most communities, the banker, Representative Fernand St. Germain, Democrat of Rhode Island, said, "is a leader in church. He is the source of credit to the car dealer and all other businessmen. He is the adviser. Politically, he has great power—and that is something to contend with. What other group has that kind of power?"

"The bank lobby is a growth industry in Washington. The venerable American Banking Association, founded in 1875, now has a professional staff of 350, an annual budget of $24 million, and 16 registered lobbyists, 4 of whom are said to specialize in maintaining the A.B.A.'s contacts with the regulatory agencies. Another bank lobby is the Independent Bankers Association, which tends to represent small and medium-sized banks, sometimes at odds with the A.B.A. Then there are more specialized lobbying groups. The Mortgage Bankers Association of America, with 76 staff members and a $4 million annual budget, represents companies that specialize in financing real estate transactions. The nation's largest banks recently formed the Association of Reserve City Bankers to look out for their special concerns. The savings and loan associations also have several Washington-based trade associations that divide their time between Capitol Hill and the regulatory agencies. "Banks' Influence in Capitol Called Strongest of Any Regulated Industry," *New York Times,* December 23, 1977, pp. Al, D3.

That a 1978 law tightening regulation slipped by Congress shows that the control is not perfect. But this was an exception, and a modest one at that.

[12] On basic conditions, see the sources noted in footnote 1 above; W. J. Baumol, *The Stock Market and Economic Efficiency* (New York: Fordham University Press, 1965); Sidney Robbins, *The Securities Market* (Glencoe, Ill.: Free Press, 1966); and Robert Sobel, *NYSE* (New York: Weybright & Talley, 1975). On the turbulent conditions of the 1960s, see John Brooks, *The Go-Go Years* (New York: Weybright & Talley, 1973).

The Brokerage Function. Brokerage is handled by a hierarchy of stock exchanges. The New York Stock Exchange has the leading firms; the American Stock Exchange has lesser ones; while the regional and over-the-counter market includes the mass of small and new firms. They are the trading arena used by the hundreds of private brokerage firms.

Transactions are essentially simple housekeeping actions: finding the price, conducting a trade, recording the terms, and transferring the certificate. There must be an information network, so that traders at a distance can learn the going prices. The whole process is simple, standard, and increasingly computerized. Yet ordinary traders must have the transaction done—for a fee—by a broker, who has access to the exchange. This is usually a brokerage house, which has one or more memberships in (or "seats on") the exchange, through which the trades are funnelled. Since NYSE members can only do brokerage business (by NYSE rule), they are neatly immunized from takeover by other firms.

The broker provides the access, the instant information, and the handling. The brokerage firms range from the dominant Merrill Lynch, Pierce, Fenner & Smith down to many scores of small firms. Their ranks have been thinning with the fluctuations since 1966, by failure and mergers. The larger firms also do some market research and circulate advice to investors, but this printed material is of limited value to most customers. The basic objective is to outguess the rest of the market. This involves much sheer gambling, since the impact of any new information depends on how well it has already been anticipated, plus many other influences; and those are anybody's guess in many cases. (However, brokerage firms also try to get all possible inside information for their clients; some of this is important and also poses major policy questions.)

Until 1975 brokers' fees were fixed in a structure illustrated roughly by Figure 20–3.[13] The cost per transaction was relatively uniform. Yet the fee varied by the total value of the sale, reflecting both the price of the shares and the number of shares of the stock. Therefore, the pricing mixed cost criteria and price discrimination. The fee schedule was set by the Exchange, acting as a cartel of its members. Fees were made competitive in 1975, and so their basic shape is now similar to the average cost line in Figure 20–3.

The long trend is toward computerizing and linking trades in one unified market. The separate stock exchanges would fade away in the process, and so would the cartel controls they maintain. Therefore they are tending to retard this evolution, in their members' behalf. Yet the members were also losing from the long-term shrinkage of business which the price fixing itself

---

[13] On pricing, costs, and competition, see H. M. Mann's chapter 9 in A. Phillips, ed., *Promoting Competition;* Subcommittee on Securities, *Securities Industry Study;* and Irwin Friend and Marshall E. Blume, *The Consequences of Competitive Commissions on the New York Stock Exchange,* an excellent analysis included as Appendix A in "Stock Exchange Commission Rates," Hearings before the Senate Subcommittee on Securities, 93d Cong. 2d Sess. (Washington, D.C.: U.S. Government Printing Office, 1972), pp. 259–404.

492

FIGURE 20–3
The Basic Patterns of Costs and Fees in Brokerage before 1975, Illustrated

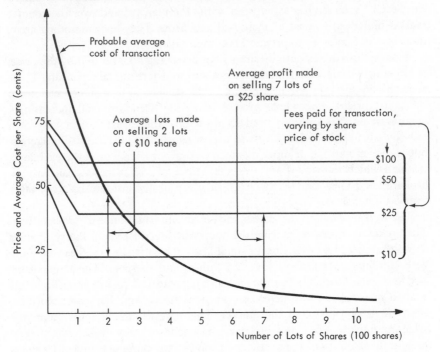

caused. The outcome has been a vector of these cross-incentives: some retardation, but with complex struggles among the various members, independents, and other trading groups.

In its essentials, stockbroking is a potentially competitive industry. Stock exchange, officials claimed instead during 1968–75 that it tends toward "destructive" competition, so that price fixing gave social benefits. Yet that view has little merit. Stock-exchange price-fixing existed for over a century, only encountering policy resistance before the SEC in 1968. It was abolished in 1975, causing most fees to drop sharply toward cost levels (thus, the average fee on large orders fell from about 22 cents a share to 5–7 cents a share.)[14] Brokerage firms have had financial stress, especially since 1963; some have failed and some have been merged as "failing" firms. The severity of these problems has not been caused by the freeing of fees.

The Market for Capital and Control. Now we turn to the deeper role of stock trading, in fostering efficient capital flows and giving fair access to information. U.S. conditions are known to be perhaps the best among the

---

[14] The effects are appraised in Aharon R. Ofer and Arie Melnick, "Price Deregulation in the Brokerage Industry: An Empirical Analysis," *Bell Journal of Economics* 9 (Autumn 1978), 633–41.

world's stock exchanges, but they are still improvable. Stock-holding and trading are by diverse units, including *(a)* large institutional investors (insurance firms, pension funds, endowments, bank trust officers, and so on); *(b)* small professional traders (expert, well placed, often specializing in esoteric operations); and *(c)* personal investors, ranging from large, experienced holders down to the masses of small investors. Institutions now do over 70 percent of all trading (in 1974 the share reached about 85 percent). The largest bank trust departments play a large role. Small investors tend to earn small or negative gains, since *(a)* they are ignorant of basic trends, methods of evaluation, and timing strategy; *(b)* they get news after the professionals have already learned, acted upon, and discounted it;[15] and *(d)* brokerage fees are a higher proportion of the value of their trades.

The whole process performs several functions. It evaluates management. It allocates capital among the whole range of firms. It rewards good and timely investment decisions and penalizes incorrect ones. In a well-functioning capital market, stock values move smoothly in line with actual performance and prospects of the firm. There is an inherent gambling element, but it operates moderately, as a form of arbitrage to keep stock prices in line with the underlying industrial values.

Actual conditions diverge from this ideal in certain ways. The basic flaw is *insiderism:* the disparity in access to key information. There are layers of access to data, which systematically favor larger, well placed investors. Brokerage firms (and others) often discriminate in using the inside information they do get. There is a steady stream of cases involving favors to large clients: this is probably the small visible tip of a large iceberg. Such insider problems are widespread and have real effects. The small investor is forced to rely, on the whole, on mediocre advice and late information.[16]

As for efficiency, stock markets deal in portfolio assets, not directly in productive investment. Their allocative effect is indirect and can be compromised by imperfections and extraneous disturbances. Market psychology can put whole classes of productive firms into disfavor, pushing their stock prices below levels at which efficient amounts of new capital can be raised. It is

---

[15] The advantages of professional stock specialists were summarized by one successful trader: "As a trader, I had a terrific edge over the average investor because of all the electronics and direct lines to trading desks at my disposal. It gave me total information and market feel about various stocks, which is invaluable. Mainly I could get people to tell the truth about stocks." (*The Wall Street Journal,* October 4, 1974, p. 1.)

[16] This is widely agreed among expert observers, and is frequently discussed in *The Wall Street Journal, Business Week, Forbes,* and the like. As the small investor has realized that the market "is rigged against him in favor of the big institutional customers," (*Business Week,* November 17, 1973, p. 27), participation has decreased. In 1970 30 percent of U.S. families owned some stock; in 1977 only 19 percent did. Companies routinely hold private meetings for institutional stockholders and security analysis at which advance information is given. This is used first for the best clients and then, if ever, disseminated. Repeatedly, the large traders' actions change the price by 25 percent or more before small investors have a chance to hear.

not clear that stock prices are brought into line with intrinsic values. Many experts believe that the allocative function is not performed well.[17]

In short, there are serious doubts about the structure, behavior, and performance of the stock market. There may be sizable social losses under present conditions.

C2. SEC Actions

The Securities and Exchange Commission, created in 1934, is the main regulating agency. It deals mainly with honesty in information, but it also acted in 1975 to stop the fixing of brokers' fees. There are three topics to consider: *(a)* fixed commissions, *(b)* insiderism, and *(c)* the SEC's role.

Fixed Commissions. Policy long tolerated cartel behavior by the stock exchanges, which held brokerage prices above their long-run levels. This fostered inefficiency in the brokerage houses, which the stresses of the 1960s quickly exposed. The exchanges also retarded evolution toward an efficient unified market. The SEC's shift toward the 1975 termination of fixed rates was partly a shift toward improved regulation. But mostly it reflected the shift in the basic interests, as trading moved off the exchange floors into the large-volume third market and the NYSE's members' own interests altered. The SEC acted: it also was carried along by the underlying realities.

Insiderism. The SEC abates gross instances of insider trading, via its "Insider Report" and occasional cases. But the basic problem remains, with no new policy treatment in prospect. And even the occasional suits usually rely on special tips and complaints, so that many unreported offenses slip by. Experts regard the volume of unprosecuted insider abuses as extensive. The SEC has also acquiesced in other practices (such as special briefings for institutions and analysts) which favor some investors at the expense of others. Nor has it studied the problem in depth.

Long-term secrecy has been reduced by the SEC's recent requirements for divisional reporting. Since 1970 firms must disaggregate on "Form 10-K" all "lines of business" over 15 percent of company revenues. The definition of "line of business" is often slippery, and the costs and assets can often be freely allocated among lines of business to fit company objectives. Form 10-K has therefore reduced secrecy only moderately. The net effect has fallen well short of full disclosure.

The SEC's Role. The SEC emerges as part mediator, part innovator. It is widely regarded as superior to most other regulatory commissions, though it treats some problems only moderately and others not at all. This good reputation can be credited to several factors. *(a)* The SEC has a diverse constituency; large and small investors, the exchanges and brokers, industrial and other firms, etc. It can balance among these, nudging toward changes

---

17 See Irwin Friend, "The Economic Consequences of the Stock Market," *American Economic Review* 62, 2 (May 1972), 212–19, and sources cited there.

which are latent or already in progress. It need not become dependent on just one regulatee.

(b) It focuses its efforts. Since its resources are thin compared to its ultimate tasks, this means that large problems go untreated. But it also preserves the SEC from entering various troubled waters. *(c)* The tradition of high-quality chairmen has become fairly firm. As in antitrust, the constituency has come—since 1960 especially—to expect sophistication, honesty, and energy in the appointed chairman.

D. INSURANCE

D1. Basic Conditions

Insurance operations have two sides: *(a)* insurance (coverage of risks to life and property), and *(b)* investment (large-scale portfolio operations). Small net losses on the insurance are often more than off-set by profits on the investment function (mutual firms have roughly zero net profits). The industry is on a large scale, with a range from large to medium-size firms. Life and property insurance are the main parts. To most consumers, life, home, and automobile insurance pose the main problems.[18] Though most operations are national, insurance is regulated only at the state levels.

As is common elsewhere, there are some economies of scale, but not beyond moderate size. The risk of the firm arises both in insurance and in investment operations, and so sheer size does not add greatly to stability.

Structure ranges between loose and tight oligopoly, with some variation among states. This is usually tighter than minimum efficient scale requires. Competition is also limited by various regulatory rules and by the life insurance firms' practice of using the same mortality table as a basis for rates.

There are four main criteria of social performance for insurance: *(a)* breadth of coverage, *(b)* efficient management, *(c)* reducing the cost of insured losses, and *(d)* security of coverage. *Breadth* of coverage need not be universal, but in a decent society it will not exclude large groups of needy and high-risk persons. This inherently conflicts with the economics of private insurance; to maximize profits, the firm will tend precisely to exclude persons with known high risks who are unable to pay premiums. This exclusion is not complete, but it is substantial. The large minority of the population which is left unprotected is primarily those who most need coverage, both on private criteria and social criteria.

Costs are substantial. Between 20 and 50 percent of premiums are absorbed in company costs (though much less for Blue Cross and Blue Shield). The sales costs are substantial, including about 600,000 salespeople. The better firms hold sales and administrative costs to low levels; public, universal-coverage systems have especially low cost ratios.

---

[18] Health insurance is dominated by the Blue Cross-Blue Shield, Medicare, and Medicaid systems. Unemployment and accident insurance are largely public systems.

Constraints can be exerted by insurance firms on such costs as medical care and automobile design and repair. Special rates can be offered for healthy living and driving habits, and better automobile design. Hospitals can be pressured to increase efficiency and to price their services more efficiently. Instead, insurance firms have mainly been passive.

Security is important, because the policy is a long-term commitment which becomes like a principal savings account to many policyholders. Failure of an insurance firm can cause devastating hardships for thousands of clients (unless the firm is reinsured, privately or publicly.)

Performance in the main insurance markets therefore shows certain defects. These touch both on efficiency and equity, often with sharp impacts.

D2. Policies

Insurance long claimed exemption from antitrust, on the ground that it was not truly interstate commerce. But in the 1940s there were efforts to put it either under antitrust or under federal regulation.

In 1944, the Supreme Court held that the Sherman Act did apply, since there was much interstate sending of documents, letters, and money.[19] The insurance firms then took shelter under state regulation via the McCarran Act of 1945. It gave state regulation precedence over the antitrust laws, save for certain clear price-fixing actions and mergers. Many states then passed new regulatory laws for insurance, patterned on a model statute prepared by the insurance firms.

State regulation of insurance involves a severe disparity between agency resources and tasks. The supervision tends to lag well behind events, as the few evaluators struggle with masses of material. Though California and Illinois are regarded as among the better regulatory units, it was they who conspicuously failed to detect the brazen Equity Funding abuses of 1970–73. Like other state regulators, they tend to become passive toward the larger firms they regulate and to be unable either to regulate or to achieve reform for their own awkward situation.

The regulators supervise *(a)* financial soundness, *(b)* the fairness of trade practices, and *(c)* rates.

Soundness. State insurance commissioners determine the capital a company must have, require the maintenance of adequate reserves, prescribe accounting methods, check on the value of assets, and control investment policies. They enforce these controls by requiring companies to make deposits of securities, by calling for annual reports, and by conducting examinations of company accounts. Processing often lags two years behind the filings.[20]

---

[19] *U.S.* v. *South-Eastern Underwriters,* 322 U.S. 533.

[20] In *The Wall Street Journal's* words, "The picture the audit presents has all the freshness of the Dead Sea Scrolls." The regulatory units are usually financed by the insurance firms themselves, and officials move freely between the firms and official positions. "Commissioners often negotiate for and announce new jobs in the industry

Trade Practices. Brokers and agents are required to obtain licenses, and those who cannot satisfy administrative standards are excluded from the field. Tying clauses, requiring one party to a transaction to purchase insurance from the other, and the rebating of premiums to favored purchasers of insurance, are banned. Policy forms are simplified and standardized or limited to those that the commissioner may approve. An effort is made to assure fairness in the settlement of disputed claims, some states seeking to avoid the time and cost of litigation by providing machinery to arbitrate disputes.

Rates. Here the choice lies between competition, on the one hand, and cooperation under public supervision, on the other. Cooperation has been chosen on the ground that competition might drive rates down to a level that would impair the ability of the companies to pay their claims. The laws provide only that rates shall not be excessive (whatever that may mean) and shall not discriminate among the purchasers of policies. The rates of fire and casualty insurance companies are prepared by private rating bureaus, filed with the state insurance commissioner, and made effective when approved by him. Commissioners have sometimes succeeded in preventing increases and bringing about reductions in rates. Membership in rating bureaus is required in a few states but not in most. Some states forbid agreements by the insurers to adhere to bureau rates. Independent filing is generally permitted, and deviations from bureau rates have increased. In the case of life insurance, rate bureaus are not needed. All of the companies use the same mortality tables as the basis for their rates, but those tables too are dubious.

This supervision may marginally abate the risk of financial failures and avert some sharp trade practices, but it tends more to stabilize premiums than to constrain them.[21] As in stock trading, the conditions that might cause destructive competition are absent or weak. Risks of default could be covered—as in banking—by direct insurance (or reinsurance) of the firms. Therefore the present regulation is an alternative to *(a)* genuinely strict and thorough regulation, or to *(b)* effective competition.

QUESTIONS FOR REVIEW

1. "The main activity of banks is handling personal deposits at the cashier's window." True?
2. "There are several layers of banking 'markets,' from local up to regional and national markets." True?
3. "Banking is much more competitive than the average retailing market." True?

---

while they are still in charge of regulating it." Regulation is also shallow and inefficient in various ways, and commissioners are of doubtful quality and have high turnover. And the regulation of state-size parts of large national firms is inevitably incomplete. *The Wall Street Journal,* August 2, 1973.

[21] For a lucid analysis of the reasons for removing regulation, see Paul L. Joskow, "Cartels, Competition, and Regulation in the Property-Liability Insurance Industry," *Bell Journal of Economics and Management Science* 4, 2 (Autumn 1973), 375–427.

4. "Banking relationships are usually stable and close." True?
5. "U.S. banking was often turbulent before 1929, but regulation since then has magnified the risks." True?
6. "Actual policies to make banking secure include *(a)* insurance of depositors, *(b)* tight scrutiny of operations, and *(c)* limits on bank competition." Which?
7. "To enter a banking market, you must prove that another bank is needed." True?
8. "Some states limit every bank—no matter how big it is—to just one location." True?
9. "Brokers' fees were fixed by stock exchange cartels until 1975, but since then little competition has occurred." True?
10. "Destructive competition is unlikely to occur in brokers' fees." True?
11. "Insiderism continues as a serious problem, despite the SEC's marginal effects on it." True?
12. "State regulation of insurance assures good social performance." True?
13. What banking policy "reforms" might be in order, in your best judgment?
14. If "destructive competition" were to occur in brokers' fees, how might it best be dealt with?
15. What social benefits does state regulation of insurance provide? Are they worth the costs?

chapter 21

Patents

A patent is a monopoly grant to an inventor, giving control over the production and selling of a new product or technique for 17 years. The resulting monopoly is virtually absolute and often lasts long after the patent's formal life is over. About 78,000 patents yearly are awarded in the United States. Among this flood of new ideas is a small number of sensationally successful ones, many useful ones, and thousands of stillborn flashes of genius.

The issue is important. Technical progress is the ultimate economic escape from national and global scarcity. It derives from widespread processes of invention and innovation, which involve at least $30 billion yearly in nearly every nook and cranny of the economy. Patenting may enhance or impair this effort. In any event, it creates much monopoly profits, and it poses antitrust issues in several important industries.

Patents pose basic questions about the origins of progress and their relation to market power.[1] Patents grant monopoly, which may last long. Yet patents may be an integral part of the process of progress and competition. In this chapter, we first describe the patent system. Next we analyze the basic economics of patents. Then we consider the antitrust problems raised by patent policies, and possible reforms. Trademarks are also briefly reviewed.

The wisdom of the patent system is endlessly debated, but the system

---

[1] Among the growing literature on the economic issues, see Jacob Schmookler, *Invention and Economic Growth* (Cambridge: Harvard University Press, 1966); F. M. Scherer, *Industrial Market Structure and Economic Performance* (Skokie, Ill.: Rand McNally, 1970), chap. 15; Edwin Mansfield and others, *Research and Innovation in the Modern Corporation* (New York: Norton, 1971); John Jewkes and others, *The Sources of Invention*, rev. ed. (New York: St. Martin's Press, 1968); Joseph A. Schumpeter, *Capitalism, Socialism, and Democracy* (New York: Harper, 1942); National Bureau of Economic Research, *The Rate and Direction of Inventive Activity* (Princeton: Princeton University Press, 1962); and William D. Nordhaus, *Invention, Growth, and Welfare* (Cambridge: MIT Press, 1969).

On the patent system's role, see Alfred E. Kahn, "The Role of Patents," in J. P. Miller, ed., *Competition, Cartels, and Their Regulation* (Amsterdam: North-Holland, 1962); Fritz Machlup, *The Economics of the Patent System;* and Scherer, *Industrial Market Structure,* chap. 16.

itself is highly resistant to change. Here the twin problems of progress and competition are brought together in a clear focus.

A. THE PATENT SYSTEM

The U.S. system, like most others, gives a monopoly to the inventor. It processes and stores these new ideas, validating them (after a delay when they are "pending"), and making the invention public.

Nature of the Patent. A patent is an exclusive right conferred on an inventor, for a limited period, by a government. It authorizes the inventor to make, use, transfer, or withhold whatever may be patented. This might be done in any case; what the patent adds is the right to exclude others or to admit them on the patentor's own terms. Without a patent, one might attempt to preserve a monopoly by keeping the invention secret; to get a patent, it must be disclosed.

FIGURE 21–1
Trends in Patent Activity in the United States, 1850–1976

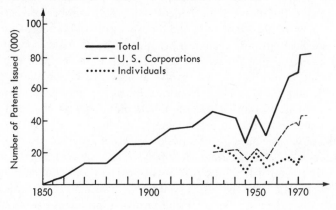

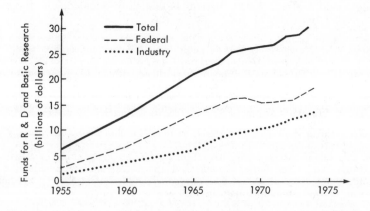

The policy of promoting invention by granting temporary monopolies to inventors, a policy that had been followed in England for nearly two centuries, was written into the Constitution of the United States.

Congress passed the first patent law in 1790, offering protection to all inventors of novel and useful processes and devices who would disclose their nature in sufficient detail to "enable a workman or other person skilled in the art of manufacture . . . to make, construct . . . or use the same."

In 1793 a second law authorized the Department of State to issue patents to everyone who might register inventions, without questioning their novelty or usefulness, leaving their validity to be determined by the courts. This act resulted in a flood of worthless patents and clogged the courts with litigation.

It was superseded in 1836 by a third law which set up a Patent Office under a Commissioner of Patents, required that applications be examined to determine whether the inventions claimed were really new, and provided that patents should be issued only when such inventions were deemed by the Commissioner to be "sufficiently useful and important." The American patent system still rests upon the foundations established by the Act of 1836.

Patents have been obtainable in the United States since 1790 on any useful "art, manufacture, engine, machine," since 1793 on a "composition of matter," since 1842 on "ornamental designs," and since 1930 on botanical plants, and on improvements to any of them.[2] Patents are not granted on methods of doing business, or on fundamental scientific discoveries. But otherwise the law is generous in its coverage.

Patents are issued to individuals, not to corporations. A patent is granted only to a person called "the sole and true inventor." But patent rights can be transferred to others through assignment. An inventor may sell rights in an invention already made. Or he may accept employment under a contract which binds him to transfer his rights in any invention that he may come to make.

In the usual case, he will file his assignment along with his application for a patent, and the corporation that employs him will be the assignee. In legal theory, patents are issued to individual inventors; in practice, 70 percent of them are assigned to corporations.

---

[2] The law thus covers processes of production (art, manufacture), the implements employed in such processes (engine, machine), and the products resulting from them (manufacture, composition of matter, and botanical plants). It covers, as a "composition of matter," not only such chemical products as dyestuffs, plastics, and synthetic fibers, but also foods and medicines—products to which the patent privilege is not generally extended under the laws of other countries.

Patents on "ornamental designs" may relate to the design of the article itself or to designs that are incorporated in it or affixed to it. Designs, however, may be protected more cheaply and for longer periods by obtaining copyrights. Design protection is afforded to products that are durable, such as jewelry and furniture. But fashions, in which the element of design is important, are neither patented nor copyrighted, not because the law exudes them, but because they change too rapidly to be protected by the usual legal processes.

The territorial scope of a patent is limited to the jurisdiction of the country that grants it. An American who wishes to protect an invention in other countries must take out patents under their laws. Foreigners may likewise take out patents in the United States. A patent may be exploited in one country, in another, or in both, and rights in different countries may be assigned to different firms. Products that are patented may not be imported in violation of domestic patent rights.

The 17-year patent life is an historical accident. In England in 1643 the duration of a patent was fixed at 14 years, a period sufficient to enable a craftsman to train two successive groups of apprentices. This term was adopted in the first patent law in the United States. In 1861, however, an effort to extend the term to 20 years resulted in a compromise that fixed it at 17, and 17 years is still the nominal duration of the monopoly conferred by the patent grant.

In most other countries the patent holder is required to put the invention to work.[3] No such obligations attach to patents issued by the United States. Within the limits laid down by the courts, the owner of a patent many refuse to work it, work it and refuse to license it to others, or license it on virtually any terms. In the lightness of its requirements, as in the breadth of its grants, the American patent law is extremely liberal.

How Patents Are Issued and Validated. It is the function of the Patent Office merely to accept or to reject the applications that are brought before it. Each application must describe, with some precision, the nature of the invention that is claimed. This description takes the form of drawings or formulae accompanied by exposition couched in technical phraseology. The monopoly awarded to an applicant will be confined within the boundaries of the claims. These claims are usually formulated by a patent lawyer employed by the inventor or, more often, by the corporate assignee.

Their preparation is an art in itself involving complex strategy decisions. The broader they can be made, without appearing to be limitless, the wider will be the area of the monopoly. The less informative they can be made, without appearing to withhold essential facts, the less is the likelihood that the technology involved will be disclosed to possible competitors. When the application is submitted to the Patent Office, it must be accompanied by a $65 fee. When the patent is obtained, another $100 must be paid. The fee or salary of the patent lawyer is the major cost of patenting. Comparative costs in various countries are given in Table 21–1.

Applications are not made public by the Patent Office. Persons who may hold patents on similar inventions are not informed of the proceedings. Persons

[3] In some countries this requirement is absolute. In others, it may be waived if the holder can show good cause or prove that a reasonable effort has been made. Failure to work an invention may be penalized by revocation or by the requirement that it be licensed to others. Licensing may also be required where enforcement of one patent would prevent the development of an invention covered by another, where refusal to license would prejudice the trade of other groups, and where the output of patented goods falls short of meeting public needs.

TABLE 21–1
Costs and Volumes of Patents Differ

Country	Minimum Amount of Fees and Other Costs of Patenting, per Patent, 1974	Numbers of Patents, 1971	
		Applied for	Granted
United States	$165	105,000	82,000
Britain	8	62,000	42,000
Holland	400	19,000	3,000
Sweden	130	18,000	11,000
Germany	165	64,000	19,000
Austria	14	13,000	10,000
Japan	43	107,000	38,000

who might be injured by a grant of monopoly are not notified. Agencies of government charged with the maintenance of competition are not represented. Interests adverse to the grant are given no opportunity to protest. Whether a patent shall be issued is determined as a matter not of public interest but of private privilege.

An invention is not supposed to be patented unless it is new and useful and actually works. But the number of applications presented to the Patent Office is so large, and the resources available for handling them are, by comparison, so small, that rigorous standards of appraisal cannot be maintained. The Office does not undertake to determine whether an invention is workable. With respect to usefulness, it adheres to the standard established by Justice Story in 1817. The word "useful," he said, "is incorporated in the Act in contradistinction to mischievous or immoral.[4] An invention is thus presumed to be useful unless there is evidence that it would do positive harm. Nor is there real assurance that the invention covered by a patent is new.

Applications for patents run around 110,000 per year, with more than 200,000 pending at any one time, each of them being taken up in its turn. The Patent Office has a staff of about 70 examiners and 1,000 assistant examiners. The typical assistant examiner is an engineering graduate who is studying law at night, preparing to become a patent attorney. The turnover in this group, amounting to 20 percent per year, is one of the highest in the government. The Patent Bar is a thriving small army clustering in Washington, D.C., but also extending into every sizable town.

Each assistant examiner handles 70 to 80 patent applications per year. In each case, he must analyze the application and search the prior art as revealed in Patent Office files and in scientific publications in the United States and abroad. In the case of certain chemicals, this process has been speeded by computerizing some of the relevant data; in other fields, however, mechanization is more difficult and has not yet been undertaken.

---

[4] *Lowell* v. *Lewis,* 15 Fed. Cases, 1018, 1019.

An examiner typically rejects one or more claims in an initial application, giving the applicant six months in which to file an amended application, which he then considers in its turn. He has, on the average, three working days in which to take all the steps that may be required from his first receipt of an application until a final determination can be made. Two out of five applications are finally abandoned or rejected; three are allowed. The typical patent, when granted, has been pending more than three years.[5]

If the examiner rejects an application, it may be carried to the Board of Appeals in the Patent Office where, in a third to a half of the cases, he is likely to be reversed. If the examiner is sustained, the applicant may go on to the Court of Customs and Patent Appeals where his chance of obtaining a patent may be one in five. Out of this flood of claims to monopolistic rights, granted as carelessly as must be the case, there will be many that will overlap.

The Patent Office does not guarantee its product. It does not warrant that the patentee is the true inventor or insure that his claim will be upheld. If he is sued for infringing another patent, he can argue that his own is different or superior. But the Patent Office will not come to his assistance. It leaves to him the burden and the cost of his defense. All that it gives him is a claim upon which he himself can enter suit. If another uses his invention without permission, he can seek an injunction and ask for damages. But the defendant may counter with a patent of his own, or may argue that the plaintiff's patent covers a process or a product that has long been common property. The resolution of such conflicts is the duty of the courts.

In about 60 percent of the cases decided, the courts have found that the plaintiff's patent was not infringed or that it was lacking in validity. It is a rare patent, however, that is taken to court, and an even rarer one that is appealed to the higher courts. The currency that is issued by the Patent Office thus passes at face value, save in those cases where the courts have found it to be counterfeit.

The decision to patent often involves close choices, and in numberless cases the choice is for secrecy or some other strategy instead. The choice depends on many things. Patents are a specific strategy fitted to certain conditions, *not* a universal stimulant to progress.

They cluster tightly in certain industries, especially in drugs, photocopying, aerospace, and electrical equipment. Over large areas of industry, patents are virtually absent and irrelevant.

Some patents are astronomically profitable. Often the inventor is so enriched that he ceases inventing altogether. Occasionally a patent serves to create a near-permanent monopoly.

---

[5] U.S. Senate, Committee on the Judiciary, Subcommittee on Patents, Trademarks, and Copyrights, Study No. 29, *The Examination System in the U.S. Patent Office* (Washington, D.C.: Government Printing Office, 1961). Each new Patent Commissioner vows to revolutionize (that is, computerize, expand, and so on) the process, but the basic process remains the same.

B. ECONOMIC ISSUES

Concepts.   Does the system make good economic sense? One begins with the basic economics of technical progress.[6] The process divides into various categories:

1. *Invention;* the new idea conceived and tested.
2. *Innovation;* the first application of the idea in production.
3. *Imitation;* spreading of the innovation to other producers.

Innovations are of two types:

a. *Product* innovations; a new product, the same production methods.
b. *Process* innovations; the same product, produced differently (so that the average cost curve shifts down).

These conceptual distinctions often have blurred edges in practice, but they clarify the stages and incentives in the process.

Also, new ideas differ in scope. Some are small and specialized: a knob here, a notch there, or a stripe in toothpaste. At the other extreme, some are broad and basic concepts, such as the wheel and interchangable parts. Patents cluster in the middle range; significant ideas whose gains can be temporarily monopolized without intolerable social effects. Society must decide how far up the range of bigness it will let ideas be monopolized.

Autonomous versus Induced Inventions.   Much progress is autonomous, seeming to materialize from thin air as part of the great evolution of new ideas and technology. When the Patent, Trademark, and Copyright Foundation asked a long list of inventors if the availability of patent protection had stimulated their inventive activity, one fifth of those who replied said yes; four fifths said that it was not essential or made little difference. The nature and the motivation of invention have been something other than the law assumes. More commonly, there is a mixture of incentive, eccentricity, opportunism, and random chance.

Invention requires *thought,* above all, plus large research resources in some cases. Despite recent rhetoric about team and large-scale research, invention is usually a small-scale personal activity. Innovation differs: it requires business skills and resources, sometimes on a large scale. Innovation therefore is usually done by firms, which may be entirely separate from the inventors who feed in the new ideas. *The incentives and resources needed for invention often differ from those for innovation.*

The *net* gains are the social criterion. Innovation creates new products, and it lowers costs. These allow a greater supply of consumer goods at lower prices. Yet innovation can have its costs, also. Innovation destroys the old in creating the new. It can be too rapid. Its damage to one private group can exceed the private gains to another. And there may be wider external

---

[6] See the sources noted in note 1 above.

costs. The social goal is to optimize the net benefits from creative activity. This is more sophisticated and difficult than the usual goal of patents: getting as much innovation as fast as possible.

If all inventions were autonomous, there would be no social purpose in patents or related devices. Too, if capital markets functioned perfectly, no idea or inventor would lack the resources needed to optimize it. Therefore patents would be irrelevant or directly harmful. The case for patents rests on capital-market imperfections and on *inducement;* that the rewards of the temporary patent monopoly will induce the optimal rate and direction of invention and innovation.

It is often urged that modern industry provides a new rationale for patents. Instead of the old handicraft economy, there is now large-scale, professional, "corporate" research underlying most new ideas. This R&D must be financed by profits on earlier successes, to keep progress going. Since patents yield profits, they are necessary to innovation.

This argument actually contains *non sequiters.* Some—not all—large corporate research is now realized to be bureaucratic and anti-creative. The profits under patents may stray far from the optimum rewards that might be necessary. It is *future* gains that should properly induce R&D, not the financial flows from past actions.

An "optimal" patent system will contain just the right *(a)* standards of patentability, *(b)* length of patent life, and *(c)* degree of control by the patent owner. These optimal conditions then depend in turn on three factual elements:

1. How strongly invention and innovation are actually induced by rewards,
2. How extreme the monopoly exploitation of patents is, during their lives, and
3. How rapidly the monopoly fades after the patent life ends.

In short, there may be a social trade-off between net progress and monopoly. The trade-off may be constant in all markets, or it may differ sharply among sectors (with patents giving progress and competition in some sectors but stagnation and monopoly in others).

Around the core of simple issues are evidently a lot of complex relationships. All of them, simple and complex, may be hard to measure. The basic issues have been understood for generations, but there has been little clear analysis or estimation of the trade-offs.

Patent Life. The optimum patent life has been analyzed, under simplified assumptions.[7] Very roughly speaking, the more sharply a prospective innovation reduces costs, the shorter the optimal life of a patent will be. For a

---

[7] The analysis is not simple. See William D. Nordhaus, *Invention, Growth, and Welfare* (Cambridge: MIT Press, 1969); and F. M. Scherer, "Nordhaus' Theory of Optimal Patent Life: A Geometric Reinterpretation," *American Economic Review,* 62 (June 1972), 422–27.

cost reduction of 10 percent and elasticity of demand anywhere in the range of 0.7 to 4.0, the optimal patent life appears to be in the range of three to seven years. Broadly speaking, a long patent life is only optimal for the very largest and costliest innovations.

Yet such large innovations are precisely those which tend to create or recast an industry with full monopoly which may long outlast the patent. A correct analysis replaces *patent* life with *monopoly* life; an optimal patent life will be shorter—possibly much shorter—than optimal monopoly life.

Patent *life* and the degree of patent *control* are substitutable elements, for they both define the present value of—that is, the inducement for—the invention. The present patent system maximizes the control. It also makes the profits more secure, by giving a guaranteed monopoly. These profits may well exceed the optimal incentive by a large margin. Instead, there could be limits on the degree of profit, the terms of licensing, or other patent actions. In various countries, they are constrained.

Market Position.   Generally, monopoly yields less inventive activity than does competition.[8] And firms with large market shares have incentives to follow rather than to innovate first.[9] They choose between speed and economy in innovation, often under conditions described by the curves in Figure 21–2. The dominant firm can get a long stream of high revenues from the innovation, as shown by its high flattish benefits curve. A small competitor, by contrast, will be able to gain lower revenues and for a short time, before other firms move in on it. Its benefits curve is lower (and possibly steeper). Each firm selects the time-cost result where the cost per time unit just equals the benefit per time unit. A rational dominant firm tends to go slow, imitating when forced to by lesser firms. A patent creating a dominant firm therefore tends to breed imitation rather than future innovation.

Moreover, patentable activities are often related so that one patent gives advantages in forming a cluster of newer patents which maintain or increase the firm's market share.

In short, there are often added costs of the patent monopoly beyond the direct profit rewards during the formal patent life. One should be alert for real cases where monopoly is extended. This accords with the research consensus that at market shares above 25 percent the degree of technical progress tapers off (recall Chapter 2).

The patent system exists on *(a)* an intuition that incentives breed progress, and *(b)* inertia, reinforced by interested groups. But we have now seen that incentives are a complex matter, where the net benefits are easy to overstate and the total costs extend in time and space. There are plausible grounds for abolishing patents outright or modifying them sharply. There are good preliminary grounds for shortening patent life and limiting patent rights.

---

[8] See Kenneth J. Arrow's chapter in National Bureau, *The Rate and Direction,* and Scherer, *Industrial Market Structure,* chap. 15.

[9] Scherer, ibid.

508

FIGURE 21-2
Typical conditions for innovations: dominant firms tend to follow.

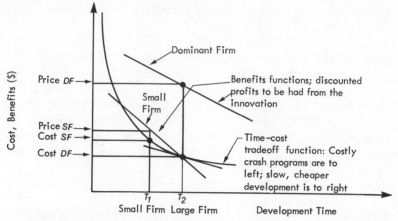

Source: Adapted from F. M. Scherer, *Industrial Market Structure and Economic Performance* (Skokie, Ill.: Rand McNally, 1970), p. 367.

Innovators maximize the gap between benefits and costs. The small firm normally innovates faster than the dominant firm and supplies the product at a lower price.

C. ABUSES OF PATENTS

So far the analysis has not considered the ways in which patents can be used deliberately to suppress competition. These abuses are of several sorts, as follows.

Patents without Inventions. The volume of patents has clearly been greater than the quantity of significant invention. Patents have been granted on mere gadgets, on contrivances expressing the lowest order of mechanical ability, and on ideas involving little in the way of novelty.[10]

When such patents reach the courts, they will rarely be allowed to stand. But until they do, they continue to afford a basis for market power.

Suppression of Technology. Under American law the patentee is not required to work his patent. As a consequence, the law may be employed not to promote but to retard the introduction of advances in technology. It has frequently been charged—and as frequently denied—that new inventions are deliberately suppressed.

While proof is not sufficient to support this charge, it is certain that patents

---

[10] Patents have covered an indentation on the head of a screw, an eraser on the end of a pencil, rubber hand grips on bicycle handlebars, a bosom or dickie sewn onto the front of a shirt, the use of flat cord instead of round cord in the loop at the ends of suspenders, and the use of an oval rather than a cylindrical shape in a roll of toilet paper.

outnumber the inventions that are put to work. At any time, about half to three quarters of the outstanding patents are not in use. Failure to work a patent need not involve suppression of technology. But a patentor's judgment as to these matters may well be influenced by the fact that he has substantial sums invested in a competing product or in a process that embodies an earlier technology. Under active competition, the rate of change is determined by the market. Under the patent monopoly, it is determined by the patentor. When suppression of patented inventions does occur, it clearly defeats the fundamental purpose of patent law.

The Monopolization of Patent Monopolies.   Many related patents may be accumulated by one or a few large firms or brought together by agreement among them. There is no limit to the number of patents that may be held by a single company. The large corporation will usually obtain a steady flow of patents through assignment from members of its own research staff and will supplement them by purchases from outsiders.[11]

Concentration of patent ownership may place in the hands of a single firm control over each of the possible methods by which a good may be produced, enabling it to monopolize the technology of an entire industry.

Where a few large corporations hold patents that overlap, each is likely to share its rights with the others through cross-licensing. Such agreements may call for exclusive or nonexclusive licensing, and may cover future as well as present patent rights. The companies participating will usually agree to refrain from attacking the validity of patents held by other members of the group. In this way all of the technology in the field may be brought under unified control.

Patent Warfare.   Large firms have sometimes undertaken to fortify a position of monopoly by accumulating an arsenal of patents to be used in attacking possible competitors. Their lawyers have flooded the Patent Office with a stream of applications to cover every process, every machine, and every product that their technicians have invented or might conceivably invent.

In addition to "blocking" and "fencing" patents, there are "umbrella," "accordion," and "drag-net" patents, drawn up with claims so broad, so expansible, and so effective as to cover and seize upon extensive areas of industrial technology. In one view, "The great research laboratories are only incidentally technological centers. From the business standpoint they are patent factories; they manufacture the raw material of monopoly. Their product is often nothing but a 'shot-gun,' a basis for threatening infringement suits and scaring off competitors; or a 'scare-crow,' a patent which itself

---

[11] For example, among the companies receiving patents from 1939 to 1956, there were 39 with more than 1,000 and 15 with more than 2,000 each; duPont received 6,338; Westinghouse, 7,567; RCA, 7,894; AT&T, 8,539; and GE, 10,757. U.S. Senate, Committee on the Judiciary, Subcommittee on Patents, Trademarks, and Copyrights, Study No. 3, *Distribution of Patents Issued to Corporations* (Washington, D.C.: Government Printing Office, 1957).

represents little or no contribution but seems . . . to cover an important part of a developing art and hence permits threat of suit."[12]

Litigation has been deliberately employed as a weapon of monopoly. Between 1877 and 1893, when the first Bell patent expired, the telephone company initiated more than 600 infringement suits. Patent warfare was similarly employed to build the power of National Cash Register, Eastman Kodak, United Shoe Machinery, and many drug firms.

In patent warfare there is no assurance that the adversary with the better claim will be victorious. Litigation is costly, and the outcome is likely to favor the party with the larger purse.[13] In many cases, suits have been settled before the courts have passed upon the rival patent claims. A weaker firm with a valid patent may thus sell out to a stronger firm with a patent of dubious validity. Or it may recognize the latter's patent as valid, take out a license, and agree to abide by its terms. Exclusive rights thus tend to gravitate to large concerns, regardless of the legal status of their claims.

Extending the Boundaries of Monopoly. The normal duration of the formal monopoly conferred under the patent system is not 17 years but over 20. An invention may be worked for a year before a patent is applied for, and the usual application remains pending in the Patent Office for three years or more. The period of pendency has been further extended by the withdrawal and amendment of applications and through the initiation of interference proceedings by the Patent Office when two applications appear to cover the same ground.

The duration of monopoly has also been prolonged by dividing a complicated invention into several parts—the steps in a process, the elements in a compound, or the sections of a machine—and applying for separate patents at judicious intervals. During the life of a basic patent, its owner will seek to develop and patent improvements. When one grant of monopoly has expired, another will be ready to take its place. During its period of patent protection, moreover, a firm may have developed a productive organization, market outlets, control over materials, and a monopoly of skilled personnel that will make it difficult, if not impossible, for others to enter the field when its patents have expired. The patent system, in its operation, thus provides more than 17 years of monopoly.

The monopoly power afforded by patents has been extended in space as well as in time. Monopoly has been extended horizontally from one patented product to another and from patented to unpatented goods. Monopoly has

---

[12] Kahn, in Miller, *Competition.*

[13] Suits may be brought in different jurisdictions and under many different claims. A firm may see its markets vanish as suits are brought against its customers. Such litigation, moveover, may drag on for years. Its victim may well conclude that capitulation is preferable to bankruptcy. When Eastman Kodak sued the Boston Camera Co. in 1894, obtaining a temporary injunction against the sale of Boston's wares, Eastman was finally adjudged the real infringer, but Boston had by then been broken and was thereupon absorbed. When the predecessor of the Aluminum Company of America sued the Cowles Brothers, it was found, after ten years, to have infringed their patents, but they agreed to accept a cash settlement and retired from the field.

also been extended vertically from one stage of production and distribution to the next.

Restrictive Licensing. The patent holder may fail to work his patent himself; he may refuse to license others to do so. Even if licenses are given, they may be restrictive. Output may be limited by imposing quotas or by charging graduated royalties. A patent holder may also undertake to fix the prices that are charged by subsequent distributors. Thus, U.S. Gypsum required its licensees to sell on a delivered basis under a multiple basing point system and to observe the minimum prices which it prescribed, and Masonite licensed competing manufacturers of hardboard and fixed the prices they could charge. In each of these ways the patentee imposes restraints on competition.

Patent Pools. In industries where essential patents are controlled by many firms, they may be brought together in a common pool. Under such an arrangement, patents may be assigned to a trade association or to a corporation set up for the purpose, and licenses granted to each of the participants under all of the patents in the pool. Licenses may be restricted or unrestricted; royalties may be collected and distributed, or patents may be licensed royalty free. Whatever its characteristics, the patent pool in every case will centralize control over a substantial segment of industrial technology.

Patent pooling may be employed either to liberate competition or to intensify monopoly. Improvements resulting from invention are made available to all of the participants and costs are reduced by eliminating litigation within the group. If unrestricted licenses are granted to all applicants on reasonable terms, outsiders are afforded access to the industry's technology.[14]

But agreements combining patents may also be administered with less liberality. A pool controling all of the inventions in an industry will be the only purchaser of future patents and the only source of patent licenses. By refusing to license, by charging exorbitant royalties, and by drawing upon the combined resource of its members in prosecuting and defending patent suits, it may eliminate outsiders from the field. By including in its contracts provisions which restrict the quantity a licensee may produce, the area in which he may sell, and the prices he may charge, it may regiment an entire industry. Whether cross-licensing and patent pooling make for competition or for monopoly depends therefore upon the purposes for which they are established and the way in which they are administered.

D. POLICIES AND PRECEDENTS

Most of these abuses have been presented in cases brought before the courts. In general, the earlier decisions were favorable to the patent holder.

---

[14] In the automobile industry since 1915, patents have been pooled and licenses freely given without restriction and without charge. Patents covering all but the more recent inventions are thus thrown open to the entire industry, and smaller and newer firms may use them without contributing inventions of their own. Since the pool was first established, no manufacturers of automobiles have appeared as plaintiff or defendant in an infringement suit.

But the courts have come increasingly, in recent years, to limit the scope and check the abuses of patent monopoly.

The Standard of Patentability. Until 1835 no patent was found invalid for want of novelty. Thereafter a succession of cases involving patents on gadgets led to the development of a judicial standard of patentability. In 1850 the Supreme Court held that a doorknob made of clay or porcelain rather than metal or wood was "the work of the skilled mechanic, not that of the inventor."[15] This distinction continued to govern the decisions handed down for the better part of a century, and patents were upheld if they were deemed to embody a degree of skill that was greater than that of the artisan. But as invention came increasingly to be the product of corporate research, the standard of patentability was raised.

The broad rule is that a patent is to be issued if the differences between an invention and the prior art are substantial. But the obviousness of inventions and the substantiality of their differences from the prior art is still a matter of judgment. Whether an invention is patentable depends, as it has always depended, on the opinion of the courts.[16]

Concentration of Patent Ownership. Where a single company has clearly sought to monopolize an industry's patents as a means of monopolizing the industry itself, its action has been condemned. In itself, however, the ownership of many patents by a single company has not been found to violate the law.[17]

---

[15] *Hotchkiss* v. *Greenwood,* 11 How. 248.

[16] In three cases decided in 1966, the Supreme Court found patents on two inventions (one that placed the shank on a vibrating shank plow above the hinge plate, and one that provided a leak-proof cap for a finger-operated spray dispenser) to be invalid, and a third patent (on a water-activated battery of a radically new design) to be valid, on the ground that the first two would have been obvious to an artisan having ordinary skill in the prior art, while the third would not. *Graham* v. *John Deere Co.* and *Calmar, Inc.* v. *Cook Chemical Co.,* 383 U.S. 1; *U.S.* v. *Adams,* 383 U.S. 39.

[17] The issue was raised in the United Shoe Machinery case. The company held nearly 4,000 patents, about 95 percent of them the product of its own research, only 5 percent of them purchased from others. The government charged that the company "has been for many years, and is now, engaged in a program of engrossing all patents and inventions of importance relating to shoe machinery for the purpose of blanketing the shoe machinery industry with patents under the control of United and thereby suppressing competition in the industry."

This was one among the factors that led to a finding of illegality. Here, the court found no evidence that the patent right had been abused. United had put a third of its patents to work; it had not suppressed the others or used them to threaten possible competitors. It had not offered or been asked to grant licenses, but it had not refused to do so. It had not resorted to litigation as a means of harassing competitors but had acted in good faith in bringing infringement suits.

It had adopted certain policies, however, that operated to handicap competitors. It had refused to sell its machines, making them available only on long-term leases. It had included in its leases provisions that discriminated against customers who might install competing machines. It had required them to use its own machines at full capacity on all the shoes they made. It had entered into blanket contracts covering services. None of these policies was held to be illegal per se. But their combined

The issue of concentration of patent ownership was also raised in the 1950s Section 2 cases involving Western Electric and International Business Machines. But here the legality of such concentration was not determined, each of the cases being settled in 1956 by a consent decree. Apart from coercive tactics or a complex of anticompetitive practices which extend the patent monopoly, a monopoly of patents is yet to be condemned.

Tying Contracts. Many decisions of the courts have dealt with the efforts of a patentee to extend the scope of his monopoly beyond the boundaries of the patent grant. Since the passage of the Clayton Act, such tying contracts have consistently been condemned. The courts have struck down contracts, among others, requiring radio manufacturers licensed under RCA patents to buy their tubes from RCA;[18] requiring lessees of International Business Machines to buy their tabulating cards from IBM;[19] and requiring the purchase of rivets by lessees of patented riveting machines.[20] In these cases the contracts were found substantially to lessen competition, within the meaning of the Clayton Act, because the patentee dominated the market for the process or product to which the unpatented commodity was tied. But tying contracts have also been invalidated in cases where the patentee was far from having a monopoly. Thus, in the International Salt case,[21] the Supreme Court held that a contract requiring the users of a patented salt dispenser to purchase salt from its producer was unreasonable per se. It is evident that the courts will not now tolerate the use of tying clauses, under any circumstances, to extend the boundaries of a patent monopoly.

Restrictive Licenses. Where a patent owner grants a license to use a patented machine or process or to make and sell a patented product, the courts have generally upheld his right to limit the licensee to a certain geographic area[22] or a certain field of industry,[23] to restrict his output,[24] and to fix the price that he may charge when he sells the patented goods.[25]

Surrender of title to a patented good, however, has long been held to

---

effect, given United's dominant position in the field, was found to prove monopolization, in violation of Section 2 of the Sherman Act. *U.S.* v. *United Shoe Machinery Corp.,* 110 F. Supp. 295.

[18] *Lord* v. *Radio Corp. of America,* 24 F. 2d 505 (1928).

[19] *International Business Machines Corp.* v. *U.S.,* 298 U.S. 131 (1936).

[20] *Judson Thompson* v. *FTC,* 150 F. 2d 952 (1945).

[21] *International Salt Co.* v. *U.S.,* 332 U.S. 392 (1947).

[22] *Providence Rubber Co.* v. *Goodyear,* 9 Wall. 788 (1869).

[23] *General Talking Pictures Corp.* v. *Western Electric Corp.,* 304 U.S. 175 (1938).

[24] *Rubber Tire Wheel Co.* v. *Milwaukee Rubber Works Co.,* 154 F. 328 (1907), 210 U.S. 439 (1908).

[25] The leading decision on the latter point was handed down by the Supreme Court in the General Electric case in 1926. One of the issues raised in this case related to the right of General Electric, under its basic patents on the electric lamp, to fix the prices charged by Westinghouse. This right was upheld by the Court, and license contracts fixing a licensee's prices on patented products are still permitted by the law. *U.S.* v. *General Electric Co.,* 272 U.S. 476.

terminate the patentee's authority over its subsequent use and sale. His right to control the price at which patented products, once sold by him, are resold by others has therefore been denied. In the case of *Bauer* v. *O'Donnell*[26] in 1913, it was held that O'Donnell had not infringed Bauer's patent on Sanatogen when he resold it for less than the price that Bauer had printed on the package. This precedent has generally been followed since that time.

Restrictive licensing of another manufacturer has been permitted where it applied to a single licensee. But it has been held to be illegal when employed for the purpose of eliminating competition among many licensees.[27] When each of several licensees accepts restrictive terms on the condition or with the knowledge that others will do so, they are guilty of conspiracy in restraint of trade.

On a number of occasions, the government has asked the Court to reverse the rule permitting a patentee to fix the prices that may be charged by a single licensee. In the Gypsum case in 1948, four of the judges were willing to do so, but this fell short of a majority. In the Huck case[28] in 1965, the Court split 4 to 4 on a similar request. Sooner or later, it is likely that the rule will be reversed.

Remedies in Patent Cases. Employment of patents to eliminate competition has repeatedly been restrained by the courts. This has been true, of course, in the many cases in which a court has found that a patent was not valid or was not infringed. In a number of cases, too, the Supreme Court has permitted defendants in infringement suits to show that patents had been used to violate the antitrust laws and then refused, on that ground, to enforce them.[29] The patents, though not invalidated, were rendered ineffective, and their use as an instrument of monopoly destroyed. The Court has also held that a defendant in an infringement suit, brought to enforce a patent that had been obtained through fraudulent representations, could sue the patentor for treble damages.[30]

Judicial actions have also sought to remove barriers to entry. In the Hartford-Empire case[31] the Supreme Court required compulsory licensing for the first time in history.

---

[26] 229 U.S. 1.

[27] In the Gypsum case in 1948, the Supreme Court condemned the establishment of common prices for manufacturers of gypsum board through provisions contained in separate contracts for patent licensing. The General Electric precedent, said the Court, "gives no support for a patentee, acting in concert with all members of an industry, to issue substantially identical licenses . . . under which industry is completely regimented." *U.S.* v. *U.S. Gypsum Co.*, 333 U.S. 364.

[28] *Huck Manufacturing Co.* v. *U.S.*, 382 U.S. 197.

[29] *Morton Salt Co.* v. *G. S. Suppiger Co.*, 314 U.S. 488 (1942); *B. B. Chemical Co.* v. *Ellis*, 314 U.S. 495 (1942); *Mercoid Corp.* v. *Mid-Continent Investment Co.*, 320 U.S. 661 (1944).

[30] *Walker Process Equipment Co.* v. *Food Machinery and Chemical Corp.*, 382 U.S. 172 (1965).

[31] *Hartford-Empire Co.* v. *U.S.*, 323 U.S. 386 (1945). This precedent was followed two years later in *U.S.* v. *National Lead Co.*, 332 U.S. 319 (1947).

Royalty-free licensing was first required by a district court in the case of the General Electric Company in 1953.[32] The court refused to dismember the company or to ban the agency system, but it did order the licensing of patents, with future patents to be made available at reasonable royalties and existing patents royalty-free.[33]

Similar provisions have been incorporated in consent decrees. Scores of such decrees have been accepted, providing for the licensing of all applicants, many of them for licensing without royalties. Under the typical decree, existing patents must be licensed royalty-free and future patents at reasonable royalties. Royalty charges are determined by agreement between the patent owner and the licensee or, failing this, are established by the courts. A consent decree accepted by General Motors in 1965, in a suit attacking its control of 85 percent of the output of buses, provided for royalty-free licensing of future as well as existing patents. The Xerox settlement in 1975 was similar (recall Chapter 5).

Decrees in antitrust suits have also called for the provision of necessary know-how. Owens-Corning Fiberglas was required to furnish its licensees, at nominal charge, with written manuals describing its machinery, materials, and processes. American Can was directed to provide technical specifications and, if necessary, expert assistance.[34] Eastman Kodak agreed to provide other finishers of amateur color film with manuals describing its processing technology, to keep the manuals up to date by issuing annual supplements, and to provide technical representatives to assist competitors in using the methods described.[35] International Business Machines agreed to train outsiders in the techniques of making and using tabulating equipment and to provide the trade with its basic designs.[36] And General Electric was ordered to take similar steps to provide other manufacturers with the know-how required for the production of electric lamps.

E. PATENT REFORM

Patent "reform" is always just around the corner. The courts have shaped the content of the law and limited many abuses. Congress has only made small changes, in 1939 and 1952. A large task force study proposed in 1967

---

[32] Following the company's conviction in a criminal suit in 1949, the government asked that it be required to dispose of half of its productive facilities; to abandon the agency system under which it controlled the prices charged by its distributors; to dedicate to public use all of its existing patents covering the manufacture of electric light bulbs and parts; and to grant licenses under future patents in this field, on a reciprocal basis, at reasonable royalties.

[33] *U.S.* v. *General Electric,* 115 F. Supp. 835.

[34] *U.S.* v. *American Can Co.,* Civil Action 2643-H, District Court of the U.S., Northern District of Cal., Final Judgment, June 22, 1950.

[35] *U.S.* v. *Eastman Kodak Co.,* 1954 Trade Cases, Par. 67, 920.

[36] *U.S.* v. *International Business Machines,* Civil Action C-72-344, District Court of the U.S., Southern District of N.Y., Consent Decree, January 25, 1956.

mainly *(a)* a first-to-file standard and *(b)* confining Patent Office decisions to contested patents. Even these mild changes have been blocked—primarily by the Patent Bar, whose income they would reduce. Efforts at patent reform usually exhaust all the participants and leave the system nearly untouched.

Still, patent reforms might offer large economic gains. Obvious ones include first-to-file and the obligation to use a patent or lose it (like the old homestead grants).[37] These have now been adopted in a number of countries.

Patent Life. The issues are complex, but a shorter life—perhaps down to five years—now seems more efficient than the present 17 years. The precise change requires close study, and a range of lives—depending on the industry, subject, scope of patent, and so on—might be better than a single period. Patentors might be given a choice between long constrained patents and short unfettered ones. Or the limits might automatically begin after an initial period. One beauty of changing patent lives is that it could be applied to all new patents and soon (that is, five or ten years) come to be universal without destroying present vested patent values.

Patent Restrictions. The patentor could be required to license all comers at a reasonable royalty fee. Such compulsory licensing is practical: it has been used in many consent decrees, and rarely have the courts needed to set the royalty rate. When the would-be user can threaten court action, a "reasonable" royalty is agreed privately.

But there would often be some burden on the courts or agencies. And compulsory licensing is a blade with two edges, not only making the strong firm license the weak one, but also the other way round. The proposal is a perennial, but its optimal use needs careful analysis.

Altogether, an optimal policy might be a sophisticated mix of periods and restrictions, perhaps with differing scope by types of inventions, etc. Yet a proliferation of "ideal" adjustments risks creating—in practice—a honeycomb of distortions by special interests. Somewhere between this and the simplicity of abolition is a yet-to-be-defined optimal patent system. Its conditions probably evolve as industrial conditions change.

F. TRADEMARKS

Readers will naturally be familiar with the trademarks of hundreds of goods. Specific company and product names can be made to signify extra

---

[37] The number of patent monopolies might be reduced by legislative changes in the standard of patentability. Patents might well be confined to inventions representing really significant advances in technology or granted only to persons who could show that substantial sums had been spent on research and development. Designs might better be left to protection through copyrights. And the patent privilege might be withdrawn from foods and medicines. The multiplicity of patents might also be reduced through changes in procedure. Patent applications might be published and hearings given to competitors, consumers, and antitrust officials in opposition to the patent grants. The Patent Office might be equipped with a larger staff at higher salaries and thus enabled to take more time and exercise more skill in passing on applications. Larger appropriations for this purpose might be financed by increasing patent fees. All of these measures, or any of them, should operate to check the excessive creation of legal monopolies.

product value, as well as simply to jog the memory. Trademarks are often built up by large volumes of advertising, and they often yield a large price premium. Like advertising generally, trademarks may serve as an entry barrier.

Trademarks are among all the kinds of identifying signs and words which firms try to use. By registering a trademark at the Patent Office, a person or firm gets 20 years (renewable) of formal evidence of ownership. After five years on the register, a mark cannot be contested. Some 30,000 new trademarks are validated each year, while about 6,000 renewals are issued.

Trademark rights, like patent rights, are enforced by bringing infringement suits. At first such suits were entertained at common law. Statutory protection was subsequently given to trademarks by the legislatures of the states. The federal Constitution made no mention of trademarks. But Congress acted, in 1881, to protect marks used in foreign trade and, in 1905, to protect those used in interstate commerce. Infringement suits were still decided in accordance with the laws of the states. The first effective federal trademark law, the Lanham Act, was not passed until 1946.

Trademarks inevitably cluster in consumer-goods markets, especially those with repeated buying of moderately complex and expensive goods, whose quality matters. Cars, film, beer, TV sets, and patent medicines are examples: vegetables and bricks usually are not.

Trademarks are frequently used to extend the market power created under a patent. They often are the only name by which customers know the product (examples: thermos jug and xeroxing. "IBM machine" has come close to standing for "computer." Try to list five other such names). Where names become generic, courts can defend the right of others to use the name.[38] But this is often long, costly, and uncertain.[39]

Trademarks have been used successfully, where patents and copyrights failed, in the maintenance of resale prices. They have been used to implement discriminatory pricing: methyl methacrylate was sold by Rohm & Haas to manufacturers as Lucite and Crystalite at 85 cents per pound, and to dentists as Vernonite and Crystalex at $45 per pound. They have been used to obtain exclusive markets: General Electric persuaded procurement agencies to establish specifications requiring Mazda bulbs, permitted Westinghouse to use the name, but denied its other licensees the right to do so.[40] Trademarks have also been used to effect a division of markets among the members of international cartels. Here, a mark is advertised throughout the world, each participant is given the exclusive right to use it in his own territory, and

---

[38] Thus, in January 1978, the Supreme Court rejected an attempt by Miller Brewing Co. to keep other brewers from using the word "light" to describe their beers. Miller was attempting to extend its trademark on the word "lite" to cover the use of a common word.

[39] Thus the patent on shredded wheat expired in 1912. But not until 1938 was the name found to be in the public domain: *Kellogg Co.* v. *National Biscuit Co.,* 305 U.S. 111. The case had been dragged out for more than a quarter of a century.

[40] See S. Timberg, "Trade Marks, Monopoly, and the Restraint of Competition," *Law and Contemporary Problems* 14 (1949), 323–61.

anyone who oversteps the boundaries assigned to him is driven back by an infringement suit.

Trademarks are more widely spread but usually weaker than patents. They reflect the underlying sales effort, which is often costly and must be refreshed by continuing efforts. Trademark reform is not a major topic or need, as long as abuses can be challenged in court. Any basic problem with trademarks arises from the advertising process which creates and maintains them.

Monopolistic practices involving trademarks have been enjoined in many cases by the courts. Contracts maintaining the resale price of trademarked goods were held to be unlawful in the Dr. Miles case[41] in 1911; their subsequent legalization has been discussed in Chapter 6. Decisions were rendered against the use of trademarks to promote discriminatory pricing in the Rohm & Haas case[42] in 1948 and against their use in excluding competitors from markets in the General Electric case[43] in 1949. In a number of cases involving the sharing of markets for trademarked goods by international cartels, decided from 1945 to 1950, the courts found such arrangements to be in violation of the Sherman Act, rejecting trademark licensing as a defense.[44]

G. SUMMARY

Patents are a specialized device with obscure origins and many alternative forms. In the United States, they grant 17 years of monopoly to any invention, small or great, often yielding huge returns. They are subject to abuse, and the resulting monopolies often last much longer than 17 years. Indeed, they have helped create some of the greatest and longest-lasting dominant positions in modern industry.

Yet literally nobody knows if they do induce invention and/or innovation. The optimal patent system—somewhere between abolition and a special grant tailored to each invention—is a matter for complex analysis of incentives, monopoly life, and monopoly effects. It may differ among sectors or types of inventions. It probably involves shorter patent lives, a first-to-file basis, and requirements to use the patent (directly or by licensing) or lose it.

Trademarks pose similar but less severe problems. They can extend the life of patent monopolies and impede entry. But their power arises mainly from the sales effort which builds and maintains them, rather than the official grant itself.

QUESTIONS FOR REVIEW

1. "If inventions are mostly induced, then a patent system will have little value." True?

[41] *Dr. Miles Medical Co.* v. *John D. Park & Sons Co.,* 220 U.S. 373.

[42] *U.S.* v. *Rohm & Haas,* Civil Action No. 9068, District Court of the U.S., Eastern District of Pa.

[43] *U.S.* v. *General Electric Co.,* 82 F. Supp. 753.

[44] *U.S.* v. *Timken Roller Bearing Co.,* 83 F. Supp. 294 (1949).

2. "The optimal patent life will differ among inventions, rather than be the same for each." True?

3. "Patents are generally appropriate for really big or really little inventions, not the medium range of new ideas." True?

4. Patent abuses include *(a)* suppression of technology, *(b)* patent warfare, *(c)* restrictive licensing, *(d)* rapid innovation, and *(e)* patent pooling. Which?

5. "Some court decrees require licensing of patents, but no general requirement for using patents exists." True?

6. What directions of patent reform might be needed?

chapter 22

Conserving Natural Resources

Each generation inherits a finite set of resources. It exploits and/or conserves them, in varying degree, using its own rates of time discount and technology. To *conserve* resources is to use them economically, in line with the whole future set of probable needs. The extreme degree is *preservation;* nonuse, hoarding. Economic criteria usually suggest using resources, at carefully set rates which optimize their total value over present and future time. But unfettered private markets often use them faster than this. The degree of monopoly can also affect the rate and pattern of usage. Meanwhile, social interests—in abundant resources, amenity, maintaining traditional patterns, or fairness—often require an even slower usage than the efficient economic rate.[1]

Therefore, reaching the optimum rate and pattern of use for each resource can be a complex and uncertain task. The stakes are big. Resources include *(a)* minerals (oil, ores, coal), *(b)* soil, terrain, and sea to support life, *(c)* fresh water, air, and tranquility, and *(d)* natural wilderness and beauty (see Table 22–1).[2] They affect all corners of our lives—what we eat, breathe, smell, see, and touch—and will continue doing so for our descendants.

We will treat several groups of these problems. Section A presents the economic analysis of conservation, by markets and policy choices. Next, the use of land resources is reviewed in Section B, followed by a discussion of

---

[1] Good basic sources include S. V. Ciriacy-Wantrup, *Resource Conservation: Economics and Policies,* 3d ed. (Berkeley: University of California Press, 1968); J. H. Dales, *Pollution, Property, and Prices* (Toronto: University of Toronto Press, 1968); E. J. Mishan, *The Costs of Economic Growth* (New York: Praeger, 1967). Gerald Garvey, *Energy, Ecology, Economy* (New York: Norton, 1972), gives a lucid introduction to environmental problems. See also the excellent review of external effects in E. J. Mishan, "The Postwar Literature on Externalities: An Interpretative Essay," *Journal of Economic Literature* 9, 1 (March 1971), 1–28, and the sources cited there.

[2] Appraisals of actual resources are given in H. H. Landsberg, *Natural Resources for U. S. Growth* (Baltimore: Johns Hopkins Press, 1964); R. G. Ridker, *Economic Costs of Air Pollution* (New York: Praeger, 1967); and D. H. Meadows et al., *The Limits to Growth* (New York: Praeger, 1972).

TABLE 22-1
The Main Natural Resources

Nonrenewable
   Fuels (coal, oil, gas), land, ores, chemical deposits; natural beauty sites
Replaceable at great cost
   Soil, wilderness, certain rivers and lakes, clean shorelines
Renewable
   Other rivers and lakes; urban fresh air
Self-renewing
   Forests, fisheries, other "crops"
Virtually inexhaustible
   Rural fresh air, solar energy

---

oil in Section C. Then the problem of pollution occupies Section D. Finally, fish resources are treated in Section E.

A. ECONOMIC CONCEPTS AND ISSUES

A1. The Need for Conservation

Private market choices can destroy renewable resources. They may wash off the topsoil, denude forests, lower the water table, pollute air and streams, and destroy the stock of fish. All these harms have happened in the United States, changing many of its rich resources into ugly wastelands. Many nonrenewable resources are also being rapidly depleted: oil and gas are only the most obvious example of these.

In coming decades, the growth of population and production will encounter increasing scarcity of resources of this "spaceship earth." Past technological progress has relieved some of the Malthusian pressures. But in fuels, ores, space, and ecology, the next 50 years appear to pose newly severe scarcities. The natural economic solution is simply a rising trend in resource prices, with perhaps sharp future rises. But some analysts predict stresses and pollution so great as to cause worldwide social collapse. Others see only a glut of oil and many new sources of energy and materials, as technology advances. Whether the Doomwatchers or the technological optimists are correct it is too early to say. But severe individual problems will continue to arise and provoke conservationist efforts, as in 1890–1910 and since 1967. Resources and clean environment will, at the least, require hard choices about large costs.

A2. Economic Issues

To evaluate these issues, we apply the basic economics of conservation. The objective is to use efficiently—and equitably, within each generation and among generations—a physically limited, depletable resource. Some resources are renewable, such as forests, fish, and clean rivers. Others, such as oil, ores, and coal, are nonrenewable: once used, gone forever. Still others are in between: renewable only at great cost (topsoil, wilderness). For all of them, the basic aim is identical: to use the resource at the rate which maximizes the total social value of its use, over the whole span of time.

Each resource is an asset, a stock (possibly renewable). It can be held in its present form or used—at some rate—either for consumption or investment purposes. Decisions affecting the use of resources are basically speculations on their future worth, either in their natural state or in some converted form. Physical *preservation* is only one alternative among the ways to *conserve* a resource. To avoid economic waste often requires physical *usage* of a resource.

One popular fallacy is to regard our resource base as a fixed inventory which, when used up, will leave society with no means of survival. A related fallacy is that physical waste equals economic waste: the feeling that it is wasteful to use materials in ways that make them disappear. This attitude can lead to devoting a dollar's worth of work to "saving" a few cents' worth of waste paper and old string. These fallacies together lead to a hairshirt concept of conservation which makes it synonymous with hoarding.[3]

For each asset, and for the whole bundle of natural resources, the optimum rate of use is not precisely determinate. It depends on the current rate of interest, on the length of time horizon which society and/or the owner of the asset applies, and on the ethical weights used in comparing the value of use between present and future generations. Costs of finding, using, and renewing resources also affect the optimum. Also, the expected rate and direction of technological change may be decisive, for it may require more— or less—of the natural resource in question, as time passes.[4]

These are matters of social preference and of simple economic scarcity. The longer the time length of a horizon and the lower the social rate of time preference and interests rates, the slower will be the optimum rate of using natural resources. By contrast, if interest rates are high, the time horizon is short, and the interests of current citizens are considered urgent, then a

---

[3] "Conservation is something very different from simply leaving oil in the ground or trees in the forests on the theory that by sacrificing lower value uses today we will leave something for the higher value uses of tomorrow when supplies will be scarcer. Using resources today is an essential part of making our economy grow; materials which become embodied in today's capital goods, for example, are put to work and help make tomorrow's production higher. Hoarding resources in the expectation of more important uses later involves a sacrifice that may never be recouped; technological changes and new resource discoveries may alter a situation completely. It may not be wise to refrain from using zinc today if our grandchildren will not know what to do with it tomorrow." President's Materials Policy Commission, *Resources for Freedom* (Washington, D.C.: Government Printing Office, 1952), vol. 1, p. 21.

[4] For example, there might be a fixed and small stock of natural gas available, so that scarcity and rising gas prices are imminent. But if nuclear power replaces gas entirely within 20 years, then the value of the gas will tend toward zero.

society may choose to "use up" its resources here and now. The solution turns closely on predictions about many technical factors, and on judgments about the social rate of time preference.

There is one additional wrinkle for renewable resources (such as fish). The rate by which they are cropped depends on the same basic factors, but there is a range of choice in establishing the best steady-state harvesting levels. There is usually a yield curve given technically, as is shown roughly in Figure 22–1. The optimum yield as illustrated at point A, where the marginal value of the fish is just equal to the marginal cost of catching them. Only if the harvesting were costless would the maximum physical yield be the best outcome. The resource will sustain a physically more intensive harvesting than this optimum yield, as shown by point *B,* but the total net value of the operation there is smaller than at *A.* The optimum rate as shown depends, again, on several factors. Of course, optimal conservation may require the resource to be gradually exhausted over time, even if it is cropped efficiently during that decline.

A further peculiarity is that resource values are partly economic rents, set by factors other than cost of production. These rents rise with scarcity, but they often are strictly residual and contain windfall elements. Being capitalized values of future benefits, they are influenced by expectations, by psychology. Any significant policies will affect these values.

A3. Private Markets Optimize, Except . . .

These hornbook points about conservation are of long standing among experts, though not in common debate. Two main policy issues will be germane here. *(a)* The time discounts applied by private owners may diverge from

FIGURE 22–1
Optimizing the Use of a Renewable Resource

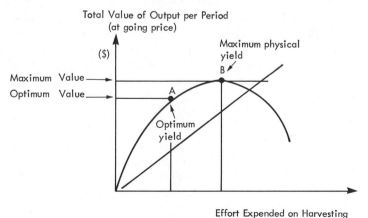

the "true" social time preference, and *(b)* the degree of monopoly in resource markets may affect the outcome.

The Conventional Economic Lesson. This is quite clear and optimistic: *private markets operating with relatively perfect conditions of mobility, knowledge, and rationality can fit the social criteria for conservation of resources over time.* The owners will be guided both by their profit-maximizing motivation and by the objective conditions prevailing in financial and industrial markets. These will usually tend to reflect precisely those social valuations of time preference, productivity, and expected innovation which determine the optimum rate. Moreover, it is in the interests of the resource owners to seek out accurate information on these magnitudes and apply them in their own decisions. Therefore, the private-market disposal of natural resources can optimize their use.

This holds for competitive markets under perfect assumptions. Monopolists will usually hold the rate of resource use lower, by restricting output and raising price in the present. Yet monopolists too will wish to maximize the value of resource use in the long run, and so the restrictive effect may distort their choices only slightly.

In well-functioning markets, with rational choices, the prices of natural resources will tend to anticipate further scarcities, so that the users of resources will act in accord with the genuine social costs of their use of resources. Further, as unexpected changes occur in these predicted future scarcities, the prices of resources will adjust quickly and automatically. Therefore both the present and future scarcities—even if they are changing and uncertain at each point—will be fully reflected in the prevailing prices and the rates of usage. This will occur spontaneously, without conscious or detailed social planning. In short, the "invisible hand" extends to conservation.

Limits and Biases. But this optimality is limited, and there may be specific biases. Six of these possible limits and biases follow.

1. *Multiple access.* If a resource can be used by several separate extractors, then the shared access will invariably lead the resource to be depleted too fast. Classic instances include many now-extinct species of animals and others verging on extinction, oil fields, fisheries, and other oceanic resources, which have been open to multiple extractors. As with several people with straws in one milkshake, each owner's private interest is in taking it out as fast as possible, and so the private choices may depart radically from the social optimum. The corrective is to unitize the control of each such resource, so that the optimum technical pattern and rate of usage can be designed and applied.

2. *Time preferences and myopia.* The private rate of time preference (influenced by specific opportunities, time horizons, and personal attitudes) may be too high. Firms often have short time horizons, under the stress of commercial competition. This may under-represent the legitimate interests of future generations. Ultimately, a negative rate of time preference should perhaps be applied to some inter-generation choices. If population and income levels

continue growing, and technology fails to provide magic new methods, then the pressure on resources may far exceed anything now imagined. Therefore, in a long perspective, it might be optimal for us now to set the value of future use higher than that of present use. At any rate, the social rate of time preference may be lower, perhaps much lower, than the rate established by private choices.

3. *Inadequate forecasting.* Present users may simply fail to foresee future developments. This may reflect a lack of sufficient research interest and ability to discern future changes. There may be close interactions among the uses of resources which are not presently apparent to the individual users of each (that is the crux of the Doomwatch projections). And some users may simply be careless or superficial in their judgments.

4. *Special influences.* Specific taxes and other incentive devices may encourage overly rapid use of resources. In fact, the use of almost every resource *is* affected by one or several artificial incentives. There are special tax provisions for almost all natural resource uses, such as oil, ores, and the like. The use of land surrounding cities has been intensified by special tax provisions which favor creating suburban developments as investment tax shelters. Farm policies affect the extent and intensity of cultivation. National policies affect the exhaustion of oceanic fish resources. These incentives almost invariably induce a more rapid use of resources, often drastically higher and perhaps extinguishing the resources in the end.

5. *External effects.* There are important externalities in the uses of many resources, so that private users ignore major degrees of pollution and other external costs.[5] This affects both the rate of withdrawal of earth resources and the degree to which the common environment of air, water, and habitat are degraded. Almost always, a recognition of such externalities will cause a slower and altered use of natural resources. Note that this problem is only one of six, though it has been the main focus of the "environmental movement" since 1967.

6. *Distribution.* Finally, private market decisions are based on the existing distribution of wealth and income. As resource users vote with their dollars, market demand will more strongly reflect the interests and preferences of the wealthy. This may conflict with broader social criteria, especially where amenity is differently affected among neighborhoods or locales. Thus, the best land may be held by the rich and used exclusively, even though it would be socially preferable to open it to all as parkland. Some impacts—such as congestion and pollution—may affect the poor more acutely. And the poor have a greater need for common recreational space and facilities.

Directions for Policy Action. In all, private maximizing may fail to yield true conservation of natural resources, in several ways. Explicit social choices and controls may need to be applied in many situations, perhaps sharply

---

[5] This was stressed in the great work of A. C. Pigou at Cambridge; see *The Economics of Welfare,* 4th ed. (London: Macmillan, 1946).

altering the rate and directions in which natural resources are used. Several directions are worth noting here.

First, a lower rate of time preference may be imposed, using any of several tactics. Physical limits may be set on uses or pollution levels. Special loans may be provided. Tax subsidies or stockpiling may be tried. Resources may be put under public ownership—entirely or in part—for direct treatments. In short, many devices which have appeared earlier in this book might be strictly appropriate for optimizing natural resource use (or, conversely, they may be misapplied and cause waste).

Second, external effects may be offset by a range of incentives or penalties. Since these will operate on private decision-makers (as well as some public managers), their design may intimately relate to market structure and profit-maximizing behavior. The externalities may arise either in production or in use. Therefore, they may be involved with other choices of industrial policy.

Third, resource-managing industries may need to be restructured so as to avoid biases. This may include unifying control over shared-access resources, such as oil fields. Or it may involve creating greater degrees of competition; or, in other cases, changing the degree of monopsony power. Or it may involve establishing public enterprises for all or part of the market.

Hazards. Public policies may also distort resource use. Resource owners are usually a focal group with strong economic interests, since they hold title to part or all of a specific scarce resource. If properly combined, they can obtain large windfall gains from their ownership. They can be expected to seek these gains, both by market controls and in political efforts. "Conservation" campaigns can cloak *anti-*conservation and selfish strategies. In practical terms, this often means the creation of a government agency which manages and controls the use of the resource. This department will often be effectively controlled by the resource owners and will set restrictions and direct subsidies. Conceivably, these choices will turn out to fit the social optimum. But that is unlikely, and capital gains will also normally accrue.

One should not assume that the creation of a public agency to manage a resource sector will promote conservation. Natural resource policies and agencies need the closest possible scrutiny. The solutions are usually debatable, and the possibility for abuse and confusion is great. By the same token, there will often be large gains from correcting previous policies.

B. LAND

Conservation activities have come in two main waves—during 1890–1910 and since 1967—and have spread to many sectors, using a profusion of devices.[6] In the earlier actions public lands were a prime focus. More recently,

---

[6] See S. P. Hays, *Conservation and the Gospel of Efficiency* (Cambridge: Harvard University Press, 1959), and the many sources cited there. There was also a variety of lesser actions during 1910–67.

attention has centered on external effects and the conservation of the whole set of resources, public and private.

Meanwhile, a long series of actions have affected the use of land resources, but often in wasteful and inequitable ways. Changes are slow and often reversed. Controls turn out to have loopholes and surprising beneficiaries. Huge pieces of public land and resources have been given away, often under seamy conditions, even up to the present. A large domain of public lands and forests has been retained, but parts of it have been opened to private exploitation under dubious conditions.

The public holdings of lands have been very large. Of the 1.8 billion acres that once constituted the public domain, a billion acres have been transferred from federal ownership, while 761 million acres, a third of the nation's area, remain in federal hands.[7]

Disposal has taken several routes. Large tracts were given to states and to railroad companies. Before 1862 private disposal was a revenue-raiser. Then homesteading became the main objective. This was widely abused, in forming large commercial tracts with rich forest stands and mineral beds.

After 1891 this was reversed and public lands were increasingly reserved and expanded. But 96 percent of public land lies within just 11 states, where it is more than half of their area. Strong sectional and industry interests have therefore borne on the uses of these lands. The continental shelf also has involved intense stresses between local and national interests.

Accumulation of recreational and scenic lands has been slow and complex. Most are far away from population centers, and many are still encumbered by private rights and limits. Adding lands closer to the cities is arduous, expensive, and slow.[8]

Access to the public domain has been under a great variety of rules and incentives, some of them intensely controversial. Forest cropping is permitted under diverse conditions, on a sustained-yield basis. After decades of modest harvest, the cut was sharply increased in the 1960s and now brings about $400 million per year. The terms do not maximize the public revenue and often are not openly let, but the basic management is along efficient lines.

Grazing on public lands and forests occurs on a large scale under permits and at modest prices. For decades ranching groups set policies for grazing lands. Fees were nominal; permits were capitalized and sold. Supervision was cut to derisory levels in 1945–48. Management of the process has now improved, and the fees have been raised toward economic levels.

---

[7] Of this total, only 186 million acres are in national forests, and only 24 million acres in national parks. Most of it is in Alaska.

[8] Under the Land and Water Conservation Act of 1965, money received by the federal government from several sources (receipts from the sale of surplus lands, entrance fees at national recreational areas, charges for the use of camp sites, and a tax on fuel used by motor boats) is kept in a separate fund. Two fifths of this fund is to be used by the government to purchase outdoor recreational facilities near urban areas. Three fifths of it is to be granted to the states, on a matching basis, for the same purpose. But the amounts involved under this and later provisions remain small.

Mining on public lands is under the Mining Act of 1872, except for oil, gas, coal, and certain others which are under the Mineral Leasing Act of 1920. The most important of the current issues of minerals policy is the possible exploitation of oil shale in Wyoming, Colorado, and Utah.

C. OIL

Beneath the intense debates about the oil industry, the underlying issue is the management of a crucial nonrenewable resource whose location entangles it in international politics. The "age of oil" has had abundance for a century, but it now faces rising scarcities. This natural scarcity is also overlain by the artificial scarcities of OPEC cartel pricing, and by actions of the major oil companies.

World Oil Markets.[9] There are two cardinal facts: (1) the lop-sided patterns of world oil supply and consumption, and (2) the remarkable 1973–74 rise of the OPEC cartel. The posted price of Middle East crude oil had long been just below $2 per barrel. The large oil companies dominated the market, acting as a noncompetitive cartel in setting prices and planning production and exploration. The oil countries chafed under oligopsony limits which kept the countries' royalties low, at about 25 cents per barrel. Also, the world oil price was held down by new discoveries and improved shipping methods (pipelines, "supertankers," and so on).

OPEC was formed in 1960, but a 1960s oil glut limited its bargaining power. Small gains were made by OPEC after 1965, but it was the 1973 war with Israel that triggered OPEC's assertion of monopoly power. Oil prices were pushed up to $11 and then $13 per barrel and seemed likely to stay at least that high into the 1980s. Meanwhile the major U.S. oil firms had fitted oligopoly behavior by restricting their refinery capacity in the United States. This accented the crisis further, helped cause gasoline prices to rise from about 38 cents to 60 cents per gallon, caused long lines at service stations, put many thousands of independent stations out of business, and swelled oil-company profits by many billions.

The cartel's prospects depend on complex supply and demand conditions, and on the policy steps that may be taken. The main parts of this interaction are as follows.

Supply. Oil occurs under special conditions (see the next section), in all sorts of odd places. The locations vary. Costs also differ, from about 12 cents per barrel in Saudi Arabia to 60 cents in Venezuela and $2.50 and much higher in the United States and other locations. (U.S. costs are enhanced by the U.S.'s own policies). Currently the Arab oil states dominate the holdings of low-cost proven reserves. They also consume little.

Therefore these OPEC countries *(a)* hold monopoly power in selling to

---

[9] See especially Morris A. Adelman, *The World Petroleum Market* (Baltimore: Johns Hopkins Press, 1972), for a review of basic conditions.

consuming nations (such as Europe, Japan and the United States), and *(b)* earn large economic rents. Their rents are so large, indeed, that some OPEC members can easily cut production and forego current revenues.

Potential reserves are much larger, lying in widely disparate sites. They will greatly augment present *proven* reserves, perhaps reducing the relative importance of OPEC supply. Yet discovery is often difficult and full of surprises. New reserves may have high production costs; current estimates are at $8 per barrel and up. Other substitutes (shale oil, tar sands, nuclear breeder reactors, and so forth) are also costly and speculative.

Accordingly, the long-run supply of oil is only partially elastic. For the next decade at least, OPEC oil is likely to gain high rents and to bulk large in world oil sales.

Demand.   Several large oil users—the United States, Russia, and Britain—also have large reserves. By contrast, continental Europe and Japan require large imports. Yet all industrial economies face rises in oil demand so great that imports are likely to grow more critical. Demand is generally income-elastic (motoring, home heating, plastic products, and so forth), but only moderately price-elastic. The growth of consumption has been rapid and seems likely to continue so.

Since 1973 industrial countries have groped for methods of abating this growth. These efforts will continue, for growing demand will tend to keep OPEC cartel prices firm. The margin of reduction need not be large, especially for the United States. A reduction to about 2 percent per year—*plus* the onset of new North Sea, Alaskan, and other oil—could sharply cut their reliance on the 20 million barrels per day that OPEC countries sell.

The importing countries differ widely, in oil reserves, growth rates, balance of payments stresses, and the like. Therefore, a buyers' cartel among them is difficult to form. Beyond a minimal level, concerted action to offset the OPEC cartel is likely to be unstable. The Israeli-Arab issue adds further complications, tending to crystallize Arab unity and divide the consuming countries.

Cartel Prospects.   OPEC appears able to maintain the price of oil above $11 for many years. The consuming nations may try to factionalize the OPEC members, by diplomatic, commercial, and other means.[10] A range of threats and incentives may be used. The outcome will reflect a complex but classic bilateral oligopoly process, operating under uncertain and changing conditions.

---

[10] Within OPEC there are two groups. Group One includes the seven populous, poor, and developing countries: Iran, Venezuela, Indonesia, Iraq, Nigeria, Algeria, and Ecuador. They need the funds and will be loath to restrict production significantly. The other six, in Group Two—Saudi Arabia, Libya, Kuwait, Abu Dhabi, Dabai, and Qatar—are lightly populated and are collecting far more money than they can spend. They are also most deeply involved in the Israeli-Arab conflict, by proximity and religious conviction. Future restrictions will devolve mainly upon Group Two, while Group One is more likely to "chisel" or leave the cartel ranks. Iran, Venezuela, and Nigeria are the critical swing sellers, who may eventually weaken OPEC's price front.

Controls in the United States. Instead of letting prices rise to reflect the higher world price for oil, the United States created in 1973 an agency for allocating oil supplies at controlled prices. The Federal Energy Office (which became in 1977 the core of the new Department of Energy) installed a complicated system of allocations, based on past usages. The effort was to maintain production while avoiding large windfall gains for owners of U.S. oil reserves. Domestic crude oil was now artificially scarce, and its products were competing against those from high-priced imported oil. This led to an "entitlements" system. Refiners depending on expensive imported oil were "entitled" to payments from those using a greater than average amount of cheap domestic oil. The net effect was to subsidize imports.

The new Carter administration chose to develop the controls further, rather than abolish them and let market forces operate freely. Abolition would have reduced imports automatically, possibly reducing the long-term ability of OPEC to raise oil prices. It would also have given large windfall gains to oil and gas owners. In late 1978, portions of the Carter proposals were enacted, after much dilution. Their enforcement leaves much room for discretion and for doubt about their effects.

D. THE PROBLEM OF POLLUTION

Conservation of the environment touches on living conditions which, for many people, are degraded by air, water, and noise pollution and other forms of blight. There are two broad subtopics. One is the dispersal of pollutants, especially in urban areas. The other is the maintenance and use of natural wildlife and terrain, much of it away from cities. The first question relates most closely to the industries which produce the pollution and the urban policies dealing with them. The second set of issues is primarily in a regional and federal context.

Urban Pollution and Congestion. These arise primarily from the operation of factories and vehicles which emit fumes and particles. The problem resides mainly in the design of the factories and vehicles. It also relates to the urban balance between pollution-intensive devices, particularly the private automobile, compared to pollution-minimizing systems such as public transit. These further relate to the pricing of urban transport services and of other public-enterprise activities (water, housing, and so on; recall Chapter 18). We will look primarily at the industrial side of these issues.

By 1968 pollution had become an sharp problem, surfacing for sharp national debate. Many of the nation's streams have been polluted with wastes discharged by steel and paper mills, oil refineries, packing plants, canneries, and the like, with pesticides and herbicides washed off the farmer's fields, with detergents discharged by households, and with sewage dumped by local governments. Normally, the streams would have cleansed themselves of such pollutants. But now their quantity is so great that this cannot occur. The consequences are serious. The fisheries of Lake Erie, it is said, are gone beyond recovery. Ponds and lakeshores are coated in green slime. The beds of rivers lie deep in oily muck.

There is also pollution of the air. Clouds of smoke and soot, noxious fumes, and deadly chemicals are discharged into the air by factories and power plants, by incinerators and burning dumps, by commercial and residential buildings, by automobiles, trucks, and airplanes. They damage health, crops, livestock, property, and the whole quality of life. Also, much of the natural landscape has been spoiled: loggers denuding the hillsides, mines building up slag heaps, stripmines cutting great gashes through the landscape. There is the assault on the wilderness: superhighways driven through the forests, jet ports built in wildlife refuges. There is the creation of ugliness: the mountains of industrial and household wastes, the junk yards, billboards, and neon-strip commercial enterprises that line our roadsides. And there is noise—unceasing and increasing noise.

The costs of this spoliation are heavy, and curing it is a costly process. Since 1965 large federal programs to abate them have sprung up: the Water Quality Act of 1965, the Clear Air Act of 1967, the National Air Quality Act of 1970, and so on. They are imposing upwards of $250 billion in extra costs during the 1970–85 time period. These policies have stirred lively debate, and some are only getting underway.

Efficient abatement of pollution often requires applying direct limits, or incentives and penalties. The objective is not zero pollution, but rather the optimum degree consistent with other economic costs and benefits. Determining that optimum level is itself a major problem, and the practical effectiveness of alternative incentives and compulsions is not thoroughly known.

In practice, a rough process of negotiation and learning has occurred, involving a variety of inducements. There are flat prohibitions; quantitative standards; fines and other incentives; tax remissions (e.g., pollution control bonds, and so on); and others. The normal regulatory bargaining process has occurred in scores of industries, with frequent overstatements looking toward a compromise. Any appraisal of this complex process is beyond this book, but there is one strong industrial aspect: the controls and penalties almost always bear harder on small and marginal producers than on the major firms. With their survival threatened; these lesser firms have special incentives to resist pollution controls. When applied, the controls can increase concentration, unless they are carefully designed to avoid it.

Industrial structure may also play a causative role. Does the degree of monopoly affect the degree of polluting? The problem subdivides again into two parts. First, there are externalities among firms which are still *internal* to the industry. These will tend, of course, be greater under competition than monopoly. "Unitizing" the industry under single control will apply incentives to eliminate such external effects, though anything less than pure monopoly will not suffice.

Second, the greater mass of externalities are *external* to the entire industry. These will be affected primarily by the level of output in the industry. This will be greater under competition than under monopoly, and so competition gives more pollution than monopoly. But monopolizing will only slightly abate the effect. And oligopoly may tend to maximize pollution, when the design of the product itself is concerned. Innovations to reduce the emission of pollution are usually optional to the manufacturer, and the shared-monopoly outcome may minimize such innovations.

Parks and Scenic Resources.   This poses issues of public ownership. Inherently, private market processes will always adjust to equalize the degree of use and amenity, so that no substantial tract of land or natural scenic beauty will remain untouched. The best parts will be picked out and the character of the whole will be eroded; the greater the value, the greater the incentive. Furthermore, if private owners do maintain a natural landmark, they will still rationally restrict and sell access to it so as to maximize their private gain.

Therefore, public ownership and management are usually necessary in order to maintain the minimum stock of natural terrain and landmarks and to make them fairly available.

Yet public ownership of cultural and national assets should not be immune from all economic considerations. Maintenance is often costly and should be set at the right level and format. Timber and other resources often can be harvested without destroying or altering the significant features. And those who visit such landmarks can be charged some form of price related to their usage and costs. In the United States this fosters endlessly debatable policies on granting mineral and forest rights to private interests on public lands. There is also the hidden but important converse problem that portions of many "public" lands and parks are in fact still held by private owners.

The problems of setting the capacity, format, and charges for park use are intricate. Even the publicly owned lands and monuments will tend to be overused if treated strictly on economic grounds. The development and use of natural and cultural landmarks usually erodes their character. The evaluations which determine capacity and prices for using them should usually lean towards less use. This is heightened because most public conservation agencies dealing with natural areas are nearly always below their optimum budget levels and lack adequate powers.

There is one added proviso: the criterion of fairness is often neglected in these evaluations. Therefore efficient prices reflecting true social cost may have a regressive incidence. As in so many other policy treatments, special adjustments in format and pricing may be necessary to serve equity.

E. FISH

The taking of fish is an increasingly important activity, using oceanic resources. It fits within our analysis of optimum yield. The optimum harvesting conditions are complicated by the mobility of the fish themselves, and so there are deep problems in management and pricing, as well as in international diplomacy.

The optimum harvest can often be determined precisely, in technical terms. One estimates the inital stock of fish, the technical costs involved in cropping the fish, and the conditions for maintaining the fish population. The optimum rate of take can be derived, and the efficient set of fishing technology can be applied so as to reach the optimum. Conditions may vary from year to year as unexpected changes occur, but these can be readily accommodated in the analysis. The manager of the unified fishery would, of course, need to be placed under appropriate constraints, if the position involved a high degree of monopoly. This can be done along conventional lines.

International fishing poses the unification problem in acute form. The efficient answer is a joint agency with powers to compel cooperation. However, this has anciently been a difficult task. There are the classic mixed cartel incentives for each claimant either to stay outside or to break ranks. This often is enough in itself to avert any joint controls. It is sharpened by the differences in economic status and interests among the countries. One claimant country is often much poorer and militarily less powerful than others. Such discord of motives further undermines fishing agreements, to the point of armed conflicts around Iceland and off South America in recent years. Such conflicts have occurred throughout human history. The modern instances confirm the continuing power of the incentives and the difficulty of reaching solutions.

Several Actual Cases Illustrate the Problems. For fisheries within countries, prime examples are oyster fishing off the East Coast and salmon fishing on the Northwest Coast. In both cases, unified management is needed and feasible. But competitive fishing is permitted and runs to excess. The technology of boats and tackle is increasingly powerful, so that the race for catch has quickened. The public interest requires reducing the rate of take. Yet as long as entry is permitted, this can only be done by limiting the size of nets, the power of motors, the size of boats, the time period permitted, and so forth. This has been done, but the limits induce further adaptation and innovation and so the controls must be continually tightened. The result is an increasingly wasteful technology, which nonetheless results in a continuing depletion of the fish population (even past point B in Figure 22–1.

Salmon harvesting in the U.S. northwest is the classic case where unification is needed in order to reach efficiency.[11] Quotas were imposed in 1966 on the major yellowfin tuna ground in the eastern Pacific. These encourage

---

[11] Each year salmon go upstream in clear-water rivers to breed. In some rivers they pass over salmon ladders which bypass dams and other obstructions. In others there are precise points where netting could be managed. There can be complete control over the cropping of salmon, by replacing salmon fishing with unified harvesting. Instead, state regulations ban this, and so private fishing engenders extra fishing equipment and costs, distorted innovation, and the depletion of the fish population itself.

the fastest rate of catch; by 1973 the rate was so high that the season lasted only 69 days. Controls on fishing equipment often approach the bizarre.[12] Federal efforts to reform the rules have been stalled because they threaten the large number of inefficient operators which state regulation has protected.

The U.S. Fishing Industry has declined sharply in recent decades, owing to misguided policies as well as innate inefficiency. The U.S. catch has stayed about constant during 1948–76, while world production rose from 18 to 76 million tons. Foreign ships handle about 10 times as much fish per man-day as do U.S. ships. The U.S. haddock catch has dropped from 40 to 5 million pounds between 1965 and 1972. Almost all economy fish (frozen fillets, fish sticks, and the like) are now imported. Foreign technology stresses large factory ships on long tours with advanced freezing and processing capability. The Soviets and Japanese have led this progress. Except for tuna, U.S. fishing technology involves old, small, and specialized ships, on short trips and bound by wage agreements which often discourage effort. There is little innovation or effort to develop markets for new, cheaper kinds of fish.

Two U.S. policies have deepened the decline. One has required all U.S. fishing ships to be built in U.S. shipyards. This doubles the cost. The second policy permits only U.S.-built ships to land fresh seafood in this country. This has induced U.S. fishers to specialize in high-cost fresh fish, and to neglect the more efficient and fast-growing frozen fish markets.

Open-Seas Fishing. This involves large degrees of overfishing, which threaten the whole supply. At present practices, the potential sustainable yield of major species is about 110 million tons; recent growth rates would reach that by 1980.[13] Better management might triple this yeild, and the use of less familiar species could further double or triple the yield. Most of the species and fishing grounds are now overfished. Unified and efficient management is therefore a critical task. There is now a race between decentralized economic interests and the effort to organize this complex industry, so as to restore incentives for conservation. The world stakes are very high.

In 1977 the United States and other nations extended to 200 miles the area of exclusive national fishing rights. This immediately stopped international competition in some major fishing areas. U.S. fishing underwent a small boom. Yet the danger of depletion by competitive fishing remains and will require effective policies.

---

[12] Virginia oysterfishers must employ cumbersome 20-foot tongs to raise oysters laboriously from public waters, instead of using efficient dredges towed by boats. In Maryland dredges can be used, *if* they are towed by *sailboats; except* that motorized push-boats can be used—on Mondays and Tuesdays only. T. Alexander, "American Fishermen are Missing the Boat," *Fortune* (September 1973), pp. 192–98.

[13] J. A. Gulland, ed., *The Fish Resources of the Oceans* (Rome: U.N. Food and Agricultural Organization, 1971).

QUESTIONS FOR REVIEW

1. "Conservation may involve strict physical preservation or it may require using a resource up." True?

2. "Private markets usually optimize the use of resources except where *(a)* there is multiple access, *(b)* private forecasts are wrong, *(c)* external effects are absent." Which?

3. "U.S. public lands are small in area but spread evenly among the states." True?

4. "OPEC is not wholly unified, but the consuming nations are even less coordinated. Therefore, countervailing power to break the OPEC cartel has been weak." True?

5. "Abolition of oil price controls in the United States would *(a)* improve allocation but *(b)* give large windfall gains to a few." True?

6. "Pollution controls often hit the smaller firms hardest, thereby causing increased concentration." True?

7. "Competition in fishing is destructive because each operator has incentives to take out too much." True?

8. Which resources are probably being too rapidly exploited? What do you compare in reaching such judgments?

9. Do large tracks of wilderness ever make good economic sense?

10. How can the harvesting of fish in the U.S. 200-mile coastal waters be reconciled with free access to all U.S. ships?

chapter 23

Regulating Advertising, Products, and Production

There are several types of policies to promote consumers' and workers' interests. They have developed since 1960 in a number of directions, with several new agencies. Some writers see them as part of a "new wave" of regulation, but they are so new that any assessment is hazardous. They are controversial and have uncertain effects.[1]

They try to set limits on the way the product is designed or advertised or on the way production is organized. These policies reach *inside* the firm *(a)* to set limits on its use of factors and its offerings to consumers, or *(b)* to require extra safety devices or consumer warnings. By contrast, the other policies in this book deal only with more *external* matters, such as price, profit, volume of output—leaving production and marketing to the firms' own choices. The newer, seemingly more intrusive regulations have stirred sharp resistance. They have also developed haphazardly, often with little economic clarity or validity. Most of them are too new to offer clear effects or lessons. Though they get much attention in the press, they have so little definite content so far that this chapter will not be a long one.

The recent spread of this activity is suggested by Table 23–1. It shows new laws of this sort during 1962–74 (other than those covered in other chapters, such as laws on pollution and banking). Some of these laws merely extend pre-existing programs, such as for safe foods and for consumer information. Perhaps the most important new Acts have been those affecting occupational safety (1970) and consumer product safety (1972). The main agencies are summarized in Table 23–2. Some are new, some old. Taken altogether, the "new" regulation fits within the longer growth trend in protective laws. Some of the recent actions appear to have been overdue.

---

[1] For good analysis of some of the economic problems, see Richard E. Caves and Marc J. Roberts, eds., *Regulating the Product: Quality and Variety* (Cambridge: Ballinger, 1975). For a view that the "new" regulation is a drastic departure which is taking away managers' area for choice, see Murray L. Weidenbaum, *Business, Government, and the Public* (Englewood Cliffs, N.J.: Prentice-Hall, 1977).

TABLE 23–1
Extension of Government Regulation of Business, 1962–1974

Law and Year of Enactment	Formal Purpose and Function
1962 Food and Drug Amendments	Requires pretesting of drugs for safety and effectiveness and labeling of drugs by generic names
1963 Equal Pay Act	Eliminates wage differentials based on sex
1964 Civil Rights Act	Creates Equal Employment Opportunity Commission (EEOC) to investigate charges of job discrimination
1965 Cigarette Labeling and Advertising Act	Requires labels on hazards of smoking
1966 Fair Packaging and Labeling Act	Requires producers to state what a package contains, how much it contains, and who made the product
1966 Child Protection Act	Bans sale of hazardous toys and articles
1966 Traffic Safety Act	Provides for coordinated national safety program, including safety standards for motor vehicles
1966 Coal Mine Safety Amendments	Tightens controls on working conditions
1967 Flammable Fabrics Act	Broadens federal authority to set safety standards for inflammable fabrics, including clothing and household products
1967 Wholesome Meat Act	Offers states federal assistance in establishing interstate inspection system and raises quality standards for imported meat
1967 Age Discrimination in Employment Act	Prohibits job discrimination against individuals aged 40 to 65
1968 Consumer Credit Protection Act	Requires full disclosure of terms and conditions of finance charges in credit transactions
1968 Wholesome Poultry Products Act	Increases protection against impure poultry
1969 National Environmental Policy Act	Requires environmental impact statements for federal agencies and projects
1970 Public Health Smoking Act	Extends warning about the hazards of cigarette smoking
1970 Poison Prevention Packaging Act	Authorizes standards for child-resistant packaging of hazardous substances
1970 Occupational Safety and Health Act	Establishes safety and health standards that must be met by employers
1972 Consumer Products Safety Act	Establishes a commission to set safety standards for consumer products and bans products presenting undue risk or injury
1972 Noise Pollution and Control Act	Regulates noise limits of products and transportation vehicles
1973 Vocational Rehabilitation Act	Requires federal contractors to take affirmative action on hiring the handicapped
1973 Safe Drinking Water Act	Requires EPA to set national drinking water regulations
1974 Employee Retirement Income Act	Sets new federal standards for employee pension programs

Source: Adapted from Murray L. Weidenbaum, *Business, Government, and the Public* (Englewood Cliffs, N.J.: Prentice-Hall, 1977), Table 1–1.

TABLE 23–2
The Main Agencies Regulating Products and Jobs

Name and Year of Origin	Budget 1978–79 ($ million)	Staff Size	Its Formal Purpose Is:
Federal Trade Commission (1914)	31*	1,716	To stop unfair practices, fraud, and deception
Food and Drug Administration (1931)	294	7,583	To insure the safety of foods, drugs, medical devices and radiological practices
Consumer Product Safety Commission (1972)	42	899	To reduce product-related injuries to consumers, by requiring better design and instructions
National Highway Traffic Safety Administration (1970)	121	900	To reduce traffic accidents, by requiring better design of motor vehicles
Occupational Safety and Health Administration (1971)	163	2,860	To protect safety and health on the job
Equal Employment Opportunity Commission	116	3,219	To prevent job discrimination by race, sex, religion or other unfair bases

* The part of the FTC budget for "consumer protection."
Source: U.S. Government, *Budget, Fiscal Year 1979,* Appendix.

They occasionally overlap or conflict, but that too is often normal among policies as they develop. Some of the new agencies have tried to do more than their resources permit. Others have had teething problems, delays, and mistakes. Yet the whole development is normal and—after a sorting-out period—will probably fit reasonably efficient lines.

This chapter focuses on consumer information in Section A, product design in Section B, and occupational conditions in Section C. In such a formative area, one aims only to draw the main lessons rather than set out the details. Since the regulation does not deal in the familiar regulatory quantities of prices and profits, its economic effects are bound to be diffuse. Moreover, the subject attracts polemics and rhetoric, so that the wise student adopts an especially skeptical stance. There are important social interests involved. But the economic content is often obscure.

A. CONSUMER INFORMATION

The social interest in good consumer information lies in two directions: *(a)* getting full, accurate disclosure of the nature of the product, and *(b)* preventing deceptive claims and exploitative advertising.

Caveat emptor (let the buyer beware) has been a valid rule for several millenia. It still suffices for most consumer purchases, which are small, simple, and repetitive (for example, most foods and clothing). But some goods are complex and infrequently bought, and so consumers may be fooled and cheated. They include the larger consumer durables (houses, automobiles, appliances), medical care, mortgages, and other credit. Large numbers of consumers may be routinely deceived in these consumption choices and suffer lasting hardship because of contrived ignorance. The social losses are likely to be regressive in incidence, focusing on lower income and educational groups. Better information would therefore provide social benefits.

The main agency to promote this interest is the Federal Trade Commission. About half its budget goes to consumer protection in three main kinds of activities. Various state agencies also provide some consumer support, usually by investigating and by pursuing actions in the courts.

A1. Information

The FTC enforces a series of laws requiring fair labeling of products. For example, the facts on the tags in clothes and furs are under its regulations. "Hazardous substances" and various other products must be labeled in line with its rules. The FTC also measures cigarette tar content and supervises the health warning notes in cigarette advertisements and on the package. There are also "truth-in-lending" provisions, requiring full data about true interest costs. These enforcement actions are simple and repetitive. They have greatly improved the reliability of information about products.

A2. Deception and Fraud

The FTC also handles thousands of individual complaints about deception and fraud by sellers. These cover all kinds of markets, and most are settled by compromise rather than pursued at length. Most of them are small-change matters, with small yields. For such cases, the main social value may be the general benefit of knowing that a sympathetic agency is ready to handle even very small consumer complaints. State agencies also are active in this direction, at a grass-roots level.

A recent major case involved "engine switching" by General Motors in the 1960s and 1970s. GM had long shared various automobile parts among its five main divisions, but in 1977 the undisclosed use of Chevrolet engines in Oldsmobiles provoked a storm of protests by angry customers.[2] (The "regular" Oldsmobile engine was in fact made by Buick.) Legal actions by several states sought large damages for purchasers. GM negotiated costly settlements in some states, paying owners up to $1,000 per car for the mislabeling. Other states sought more punitive damages for the deception, and their cases were settled in 1978 for higher amounts.

---

[2] By contrast, Ford and Chrysler did not claim differences among their engines according to their divisions.

A3. Advertising

The FTC routinely monitors advertising, in order to find and stop deceptive claims. In the course of a year the FTC receives thousands of complaints concerning deceptive advertising and, among these, investigates a few hundred. It examines hundreds of thousands of printed advertisements and radio and TV commercials, and questions one in 15 or 20. From all this, less than 500 items may lead to action.

During 1970–75, the FTC enlarged this program, as part of the effort to "revitalize" the FTC.[3] A large variety of cases of alleged deceptive advertising was quickly built up, evoking in turn strong denunciations by sellers and advertising firms.

In the majority of cases the FTC did establish that the contested claims had been deceptive. The net result may have been a modest rise in the standards of honesty in nationally advertised brands. But the whole economic gain was modest, and the FTC impact on advertising remains slight.

The usual case is closed by an assurance of discontinuance, which is nothing more than a slap on the wrist. An order carries no penalty for past deceptions and does nothing to prevent future ones. In one notorious case, the FTC, beginning in 1959, investigated claims by the manufacturer of Geritol that his product cured tiredness, loss of strength, run-down feeling, nervousness, and irritability by providing iron to "tired blood." In 1962 the Commission issued a formal complaint. In 1965 it issued an order to cease and desist. In 1967 this order was upheld by a circuit court, making it final and binding. In 1968 the Commission ruled that the manufacturer had violated the order. In 1969 it asked the Department of Justice to bring suit to compel compliance. In 1970 the Department sued, asking that the manufacturer be fined $500,000 and his advertising agency another $500,000 for violations of the Commission's order. In all this time the company continued to advertise the iron in Geritol as a remedy for bad blood.

The FTC has an uphill fight. The Commission, rather than the advertiser, bears the burden of proof. It must draw a difficult line between harmless exaggeration and harmful deception. It must base its orders on evidence that the advertiser's claims are false and on testimony that they are, in fact, deceptive. When orders are issued, cases won, and sanctions imposed, moreover, they apply only to the company that makes the advertised product, not to the advertising agency that prepares the misleading copy, to the publisher who prints it, or to the station that broadcasts it. And then the advertiser need only drop the old campaign and embark upon a new one as deceptive as the last. The Commission cannot require the publication of retractions. It cannot censor copy in advance. And it can scarcely be expected to keep

---

[3] For the rationale of the FTC's type of advertising program, see Robert Pitofsky, "Beyond Nader: Consumer Protection and the Regulation of Advertising," *Harvard Law Review* 9 (February 1977), 661–701.

pace with the inventive copywriters in the advertising agencies. The control that it exerts may moderate some of the more serious abuses of advertising. But it is not to be described as rigorous.

In 1977 the FTC turned to advertisements directed at children. On average, U.S. children watch about 20,000 television commercials per year, most of them designed to stir the child to ask its parent to buy the product. It is big business, involving advertising revenues over $500 million per year. (Of this total, the three leading cereals firms—Kellogg, General Foods, and General Mills—alone do about 25 percent.) At issue was whether children are inherently vulnerable and need protection. The issue divided into two parts. First, certain harmful products might need special action in any case: sugary cereals which erode teeth were the leading example. Second, possibly all advertising exploiting children's trusting nature should be limited, in a civilized society.

There were several alternative methods for treating the problem. One was an outright ban on commercials for "harmful" products. Another was a requirement that time be set aside for "counter-commercials" (such as the antismoking ads presented by health groups in the early 1970s before all cigarette advertising on television was banned). A third alternative was to set strict guidelines for selling on children's programs.

The issue was a complex test of the correct margin for limiting advertising. Actually only 16 percent of children's total viewing hours occurs during the times (such as Saturday mornings) when most programs are directed at children. FTC action would require lengthy hearings and revisions, and any final rule would probably be challenged by advertisers in court. The FTC's best hope might be in pressuring industry to adopt its own restrictions to lessen the exploitation of children. The FTC's power is evidently limited, even though its statute seems to give it full authority.

B. PRODUCT DESIGN

Certain products are unsafe *and* involve a public interest in exclusion, because *(a)* they are too complex or hazardous to be evaluated properly by the consumer and/or *(b)* their failure would harm not only the owner of the product but also other people. In practice, it is in pharmaceutical products and automobiles that the most direct public controls have been established, to exclude "unfit" products. The FDA and NHTSA deal with these industries. The new CPSC is the agency with general coverage of consumer products.

The objective is simple—safer products—but it can pose difficult economic issues. First, the *correct* degrees of safety is needed, not the ultimate of *perfect* safety. (Thus using a ladder, a knife, or a bicycle always poses some risk.) This correct margin is usually debatable. Second, setting strict standards can freeze the nature of the product too narrowly in one mold and stop innovation. Usually, it is good to have variety among products, even in their degree of safety. Some users need more protection than others. Setting safety standards too high would be like requiring all cars to be of Rolls-Royce quality.

In practice the agencies have groped for the right margins of safety. They have often sunk into trivia and bureaucratic rules. For some products, little has been done. For others, the standards have probably been too tight.

The FDA is a large agency with a wide range of tasks. It has grown and added powers mainly when a scandal proves the need for new powers and staff. It covers such diverse industries as drugs, foods, agricultural production, pesticides, cosmetics, and other household substances. It inspects thousands of premises, and tests other thousands of goods. It has gone through ups and downs of militancy and strictness, and it is under severe pressure, especially from those industries which it is intended to regulate. It is most successful where it is able to set the burden of proof against risky products, so that producers have to prove them safe. It keeps some products off the market until their safety is clearly established, but the standards it should apply are controversial. Often its exclusions and penalties are repeatedly violated by the same offenders, and often its controls appear ineffective.

The work load of the FDA is large and varied. Within a year it examines hundreds of applications to certify new drugs and new food additives and tests thousands of batches of antibiotics and color additives, rejecting a minor fraction and clearing the rest for sale. In the same period it inspects half of the 14,000 drug establishments in the United States and more than a third of the 88,000 food establishments. It examines thousands of lots of raw agricultural products, checking on residues of pesticides. It prepares standards by which to judge adulteration of foods, holds hearings on them, modifies them where necessary, and adopts them for use. It investigates tens of thousands of reports of poisonings attributed to drugs, chemical additives, cosmetics, pesticides, and hazardous household substances. It maintains surveillance over drugs after they have been cleared for use, recalling hundreds of them from the market and sending warning letters to physicians where it finds them to be unsafe. It undertakes to prevent illegal sales of prescription drugs by pharmacists and by dope peddlers.

The FDA was long underfinanced, but its personnel in 1978 stood as high as 7,583 and its appropriation at $294 million. Its leadership, since 1966, has been strong but rapidly changing, with three different commissioners in four years. It has been repeatedly reorganized but has never had the active interest and support of the head of its Department. In 1969 a study panel appointed by the Commissioner reported that the agency was unable to develop the kind of concerted and coordinated efforts needed to deal adequately and simultaneously with its myriad problems. "We are currently not equipped," it said, "to cope with the challenge." This problem has not changed.

Since 1962 the FDA has set higher standards for reliability and efficiency in drugs. This has entailed careful testing of new drugs, to discover side effects and establish their curative value. Concurrently, the rate of introduction of new drugs has declined. Though a decline was natural after the peak period of new "miracle" drugs in the 1950s, this led to charges that the FDA was stifling innovation.[4] In the 1970s, the testing requirements have been moderated to permit faster introduction of new drugs.

The Highway Safety Bureau has set a series of requirements for automobile safety equipment, dealing with bumpers, seat belts, structure, and the like. These have improved safety *and* had the predictable side effect of putting the smaller and less conventional automobile sellers at a disadvantage. The additional costs of mandatory safety equipment have been proportionally higher for smaller car manufacturers, again tending to benefit the larger producers relatively. As in setting high standards for medicine, setting costly safety standards for cars has tended to exclude whole ranges of lower-cost supply from the market. Against the benefits for public safety which this gives must be laid the higher costs of automobiles and a reduction in consumer choice. This reduction bears most heavily on the poorer part of the population, many of whom would prefer to make do with cheaper automobiles.

The Consumer Product Safety Commission has had a weak start. Its mandate is large, covering at least 10,000 products. It focuses on getting firms to redesign products along safe lines.

Managed at first by conservatives, the CPSC accomplished little in its first five years. It was unable to set priorities, and so it merely responded to complaints and studied products more or less at random. Its resources have been tiny and poorly used. It has been slow in developing product standards, partly because it gets mired in vast detail about the nature of the product and the features it must have. By 1978 it had issued few standards, and these had been greeted by strong business criticism for being too detailed.[5] It has taken several years to act on some clearly unsafe products. Even its few bannings have usually been qualified by letting merchants dispose of their existing stocks of the unsafe products.

The CPSC did little in its first five years to meet the genuine need for safer products. Yet its powers and resources were by 1978 large enough to

---

[4] For views critical of FDA's effects on innovation, see David Schwartzman, *Innovation in the Pharmaceutical Industry* (Baltimore: Johns Hopkins University Press, 1976); Martin Baily, "Research and Development Cost and Returns: The U.S. Pharmaceutical Industry," *Journal of Political Economy* 80 (January/February 1972), 78; Sam Peltzman "An Evaluation of Consumer Protection Legislation: The 1962 Drug Amendments," *Journal of Political Economy* 81 (September/October 1973), 1067; and Henry G. Grabowski, John M. Vernon, and Lacy G. Thomas, "Estimating the Effects of Regulation on Innovation: An International Comparative Analysis of the Pharmaceutical Industry," *Journal of Law and Economics* 21 (April 1978), 133–64.

[5] Detailed regulations concerning ladders, lawn mowers, and bicycles drew the most prominent criticism. The ladder regulations clearly did go too far, but the lawn mower standards were within reason, even though they would be costly. The bicycle standards soon were accepted as reasonable.

make large progress, if they were used efficiently. The need was to focus on the main cases, force reasonable standards through, and be stricter in enforcing the standards.

C. OCCUPATIONAL CONDITIONS

These divide into two categories: job safety and equal job opportunity. Both were recently given major new agencies to enforce higher standards. In both cases, the regulation has stirred sharp controversy and moderate change.

C1. Job Safety

Some 14,000 U.S. workers are killed each year at work and far more are injured in various ways, despite a long history of safety regulations. In 1970 the OSHA was created to reduce job hazards, by developing and enforcing higher standards. It has only 800 inspectors in the field, and it has only imposed small fines in a few cases. The main effort has gone into setting specific standards for safety from physical, biological, and noise damages. This has stimulated a higher level of safety expenditures by businesses, on the order of several billion dollars in a wide range of industries. But OSHA itself has been slow to develop efficient criteria for its standards. Its approach is to require the firm to change its machinery to be safer, rather than to rely on self-protection by workers. This may impose excessive costs. Thus, it tried to make a fuel-cylinder company install noise-reducing engineering controls costing $30,000, rather than rely on soundproof earmuffs for a few workers, costing $12 each. By 1978 OSHA was at last beginning to apply cost-benefit criteria to its rules, but many of its individual actions had been dubious.

OSHA is able to enforce safety directly in only a relatively few premises. Its rules and standards may have a much wider effect, as firms act so as to avoid problems with OSHA. The new agency has taken too long to work toward efficient regulations, and it does impose extra paperwork burdens. But it may have helped to increase company efforts at job safety, enough to justify its costs.

C2. Equal Job Opportunity

Job discrimination against minorities and women has been deeply rooted in the U.S. economy. It has caused both inefficiency and inequity. The U.S. Equal Employment Opportunity Commission was created in 1964 to abate the problem, and by 1977 it had become the main U.S. agency dealing with the issue. By all accounts it has not been efficiently run, and so its effect has been limited.

At first it merely responded to complaints. These soon grew to a backlog of over 100,000, and so by 1972 the EEOC was trying to select a few large firms as targets, in order to get as much effect as possible for each action. AT&T and other large firms quickly settled with small payments to compensate for past discrimination. Restricted job classes were opened to women, and minorities were promised even chances. The mass of individual cases still moved slowly, and by 1978 the EEOC had still made little headway in opening up the upper-level jobs to minorities and women. It could not apply quotas, and it could not handle individual cases briskly. It is not clear that the EEOC can do much more for disadvantaged groups than the general trend toward women's liberation and minority rights is already doing.

D. SUMMARY

Recent growth in regulating products and production has been part of the longer development of protective regulation in the Unites States. The new agencies have had the usual problems in setting priorities and designing efficient controls. There have been mistakes, some of them large. These errors have been publicized and the agencies' positive actions have been resisted. Their resources are usually too small. Yet some of the policies have stirred improvements in a wide range of firms.

QUESTIONS FOR REVIEW

1. "Business is being engulfed in a tide of new, useless regulation which is taking over its domain of choice." True?
2. "Consumers can protect themselves from false claims in many products, especially the simpler, smaller ones which are purchased frequently." True?
3. "Getting truth in advertising is a never ending struggle." True?
4. "You can't just place a dollar value on a human life, so one can't use cost-benefit analysis to set product safety criteria." True?
5. "The FDA's tighter testing standards for new drugs after 1962 were followed by a decline of innovation in drugs. This proves that the standards were a mistake." True?
6. "If it costs $100 to make the machine quieter and $12 for a pair of soundproof earmuffs, then the earmuffs are the only correct choice." True?
7. How *should* the FTC try to go about preventing deceptive and harmful advertising?
8. Should drugs have to be efficacious or merely not harmful?
9. Should cars have to be equipped with "airbag" safety devices? What categories of cost and benefit do you use in appraising this?
10. Identify several products you consider hazardous and try to define standards for safety design for them.
11. What should OSHA's rules be for protecting safety in the work of *(a)* professional football and hockey players, and *(b)* construction workers in skyscrapers?

chapter 24

Other Departures from
Standard Policy Treatment

$W_{\text{e now}}$ finish up the coverage of policies which permit or promote monopoly. Section A reviews the exemptions from antitrust and the policies which restrict competition or enforce cartels. Then come labor unions in Section B and military purchases in Section C.

A. EXEMPTIONS AND ANTICOMPETITIVE POLICIES

About half of the economy is exempt from antitrust and utility regulation, as Chapter 1 noted. In some sectors the government openly supports monopoly without regulating it.

Trade Restrictions.   The most ancient and extensive restraints are those on foreign trade. For the United States, leading features of these tariffs and physical limits are shown in Table 24–1. Some approach a total exclusion of import competition. The degree of actual protection is often difficult to assess, for it reflects both output tariffs and tariffs on imported inputs. In part, many tariffs can be regarded merely as equalizers against corresponding tariffs set by foreign countries. Such opposed tariffs make it difficult to cut tariffs unilaterally as a means of fostering competition in domestic markets. Still, the net effect of a tariff is to exclude competition, and the benefits are reaped by producers at the expense of consumers.

Supplementing or substituting for tariffs often are quotas or other physical limitations on imports. These have been most prominent in the oil and steel industries, especially since the middle 1950s. The oil import quotas lasted for about 14 years during 1959–73 when there were surplus oil supplies both internationally and domestically. Since 1973 such quotas have been superfluous as U.S. oil supplies have tightened, and so the import quotas were suspended. In periods of boom, restraints on steel imports have also had little force. Yet there has existed since 1968 an effective international

TABLE 24–1
Selected Trade Restrictions, 1978

Tariffs	Rate of Tariff as Percent of Value	Tariffs	Rate of Tariff as Percent of Value
Distilled liquors	18	Steel products	5–15
Wool fabrics	47	Machinery	5–15
Clothing	20–30	Motors	12
Furniture	11	Appliances	10–12
Organic dyes, etc.	37	Automobiles	6
Shoes	15	Cycles	13
Flat glass	17	Sporting goods	19
Glassware	17	Musical instruments	21

Other Restrictions

Steel	"Voluntary" restrictions on steel sales to the United States. Also, a system of "reference" prices which trigger extra duties on imported steel (first imposed in 1977).
Ships	Foreign-made ships cannot (a) ply U.S. coastal routes nor (b) get shipping subsidies
Cotton	Restrictions are negotiated by governments. Japanese sales have dropped 60 percent.
Sugar, wheat, cotton	Restricted.
"Buy American"	Excludes foreign suppliers in a wide range of major industrial products.
Nuclear fuel cores	Banned, unless enriched in AEC plants.

Source: Commission on International Trade and Investment Policy, *U.S. International Economic Policy in an Interdependent World,* Vol. I (Washington, D.C.: U.S. Government Printing Office, 1971), and other sources.

cartel limiting imports of steel from Japan and Europe to the United States (recall Chapter 7).[1]

Agricultural and Fisheries Cooperatives. These dominate the trade in most crops, livestock, and seafoods. Some of them are big businesses and hold a high degree of market power. A wave of mergers during the 1970s increased concentration among them further, and some have moved into large-scale production of fertilizers and chemicals. Since 1922, under the Capper-Volstead Act, farmers can use cooperatives as common agencies in sorting, grading, and packaging their crops; in producing such foodstuffs as butter, cheese, and canned goods; in marketing their output; and in fixing prices and terms of sale. Under various other side limits, such cooperatives are permitted to operate even where they might violate the antitrust laws. In the most basic agricultural goods, they usually have little market power. But where producers are geographically concentrated as they are in the cases of fruits, vegetables, nuts, and milk, a cooperative may possess much market power. In some cases, cooperatives equalize the bargaining powers of sellers

---

[1] On other aspects of steel import restraints, see Walter Adams and Joel B. Dirlam, "Import Competition and the Trade Act of 1974," *Indiana Law Journal* 52 (Spring 1977), 535–99.

and buyers. But in others they are simply a license to monopolize. A similar exemption resides in the Fisheries Cooperative Marketing Act of 1934. Under it fisheries can form cooperatives, some of which are able to affect the prices and terms of sale.

Newspapers are another major exemption from antitrust. In recent decades their numbers have been dwindling, partly because the economies of scale in production and distribution have risen. (Also the profit gains from increasing the share of local advertising have risen.) In 1970, after a series of adverse court decisions against newspaper mergers, the newspapers succeeded in getting Congress to pass an act exempting joint arrangements between pairs of papers for mutual printing and business organization of newspaper production. This is, in effect, a large special application of the "failing-firm" criterion (recall Chapter 6). Genuine economies of scale (plus the gains from monopolizing advertising) might lead to a virtually complete situation of one-paper cities throughout the country. Therefore the exemption may marginally promote variety and competition. Yet it does acquiesce in an extraordinary degree of monopoly in most newspaper markets.

Chapter 13 noted that many transport price-fixing groups are permitted. These affect ocean shipping rates, international airline fares, trucking, and railroad rates, and—in effect—domestic airline fares. Still other exemptions—banks, insurance, professions, etc.—are discussed in other chapters.

Interstate Limits. Various state laws have restricted the sales of beer, wine, and various food products across state lines. Eggs, chicken, fruits, and vegetables are among those which have been affected. State laws have handicapped out-of-state truckers. Some states have discriminated against trucks that come in loaded, prepared to sell, in favor of those that come in empty, prepared to buy. The Buy American Act has its counterpart in state law. Nearly every state requires that some sort of preference be shown to residents in making public purchases. State agencies and institutions have thus been forced to hire local labor, award contracts to local bidders, and purchase supplies from local firms. City councils have taken similar actions affecting milk and construction.

These measures have the same defects as do the barriers to international trade. In fact, they may be more harmful, since the area they leave open to freedom of competition is a smaller one.

Milk. Markets for milk are essentially the areas around the largest 60 or so cities in the United States. Each is limited by local health laws and price controls authorized by the U.S. Department of Agriculture. There are usually only two or three milk suppliers, competing by brands and service rather than by price. A complicated set of formulas is applied in fixing local milk prices, involving discrimination as well as cartel results.

In 20 states prices paid to milk producers are fixed by public agencies. Covering intrastate markets, they are generally similar to federal controls but tighter. Resale prices are fixed for milk under the laws of 15 states. Sales below cost are forbidden by the laws of 10 other states. They too restrict sales and raise prices.[2] Distributors' margins are also protected by regulations that restrain competition.

These official cartels have cost consumers over $500 million per year, at a net social cost of $200 million per year.[3] They could be replaced by free-market processes, giving a much more efficient outcome.

The NRA. It is difficult now to convey fully the trauma of the Great Depression of the 1930s, but it does explain the oddity of some policy treatments tried then. One was the National Industrial Recovery Act, rushed through in June 1933 as an early Rooseveltian effort to stabilize prices and promote industrial production. The episode was quickly recognized as a bizarre economic failure. But it graphically illustrates the effects of suspending antitrust, and it immunized at least a generation of Americans against such self-regulation by industry.

Industries were permitted to draw up codes of conduct, under a blanket immunity from the antitrust laws. Draft codes were drawn up by industry trade associations, revised by committees of industry and labor representatives, and then given the force of law.

The NRA approved 557 basic codes, 189 supplementary codes, 109 divisional codes, and 19 codes entered into jointly with the Agricultural Adjustment Administration—a grand total of 874. The codes spelled out more than a thousand different kinds of provisions for the regulation of 150 different types of competitive practices. They controlled terms of sale, prices, markets, production, capacity, and the channels of distribution. In the name of fair competition, they required adherence to practices that the Federal Trade Commission and the courts had held to be unfair. Industry by industry, they were designed by a majority to curb the competitive propensities of an obstreperous minority. Item by item, they copied the pattern of the standard European cartel.

More than 85 percent of the codes contained some provision for the direct or indirect control of price. In iron and steel, and in a few other industries, the codes legalized basing-point systems of delivered pricing, specifying each of the elements of the pricing formulas and prescribing their use.

The fixing of prices was usually less overt. Some 200 codes permitted code authorities to establish minimum prices only to prevent "destructive price cutting" and to do so only in the event of an "emergency." These limitations, however, had little significance. The concepts were never clearly defined. "An emergency," it was said, "is something that is declared by a code authority." As the coal dealers put it, "We have always had an emergency in retail solid fuel."

---

[2] U.S. Department of Agriculture, Economic Research Service, Agricultural Economic Report No. 152, *Government's Role in Pricing Fluid Milk in the United States* (Washington, D.C.: Government Printing Office, 1968).

[3] Reuben A. Kessel, "Economic Effects of Federal Regulation of Milk Markets," *Journal of Law and Economics* 10 (1967), 51–78; and Richard A. Ippolito and Robert T. Masson, "The Social Cost of Government Regulation of Milk," *Journal of Law and Economics* 21 (April 1978), 33–66.

Ninety-one codes provided for the restriction of output and the sharing out of available business. Sixty codes, most of them in the textile industry, imposed limitations on the number of hours or shifts per day, or the number of hours or days per week, during which machines or plants might be operated, thus curtailing production and allocating the resulting volume of business on the basis of capacity. A half dozen codes, including those for the petroleum, lumber, copper, and glass container industries, provided for the limitation of production in accordance with estimates of total demand, and for the assignment of production quotas on the basis of present capacity or past production or sales.

This wave of cartelization soon drew criticism and doubt. In the spring of 1934, the President appointed a committee, under the eminent lawyer, Clarence Darrow, to investigate. The committee's report condemned the whole undertaking, denouncing it as "monopoly sustained by government" and as "a regimented organization for exploitation." The Supreme Court settled the matter in 1935, by its decision on the *Schechter* case.[4] The Court was unanimous. The law involved an unconstitutional invasion of intrastate commerce and an unconstitutional delegation of legislative power. The NRA was put to death on May 27, 1935.

The National Industrial Recovery Act contributed little, if anything, to recovery. But it did serve one useful purpose. It provided the country with a demonstration of the character and the consequences of cartelization. It showed that industry, when given the power of self-government, could not be trusted to exercise it in the public interest; that enterprise would be handicapped and vested interests protected, progress obstructed, and stagnation assured.

The NRA was like a vaccination, giving the United States a mild case of the cartel disease and immunizing it against the disease itself.

Price Controls.   Formal price controls have been tried in the U.S. mainly during World War II, the Korean War, and 1971–74.[5] Many U.S. economists have been part of the effort, and most of them regard it as frustrating and only partially successful. Since 1955 there have been many informal "jawboning" attempts—and quasi-formal "wage-price guidelines"—to abate price rises.[6] Expert opinion divides on the issue. Some economists regard controls as worth trying, at least during crisis periods. Others liken them to bandages applied to cure a fever. Price-wage controls during peace-time seemed necessary for the first time in many North Atlantic economies in 1971–73. Yet they now seem to have had slight effects and have once again gone out of style.

Four basic lessons hold *(a)* Controls work best during a crisis, especially in war. Loyalty is high, and the situation seems to be temporary. *(b)* Price-

---

[4] *Schechter* v. *U.S.,* 295 U.S. 495 (1935).

[5] An excellent analysis of World War II experience is given in J. K. Galbraith, *A Theory of Price Control* (Cambridge: Harvard University Press, 1952).

[6] John Sheahan, *The Wage-Price Guidelines* (Washington, D.C.: Brookings Institution, 1968).

wage controls fail when any important groups (especially upper groups: top executives, capital-gains receivers, speculators) are exempted from controls, while ordinary citizens are made to sacrifice. *(c)* Controls are most effective on major concentrated industries. *(d)* Price-wage controls are cumbersome, costly, and unfair to some groups. Inspired leaders can minimize these flaws.

In short, controls are best used selectively for selected situations. There are good reasons for focusing upon major tight oligopolies. Fewness makes for ease of measurement and control. It also lends theatrical drama to the event, by holding up for public attention those largest firms which might have a large impact. In contrast, attempts to control the decentralized, competitive markets in clothing, furniture, or similar secondary products are likely to be futile. This was learned first in World War II, where price controls on major firms in large industries were the most successful. The Korean War effort—on a smaller scale—confirmed this tendency. Perhaps no controls could arrest the long-term upward movement of such prices. Still, the will to believe that an extensive apparatus must be accomplishing something has led some observers to conclude that the effort during 1971–74 did have at least some effect. The formal end of controls in 1974 brought a reversion to "jaw-boning." Price-wage controls no longer seemed a necessary treatment for industrial economies in peacetime. Yet a variety of more selective limits on a relatively few large industries were likely to be tried.

The controls were not a proper experiment but only a superficial half-effort.[7] There were a variety of major technical gaps and flaws. Profits, capital gains, dividends, and top executives' pay were effectively exempt. It took much time simply to assemble the staff and set rules. Decisions were often hasty and crude—and easily avoided.

In smaller economies such as Britain, price controls can be more pointed and effective. During 1965–70 a Prices and Incomes Board was able to stop or modify price increases in scores of industries. Since 1976, a Price Commission has dealt both with price increases and parallel pricing in tight oligopolies. The Commission has adequate powers, staffing, and technical skill. It may succeed in restraining market power in many of the major problem industries, by forcing prices down toward cost levels.

B. LABOR MARKETS

B1. Economic Issues

There are two related policy issues. One is the exemption of unions from antitrust: this affects a wide range of industrial labor markets for unskilled and skilled blue-collar labor. The other issue is self-regulation and restrictions in professional trades (doctors, lawyers, embalmers, accountants, beauticians,

---

[7] See the revealing analysis of these defects by C. Jackson Grayson, the head of the Price Commission, and the excellent analysis by R. F. Lanzillotti, Mary Hamilton, and Blaine Roberts, *Phase II in Review: The Price Commission* (Washington, D.C.: Brookings Institution, 1975).

barbers, and the like). The two are parts of the same process: the effort of workers to use bargaining power to better their income and working conditions.

The market power held by labor groups may be large enough to affect national economic performance. It may help cause a wage-price spiral. It may also rigidify labor practices and impede productivity. Strikes may reduce output sharply. At the upper end, professional services may be misallocated and restricted. These are only possibilities, and there are counter-arguments.[8] Yet they stir frequent proposals to restore free competition in labor markets.

Labor monopoly varies greatly in its incidence, forms, and effects. We need first to analyze how it works.

Labor Markets differ in no less than six important directions, which together define their structure and importance.

1. *Type of industry.* The range stretches from basic industry over to trade and commerce, finance, utilities, public agencies, and civil service sectors.

2. *Range of skills.* These go upward from raw manual labor to skilled, white-collar, managerial, and professional qualifications.

3. *Geographic scope.* The range is from local hiring points, on up to regional, national, and international scope.

4. *Potential for innovation.* This attribute arises partly from industry type, but it is an important trait on its own. The range is from a high potential for innovation and change in workers' activities, down to zero change in static industries.

5. *Range of buyer types.* The buyers of labor services are of many types. At one extreme is the informed monopsonist (utility, civil service). Intermediate is the partially competitive employer, on roughly equal terms with the employee. At the other extreme are customers who are—or can be made to be—inexpert and passive (such as some of those buying medical, legal, and educational services).

6. *Leverage.* Above all, markets differ in the degree of damage which labor sellers can inflict on their customers and others by *striking.* This depends partly on the other five conditions. The range is great: from small specialized groups with virtual life-and-death power over many others, down to large groups with no capability of inflicting damage on anyone but themselves. Such leverage is the ratio between *(a)* the damage which this group can inflict on others and *(b)* the cost it suffers from taking such actions. Leverage is one element of market power in labor markets.

These conditions determine how much labor market power can be created and how it may affect performance. Unions or other formal bargaining groups are superimposed on these basic conditions, but it is the conditions which largely determine the outcome. There will be large labor sectors where market

---

[8] Instead, it may induce greater effort and willingness to cooperate by workers. It may provide a means for negotiating and speeding change. Or, at the least, it may simply have few effects of any kind on efficiency.

power in labor services simply cannot be established or—if it does arise formally—will still be inconsequential. And if there are effects, the conditions influence whether they will be socially positive or negative.

Effects.   The economic effects of such power are likely to be:

1.   Higher payments for labor, and more favorable working conditions.
2.   Exclusion of nonmembers from at least part of the market.
3.   Retardation of labor-saving innovation (both autonomous innovation and innovation induced by the increase in labor payments).
4.   Occasional withdrawal of services from this and other markets (strikes).
5.   Ultimately, an increase in the macroeconomic problems of inflation and unemployment.
6.   Possibly deep changes in the content of enterprise activity.

The process is basically simple. A labor group first establishes itself as the exclusive provider of the labor services, by legal or other devices. This involves *(a)* excluding alternative providers (for example, doctors excluding osteopaths), and *(b)* setting controls on entry into its own ranks. The resulting market power is then exerted in a general or specific threat situation. The union seeks changes in the job content and supply-wage terms so as to optimize the total job-related welfare (including income) of its members. The degree of restriction depends on the power to exclude and the relative monopsony power of the customers.

Therefore, the costs of labor monopoly divide into two broad classes: *(a)* restrictions on supply and technical change, and *(b)* strike-related costs. An actual strike (or similar punitive action) may be infrequent, no more than is necessary to reaffirm that the threats mean business. Frequency of strikes is an ambiguous signal: it can reflect the application of great power, or it can indicate that implicit threats have not been effective.

The range of possible net benefits or costs is wide. Equity and efficiency may both be increased, if members are at below-average income and if membership reduces alienation and increases effort. But they may both be reduced, if members are already at high income levels and if their combined activities cause obstruction and disruption for this and other industries.

In this light, union monopoly may be most harmful when *(a)* members are above-average in initial incomes and opportunity, so that their future gains have a regressive effect, *(b)* work conditions are made rigid, *(c)* potential growth and innovation in the industry are high, and so the retardation or distortion of innovation may be large, and/or *(d)* the leverage or damage inflicted on others by strikes is high. These are mainly certain professional "unions," or specialized workers at upper levels, who can cause whole industries to close down; key unions which can endanger leading sectors; and major unions which face highly concentrated employers.

Treatment.   The optimal treatment would focus on the problem cases, not on all labor organizations or even just formal ones. It is not optimal policy to ban all unions, any more than it is optimal to ban all corporations.

The union problem arises in upper-level associations, as well as in certain industrial unions. Unions of *lower*-level workers are likely to cause net *benefits* of job content, equity, and—though the answers are still obscure—at least no large efficiency losses. On balance a small loss in efficiency (if any) may be offset by the probable gain in job content and equity. But in the *upper*-level labor groups, the effects are more likely to be negative.[9]

B2. Barriers to Certain Occupations: The Guilds of Today

We can now turn to actual policies. First, we will consider various restrictions of "professional" trades. These are entry barriers, formal rules against competitive practices, and informal limits or behavior. Often this self-regulation is enforced by public power.

Entry into professions affecting public health and safety—medicine, nursing, pharmacy, and the like—has long been restricted by groups operating under state laws. Qualifications have been established, examinations given, and licenses required. Over the years, this form of control has gradually been extended until, today, there are as many as 75 trades where entry is restricted by law. All of the states require licenses of accountants, architects, attorneys, chiropodists, dentists, embalmers, engineers, nurses, optometrists, osteopaths, pharmacists, physicians, teachers, and veterinarians, and most of them license barbers, beauticians, chiropractors, funeral directors, surveyors, and insurance and real estate salespersons. A number of states also license such tradsemen as plumbers, dry cleaners, horseshoers, tree surgeons, automobile salespeople, and photographers. Altogether, there are more than 1,200 occupational license laws, averaging 25 per state. Every state has at least 10 licensing boards for such trades; some have as many as 45.

Most of these laws reflect "self-regulation" for self-interest. The boards that administer the laws are usually composed predominantly of members of the trades concerned. In general, the states exercise little or no control. Instead, the main effect is to reduce entry and raise incomes. For example, extensive educational requirements have been set up for barbers, and 10 years of experience or a college degree asked for plumbers. Also, the trade groups are often able to fix fees and prices.[10] Though competition is being injected into some professions by recent court rulings (recall Chapter 7), the main effect of the state laws continues.

---

[9] This has long been pointed out by such classical liberal economists as Henry C. Simons, George J. Stigler, Milton Friedman, and Reuben Kessel.

[10] One result is a "Cadillac effect," which provides high-quality service for those that can afford it but cuts out all "economy grade" service. Stricter licensing forces more people into do-it-yourself plumbing and electrical wiring, often with increased danger. Licensing also excludes minorities and the poor, by stressing written tests rather than practical skills. It has been shown to raise the dental fees by about 15 percent. See Lawrence Shepard, "Licensing Restrictions and the Cost of Dental Care," *Journal of Law and Economics* 21 (April 1978), 187–202. The net social cost may be $700 million per year.

B3. Labor Unions

Policy toward industrial labor has evolved slowly, but with a shift during the 1930s toward permitting unions. Work conditions have been improved and abuses abated, since the 1830s. Government resistance to unions shifted in the 1930s to promotion of unions, under the Wagner Act. This was modified by Taft-Hartley in 1949 and Landrum-Griffin in 1959. Membership boomed and then, since about 1955, has stabilized. Industrywide bargaining in certain major industries is a fact of life.

Antitrust Exemption. Legal exemption from antitrust came slowly. In fact the first use of the Sherman Act was to help break the Pullman Strike in 1892. In the Danbury Hatters' case in 1908, the Court awarded damages to an employer who had been injured by a secondary boycott.[11] This led to the inclusion in the Clayton Act of a section providing that unions, as such, shall not "be held or construed to be illegal combinations or conspiracies in restraint of trade." The courts also began in 1940 to permit unions to act in concert with others to enforce boycotts and controls on prices.[12] The immunity now granted to labor by the law extends beyond the market for labor to the markets for other goods and services. This privilege, denied to business, is not essential to unionization or to collective bargaining.

While identical terms governing labor costs are written into the contracts that a union signs with competing employers the line between legality and illegality is the same. If a union, acting independently, undertakes to obtain identical terms in its contracts with each of the firms in an industry, its behavior is legal, whatever the consequences may be. But if it conspires with some firms to impose on others conditions that will make it difficult for them to compete, it will be found to violate the Sherman Act.[13]

Unions in various industries have attempted to make work for their members by adopting practices that have operated to reduce the productivity of labor and thus to increase its cost.[14] Yet there are ways in which unions make for greater productivity.[15] The net effect of these influences cannot

---

[11] *Loewe* v. *Lawlor,* 208 U.S. 274.

[12] *Apex Hosiery Co.* v. *Leader,* 310 U.S. 469; *Allen Bradley Co.* v. *Local Union No. 3.* 325 U.S. 797.

[13] *United Mine Workers* v. *Pennington,* 381 U.S. 657.

[14] First, they have resisted technological innovation, obstructing the adoption of new methods and refusing to work with new tools. Second, unions have limited the amount of work that a man is permitted to do. Third, unions have required the employment of unneeded labor. Fourth, unions have required the performance of unnecessary work. The practices described are confined, in the main, to fields where traditional skills are vulnerable to technical change. They are particularly notorious in railway transport, in building construction, and in printing.

[15] By giving assurance of security, unions may reduce the need for restrictive practices. By providing machinery for the settlement of grievances, they may improve the worker's morale. By exerting pressure for higher wages, they may stimulate the employer to find new means of increasing efficiency and cutting costs.

be ascertained. At any rate, the growth of labor organization has coincided with industrial growth and continuing productivity gains.

Effects. The effects of unions on economic performance are not well known. One would expect this monopoly power of unions to be reflected in the level of wages, but empirical studies of the influence of unions on wages have yielded inconclusive results. Wages in union industries are higher than those in nonunion industries, but the significance of this comparison is obscured by the fact that unions are found in dynamic industries in the North, compared to unorganized workers in traditional industries in the South. When union wages are compared with nonunion wages for workers in the same occupation, industry, and region, it is found that union wages generally are higher, but they are not invariably so, and the difference is slight. Some unions, in particular fields, have made extraordinary gains. This is true in building construction and in trucking, where the unions are large and powerful and the employers, by comparison, small and weak. It is also true in such large-scale manufacturing industries as steel and automobiles, where the unions are strong enough to extract a share of the profits of oligopoly. But for unions in general, the measurable gains are small.[16]

The process of collective bargaining creates the impression that union gains are greater than they really are. In the very nature of the process, the extent of disagreement between the union and the employer is exaggerated. The final bargain may set a wage no higher than would be obtained if the market were competitive. But it exceeds the employer's offer and enables the union to claim a victory.

Some critics of unions blame them for continued "cost-push" inflation. The issue is too large to be treated here. The scientific evidence so far is not clear. In any event, we have seen that the impact is selective rather than universal.

C. MILITARY PURCHASES

The supply of weapons is an ancient and universal problem, which can be solved in many ways, none of them satisfactory.[17] The issues include monopoly, profitability, public subsidy, the costs of innovation, and world

---

[16] See H. Gregg Lewis, *Unionism and Relative Wages in the United States* (Chicago: University of Chicago Press, 1963), chaps. III and IV; and Frank C. Pierson, *Unions in Postwar America* (New York: Random House, 1967), chaps. 3–5.

[17] Good basic sources include M. J. Peck and F. M. Scherer, *The Weapons Acquisition Process* (Boston: Harvard University School of Business 1962); C. J. Hitch and R. N. McKean, *The Economics of Defense in the Nuclear Age* (Cambridge: Harvard University Press, 1960); and F. M. Scherer, *The Weapons Acquisition Process: Economic Incentives* (Boston: Harvard University School of Business, 1963). See also J. K. Galbraith, *The New Industrial State* (Boston: Houghton Mifflin, 1968) on the mutual process of military and industrial planning. On World War II, see J. P. Miller, *The Pricing of Military Procurement* (Cambridge: Harvard University Press, 1949).

The practical features of procurement are laid out fully in J. Ronald Fox, *Arming America: How the U.S. Buys Weapons* (Boston: Harvard University Press, 1974).

survival. The capacity for waste and damage is great, and so "correct" public policies offer high yields. Yet the degree of monopoly and inefficiency are actually high.

The Sector. The weapons trade is a major sector, in both the United States and the world economy. Since 1940 a large armaments sector has become established, with several score major suppliers plus thousands of smaller subcontractors relying on military orders. Previously a small core of military facilities plus a few producers was supplemented—whenever major wars came—by a rapid build-up from private suppliers. Now the private producers are more permanent. The international trade in weapons is also brisk and growing.

Military supplies embrace a remarkable variety, from pencils, tomatoes, and uniforms to complex electronic defense and attack systems. During 1955–70 large advanced systems were a main focus. They seemed inevitably to involve (a) rapid development, even at high extra costs, (b) high degrees of discovery, innovation, and risk, and (c) rapid obsolescence and replacement with new systems. This attitude bred a tolerance for waste and error, because speed and new technology appeared to be worth great costs. More recently a reversion toward conventional weapons and careful purchasing policies has occurred. Less than half of current weapons buying concerns the high technology items.

The flow of purchases is large, and its treatment has repercussions in many markets. Pentagon decisions set or eliminate competition, both in weapons and in adjacent markets. Some firms are dependent on weapons orders (see Table 24–2): altogether, perhaps 15 major companies are primarily weapons producers. Most of the very largest firms keep military contracts to a small fraction. There is much instability in the orders: (a) There are shifts in weapons types, and military crises come and go; and (b) orders shift or rotate among firms. Defense firms generally are not among the core of established firms, and some of them have been part of the conglomerate, outsider group of the 1960s (recall Chapters 2 and 6).

Beneath the narrow focus of primary contracts in a few firms and regions, the subcontracting of components is widely spread across industries, company sizes, and regions of the country. This substructure does ensure that the motivation for high weapons spending is much wider than the narrow focus of prime contracts on a score of firms would suggest. Much the same has been true also of the programs for space flight and nuclear energy.

Most military contracts are sought by at least several firms. For firms reliant on defense orders, the key economic fact is that their short-run *marginal* cost for new orders is quite low when the order back-log is small. Yet the revenue from contracts must eventually cover their average cost. Each supplier therefore tends to bid aggressively when short of orders but only nominally when its order backlog is long.

There is also a pooling of overhead costs among contracts. The larger defense firms often hold many research, development, and production con-

TABLE 24–2
Leading U.S. Producers of Weapons and Related Products, 1976 (dollars in millions)

			Main Federal Prime Contracts*			
Sales Rank	Firm	Firm Sales	Supply	R&D	Supply as a Percent of Total Sales	Supply and R&D as a Percent of Total Sales
22	Westinghouse Electric	$6,145	$ 482	$404	7.8%	14.4%
34	Rockwell International . . .	5,220	1,871	709	35.8	49.4
35	United Technologies	5,166	1,233	113	23.9	26.0
47	Boeing	3,918	1,231	436	31.4	42.5
51	McDonnell Douglas	3,543	2,589	346	73.0	82.8
60	Litton Industries	3,365	978	22	29.1	29.8
61	Lockheed Aircraft	3,203	1,577	652	49.2	69.7
62	Sperry Rand	3,202	536	47	16.7	18.1
85	General Dynamics	2,553	1,148	446	45.0	62.6
88	Honeywell	2,495	395	50	15.8	17.9
90	Raytheon	2,462	784	243	31.9	41.8
97	FMC	2,298	417	18	18.1	18.9
148	Grumman	1,502	995	36	66.2	68.5
179	Northrop	1,265	1,496	120	118.3	127.5

* Includes contracts from the Department of Defense, the National Aeronautics and Space Administration, and the Energy Research and Development Administration.
Source: U.S. Defense Department, "100 Companies Receiving the Largest Dollar Volume of Military Prime Contract Awards, Fiscal Year 1976," and "500 Contractors Receiving the Largest Dollar Volume of Military Prime Contract Awards for Research, Development, Test, and Evaluation Work, Fiscal 1976" (Washington, D.C., issued annually); National Aeronautics and Space Administration, "Annual Procurement Report, Fiscal Year 1976"; and data supplied by the Energy Research and Development Administration.

tracts at any time, in varying stages of completion. Often funds, staff, and facilities mingle among the projects, so that costs, deficits, and performance are hard to define.

Many markets for the larger weapons are tight oligopolies or virtual monopolies. This reflects several factors, including the willingness of military purchasers to deal with only a few firms.

Special Conditions of Purchasing Decisions. *The cardinal fact is that weapons purchases are essentially made at the grass-roots level of the Pentagon,* by middle-level officers (colonels, majors, captains) who are intimately familiar with their suppliers. These people—working closely with company personnel—prepare the contracting information about needs, capabilities, and costs. This information, when processed on up to higher levels, usually defines the areas for choice. Most of these officers have been trained as engineers, and so their decision criteria are usually narrow, mingling engineering standards with aversions to risk.

These officials have little conception of, or interest in, competition in the wider range of the economy. Indeed, broadening the field of suppliers mainly adds to their tasks and insecurities. If their decisions tend to foster monopoly, that is only of incidental importance to them. Also their training and incentives favor high quality and maximum reliability as criteria, rather than the minimum cost.

Despite past experience with war profiteering, the degree of profits earned on defense contracting is often said to be small. Reported profits tend to average about three or four percent of the total costs of supply. Yet such small profit margins are often deceptive. It is profits on investment which matter. These have been much higher, in some cases extremely high.

The competitive status of weapons contracting is indicated in Table 24–3 (patterns since 1967 are similar). Approximately two thirds of purchases occur under conditions with virtually no competition at all. The military mind prefers usually to pick out a preferred supplier and then work with it; or to consider only several familiar candidates. The uncertainty and fluidity of competitive conditions are generally regarded as unreliable and troublesome.

The Antitrust Division and related agencies concerned with competition have had virtually no role in monitoring or influencing military procurement. Yet the choices may affect or exclude competition in large markets. This de facto lack of antitrust jurisdiction is virtually complete. It occurs partly because effective decisions are made so early and so deep in the military hierarchy.

Economic Incentives.   The basic economic objectives are part of a broad optimizing *(a)* to get the efficient balance among the performance criteria of *each* weapon system, and *(b)* to evolve these into the optimal bundle of

TABLE 24–3
Competitive Status of Defense Contracts, 1967

	Basis of Contracting ($ million)						
				Negotiated			
	(1)	*(2)*	*(3)*	*(4)*	*(5)*	*(6)*	
			Design and Technical compe- tition	*Exten- sion of a (2) Contract*	*Exten- sion of a (3) Contract*		*Type (4), (5), and (6) Contracts*
	Competi- tive Bids	*Price Compe- tition*				*Single Source*	
Airframes	$ 65	$ 632	$ 330	$477	$2,394	$1,596	81%
Aircraft engines	1	183	68	42	921	332	84
Missile systems	34	153	183	11	1,652	1,678	90
Ships	960	59	33	1	33	425	30
Combat vehicles	149	42	—	—	20	230	57
Noncombat vehicles ...	351	157	12	1	—	63	11
Weapons	21	55	3	—	4	243	76
Ammunitions	146	575	32	85	12	2,177	75
Electronic, communications	250	377	210	48	288	1,376	67
Total (these and other items)	3,465	4,713	1,451	747	5,647	9,632	62

Source: Defense Department compilations, given in W. G. Shepherd, *Market Power and Economic Welfare* (New York: Random House, 1970), pp. 260–61.

all weapons systems. This will yield the right degree of cost-minimizing versus weapon quality, and it will provide only the minimum equitable reward to the suppliers.

The main difficulty arises from the gap between marginal and average cost. This was noted earlier; firms hungry for new orders have low marginal cost, and they are therefore willing to bid at prices which they know are below their eventual average costs. The net effect is to reduce competition and cause a tendency to the "buying-in" of contracts. Firms bid knowingly below average costs—but at or above marginal costs—expecting to be able to push up the effective price at later stages. This simulacrum of competition creates illusions of low weapons costs at the time when contracts are prepared and let. It also prevents effective minimizing of costs. It encourages weapons markets to evolve a limited set of suppliers, each heavily reliant on weapons orders.[18]

These special cost incentives interact with the basis on which suppliers are paid. This basis can be summed up in the following formula for the actual profit realized on a contract:

$$\text{Realized profit} = \text{Target profit} + \alpha \, (\text{Target cost} - \text{Actual cost})$$

The key element here is α.[19] When α is zero, the firm realizes the target profit regardless of the costs it incurs in supplying the weapons. At the other extreme, if α is 1, the firm keeps whatever cost-saving it manages below the cost target, but it has to pay out of its own pocket any excess of actual cost over target cost. Therefore α is the degree of incentive felt by the supplier in trying to minimize cost. Typically α has been in the range of zero to 0.25. The strongest possible incentive is when α is 1. This is called a "firm fixed-price" contract. At the other extreme the notorious "cost-plus" incentive basis tends to eliminate incentives for efficiency and may even induce a preference for higher costs.

Getting α right is therefore part of optimizing the trade-offs among the various performance criteria for each project. In fact α has often not been right, and a large majority of contracting has been done—and continues to be—essentially on a cost-plus basis. The natural result includes cost overruns, a degree of X-inefficiency, and an imbalance among weapons systems.

Yet it is not enough just to set α at a tight incentive level. For α is

---

[18] A striking instance of this has been aircraft production. Successive models of military aircraft have been timed and allotted as if they had been designed, with remarkable precision, to keep the eight main private aircraft assembly lines in operation. This has amounted to de facto rotation, despite appearances (and some genuine degree) of competition and cost controls. The unusually large cost overruns in these programs have been a natural result. J. A. Kurth, "The Political Economy of Weapons Procurement: The Follow-on Imperative," *American Economic Review* 62 (May 1972), 304–11.

[19] This is lucidly explained in Scherer, *The Weapons Acquisition Process.* Compare with utility regulation, where α tends to be a zero during Stage 2 and much of Stage 3.

only one of the elements in the choices being made both by the buyers and the suppliers. If α is set higher—therefore putting stronger cost incentives on the supplier—then company effort will be shifted to getting the cost target itself higher, perhaps inflating it so as to enable illusory cost cutting.

Probable Costs.   Altogether, the weapons sector is managed in ways likely to generate appreciable net costs. Inefficiency in production is substantial, probably on the order of 20 percent of costs for the more complex systems, and in some cases reaching much higher. This reflects both cost overruns and routine inefficiency.

Further, weapons quantities and quality both tend to exceed the optimum. There is excess ordering of many items, in part because of the cost illusions fostered by underbidding. And armaments often embody service qualities which exceed the levels of efficient design. These added costs are likely to be on the order of 10 percent of actual costs.

More Competition.   The need for improvement is obvious. One long-standing proposal is to apply a greater degree of competition in contracting. Although at each juncture the contracting officials commonly believe that a more direct (that is, bilateral monopoly) approach is essential, in the long run a reliance upon a more flexible and competitive range of suppliers would tend to correct much of the inefficiency.

Yet the corridors of the Pentagon are stony ground for cultivating more reliance on competition. Military officials profess uneasiness at having only one supplier, but they behave as if averse to having more than two or three. Past efforts have only brought competitive contracting up to minor levels (perhaps 15 to 25 percent of purchases). Further marginal increases will be difficult to get and are likely to remain on the fringe.

Incentive Contracting.   Much can be done to improve contract design in order to reward efficient performance. But the practical gains will be the least precisely in those cases—complex systems which explore new technology, and so forth—where performance is chronically worst. The two most promising tactics are *(a)* to adjust α to optimize incentives for cost-minimizing, and *(b)* performance contracting (in which good past performance gives a firm priority in getting future contracts).

In principle, α can be optimized and then applied so as to induce efficiency. In practice, it interacts with the other contract variables (profit rate, time deadlines, renewal prospects) and has little force where it is most needed. In fact fixed-price contracts—with α at 1.0 for a maximum incentive effect—are workable mainly in the simpler, routine items. On those, such contracts are already common. But for complex systems, many parameters are uncertain. Raising α then causes firms to seek and get compensating adjustments in the other contract terms. And still later, when large losses nevertheless result, there ensues a semi-political struggle in which the firm has good odds of winning a price adjustment after all.

Therefore, incentive contracting may offer new yields only for certain moderate-size contracts for intermediate weapons: those which are neither simple nor extremely complex. And the grass-roots contracting process will tend to erode even these yields, by permitting other compensatory adjustments. Incentive contracting (like incentive regulation: Chapter 11) is at most a supplement to other treatments.

Renegotiation. Where excess profits are earned on defense contracts, they might be recaptured under a review process. Since World War II the Renegotiation Board has had that task.[20] It reviews contracts and, in cases where it identifies excess profits, attempts to renegotiate them with the supplier. The actual recapture is minimal. The Board has scant funds and resources, weak legal powers, and little political standing. Its renegotiations affect mainly the smaller, simpler contracts. Even on those, the profits left after refunds have often still been excessive.[21] The Board also makes technical errors; thus, it uses return on sales as a criterion, rather than return on capital. Yet perfecting the inner technique of such systems of recapture will be largely fruitless unless the Board is given sufficient powers, resources, and political backing.

In fact, the basic problem is virtually insoluble by this method. Excess profits are often converted into costs, in various forms of inefficiency. They also mingle with the other contracts and activities of the firm, often so much so that they are virtually impossible to trace. The more weight is put on renegotiating profits, the more an adaptive response occurs, to pool them with the other operations of the firm. Therefore, renegotiation offers only slight possible benefits. Once the profits arise, they can rarely be recaptured, even in part.

QUESTIONS FOR REVIEW

1. "Tariffs and quotas reduce competition by reducing the 'entry' of imports." True?
2. "The NRA tried to set price ceilings but was unable to get compliance of industry members, except in tight oligopolies." True?
3. "Labor unions have had little clear effect on wage rates. But professional 'unions' are able to raise their members' incomes appreciably." True?
4. "Military goods often involve many dimensions, of which cost is only one." True?
5. "To get the maximum incentive effect for efficient supply of weapons, α should be set at 1." True?

---

[20] See Miller, *The Pricing of Military Procurement.*

[21] During 1971–72 the Board required refunds from 131 firms, mostly in bombs, fuses, ammunition, and other ordnance. Yet even after the refunds, returns on net worth for the contract—as a percent of net worth—still were: four firms over 500 percent, 22 over 200 percent, and 94 over 50 percent. None of the contracts was over $5 million: the Board touches only the fringes of the problem. (*New York Times,* May 16, 1973.)

6. "The bulk of military purchases is made under conditions that are basically noncompetitive." True?
7. Which trade barriers are probably justified?
8. What professions should have licensing restrictions?
9. How could you make "renegotiation" of military contracts work well? Is it bound to be futile?

chapter 25

Promotion and Subsidies

A subsidy is the opposite of a policy constraint. Rather than limit a firm's profit opportunities, subsidies increase them. Subsidies and promotion take many forms, under four main categories: direct payments, tax forgiveness, risk-absorption, and various promotional devices. We will look mainly at subsidies to firms. They often relate closely to the structure and performance of industries. Some yield high benefits, while others cause social harm. They touch nearly every market, and in some cases they sustain whole sectors. The total is large and deeply woven into the industrial fabric.

We first summarize their scope and properties, and next consider their economic merits. Then separate sections are devoted to agriculture and maritime subsidies.

A. SCOPE AND VARIETY

The nation has subsidized a variety of private enterprises throughout its history, and the totals continue to grow.[1] The flow of federal subsidies is now deep and diverse, as Table 25–1 shows. A large share goes to specific firms and industries. The precise extent cannot be defined, because many consumption subsidies are indirect subsidies to the suppliers of the service. Also Table 25–1 omits many subsidies given when public agencies pay extra-high prices or provide items at prices below costs.

Types of Subsidies. Some subsidies are direct and visible; others are indirect and hidden. *Direct payments* occur in cash and in kind. The recipients often prefer indirect payments, which are less visible, harder to evaluate, and less liable to be stopped. Both kinds are shown in Table 25–2.

Tax subsidies occur for special exceptions from general tax burdens. They are for a variety of stated purposes, those for oil being perhaps the steepest. Table 25–3 shows some of them.

---

[1] An excellent source on the nature and scope of subsidies is U.S. Joint Economic Committee, *The Economics of Federal Subsidy Programs,* 93d Cong., 2d Sess. (Washington, D.C.: U.S. Government Printing Office, 1974).

TABLE 25–1

Gross Budgetary Costs of Selected Major U.S. Federal Subsidies, 1975 (in billions of dollars)

	Direct Cash Subsidies	Tax Subsidies	Credit Subsidies	Benefit-in-Kind Subsidies	Total
Agriculture and food	0.6	1.1	0.7	5.9	8.4
Health	0.6	5.8	—	10.2	16.6
Manpower	3.3	0.7	—	0.1	4.1
Education..............	5.0	1.0	0.1	0.4	6.5
International	—	1.5	0.9	—	2.4
Housing	1.7	12.9	1.1	—	15.7
Natural Resources	0.1	4.1	—	0.1	4.4
Transportation	0.6	0.1	—	1.7	2.3
Commerce	0.3	19.3	—	1.9	21.5
Other	—	13.1	0.1	—	13.2
Total	12.3	59.7	2.9	20.2	95.1

Source: Joint Economic Committee, *Federal Subsidy Programs,* a staff study, 93d Cong., 2d Sess. (Washington, D.C., U.S. Government Printing Office, 1974), p. 5.

TABLE 25–2

Selected Federal Cash Payment Subsidies, Fiscal Years 1970 and 1975 (dollars in millions)

	Amounts	
Program	1970	1975
Agriculture:		
Commodity purchase	$ 688	$ 320
Cotton production stabilization	828	79
Feed grain production stabilization	1,644	25
Sugar production stabilization	93	92
Wheat production stabilization	863	75
Agricultural conservation program (REAP)	185	0
Cropland adjustment program	77	49
Medical Care:		
Health manpower training	202	237
Community nursing home care	20	52
Health facilities construction (Hill-Burton)	201	189
International:		
Export payments...............................	101	0
Housing:		
Public housing assistance	0	1,473
Rent supplements for low-income families	21	192
Transportation:		
Air carrier payments	38	73
Operating differential subsidies	194	220
Construction differential subsidies	68	281

Source: Tables 25–2 through 25–5 are from the same source as Table 25–1.

TABLE 25–3
Selected Federal Tax Subsidies, Fiscal Years 1970 and 1975 (dollars in millions)

	Amounts	
Program	1970	1975
Agriculture:		
Expensing and capital gains for farming..................	$ 880	$1,100
International trade:		
Western hemisphere trade corporations	55	100
Exclusion of gross-up on dividends of less		
developed country corporations	55	80
Deferral of foreign subsidary income	170	375
Deferral of income of domestic international		
sales corporations	0	920
National resources:		
Capital gains treatment for cutting timber	140	260
Expensing mineral exploration and development	340	860
Excess of percentage over cost depletion	1,470	2,960
Commerce and economic development:		
Excess depreciation on buildings	550	600
Investment credit.....................................	2,630	4,900
Corporation capital gains	525	390
Excess bad debt reserves of financial institutions	680	360
Exemption of credit unions	45	110
Expensing of research and development expenditures	565	650
Corporate surtax exemption	2,300	3,700
Exclusion of interest on life insurance savings	1,050	1,450

Source: Tables 25–2 through 25–5 are from the same source as Table 25–1.

Tax subsidies also have a marked incidence among corporations. The standard corporation tax rate has been roughly 50 percent. Yet many large industrial firms (especially in oil and steel) have effective tax rates well below that, with some at zero. Much of this arises from special minerals industry tax laws, and from the treatment of profits from operations abroad.[2] The effects of tax forgiveness on corporate profits, on resource allocation, and on the market positions of leading firms, can be large.

Risk absorption is another indirect form of subsidy. It is focused in housing, agriculture, and foreign trade (see Table 25–4).

Other *promotional devices* are numerous. Some (official cartels, mail, and nuclear-power subsidies) have been analyzed in earlier chapters. Others involve direct programs by agencies promoting growth, employment, and the like (see Table 25–5).

Past Instances and Sectors. We now consider a variety of actual subsidies, to give more concrete detail.

---

[2] The favorite of the tax law is the mining industry. Not only may mining companies deduct the costs of exploration and development—successful and unsuccessful, tangible and intangible—as current expenses in computing taxable income. They are also given the option of making arbitrary deductions, up to half of net income, for depletion of wasting assets instead of deducting the depletion that actually occurs. The depletion allowance, moreover, may be deducted year after year even though every dollar invested in the property has long since been written off.

TABLE 25–4

Selected Federal Credit Subsidies, Fiscal Years 1970 and 1975 (dollars in millions)

	Subsidy Costs	
Program	1970	1975
Agriculture:		
Commodity price support	$ 40	$ 18
Rural electrification	239	220
Rural telephone	0	81
Miscellaneous	95	176
International:		
Export-import bank; direct	108	231
Development loans—Revolving fund	233	301
Public Law 480..................................	211	331
Housing:		
Mortgage insurance	1,698	855
Low-rent public housing	1,174	283
Commerce and economic development:		
Small business economic injury disaster loans..........	18	8
Small Business Administration loans	17	10

Source: Tables 25–2 through 25–5 are from the same source as Table 25–1.

Free Services. Governments give out vast amounts of free data. They are the principle source of the statistical reports that are used by businessmen in their daily operations. The *Statistical Abstract of the United States,* its annual editions containing fifteen hundred pages of fine type, serves as little more than an index to the vast quantities of statistics that are prepared,

TABLE 25–5

Selected Federal Benefit-in-Kind Subsidies (dollars in millions)

	Amounts	
Program	1970	1975
Food:		
Food distribution	$ 558	$ 301
Food stamps	551	3,985
School lunch program	301	1,212
Medical care:		
Medical assistance program (Medicaid)	2,638	6,592
Health insurance for the aged (Medicare)	1,979	3,586
Education:		
Surplus property utilization	409	400
Natural resources:		
Water and waste disposal systems for rural communities	45	100
State and private forestry cooperation	26	23
Resource conservation and development	11	24
Transportation:		
Airport development aid	0	310
Urban mass transit capital improvement grants	133	1,255
National Rail Passenger Corporation	80	143
Commerce and economic development:		
Excessive tax and loan account balances	300	300
Postal service	1,510	1,553

Source: Tables 25–2 through 25–5 are from the same source as Table 25–1.

analyzed, and published by scores of agencies.[3] Many of these are of use only to specific trades and firms.

Sales at Low Prices. Such sales are common. During the 19th century, valuable mining and timberlands were sold for a song. Merchant ships built by the government during the two world wars were subsequently sold to private operators at a fraction of their cost. After World War II, other property that had cost the government $15 billion was sold by the War Assets Administration for $4 billion. Great amounts of surplus military material are still routinely disposed of at extremely low prices.

So, too, with the sale of public services. When government engages in lending, guaranteeing, and insuring operations, the fees it charges frequently fail to cover its total costs, the administration of such programs being financed by the taxpayers.[4]

High Prices. Purchases at high prices are endemic in military procurement (recall Chapter 24). Stockpiling of strategic materials also involves a degree of subsidy. For example, in 1965 these stockpiles consisted of 76 commodities, ranging from asbestos to zirconium and including goose feathers and castor oil, many of them bought in quantities well in excess of probable needs. Holdings acquired at a cost of $8.5 billion were then valued at $7.8 billion, representing a paper loss of $700 million.

Transportation has been perhaps the most heavily subsidized of all sectors. American railroads, during the 19th century, were the recipients of grants amounting to 183 million acres of public lands, some of them valuable mining and timber properties. They were also aided by cash contributions, by tax exemptions, and by governmental subscriptions to their securities. Altogether, the aid extended to railroads by federal, state, and local governments is said

---

[3] Special studies, covering many phases of business activity, are listed in each number of the *Monthly Catalogue of Governmental Documents*. Maps, charts, and other aids to navigation are published by the Coast and Geodetic Survey. Estimates of prospective crops are released by the Crop Reporting Service. And weather forecasts—of great importance not only to agriculture but also to shipping, aviation, and other businesses—are issued daily by the Weather Bureau.

Government also carries on research and releases its findings for commercial use. The Geological Survey and the Bureau of Mines, the Forest Service, and the Fish and Wildlife Service, together with similar agencies in many states, function in effect as laboratories for the mining, lumbering, and fishing industries. The Tennessee Valley Authority has developed new chemical fertilizers and given its formulas to the fertilizer industry. The National Bureau of Standards engages in physical research, conducts tests, and establishes industrial standards when requested to do so by two thirds of the members of a trade.

[4] Government has subsidized private forestry, not only by supporting research and education, but also by providing it with fire protection, with planting stock, and with technical assistance for less than cost. Government has subsidized the livestock industries by permitting sheep and cattle to graze in national forests and on other public lands for fees below those charged on private ranges. It has subsidized advertisers and the publishers of newspapers and magazines by delivering their products at a loss. In 1977, for instance, the subsidy involved was more than $1 billion. In the postal carrier's bag are pounds of periodicals that denounce the government for paying subsidies, but not (it may be assumed) for subsidizing publishers.

TABLE 25-6
Public Subsidies to the Performing Arts (current operating expenditures only)

Country		Amount (in millions)	As Percent of GNP
United States (1969–70)		$30	0.003%
United States (public subsidies plus private contributions from foundations, business and individuals) (1969–70)		$80	0.008
United Kingdom (1970)		£ 6.6	0.015
West Germany (1968)	DM	505.5	0.09
France 1968	Fr	83.5	0.013
Sweden (1969–70, 1965–66)	Kr	222.6	0.15
Norway (1968, 1970)	Kr	29.2	0.04

Source: Tibor Scitovsky, "What's Wrong with the Arts Is What's Wrong with Society," *American Economic Review* 62, 2 (May 1972), 62–69.

to have amounted to $1,282 million. Though government traffic was later carried at lower rates, this offsetting subsidy was much smaller than the original subsidies (with their accrued value over time.)

Since 1950 programs to rescue passenger service have been subsidized. And since 1970 Amtrak has been subsidized at over $100 million per year ($500 million in 1977–78). From 1940 to 1978 the federal government spent more than $150 billion on highways, waterways, and airways, more than half of it on highways. Passenger cars have been required to pay more and trucks less than their proper share of these costs. As a result the trucking industry has been subsidized. Maritime subsidies are of two kinds: *(a)* ship-building and *(b)* shipping (see Section D below).

Atomic power has been deeply subsidized (recall Chapter 18). Government has put over $3 billion into research. In a few cases it contributed to the cost of building the reactors. In every case it supplied atomic fuel at a rental charge so low as to involve a subsidy. A further subsidy may have been hidden in the price it paid for by-product plutonium. The cost of insurance against catastrophic accidents, finally, was largely borne by the government.

Oil. The oil industry has vied with agriculture as the most heavily subsidized industry in recent years (see also Chapter 22). During 1959–73 the subsidies were over $6 billion yearly, and the industry also has been partially exempt from antitrust. Only the onset of the energy crises has superseded some of these subsidies.

The Arts. By contrast, the performing arts have been lightly subsidized.[5] The situation is summarized in Table 25–6, with international comparisons. There are certain indirect subsidies (by tax exemption) which would increase

---

[5] W. J. Baumol and W. G. Bowen, *Performing Arts: The Economic Dilemma* (New York: Twentieth Century Fund, 1966); Tibor Scitovsky, "What's Wrong with the Arts Is What's Wrong with Society," *American Economic Review* 62, 2 (May 1972), 62–69; and T. G. Moore, *The Economics of the American Theater* (Durham: Duke University Press, 1968).

the true U.S. total, but it is still relatively slight. In fact, public support of the arts in the United States scarcely existed until 1965. It has been a preserve of private contributions, in a mixture of charitable, civic, and selfish motivations. Throughout Western and Eastern Europe, the degree of public support is much higher. This reflects the broader interest in the arts in these and other countries.

B. ECONOMIC ISSUES

Which subsidies are optimal? They all arise from the real political process (recall Chapter 3), and so one may expect many of them to be inefficient, or inequitable, or both. They may also have side effects, depending on their forms and conditions. Often their formal purposes bear little relation to their true nature and effects.

The political efforts to gain subsidies go on continually. The outcome reflects the underlying pattern of interests and power. Rarely are full, explicit data on costs and benefits used in settling subsidies. Continuity and inertia are also important. Once begun, subsidies become part of the structure of values and expectations; to stop them usually requires a strong affirmative act. Investments, workers' lives, locales, managers' ambitions, and other interests come to rely on the subsidy.

The economic performance of a subsidy obviously turns on the allocative value of its effects, and on the fairness of its incidence. These often hinge in turn on several technical features, especially openness, permanence, financing, specific duties, incidence, and incentives. *Open subsidies* are more likely to be known and screened adequately. Hidden subsidies (which the recipients naturally prefer) are likely to grow and persist without a fair appraisal.

Temporary subsidies are preferable to open-ended or permanent ones. The social need is usually temporary, and so the burden of proof should usually go against continuance. Renewal procedures should involve a genuine reappraisal: this requires independence and staff resources. *Financing by taxes* rather than higher consumer prices is preferable. Price-raising usually has a regressive incidence. Taxes can be arranged to fit ability to pay. *Specific duties* can be required of the recipients. These limit the net giveaway and provide a basis for monitoring the value of the subsidy. Simple grants to categories of recipients tend to lack constraints on the amounts taken and the ease of abuse.

Incidence among firms also can be important. Subsidies can favor firms against their competitors and potential competitors. Where dominant firms gain subsidies, the entrenching effect can deeply affect structure and performance. This effect needs to be anticipated carefully in designing subsidies, for the tendency to favor the established firms is a general one.

Finally, *incentives* are often critical. Since subsidies come, not from markets, but from the public purse, they may divert the attention of managements from the cultivation of customers to the cultivation of Congress. Being paid, in general, when losses are incurred and not when profits are shown, they reward incompetence and penalize efficiency. Instead of encouraging the producer to stand on his own feet, they invite him to lean upon the state. They make for lethargy, rather than progress.

Subsidies commonly chill incentives, by rewarding recipients for staying in the subsidized condition. Incentives for efficiency can be built in, by hinging payments on specific actions, on performance criteria, or on a sharing of cost reductions. Every subsidy does apply a set of incentives: the question is whether they will be optimal or distorted.

Ideally, the subsidy's purpose will be clearly identified, and the likely direct and indirect effects of the subsidy will be known. Next, an optimal incentive structure is derived, to fit the criteria. Then the best level and design of the subsidy can be set, in open/and full discussion. The optimal incentives will often be complex, to induce specific actions, to avoid fostering inefficiency, and to phase out the subsidy unless the burden of proof for continuance is fully met.

These attributes can be compared with actual subsidies, in this chapter and elsewhere in the book. The endless effort to minimize inefficient subsidies deals both in technical features and in the realities of political life.

C. AGRICULTURE

Government, in the United States, has aided agriculture for a century and more. Since the 1930s, its assistance has taken the form, in part, of cash payments from the Treasury: payments to producers of particular crops such as sugar and wool, and payments to farmers in general for retiring acreage, restricting output, and using soil-conserving practices. It has also taken the form, in larger part, of measures designed to raise the prices of the things the farmer sells. This has been done by making loans and purchases, by restricting imports and by subsidizing exports, by curtailing the quantities produced, and by imposing controls on marketing. Public expenditures on such programs have run to more than $5 billion a year. But this is not all: government has also extended aid in other ways. It has supplied free land and services, financed research and education, provided water for irrigation, increased the supply of credit, promoted rural electrification, insured crops, and ameliorated rural poverty. Expenditures on these activities have approached another $1 billion a year.

The quantum rise in agricultural prices during 1972–74 suggested that some restrictive policies and subsidies might now end. But the basic pattern is more likely to continue. And even if price-raising policies were abolished, other large subsidies would continue or grow. Therefore we will look in detail at the whole set of farm policies.[6]

---

[6] For a basic review, see Geoffrey S. Shepherd, *Farm Policy: New Directions* (Ames, Iowa: Iowa State University Press, 1964).

C1. Basic Conditions in Farming

Migration. The larger setting is the long-term migration from farms to towns, as farm efficiency rose and the economy became industrialized (see Figure 25–1). This shrinkage continues, but it has a complex pattern among regions, age groups, and racial types. The political structure also favors subsidies, since the rural districts have been over-represented. There are also the old-time values and images of rural life as wholesome and upright.

FIGURE 25–1

The migration from the farms continues.

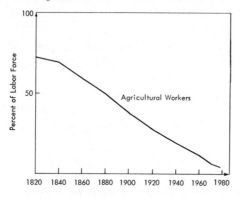

FIGURE 25–2

Farm land has benefited from farm policies.

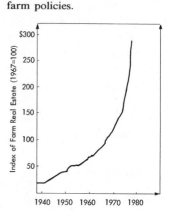

Source: U.S. Department of Commerce, *Historical Statistics of the United States* (1957), and *U.S. Statistical Abstract,* annual.

The main present programs were set during 1920–40, when fluctuations bankrupted farmers by the millions and crop failures caused desperate farm poverty.[7] Yet farming includes many differing parts, by crops, regions, size, riskiness, and so on. Moreover, it is increasingly integrated with world markets and their instabilities. The byzantine complexity of farm programs reflects all of these background factors.

---

[7] The two decades before World War I were a golden era for American agriculture. Markets grew as industry expanded. On the farms, prices and incomes rose. Prosperity was sustained, uninterrupted, for the longest period the farmer had ever known. With the outbreak of war, production of foodstuffs in Western Europe suffered, and supplies from the Argentine and Australia were cut off by a shortage of shipping. The United States was called upon to feed her allies. Farm prices rose sharply, farm output was expanded, and farm debt grew, as new acres were bought on credit and the prices of crops were capitalized in the price of land. When the war ended, the farms of Europe came back into production and shipments from Argentina and Australia were resumed. Markets disappeared and prices dropped.

American agriculture did not participate in the prosperity that followed the war. And when the Great Depression struck, agriculture went from bad to worse. Demand at home collapsed, and prices continued to fall. The cash income of farmers dropped from $11 billion in 1929 to $5 billion in 1933. Farm wages sank to 10 cents per hour or a dollar a day, if one could find work at all.

Supply and Demand.   The basic economic fact is that short-run demand and supply are *inelastic* for many farm products. Therefore, small shifts cause big price jumps, sharper than most other economic groups have to face. There is a strong case for insulating farmers from severe jolts, but their income depends on farm prices *and* other factors:

$$\text{Net farm income} = \text{Revenues} - \text{Costs}$$
$$= \underset{\text{Outputs}}{\Sigma \, P_i \cdot Q_i} - \underset{\text{Inputs}}{\Sigma \, P_n \cdot Q_n}$$

and the rate of return for farming is

$$\text{Rate of return} = \frac{\underset{\text{Outputs}}{\Sigma \, P_i \cdot Q_i} - \underset{\text{Inputs}}{\Sigma \, P_n \cdot Q_n}}{\text{Capital invested}}$$

just as for all firms (including regulated firms: recall Chapter 11). Farmers have to make complex speculative decisions, involving production techniques, future prices, costs of capital, weather risks, and public policies. A high order of skill is needed in several fields, plus a large chunk of capital (on the order of $1 million in average grain-belt farms).

The long-trend rise of productivity for agriculture has been rapid and sustained. This reflects the creation of massive agricultural investment down the decades, plus a high technological opportunity in the sector. With newer hybrid strains, breeds of livestock, methods of crop rotation, fertilizers, insecticides, and equipment types, the potential for rising farm productivity has been very great indeed. Yields per acre and per worker have doubled and redoubled. In 1940 a farmer fed 10 people; now he feeds over 40.

This has operated to raise the capital invested in farming, to reduce the labor inputs required, and constrain the long-term rise of farm prices. In this context, the trends and configurations of farm incomes—on a per-farmer basis—have been the vector of several powerful forces working through the basic economic equations. The level of farm output *prices* is only one determinant of farm income. Yet farm policy has focused on it.

Farmers have always seen themselves as victims. Their incomes are below average. They buy from industrial suppliers (of equipment, construction, gasoline, mortgage credit, and so forth) who can add in a margin of monopoly profit. But they must sell on purely competitive markets, where no such profit arises. This sense of injustice is aggravated by the demands of new technology, which require ever larger scale and investment (and debt). And farm income fluctuates from year to year as weather, the economy, and other factors shift.

This view oversimplifies. Many markets farmers buy in are reasonably competitive. Where they are not, it would be better to make them so rather than monopolize farming. The key point is that incomes differ sharply among farmers and fluctuate from year to year.

Scope. Farming includes those who raise feed grains and livestock in the Corn Belt, wheat on the Great Plains, cotton and tobacco in the South, and range livestock in the Southwest. It covers the dairy farms of New England, the Middle Atlantic, and the Lake States; the citrus groves of Florida and California; and the apple orchards of Virginia and Washington. It includes the producers of ducks on Long Island, sugar cane in Louisiana, and tree nuts on the Pacific Coast. With 200 different products, grown under widely differing conditions, there is no such thing, in actuality, as a typical farmer or an average farm.

Nine-tenths of all farms, or about 2 million, are operated by their owners, three fifths of them debt-free, two fifths encumbered with mortgages. One tenth, or less than 250,000, are operated by tenants, rents being paid by some of them in cash, by others in shares of agricultural products.

The Family Farm. A few thousand farms are operated by salaried managers. The great majority are family farms. A family farm is usually defined as an enterprise of such size that it can be financed, managed, and operated, with little or no hired help, by a farmer and the members of his family. The farmer is owner, manager, and worker, his residence is both a home and an office, his wife and children are partners and fellow laborers. His income from farming and other sources may go into a common pool; his operating costs and his living expenses may be met from the same account. The family farm thus differs in character from other businesses. It combines a productive enterprise with a mode of life.

As farms are defined by the Census, they include suburban homes whose occupants have industrial employment and do a little farming on the side and farms occupied by aged owners who are in semiretirement. More than a third of the 2.3 million farms in the country fall into this category, their operations being part-time or nominal. When these are subtracted, there remain 1.4 million full-time farms. In this group, however, there are more than 300,000 farms that afford little more than subsistence to the farmer and his family. This leaves around 1,100,000 commercial farms. And of these, three-fifths account for nine-tenths of agricultural output. This is commercial agriculture. And it is to serve the interests of commercial agriculture that price and production legislation has been devised.

There are pockets of rural poverty, especially among the smaller, part-time, and subsistence farmers. But among normal-sized and larger farms, farmers' real incomes are equal or much higher than the averages elsewhere. Also, farmers make capital gains as the value of their holdings rises (farm land prices have quintupled in the last 20 years). But these are not included in farm income statistics.

In short, rural poverty is a genuine problem, scattered in a number of states and lines of farming. But it is quite distinct from the mainstream of commercial farming, where the only legitimate social issue is short-run instability.

C2. Farm Policies

In this perspective, farm programs have had three directions: *(a)* stabilizing farm prices in the short-run, *(b)* raising farm prices in the long-run, and *(c)* directly subsidizing specific parts of farming. They have been highly complex and, in many ways, drastically inefficient and inequitable. They are the classic instance of competitive markets being controlled along monopoly lines, for purposes which could be met by direct policies at a small fraction of the present costs.

Stabilizing Prices.   As Table 25–7 shows, the stabilizing effort really began in 1933–38. At that point, stabilizing incomes was integral with raising farm prices. By 1938, prices were being supported as well as smoothed, and that has continued down to the present (see below). Stabilizing is provided both by *(a)* price supports, which set a guaranteed price for the coming year, and *(b)* various insurance and lending programs. The CCC has provided storage space and services on a large scale, so as to smooth fluctuations as well as to maintain price levels.

Price Supports.   By 1938, the price support program was firmly in place. World War II restored farm prosperity, but parity and price supports had taken root. Coverage included scores of crops and livestock. Parity was the criterion for settling price floors. The formula has evolved, but the basic idea is the same; that farm output prices should not decline relative to farm input prices. It is managed by the Department of Agriculture, in ways which naturally benefit farmers.[8]

Parity Price Is Said to Be a "Just" Price.   But, at best, the figure rests on fallible human judgment. And, at worst, it is subject to deliberate manipulation.[9] Since World War II prices have usually been pegged at 75

---

[8] The process involved in computing a parity price may be illustrated by showing how such a price was determined for hogs, per 100 pounds, in January 1958:

a. Determine the average price received by farmers for the commodity during the preceding 10 years. For hogs, this was $18.90

b. Compute an index of the average prices received by farmers for all agricultural commodities during the same 10 years, using the prices received in 1909–14 as 100. In January, 1958, this index stood at 262

c. Divide *(a)* by *(b)*. This gives an "adjusted base price" for hogs of $7.21

d. Compute an index of prices paid by farmers, taking those paid in 1909–14 as 100. In January, 1958, this index stood at 301

e. Multiply *(c)* by *(d)* and divide by 100. The parity price for hogs is.... $21.70

Parity, or $21.70, was the price to which the farmer was held to be justly entitled. Support prices, however, were set at less than parity. If fixed, in this case, at 80 percent, the price would be $17.36.

[9] Parity can be raised by shifting the base date from 1909–14 to some other period when price relationships were more favorable, and this has been done in the case of certain commodities. It can be raised by boosting the index of prices paid, and this was done when Congress required, at one time or another, that interest, taxes, freight rates, and wages be added. Before 1950 this index included 170 commodities used in farm production and in farm family living. Since then it has included some

TABLE 25–7
Milestones of Farm Policy

1921–22	Tariffs on agricultural imports; ineffective.
1929–31	Federal Farm Board, with $500 to stabilize prices; swamped by the collapse of farm prices.
1933–36	Agriculture Adjustment Act, to restore farm price parity on seven "basic" products (wheat, cotton, corn, hogs, rice, tobacco, milk). Commodity Credit Corporation created to channel loans; acreage is restricted.
1938	Second AAA makes controls and price supports permanent.
1940–45	World War II restores farm prosperity.
1945–72	Prices supported near parity. Surplus grows, despite various acreage restrictions. Calls for abolition of controls have little effect.
1972–76	Worldwide food and commodity scarcities elevate prices, render most controls superfluous. Payments shift toward a direct basis, and most controls are removed. Yet the basic control apparatus remains.
1978	New price supports are applied for selected products.

to 90 percent of parity. Some 200 different commodities are produced on American farms. Of these only six—wheat, corn, cotton, tobacco, rice, and peanuts—are designated as "basic" and these, together with certain nonbasic products, receive supports. The supported commodities accounted for 42 percent of farm market sales in 1967; the nonsupported commodities for 58 percent.

With Prices Supported, Surpluses Result. These have been stored, in amounts which had grown mountainous by the 1960s, costing $3 billion yearly.[10] Surplus disposal became a major problem. Large amounts have been "dumped" abroad, as part of foreign aid. This harms foreign farmers, of course, and invites retaliation, and so ingenious ways to present it as disaster relief and soft-currency sales have been used.

Surpluses are also dumped at home. School lunch programs subsidize 20 million school children, mainly from poor families. Various welfare distributions occur, through institutions and a food stamp plan. Much of this simply replaces food that would have been bought commercially. Therefore it has reduced the surpluses only marginally, while costing nearly $4 billion yearly.

Reducing Production. Production controls therefore became critical. First, farmers were limited by acreage. But farmers naturally used their best

---

340. Each of these commodities is given a weight in making the computation. The index of prices received has included 52 agricultural commodities, each of which is given its own weight. The height of a parity price is influenced by the items chosen for inclusion in these indexes and by the weights assigned them. These decisions are made by the statisticians of the Department of Agriculture.

[10] See Shepherd, *Farm Policy.*

acres and cultivated them more intensively. Output was scarcely reduced.[11] Output controls would be technically more effective for each crop, but they would also be costly.

There have also been programs to retire land entirely. During the 1930s the government purchased and retired 12 million acres of marginal farm lands. The effect of this operation on agricultural output was imperceptible. A second land retirement effort was made under the Soil Bank Act of 1956. Under this law the government offered to make rental payments to farmers who would enter into contracts to take land out of production. These payments covered the farmer's normal profit on the acres under contract, an incentive bonus, and the cost of conservation practices. The law set up two programs: an "acreage reserve" and a "conservation reserve." Both were costly, inefficient, and inequitable. They harmed consumers while benefiting mainly the richest farmers.[12]

The price support program has been riddled with inconsistencies and costly effects. It has been based on statistical deceptions about low farm incomes. The aim of fixing farmers' income at a prior level has little sense. Parity itself verges on a nonsense concept. Equity among farmers is not served, for benefits vary strictly with farm size, which is *inversely* related to need. The one million large farmers, already better off, got 80 percent of the subsidy. The two million smaller farmers got the rest. The price of farm land has capitalized these benefits (See Figure 25–2), again enriching mainly the large owners.

The efficiency effects have been serious. Prices and crop patterns have been distorted.[13] Substitute goods have been encouraged; for cotton, wool, and butter, the effects have been sharp. Some crops have been increased, others cut, and misallocation within farming has been substantial. The programs have been costly, toward $100 billion from 1932 to 1974 and $5 billion per year in the 1960s. Productivity may have risen faster because farmers were given incentives and security. But much of the gain has come autonomously from technical opportunity.

---

[11] From 1953 to 1963 a cut of 33 percent in acres planted caused a drop of only three percent in the output of wheat; a cut of 45 percent in acres caused a drop of only six percent in the output of cotton; a cut on 40 percent in acres failed to change the output of tobacco; a cut of 14 percent in acres was followed by an increase of 42 percent in the output of corn.

[12] In 1974, when 13 million acres were freed to return to production, only 7 million acres actually came back into use. The other 6 million acres had been phantom acres, falsely claimed as reserves by the farmers.

[13] With tobacco, for instance, where an acre yields a gross income of 20 times that yielded by an acre of wheat or corn, farmers have crowded in to share in the profits; allotments are now given to nearly 100,000 farms. As a consequence the size of the individual allotment has declined, the average for Burley tobacco dropping from 1.58 acres in 1948 to 1.16 in 1963. Where an advantage remains, it is capitalized in determining the prices charged for land. Without a quota, tobacco land may sell for $50 an acre; with a quota it will bring $2,500 or more.

Direct Payments. These are a parallel form of farm subsidy. They make up the gap between the market price and some target price; evidently they too go mainly to larger farmers. During the 1960s direct payments increasingly replaced price supports, and in 1973 they became the central basis of farm policy.

Direct payments are more efficient than price supports. The cost to the community may be lower. The expenses incurred in storing commodities are avoided; the whole supply moves into consumption; none of it spoils in storage; none of it is destroyed. The method can be used with commodities that are perishable as well as with those that are durable. Prices on the domestic market are lower; the consumer's burden is reduced. Commodities are sold on world markets on the same price basis as at home; the appearance of export dumping is avoided. The subsidy is made visible; it must be debated and voted each year.

But there are also disadvantages. A system that makes it easy to subsidize perishables may make for larger costs. A subsidy paid directly will be fully as powerful as one paid indirectly in stimulating increased output. The consumer's burden may go down; the taxpayer's burden will go up. There will still be surpluses to export; they will still cause international friction; they will still be attributable to artificial stimulation of production by the government. The largest farmers will get huge subsidies, while most farmers will get little.

Other Subsidies. Now we consider several of the older subsidies to farming. They have tended to increase output (clashing therefore with the price support and direct payment programs).

Government stimulated agricultural settlement for more than a century, by selling land to farmers at low prices and by giving it away. Government also provides the farmer with a number of free services. It delivers the mail to his home, however remote, with no extra charge. It supplies him with current market information through its crop and livestock reporting service. It facilitates the distribution of his products by establishing standards and grades of quantity and quality. It protects him against loss from insect pests and plant and animal diseases. It finances agricultural research and education. These are large programs.

Irrigation has conveyed extensive subsidies. Half of the cropland in the West is now irrigated and, of this, a fourth is irrigated by water from federal projects. This irrigation is 80 percent of all water use in the entire nation. Owners do not pay interest on the irrigation investment, and they repay capital only during the 10th and 50th year after the work is done. The subsidy to the farmers of irrigated lands is about 90 percent of the costs.[14]

---

[14] See Otto Eckstein, *Water Resource Development* (Cambridge: Harvard University Press, 1958), chap. 8; and National Water Commission, *Fiscal Report* (Washington, D.C.: U.S. Government Printing Office, 1973). Thus the Manson unit being constructed in Washington will cost $414 per acre *per year* (compared to annual charges at present rates of $32.50 per acre). The annual *gross* crop receipts per acre are likely to be

A complex of lending agencies was created during 1916–33, supervised by a Farm Credit Administration. It now is largely self-financing and stands as an internally efficient program.[15] There has been federal crop insurance for some farmers since 1939, on a modest scale. There were losses and revisions during 1940–47, and coverage has shrunk to 24 crops in 1,363 counties. The subsidy is small, and the poorer risks tend to be overrepresented.

Only the Farmers Home Administration has, since 1946, specifically given help to small, poor farmers. It provides loans plus careful supervision for nearly all operations which will improve small farmers' prospects. Remarkably, only 1 percent of the loans are not repaid. For $70 million in administrative costs per year, the FHA provides at least some help to needy farmers. This is, of course, only a trifle compared to the subsidies for the well-to-do commercial farmers.

In a larger perspective, farm programs have eased the rural impact of the long-term migration from farms to cities. The rate of migration was increased, especially the small farmers and sharecroppers in the southeastern region. Farm programs have therefore intensified the urban problems of ghettos and decay.

The 1970s have brought large changes in these programs, some of it toward more efficient and fairer lines. A limited program of stabilizing and crop insurance plus expanded FHA operations would probably be about optimal. But the older programs are part of a deep political equilibrium and are likely to persist.

D. MARITIME SUBSIDIES

There are five main forms of aid to U.S. maritime industries. They are summarized in Table 25–8.

Subsidies to Shipbuilders. Under the Merchant Marine Act of 1936, shipping companies receiving operating subsidies were required to have their ships built in American yards. This put them at a competitive disadvantage, since the cost of building ships in the United States was twice as great as that of building them abroad. The law therefore authorized the government to contribute, as a "construction differential subsidy," the difference between American and foreign costs. Until 1960 the government's contribution normally could not exceed half of the cost. In 1960 its share was raised to 55 percent; in 1962 to 60 percent. The largest ship to be subsidized under this law was the liner "United States," built at a cost of $76.8 million. Of this,

---

about $200, less than half of the true cost of the irrigation. Such projects are wildly uneconomic.

[15] The Rural Electrification Administration provided loans at 2 percent, plus all other technical support, to bring electricity to farms. From 10 percent in 1934, farms with electricity are now 98 percent of the total. There are over 1,000 REA cooperatives, with 6 million customers in 46 states. Telephones, too, have been extended by the REA, from one third of farms in 1949 to four fifths.

TABLE 25–8

Maritime Subsidies

	Since	Estimated Total, to 1977	Annual Amount, Recent Years
Operating differential	1936	$4 billion	$230 million
Construction differential	1936	2 billion	300 million
U.S. flag shipping rules (sabotage laws)	1950	3 billion	150 million
Tax subsidies	1936	0.5 billion	40 million
Cargo preference	1950	6 billion	200 million

Source: Joint Economic Committee, *The Economics of Federal Subsidies,* and other more recent industry sources.

$32.9 million was put up by the United States Lines, $43.9 million by the taxpayers.

From 1937, when the program began, to 1968, the government paid out nearly $1 billion in construction subsidies; in 1968 more than $100 million. At that time the Johnson Administration proposed that the American construction requirement be dropped, permitting shipping companies to purchase ships built in foreign yards. The Nixon Administration rejected this proposal. Under a new law, enacted in 1970, cargo liners are to be built in American yards at the rate of 30 ships a year for the next 10 years, with the government's contribution to their cost dropping from 55 percent at the beginning to 35 percent in the mid-seventies. The law is likely to cost the taxpayer $2.7 billion for construction subsidies during the 1970s.[16]

Subsidies to Shipping. Coastwise and intercoastal shipping has been reserved, since the early days of the republic, to vessels flying the American flag. Such protection has also been afforded, since the turn of the century, to trade with noncontiguous possessions of the United States. Exclusion of competitors thus operates indirectly to subsidize American concerns.

Transoceanic shipping has been subsidized in four different ways. *First,* it has been granted "cargo preferences." In 1904 Congress required that goods purchased for the Army or Navy be carried in American vessels. In 1934 it expressed its desire that exports financed by government loans be carried in such vessels. And in 1954 it required that at least half of the tonnage of all goods procured by the government or supplied by it, through loans or grants, to other governments be transported under the American flag. American shipping companies, protected from foreign competition, have thus obtained a subsidy in the form of higher freights, paid from funds that were nominally appropriated for other purposes, such as the provision of foreign aid. This subsidy has amounted to $100 million a year.

Second, the transoceanic lines have been enabled to acquire ships on terms

---

[16] On subsidies to shipping and shipbuilding, see Samuel A. Lawrence, *United States Merchant Shipping: Policies and Politics* (Washington, D.C.: Brookings Institution, 1966); and *The Economics of Federal Subsidy Programs,* Part 6.

that have cut their capital costs. Ships that were built for the government have been sold to private operators at a few cents on the dollar. After World War II, 843 ships that had cost $4,400 million were sold for $1,776 million, representing two fifths of their original cost and a fourth to a fifth of their replacement cost. Moreover, the government gives generous trade-in allowances on old vessels and offers easy-payment plans. Three fourths of the price a company must pay may be loaned to it by the government, these loans being made on terms that themselves involve a subsidy.

Third, the shipping companies are given a tax subsidy, being permitted to put part or all of their earnings and capital gains into reserve funds on which they can draw to purchase new ships. The income thus sequestered is exempted from the corporate income tax.

Fourth, the operating costs of passenger and cargo liners providing scheduled service on established routes are also subsidized. For many years, a subsidy was hidden in excessive payments made for carrying the mails. Under the Merchant Marine Act of 1936, it was brought into the open. An "operating differential subsidy" has since been paid to cover the difference in cost in operating under the American rather than a foreign flag. In 1969, this subsidy was being paid to 15 companies operating 13 passenger liners and some 300 cargo ships. It met a fourth of their operating costs. From 1954 to 1969, the subsidy paid to keep these ships afloat rose from $100 million a year to $200 million. Under legislation enacted in 1970, the operating differential subsidy will be $6 billion during the 1970s.

These subsidies are widely agreed to have been costly and deadening to efficiency. Shipping, under more progressive management, might have been able to pay its own way. Ship design, port facilities, and cargo-handling devices all could be improved. More freight could be pre-packed for loading in containers. Ships could be loaded to a higher fraction of capacity, sailing full and down. Time in port standing idle could be reduced, and time at sea earning money could be increased. Subsidization has not sufficed to keep American merchant ships afloat. The number of ships flying the American flag has steadily declined. Since World War II, the share of American trade carried by such vessels has fallen from 60 percent to less than 10 percent. What has been needed is less an infusion of funds from the Treasury than a revolution in management. Some subsidies are also siphoned in exotic ways into pockets far outside the officially eligible groups.

On the whole, maritime subsidies exhibit the worst features of subsidies. They are too large. They yield small, narrow and inequitable benefits. And they have set a dead hand upon efficiency in the sector for nearly 40 years.

QUESTIONS FOR REVIEW

1. "Subsidies are extensive, but at least they are rationally decided and equitably distributed." True?
2. "If the government merely guarantees somebody's private loan, that is not costly to the public." True?

3. "The arts are heavily subsidized and the benefits are widely spread among the populace." True?
4. "A good subsidy is one which applies strong economic incentives for inefficiency. Most subsidies do not in fact meet this criterion." True?
5. "Price supports for farm products are likely to cause distortions, for they affect only one part of the whole farm income equation." True?
6. "Farming is a homogeneous sector, with only a few major markets." True?
7. "Acreage controls have driven down the value of farm land." True?
8. What conditions make for rational and fair subsidies?
9. What sort of farm policy is needed now: supporting prices, incomes, exports, and so forth?

chapter 26

Balance among Policies

We end where we began, but wiser. There is a set of basic concepts which define policy choices and their probable effects. These can be used to define "optimal" choices—at least approximately—and to appraise actual policy treatments. The analysis rarely yields precise answers, but it does usually identify the problem areas. There is often a wide range of plausible policies to choose among, since the evidence about markets and policy instruments is usually soft. But whatever policies one actually favors, the real task is to use the concepts rationally and fairly. Illusions and deceptions are common, and so we need to practice a clear, analytical skepticism. Otherwise we trap ourselves in our own—or worse yet, other people's—biases.

This chapter first restates the main lessons which have recurred throughout the book. Then it reviews the problem of balance among the main policy treatments.

A. THEORY AND PRACTICE

A1. Principle

In principle, reaching optimal policy choices is quite straightforward. One defines and estimates the costs and benefits of alternative treatments, using standard categories for the various elements in the comparison. If a policy's yields are positive and higher than those of all alternatives, then that treatment is optimal. The magnitudes included in the appraisal are reasonably well-known and agreed. They must be discounted and adjusted in various ways, but these are also matters for reasonable judgment. It is important to get the burden of proof set neutrally and to avoid biases in the advantages of time. Also, an incentive structure to induce optimal behavior will usually be more effective than enforced restorative actions which go against the interests and expertise of the main actors.

Policy evaluation therefore requires skill and good sense, and it can be baffled in some cases. Yet the main elements are relatively clear and logical, and they are basically the same for all industrial policy choices. This unity knits the whole subject together. Policies are not separate boxes, each belonging in certain sectors. They are alternatives, supplements, and packages, which evolve and need adjusting. Their content and effects are often misunderstood, and deviant policies often persist even when their harms are manifest. Yet the logical core of optimal policy is quite clear and general for all sectors.

Policy choices often go astray for lack of good data. The most critical data are usually highly sensitive, and so there are strong interests in secreting or biasing them. Some key data may never be available in reliable forms, either for technical reasons or because the interests at stake are so powerful. A further problem is that certain broader costs and benefits are hard to measure and easy to neglect—and so they are frequently excluded altogether. Data about them are often soft or absent. If these elements are indeed important, then narrow technical appraisals of costs and benefits may often reach incorrect answers.

Still, on the whole, cost-benefit analysis can be a useful and consistent approach, to which all industrial policies should be subjected. This book has offered practice in using it, both to illumine the character of sound policies (and to display the variety of deviant ones) and to show how difficult it can occasionally be to decide whether a policy is sound or deviant.

Even if the method were unequivocal and data were ample, the prospects for rational policy would face practical limits. The democratic process is encased in the larger tissue of past patterns. These include vested property rights, precedents, expectations and concrete social patterns. Revision comes slowly and often with a lag of decades. The political economy frequently blocks policy reform quite directly and predictably. Policy agencies themselves evolve biases in their own procedures and incentives. Often they come in due course to perpetuate deviant policies. In light of this, the minimum hope is that policy choices can at least be understood, be revised in the right directions, and be kept from being merely deceptive or worse.

This is a main reason why competition is a reasonable norm—a basis for avoiding or moderating the abuses that can arise under direct manipulation of public policies. Such competition is not the arcane, extreme version of perfect competition. Rather, it involves the intermediate degrees of reasonable and effective contending among genuine competitors, whose striving tends to neutralize each others' independent power. As in religion, politics and other social affairs, a system of neutral balances and checks may be the best single method for getting reasonably efficient and fair outcomes. The burden of proof correctly rests against excluding competition.

A2. Practice

Now consider briefly how the main policies have worked out in practice.

Antitrust is the main line of policy, though large areas of the economy are exempt from it. Against collusion and mergers, it is strict; toward existing structure it is relatively permissive. The net effect may be a basic twist, which hardens structure and benefits dominant firms. Or, conceivably, innovation and oligopoly rivalry may be fostered. Perhaps the main favorable sign since 1960 has been the extension of antitrust constraints into regulated sectors and others previously untouched. ·

Regulation of utilities is often shadow rather than substance. It tends to tighten, rather than to shift toward competition, as the utility evolves back toward normal conditions to Stages 3 and 4. A good long-run regulatory treatment may require a forceful lifting of the franchise barriers and regulatory constraints, so that the utility can revert back to a competitive status.

In the short run, the direct effects of regulatory action are often weak, while the side effects—many of them negative and socially costly—often are strong. These side effects are of several varieties, tending to undermine the total efficiency of utilities in defining their output mix and producing it. By the most reasonable guesses, regulation often induces substantial inefficiency, though its benefits may also be large. Since good evidence is usally lacking, the appraisals are usually controversial.

Public Enterprise.   Even less is known about public enterprise. It is extensive and diverse, both in the United States and abroad, though it tends to be confined to the conventional form of a fully owned, national, partly subsidized utility monopoly. The common fear that public enterprises will be bureaucratic and rigid has not been borne out in practice. Rather, their behavior seems to approximate that of other enterprises of their size. The ideological bias against public enterprise in the United States is now fading, as experience grows. Therefore, on the whole, public enterprise offers a wide set of lessons and openings for future experimenting. It still needs regulating as much as comparable private firms do.

Then there is the wide range of **special treatments** and ad hoc cases. These, regrettably, include many dark corners of policy choice, where the social results are quite negative. Inherently, such special cases tend to generate inequity and inefficiency, because each has its own rules and subsidies. The rehabilitation of these parts will require a return to the more general criteria; this will usually involve more competition and a more open and skeptical review of the results than now occurs. In these sectors, applying the concepts of industrial organization anew might yield high social benefits.

B. BALANCE AND EXPERIMENT

For the future, the main lessons are *(a)* use the concepts of industrial organization across the whole range of industry types, and *(b)* rely on a degree of competition, wherever it is at all possible. Loose oligopoly is the main standard of reference, even for sectors where entrenched groups claim that it is not "feasible." Even where little competition seems possible, it should usually be nurtured carefully.

This sort of unified approach to industrial economics in all sectors is an essential for defining good treatments and evaluating actual policies. Individual markets will differ, of course, in their own inner conditions of demand and technology. Therefore the unified treatment needs to be fitted to actual cases. But all markets share the same underlying conditions, and they tend to evolve through the same basic conditions. Therefore, no sector should routinely be declared a natural monopoly—or exempt from competitive conditions for a variety of reasons—except under close conditions of proof. This is especially important for "utility" sectors, which actually share basic conditions with many industrial markets. Conversely, many near-monopolies in industry may be suited to some degree of regulation. Another attribute of optimal policy is that it will *anticipate* changes, so that current policy design can fit the evolving conditions of markets. In the utilities especially—but also in antitrust and other treatments—good policy must look ahead, anticipate unavoidable lags, and design solutions around what is *coming to be,* rather that what *is.*

The general principle is that unconstrained high market power is not tolerable in the modern economy, and that rational policy can deal effectively with it. There are adequate analytical tools to define the main lines of good treatments reasonably well, even for the most complex cases. There are certain biases, and they can be expected to continue to make optimal policy difficult. Yet the lessons need to be pursued apart from—or rather, anticipating—these biases, for without clear guidelines no technical improvements in policies will matter in any event.

The need is for new experiments and new policy types, as well as a better balancing among the old ones. Policies need to apply better incentives to firms, and they need to engage company skills and interests rather than run squarely against them. There are high stakes; failing to solve these problems may leave us with heavy and increasing economic burdens as the decades pass. The conventional policy treatments have their own momentum, which makes careful revision difficult. Once one sees the traditional policies for what they are—fallible treatments, mostly designed long ago, and shaped by the evolving political economy—one can then think clearly and skeptically about them and about newer techniques.

None of them will solve all problems at a stroke. But with care and logic, the evolving older treatments can be adjusted or—in some cases—replaced so as to reduce the costs and improve the benefits. This book has tried to bring you to the point where you can perceive the new possibilities as well as anyone else can.

ANSWERS TO TRUE-FALSE AND MULTIPLE-CHOICE REVIEW QUESTIONS

If a statement or question is incorrect in any part, it is answered as "false." Thus, the conclusion may be correct but the premise false; or vice versa. Or the logic may be correct but the facts wrong; or vice versa. Inspect each question carefully. The answers to the essay questions are for you to provide.

Chapter 2.

1. True **2.** True **3.** True **4.** False **5.** *a, b, ·d* **6.** False **7.** False **8.** *a, c, d* **9.** False **10.** False **11.** True.

Chapter 3.

1. True **2.** False **3.** False **4.** All **5.** True **6.** True **7.** False **8.** True **9.** False **10.** False **11.** False **12.** False.

Chapter 4.

1. False **2.** False **3.** True **4.** All **5.** False **6.** False **7.** False **8.** False **9.** *d* **10.** False **11.** False **12.** True **13.** True.

Chapter 5.

1. False **2.** True **3.** False **4.** False **5.** True **6.** False **7.** False **8.** True **9.** False **10.** True **11.** True **12.** False **13.** True **14.** False.

Chapter 6.

1. False **2.** True **3.** True **4.** False **5.** False **6.** False **7.** True **8.** True **9.** True **10.** True **11.** False **12.** True.

Chapter 8.

1. False **2.** True **3.** False **4.** True **5.** False **6.** True **7.** True **8.** False **9.** False **10.** True **11.** True **12.** True.

Chapter 9.

1. False **2.** False **3.** False **4.** False **5.** True **6.** True.

Chapter 10.

1. False **2.** True **3.** False **4.** True **5.** False **6.** True **7.** False **8.** False **9.** True **10.** False **11.** True **12.** True **13.** True **14.** True.

Chapter 11.

1. True **2.** True **3.** True **4.** False **5.** True **6.** True **7.** False **8.** False **9.** True **10.** True **11.** True **12.** True **13.** True **14.** True **15.** True **16.** True **17.** False.

Chapter 12.

1. False **2.** False **3.** False **4.** True **5.** True **6.** True **7.** True **8.** True **9.** False **10.** False **11.** False **12.** False **13.** False.

Chapter 13.

1. True **2.** False **3.** True **4.** True **5.** True **6.** False **7.** True **8.** False **9.** True **10.** True **11.** False **12.** True **13.** True **14.** True.

Chapter 14.

1. False **2.** True **3.** True **4.** False **5.** False **6.** True **7.** False **8.** False **9.** False **10.** True.

Chapter 16.

1. True **2.** False **3.** True **4.** True **5.** False **6.** False **7.** True **8.** True **9.** True **10.** True **11.** False **12.** True **13.** True **14.** True **15.** False.

Chapter 17.

1. True **2.** False **3.** True **4.** False **5.** True **6.** False **7.** True **8.** False.

Chapter 18.

1. False **2.** False **3.** True **4.** False **5.** True **6.** True **7.** True **8.** True **9.** True **10.** True **11.** False.

Chapter 20.

1. False **2.** True **3.** False **4.** True **5.** False **6.** All three **7.** True **8.** True **9.** False **10.** True **11.** True **12.** False.

Chapter 21.

1. False **2.** True **3.** False **4.** *a, b, c* **5.** True.

Chapter 22.

1. True **2.** *a, b,* **3.** False **4.** True **5.** True **6.** True **7.** True.

Chapter 23.

1. False **2.** True **3.** True **4.** False **5.** False **6.** False.

Chapter 24.

1. True **2.** False **3.** False **4.** True **5.** True **6.** True.

Chapter 25.

1. False **2.** False **3.** False **4.** False **5.** True **6.** False **7.** False.

Index of Cases

Index of Persons

A

Aaron, Henry J., 469 n
Adams, Walter, 54 n, 77, 101 n, 151 n, 167 n, 258 n, 268 n, 269 n, 547 n
Adelman, Morris A., 234 n, 242 n, 528 n
Alexander, T., 534 n
Alhadeff, David, 425 n, 477 n, 488 n
Allen, F. L., 170 n
Andreano, Ralph, 482 n
Areeda, Philip, 233 n, 240 n
Arigo, Michiko, 212
Arnold, Thurman, 24, 111
Arrow, Kenneth J., 47 n, 68 n, 464 n, 507 n
Auerbach, C., 71 n
Averch, Harvey A., 303 n

B

Backman, Jules, 47 n
Bailey, Elizabeth E., 303 n
Baily, Martin, 543 n
Bain, Joe S., 27 n, 40 n, 46, 48 n, 196 n
Baker, Donald I., 111, 151 n
Balassa, Bela, 159 n
Bane, Charles A., 203 n
Baratz, Morton, 453 n
Barnett, Harold J., 371 n
Bassett, Lowell R., 167 n
Bauer, John, 269 n, 288 n
Baumol, William J., 242 n, 313 n, 490 n, 569 n
Becker, Gary S., 464 n
Beelar, Donald C., 360 n
Bell, Alexander Graham, 350–51
Berle, Adolf A., 30 n
Bernstein, Marver H., 286 n
Berry, Charles H., 38 n
Bisson, Thomas A., 158 n
Blair, John M., 35 n, 151 n
Blake, Harlan M., 167 n
Blaug, Mark, 464 n
Bloom, Benjamin S., 464 n

Blume, Marshall E., 491 n
Boeckh, A., 419 n
Bonbright, James C., 267 n, 293 n, 310 n
Borgsdorf, Charles W., 187 n
Bork, Robert H., 129 n, 167 n
Borkin, Joseph, 158 n
Bowen, William G., 509 n
Bowman, Ward S., 247 n
Bradford, David F., 242 n, 313 n
Bradley, Joseph F., 220 n
Breit, William, 100 n, 260 n
Breyer, Stephen G., 335 n, 338 n, 339 n
Brock, Gerald S., 55 n, 147 n, 153 n, 239 n, 240 n
Brooks, John, 345 n, 350 n, 490 n
Burn, Duncan L., 438 n
Burton, John F., 101 n
Bussing, L., 288 n
Buzzell, Robert D., 50 n
Bye, Maurice, 405 n

C

Campbell, James S., 185 n
Capron, William M., 315 n, 345 n
Caves, Richard E., 27 n, 385 n, 392 n, 536 n
Caywood, Russell E., 320 n
Chamberlin, Edward H., 195 n
Chandler, Alfred D., 56 n, 139 n
Cicchetti, Charles J., 328 n
Ciriacy-Wantrup, S. V., 520 n
Clabault, James M., 101 n
Clapp, G. R., 448 n
Clark, John M., 22 n, 217 n
Coase, Ronald A., 366 n
Cole, Charles W., 23 n, 420 n
Colenutt, D. W., 187 n
Collins, Norman R., 36 n
Comanor, William S., 47 n, 52 n, 249 n
Courville, Leon, 334 n
Cox, E. F., 114 n
Cramton, Roger, 269 n
Crandall, Robert W., 371 n

593

594

D

Dahl, Robert A., 68 n
Dales, J. H., 520 n
Dalton, James A., 99 n
Davidson, Ralph K., 328 n
Davidson, Sidney, 300 n
DeAlessi, Louis, 449 n
de Jong, H. W., 187 n
Demsetz, Harold, 272 n
Dennison, Edward, 465 n
Dewey, Davis R., 483 n
Dewey, Donald J., 24 n, 25 n, 81 n, 196 n, 269 n
Dickieson, A. C., 360 n
Dirlam, Joel B., 167 n, 242 n, 439 n, 547 n
Donnison, David V., 469 n
Douglas, George W., 374 n, 385 n, 386 n, 392 n, 393 n, 394 n
Downs, Anthony, 68 n
Dystel, John J., 355 n

E

Eads, George, 384 n, 393 n
Eckstein, Otto, 578 n
Edelstein, David N., 227 n
Edwards, Corwin D., 184 n, 235 n, 237 n, 244 n
Edwards, Franklin R., 482 n
Eichner, Alfred, 138 n
Einaudi, M., 405 n
Elliot, D. C., 187 n, 211 n
Elzinga, Kenneth G., 100 n, 101 n, 238 n, 258 n, 260 n
Etra, Donald, 480 n

F

Fellmeth, Robert G., 114 n, 384 n
Fellner, William J., 195 n
Fetter, Frank A., 217 n
Fischer, Gerald C., 477 n
Fisher, I. N., 51 n, 480 n, 483 n
Fleming, M., 72 n, 468 n
Foster, Christopher D., 405 n
Fox, J. Ronald, 556 n
Fray, L. L., 371 n
Friedlaender, Anne F., 374 n
Friend, Irwin, 477 n, 491 n, 494 n
Fusfeld, Daniel R., 220 n

G

Gabel, Richard, 305 n, 355 n
Galatin, M., 325 n
Galbraith, John K., 47 n, 197 n, 550 n, 556 n
Gale, Bradley T., 50 n
Garfield, Paul J., 401 n
Garrison, L., 71 n
Gaskins, Darius, 123 n
Gibbon, Edmond, 419 n
Gies, Thomas G., 355 n, 375 n
Glaeser, Martin G., 288 n, 401 n

Grabowski, Henry G., 543 n
Gray, Horace M., 269 n, 286 n
Grayson, C. Jackson, 551 n
Green, Mark J., 136 n, 146 n, 256 n
Gribbin, J. D., 187 n, 211 n
Gulland, J. A., 534 n
Guttentag, J. M., 480 n

H–I

Hadley, Eleanor T., 158 n, 188 n, 212 n
Hale, Matthew, 287 n
Hall, George F., 51 n
Hamilton, Mary, 551 n
Hamilton, Walton, 88 n, 105 n, 108 n
Hand, Learned, 123
Hanson, W. L., 465 n
Hay, George A., 199 n
Hays, S. P., 526 n
Heggestad, Arnold A., 480 n
Hellman, Richard, 448 n
Herman, Edward S., 480 n
Hitch, Charles J., 556 n
Hogarty, Thomas F., 238 n
Holland, Stuart, 409 n, 421 n, 427 n, 428 n
Hotelling, Harold, 318 n
Houghton, Harrison F., 176 n
Howe, W. Stewart, 115 n, 211 n
Hunter, M. H., 287 n
Hurst, W., 71 n
Ippolito, Richard A., 549 n
Iulo, William, 334 n

J

Jacobs, D., 480 n
Jacobs, Sanford L., 354 n
Jacquemin, Alex P., 187 n
Jencks, Christopher, 464 n
Jenny, Frederick, 211 n
Jewkes, John, 47 n, 499 n
Johnson, Leland L., 303 n
Johnson, Nicholas, 355 n
Jones, David P., 212 n
Jordan, William A., 385 n, 386 n, 392 n, 393 n
Joskow, Paul L., 281 n, 497 n
Jurewitz, John, 328 n

K

Kahn, Alfred E., 77 n, 230 n, 242 n, 267 n, 268 n, 269 n, 293 n, 297 n, 310 n, 312 n, 313 n, 314 n, 315 n, 316 n, 330 n, 499 n, 510 n
Kami, Michael, 356 n
Kaplan, A. D. H., 133 n, 134 n
Kauper, Thomas E., 111
Kaysen, Carl, 40 n, 214–15, 244 n, 262 n
Keeler, Theodore E., 386 n, 392 n, 393 n
Kelley, Daniel, 199 n
Kessel, Reuben A., 549 n
King, C. L., 287 n, 288 n
Kingsbury, Nathan C., 350 n

Index of Subjects

This book has been set Videocomp in 10 and 9 point Times Roman, leaded 2 points. Part numbers are 20 point Compano and part titles are 16 point Compano. Chapter numbers are 16 and 18 point Compano and chapter titles are 16 point Compano. The size of the type page is 27 by 46½ picas.